THE AMERICAN PRESIDENTS

THE AMERICAN PRESIDENTS

BY

David C. Whitney

AND

Robin Vaughn Whitney

EIGHTH EDITION

Doubleday Book & Music Clubs, Inc.
GARDEN CITY, NEW YORK

Published by The Reader's Digest Association, Inc., 1993,
by permission of Doubleday Book & Music Clubs, Inc.

Photographs in this volume are courtesy of the Library of Congress, except for the following: George Washington, the Pennsylvania Academy of Fine Arts; John Quincy Adams, *John Quincy
Adams*, Thomas Sully, courtesy of the National Gallery of Art,
Washington, D.C., Andrew W. Mellon Collection; George
Bush, courtesy of Dave Valdez, The White House; and Bill Clinton, copyright © 1992 Rick Friedman, Black Star.

ISBN: 1-56865-031-0

Printed in the United States of America

Contents

CONTENTS

Foreword

EACH OF THE MEN who has been President of the United States has played the starring role in the drama that was the history of his time. No actors ever dared to rewrite their parts to fit their own abilities and ambitions as have the men who have been President. And no playwright ever has conceived a work so filled with suspense, tragedy, comedy, and unexpected turns of fate as that viewed with the White House as the stage.

When created two centuries ago, the office of the President of the United States was unique—a ruler to be elected and to be judged by his electors every four years; a ruler combining the powers of a king, a prime minister, and a commanding general. The statesmen of Europe, wise in the politics of royal courts, knowingly winked at each other and predicted that the peculiar American experiment would last a few years at the most—that a strong President would refuse to bow to the wishes of the electors and would make himself king for life, or that a weak President would be cast out of office by revolution before his four years were up. They were wrong. And the reasons why they were wrong can only be understood by studying the lives of the Presidents and their part in the evolution of American political democracy.

The American system of government—with its checks and balances, its constitutional restrictions of power, and its unwritten complexities of two-party politics—is exceedingly complicated. But at the heart of the system lies a simple idea—that the people have the right to change their leaders at regular intervals. Every four years the people can retain or remove the President. And every two years they can pass judgment on his policies by supporting or rejecting the congressional candidates of his party. Congress, moreover, has the power to remove the President if he is guilty of treason, bribery, or "other high crimes and misdemeanors." One day a man can hold the most powerful office in the world, and the next he can be out of office with no more power than that held by any other private citizen. The universal acceptance of this simple idea, first demonstrated by George

Washington when he turned the presidency over to John Adams, has given the American system a resilient vitality, enabling the people to tolerate a President they merely dislike in the knowledge that they do not have long to wait until they can be rid of him.

Of even more importance has been the acceptance of the idea that both the President and his party can be turned out of office and replaced with a new leader *and* a new party by means of an election instead of an insurrection. The first such "election revolution" took place when liberal Thomas Jefferson and his Democratic-Republican followers won out over conservative John Adams and his Federalists. At the time, doom-sayers forecast that blood would run in the streets if the Democratic-Republicans were allowed to assume control of the government. But when Adams peacefully stepped down and Jefferson demonstrated that an opposition party could assume power in a responsible manner, the tradition of revolution by election was established.

Throughout the early days, however, the election of the President was by no means in the hands of the man-in-the-street voter. From Washington to John Quincy Adams, presidential candidates were chosen by caucuses of senators and congressmen. In turn, state legislatures indirectly chose the President by appointing electors to the Electoral College. Because of this system, the early Presidents did not have to strive for great popular appeal with the masses of voters, but instead were more concerned with staying in the good graces of Congress and the state legislatures. Presidential political campaigns in the modern sense were unknown. And the Presidents themselves—Washington, Adams, Jefferson, Madison, and Monroe—were able to emphasize their roles as statesmen rather than as popular politicians.

The disputed election of 1824 broke this pattern. None of the candidates had a majority of votes in the Electoral College, so the President was chosen by the House of Representatives. Although Andrew Jackson had received the largest number of electoral votes, the supporters of John Quincy Adams and Henry Clay united to award the presidency to Adams—who in turn appointed Clay as his Secretary of State. Jackson's followers cried "foul!"

By the time of the election of 1828, the power to name the presidential electors had been taken out of the hands of the state legislatures in all states except South Carolina and had been given directly to the voters. When Jackson soundly defeated Adams in their return engagement in 1828, he became the first President to be popularly elected in the modern sense. Members of the older order were horrified when Jackson rewarded his backwoods followers by opening the doors of the White House to them and by cutting them in on the "political spoils" of victory.

Jackson next broke the power of the congressional caucus to name presidential candidates. The first national convention of the Democratic party in 1832, which brought together local politicians from all states, renominated Jackson for President and ratified his choice of Martin Van Buren for Vice President.

The whoop-and-holler style of national political campaigns came into its own in 1840 when the Whigs learned the importance of appealing to the common man by portraying their candidate, William Henry Harrison, as a national hero who had been born in a log cabin. Torchlight processions, campaign slogans, and campaign songs roused the electorate and brought 60 percent more voters to the polls than in the previous election.

From that time on, the major political parties began to choose their presidential candidates for their popular appeal as much as for their abilities. Candidates campaigned more and more aggressively, trying to be seen and heard by as many voters as possible. Eventually radio and television carried the presidential campaigns directly into the voters' homes.

After Jackson had demonstrated that a man did not need to be a member of the aristocracy or even a college graduate in order to be elected President, it became the American dream of many mothers that their sons would "grow up to be President." And many later Presidents were to attribute their success to their mothers' encouragement.

With few if any exceptions, the men who have been President have wanted the office very badly, and they have worked hard to get it. Some were rich men who devoted their lives to public service. Some were poor boys who struggled to the top in the Horatio Alger tradition. Others were men who won their fame on the battlefield. The majority have been lawyers—the law profession being a natural entrée to local politics. Almost all held lesser political offices before climbing to national stature.

The men who have been our most successful Presidents have had the ability both to administer the government as statesmen and to lead their political parties as politicians. Through experience before becoming President they have had a clear understanding of the legislative process—of the necessity of internal leadership of their party and external appeal to the popular imagination of voters—in order to accomplish their programs.

Generally, historians have given the accolade of "great" to those Presidents who have strengthened the office by acquiring powers previously left to the legislative branch or to the states. Such judgments often reflect the party biases of the historians making the selection.

Since the success of a President is evaluated by his contemporaries in political conventions and at the polls, it might be fairer to weigh later judgment on the basis of renomination and re-election. In other words, perhaps the most successful—if not necessarily the "greatest"—Presidents were those who served one term of office well enough to satisfy first their own party and then the voters that they should be reelected to a second term. Fewer than half of the Presidents—only fourteen—meet this criterion: George Washington, Thomas Jefferson, James Madison, James Monroe, Andrew Jackson, Abraham Lincoln, Ulysses S. Grant, Grover Cleveland, William McKinley, Woodrow Wilson, Franklin D. Roosevelt (who was elected four times), Dwight D. Eisenhower, Richard Nixon (who perhaps was the exception that proves the rule), and Ronald Reagan. Also to this list could be added the four Presidents who succeeded to the office on the death of a predecessor and served part or most of a term in a satisfactory enough manner to win nomination and election to a full term on their own—Theodore Roosevelt, Calvin Coolidge, Harry Truman, and Lyndon Johnson.

The majority of Presidents—twenty-two in all—have served as President for four years or less, sometimes leaving such a faint mark on history that even their names have been forgotten by most Americans.

More than half of the Presidents had military service before coming to the White House. Eleven were generals: Washington, Jackson, W. H. Harrison, Taylor, Pierce, Grant, Hayes, Garfield, Arthur, Benjamin Harrison, and Eisenhower. Twelve others held lesser ranks: Monroe, Tyler, Lincoln, McKinley, Theodore Roosevelt, Truman, Kennedy, Lyndon Johnson, Nixon, Ford, Carter, Reagan, and Bush. The latter seven all served in World War II.

Two-thirds of the Presidents had congressional experience. Twenty-two had been representatives and fifteen senators, with nine having served in both houses of the U. S. Congress: Jackson, W. H. Harrison, Tyler, Pierce, Buchanan, Andrew Johnson, Kennedy, Lyndon Johnson, and Nixon.

Nineteen of the Presidents had been governors of states or territories: Jefferson (Virginia), Monroe (Virginia), Jackson (Florida), Van Buren (New York), W. H. Harrison (Indiana), Tyler (Virginia), Polk (Tennessee), Andrew Johnson (Tennessee), Hayes (Ohio), Cleveland (New York), McKinley (Ohio), Theodore Roosevelt (New York), Taft (Philippines), Wilson (New Jersey), Coolidge (Massachusetts), F. D. Roosevelt (New York), Carter (Georgia), Reagan (California), and Clinton (Arkansas).

Four Presidents died in office of natural causes—W. H. Harrison, Taylor, Harding, and Franklin D. Roosevelt. Four have been assassinated—Lincoln, Garfield, McKinley, and Kennedy. One resigned—Nixon. As a result, nine men succeeded to the office because they were Vice Presidents at the death or resignation of their predecessors—Tyler, Fillmore, Andrew Johnson, Arthur, Theodore Roosevelt, Coolidge, Truman, Lyndon Johnson, and Gerald Ford.

Twelve Presidents or former Presidents tried to win another term of office and were defeated—John Adams, John Quincy Adams, Van Buren, Fillmore, Cleveland, Benjamin Harrison, Theodore Roosevelt, Taft, Hoover, Ford, Carter, and Bush. After completing their first term in office, seven Presidents did not take or were not given a chance to run for a second term—Tyler, Polk, Pierce, Buchanan, Andrew Johnson, Hayes, and Arthur. Five Presidents have won the office after being previously defeated in a presidential election—Jefferson, Jackson, W. H. Harrison, Cleveland, and Nixon. One man—Cleveland—served discontinuous terms, resulting in the anomaly that, although only forty-one men have been Chief Executive, there have been forty-two Presidents.

The average age of the Presidents upon taking the oath of office has been fifty-four. The youngest to become President was Theodore Roosevelt, who succeeded to the office at the age of forty-two upon the death of McKinley. But the youngest to be elected President was forty-three-year-old John F. Kennedy. The oldest to be elected to the White House was Ronald Reagan, who was sixty-nine when first elected and seventy-three when reelected. Of all the men who have been President, the one who lived to the greatest age was John Adams, who died after attaining ninety years and eight months.

Since the Republican party began contesting with the Democratic party for the presidency in 1856, Republicans have won twenty-one of the thirty-five presidential elections, while Democrats have won fourteen.

The forty-one men who have been President have all viewed their roles differently. Some have accepted the office as a reward for past services to their country. Some have been frightened by the responsibilities, particularly some of the Vice Presidents who were plunged into the office by the death of a predecessor. Some of them have regarded the presidency as a burdensome chore and have literally worked themselves to death. Others, such as Theodore Roosevelt, have thought it was fun. But none has described it more eloquently than Thomas Jefferson, who called it a "splendid misery." All forty-one could agree to that.

David C. Whitney
Robin Vaughn Whitney

THE AMERICAN PRESIDENTS

George Washington
The First President of the United States
1789–97

1732 (February 22) Born at Wakefield on Pope's Creek Farm in Westmoreland County, Virginia.

1747 Became a surveyor after leaving school at fourteen or fifteen.

1753 Took oath as major in Virginia militia.

1753–54 Carried message to French in western Pennsylvania warning them to leave Ohio Valley.

1754 (July 4) Forced to surrender Fort Necessity to French attackers.

1754–58 Fought in French and Indian War, rising to rank of colonel in command of Virginia militia.

1759 (January 6) Married Martha Dandridge Custis.

1774–75 Member of Virginia's delegation to First and Second Continental Congresses.

1775–83 Commander of Continental Army throughout Revolutionary War.

1787 President of Constitutional Convention that drew up Constitution of the United States.

1789–97 First President of the United States.

1798 (July 4) Commissioned lieutenant general and commander in chief of the United States Army when war threatened with France.

1799 (December 14) Died at Mount Vernon, Virginia.

E lected by the unanimous vote of his countrymen, George Washington brought to the newly created office of United States President such enormous prestige that he easily set lasting precedents that made it the most powerful elective office in the world.

Although reluctant to leave retirement at his beloved Mount Vernon, he felt it was his duty to guide the first steps of the new Republic, whose struggle for independence he had led. Later insinuations by political enemies that he had accepted the office to please his vanity sent him into a rage, for he knew, as did his associates, that a single hint from him at the end of the Revolutionary War would have caused him to be crowned King of America.

His sense of destiny had led him to accept the hazardous command of the Continental Army in 1775 and hold together his troops through every hardship until freedom had been won. In 1787, when he saw that the new nation was threatened by discord under the weak Articles of Confederation, he brought together and inspired the delegates who wrote the Constitution.

Washington was a towering figure, both in physique and accomplishments. The aristocratic bearing of his six-foot-two-inch figure and the calm nobility of his face created awe in those who saw him. His presence, coupled with the battlefield miracle he had accomplished, made him an idol among his contemporaries. But idolatry brought with it a difficulty. People both then and now refused to accept the truth that Washington was mortal, a man with normal appetites and frailties—a man who loved women, enjoyed gambling, liked to dance all night, and prided himself on his fine horses. They interpreted as a god-like coldness his self-conscious determination not to make any blunders that would reveal the background of a poorly educated orphan who had achieved success and riches by a combination of luck, ingenuity, and resolution. Legends about his strength and honesty won more ready acceptance as fact than understanding of the human qualities that both hindered and helped him on his path to immortality.

No man knew Washington's strengths and weaknesses better than Thomas Jefferson, who served as his first Secretary of State. Fifteen years after Washington's death, Jefferson wrote:

"His mind was great and powerful, without being of the very first order; his penetration strong, though not so acute as that of a Newton, Bacon, or Locke; and as far as he saw, no judgment was ever sounder. It was slow in operation, being little aided by invention or imagination, but sure in conclusion. . . .

"Perhaps the strongest feature in his character was prudence, never acting until every circumstance, every consideration, was maturely weighed; refraining when he saw a doubt, but, when once decided, going through with his purpose whatever obstacles opposed. His integrity was most pure, his justice the most inflexible I have ever known, no motives of interest or consanguinity, of friendship or hatred, being able to bias his decision. He was indeed, in every sense of the words, a wise, a good and a great man. . . .

"On the whole, his character was, in its mass, perfect, in nothing bad, in few points indifferent; and it may truly be said, that never did nature and fortune combine more perfectly to make a man great, and to place him in the same constellation with whatever worthies have merited from man an everlasting remembrance. . . ."

Washington's Boyhood

THE ELDEST CHILD of a second marriage, George Washington was born on February 22, 1732 (February 11 by the Old Style Calendar). When he was two, his family moved from his birthplace, Wakefield on Pope's Creek Farm in Westmoreland County, Virginia, to a new farm about fifty miles north along the broad, curving Potomac River. This new plantation, later to become part of the huge estate of Mount Vernon, was called Little Hunting Creek Farm. During Washington's childhood there was neither the wide expanse of meticulously trimmed lawn nor the gleaming white-pillared colonial mansion. There was only a rustic tobacco farm with few neighbors in the surrounding countryside.

When Washington was six, his father, Augustine, decided to move again, to be closer to an ironworks in which he had a part interest. This time the move was to the 260-acre Ferry Farm on the east bank of the Rappahannock River. There young George grew up enjoying hunting, fishing, and horseback riding.

Washington's father died when the boy was eleven, leaving a substantial estate of about 10,000 acres of land and about fifty slaves. The largest share of the inheritance went to Lawrence Washington, the eldest son of Augustine's first marriage; George was to receive Ferry Farm as his share when he reached the age of twenty-one. George and his five younger brothers and sisters were left to grow up under the guidance of their widowed mother, Mary Ball Washington.

Little is known of Washington's formal education. Historians have speculated that he may have gone to school in the small town of Fredericksburg, which lay just across the Rappahannock from Ferry Farm, or he may have been tutored by an indentured servant. In either case, it is certain that what little education he received was closely supervised by his possessive mother, who was determined to keep her eldest son as close to her as possible. Perhaps the learning that had the most effect upon him was his copying, as a schoolboy of thirteen, of 110 "Rules of Civility and Decent Behaviour in Company and Conversation." All his later behavior as a man seems to have been guided by these principles, a few of which are listed below as he wrote them:

Use no Reproachful Language against any one neither Curse nor Revile.

Every Action done in Company ought to be with some Sign of Respect to those that are Present.

While you are talking, Point not with your Finger at him of whom you Discourse nor Approach too near him to whom you talk especially to his face.

Strive not with your superiors in argument, but always submit your Judgment to others with Modesty.

Be not Curious to Know the Affairs of Others neither approach those that Speak in Private.

Washington was never a scholar. Even in his latter years he seldom read books unless they could serve some practical purpose, such as helping him learn more about farming methods. But he had respect for books and once wrote: "I conceive a knowledge of books is the basis upon which other knowledge is to be built." Throughout his life Washington wrote extensively in diaries and letters, leaving a wealth of material that gives historians much information about his life and his beliefs.

A Youthful Surveyor

YOUNG GEORGE WASHINGTON hero-worshiped his stepbrother Lawrence, fourteen years his senior. He spent as much time as his mother would allow visiting Lawrence at the handsome new mansion at Mount Vernon, which Lawrence had built and named for a British admiral under whom he had served in a brief war with Spain in the 1740s. Lawrence encouraged George to join the British Navy, but Mary Washington refused to give her consent.

When George was fifteen, he decided he must find some way of bringing more money into his household—under his mother's management Ferry Farm was accumulating more debts than income. So he dusted off an old set of surveying instruments that his father had owned, and began work as an assistant surveyor. When he was sixteen, he made his first trip into the wilderness of western Virginia to help survey the huge landholdings of Lord Fairfax, a relative of Lawrence Washington's wife. By 1749, when he had established enough of a reputation to be appointed official surveyor of Culpeper County, he began using his income to buy land, a practice he continued throughout his life, gradually becoming one of the largest landholders in the country.

When Washington was nineteen, he accompanied Lawrence on a trip to Barbados that his brother undertook for his health. It was the only time he ever left America's shores. But in Barbados, Washington contracted smallpox. He noted in his diary: "Was strongly attacked with the small Pox: sent for Dr. Lanahan whose attendance was very constant till my recovery, and going out which was not 'till thursday the 12th of December."

After returning from Barbados, George fell deeply in love with a pretty sixteen-year-old by the name of Betsy Fauntleroy. But she rejected his marriage proposals, even though George enlisted the help of her father "in hopes of a revocation of the . . . cruel sentence."

Lawrence Washington died of tuberculosis in 1752. His will provided that the Mount Vernon estate should go to George if his only daughter, Sarah, died without having any children—an event that came to pass two years later.

The French and Indian War

IN AN EFFORT TO EMULATE his beloved Lawrence, George applied to the governor of Virginia for an appointment as adjutant in the militia, a post Lawrence had held. After considering the matter, the governor decided to apportion the position among four persons, and chose George as adjutant for the southern part of the colony. Accordingly, on February 1, 1753, George was sworn in as a major in the Virginia militia, a twenty-year-old with great ambition but little more knowledge of military affairs than had the men he was to command.

In the autumn of 1753, George read reports in the Virginia newspapers that French troops had invaded the Ohio Valley near Lake Erie, an area claimed by Virginia. When he learned from a friend that Governor Robert Dinwiddie was planning to send a warning message to the French commander, he realized that this might be the chance of a lifetime to have a look at the western frontier. Hurrying to the capital at Williamsburg, Washington volunteered his services as messenger and was gladly accepted.

Setting out from Williamsburg on October 31, 1753, Washington collected supplies, horses, and a party of six frontiersmen. In the teeth of extreme cold, much snow, and unfriendly Indians, he made the hazardous 800- to 1,000-mile round-trip journey to the French Fort Le Boeuf on Lake Erie. It took two and a half months. Once he had to swim for his life amid chunks of ice in a flooded river; he was shot at by an Indian; and he had to walk hundreds of miles when his horses grew too weak to go farther. In his report on the journey he wrote: "From the first Day of December to the 15th, there was but one Day on which it did not rain or snow incessantly: and throughout the whole Journey we met with nothing but one continued Series of cold wet Weather . . ."

The message that Washington brought back from the French rejected Dinwiddie's request that they leave the Ohio Valley, and Dinwiddie immediately set about raising money and troops to push them out.

Four months after returning from his journey as a messenger, the twenty-two-year-old Washington commanded a British force in the first engagement of the French and Indian War. Promoted to lieutenant colonel, and leading a small body of Virginia troops, he ran into a French scouting party in southern Pennsylvania on May 27, 1754. Washington and his men captured twenty-one of the enemy and killed ten in the skirmish, losing only one man. He later wrote that he "heard the bullets whistle" and felt that there was "something charming in the sound."

Early in June, Washington was promoted to colonel in command of all Virginia troops in the field. Expecting a retaliatory attack from the French, he prepared for it by building Fort Necessity, near the site of present-day Uniontown, Pennsylvania. True to his predictions, several hundred French and Indians surrounded the fort on July 3, forcing Washington and his 400 troops to surrender on the early morning of July 4. He and his men were allowed to return to Virginia with their arms and ammunition.

Shortly after his return, the British government ordered all militia officers commissioned by the colonial government reduced in rank so that none would outrank captains commissioned by the British king. Washington resigned as colonel in October 1754 and returned to Mount Vernon. But the next spring, he volunteered to serve as aide-de-camp to British Major General Edward Braddock, who was planning to attack the French at Fort Duquesne (now Pittsburgh). Although Washington warned Braddock about Indian ambush tactics in frontier fighting, the British Army marched toward the fort as though on parade before the king in London. On July 9, 1755, the French and Indians fell on the British troops with murderous war whoops, and the terrified redcoats broke and ran. Almost a thousand British soldiers were killed and Braddock was fatally wounded. Washington later wrote: "I had four bullets through my coat, and two horses shot under me, yet escaped unhurt, altho' death was levelling my companions on every side!"

With mounting fear of a French and Indian attack on Virginia's western settlements, Governor Dinwiddie appealed to Washington to resume command of the Virginia militia with the rank of colonel. At first Washington rejected the offer, but after persistent urging he agreed. He continued in this command until the end of the war.

Planter and Legislator

IN THE MEANTIME, Washington proposed to and was accepted in marriage by Mrs. Martha Dandridge Custis. But at the same time he apparently was involved with his neighbor's wife, Mrs. Sally Fairfax. A letter to Sally from the frontier in September 1758 reads: "The world has no business to know the object of my love, declared in this manner to you, when I want to conceal it." No reply has ever been found, and the affair remains a mystery. Relations between the Fairfaxes and the Washingtons continued to be cordial, and Washington duly married Martha Custis on January 6, 1759. She brought to the marriage a fortune in land and money as well as two children by her first marriage. The Washingtons never had children of their own.

Meantime, he had been elected to the Virginia House of Burgesses. After a short honeymoon, Martha accompanied him to Williamsburg for the session. In the following years he was regularly re-elected, gaining a fine schooling in representative government.

During these same years, Washington acquired more and more land, traveling deep into the Ohio Valley in 1770 looking for sites to purchase for future development. He rented thousands of acres to tenant farmers, but he devoted his greatest attention to the management of Mount Vernon. He enjoyed experimenting in agriculture, trying new crops, and breeding better livestock, and took pleasure in the social life and recreation of the plantation —the dances, games, fox hunts, and sports.

The Revolutionary War

BECAUSE HE WAS A MILITARY MAN, it was natural that Washington's thoughts turned to the use of force when actions of the British government interfered with the rights of colonists. When the governor of Virginia disbanded the House of Burgesses in 1769 because its members protested the British Stamp

Act, Washington wrote privately to a friend of his conviction that the colonists must "maintain the liberty which we have derived from our ancestors" even if it meant resorting to arms.

As a delegate to the First Continental Congress in Philadelphia in 1774, Washington impressed his colleagues from other colonies with his assurance and wisdom. When Patrick Henry was asked to name the greatest man in the Congress, he replied: ". . . if you speak of solid information and sound judgment, Colonel Washington is unquestionably the greatest man on that floor."

When the Second Continental Congress opened in May 1775, just after Lexington and Concord, the forty-three-year-old Washington wore his bright colonel's uniform to the sessions to dramatize his belief in the necessity of concerted military action by all the colonies. On June 15 the delegates unanimously elected him commander in chief of the armed forces. He accepted with modesty, rejecting any pay for the position, and expressed his willingness to accept only repayment of his expenses.

By July 2, 1775, Washington had taken command of the troops in Massachusetts at headquarters in Cambridge. He organized the siege of the British forces in Boston, despite a serious shortage of ammunition, and succeeded in forcing the British to sail away from Boston in March 1776, leaving the city in the hands of American forces.

Guessing that the British probably would attack New York City in an effort to drive a wedge between the northern and southern colonies, Washington was there to meet them when they landed in force in July. Lack of supplies, undisciplined troops, and inexperienced officers brought defeat, forcing Washington to retreat into New Jersey by November.

Desertions and the refusal of "sunshine patriots" to re-enlist weakened Washington's army to a total of about 5,000 men by December, and many began to fear the war was lost. Hope revived with Washington's brilliant surprise attack on Hessian troops at Trenton the day after Christmas, 1776. He followed this victory with another at Princeton the first week of January 1777.

Washington spent the summer of 1777 anticipating a British land assault on Philadelphia from New York. But the British used their superior naval power to bypass the American army and land troops south of Philadelphia. Washington, hurrying south to oppose them, was defeated at the battle of Brandywine Creek in September, losing Philadelphia to the British. The American cause was strengthened in October when General Horatio Gates won a major victory at Saratoga, New York, capturing the British General John Burgoyne and about 5,000 British troops.

Washington and his men spent the bitterly cold winter of 1777–78 at

Valley Forge, Pennsylvania. Their misery was made doubly hard with the knowledge that the British were wintering in comfort in Philadelphia. Washington's steadfastness to the American cause and his closeness to his men held the army together, even while some of the leaders of Congress were wondering whether he should be replaced. Of his troops, Washington wrote: "Naked and starving as they are, we cannot sufficiently admire the incomparable patience and fidelity of the soldiers."

Good news came in the spring of 1778. The kingdom of France had decided to join in open alliance with the Americans and would send money, troops, and a fleet. When they learned of the French alliance, the British decided to consolidate their position, quitting Philadelphia to march across New Jersey to New York. Washington planned an attack on the British column for June 28 at Monmouth, but the cowardice and insubordination of his second in command, Major General Charles Lee, lost him the opportunity. Lee was found guilty of disobedience by a court-martial and was discharged from the army.

From the summer of 1778 through the summer of 1781, Washington kept the main part of the British Army sealed in New York City. During these years he faced and overcame one discouragement after another as inaction led to grumbling and desertions by his soldiers, while a weak Congress had to be continuously prodded to supply necessary money and supplies. Late in 1780, Washington wrote:

"We have been half of our time without provision, and are likely to continue so. We have no magazines, nor money to form them; and in a little time we shall have no men, if we had money to pay them. We have lived upon expedients till we can live no longer. In a word, the history of the war is a history of false hopes and temporary devices, instead of system and of economy. . . ."

Washington's patience was rewarded in the summer of 1781 when he received word that the French finally were sending the main part of their fleet, thousands of troops, and a substantial loan to aid the Americans. At once he resolved to take the offensive. When word came that a large British force led by Lord Cornwallis had invaded Virginia, Washington and Count Rochambeau, the French commander, marched their combined armies rapidly to Virginia, where they joined smaller forces under the young Marquis de Lafayette and troops from the French fleet that had sealed off Chesapeake Bay. From the end of September to the middle of October, Washington besieged Cornwallis at Yorktown. On October 19, 1781, Washington experienced the greatest triumph of his military career when Cornwallis surrendered his entire army of more than 7,000 men. The blow was decisive.

The fighting was over, although it took nearly two years for a formal peace treaty to be written and signed. In this interlude between war and peace, Washington had many problems with his army, which was again growing disgruntled with the reluctance of Congress to vote adequate reimbursement. One of his colonels, Lewis Nicola, openly advocated in May 1782 that America should become a monarchy with Washington as king. To this proposal Washington reacted in typical fashion:

"With a mixture of great surprise and astonishment, I have read with attention the sentiments you have submitted to my perusal. Be assured, Sir, no occurrence in the course of the war has given me more painful sensations, than your information of there being such ideas existing in the army, as you have expressed, and I must view with abhorrence and reprehend with severity. . . .

"I am much at a loss to conceive what part of my conduct could have given encouragement to an address, which to me seems big with the greatest mischiefs, that can befall my Country. . . . you could not have found a person to whom your schemes are more disagreeable. . . ."

When the officers of the army were on the verge of overthrowing Congress and setting up their own government, Washington called them together in March 1783 and persuaded them that they must have patience. The emotional climax of his talk came when he put on eyeglasses and commented: "Gentlemen, you must pardon me. I have grown gray in your service and now find myself growing blind."

On the day the British fleet sailed out of New York Harbor, December 4, 1783, Washington met with his few remaining officers in Fraunces Tavern, embraced them individually, and left the city at once in his eagerness to return to Mount Vernon. Each city he passed through on his homeward journey made the event a celebration. At Annapolis, Maryland, where Congress then was meeting, he addressed the representatives on December 23, 1783, turning back to them his commission as commander in chief. At the close of his brief talk, he said:

"Having now finished the work assigned me, I retire from the great theater of action, and bidding an affectionate farewell to this august body, under whose orders I have so long acted, I here offer my commission, and take my leave of all the employment of public life."

Helping Redesign the Government

NOW IN HIS EARLY FIFTIES, Washington happily resumed the life of a Virginia planter confident that his days of public service were concluded. But, as the next few years went by, he became more and more concerned with the inability of Congress to solve national problems because of its lack of authority under the Articles of Confederation. News of Shays' Rebellion in Massachusetts increased his fears that the independence he had so long struggled for might be destroyed unless he took a hand in strengthening the national government. In May 1786, he wrote:

"That it is necessary to revise and amend the articles of Confederation, I entertain no doubt; but what may be the consequences of such an attempt is doubtful. Yet something must be done, or the fabric must fall, for it certainly is tottering."

His friends convinced Washington that he must lend his prestige to the Constitutional Convention called in Philadelphia in 1787, so he reluctantly accepted election by the Virginia legislature as a delegate to the meeting. On May 25, the day the convention opened in Philadelphia, Washington was unanimously elected its president. From a chair with a rising sun painted on its back, he presided over the convention throughout the summer, while the debates that raged were as hot as the weather. He never expressed his own views from the chair; but his continued presence, and his privately stated determination that all obstacles could be overcome, became dominant factors in its success.

On the final day of the convention, September 17, 1787, Washington made his only formal request to the delegates. He asked that they adopt an amendment increasing the number of representatives in Congress to provide a broader base for the democracy. The amendment was quickly written and approved. Washington and most of the other delegates then signed the new Constitution.

In the months that followed, Washington waited anxiously at Mount Vernon as the various states argued the question of whether or not to ratify the Constitution. He did not enter the public debate and issued no statements, but he kept in close correspondence with his friends who were taking an active part in the individual ratification conventions. Within nine months New Hampshire became the ninth state to ratify the Constitution, putting the new government into operation.

Washington's First Term

THROUGHOUT THE STATES there was a general assumption that Washington would be the first President under the Constitution. This belief made it easier for the states to accept the idea of a strong national executive, because they were sure that Washington never would abuse the great powers granted to the office. When the first Electoral College met in New York City on

February 4, 1789, Washington was unanimously elected President. He accepted, although "with more diffidence and reluctance than I ever experienced before in my life."

From the day of his inauguration, April 30, 1789, Washington began setting precedents and traditions that were to be followed by each of his successors. The inauguration took place on a balcony at Federal Hall in New York City, then the capital of the United States. When he took the oath of office, administered by Chancellor Robert Livingston of New York, Washington spontaneously added the words "So help me God" and kissed the Bible on which his right hand had rested. After receiving cheers from the crowd that filled the streets and adjacent rooftops, the new President went inside the building, where he delivered a twenty-minute inaugural address to the assembled members of the Senate and the House of Representatives.

In his address he appealed somewhat indirectly to Congress to amend the Constitution with a Bill of Rights, the lack of which had prevented Rhode Island and North Carolina from approving ratification. In this regard he remarked: ". . . a reverence for the characteristic rights of freemen and a regard for the public harmony will sufficiently influence your deliberations on the question how far the former can be impregnably fortified or the latter be safely and advantageously promoted." He also declared that he would accept nothing more than expenses during his term of office.

Shortly after his inauguration, the fifty-seven-year-old President wrote to a friend concerning his feelings of uncertainty in his new position: "I walk, as it were, on untrodden ground, so many untoward circumstances may intervene in such a new and critical situation, that I shall feel an insuperable diffidence in my own abilities."

Washington faced four major problems upon assuming the presidency. These were: (1) organizing the new government and making the many necessary appointments; (2) straightening out the tangled financial affairs of the nation; (3) obtaining better relations with Great Britain; and (4) negotiating treaties of friendship with the Indian tribes on the frontiers. He successfully achieved solutions to each during the course of his administration.

Nearly five months went by before Congress approved all the legislation necessary to set up the main departments of the federal government. Washington placed great reliance in the advice of his department heads, but it was not until his second term that this group began to be called the Cabinet.

In the realm of finance, Secretary of the Treasury Alexander Hamilton worked out a plan approved by Congress in which the national government took over the debts accumulated by the states during the Revolutionary War. In turn, money was borrowed from foreign countries to meet the debts.

In an effort to improve relations with Great Britain, Washington asked

Gouverneur Morris to act as diplomatic representative in London. Washington particularly hoped that Morris could arrange a trade treaty with the British, but this was not accomplished until his second term.

Treaty negotiations with the frontier Indian tribes went on throughout Washington's eight years as President. He insisted on fair treatment of the tribes and won their friendship in return.

Under the leadership of James Madison, then a U.S. representative from Virginia, Congress approved the ten Bill of Rights amendments to the Constitution. After ratification by the states, these amendments became effective in December 1791. Meanwhile, the two states that had held out for more guarantees of freedom joined the Union, North Carolina in November 1789, and Rhode Island in May 1790. Three other states were created during Washington's presidency: Vermont in 1791, Kentucky in 1792, and Tennessee in 1796.

Washington established the presidential veto in April 1792, when for the first time in American history a President turned down legislation passed by Congress. The bill in question was a re-apportionment of Congress based on the census of 1790, which showed that the population of the country was nearly 4,000,000 persons (including close to 700,000 slaves). The measure seemed to give a disproportionate share of new seats in Congress to the northern states, so Washington vetoed it. The House of Representatives failed to override the veto. Several months later new legislation that provided a more equitable apportionment was passed and signed by Washington.

Although Washington believed the President should be a strong leader, he also felt that the three main branches of the government should be as separate as possible. Therefore, he did not personally endeavor to sway Congress to pass legislation that he favored. Instead, he left this to his department heads, particularly Secretary of State Jefferson and Secretary of the Treasury Hamilton.

Because Jefferson represented the agrarian South and Hamilton the commercial North, it was natural that their views were often opposed to each other on important national issues. It distressed Washington to see this division between two men that he admired, and he was deeply concerned that the political parties they fostered were likely to divide the country. Hamilton and his supporters promoted the Federalist party, while Jefferson and his followers became known as Anti-Federalists or Democratic-Republicans.

Washington's Second Term

ALTHOUGH WASHINGTON had planned to retire at the end of his first term and had even begun to prepare his Farewell Address as early as 1792, he bowed to demands that he accept four more years as President. Jefferson told him, "North and South will hang together if they have you to hang on." He was again elected unanimously when the Electoral College met on February 13, 1793, in Philadelphia, to which the national capital had been transferred in 1790.

Washington's second term was vastly different from his first. He felt betrayed when his two closest advisers resigned from his Cabinet—Jefferson in the summer of 1793 and Hamilton early in 1795. Political invective began to be directed at Washington himself by the Democratic-Republican newspapers—sniping criticisms that wounded him deeply, partly because he had grown so used to universal adulation. The excitement of forming the new government was over, and he found it increasingly difficult to find good men to replace those who retired.

In the area of foreign relations, Washington's task was made exceedingly difficult by the general war in Europe, in which Great Britain and the other monarchies fought against the new French republic. Washington proclaimed a policy of "strict neutrality" that was opposed by Jefferson and the Democratic-Republicans who favored aid to the French revolutionaries. Criticism of Washington by the Democratic-Republicans reached a peak in 1795 when he signed the Jay Treaty, a trade agreement with Great Britain that had been negotiated by Chief Justice John Jay. Washington had been strongly influenced to sign the treaty when documents came into his hands that indicated Secretary of State Edmund Randolph had been bribed by the French to speak against the treaty. Randolph denied he had been in the pay of France, but he resigned from the Cabinet.

On the domestic scene, the greatest crisis of Washington's second term was the Whisky Rebellion in Pennsylvania. In the summer of 1794 riots broke out in western Pennsylvania when farmers refused to pay federal excise taxes on the whisky they distilled from their grain. The whisky provided the largest share of their income, and they felt that the federal government had no right to collect taxes on it. To prove that the federal government could enforce its power of taxation, Washington called up 15,000 militia and went with them to Pennsylvania. The leaders of the revolt were arrested and the rebellion ended.

The last year of Washington's administration was relatively quiet and uneventful. Economic conditions improved as a result of the trade stimulated by the Jay Treaty. Attacks on Washington by the Democratic-Republicans diminished both in violence and in frequency. Efforts were underway to persuade him to accept a third term, but he published his eloquent Farewell Address on September 19, 1796, ending talk of his candidacy and setting the important two-term precedent.

Washington's Last Years

AFTER TURNING THE PRESIDENCY over to John Adams in March 1797, Washington and his wife set off for Mount Vernon as quickly as they could. He wrote of his retirement in May 1797:

"To make and sell a little flour annually, to repair houses (going fast to ruin), to build one for the security of my papers of a public nature, and to amuse myself in agricultural and rural pursuits, will constitute employment for the few years I have to remain on this terrestrial globe. If . . . I could now and then meet the friends I esteem, it would fill the measure and add zest to my enjoyments; but, if ever this happens, it must be under my own vine and fig-tree. . . ."

But Washington was not to be left in the peaceful retirement he had contemplated. In 1798 war threatened with France. As the nation prepared to defend itself, President Adams asked Washington to accept a new commission as lieutenant general and take command of the new United States Army to be raised. For the next several months he was busy helping choose the generals and other officers for the army. Then, in 1799, the French crisis subsided, and Washington once more relaxed into plantation life. Nearly two centuries later, in 1978, the U. S. Army promoted Washington to the rank of General of the Armies of the United States so that he would be the senior general officer on army rolls.

On the snowy morning of December 14, 1799, he awoke with a throat so sore that he could hardly speak. He had noticed the sore throat the day before, but thought it would quickly pass. Doctors came and employed the traditional remedy of bleeding. Washington quickly grew weaker, and at about 10 P.M. he died. Four days later his body was buried in the family vault at Mount Vernon.

Memorial services were held in scores of towns and cities. On the day after Christmas, one of the most elaborate ceremonies took place in the nation's capital, Philadelphia, where one of Washington's former officers, Henry

"Light Horse Harry" Lee, gave the eulogy that contained the famous description of Washington:

"First in war, first in peace and first in the hearts of his countrymen, he was second to none . . ."

John Adams

The Second President of the United States
1797–1801

1735 (October 30) Born in Braintree (now Quincy), Massachusetts.

1755 Graduated from Harvard College.

1758 Started practicing law.

1764 (October 25) Married Abigail Smith.

1774–77 Attended Continental Congress as delegate from Massachusetts.

1779 Wrote constitution for state of Massachusetts.

1778–88 U.S. diplomat in Europe.

1789–97 First Vice President of the United States.

1797–1801 Second President of the United States.

1826 (July 4) Died in Quincy, Massachusetts.

Because he lived in an age of very great men, John Adams, despite extraordinary accomplishments, stood second in almost everything he did. As a patriot in Massachusetts in the days before the Revolutionary War, he was overshadowed by his fiery cousin, Sam Adams. In the Continental Congress when he was assigned to the committee to write the Declaration of Independence, he had to bow to Thomas Jefferson's greater literary ability. As a diplomat in Europe during the Revolutionary War, he was outshone by Benjamin Franklin. And, finally, as the first Vice President and second President of the United States, he worked in the shadow of George Washington.

A scholar and proficient writer in the theory of government, Adams brought to the presidency a greater knowledge of political science than any other President, with the possible exception of Woodrow Wilson. He regarded himself as a strong President but was handicapped by his obligation to carry on his predecessor's Cabinet, a group of men who not only were not devoted to him, but actually worked to defeat him in his bid for re-election.

Adams' most important accomplishment as President was his avoidance of war with France. But, in preserving peace, he broke with his own party's policy, causing a rupture that destroyed his career.

A short, plump New Englander, Adams believed in plain clothes and plain talk. He tried to do what he believed was right for his country, rather than what was politically expedient. His blunt frankness sometimes lost him friends, but he was respected for his honesty even by his political enemies. His diaries and letters are livelier and more entertaining than was his personality, which often was rude and irascible.

An Adams of Massachusetts

A FIFTH-GENERATION AMERICAN, John Adams was born the son of a farmer and part-time cobbler on October 30, 1735 (October 19 by the Old Style Calendar). The small frame house where he was born still stands in Quincy (then Braintree), Massachusetts.

His father was a Harvard graduate who believed in education, and John entered Harvard at the age of sixteen. He was regarded as one of the best students in his class of twenty-four, but was ranked fourteenth in the class according to his social position.

After graduation, Adams taught school for a year in Worcester, Massachusetts, and then decided to become a lawyer. He studied for two years in the office of a Worcester attorney, James Putnam, and in October 1758 was admitted to the bar. Shortly after, he began law practice in Braintree.

While still a struggling small-town lawyer of twenty-nine, he married Abigail Smith, the daughter of a clergyman. Ten years his junior, Abigail matched Adams in wit and love of books. In later years when they were often separated for long periods by his public duties, she kept him informed of happenings at home in clever, perceptive letters that are a treasure house to historians. John and Abby, as he called her, had five children; their eldest son, John Quincy Adams, became the sixth President of the United States.

Lawyer, Legislator, and Patriot

WHEN THE BRITISH PARLIAMENT passed the Stamp Act in 1765, John and his older cousin Sam Adams took active roles in urging opposition to it. Sam Adams helped organize the Sons of Liberty, a patriotic organization that stirred up mob action against the British, while John Adams prepared resolutions against the tax that were approved by Braintree and other Massachusetts towns. John also wrote a series of anonymous articles in the Boston *Gazette* urging the people to defend America's liberties.

In 1766 Adams moved his family to Boston in order to improve his law practice. His most famous case came with the defense of a British captain and eight soldiers who fired into a mob in the Boston Massacre of March 5, 1770. In taking the case, Adams realized that it might lose him popularity; but he felt strongly that the British authorities who had stationed the troops in Boston were more guilty of the murder of Boston citizens than the soldiers who actually fired the shots. Adams and his associate, Josiah Quincy, succeeded in winning the acquittal of the British captain and six of his soldiers. Two were convicted of the lesser charge of manslaughter. Although many Boston patriots, including Sam Adams, denounced John for defending the British soldiers, he also won wide respect for the sense of justice that had led him to take the case. He was elected late in 1770 to the Massachusetts legislature, the General Court.

John Adams did not happen to be in Boston on the night of December 16, 1773, when Sam Adams helped organize the Boston Tea Party, protesting a British tax on tea; but he rejoiced in the action, noting in his diary: "This destruction of the tea is so bold, so daring, so firm, intrepid and inflexible, and it must have so important consequences, and so lasting, that I can't but consider it as an epoch in history!" Subsequent events bore him out, for the British soon retaliated by closing the port of Boston, which in turn led to the convening of the first Continental Congress in Philadelphia in 1774.

Apostle of Independence

BOTH JOHN AND SAM ADAMS were elected as delegates from Massachusetts to the Continental Congress. Both were eager to unite the colonies to fight Great Britain, but they soon learned at the convention that many delegates from other colonies were too conservative to support strong measures. They had to be satisfied with such mild actions as an appeal to the British king to grant the colonies the right to determine their own taxation and the creation of an association to boycott trade with Great Britain. John Adams vented his irritation by writing in his diary:

"In Congress, nibbling and quibbling as usual. There is no greater mortification than to sit with a half a dozen wits, deliberating upon a petition, address or memorial. These great wits, these subtle critics, these refined geniuses, these learned lawyers, these wise statesmen, are so fond of showing their parts and powers, as to make their consultations very tedious."

After returning home from the Congress, Adams contributed articles to the Boston *Gazette,* over the signature *Novanglus* (New England), in which he detailed the legal position of the American patriots in their controversy with Britain. But the articles were interrupted by the battles of Lexington and Concord.

At the second Continental Congress in May 1775, Adams expected the other delegates to be as fired with zeal for independence as he was; but days dragged into weeks as the Congress talked and did little. Fearing that an irreparable split was developing between North and South that might leave Massachusetts to fight alone, Adams thought of a solution that might anger some New England generals but would help unite the country. On June 14 he nominated a Virginia militia colonel, George Washington, to be commander in chief of an army to be formed with troops from all the colonies. Sam Adams enthusiastically seconded the nomination. The next day the delegates unanimously elected Washington to the post, and the fighting became the American Revolution instead of the Massachusetts Rebellion.

For the next several years Adams worked tirelessly in Congress, noting in his diary that he "unquestionably did more business than any other member of the house." Throughout 1775 and into the spring of 1776, he was particularly concerned with efforts to get the Congress to declare independence from Great Britain. Finally, in June, while Washington's troops were preparing to defend New York City from an imminent British invasion, Congress elected a committee, with Adams as a member, to write the Declaration of Independence. Although Adams was noted for his writing, he deferred the authorship of the Declaration to Thomas Jefferson, later giving his reasons in his *Autobiography:* "(1) that he was a Virginian and I a Massachusettensian. (2) that he was a Southern Man and I a northern one. (3) that I had been so obnoxious for my early and constant Zeal in promoting the Measure, that any draught of mine, would undergo a more severe Scrutiny and Criticism in Congress, than one of his composition. 4thly and lastly, and that would be reason enough if there were no other. I had a great opinion of the Elegance of his pen, and none at all of my own."

But when the time came in the first week in July for the final debate on whether the colonies would declare themselves independent, Adams stepped to the fore to lead the argument for freedom, speaking—as Jefferson later described—"with a power of thought and expression that moved us from our seats." When the Congress finally did vote for independence, with only New York abstaining, Adams wrote jubilantly to his wife that the event "ought to be solemnized with pomp and parade, with shows, games, sports, guns, bells, bonfires, and illuminations, from one end of this continent to the other, from this time forward, forevermore."

In Adams' last year in Congress, 1777, he presented the resolution establishing the United States flag with thirteen red and white stripes and a union of thirteen white stars on a blue field "representing a new constellation."

Diplomat in Europe

ALTHOUGH MORE NOTED for his bluntness than his diplomacy, Adams was appointed by Congress as one of its commissioners to France to try to negotiate military and monetary aid. He arrived in Paris in 1778 to discover that a treaty already had been negotiated by Benjamin Franklin. While awaiting a decision from Congress on his next assignment, he remained in France for about a year with few other duties than sightseeing with his ten-year-old son, John Quincy Adams, who had accompanied him.

Returning home for a few months in 1779, he did most of the work in writing a new state constitution for Massachusetts, sections of which were widely copied by other states; then he returned to France in 1780 as one of the commissioners to negotiate a peace treaty with Great Britain. Because the British were not yet ready to talk about peace, Adams spent most of the next two years in the Netherlands, where he persuaded the Dutch to recognize and loan money to the United States. Late in 1782 he took part in discussions with the British that resulted in the peace treaty ending the Revolutionary War, but Benjamin Franklin won most of the credit for the agreement.

Adams remained in Europe until 1788, spending the last three years as minister to Great Britain, where he was received with cool politeness and a rebuff to all his efforts toward obtaining a trade treaty. During this period Adams helped fill his time by writing an erudite three-volume work of political science entitled *The Defence of the Constitutions of Government of the United States of America.* He sailed back to the United States in the spring of 1788.

Vice President Under Washington

As THE STATES PREPARED for the first presidential election under the new Constitution, it was clear that no one but George Washington had any chance of being named to the nation's highest office, so Adams' friends pushed him as a vice-presidential candidate to represent the North. Under the Constitutional provision as it then stood, each elector cast two votes. When the Electoral College met in February 1789, all sixty-nine electors named Washington. Second choices were numerous, and Adams barely squeaked into office with thirty-four of the sixty-nine votes cast.

In performing his official duties as presiding officer of the new United States Senate, Adams took part in discussions and tried to guide the deliberations of the body. His ten years abroad in the capitals of kings had led him to respect pomp and protocol, but his efforts to introduce in the new government what he regarded as a proper ceremoniousness merely won him an undeserved reputation as a monarchist. "My office," he wrote, "requires rather severe duty, and it is a kind of duty which, if I do not flatter myself too much, is not quite adapted to my character—I mean it is too inactive and mechanical." Adams used his tie-breaking vote in the Senate to support the President and to strengthen the powers of the presidency, most notably the presidential right to remove from office appointees who had been confirmed by the Senate.

Somewhat bored by the vice presidency, which he described as "the most insignificant office that ever the invention of man contrived or his imagination conceived," Adams again turned to writing, publishing a number of articles called *Discourses on Davila*, which upheld the advantages of the United States governmental structure as opposed to that set up in France by the French Revolutionists. These articles offended Thomas Jefferson, an enthusiastic supporter of the French Revolution, and led to a break in friendship between the two patriots.

By the time of the second presidential election, the country was clearly divided into two political parties, the Federalists and the Democratic-Republicans, or Anti-Federalists. The Democratic-Republicans, recognizing that it was impossible to overcome Washington's prestige, concentrated their fire on Adams in an effort to defeat his bid for a second term as Vice President. The opposition ridiculed Adams' rotund figure and excoriated him for his supposed monarchial views; but when the electoral votes were tallied in February 1793, Adams won easily with seventy-seven votes to fifty for the opposition candidate, Governor George Clinton of New York.

Throughout his second term as Vice President, Adams stood solidly in support of President Washington, particularly as the attacks of the Democratic-Republicans increased in fury with ratification by the Senate of the Jay Treaty with Great Britain.

The publication of Washington's Farewell Address in September 1796 set off the first real contest in American history for the nation's highest office. As Washington's heir-apparent, Adams was accepted at once by the Federalists as their candidate, while the Democratic-Republicans pressed the candidacy of Jefferson. Neither candidate took an active part in the campaign, in which the Democratic-Republicans accused Adams of desiring to set up a hereditary monarchy in the United States and the Federalists denounced Jefferson as an advocate of overthrowing the Constitution. Adams was particularly angered when his cousin Sam Adams, now governor of Massachusetts, opposed his candidacy and supported Jefferson. Even after the presidential electors were chosen, the election remained in doubt. At this date the custom of electors voting for their party's candidate was not yet an ironclad tradition. Alexander Hamilton, the acknowledged leader of the Federalist party, plotted to get certain electors to switch their votes in an effort to win the presidency for the more tractable Thomas Pinckney, the Federalist candidate for Vice President. The maneuver almost lost the election for the Federalists. The count of the electoral vote gave Adams the presidency by the narrow margin of three votes—seventy-one for Adams to sixty-eight for Jefferson.

Second President of the United States

WHEN THE SIXTY-ONE-YEAR-OLD ADAMS was sworn in as President in Philadelphia on March 4, 1797, the ceremony notified the world that the republican form of government had successfully carried out a peaceful and orderly change in Chief Executives. Most of the crowd's cheers were for Washington. Because Abigail Adams had been unable to get to Philadelphia for the inauguration, John wrote to her describing it, commenting that Washington "seemed to enjoy a triumph over me. Methought I heard him say, 'Ay! I am fairly out and you fairly in! See which of us will be the happiest!' "

Adams carried over into his administration all the members of Washington's Cabinet—a grave mistake because these men were not of his choosing nor he of theirs, and behind his back they wrote to Alexander Hamilton for guidance on the nation's affairs. Not until after the death of Washington in 1799 did Adams feel free to rid himself of them.

More seriously yet, from the moment he assumed office he was confronted with a crisis in relations with France that dominated his entire administration. The leaders of the French Revolution wanted the United States to join them in their war with Great Britain. They imperiously refused to recognize the American diplomats sent to them and threatened to hang any American seamen they captured on British ships. Adams called a special session of Congress in May and in a ringing address asserted his intent to prove that the United States would not permit itself to be "humiliated under a colonial spirit of fear and a sense of inferiority." He called for the support of Congress in preparation for national defense.

Early in 1798, Adams received dispatches from the new commissioners he had sent to France revealing that agents of the French government, referred to simply as X, Y, and Z, had demanded a bribe before the American envoys would be received by the foreign minister, Talleyrand. At first inclined to call for a declaration of war, Adams restrained himself, keeping the dispatches secret, and asking Congress instead to revoke Washington's policy of neutrality only enough to permit American merchant ships to arm themselves. When his request was met with violent opposition by the Democratic-Republicans, Adams made the dispatches of the XYZ affair public. The country soon took up the cry, "Millions for defense, but not one cent for tribute."

Preparations for war moved ahead rapidly. Adams called Washington back to active duty as commander in chief of a new United States Army, and, at Washington's insistence, appointed Alexander Hamilton as second in command. When Congress established a Department of the Navy, Adams named Benjamin Stoddert as the first Secretary of the Navy. The frigates *United States, Constitution,* and *Constellation* were the first warships of a new United States Navy that grew to a fleet of forty-nine vessels by 1799.

As part of the war scare, the Federalist-controlled Congress in 1798 passed the Alien and Sedition Acts that gave the government unusual powers to imprison aliens and citizens who threatened or opposed the federal government. These acts were used by the Adams administration to shut down opposition newspapers and silence opponents in a manner that threatened the Bill of Rights.

Dropping a bombshell on both his Federalist supporters and his Democratic-Republican opponents, Adams proposed early in 1799 a new attempt to establish diplomatic relations with France. When Federalist senators told him they would refuse to go along with the plan, Adams threatened to resign and leave the presidency in the hands of Vice President Jefferson. In the end, three commissioners were dispatched to France, and the threat of war abated.

As the presidential election of 1800 approached, the Federalist party was split over Adams' actions in avoiding war with France. Hamilton, who had become commander in chief of the U. S. Army after Washington's death, had fancied that he would attain military glory in such a war. Now he sabotaged Adams' chances for re-election by circulating a letter to party leaders declaring that Adams was unfit to continue in office and utilizing secret information about Adams' actions that he had obtained from the treacherous members of the Cabinet. Not surprisingly, Adams was defeated by Jefferson and his running mate, Aaron Burr, who each won seventy-three electoral votes to Adams' sixty-five.

The last few months of Adams' administration were conducted from Washington, D.C., the new federal capital. The Executive Mansion, designed by Irish-born architect James Hoban, was still unfinished, but Adams moved into it on November 1, 1800. A few days later Adams was defeated in his bid for a second term as President. Then he spent several unpleasant months waiting for the House of Representatives to decide whether Jefferson or Burr would succeed him.

Almost alone in the gray sandstone structure, not yet called the White House, Adams wrote to his wife, expressing the prayer that nearly a century and a half later came to be carved on the mantel in the State Dining Room: "I pray to Heaven to bestow the best of Blessings on this House and all that shall hereafter inhabit it . . . May none but honest and wise men ever rule under this roof."

Before his administration ended, Adams had the satisfaction of receiving a peace agreement with France and seeing it approved by the Senate.

On the last night of his presidency, Adams spent some time signing the commissions of a number of eleventh-hour appointments of federal judges, and then early next morning left Washington for his home in Massachusetts. Historians are not sure whether he refused to attend Jefferson's inauguration from bitterness, or whether he simply had not been invited to the ceremony.

Although toothless, palsied, and old beyond his sixty-five years, Adams lived another quarter of a century, attaining the greatest age of any man who ever has served as President—ninety years and eight months. A year before his death Adams was overjoyed at having his son, John Quincy Adams, become the nation's sixth President. After Jefferson's retirement from the presidency, he and Adams resumed a cordial correspondence, and on his deathbed Adams' last words were of his old friend: "Thomas Jefferson still survives." But by an extraordinary quirk of fate, Jefferson died the same day, July 4, 1826—the fiftieth anniversary of the Declaration of Independence for which they had both struggled so hard.

Thomas Jefferson
The Third President of the United States
1801–9

1743 (April 13) Born at Shadwell in Albemarle County, Virginia.

1762 Graduated from College of William and Mary.

1767 Began practicing law.

1769–79 Served in Virginia legislature.

1772 (January 1) married Martha Wayles Skelton.

1775–76 Member of Virginia's delegation to Congress; wrote Declaration of Independence.

1779–81 Governor of Virginia.

1783–84 Member of Virginia's delegation to Congress.

1784–85 Diplomatic commissioner of Congress in Europe.

1785–89 U.S. diplomatic minister to France.

1789–93 Secretary of State under George Washington.

1797–1801 Vice President under John Adams.

1801–9 Third President of the United States.

1816–25 Founder and first rector of the University of Virginia.

1826 (July 4) Died at Monticello in Albemarle County, Virginia.

I have sworn upon the altar of God eternal hostility against every form of tyranny over the mind of man."

This quotation from Thomas Jefferson, carved on his memorial in Washington, D.C., epitomizes the philosophy to which he dedicated his life, his mind, and his eloquent pen.

Master of any talent or profession to which he turned his hand, the redhaired Jefferson won undying fame at the age of thirty-three as author of the Declaration of Independence. His public service spanned forty years as a legislator, governor, congressman, diplomat, Secretary of State, Vice President, President, and university founder; but he also found time to achieve success as a lawyer, farmer, philosopher, writer, architect, scientist, musician, and inventor.

Denounced as a radical and an atheist by his conservative political opponents, Jefferson became the first leader of an opposition political party to wrest control of the national government from the party in power. Despite grim prophecies by the outgoing Federalists that the Constitution would be overthrown by Jefferson's Democratic-Republicans, he proved to the world the strength and staying power of the American republic and its democratic system under a changing political philosophy. Jefferson believed that the United States should remain an agricultural country of small farms with a national government that interfered as little as possible in the lives of its people; but as President he, in his own words, "stretched the Constitution till it cracked," in using the presidential treaty-making powers to double the size of the nation with the Louisiana Purchase. He established the right of an incoming President to discharge major political appointees of his predecessor, but was restrained by Chief Justice John Marshall from applying the same principle to federal judges.

Jefferson believed his presidential accomplishments were among the least of his contributions. This was evidenced by his epitaph; he asked that "not a word more" than the following be engraved on his monument at Monticello:

Here was buried
Thomas Jefferson
Author of the Declaration of American Independence,
Of the Statute of Virginia for Religious Freedom,
And Father of the University of Virginia.

A Virginia Plantation Owner

THE SON OF PETER JEFFERSON, a planter and surveyor, Thomas Jefferson was the third child in a family of ten. His mother, Jane, was a member of the Randolph family, one of the oldest and most distinguished in Virginia. He was born at his father's farm, Shadwell, in Albemarle County, Virginia, on April 13, 1743 (April 2 by the Old Style Calendar).

Jefferson, as a boy, took easily to learning. He knew Latin and Greek by the age of fourteen, when his father died, leaving him, as the eldest son, the head of the family with an estate of about 2,500 acres and thirty slaves. Two years later he enrolled at the College of William and Mary in Williamsburg.

While attending William and Mary, young Jefferson was stimulated by the hustle, bustle, and culture of the Virginia capital. He became a friend of Governor Francis Fauquier and of two scholars: William Small, professor of mathematics at the college, and George Wythe, a learned lawyer and judge. Jefferson played violin with a chamber music group organized by the governor, and was treated as an equal at intimate dinners with the three older men, later writing that "at these dinners I have heard more good sense, more rational and philosophical conversations, than in all my life besides."

After graduation from William and Mary in 1762, the nineteen-year-old Jefferson took up the study of law, which he continued for five years under Wythe's direction, until being admitted to the Virginia bar in 1767. Often attending sessions of Virginia's House of Burgesses, Jefferson became acquainted with the great Virginia lawmakers of the day, including Patrick Henry. He was particularly impressed with Henry's famous "Give Me Liberty" speech denouncing the British Stamp Act in 1765, saying that Henry's forensic talents were "such as I have never heard from any other man."

All was not seriousness and study for the redheaded young bachelor. Much of his time was occupied with romance, fox hunts, shooting matches, violin-playing, and theater-going. To a friend who wrote suggesting that he marry, he replied: "No, thank ye; I will consider of it first. Many and great are the comforts of a single state."

But like many young bachelors, Jefferson presently changed his mind. In 1772 he married a well-to-do widow, Martha Wayles Skelton, whose fortune practically doubled Jefferson's already sizable estate. His birthplace, Shadwell, had burned down two years earlier, and he had begun building his handsome mansion, Monticello. While awaiting its completion the young couple moved into a one-room cottage. The marriage was a congenial one, but darkened by the loss of four of the six children born in the next ten years, and tragically ended in 1782 by Martha's own death. Jefferson never remarried.

In 1769, when he was only twenty-six, he had already entered politics, winning election to the Virginia colonial legislature. For the next ten years he was regularly re-elected, adding steadily to a reputation for patriotic views and a skill in expressing them in writing.

In 1773 he was appointed by the Virginia legislature as a member of the Committee of Correspondence to keep in touch with patriotic leaders in the other colonies. When the governor of Virginia dissolved the colonial legislature because of its patriotic activities, Jefferson wrote a strongly worded pamphlet for a Virginia convention of legislators called to meet in August 1774. Entitled *A Summary View of the Rights of British America, Set Forth in some Resolutions Intended for the Inspection of the Present Delegates of the People of Virginia, now in Convention,* it won fame for its author as "Mr. Jefferson's Bill of Rights."

The Declaration of Independence

BARELY TWO YEARS LATER the gifted pen of the tall young Virginian was drafted for the most important piece of writing in American history. The Continental Congress, which had gathered in Philadelphia in 1775 to the sound of the guns of Lexington and Concord, had moved steadily toward a final break with the British monarchy. A five-man committee, including Roger Sherman, Robert Livingston, Benjamin Franklin, John Adams, and Thomas Jefferson, was chosen to write a suitable "Declaration of Independence" from the crown.

His older colleagues, although noted for their literary skill, promptly deferred to Jefferson, possibly feeling that if written by a Southerner it more likely would be approved by Congress. Seating himself at the portable writing desk he himself had invented, Jefferson "turned to neither book nor pamphlet" for inspiration. From its stirring opening, "When in the course of human events," to its end, the Declaration bears the stamp of a remarkable originality. The three-day debate and extensive editing that followed its presentation irritated the author, but in the end the most important of his ringing words survived. They were finally approved on July 4, making "Life, Liberty and the pursuit of Happiness" a lasting proclamation of the rights of man.

Less than two months later Jefferson resigned to return to Virginia and take his seat in the state legislature. It was supremely important to him that the new laws of his state provide adequate safeguards for the rights of its citizens. As he explained it: "I knew that our legislation under the regal government had many very vicious points which urgently required reformation, and I thought I could be of more use in forwarding that work."

Within a week after returning to Virginia, Jefferson drew up legislation establishing a new system of state courts. Next, he introduced bills to abolish entail and primogeniture, the feudal hereditary restrictions on property. Although himself a slave-owner, he endeavored to abolish slavery, but succeeded only in outlawing further importation of slaves. Tirelessly writing bill after bill, he drew up plans for a system of free public schools, a state library, and many other measures, some of which were not adopted by the legislature until years later.

But Jefferson regarded his greatest accomplishment during this time to be the establishment of religious freedom in Virginia. The Church of England had always been the state church of the colony, established as such in the original land grant to Sir Walter Raleigh; and expenses had been paid by taxation of both members and non-members. Jefferson fought for three years, from 1776 to 1779, to disestablish the church, taking part, in his own words, in "the severest contests in which I have ever been engaged." The statute for religious freedom that he wrote said in part: ". . . no man shall be compelled to frequent or support any religious worship, place or ministry whatsoever, nor shall be enforced, restrained, molested or burdened in his body or goods, nor shall otherwise suffer, on account of his religious opinions or beliefs; but that all men shall be free to profess and by arguments to maintain their opinions in matters of religion, and that the same shall in no wise diminish, enlarge or affect their civil capacities." This Virginia statute later became the basis for the First Amendment to the Constitution.

At thirty-six, Jefferson was elected by the legislature to succeed Patrick Henry as governor of the state. He served for two years, from 1779 to 1781, during the most desperate period of the Revolutionary War in Virginia, when British forces under Lord Cornwallis ravaged the countryside, plundering, looting, and killing. Jefferson himself barely escaped capture at Monticello, where the British burned his barns, ate his livestock, and carried off his slaves.

Most of Jefferson's energies as governor were devoted to raising troops and supplies for Washington's Continental Army, while at the same time trying to organize the defense of Virginia. During this time he wrote: "The nakedness of the militia on service near Williamsburg and want of shoes is such as to have produced murmurings almost amounting to mutinies . . ." Jefferson declined re-election, recommending that the legislature choose a soldier, General Thomas Nelson, to replace him.

Temporarily retiring from public service, he devoted considerable time to writing *Notes on Virginia*, a book on natural history that won him a reputation in Europe as a scholar and scientist. For the French edition of his book he drew a new map of Virginia.

The death of his wife in 1782 threw Jefferson into such desolation that his family feared he might never recover. He destroyed all the letters they had written each other, and for weeks remained in what he later described as a "stupor of mind which had rendered me as dead to the world as she was whose loss occasioned it."

Congressman and Diplomat

RETURNING TO PUBLIC LIFE IN 1783, with his election to Congress by the state legislature, Jefferson again began to utilize the great resources of his mind for his country's benefit. He served as chairman of the committee handling the peace treaty with Great Britain and recommended ratification. He invented the decimal system of coinage adopted by the national government. He also wrote a bill for organizing the Northwest Territory which was later largely adopted. The bill prohibited slavery in the future new states (Michigan, Ohio, Indiana, Illinois, Wisconsin). Jefferson sought to bar slavery from *all* future new states, a measure which, had it been passed, might have prevented the Civil War. This sweeping proposal was defeated by one vote. Jefferson, who was keenly disappointed, wrote:

"The voice of a single individual . . . would have prevented this abominable crime from spreading itself over the new country. Thus we see the fate of millions unborn hanging on the tongue of one man, and Heaven was silent in that awful moment! But it is to be hoped that it will not always be silent, and that the friends to the rights of human nature will in the end prevail."

Deploring the national government's weakness under the Articles of Confederation, Jefferson wrote to George Washington in 1784: "The crippled state of Congress is not new to you. We have only nine states present, eight of whom are represented by two members each, and of course on all great questions not only a unanimity of states but of members is necessary—a unanimity which can never be obtained on a matter of any importance. The consequence is that we are wasting our time and labor in vain efforts to do business."

In July 1784, Jefferson sailed to Europe as a special envoy of Congress, remaining there for the next five years. He first joined Benjamin Franklin and John Adams in negotiating trade treaties for the new United States government and afterward became United States minister to France.

"Behold me at length on the vaunted scene of Europe!" Jefferson wrote exuberantly. He enjoyed the culture of France and traveled extensively on the

Continent, visiting John Adams, United States minister to Great Britain, in London. He was presented to King George, against whom the Declaration of Independence had been directed scarcely a decade earlier, and about whom he did not alter his views on this occasion, describing him afterward as a "mulish being" with a "narrow mind."

Jefferson was intrigued with the invention of phosphorus matches and with the experiments he observed in the use of balloons to carry men. He also noted the first use of mass production methods by the French in 1785, the making of muskets with parts that were interchangeable from one gun to another. He himself invented a small hand-printing press, and drew the designs for the new Virginia capitol to be built in Richmond.

Because he was in Europe, Jefferson took no part in the writing of the new United States Constitution, but he welcomed the reorganization of the government, writing: "I approved, from the first moment, of the great mass of what is in the new Constitution." But he was dismayed by the absence of a Bill of Rights guaranteeing the freedoms of the people, and disapproved the provision that permitted a President to be re-elected, fearing it could lead to monarchy. His views on the Bill of Rights later prevailed when the first ten amendments were added to the Constitution.

Living in Paris during the early stages of the French Revolution, Jefferson heartily endorsed its democratic principles and followed its progress with hope. "I was much acquainted with the leading patriots of the Assembly," he wrote. "Being from a country which had successfully passed through a similar reformation, they were disposed to my acquaintance, and had some confidence in me." He was present at the first clash between a French mob and troops of the king on July 11, 1789, and closely followed the events that led to the storming of the Bastille three days later. By the time he left France to return home in the autumn of 1789, Jefferson had acquired a fondness for the French people that was to influence his judgment in international relations for the rest of his life.

Secretary of State

ON HIS RETURN TRIP, Jefferson received a letter from President Washington asking him to serve as first Secretary of State under the Constitution. He accepted the appointment in December 1789, and arrived in New York, then the national capital, in March of 1790. The political atmosphere of the capital discouraged him. He later wrote: "Here, certainly, I found a state of things which, of all I had ever contemplated, I the least expected. I had left France in the first year of her revolution, in the fervor of natural rights and zeal for reformation. . . . But I cannot describe the wonder and mortification with which the table conversations in New York filled me. Politics were the chief topic, and a preference of kingly over republican government was evidently the favorite sentiment. . . . I found myself for the most part the only advocate on the republican side of the question."

Shortly after joining Washington's administration, Jefferson took part in a "deal" with Alexander Hamilton in which he later claimed that he was "duped" and "made to hold the candle." Hamilton's plan that the national government should assume the war debts of the states had been defeated by a close vote in the House of Representatives, so the Secretary of the Treasury came to Jefferson and asked his aid in switching the votes of some of the southern congressmen. Jefferson agreed to assist on the condition that Hamilton would help him win congressional approval of a plan to move the national capital to Philadelphia temporarily, and then to Georgetown, Virginia, permanently. With Jefferson and Hamilton in accord, both measures passed.

But Jefferson soon fell out with Hamilton, when the latter proposed and won approval of a Bank of the United States, which Jefferson believed was an evil instrument of power not authorized by the Constitution. Because Hamilton spoke favorably of the British system of government, Jefferson concluded that Hamilton "was not only a monarchist but for a monarchy bottomed on corruption." Jefferson became the acknowledged leader of the Democratic-Republican party and Hamilton the leader of the Federalist party, the members of which Jefferson described as "monarchists in principle" and a "mercenary phalanx."

As Secretary of State, Jefferson was occupied with moving the infant nation's foreign policy along a path in which it would not be endangered by the power politics of Great Britain, France, or Spain, and sought to establish peaceful relations with the Indians on the southern and western frontiers. At the same time he continued to pursue his many other interests. In 1791 he took time off for a trip to Lake George in New York with his friend James Madison, communing with nature, fishing, and collecting botanical specimens. He helped plan the new federal city that was to become Washington, D.C., insisting on streets at least 100 feet wide and suggesting that eight-acre parks be located every 200 yards along the avenues. He corresponded with Eli Whitney about buying one of the inventor's new cotton gins for Monticello. And he drew up a plan for a decimal system of weights and measures that he tried to have ratified in Congress.

When news came in March 1793 that the French had guillotined the king and had established a republic, Jefferson commented that "should the present foment in Europe not produce republics everywhere, it will at least soften the monarchical governments by rendering monarchs amenable to punishment like other criminals." With American recognition of the new French Republic, an important precedent was set: the American government would deal with any new government based on the will of its people. In this regard, he wrote to Gouverneur Morris, the American representative in Paris, "We surely cannot deny to any nation that right whereon our own government is founded, that every one may govern itself according to whatever form it pleases, and change these forms at its own will."

When Great Britain and the other monarchies of Europe went to war with the new French Republic, Jefferson felt that the United States should aid France in accordance with the treaty signed between the two countries during the American Revolution. However, Washington, at Hamilton's urging, decided that because the treaty had been made with the royal government of France it no longer was binding. Jefferson reluctantly went along with Washington's decision to proclaim the neutrality of the United States, but noted in the discussions that led to this decision, "Hamilton and myself were daily pitted in the Cabinet like two cocks."

After the French sent Citizen Edmond Genet as their ambassador to the United States, Jefferson was further embarrassed in his efforts to win support for France. The hotheaded Genet disregarded all rules of diplomacy in trying to stir up war between the United States and Great Britain. "He renders my position immensely difficult," Jefferson wrote. In July 1793, Washington requested that France recall Genet. The neutrality crisis then subsided somewhat.

For more than a year Jefferson made repeated efforts to resign his cabinet post, but each time was persuaded by Washington to remain. Finally, on the last day of 1793, he prevailed on Washington to accept his resignation, and immediately set off for his beloved Monticello in the belief that he was retiring forever from public office.

Vice President Under Adams

ALTHOUGH HE TURNED ENTHUSIASTICALLY to farming and the invention of a new plow, Jefferson could not disregard politics. When the terms of the Jay Treaty with Great Britain were revealed in 1794, Jefferson led the Democratic-Republicans in denouncing it as an "execrable thing" and an "infamous act." He inveighed against the Federalists as "an Anglican monarchical aristocratical party . . . whose avowed object is to draw over us the substance, as they have already done the forms, of the British government."

In the presidential election of 1796, Jefferson did little to promote his candidacy against that of John Adams, but, as the electoral votes were counted, it was discovered that he had lost to Adams by only three votes—seventy-one to sixty-eight. Because he had received the second largest number of electoral votes, Jefferson became Vice President. "A more tranquil and unoffending station could not have been found for me," he commented. "The second office of the government is honorable and easy, the first is but a splendid misery."

At the outset of his term as Vice President, Jefferson received overtures from Adams suggesting that the two old friends could work closely together. But the Federalist Cabinet that Adams inherited from Washington quickly put a stop to any such co-operation. As time went by, the breach widened between the President and Vice President as Jefferson became more and more convinced that Adams wanted war with France.

With the Federalists firmly in control of the government, Jefferson's role as Vice President was largely that of a frustrated and disapproving spectator. The passage of the Alien and Sedition Acts convinced Jefferson that the Federalists had no regard for the Bill of Rights. He wrote that he next expected them to pass "another act of Congress declaring that the President shall continue in office during life, reserving to another occasion the transfer of the succession to his heirs, and the establishment of the Senate for life." In an effort to counter the Alien and Sedition Acts, Jefferson secretly wrote the Kentucky Resolutions, which declared that the acts were unconstitutional and a violation of states' rights—he would have been horrified had he known that these principles would later be used as arguments for nullification and secession in the slavery issue.

As the presidential election of 1800 approached, the attacks on Jefferson by the Federalists increased in fury and intemperance, for it was evident that he would be the Anti-Federalist candidate. To his good friend James Monroe, Jefferson wrote: "As to the calumny of atheism, I am so broken to calumnies of every kind . . . that I entirely disregard it. . . . It has been so impossible to contradict all their lies that I have determined to contradict none, for while I should be engaged with one they would publish twenty new ones."

On the day of Democratic-Republican victory, Jefferson visited Adams at the White House and later described their conversation as follows: "He (Adams) was very sensibly affected, and accosted me with these words:

" 'Well, I understand that you are to beat me in this contest, and I will only say that I will be as faithful a subject as any you will have.'

" 'Mr. Adams,' said I, 'this is no personal contest between you and me. Two systems of principles on the subject of government divide our fellow-citizens into two parties. With one of these you concur, and I with the other. As we have been longer on the public stage than most of those now living, our names happen to be more generally known. One of these parties, therefore, has put your name at its head, the other mine. Were we both to die today, tomorrow two other names would be in the place of ours, without any change in the motion of the machinery. Its motion is from its principle, not from you or myself.'

" 'I believe you are right,' said he, 'that we are but passive instruments, and should not suffer this matter to affect our personal dispositions.' "

When the electoral votes were counted, Jefferson had indeed defeated Adams, but a curious defect in the wording of the Constitution was uncovered. All seventy-three electors favoring Jefferson wrote down two names, in accordance with the directive of Article II. The names they wrote down were those of Jefferson and Aaron Burr, a New York Anti-Federalist. It was clear that the popular mandate was for Jefferson to be President and Burr Vice President, but according to the terms of the Constitution the decision was now turned over to the House of Representatives. The House, owing to another quirk of the Constitution, was controlled by the outgoing Federalists, who hoped to extract concessions from Jefferson. Various Federalists, including President Adams, told Jefferson they would swing the election to him if he would give assurances that Federalist officials would not be turned out of office, that he would not disband the new navy, and that he would not erase the public debt. Jefferson later wrote that he replied "that I should certainly make no terms; should never go into the office of President by capitulation, nor with my hands tied by any conditions which should hinder me from pursuing the measures which I should deem for the public good." Finally, fearing the opportunistic Burr more than Jefferson, the Federalists granted the presidency to the sage of Monticello on the thirty-sixth ballot.

Jefferson's Administration

JEFFERSON WAS FIFTY-SEVEN YEARS OLD when he was sworn in as President on March 4, 1801, at a simple ceremony in Washington, D.C.—the first President to take office in the new capital, then a city of about 6,000 population. Aware of the drama in being the first Democratic-Republican President and of widespread apprehension that he would destroy the Constitution, he endeavored to allay fears in an eloquent inaugural address.

"Let us restore to social intercourse that harmony and affection without which liberty and even life itself are but dreary things," he said. "And let us reflect that having banished from our land that religious intolerance under which mankind so long bled and suffered, we have yet gained little if we countenance a political intolerance as despotic, as wicked, and capable of as bitter and bloody persecutions."

Moving immediately to correct the Federalist abuses of power, he freed all persons who were imprisoned or under prosecution by the Alien and Sedition Acts, "without asking what the offenders had done, or against whom they had offended." He ordered reductions in the size of the army, the navy, and the diplomatic service, and pushed Congress "to the uttermost in economizing" and in the reduction of taxes.

When Jefferson learned in 1802 that Spain had turned over to France the vast Louisiana Territory, he wrote to Robert Livingston, the American minister in Paris, that this event "reverses all the political relations of the United States." He warned that "the day France takes possession of New Orleans fixes the sentence which is to restrain her forever within her low-water mark. . . . From that moment, we must marry ourselves to the British fleet and nation." He then asked Livingston to urge the French to sell New Orleans to the United States. He also dispatched James Monroe to France to aid in the negotiations.

To Jefferson's amazement, his commissioners reached agreement with Napoleon to purchase the entire Louisiana Territory for $15 million (about three cents an acre). Because the Constitution made no provision for incorporating foreign territory into the United States, Jefferson believed that a constitutional amendment was needed to insure the legality of the agreement; but fearing it would take so much time to amend the Constitution that Napoleon might change his mind, he urged Congress to approve the treaty quickly and appropriate the necessary money. "The less said about any constitutional difficulty, the better," he wrote. With a minimum of discussion Congress approved the purchase in the autumn of 1803. Soon Jefferson sent Meriwether Lewis, his private secretary, and William Clark on their famous expedition to explore the new territory.

The peace, prosperity, and expansion of the country during Jefferson's first term helped win him an overwhelming victory in the 1804 election. He received 162 electoral votes to 14 for the Federalist candidate, Charles Cotesworth Pinckney.

The Aaron Burr treason scandal rocked the nation during Jefferson's second term. Burr, who had killed Alexander Hamilton in a duel in July 1804, was dropped from the Democratic-Republican national ticket in the 1804 election. After leaving Washington, Burr became involved in a scheme to lead a private army in an attack on Mexico, and then to force the western states to secede from the Union and join Burr's new empire. Jefferson ordered Burr's arrest for treason, and considered it a direct slap at himself when Chief Justice John Marshall, a Federalist, acquitted Burr.

The forcible impressment of American seamen into the British Navy brought a new threat of war in 1807. In an effort to preserve neutrality,

Jefferson persuaded Congress to pass an embargo act that forbade the shipping of American products to any foreign country and outlawed the sailing of American ships to foreign ports, describing the act as "the last card we have to play, short of war." Despite opposition by New England merchants, the act remained in force to the end of Jefferson's administration, and war was avoided.

During the eight years he lived in the Executive Mansion, Jefferson decorated it with French furniture he imported. With the help of Benjamin Latrobe, the surveyor of public buildings, Jefferson expanded the building to include one-story east and west wings that included servants' quarters, woodsheds, and a wine cellar. He also provided a water supply by digging a well and a cistern. Adams, his predecessor, had been forced to obtain water by having it hauled from a spring some distance away.

Refusing all pleas that he run for a third term, Jefferson supported his friend and Secretary of State, James Madison, as his successor. When Madison won the election, Jefferson was gratified both at his friend's success and at his own approaching retirement. He wrote: "Never did a prisoner released from his chains feel such relief as I shall on shaking off the shackles of power. . . . I thank God for the opportunity of retiring from them without censure, and carrying with me the most consoling proofs of public approbation."

Philosopher and College President

FOR THE REMAINING seventeen years of his life, Jefferson lived as a farmer-philosopher at Monticello, corresponding prolifically with statesmen, scientists, inventors, and old friends. When the Library of Congress was destroyed by the burning of Washington in 1812, he turned over his own large collection of books as the nucleus of a new national library. But the greatest accomplishment of his old age—one of the three achievements that he asked to be remembered for—was the founding of the University of Virginia at Charlottesville, near Monticello. He designed the school's buildings, planned the courses of study, employed the academic staff, and acted as rector, or head of the governing body of the school. In the year before he died he saw the university open its doors to its first classes.

After an illness of about a month, Jefferson died at the age of eighty-three on the fiftieth anniversary of the adoption of the Declaration of Independence—July 4, 1826.

James Madison
The Fourth President of the United States
1809–17

1751 (March 16) Born at Port Conway, Virginia.

1771 Graduated from College of New Jersey at Princeton.

1776 Helped write Virginia state constitution.

1776–77 Member of Virginia legislature.

1778–79 Member of Virginia governor's advisory council.

1780–83 Delegate to Congress.

1784–86 Member of Virginia legislature.

1786 Delegate to Annapolis Convention.

1787 Delegate to Constitutional Convention.

1787–88 Member of Congress of the Confederation; wrote many of *The Federalist* essays.

1789–97 U.S. representative in Congress.

1794 Married Dolley Payne Todd.

1799–1800 Member of Virginia legislature.

1801–9 Secretary of State under Thomas Jefferson.

1809–17 Fourth President of the United States.

1826 Succeeded Jefferson as rector of the University of Virginia.

1829 Co-chairman of Virginia state constitutional convention.

1836 (June 28) Died at Montpelier, Orange County, Virginia.

T he last of the Founding Fathers to serve as President, James Madison served two terms in the White House, but his greatest contributions to American history already lay behind him in the Constitution and the Bill of Rights. In many ways his career, as well as his political philosophy, paralleled that of his friend and mentor, Thomas Jefferson. Their mutual political adversary, John Quincy Adams, regarded Madison as "in truth a greater man."

Shorter than average height in a time of short men, Madison relied more upon his brilliant mind than on a commanding presence to lead others to his way of thinking. As a co-founder, with Jefferson, of the Democratic-Republican party, he was vilified by the Federalists, whose chief spokesman, his former friend Alexander Hamilton, said of him: "Mr. Madison, co-operating with Mr. Jefferson, is at the head of a faction . . . subversive of the principles of good government and dangerous to the Union, peace, and happiness of the country."

A Rising Young Virginian

THE SON OF A VIRGINIA PLANTER, James Madison was born at his grandparents' home in Port Conway, Virginia, on March 16, 1751. He grew up at his family's plantation, Montpelier, becoming, in Jefferson's words, "the best farmer in the world." At the age of eighteen, he went to the College of New Jersey at Princeton, graduating two years later.

Returning home from college in 1771, he plunged into the political storm that was gathering. When Virginia declared itself independent of Great Britain in 1776, the twenty-five-year-old Madison served as a delegate to the patriotic convention called to form a new state government and helped write the Virginia constitution. Elected to the first state legislature, he met the already-famous Jefferson, just returned from writing the Declaration of Independence in Philadelphia. A lifelong friendship began on the spot. Madison was not re-elected to the legislature because he refused to follow the custom of providing free rum for voters, but Governor Patrick Henry appointed him to the council of state. On this advisory council Madison continued to serve in the following administration of his friend Jefferson.

As a member of Virginia's delegation to Congress from 1780 to 1783, he helped organize the national government under the newly adopted Articles of Confederation. Despite his affinity for Jefferson's democratic ideals, Madison found himself attracted to one of the principal doctrines of Alexander Hamilton, a man of his own age. That was the need for a strong central government. The two young men—Madison was in his early thirties, Hamilton even younger—agreed to work together. It was one of the most fruitful collaborations in United States history.

A little later Madison was able to bring his views on a federal government to the attention of George Washington. Washington was impressed with his young fellow Virginian and applauded his election as a delegate to the Annapolis Convention in 1786. This was a meeting of several states to study interstate commercial problems. Few delegates appeared, but two—Madison and Hamilton—made the unsuccessful conference a turning point in the nation's history. They prevailed upon the meeting to call for a convention of states to revise the Articles of Confederation. Washington approved, writing to Madison: "Without some alteration in our political creed, the superstructure we have been seven years raising at the expense of so much blood and treasure, must fall."

Father of the Constitution and the Bill of Rights

As a delegate to the Constitutional Convention in Philadelphia, the thirty-six-year-old Madison played a major role. He took it upon himself to keep a complete record of the debates during the secret meetings of the convention, stationing himself at the front of the room near the chair of the presiding officer, Washington. Further, he had drafted a complete plan for a new national government. Madison's "Virginia Plan," as it was called, became the main basis for the Constitution, ultimately approved four months later. Throughout the convention Madison repeatedly spoke out on the necessity of providing a democratic basis for the government with election of congressmen directly by the people. As a member of the committee on style, Madison helped write the final version of the Constitution that was signed on September 17.

At the close of these sessions, Madison set to work on a series of essays designed to explain the new Constitution to the people. These brilliant tracts, along with others written by Hamilton and John Jay, are collectively known as *The Federalist* and continue to this day to provide an unequaled interpretation of a federated national government. At the time, they were invaluable in winning support for the new Constitution.

Fearing that the opposition of Patrick Henry, Virginia's political boss, might cause their home state to reject the Constitution, Washington appealed to Madison to run for election to the state ratification convention and lead the floor fight there. He wrote: "Explanations will be wanting, and none can give them with more accuracy and propriety than yourself."

Madison attended the convention and helped win ratification by a narrow eighty-nine to seventy-nine vote. In doing so he also won the lasting enmity of Henry. When Madison's name was proposed as one of the state's new U.S. senators, Henry declared that Madison's election would bring a revolution with "rivulets of blood throughout the land." Defeated for senator, Madison ran for U.S. representative. Again Henry tried to thwart him by redistricting, and by putting up the young, well-liked James Monroe to oppose him; but, after a hard-fought campaign, Madison was elected by a small margin.

Congressman and Secretary of State

IN CONGRESS, Madison distinguished himself by preparing the Bill of Rights amendments to the Constitution and much of the legislation forming various departments of the new government. He also acted as an adviser to Washington, helping prepare both his Inaugural Address and his Farewell Address.

In 1794 Madison married a pretty widow, Dolley Payne Todd, seventeen years younger than himself. Her social charm aided him immeasurably in his later career as Secretary of State, when she often acted as hostess for the widowed President Jefferson, and as President, when she sustained him during the difficult war years. They had no children of their own, but reared her son by a previous marriage.

When Federalist John Adams became President, Madison retired from Congress, returning to plantation life at Montpelier. But when the Federalist administration threatened the freedoms guaranteed in the Bill of Rights, Madison angrily wrote the Virginia Resolutions, denouncing the unconstitutionality of the Alien and Sedition Acts. To further his fight for the defense of civil liberties, Madison again won election to the state legislature, serving from 1799 to 1800.

Madison campaigned for Jefferson's election in 1800, and afterwards accepted appointment as Secretary of State. During the next eight years the two worked together so closely on foreign policy that it is difficult to separate their individual contributions in helping to preserve American neutrality in the European wars and in negotiating the Louisiana Purchase.

As Jefferson's choice to succeed to the presidency, Madison easily won the election of 1808, defeating the Federalist candidate, Charles Cotesworth Pinckney, with 122 electoral votes to 47.

Madison's Administration

MADISON CAME to the nation's highest office at a time of crisis in foreign relations. Both Great Britain and France were riding roughshod over American rights as they fought the Napoleonic wars, and American public opinion was sharply divided. The Federalists and the North favored Great Britain while the Democratic-Republicans and the South and West sympathized with France. Jefferson and Madison tried to steer a course of neutrality. One of Jefferson's last decisions as President was to sign the repeal of the Embargo Act, substituting for it the new Non-Intercourse Act, which permitted trade with any countries except France and Britain. The new act failed to influence the warring powers, and friction with Britain was augmented by a major Indian uprising, widely blamed on the British. The Indians were crushed by William Henry Harrison in the battle of Tippecanoe.

Another element making for war was a coterie of American expansionists who dreamed of the annexation of Canada. In Congress the leaders of the "war hawks," as Jefferson called them, were Henry Clay of Kentucky and John Calhoun of South Carolina. This group also hoped that Florida could be wrested from Britain's ally, Spain.

Bowing to external and internal pressures, Madison asked Congress on June 1, 1812, for a declaration of war on Britain. On June 18 the measure passed by the narrow margin of nineteen to thirteen in the Senate and seventy-nine to forty-nine in the House. Ironically, two days earlier the British had repealed a set of blockade orders which had been a major provocation to war, but word did not reach America until the war was well underway.

The military and naval forces of the United States were hardly prepared for what became known by the Federalists as "Mr. Madison's War." The U. S. Army had only about 10,000 troops and the U. S. Navy fewer than two dozen ships.

The initial military strategy approved by Madison called for a three-pronged American attack on Canada. This plan ended in a series of disasters, the worst of which was the surrender without a shot being fired of an entire 2,000-man American army at Detroit on August 16, 1812. In the East, state militia refused in the fall of 1812 to cross the border into Canada.

Much of the war was fought at sea. The British Navy blockaded the East Coast, cutting off manufactured goods from Europe. In turn American privateers preyed on British shipping, capturing more than 800 vessels during the war. Heroic sea battles by the frigate U.S.S. *Constitution* won it the nickname "Old Ironsides." The dying words of U. S. Navy Captain James

Lawrence of the U.S.S. *Chesapeake* in 1813 gave Americans a rallying slogan: "Don't give up the ship!" And on September 10, 1813, U. S. Navy Captain Oliver Hazard Perry won the battle of Lake Erie, reporting: "We have met the enemy and they are ours."

Perry's victory opened the way for future President William Henry Harrison, the commander of U.S. forces in the West, to move his 4,500-man army across Lake Erie and defeat the British at the battle of the Thames River in Ontario on October 5, 1813. Two months later a British army invaded western New York, burning the village of Buffalo and nearby communities.

In the South an uprising by Creek Indians brought massacres of settlers along the frontier. Future President Andrew Jackson brought an end to Indian raids, leading Tennessee militia to victory over the Creeks in the battle of Horseshoe Bend in Alabama on March 27, 1814.

The defeat of Napoleon in Europe in 1814 freed Britain to send an army of 4,000 veterans to invade the Chesapeake Bay area. After routing a larger American army at the battle of Bladensburg, the British troops captured Washington, D.C., on August 24, 1814, while President Madison, his Cabinet, and members of Congress fled to safety in Virginia. Dolley Madison escaped just ahead of the British troops, pausing only long enough to carry away Gilbert Stuart's portrait of George Washington. British soldiers ate the hot meal she had been cooking before she fled. The British proceeded to burn the Capitol, the Executive Mansion, and most other public buildings. They abandoned the burning city the next day because of a storm that threatened their ships.

Britain and the United States agreed to end the War of 1812 by signing the Treaty of Ghent on December 24, 1814, which called for each side to give up captured territory. Slow communications prevented news of the peace from crossing the Atlantic in time to prevent the war's biggest battle, at New Orleans on January 9, 1815, in which General Andrew Jackson won both victory and undying fame.

During the war, Madison had decisively won a second term over the fusion presidential candidate, De Witt Clinton, achieving an electoral vote of 128 to 89. Clinton, a disaffected New York Democratic-Republican, had been chosen as the best hope of the dying Federalist party.

When the Madisons returned to Washington after the War of 1812, they lived in temporary quarters while the Executive Mansion was rebuilt. Architect James Hoban decided to use white paint to cover the fire-blackened sandstone exterior. Henceforth, it became known as the *White House.*

With the end of the war, the westward movement of settlers resumed, bringing the country new prosperity and Madison new popularity. He now accepted in large measure the economic principles of the Federalist party, putting his signature to a law chartering a new United States Bank and calling for higher tariffs to protect American manufacturers.

Although he had revised his economic thinking. Madison refused to change his belief that the Constitution should be strictly interpreted. He demonstrated this forcibly on his last day before leaving office, March 3, 1817, when he vetoed John Calhoun's "Bonus Bill" that would have used federal funds to help build a "perfect system of roads and canals" for the nation. Madison explained his veto by saying he believed "the permanent success of the Constitution depends on a definite partition of powers between the General and State governments" and that he could find no provision in the Constitution that called on the federal government to build roads and canals.

Retiring at the end of his second term, Madison left the presidency in the hands of James Monroe, whom he had designated as his successor, and whose overwhelming victory over the Federalist candidate, Rufus King, was taken by Madison as a personal tribute.

A Ripe Old Age

SURVIVING ALL HIS OLD COLLEAGUES of the Constitutional Convention, Madison lived on to the age of eighty-five, seeing the transportation revolution that came with railroads and steamboats and the expansion of the United States to twenty-five states stretching to the Mississippi. After Jefferson's death in 1826, Madison carried on his friend's work in education by assuming the office of rector of the University of Virginia. He also maintained his interest in constitutional affairs to the end of his life, serving as co-chairman of a Virginia convention in 1829 that revised the state constitution he had helped write more than fifty years earlier. After his death on June 28, 1836, at Montpelier, his wife sold to the government his invaluable, and until then secret, notes on the Constitutional Convention of 1787. In the introduction to these notes, Madison wrote perhaps his own best eulogy:

". . . whatever may be the judgment pronounced on the competency of the architects of the Constitution, or whatever may be the destiny of the edifice prepared by them, I feel it a duty to express my profound and solemn conviction, derived from my intimate opportunity of observing and appreciating the views of the Convention, collectively and individually, that there never was an assembly of men, charged with a great and arduous trust, who were more pure in their motives, or more exclusively or anxiously devoted to the object committed to them, than were the members of the Federal Convention of 1787, to the object of devising and proposing a constitutional system which should best supply the defects of that which it was to replace, and best secure the permanent liberty and happiness of their country."

James Monroe
The Fifth President of the United States
1817–25

1758 (April 28) Born in Westmoreland County, Virginia.

1776–80 Fought in Revolutionary War, rising to rank of lieutenant colonel.

1782 Member of Virginia legislature.

1783–86 Member of Virginia's delegation in Congress.

1786 (February 16) Married Elizabeth Kortright.

1786–90 Member of Virginia legislature.

1790–94 U.S. senator from Virginia.

1794–96 U.S. minister to France.

1799–1802 Governor of Virginia.

1803 Helped negotiate the Louisiana Purchase.

1803–7 U.S. minister to Great Britain.

1811 Governor of Virginia.

1811–17 U. S. Secretary of State.

1814–15 U. S. Secretary of War.

1817–25 Fifth President of the United States.

1829 Co-chairman of Virginia state constitutional convention.

1831 (July 4) Died in New York City.

Bringing the country such peace, prosperity, and growth that his administration won the nickname of the "Era of Good Feeling," James Monroe became so popular with voters and politicians that he was unopposed for his second term as President—an honor accorded only one other Chief Executive, George Washington. A hero of the Revolutionary War, described by Thomas Jefferson as "a man whose soul might be turned wrong side outwards without discovering a blemish to the world," he left the country in political turmoil largely because he did not want to hurt the feelings of any of his friends by supporting only one of them as his presidential successor.

Monroe did much to expand the size of the United States. He made the key on-the-spot decision that resulted in the Louisiana Purchase, and as President succeeded in negotiating the acquisition of Florida. His approval of the Missouri Compromise that admitted Missouri as a slave state helped postpone the crisis over slavery between the North and South. And his conclusion of a treaty demilitarizing the boundary between the United States and Canada insured history's first continuing peace between two large neighboring countries.

His most remembered act, the Monroe Doctrine, conceived as a warning to the European powers to keep hands off the new Latin American republics, became an abiding cornerstone of American foreign policy.

A contemporary description of Monroe by William Wirt, who served under him as Attorney General, follows:

"In his stature, he is about the middle height of men, rather firmly set, with nothing further remarkable in his person, except his muscular compactness and apparent ability to endure labor. His countenance, when grave, has rather the expression of sternness and irascibility; a smile, however (and a smile is not unusual with him in a social circle), lights it up to a very high advantage, and gives it a most impressive and engaging air of suavity and benevolence. His dress and personal appearance are those of a plain and modest gentleman. He is a man of soft, polite, and even assiduous attentions . . . there is often in his manner an inartificial and even an awkward simplicity, which, while it provokes the smile of a more polished person, forces him to the opinion that Mr. Monroe is a man of a most sincere and artless soul."

A Revolutionary War Hero

LIKE WASHINGTON, JEFFERSON, AND MADISON, James Monroe was the son of a Virginia planter. He was born on April 28, 1758, in Westmoreland County, the eldest of five children of Spence and Elizabeth Jones Monroe. When he was sixteen, young Monroe was sent to attend the College of William and Mary at Williamsburg, where one of the other undergraduates at the time was John Marshall, a future Chief Justice of the United States.

With the outbreak of the Revolution, Monroe quit college to join a Virginia regiment of the Continental Army, receiving a commission as lieutenant at the age of eighteen. His regiment joined Washington's troops in New York, where he fought in the battles of Harlem and White Plains. While leading the advance guard in the battle of Trenton, he was wounded in the shoulder, and for his bravery was promoted to captain by Washington. During 1777 and 1778 he took part in the battles of Brandywine, Germantown, and Monmouth. Commissioned a lieutenant colonel in 1778, he undertook to recruit a new Virginia regiment, but was unable to raise enough volunteers. In 1780 he carried out an assignment by Jefferson, then governor of Virginia, to report on the condition of the southern army.

The war ending, Monroe became a protégé of Jefferson, studied law under the older man's guidance, and won election to the state legislature in 1782. The next year he was elected with Jefferson as a member of Virginia's delegation to Congress. During his three years in Congress, he helped write the Northwest Ordinance with Rufus King, whom he was to defeat thirty years later in the 1816 presidential election, and made two trips into the Ohio Valley to gain first-hand information on conditions on the western frontier. Believing that the Articles of Confederation needed strengthening, Monroe drew up an amendment that would have given Congress the power to regulate commerce between the states, but he was unable to win its acceptance.

While serving in Congress, Monroe fell in love with and married Elizabeth Kortright, the daughter of a New York businessman. When his term of office expired in 1786 he temporarily retired from politics and established a law practice at Fredericksburg, Virginia. Later, he built Ash Lawn, near Jefferson's Monticello, where he and his wife reared their two daughters. A third child, a son, died at the age of two.

Monroe did not take part in the Constitutional Convention of 1787, and he vigorously opposed ratification of the Constitution at the Virginia convention until he received assurances that a Bill of Rights would be adopted. After ratification of the Constitution, he ran for Congress against Madison, but was defeated. In 1790, through the political influence of Patrick Henry, the thirty-two-year-old Monroe won appointment as a U.S. senator to fill a vacancy caused by the death of William Grayson.

In the Senate, Monroe became a leader of the Democratic-Republican party, and helped fight the Federalist policies of Alexander Hamilton. He formed a low opinion of Hamilton's motives, and when he made his views public a few years later he was almost forced into a duel with Hamilton.

Diplomat, Governor, and Secretary of State

BECAUSE MONROE'S SYMPATHIES for the French revolutionists were well known, President Washington appointed him in 1794 to soothe relations with France. In Paris, Monroe quickly won the friendship of the French and became the only ambassador of a foreign power invited to sit in their national legislature. In an address to the French national assembly he enthusiastically committed himself to aiding the French cause; but when word of his speech reached America he was severely reprimanded for jeopardizing United States neutrality in the war between France and the European coalition. When word of the Jay Treaty with Britain reached Monroe, he denounced it as ". . . the most shameful transaction I have ever known of the kind." Washington ordered the recall of his outspoken ambassador in 1796. Returning to the United States, Monroe published a 500-page book, *A View of the Conduct of the Executive*, in which he attempted to vindicate his conduct in France and blamed Washington's administration for damaging relations with America's former ally.

Late in 1799, the Virginia legislature elected Monroe governor. During the three years that he served in this office, he became closer friends with Madison, who served in the legislature during the first part of this time.

In 1803 Monroe again was sent to France, this time by Jefferson, who needed a special envoy to help negotiate the purchase of New Orleans. When he arrived in Paris, he learned from Robert Livingston, the regular U.S. minister to France, that Napoleon already had indicated the desire to sell all of the Louisiana Territory to the United States. Although he and Livingston were not authorized to agree to such a large transaction, Monroe enthusiastically took the responsibility on himself and helped negotiate a treaty that doubled the size of the United States at a cost of $15 million.

From Paris, Monroe was sent to London where for the next several years he tried to negotiate a treaty that would end the friction between Britain and the United States over freedom of the seas. During this time he also spent several months in Madrid trying to bargain with the Spanish for the purchase of Florida. Unsuccessful on both scores, he returned to the United States in 1807 and again resumed the private practice of law in Virginia. Some of his friends urged him to run for President, but a congressional caucus of the Democratic-Republican party overwhelmingly chose Madison.

The Virginia legislature for the second time elected Monroe governor in 1811, but when Madison offered him an appointment as Secretary of State he resigned the governorship. Monroe helped draft the recommendations to Congress that led to a declaration of war on Britain in 1812. As American defeats mounted during the war, Monroe urged Madison to appoint him as Secretary of War. Madison agreed to this appointment after the fall of the city of Washington, and for the rest of the war Monroe held both cabinet posts. He instilled new enthusiasm in the army, and American troops began to win victories. His vigor and energy are exemplified by a message to western governors before the battle of New Orleans: "Hasten your militia to New Orleans; do not wait for this government to arm them; put all the arms you can find into their hands; let every man bring his rifle with him; we shall see you paid."

With the end of the war and the expanding prosperity of the country in the last years of Madison's administration, Monroe was held in high esteem throughout the country. With Madison's support, Monroe won the Democratic-Republican presidential nomination when a congressional caucus chose him by a sixty-five to fifty-four vote over Secretary of the Treasury William H. Crawford. He then went on to win the 1816 presidential election over Federalist candidate Senator Rufus King of New York, receiving an electoral vote of 183 to King's 34.

Monroe's Administration

TAKING OFFICE AT A TIME when the United States faced no unusual problems, the fifty-eight-year-old Monroe commented in his inaugural address:

"Never did a government commence under auspices so favorable, nor ever was success so complete. If we look to the history of other nations, ancient or modern, we find no example of a growth so rapid, so gigantic, of a people so prosperous and happy. In contemplating what we have still to perform, the heart of every citizen must expand with joy when he reflects how near our Government has approached to perfection; that in respect to it we have no essential improvement to make; that the great object is to preserve it in the essential principles and features which characterize it, and that that is to be done by preserving the virtue and enlightening the minds of the people . . ."

Appointing one of the strongest and most stable Cabinets in presidential history, Monroe helped end sectional discord by choosing John Quincy Adams of Massachusetts as Secretary of State and John C. Calhoun of South Carolina as Secretary of War. Monroe also strengthened his popular support with a three-and-a-half-month tour in 1817 that took him through the New England states and as far west as Detroit—a trip that his critics called a "political jubilee," but one that was so successful that he followed it up with a similar tour of the southern states in 1819.

The war-ravaged White House was still being rebuilt when Monroe became President, so he and his wife did not move in until late in 1817. They decorated the White House with furniture and silverware purchased in France at an auction of the possessions of executed Queen Marie Antoinette. Using a special congressional appropriation for the purpose, they imported additional furnishings from France, including a set of gilt furniture custom-designed by Parisian cabinetmaker Pierre-Antoine Bellangé. The First Lady showed off the newly decorated and refurbished White House to the diplomatic corps with a gala candle-lit reception on New Year's Eve. Monroe also expanded the White House by adding a north portico and colonnade designed by Benjamin Latrobe.

By the time Monroe ran for re-election in 1820, the Federalist party was dead. Monroe received all but one of the Electoral College's 232 votes—one elector having cast his ballot for Secretary of State John Quincy Adams, supposedly to preserve for Washington the honor of having received the only unanimous vote for President.

The Monroe Doctrine

THE GREATEST SUCCESSES of Monroe's administration occurred in the field he knew best—foreign relations. The Rush-Bagot Agreement with Britain in 1817 eliminated fortifications along the Canadian border. Two years later successful negotiations were concluded to acquire Florida from Spain. But the proclamation of the Monroe Doctrine in 1823 has lived on as his most monumental achievement.

Fearing that European powers might attempt to intervene in Latin America, where various countries had just won their independence from Spain, Monroe wrote to Jefferson asking his advice as to what course to take. The elder statesman replied to his protégé: "Our first and fundamental Maxim should be, never to entangle ourselves in the broils of Europe. Our second, never to suffer Europe to intermeddle with cis-Atlantic affairs." Following this advice, Monroe established the doctrine that bears his name in his annual message to Congress on December 2, 1823, in which he said in part:

". . . we should consider any attempt on their part (that of European powers) to extend their system to any portion of this hemisphere as dangerous to our peace and safety. With the existing colonies or dependencies of any European power we have not interfered, and shall not interfere. But with the governments who have declared their independence and maintained it, and whose independence we have, on great consideration and on just principles, acknowledged, we could not view any interposition for the purpose of oppressing them, or controlling in any other manner their destiny, by any European power, in any other light than as the manifestation of an unfriendly disposition toward the United States."

In domestic affairs, Monroe made no effort to lead Congress. He followed the precepts of Jefferson and Madison in denying the constitutionality of federal financing of such public improvements as roads and canals. However, he indicated his support by calling for a constitutional amendment to allow such federal action, and by approving the Survey Act of 1824, which provided for planning of future public works. Several acts increasing protective tariffs were also approved by Monroe. He held himself largely aloof from the congressional debates that led to the Missouri Compromise, but let it be known that he favored admitting Missouri as a slave state.

Monroe's Last Years

AFTER COMPLETING his second term as President, Monroe retired to Oak Hill, an elegant mansion he had built south of Leesburg, Virginia. He then resumed at closer hand his friendships with Jefferson and Madison. He served with them as a regent of the University of Virginia, and acted as co-chairman with Madison of the Virginia state constitutional convention of 1829.

In the final years of his life Monroe suffered financial distress. He spent much time trying to collect from the government money that he said was owed him for expenses during his long public service. After his wife died in 1830, he finally was forced to dispose of Oak Hill and to go to New York City to live with one of his married daughters.

He died in New York City on July 4, 1831—the third President to die on an anniversary of the nation's independence. Upon learning of Monroe's death, his former Secretary of State, John Quincy Adams, noted in his diary:

"James Monroe, a man whose life has been marked with vicissitudes as great as have befallen any citizen of the United States since the beginning of our national existence . . . His life for the last six years has been one of abject penury and distress, and they have brought him to a premature grave, though in the seventy-third year of his age. His Administration, happening precisely at the moment of the greatest tranquility which has ever been enjoyed by this country . . . was a time of great prosperity, and his personal popularity was unrivalled. Yet no one regretted the termination of his Administration, and less of popular veneration followed him into retirement than had accompanied all his predecessors. His last days have been much afflicted, contrasting deeply with the triumphal procession which he made through the Union in the years 1817 and 1819."

John Quincy Adams
The Sixth President of the United States
1825–29

1767 (July 11) Born in Braintree (now Quincy), Massachusetts.

1787 Graduated from Harvard.

1790 Began practicing law in Boston.

1794–1801 U.S. diplomatic representative in several European countries.

1797 (July 26) Married Louisa Catherine Johnson.

1803–8 U.S. senator from Massachusetts.

1806–9 Professor of oratory and rhetoric at Harvard.

1809–14 First U.S. minister to Russia.

1814 Led negotiators that drew up the Treaty of Ghent, which ended the War of 1812.

1815–17 U.S. minister to England.

1817–25 U. S. Secretary of State.

1825–29 Sixth President of the United States.

1830–48 U.S. representative from Massachusetts.

1848 (February 23) Died in the U.S. Capitol in Washington, D.C.

Threw only man ever to win the presidency both with fewer electoral votes and fewer popular votes than his opponent, John Quincy Adams was also the only son of a President ever to succeed to the nation's highest office. Outwardly a Puritanical scholar who found it difficult to bend to public popularity, Adams revealed himself as a man of strong, though hidden, emotions in the voluminous diaries that he kept all his life. He aptly described himself: "I am a man of reserved, cold, austere, and forbidding manners: my political adversaries say, a gloomy misanthropist, and my personal enemies, an unsocial savage. With a knowledge of the actual defect in my character, I have not the pliability to reform it."

Deeply religious, Adams made it a point to read through the entire Bible at least once each year. He perused several chapters each morning before breakfast, first from an English Bible, then from one in French, and from one in German—only a few of the languages he read with ease. He loved books so much that he once wrote: "To live without having a Cicero and a Tacitus at hand seems to me as if it was a privation of one of my limbs."

A man of middle height—he was five feet seven inches tall—he believed in strenuous physical exercise as the key to fitness. He walked for several miles each day, and in the summer swam in the Potomac River—on one such occasion when a sudden squall came up, he lost his clothes and had to make his way half naked back to the White House.

A Revolutionary Boyhood

THE ELDEST OF THREE SONS of John and Abigail Adams, John Quincy Adams was born on July 11, 1767, in Braintree, Massachusetts, while his father was a struggling young lawyer. One of his earliest recollections as a boy was standing on a hilltop on "the awful day" of Bunker Hill listening to the thunder of the cannon and watching the smoke of battle.

When Adams was only ten years old, he accompanied his father on a diplomatic mission to France. As the elder Adams was assigned one diplomatic post after another, young Johnny attended schools in France and the Netherlands. At fourteen he won his father's permission to go to Russia for two years as private secretary to Francis Dana, the first American diplomat assigned to the Russian court.

Returning to America in 1785, he enrolled in Harvard and was graduated two years later at the age of nineteen. He immediately took up the study of law and began his own practice in Boston in 1790. Like most young lawyers, he had few clients, so he filled his time by writing political articles for newspapers, defending the Federalist policies of the national government in which his father was then Vice President.

Diplomat and Senator

WHEN HE WAS TWENTY-SEVEN YEARS OLD, Adams was appointed by President Washington as United States minister to the Netherlands, where he arrived in January 1795 to find the country occupied by an invading French army. The next year he was appointed minister to Portugal, but before he could leave the Netherlands, he received word that his father had been elected President, and that he was re-assigned as minister to Prussia.

Before traveling to Berlin, Adams married twenty-two-year-old Louisa Catherine Johnson, the daughter of an American diplomat. Their long and happy marriage lasted to Adams' death more than fifty years later. They had four children of whom the youngest, Charles Francis Adams, won the greatest distinction, as U.S. minister to Great Britain during the Civil War.

After spending four years in Berlin, Adams returned to the United States in 1801 when Thomas Jefferson became President. The next year Adams won election to the Massachusetts state senate, and in 1803 the legislature elected him to the United States Senate.

Considering his long training as a diplomat, Adams exhibited little tact as a senator. He had been elected to that office as a member of the Federalist party, but he refused to vote on party lines, studying each issue in light of his own conscience. As he wrote in his diary:

". . . if I cannot hope to give satisfaction to my country, I am at least determined to have the approbation of my own reflections."

In 1807 he broke completely with the Federalists, supporting President Jefferson's embargo act. As a rebuke, the Federalist-controlled Massachusetts legislature chose a successor for Adams six months earlier than was necessary. In anger, he resigned as senator in June 1808, and devoted the next year to his law practice and to teaching oratory and rhetoric at Harvard.

Two days after James Madison's inauguration as President in 1809, Adams was rewarded by the Democratic-Republicans with an appointment as the first U.S. minister to Russia. He was accompanied on the long journey by his wife, youngest son, two servants, and three secretaries. While in Russia, he turned down an appointment in 1811 as a justice of the Supreme Court of the United States. In a moment of reflection, he wrote in his diary on his birthday in 1812:

"I am forty-five years old. Two-thirds of a long life are past, and I have done nothing to distinguish it by usefulness to my country or to mankind. I have always lived with, I hope, a suitable sense of my duties in society, and with a sincere desire to perform them. But passions, indolence, weakness, and infirmity have sometimes made me swerve from my better knowledge of right and almost constantly paralyzed my efforts of good. I have no heavy charge upon my conscience, for which I bless my Maker, as well as for all the enjoyments that He has liberally bestowed upon me. I pray for his gracious kindness in future. But it is time to cease forming fruitless resolutions."

Adams was in St. Petersburg during Napoleon's invasion of Russia. Becoming good friends with Czar Alexander I, he accepted the Russian ruler's offer to help mediate the War of 1812. This led to his appointment as chief U.S. negotiator at Ghent, where a treaty was concluded on Christmas Eve in 1814. Adams then traveled to Paris, where he witnessed Napoleon's dramatic return from Elba in 1815.

From 1815 to 1817 he served as U.S. minister to London, a post once filled by his father.

Secretary of State and Presidential Candidate

APPOINTED SECRETARY OF STATE by President James Monroe, Adams returned to the United States in 1817, taking office in September. The success of Monroe's administration in the field of foreign policy has been attributed largely to Adams' skill. He wrote that he felt "the most important event of my life" was the successful conclusion of a treaty with Spain acquiring the territory of Florida. He also played an influential role in drafting the Monroe Doctrine.

Despite the prevailing "Era of Good Feeling," Adams noted in his diary as early as December 1818: ". . . political, personal and electioneering intrigues are intermingling themselves with increasing heat and violence. This Government is indeed assuming daily more and more a character of cabal, and preparation, not for the next Presidential election, but for the one after —that is, working and counter-working, with many of the worst features of elective monarchies. Jackson has made himself a multitude of friends, and still more enemies. The course pursued by the Administration has satisfied neither party, but neither can find much to attack it." The only electoral vote cast against Monroe for a second term in 1821 was given to Adams.

Among those preparing for the election of 1824 was Adams himself. He had four rivals; all Southerners: Secretary of War John C. Calhoun of South Carolina, Secretary of the Treasury W. H. Crawford of Georgia, Congressman Henry Clay of Kentucky, and General Andrew Jackson of Tennessee. Adams expressed private opinions of his opponents in his diary: Calhoun— "very sanguine in his expectations of succeeding to the presidency"; Crawford—"There has never been a man in our history, who has risen so high, of so corrupt a character or upon so slender a basis of service"; Clay—"half-educated" and "his morals, public and private, are loose"; and Jackson— "quarrelsome." Calhoun finally decided to withdraw from the presidential race, settling on the vice presidency as a sure thing by becoming the running mate of both Adams and Jackson.

The election of 1824 sounded the death knell for the old political system in the United States and opened the way to a more democratic process. Party caucuses of members of Congress previously had chosen the presidential candidates. Other members of the parties had abided by the decisions of the caucuses. But in 1824, even before the caucus met, it was generally known that Crawford would be chosen, and his rivals were sounding the theme, "Shall Congress or the people elect our President?" When the caucus did meet on February 14, 1824, for the last time in the nation's history, it did choose Crawford. State caucuses ignored the congressional dictum, putting up Adams, Jackson, and Clay as regional favorites. None of the candidates ran with party labels.

After the votes in the election were counted, none of the candidates had received a clear majority. By the terms of Article II of the Constitution, the House of Representatives had the task of choosing the new President. The electoral and popular votes stood as follows:

Jackson	99 electoral votes	153,544 popular votes
Adams	84 electoral votes	108,740 popular votes
Crawford	41 electoral votes	46,618 popular votes
Clay	37 electoral votes	47,136 popular votes

Because Clay had the fewest electoral votes, he was forced to drop out of the race; but, by throwing his support to either Jackson or Adams, he could determine the victor. On the evening of January 9, 1825, Clay visited Adams for a "confidential interview," the details of which Adams did not report, even in his diary. But shortly thereafter Clay's supporters swung their votes to Adams, while partisans of Jackson and Crawford screamed that a "corrupt bargain" had been made.

When the House of Representatives voted for President on February 9, 1825, Adams received the votes of thirteen states, Jackson seven, and Crawford four. "May the blessing of God rest upon the event of this day!" Adams wrote in his diary. Significantly, when he announced the appointments to his Cabinet, Clay headed the list as Secretary of State.

The angry Andrew Jackson wrote of Clay, "The Judas of the West has closed the contract and will receive the thirty pieces of silver."

Presidential Administration

FULLY COGNIZANT that there were "two-thirds of the whole people adverse to the actual result" of his selection as President, Adams pledged in his inaugural address to do his best under the trying circumstances:

"Less possessed of your confidence in advance than any of my predecessors, I am deeply conscious of the prospect that I shall stand more and oftener in need of your indulgence. Intentions upright and pure, a heart devoted to the welfare of our country, and the unceasing application of all the faculties allotted to me to her service are all the pledges that I can give for the faithful performance of the arduous duties I am to undertake."

Nine months later in his first message to Congress, Adams called for a broader interpretation of the Constitution than that held by his three Virginia predecessors, urging that wide-ranging public improvements be financed by Congress for "the benefit of the people." He asked Congress to establish a national university in Washington, to build an astronomical observatory, and to construct more roads and canals. "The spirit of improvement is abroad upon the earth," he said.

With little support from Congress or the people, Adams was unable to achieve his program. Discouraged, he wrote in 1827: "What retirement will be I cannot realize, but have formed no favorable anticipation. It cannot be worse than this perpetual motion and crazing cares. The weight grows heavier from day to day."

Badly defeated by Jackson in his bid for re-election in 1828, Adams noted: "The sun of my political life sets in the deepest gloom. But that of my country shines unclouded."

In his final State of the Union message to Congress on December 2, 1828, President Adams reported that government expenses during the year had exceeded revenues by about $1.5 million, but that a surplus of nearly $6 million remained in the treasury, most of which could be applied against the public debt of $58 million. He concluded the message with a mild reproof, reminding Congress it had done little to carry out previous programs he had recommended:

". . . it only remains for me to assure the Legislature of my continued earnest wish for the adoption of measures recommended by me heretofore and yet to be acted on by them, and of the cordial concurrence on my part in every constitutional provision which may receive their sanction during the session tending to the general welfare."

An Ex-President in Congress

DEEP IN DESPAIR, Adams remained in Washington after leaving the presidency. His thoughts turned to death, writing in his diary: "I have no plausible motive for wishing to live, when everything that I foresee and believe of futurity makes death desirable." Then, with no campaigning on his part, the people of his home district in Massachusetts elected him in 1830 as their representative in Congress. "No election or appointment conferred upon me ever gave me so much pleasure," he wrote.

As the first former President to return to public office as a member of Congress, Adams won increasing respect as an elder statesman in the more than seventeen years he continued in this office. Although he "abhorred slavery" he labored diligently to cool the passions on this issue that constantly threatened to split the Union between North and South. During much of this time he fought for the removal of the "gag rule" in the House of Representatives that prevented the discussion of the slavery question, finally succeeding in having it abolished in 1845.

After serving in public office through the administrations of the first eleven Presidents of the United States, the eighty-year-old Adams was at his desk in the chamber of the House when he suddenly became ill. Carried to the office of the Speaker of the House, he lay in a coma for more than two days, dying on February 23, 1848. "Where could death have found him," asked Senator Thomas Hart Benton of Missouri, "but at the post of duty?"

Andrew Jackson

The Seventh President of the United States
1829–37

1767 (March 15) Born in Waxhaw, South Carolina.

1780–81 Member of militia in Revolutionary War.

1787 Admitted to bar to practice law in North Carolina.

1791 Married Rachel Donelson Robards.

1795 Member of Tennessee state constitutional convention.

1796–97 U.S. representative from Tennessee.

1797–98 U.S. senator from Tennessee.

1798–1804 Judge of Tennessee Superior Court.

1812–15 Major general in the War of 1812.

1817–18 Commanded U.S. troops in Seminole War in Florida.

1821 Provisional governor of the Territory of Florida.

1823–25 U.S. senator from Tennessee.

1829–37 Seventh President of the United States.

1845 (June 8) Died at the Hermitage near Nashville, Tennessee.

About the only thing that Andrew Jackson had in common with the scholarly Puritan whom he succeeded as President was their year of birth. Born in a frontier log cabin, Jackson grew up as a poorly educated orphan, fought as a boy-militiaman in the Revolutionary War, dissipated a small inheritance as a wild teen-ager, and then settled down as a backwoods lawyer. The hotheaded Jackson fought countless duels, won and lost thousands of dollars on horse races, speculated in land, and became a slave-holding plantation owner. By the time he was thirty, he had achieved great political power in the newly formed state of Tennessee, rising from prosecuting attorney to U.S. representative to U.S. senator. The hawk-eyed Jackson achieved undying fame in the War of 1812 first as an Indian fighter and then as victor in the battle of New Orleans—the biggest battle fought on the continent to that time.

Like George Washington, Jackson uniquely combined the art of a seasoned politician with the decision-making ability of a successful general. His tenacious loyalty toward his friends was matched by an equally unquenchable enmity for anyone who insulted or betrayed him. And the common people loved him as their fathers and grandfathers had loved George Washington.

As President, Jackson brooked no opposition by politicians in or out of his party because he was confident that the people would follow him wherever he led. He neatly summarized his own views on the presidency when he said: "It was settled by the Constitution, the laws, and the whole practice of the government that the entire executive power is vested in the President of the United States . . ."

A contemporary described Jackson as follows:

"In person he was tall, slim and straight . . . His head was long, but narrow, and covered with thick grey hair that stood erect, as though impregnated with his defiant spirit; his brow was deeply furrowed, and his eye was one 'to threaten and command.' His nose was prominent and indicated force. His mouth displayed firmness. His whole being conveyed an impression of energy and daring."

Boyhood of an Orphan

BORN ON MARCH 15, 1767, at the settlement of Waxhaw on the border between North and South Carolina, Andrew Jackson was the son of Andrew and Elizabeth Hutchinson Jackson, who had immigrated from Ireland only two years earlier. Because his father died a few days before Andrew's birth, the boy and his two older brothers were reared by their mother. She earned their keep by helping care for the eight children of her sister, Mrs. James Crawford.

A brighter than ordinary child, Andrew learned to read by the time he was five, attending a small country school in Waxhaw. Because many of the older citizens of Waxhaw could not read, those who could, including Andy, took turns as public readers when newspapers erratically reached the backwoods community. In later years he could recall the drama of reading aloud, as a boy of nine, the ringing words of the Declaration of Independence when a copy of that document first reached Waxhaw in the summer of 1776.

At the age of thirteen, Andy and his brother Robert joined the militia company of his uncle, Major Robert Crawford. His oldest brother, Hugh, already had died fighting in the Revolution. Andy and his brother were captured in 1781. When a British officer ordered Andy to clean his boots, the boy haughtily refused, on grounds it was unfit treatment for a prisoner of war. The angry officer struck at the boy with his sabre, leaving scars on the boy's arm and head that he carried the rest of his life. After the boys became ill with smallpox in the British prison at Camden, South Carolina, they were released to the care of their mother. Robert died and so did his mother, leaving Andy in the hands of his numerous Crawford relatives.

At sixteen he unexpectedly received an inheritance of between £300 and £400 from his grandfather, a well-to-do merchant who had died in Ireland. But, instead of purchasing a farm or going to college, the boy squandered the money on clothes, horse races, dice, and the gay life of the taverns of Charleston, South Carolina.

The next year, 1784, found young Jackson visiting friends in Salisbury, North Carolina, where he took up the study of law—that is, he studied when he could take time from his activities as "head of the rowdies" of the town. The dashing, six-foot, hawk-eyed Jackson captivated the hearts of the Salisbury girls with his Irish brogue. But their mothers were happy when he was admitted to the bar in September 1787 and left town to seek his fortune by following the circuit court.

Frontier Lawyer and Politician

JACKSON WAS ONLY TWENTY when his friend John McNairy, a fellow law student in Salisbury, was appointed judge of North Carolina's Western District, as Tennessee then was called. Seeing a chance to go west and be paid for it, Jackson persuaded McNairy to name him attorney general for the district.

On the way, Jackson paused to take some cases in the local law court in Jonesborough. Feeling himself insulted by an opposing attorney, he promptly challenged the man to a duel. On the field of honor, friends urged that no blood be shed, and both participants fired in the air, but Jackson had established his reputation as a man not to be trifled with.

When the Cumberland Road opened in September 1788, Jackson joined the first party of settlers moving west. Several members of the party were killed by Indians, but Jackson reached the frontier capital of Nashville unscathed.

There he swiftly established a reputation as a fearless attorney who would help a creditor collect his debts both in and out of the courtroom. Clients flocked to his office. Because land was the currency of the frontier, Jackson soon became a large landowner, collecting fees at the rate of an acre for ten cents of service.

In Nashville, Jackson lived at the boardinghouse of a widow, Mrs. John Donelson, whose dark-haired, pipe-smoking daughter caught his eye. The girl, Mrs. Rachel Donelson Robards, was the estranged wife of Lewis Robards of Kentucky. Robards came to Nashville, patched up his problems with Rachel, and took her home to Kentucky in June 1790. But the next month, Jackson followed her there and she ran away with him to Nashville. Robards threatened to come to Nashville and carry his wife home by force, so Jackson and Rachel hurried south to Natchez, where Jackson owned some land.

Believing that Robards had obtained a divorce, Jackson and Mrs. Robards were married in August 1791. They lived for a time in a log house near Natchez and returned to Nashville later that year. When news came from Kentucky that Robards had delayed getting his divorce until September 1793, Jackson and his wife were remarried on January 7, 1794. Jackson loved his wife dearly and for the rest of his life was ready to fight at any hint of slander regarding the circumstances of their courtship and marriage. Although they never had any children of their own, both Jackson and his wife loved children and adopted several on whom they lavished their affection.

In 1795 Jackson traveled for the first time to the nation's capital, Philadelphia, where he sold several thousand acres of land to speculators, using the money to purchase supplies for a trading post on the Cumberland River. Upon his return home, he was elected a member of a constitutional convention called to organize the new state of Tennessee—a name some have said was suggested by Jackson.

After Tennessee was admitted to the Union as the sixteenth state in 1796, Jackson was elected, with no opposition, as the state's first representative to Congress. There he voted with Thomas Jefferson's Democratic-Republicans and was disappointed in John Adams' victory over Jefferson in the election of 1796. Returning to Tennessee in 1797, he refused to run for re-election.

But that year Senator William Blount of Tennessee was impeached by the House of Representatives and expelled by the U. S. Senate for conspiring to take the Louisiana Territory from Spain with British assistance. Because most land-hungry Tennesseeans favored Blount's plan, he was greeted as a hero upon his return to the state legislature to succeed him.

Serving in the Senate for only a few months, Jackson did little more in the nation's capital than establish a lasting friendship with Senator Aaron Burr of New York. He resigned from the Senate in 1798 to devote his attention to his plantation and improve his personal financial affairs. But later that same year he was elected a judge of the state's superior court at an annual salary of $800 —an office he held for six years, meting out swift justice with no written decisions.

A Political General

JACKSON WON AN HONOR in 1802 that was to be more important than any other he had received so far—the officers of the Tennessee militia elected him their commander with the rank of major general, a post that at the time was largely honorary.

Two years later when some of his business enterprises failed, Jackson resigned as judge, sold most of his possessions to pay his debts, and moved to an undeveloped plantation, the Hermitage, near Nashville. His fortunes were at low ebb, but at this point he borrowed money to buy a racehorse named Truxton. After training the horse, he bet and won $6,500 on him in a match race against a horse called Greyhound. With his winnings he purchased Greyhound, and from then on the bets and stakes he won on his racing stable formed a large part of Jackson's income. Even much later, as President, he kept racehorses in the White House stable.

Meanwhile, Jackson kept alive his reputation as a hotheaded duelist. While still a judge in 1803, he had attacked Governor John Sevier on the courthouse steps in Knoxville for a slurring remark about Rachel. A duel followed, but friends prevented the two most important men in Tennessee from killing each other. In 1806 the same cause led to more serious consequences. This time it was a Nashville lawyer, Charles Dickinson, who cast aspersions on Mrs. Jackson's past. Though Dickinson had the reputation of being the best shot in Tennessee, Jackson instantly challenged him. When the two met, Dickinson fired first, hitting Jackson squarely in the chest. Despite his wound, Jackson took careful aim and killed his opponent before collapsing. Dickinson's bullet was too close to Jackson's heart to be removed, and he carried it in his body for the rest of his life.

When former Vice President Aaron Burr came west in 1805 seeking recruits for his scheme to set up an empire in the Louisiana Territory and Mexico, he twice stayed at Jackson's home. And he won Jackson's support for his plans, which supposedly had the blessing of President Jefferson's administration. In September 1806, Jackson was sufficiently recovered from his dueling wound to play host to a reception in Burr's honor. Jackson ordered his Tennessee militia to stand ready to march against Spanish troops in the Louisiana Territory, and, with money supplied by Burr, he began building riverboats for the transport of his troops.

Jackson was unaware that the federal government had moved to indict Burr for treason in Kentucky, but he learned from one of Burr's confidants that the plan involved attacking U.S. forces at New Orleans. Jackson immediately wrote to President Jefferson and to the governor of the Louisiana Territory warning them of Burr's scheme. "I would delight to see Mexico reduced," Jackson wrote, "but I will die in the last ditch before I would . . . see the Union disunited."

A Kentucky grand jury refused to indict Burr for treason, and Jackson received new assurances by mail from Burr that the plan was not against the interests of the federal government. Then, late in December 1806, before Jackson learned that Jefferson had issued an order for Burr's arrest, Burr slipped into Nashville, obtained two riverboats from Jackson, and hurried off down the Cumberland River. After Burr's arrest, Jackson was subpoenaed as a witness at the trial in 1807 at Richmond, Virginia, but was not called to testify after he made it clear that he had a lower opinion of Jefferson than he did of Burr.

A Fighting General

WHEN NEWS CAME IN 1812 that the United States had declared war on England, Jackson at once volunteered to lead his division of 2,500 militiamen to Canada to capture Quebec. But, because he was in disfavor with President Madison owing to his involvement in the Burr conspiracy, he was not given permission to carry out his plan. When Detroit surrendered to the British, Jackson offered to recapture it—and this time his offer was ignored completely. He and his militiamen were ordered instead to Mississippi to prepare for an attack on Florida. When they arrived, after a hard march in the winter of 1813, he received orders to disband his troops. Instead, the forty-six-year-old Jackson marched them back to Tennessee, walking all the way so that sick soldiers could ride the available horses. His tough discipline and willingness to share the privations of his troops won from his men the nickname "Old Hickory."

In the summer of 1813 Jackson got involved in a feud with Jesse Benton and his brother Thomas Hart, the future senator from Missouri. Jackson had acted as second for a friend in a duel with Jesse. This angered Thomas Hart Benton, then an army lieutenant colonel, who made some unrecorded but apparently intemperate remarks about Jackson. In turn, Jackson declared he would horsewhip Benton if he ever showed his face in Nashville again. Soon after, the Bentons came to town heavily armed. In a hotel hallway Jackson waylaid Thomas Hart Benton with a whip in one hand and a pistol in the other. Before he could use either, Jesse Benton appeared behind him and opened fire, hitting Jackson in the shoulder. As Jackson fell, Thomas Hart Benton pumped more bullets into his body. For several days Jackson lay near death with doctors urging him to have his shattered left arm amputated. But the strong-willed Jackson refused to allow it, and slowly began to recover. He carried these bullets in his arm for the next nineteen years, until they were removed while he was President.

While still in bed recovering from this affray, Jackson received word that the Creek Indians under Chief Red Eagle had massacred 200 settlers in the Mississippi Territory. With his wounded arm in a sling, Jackson called his militia to arms and marched south. During the first week of November 1813, he twice defeated small groups of Creeks. Deep in the wilderness of what is now Alabama, Jackson's troops failed to receive any supplies. Cold, hungry, ill-clothed, and homesick, hundreds of Jackson's volunteers and militia began leaving for home at the end of their agreed terms of active service. But Jackson angrily declared that he personally would never retreat: "I will perish first."

After more supplies and fresh troops reached Jackson, he led about 2,000 men against 800 Creeks in the battle of Horseshoe Bend on March 27, 1814. "Arrows, and spears, and balls were flying," wrote Sam Houston, who was a young officer in the battle, "swords and tomahawks gleaming in the sun." The fighting ended at nightfall with more than 750 Indians and forty-nine of Jackson's troops dead. A few days later Chief Red Eagle surrendered and the war with the Creeks was over. As punishment for their uprising, Jackson forced the Creeks to give up 23 million acres of their land. They also gave Jackson a personal present of three square miles of land.

Returning home a hero, Jackson was rewarded by President Madison with appointment as a major general in the Regular Army and was given command of the entire southwestern part of the United States. Mistrustful of the Spanish in Florida, Jackson sent a scout to Pensacola to find out what was going on. When the scout returned with word that the British were using Pensacola as a naval base, Jackson launched a lightning raid on the Florida port and captured it after a brief fight in November 1814.

Moving his headquarters west to New Orleans, Jackson arrived just in time to learn of an impending attack by a huge British fleet and army. On December 23, the British made a successful surprise landing only a few miles east of New Orleans. Jackson attacked at night, halting the British advance, then withdrew to a defensive line along an abandoned canal four miles from the city. As the British brought up reinforcements until their army numbered 10,000 disciplined veterans, Jackson's forces of only about half as many men —including Jean Laffite's pirates—threw up a mud and log rampart that stretched from the Mississippi River to a swamp.

The British first tried to attack the line on December 28, but were driven back by cannonfire. After bringing up cannon from their warships, the British launched a huge bombardment on New Year's Day, but again were unable to crack the defenses.

Then, in a cold, foggy dawn on January 8, 1815, the British attacked in force. As the redcoats advanced in unbroken lines, Jackson's expert frontier riflemen picked them off one by one. The result was one of the worst British defeats in history, with losses of more than 2,600 dead, wounded, or captured —including the death of their commanding general—while Jackson had only eight men killed and thirteen wounded!

As news of the battle of New Orleans spread across the nation, the forty-seven-year-old Jackson was hailed as the hero of the war. More than two months later official word finally reached New Orleans that the War of 1812 was over, with a peace treaty negotiated by John Quincy Adams before the battle of New Orleans had been fought.

A Period of Trials and Triumphs

AFTER JAMES MONROE'S ELECTION as President, Jackson declined appointment as Secretary of War, confident that as long as the Spanish held Florida work remained for him to do on the frontier. In 1818 he was given command of an army to put down an uprising of the Seminole Indians, with orders to pursue them into Florida, if necessary. Jackson proposed to Monroe that he be given unofficial authorization to seize Florida from Spain. Proceeding with his plans, Jackson captured the Spanish forts in Florida, appointed one of his colonels as military governor of the area, and returned in triumph to Tennessee.

In the ensuing uproar, Spain threatened to declare war if its Florida forts were not given back. In secret Cabinet meetings John Quincy Adams defended Jackson's actions, while Secretary of War John Calhoun urged that Jackson be arrested—facts that were revealed to Jackson more than a dozen years later when he was President and Calhoun was his Vice President.

Early in 1819, the House of Representatives, led by its Speaker, Henry Clay, prepared resolutions condemning Jackson's actions in Florida. Jackson hurried to Washington to defend himself, while Clay made allusions to Caesar crossing the Rubicon. Jackson's friends beat down the House resolutions at the same time Adams negotiated a treaty acquiring Florida from Spain for $5 million.

Jackson accepted appointment as the first territorial governor of Florida in 1821. But he remained there only long enough to organize the government, then retired to plantation life in Tennessee.

As the presidential campaign of 1824 approached, President Monroe offered Jackson the post of minister to Mexico. When Jackson refused, it was taken as an indication of his willingness to run for President. He made even more clear his desire to return to politics when he accepted election by the Tennessee legislature in October 1823 as U.S. senator. When he took his seat in the Senate Chamber, the adjacent desk was that of Missouri Senator Thomas Hart Benton, with whom he had fought almost to the death ten years earlier. But now both men shook hands, and Benton ultimately became one of Jackson's firmest supporters.

Jackson's presidential candidacy received its biggest boost when a political convention in the key state of Pennsylvania nominated him for President in February 1824. Holding himself aloof from the campaign, as was the custom of candidates in those days, Jackson left the electioneering to his friends.

Although Old Hickory won the largest number of popular and electoral votes in the election, he did not receive a majority, so the selection of the next President fell to the House of Representatives. There, Clay engineered the choice of second-place John Quincy Adams as the nation's next Chief Executive.

Though he had not been an enthusiastic presidential candidate in 1824, Jackson now felt he had been cheated and resolved to revenge himself on Adams and Clay. The Tennessee legislature promptly, in 1825, nominated him for President for 1828, and he resigned as senator to devote his full attention to the campaign.

Presidential electioneering sank to new lows. Jackson could scarcely restrain himself from seizing his dueling pistols when Adams-Clay newspapers raked over details of his courtship and marriage. In 1828 Jackson made one of the first "campaign tours" of a presidential candidate, traveling to New Orleans for the thirteenth anniversary celebration of his victory. When the votes were counted, Jackson beat Adams by a clear majority with an electoral vote of 178 to 83 and a popular vote of 647,286 to 508,064.

But in his moment of vengeful glory, Jackson was plunged into sorrow. His wife, Rachel, now a middle-aged, home-loving frontierswoman who enjoyed smoking a corncob pipe as much as did her husband, and had no desire to become First Lady, died just as she and Jackson were preparing to leave for Washington. One of her last remarks was: "I had rather be a door-keeper in the house of God than to live in that palace." The sorrowing President-elect blamed her death both on his political enemies and on himself.

Jackson's First Term

LOOKING OLDER than his sixty-one years, Jackson was in poor shape to assume the burdens of the presidency in 1829. He was racked by tuberculosis, and the bullets he still carried in his body contributed to his poor health. Moreover, with Rachel dead he felt he had little to live for. Many of his friends believed he would never live to complete his first term. And, if he had died during his first two or three years in office, he might well have gone down in history as one of our least successful Presidents, for the first years of his presidency were chaotic and unproductive.

Washington swarmed with job-hunting Jackson supporters on the day of his inauguration. They had come in the belief he would make a "clean sweep" of all the federal officials appointed by Adams. And, although Jackson instituted a greater job-housecleaning than had President Jefferson, the "spoils system" that he was said to have introduced replaced only about a sixth of federal office holders during his years in the White House. Many job-hunters went home disappointed.

Upon Jackson's inauguration—a ceremony that the bitter President Adams avoided attending—the new President called for "extinguishment of the national debt" to "counteract that tendency to public and private profligacy which a profuse expenditure of money by the Government is but too apt to engender." He promised "reform" to remove federal offices from "unfaithful or incompetent hands." And he reassured those who feared the ascendancy of a general to the White House by voicing his conviction that the "military should be held subordinate to the civil power."

From his strong sense of personal loyalty to a friend, President Jackson devoted a disproportionate amount of time and effort during his first term to a social contretemps that became known as the "Affair of Mrs. Eaton." For several years Tennessee Senator John Eaton, Jackson's presidential campaign manager, had been carrying on a dalliance with the pretty, married daughter of the owner of a Washington boardinghouse where Eaton resided. Jackson had lived there, too, while he was a senator, and was fond of the flirtatious girl. When the girl's husband, a navy officer, died at sea in 1828 (some said he killed himself because of her affair with Eaton), Jackson privately urged Eaton to marry her as quickly as possible to silence the tongues of scandal-mongers. Eaton followed Jackson's advice and married her two months before Jackson took office.

But, after Jackson appointed Eaton Secretary of War, many of Washington's society leaders began snubbing Mrs. Eaton. Secretary of State Martin Van Buren and Vice President John Calhoun, who both aspired to the presidency, used the affair of Mrs. Eaton to promote their own political futures. Van Buren, a widower, insinuated himself with Jackson by promoting Mrs. Eaton's social position. On the other hand, Calhoun, whose wife refused to have anything to do with Mrs. Eaton, set himself up as the leader of morality and protector of womanhood.

Because the wives of most of Eaton's fellow Cabinet members refused to receive Mrs. Eaton in their homes, Jackson took the highly unusual step of calling a Cabinet meeting and asking for the resignation of any whose wives would not treat Mrs. Eaton with respect. The Cabinet members blandly said they were unable to control the actions of their wives and refused to resign. Jackson must have felt there was some force in their argument, because even his own official White House hostess, Mrs. Emily Donelson, wife of one of Jackson's adopted nephews and private secretary, refused to help Mrs. Eaton win social success.

Barely on speaking terms with most of the members of his Cabinet, Jackson began to rely for advice on a "kitchen cabinet" made up of loyal political supporters. In a new effort to solve the problem, Jackson had Eaton send his wife to Tennessee to live, and likewise banished Mrs. Donelson to his home state. But it was too late to heal the political split among administration officials.

In 1831 Jackson broke completely with Calhoun, and gave Van Buren assurances he would help him become the next President. Now secure in his position, Van Buren proposed to break the Cabinet deadlock by resigning as Secretary of State. This apparent self-sacrifice caused Eaton to resign as Secretary of War. Jackson then demanded the resignations of the three Calhoun supporters in his Cabinet. Shortly after, Eaton challenged each of the three to duels, but all declined. The appointment of five new Cabinet members in 1831 closed the "Affair of Mrs. Eaton" and gave Jackson's administration a new lease on life.

Jackson gave Van Buren a recess appointment as minister to England in 1831. When the appointment came up for consideration by the Senate in January 1832, the foes of Jackson and Van Buren decided this would be a good time to embarrass both. The conspirators arranged a tie vote on the appointment, giving Vice President Calhoun the pleasure of casting the deciding vote against Van Buren. But the plot backfired by winning Van Buren national sympathy and making it easier for Jackson to obtain his party's vice-presidential nomination for his friend.

An issue that smoldered and occasionally burst into flame during Jackson's first administration was that of nullification. Calhoun had made himself the leader of the movement that declared that a state had the right to decide which federal laws it wished to observe and which it wished to reject. Calhoun and his followers also felt that a state had the right to secede from the Union. Jackson had made clear his feeling about secession by publicly declaring: "Our Federal Union, it must be preserved." But he had done nothing to uphold decisions by the Supreme Court that rejected the principle of nullification in regard to the rights of federally protected Indians in southern states —as an old Indian-fighter Jackson had little regard for any rights for Indians.

But it was not on the issue of nullification that the election of 1832 was to be decided—the main issue was to be the re-chartering of the Bank of the United States. This was decided by Henry Clay, who in December 1831 won the presidential nomination of a new political party called the National Republicans. The new party's vice-presidential nomination went to John Sergeant, the chief lawyer of the Bank. From the outset of his administration, Jackson had declared his hostility to renewing the twenty-year charter of the Bank when it expired in 1836, believing that the control of the nation's monetary system should not be left in the hands of a private corporation. On the other hand, Clay believed that so many people owed money to the Bank, himself included, that they would fear having to repay these loans at once if the Bank were forced to close.

When Congress, at Clay's urging, passed a bill to re-charter the Bank in the summer of 1832, Jackson, as expected, vetoed the measure. But Jackson's veto message was such a clarion call to popular imagination that it overturned Clay's schemes. Jackson said of the Bank: ". . . when the laws undertake . . . to make the rich richer and the potent more powerful, the humble members of society, the farmers, mechanics, and laborers, who have neither the time nor the means for securing like favors to themselves, have a right to complain of the injustice of their government." Clay and his supporters could not muster enough support to override the veto. And, when the returns in the presidential election of 1832 were counted, Jackson and his Democrats, as his party members had begun to be called, won a smashing victory with 219 electoral votes to Clay's 49. The popular vote stood at 687,502 to 530,189.

Shortly after the election, South Carolina's legislature voted to nullify federal tariff laws and prepared to secede from the Union if efforts were made to collect federal tariffs after February 1, 1833. In the face of this ultimatum by Calhoun's home state, Jackson began preparing for civil war. In December 1832, he issued a Proclamation on Nullification, warning: "Disunion by armed force is treason."

Calhoun resigned as Vice President to take a seat as senator from South

Carolina, expecting that the issue would be thrashed out in Congress. But Old Hickory began mobilizing thousands of troops and let it be known that he planned to hang Calhoun if South Carolina went through with its threat. Everyone, including Calhoun, knew Jackson too well to think he was bluffing. South Carolina backed down by postponing its secession deadline. Congress supported Jackson by passing the Force Bill that authorized the President to use troops to collect federal taxes, but it also threw a bone to South Carolina by passing legislation calling for a gradual reduction of tariffs. The crisis ended when South Carolina rescinded its nullification legislation on Jackson's sixty-sixth birthday—a historic birthday present.

Jackson's Second Term

IN HIS SECOND INAUGURAL ADDRESS on March 4, 1833, Jackson declared: "In the domestic policy of this Government there are two objects which especially deserve the attention of the people and their representatives, and which have been and will continue to be the subjects of my increasing solicitude. They are the preservation of the rights of the several States and the integrity of the Union." He concluded by calling upon God to aid him "that we may be preserved from dangers of all kinds and continue forever a united and happy people." As long as Old Hickory remained President, there was no more serious talk of secession.

To solidify his popularity, Jackson made an extensive trip through the Middle Atlantic and New England states in the spring of 1833. As part of this journey, Jackson became the first President to ride on a railroad train—a twelve-mile run on the new Baltimore & Ohio Railroad. He also received an honorary doctorate from Harvard—despite the disapproval of one of its most distinguished alumni, John Quincy Adams, who muttered that Jackson could hardly write his own name.

Early in his second term, Jackson determined to crush "the Monster," as he called the Bank of the United States. As a first step, he planned to transfer federal funds from it to state banks. However, he did not have the full support of his Cabinet, and particularly not the support of his Secretary of the Treasury, William J. Duane. In September 1833, when Duane refused to carry out Jackson's plan, the President removed him and appointed Attorney General Roger Taney to take over the treasury post. Taney then carried out the plan to transfer federal deposits to the state banks.

In retaliation, Nicholas Biddle, who headed the Bank of the United States, tightened up credit, recalled loans, and generally slowed down the American economy. When delegations came to Washington to ask the President to ease the economic hard times, Jackson replied: "Go to Nicholas Biddle." In this way, Jackson brought home to the people the immense financial power of Biddle and the Bank. The Senate, controlled by Henry Clay, voted to censure Jackson for his actions against the Bank, but the House of Representatives overwhelmingly passed resolutions supporting Jackson and calling for an investigation of the Bank. Clay maneuvered another harassment of Jackson by having the Senate reject Taney's appointment as Secretary of the Treasury—the first time a presidential appointment to the Cabinet had ever been turned down.

Jackson more than made good on the pledge of his first inauguration to reduce the national debt. On January 8, 1835—the twentieth anniversary of the battle of New Orleans—the federal government completely paid off the national debt for the first time in its history. The country zoomed into a period of prosperity, prices rose, and paper money flowed. And because the federal government was collecting more in taxes than it was spending, Jackson approved, in 1836, an act to distribute surplus federal funds to the states. To curb the speculation in public land caused by the abundance of paper money, Jackson issued orders that henceforth only gold and silver would be accepted as payment for public land.

The greatest crisis in foreign relations came with France in 1835–36 over demands by Jackson that payments be made by the French for damages to American shipping during the Napoleonic wars. Diplomatic relations were broken off, and Jackson prepared for military action. But the French had no wish to tangle with the frontier general, so in 1836 Jackson received four past-due installments from the French and good relations were resumed.

Jackson left a black record in Indian affairs. He did not honor the terms of treaties that even he himself had drawn with the Indians. During his administration he forced most of the eastern Indian tribes to give up their lands to white settlers and move west of the Mississippi into Indian Territory, now Oklahoma.

In 1836 word came of the fantastic exploit of Jackson's friend Sam Houston, who at the head of a small army had unbelievably defeated and taken prisoner the Mexican President Santa Anna, winning independence for Texas. Soon Texas applied for annexation to the United States. Jackson hesitated to accept the new state because of the growing northern opposition to the extension of slavery, but, on the last day of his term of office he recognized Texas independence, setting the stage for future annexation.

The next day, the sick, tired Jackson gladly turned over the reins of government to his hand-picked successor, Martin Van Buren. Two days later he left Washington by train to return to his beloved Hermitage.

Last Years at the Hermitage

ALTHOUGH OLD, in ill health, and plagued by the debts of his spendthrift adopted son, Andrew Jackson, Jr., the aging general maintained a stronger position in the councils of his party and the administration of the government than any other former President.

When the country plunged into depression in 1837, Jackson's enemies blamed his fiscal policies. He repeatedly urged President Van Buren to stiffen his resolve and told him that prosperity would return. As the depression continued, Biddle's Bank of the United States (that had been re-chartered by Pennsylvania) closed its doors in failure, and Jackson felt that his opposition to it had been vindicated.

Jackson played an important role in secret negotiations with Sam Houston to achieve the annexation of Texas. When Van Buren came out against annexation, Jackson sent word to the 1844 Democratic Convention that Van Buren should be dumped as a presidential candidate. Jackson then helped his friend James K. Polk win the Democratic presidential nomination and the election.

At the age of seventy-eight, the old hero who had defied bullets, swords, arrows, and tomahawks died in his bed at the Hermitage. His last words, addressed to all the members of his household surrounding his bedside were: "I hope to see you all in Heaven, both white and black, both white and black."

Poet and editor William Cullen Bryant said of Jackson:

"Faults he had, undoubtedly; such faults as often belong to an ardent, generous, sincere nature—the weeds that grow in rich soil. Notwithstanding, he was precisely the man for the period, in which he well and nobly discharged the duties demanded of him."

Martin Van Buren
The Eighth President of the United States
1837–41

1782 (December 5) Born in Kinderhook, New York.

1803 Admitted to the bar to practice law.

1807 (February 21) Married Hannah Hoes.

1812–20 Member of New York state senate.

1816–19 Attorney general of New York.

1821–28 U.S. senator from New York.

1929 Governor of New York.

1829–31 Secretary of State of the United States.

1831–32 U.S. minister to England.

1833–37 Vice President of the United States.

1837–41 Eighth President of the United States.

1862 (July 24) Died in Kinderhook, New York.

Although Martin Van Buren was the carefully chosen political heir of Andrew Jackson, his personality was vastly different from that of his predecessor. Nicknamed "the Magician" because of his political adroitness in behind-the-scenes maneuvers, he lacked Old Hickory's ability to win popular support for himself or his policies. However, he did achieve the unique distinction of holding, within a span of a dozen years, the offices of U.S. senator, governor of New York, Secretary of State, Vice President, and President.

The country's first major economic depression, the Panic of 1837, ruined

Van Buren's popularity, even though he could hardly be held responsible for it—an experience that another President, Herbert Hoover, was to suffer nearly a century later.

That acidulous observer and political rival John Quincy Adams summed up Van Buren in unflattering terms:

"There are many features in the character of Mr. Van Buren strongly resembling that of Mr. Madison—his calmness, his gentleness of manner, his discretion, his easy and conciliatory temper. But Madison had none of his obsequiousness, his sycophancy, his profound dissimulation and duplicity."

Lawyer and Politician

THE FIRST PRESIDENT born an American citizen, rather than a British subject, Martin Van Buren curiously enough grew up speaking Dutch better than English. His ancestors came from the Netherlands as indentured servants, and he grew up in the old Dutch community of Kinderhook, New York. After attending local schools until he was fourteen, Martin began studying law, first in Kinderhook, and then in New York City. Admitted to the bar in 1803, when he was twenty, he began practicing law in Kinderhook.

In 1807 Van Buren married a distant cousin, Hannah Hoes. They had four sons, but Mrs. Van Buren died twelve years later, in 1819. Van Buren never remarried.

When he was twenty-nine, he won election to the New York state senate as a member of the Democratic-Republican party. Learning the ins and outs of complicated New York state politics, he swiftly rose to leadership of the "Albany Regency," a political machine that dominated the state government by means of the "spoils system."

Continuing to hold office as state senator, Van Buren served as state attorney general from 1816 to 1819. He helped his friend Rufus King, the former Federalist presidential candidate, win election to the U. S. Senate in 1820, and the next year, two days before his thirty-ninth birthday, he joined King as the junior U.S. senator from New York.

Van Buren supported the unsuccessful presidential candidacy of W. H. Crawford in the election of 1824. Four years later, he won election to the governorship, and even more important, helped swing twenty of the state's thirty-six electoral votes to Andrew Jackson for President.

Secretary of State and Vice President

AFTER SERVING ONLY TWO MONTHS as governor, Van Buren resigned to accept appointment by Jackson as Secretary of State. Competing with Vice President John C. Calhoun to win control of the Democratic-Republican party, Van Buren ingratiated himself with Jackson, even taking up horseback riding so that he could accompany the President on daily rides about the nation's capital. He particularly won Jackson's favor by his ostentatious friendship with the Eatons during the scandal that rocked Washington in Jackson's first administration. On New Year's Eve of 1829, Jackson wrote a political will, so that his choice of successor would become known if he died. In it Jackson wrote:

"Permit me to say here of Mr. Van Buren that I have found him everything that I could desire him to be, and believe him not only deserving of my confidence but the confidence of the Nation. Instead of his being selfish and intriguing, as has been represented by some of his opponents, I have found him frank, open, candid, and manly. As a Counsellor he is able and prudent, . . . and one of the most pleasant men to do business with I ever saw. He . . . is well qualified . . . to fill the highest office in the gift of the people. . . . I wish I could say as much for Mr. Calhoun. You know the confidence I once had in that gentleman. However, of him I desire not now to speak."

Assured of Jackson's support for his presidential ambitions, Van Buren resigned as Secretary of State in 1831 to make it easier for Old Hickory to clear his Cabinet of Calhoun adherents. Jackson rewarded Van Buren with appointment as minister to England. But, after Van Buren arrived in London, Calhoun succeeded in having the Senate reject the appointment, with himself casting the deciding vote and then triumphantly proclaiming: "It will kill him, sir; kill him dead. He will never kick, sir; never kick."

To Calhoun's chagrin, however, Jackson succeeded in obtaining the 1832 Democratic vice-presidential nomination for his friend even before Van Buren had returned from Europe.

While Vice President from 1833 to 1837, Van Buren resumed his role as Jackson's closest adviser. He also enjoyed the neat revenge of presiding over the same Senate that had rejected his diplomatic appointment. After an assassination attempt was made on Jackson in 1835, Van Buren regularly carried two pistols with him to the Senate.

Under the mantle of Jackson's prestige, Van Buren easily captured the Democratic presidential nomination for the election of 1836. The party's Baltimore convention, at Jackson's urging, gave the vice-presidential nomination to Kentucky Congressman Richard M. Johnson, a colorful character who claimed to have killed the Indian chief, Tecumseh, at the battle of the Thames and who angered the southern aristocracy by claiming social equality for his part-black daughters.

Opposition to the Van Buren-Johnson ticket was widespread but divided. The Whigs, remnants of the old Federalist party and of Clay's National Republican party, nominated war hero William Henry Harrison of Ohio for President; Massachusetts nominated orator and senator Daniel Webster; and Tennessee revolted against Jackson's rule by nominating Senator Hugh L. White, who had expected Jackson to obtain the Democratic presidential nomination for him instead of for Van Buren.

Against this divided opposition Van Buren won easily, even though his 765,483 popular votes barely topped the total of 739,795 of his opponents. He received 170 electoral votes to the opposition's combined total of 124. No vice-presidential candidate received a majority of the electoral votes, so for the first and only time in history the election of a Vice President was left to the Senate, which chose Johnson.

Van Buren's Administration

AT VAN BUREN'S INAUGURATION Jackson stole the cheers of the crowd, just as Washington had at John Adams' inauguration and as Jefferson had at James Madison's. In his address the fifty-four-year-old Van Buren made it frankly clear that he intended to continue to work in Jackson's shadow, saying:

"In receiving from the people the sacred trust twice confided to my illustrious predecessor, and which he has discharged so faithfully and so well, I know that I can not expect to perform the arduous task with equal ability and success. But united as I have been in his counsels, a daily witness to his exclusive and unsurpassed devotion to his country's welfare, agreeing with him in sentiments which his countrymen have warmly supported, and permitted to partake largely of his confidence, I may hope that somewhat of the same cheering approbation will be found to attend upon my path."

As further evidence of the caretaker role he intended to play, Van Buren reappointed all the members of Jackson's Cabinet.

Although in his inaugural address Van Buren had described the United States as representing "an aggregate of human prosperity surely not elsewhere to be found," two months later the economic stormclouds of the Panic of 1837 darkened the entire nation as banks suspended the payment of gold or silver for paper money.

Van Buren called a special session of Congress in September 1837 and asked that an independent treasury system be established, so that the government could retain control of the money collected in taxes, rather than deposit it in private banks. He also proposed that the government begin issuing paper money in the form of treasury notes. Van Buren warned Congress that it was not within its constitutional rights to provide "specific aid to the citizen to relieve embarrassments arising from losses by revulsions in commerce and credit." His reasoning was orthodox for the time:

"All communities are apt to look to government for too much. Even in our own country, where its powers and duties are so strictly limited, we are prone to do so, especially at periods of sudden embarrassment and distress. But this ought not to be. The framers of our excellent Constitution and the people who approved it with calm and sagacious deliberation acted at the time on a sounder principle. They wisely judged that the less government interferes with private pursuits the better for the general prosperity. It is not its legitimate object to make men rich or to repair by direct grants of money or legislation in favor of particular pursuits losses not incurred in public service. This would be substantially to use the property of some for the benefit of others."

Congress was slow in adopting the measures that Van Buren requested, and it was not until July 1840 that the independent treasury system went into effect. Although prosperity returned temporarily in the winter of 1839–40, bad times recurred at the end of Van Buren's administration and persisted until 1845.

Van Buren was responsible for one of the first widespread improvements in labor conditions when, after a protest meeting by government laborers outside the White House, he reduced the work day for federal employees to ten hours.

Seeking to maintain the status quo between North and South, Van Buren only succeeded in angering both sections of the country. Anti-slavery forces opposed his support of a war against the Seminole Indians in Florida, believing it presaged the admission of Florida as a slave state And pro-slavery forces denounced him for not promoting the annexation of Texas as another slave state.

In the field of foreign affairs, Van Buren's administration was troubled with sporadic outbreaks of warfare along the Canadian border, but the President succeeded in averting full-scale war with Britain or Canada over the issues.

At home, Van Buren, a widower, had no official hostess in the White House until 1838 when the eldest of his four sons, Abraham, married Angelica Singleton of South Carolina, a distant relative of Dolley Madison. Van

Buren then invited his pretty young daughter-in-law to manage social affairs in the household.

Although Van Buren was unanimously chosen by the Democratic Convention to run for a second term in the election of 1840, the delegates could not agree on a vice-presidential candidate, deciding to leave the choice open to the electors. This extraordinary decision left Van Buren with the unusual handicap of not having a popular running mate to bring him support. Moreover, all the forces that opposed him united behind the Whig party's candidate, William Henry Harrison.

The Whigs called the President "Martin Van Ruin," because of the nationwide depression. They portrayed him as a "lily-fingered aristocrat" who drank his wine from a silver cooler and ate his meals from gold plates. He was particularly criticized for spending public money to install a hot-water tank in the White House to warm his bath water. On the other hand, they featured their candidate, Harrison, as a man of the people who could live in a log cabin and be content with hard cider. Although the facts were that Harrison was born in a mansion as a Virginia aristocrat and Van Buren was the self-made son of a tavern keeper, the voters believed the Whig version and Van Buren was defeated.

In his final State of the Union message to Congress on December 5, 1840, President Van Buren reported that a U. S. Navy expedition headed by Lieutenant Charles Wilkes had discovered the previously unknown continent of Antarctica and that two U.S. warships were stationed off the coast of Africa to intercept American ships engaged in the slave trade. But most of the long message reviewed what he regarded as his accomplishments in preserving the fiscal integrity of the government by ending his administration with a $1.5 million surplus rather than a public debt. And he defended his refusal to spend money on public works to relieve the depression on the grounds that such expenditures were unconstitutional.

"To avoid the necessity of a permanent debt and its inevitable consequences," he said, "I have advocated and endeavored to carry into effect the policy of confining the appropriations for the public service to such objects only as are clearly within the constitutional authority of the Federal Government; of excluding from its expenses those improvident and unauthorized grants of public money for works of internal improvement which were so wisely arrested by the constitutional interposition of my predecessor, and which, if they had not been so checked, would long before this time have involved the finances of the General Government in embarrassments far greater than those which are now experienced by any of the States . . ."

Van Buren's Later Years

VAN BUREN COUNTED ON RECEIVING the Democratic presidential nomination again in 1844, but made a fatal blunder that lost him his chance. He reached an apparent agreement with Henry Clay, the prospective Whig presidential candidate, to rule out the annexation of Texas as a campaign issue—both giving out announcements denouncing annexation on the same day, April 27, 1844. This "bargain" between Clay and Van Buren so angered Jackson, a proponent of Texas annexation, that he threw his weight against Van Buren and succeeded in winning the presidential nomination for James K. Polk.

Four years later Van Buren again tried to return to power, accepting the presidential nomination of the new anti-slavery Free Soil party. He failed to win a single electoral vote in the election of 1848, but his candidacy had the important effect of splitting New York state's Democratic vote, assuring the victory of the Whigs' presidential candidate, Zachary Taylor.

The aging Van Buren made a two-year trip to Europe in the 1850s and then retired to an estate, Lindenwald, that he had purchased near his birthplace in Kinderhook, New York. He died there at the age of seventy-nine, on July 24, 1862.

William Henry Harrison
The Ninth President of the United States
1841

1773 (February 9) Born in Charles City County, Virginia.

1791–98 Served in U. S. Army, rising to rank of captain.

1795 (November 25) Married Anna Symmes.

1799–1800 Delegate to Congress from Northwest Territory.

1800–12 Governor of Indiana Territory.

1811 Defeated Shawnee Indians in battle of Tippecanoe.

1812–14 General in the War of 1812.

1817–19 U.S. representative from Ohio.

1819–25 Member of Ohio state senate.

1825–28 U.S. senator from Ohio.

1828–29 U.S. minister to Colombia.

1841 Ninth President of the United States.

1841 (April 4) Died in the White House in Washington, D.C.

Serving the shortest presidential term in American history, William Henry Harrison never had the opportunity to demonstrate his ability as Chief Executive. Like Jackson, he was elected largely on the basis of his reputation as an Indian fighter and successful major general in the War of 1812. In the presidential campaign and in his inaugural address, Harrison carefully avoided taking a stand on important national issues in order to help hold together the loose confederation of conflicting interests that made up his Whig party.

Soldier and Politician

BORN ON FEBRUARY 9, 1773, in Charles City County, Virginia, William Henry Harrison was the youngest of seven children of Benjamin Harrison, a wealthy planter and politician who signed the Declaration of Independence and was governor of Virginia at the end of the Revolutionary War. Young William entered Hampden-Sydney College at the age of fourteen, but left before graduation to take up the study of medicine under Dr. Benjamin Rush in Philadelphia.

After his father's death in 1791, the eighteen-year old Harrison gave up his medical studies to join the U. S. Army with a commission as ensign. Assigned to duty on the northwest frontier, he became an aide-de-camp to General Anthony Wayne and fought in a number of battles against the Indians.

By the time Harrison was twenty-two, he had risen to the rank of captain and was placed in command of Fort Washington (now Cincinnati), Ohio. While there, he married Anna Symmes, daughter of a well-to-do landowner. In the ensuing years they had ten children. Their son, John Scott Harrison, became the father of the twenty-third President, Benjamin Harrison.

In 1798 Harrison was appointed secretary of the Northwest Territory by President Adams. The next year, at the age of twenty-six, he was elected the territory's first delegate to Congress. When the western half of the Northwest Territory was reorganized in 1800 as the Indiana Territory, Adams appointed Harrison the first territorial governor, an office that he held for the next dozen years.

Harrison won his first national fame on November 7, 1811, when he successfully led his territorial militia in defeating a large-scale attack by Shawnee Indians in the battle of Tippecanoe. This battle made good the territory's claim to about 3 million acres of land that had been taken from the Indians.

On the outbreak of the War of 1812, Harrison was commissioned brigadier general and given command of the northwest frontier. Promoted to major general the next year, he led 3,000 troops into Canada, where, on October 5, 1813, he defeated a combined British-Indian force in the battle of the Thames River, in which the fearsome Shawnee Indian Chief Tecumseh was killed.

Harrison resigned his commission in 1814 and retired to his farm at North Bend, Ohio, but was appointed to fill a vacancy in Congress in 1816. Defeated for re-election, he entered the Ohio state senate, serving six years. In

1825 the state legislature elected him to the U. S. Senate, where he succeeded Andrew Jackson as chairman of the committee on military affairs.

Harrison resigned as a senator in 1828 to accept an appointment by President John Quincy Adams as U.S. minister to Colombia, but the next year, after Jackson became President, Harrison was recalled. Throughout the rest of Jackson's administration, Harrison lived on his farm. From 1834 he held office as clerk of the court of common pleas of Hamilton County, a position that paid him about $10,000 a year in fees.

Presidential Campaigns

In the confused national campaign of 1836 Harrison was one of several presidential candidates put up by the new Whig party against Martin Van Buren. He made a surprisingly good showing, winning seventy-three electoral votes and demonstrating national popularity. Four years later the Whig party united behind Harrison and his running mate, John Tyler of Virginia, with a catchy slogan: "Tippecanoe and Tyler Too." With the country still suffering from the economic depression following the Panic of 1837, the Whigs had a good chance. Harrison ran largely on his military record, keeping silent about national problems.

In the middle of the campaign a Van Buren supporter disparaged Harrison with the assertion "Give him a barrel of hard cider and settle a pension of two thousand a year on him and, my word for it, he will sit the remainder of his days in a log cabin." The Whigs pounced on the remark, and turned it in their candidate's favor. Overnight the country blossomed with log cabins and barrels of hard cider as "Tippecanoe" was played up as a rugged frontiersman and man of the people while Van Buren was painted as a New York plutocrat. The campaign song became:

> *"What has caused this great commotion, motion*
> *Our country through?*
> *It is the ball a-rolling on,*
> *For Tippecanoe and Tyler too, Tippecanoe and Tyler too.*
> *And with them we'll beat little Van, Van, Van;*
> *Van is a used-up man."*

In many ways it was the first modern presidential election. Almost a million more persons went to the polls in 1840 than in 1836. It was the first election in which any candidate received over a million votes. Harrison had 1,274,624 popular votes to Van Buren's 1,127,781, and swamped the New

York Democrat with 234 to 60 electoral votes. The Whigs also won control of both houses of Congress for the first and only time in the history of that political party.

Harrison's Brief Presidential Administration

INAUGURATION DAY, MARCH 4, 1841, was cold, rainy, and blustery. But the weather did not chill the ardor of Harrison's supporters, who gave him, in the words of John Quincy Adams, "demonstrations of popular feeling unexampled since that of Washington in 1789."

Standing bareheaded on the east steps of the Capitol, the sixty-eight-year-old Harrison—the oldest man elected President up to that time—read a long, meandering inaugural address that had been edited by his new Secretary of State, Daniel Webster. During the course of the address, he caught a cold that would prove fatal a month later.

Denouncing what he described as a tendency toward monarchy in the presidency, he called for a constitutional amendment to limit Presidents to a single term in office, and pledged that "under no circumstances will I consent to serve a second term."

Harrison went on to discuss what he called "the impropriety of Executive interference in the legislation of Congress," asserting that "the article in the Constitution making it the duty of the President to communicate information and authorizing him to recommend measures was not intended to make him the source in legislation, and, in particular, that he should never be looked to for schemes of finance."

"I have spoken of the necessity of keeping the respective departments of the Government, as well as all the other authorities of our country, within their appropriate orbits," he said. "This is a matter of difficulty in some cases, as the powers which they respectively claim are often not defined by any distinct lines. Mischievous, however, in their tendencies as collisions of this kind may be, those which arise between the respective communities which for certain purposes compose one nation are much more so, for no such nation can long exist without the careful culture of those feelings of confidence and affection which are the effective bonds to union between free and confederated states. Strong as is the tie of interest, it has been often found ineffectual. Men blinded by their passions have been known to adopt measures for their country in direct opposition to all the suggestions of policy. The alternative, then, is to destroy or keep down a bad passion by creating and fostering a good one, and this seems to be the corner stone upon which our American political architects have reared the fabric of our Government.

The cement which was to bind it and perpetuate its existence was the affectionate attachment between all its members. To insure the continuance of this feeling, produced at first by a community of dangers, of sufferings, and of interests, the advantages of each were made accessible to all. . . .

"It should be our constant and earnest endeavor mutually to cultivate a spirit of concord and harmony among the various parts of our Confederacy. Experience has abundantly taught us that the agitation by citizens of one part of the Union of a subject not confided to the General Government, but exclusively under the guardianship of the local authorities, is productive of no other consequences than bitterness, alienation, discord, and injury to the very cause which is intended to be advanced. Of all the great interests which appertain to our country, that of union—cordial, confiding, fraternal union— is by far the most important, since it is the only true and sure guaranty of all others. . . .

"If parties in a republic are necessary to secure a degree of vigilance sufficient to keep the public functionaries within the bounds of law and duty, at that point their usefulness ends. Beyond that they become destructive of public virtue, the parent of a spirit antagonist to that of liberty, and eventually its inevitable conqueror. . . . All the influence that I possess shall be exerted to prevent the formation at least of an Executive party in the halls of the legislative body. I wish for the support of no member of that body to any measure of mine that does not satisfy his judgment and his sense of duty to those from whom he holds his appointment, nor any confidence in advance from the people but that asked for by Mr. Jefferson, 'to give firmness and effect to the legal administration of their affairs.' "

During the next few weeks Harrison was harassed by Whig office seekers, but he refused to be pressured into dismissing government officials purely on a basis of party loyalty. Senator Clay, who had believed he could treat Harrison as a pawn, insisted that some of his friends be appointed to positions. But Tippecanoe kicked Clay out of the White House, warning him by note: "You are too impetuous." Clay left for Kentucky in a rage.

Fatigued and ill with a cold, Harrison took to his bed on March 27. The next day his physicians diagnosed his illness as pneumonia, and, at a half hour past midnight on April 4, 1841, Harrison became the first President to die in office. His last words to one of his physicians were:

"Sir, I wish you to understand the true principles of the Government. I wish them carried out. I ask nothing more."

John Tyler
The Tenth President of the United States
1841–45

1790 (March 29) Born in Charles City County, Virginia.

1807 Graduated from William and Mary College.

1809 Admitted to the bar to practice law.

1811–16 Member of Virginia legislature.

1813 (March 29) Married Letitia Christian.

1813 Captain of militia in War of 1812.

1816–21 U.S. representative from Virginia.

1823–25 Member of Virginia legislature.

1825–27 Governor of Virginia.

1827–36 U.S. senator from Virginia.

1838–40 Member of Virginia legislature.

1841 Vice President of the United States.

1841–45 Tenth President of the United States.

1844 (June 26) Married Julia Gardiner.

1861 President of Peace Conference in Washington, D.C.

1862 Member of Congress of the Confederate States.

1862 (January 18) Died in Richmond, Virginia.

The nation's first "President by act of God," John Tyler shocked many persons by taking over the presidential title along with the duties upon the death of William Henry Harrison. This was the first of a number of shocks he administered, particularly to the Whig party that had elected him Vice President, but rapidly disowned him as President. Tyler described his administration as "a bed of thorns . . . which has afforded me no repose."

The fifty-one-year-old Tyler was a headstrong slave-holding Virginia planter who had broken with the Democrats over Jackson's vigorous stand against nullification. But in the White House with a Whig Congress in power he used the veto time after time in support of his low-tariff Democratic principles. A friend commented, "When he thinks he is right he is obstinate as a bull, and no power on earth can move him."

Sixteen years after quitting the White House, Tyler had an opportunity to play an even greater role as president of a Peace Convention called in an attempt to head off the Civil War, but he was unable to lead the delegates to a workable compromise. He died a member of the Confederate Congress, denounced in the North as a traitor.

A Southern Aristocrat

TYLER WAS BORN ON MARCH 29, 1790, in Charles City County, Virginia— the same county where William Henry Harrison had been born seventeen years earlier. Like Harrison, Tyler was the son of a planter-politician who served as governor of the state.

After graduation from William and Mary College at seventeen, Tyler studied law and was admitted to the bar at nineteen. Two years later he launched his political career by winning election to the Virginia legislature. In 1813 he served briefly as a captain of militia, and on his twenty-third birthday, married Letitia Christian. They had eight children and enjoyed a marriage that lasted for nearly thirty years, until Mrs. Tyler's death in the White House in 1842.

Virginia's voters bestowed every honor at their disposal on the likable young lawyer, who for relaxation played the violin and wrote poetry. At the age of twenty-six he was elected to Congress, at thirty-five he became governor, and at thirty-six a U.S. senator.

Although Tyler supported Andrew Jackson in the elections of 1828 and 1832, he broke with Jackson in 1833 over the issue of nullification and secession. He was the only senator to vote against the Force Bill that gave the President authority to use military force, if necessary, to collect federal revenues—a threat aimed at the South Carolina nullifiers. Later that year Tyler voted with a majority of senators to censure Jackson for withdrawing federal deposits from the Bank of the United States.

In 1836 the Virginia legislature, controlled by Jackson supporters, sent instructions to Tyler that he was to vote for a resolution expunging the censure of Jackson from the Senate record. Rather than comply, Tyler resigned as senator. The Whigs promptly seized on the disaffected Democrat as a strong candidate for Vice President on their ticket. Although the Whigs lost the national election of 1836, Tyler made a good showing, gathering forty-seven electoral votes.

Winning election to the Virginia legislature in 1838 as a Whig, Tyler received the additional honor of being chosen speaker of the lower house. The next year he was unsuccessful in his bid for re-election to the U. S. Senate, the voting in the legislature ending in a temporary deadlock with no one chosen to fill the vacancy.

In December 1839, at the Whig National Convention in Harrisburg, Pennsylvania, Tyler was again nominated for Vice President, this time as running mate for William Henry Harrison. The "Tippecanoe and Tyler Too" victory made Tyler Vice President, and within a month, to his own astonishment no less than to everyone else's, he was President. After Harrison's inauguration, Tyler had left Washington for his home in Williamsburg. He took no part in discussions about Cabinet appointments, and prepared to play an unobtrusive role in the government. These plans were short-lived. Roused out of bed at dawn on April 5, he learned the startling news of Harrison's death.

Tyler rode to Washington the next day and was sworn in as President at noon. He retained all the members of Harrison's Cabinet, but made it clear at once who was boss. He refused to accept the suggestion that all decisions be put to a majority vote. "I can never consent to being dictated to," he warned Secretary of State Daniel Webster and his colleagues.

Yet Henry Clay and the other Whig leaders in Congress were confident they could control Tyler by the majority they held in both houses. As soon as a special session convened in May to deal with the national economic crisis, Clay set about pushing through legislation for a new national bank, even though Tyler warned that he did not believe it was constitutional. When Tyler vetoed the measure in August, Clay was purple with rage, because he did not have enough votes to override the veto. Clay then put through a similar measure, called the Fiscal Corporation Bill, which Tyler also vetoed.

On September 11, 1841, two days after the second veto, all the members of Tyler's Cabinet except Daniel Webster resigned. And two days after that the Whig party officially expelled Tyler. The beleaguered President quickly filled out his Cabinet with conservative Democrats, starting a chain of Cabinet appointments that gave Tyler the dubious distinction of having more Cabinet changes than any other single-term executive.

Congress continued to pass legislation that it knew Tyler would not accept. In the summer of 1842 he twice vetoed bills that called for higher tariffs, bringing cries from the Whigs that he should be impeached. Finally, when the public treasury was almost empty, he signed a tariff measure in August 1842 to raise needed revenue. This did not stop the impeachment attempt, which was brought to a vote in the House in January 1843, but was defeated twenty-seven to eighty-three.

Tyler's administration achieved more success in the field of foreign relations than in domestic affairs. Daniel Webster remained in the Cabinet long enough to conclude the Webster-Ashburton Treaty, settling a long-standing dispute over the boundary between Maine and Canada. And a treaty with China in 1844 opened that country to trade with American merchants.

An unusual tragedy struck Tyler's administration in February 1844. The President and a large party of friends were on a cruise down the Potomac River on the new steam-powered warship *Princeton* when one of the ship's guns exploded. Several of the guests were killed, including Secretary of State Abel B. Upshur and Secretary of the Navy Thomas W. Gilmer.

Among the guests aboard the *Princeton,* was twenty-three-year-old New York socialite Julia Gardiner, whose family owned 3,000-acre Gardiner's Island off the eastern tip of Long Island and who had already shocked society by letting herself be pictured in newspaper advertisements endorsing a dry-goods store. Julia's father, wealthy David Gardiner, was one of the guests killed in the *Princeton* explosion. After the tragedy, the President himself carried Julia off the warship to a rescue vessel, winning her heart with his kind attention. Four months later the fifty-four-year-old Tyler married Julia Gardiner in a private church ceremony in New York City, and then took her back to the White House to preside as First Lady. Although Tyler's enemies laughed at the May-December marriage, it was a long and happy one. Tyler had seven children by his second wife.

The election year of 1844 found Tyler in the odd position of having no party willing to nominate him for re-election; so he organized a new states-rights Democratic-Republican party and campaigned on the issue of obtaining the annexation of Texas, which was opposed both by Clay, the Whig nominee, and Van Buren, who seemed likely to be the Democratic nominee. But when the Democrats nominated James K. Polk, who favored Texas annexation, Tyler withdrew at the urging of Andrew Jackson in order to insure Clay's defeat.

After Polk had been elected, Congress passed a joint House-Senate resolution approving the annexation of Texas, and Tyler signed it on March 1, 1845. On his last day in office, March 3, he signed legislation admitting Florida as the twenty-seventh state. On the same day Congress mustered enough votes (two-thirds in each house) to override one of Tyler's vetoes on a minor piece of legislation concerning the building of revenue cutters—the first time in history a presidential veto had been overridden.

Immediately after Polk's inauguration on March 4, Tyler and his family left for Virginia.

Tyler's Last Years

FOR MORE THAN A DOZEN YEARS Tyler enjoyed the pleasant life of a southern planter with a growing young family on his Sherwood Forest estate, which bordered the James River in Virginia. Although plagued with the ailments of age, he maintained an active interest in politics, and even entertained the hope that the Democrats would nominate him for President again.

As bitterness between North and South threatened to burst into flame after Lincoln's election in 1860, Tyler proposed that a Peace Convention of border states be called to try to head off civil war. The Virginia legislature indorsed the idea and called for delegates not only from the border states but from North and South as well to meet in Washington. Tyler, a member of Virginia's delegation and special emissary from Virginia to President Buchanan, was unanimously elected president of the convention, which met in February. But he found it impossible to unite the delegates in agreement on a workable compromise. In the end he openly sided with the southern secessionists, and the Peace Conference ended in failure.

Tyler hurried home to a state convention where he urged Virginia to join the other seceding states. In November 1861, Tyler was elected a Virginia representative to the Confederate Congress. While preparing to attend the first session of this congress in Richmond, the seventy-one-year-old former President died in his hotel room a few minutes after midnight on January 18, 1862.

James Knox Polk

The Eleventh President of the United States
1845–49

1795 (November 2) Born in Mecklenburg County, North Carolina.

1818 Graduated from the University of North Carolina.

1820 Admitted to the bar to practice law in Tennessee.

1823–25 Member of state legislature of Tennessee.

1824 (January 1) Married Sarah Childress.

1825–39 U.S. representative from Tennessee.

1835–39 Speaker of the U. S. House of Representatives.

1839–41 Governor of Tennessee.

1845–49 Eleventh President of the United States.

1849 (June 15) Died in Nashville, Tennessee.

Called "Young Hickory" by his supporters, James Knox Polk came to the presidency as the protégé of Andrew Jackson. Although he did not have the glamour of "Old Hickory," Polk was an astute politician who knew what the people wanted and gave it to them. In the 1840s the United States was in an expansionist mood as huge numbers of settlers flowed West by covered wagon, railroad, and steamboat, and the majority of people believed it was the "manifest destiny" of the country to fill the continent from coast to coast. Polk fulfilled these wishes by pushing the frontier all the way to the Pacific Coast, increasing the size of the United

States more than any President since Jefferson, even though it brought war with Mexico and the threat of war with Britain.

Polk, a strait-laced Methodist, and his wife, a strict Presbyterian, banished drinking, dancing, and card-playing from the White House. Sam Houston once commented that the only thing wrong with Polk was that he drank too much water. Tart-penned John Quincy Adams found other faults: "He has no wit, no literature, no point of argument, no gracefulness of delivery, no elegance of language, no philosophy, no pathos, no felicitous impromptus; nothing that can constitute an orator, but confidence, fluency, and labor."

In his inaugural address, Polk enunciated a lofty view of the presidency:

"Although . . . the Chief Magistrate must almost of necessity be chosen by a party and stand pledged to its principles and measures, yet in his official action he should not be the President of a part only, but of the whole people of the United States. While he . . . faithfully carries out in the executive department of the Government the principles and policy of those who have chosen him, he should not be unmindful that our fellow-citizens who have differed with him in opinion are entitled to the full and free exercise of their opinions and judgments, and that the rights of all are entitled to respect and regard."

Frontier Beginnings

BORN OF SCOTCH-IRISH PARENTS on a farm on the North Carolina frontier on November 2, 1795, James K. Polk was the oldest of a family of ten children. When he was ten, the boy moved west with his family to central Tennessee, where in time his father became one of the largest landholders in the region. At nineteen, young James was sent back across the mountains to the University of North Carolina, from which he was graduated with honors three years later.

Returning to Tennessee, Polk began studying law under Congressman Felix Grundy, a friend of Jackson's and later U. S. Attorney General under Martin Van Buren. Admitted to the bar at the age of twenty-four, he began practicing law in Columbia, Tennessee.

Polk entered politics in 1823 as a successful candidate for the state legislature, and because of his small stature, earned the nickname "Napoleon of the Stump." While serving in the legislature, Polk married twenty-year-old Sarah Childress on New Year's Day, 1824. They had no children.

At the age of thirty, Polk was elected to Andrew Jackson's old seat as U.S. representative from Tennessee. He swiftly rose to prominence in Congress, serving as chairman of the powerful Ways and Means Committee and as majority leader for the Democratic party. He won Jackson's support by help-ing steer the administration's legislation through the House of Representa-tives. He was elected Speaker of the House during the last two years of Jackson's administration and the first two years of Van Buren's—the only Speaker of the House ever to become President.

In 1839 the forty-three-year-old Polk left Congress to run for and win the governorship of Tennessee. That same year the Tennessee legislature nomi-nated him for Vice President to run with Van Buren, but after the Demo-cratic National Convention failed to choose a vice-presidential candidate, he declined his state's nomination. His political star seemed to have waned when he twice lost bids for re-election as governor, in 1841 and 1843.

But another chance came when the 1844 Democratic National Conven-tion in Baltimore deadlocked between Van Buren and Lewis Cass of Michi-gan. Several ballots failed to produce a decision. Then Polk's friends began spreading the word that "Young Hickory" was Jackson's choice and that he could bring harmony to the party. After the eighth ballot, the New York delegation withdrew Van Buren's candidacy, and on the ninth ballot Polk became the unanimous choice of the convention—the first "dark horse" presidential candidate of a major party. When word of Polk's nomination was flashed from Baltimore to Washington by Samuel F. B. Morse's telegraph— the first official use of the new communication system—Washington observ-ers were sure the instrument had failed because they could not believe the news.

Henry Clay, the Whig nominee for President, upon hearing of the Demo-cratic nomination, sarcastically commented: "Who is James K. Polk?" The Whigs adopted this as a campaign slogan, but it was highly ineffective com-pared to the Democratic expansionist cries of "Reannexation for Texas and Oregon!" and "54-40 or Fight!" (the latter referring to the northern bound-ary of the Oregon Territory). Polk was further aided when Jackson used his influence to get President Tyler to withdraw as an independent candidate for re-election, thus preventing a split in the Democratic vote.

The election results were closer than any since 1824. Polk barely squeezed by in the popular vote with 1,338,464 to Clay's 1,300,097 and received 170 electoral votes to Clay's 105. Polk won New York's thirty-six electoral votes by only a 5,000-vote margin—if he had lost this crucial state the election would have gone to Clay.

Polk's Administration

THE FORTY-NINE-YEAR-OLD POLK—the youngest man ever to become President up to that time—took office on a rainy March 4, 1845, delivering his inaugural address "to a large assemblage of umbrellas" (in the words of John Quincy Adams). Although he did not mention it in the address, the "Napoleon of the Stump" already was planning to take New Mexico and California, as well as make good on his campaign promises of Texas and Oregon.

Two days after Polk became President, the Mexican minister to Washington filed a protest calling the annexation of Texas, voted by Congress in the last days of February, "an act of aggression." By the end of the month the United States and Mexico had broken diplomatic relations. The threat of war was in the air, but no hostile acts occurred during the remainder of the year. By December 29, 1845, Congress had approved the admission of Texas as a state, and Polk now pushed forward his plans to acquire New Mexico and California from Mexico. He made offers to Mexico to purchase the territory, but soon concluded that force would be required to obtain his ends. A dispute over the Texas-Mexico boundary helped bring on hostilities. Polk had already prepared a message for Congress calling for a declaration of war when word came on May 9, 1846, that Mexican troops had crossed the Rio Grande and fired on American army units. Polk added this information to his congressional message, and on May 13 Congress declared war on Mexico.

American troops advanced at once into Mexican territory, and by the end of the year U.S. forces held all of New Mexico and California. In February 1847, Major General Zachary Taylor won the brilliant victory of Buena Vista. Two weeks later Major General Winfield Scott landed an army of about 10,000 men near Vera Cruz and fought his way to Mexico City by September 1847. Although Polk was tempted to take all of Mexico for the United States, he approved a peace treaty signed in February 1848, in which Mexico ceded to the United States more than half a million square miles for a payment of $15 million.

While Polk was successfully carrying out his expansionist plans in the Southwest, he was simultaneously negotiating with Britain concerning the Oregon Territory in the Northwest. When Britain balked at U.S. claims to the entire area, he agreed to compromise on a boundary at the 49th parallel of latitude. Many Northerners were angry at this settlement, feeling that the pro-slavery Polk was willing to spill blood to add territory that would extend slavery in the Southwest but was unwilling to fight for added territory in the Northwest that would be free.

Polk made one further but unsuccessful effort to expand the United States. He offered Spain $100 million for Cuba, but Spain rejected the proposition.

During Polk's first two years in office the Democrats controlled both houses of Congress, enabling Polk to obtain passage of almost any legislation he wanted to implement his domestic program, which he called the "New Democracy." At the President's urging, Congress passed a new tariff act in July 1846 that substantially reduced import duties on such basic materials as coal and steel. Shortly after, Congress revived Van Buren's independent treasury system for control of the nation's money, a system which had been repealed in 1841 under President Tyler. But in the mid-term congressional elections, the Whigs won a majority of seats in the House, largely because of the unpopularity of the Mexican War in the northern states—thus Polk received little co-operation from Congress in the latter part of his administration.

In the field of foreign relations Polk made another important long-range gain for the United States in a Latin American treaty signed in 1847 that gave the United States the right of passage across the Isthmus of Panama for a future railroad or canal.

Although Polk had made no effort to run for a second term, he was discouraged by his party's defeat in the 1848 election, considering it to be a reflection on his administration. However, no hint of his disappointment came through in the optimistic and cheerful final State of the Union message that he sent to Congress on December 5, 1848, in which he helped set off the California gold rush of 1849 with his glowing account of the "abundance of gold" that had been discovered in the newly acquired territory. Not immodestly, Polk summarized his achievements in the message:

"Peace, plenty, and contentment reign throughout our borders, and our beloved country presents a sublime moral spectacle to the world. . . .

"In reviewing the great events of the past year and contrasting the agitated and disturbed state of other countries with our own tranquil and happy condition, we may congratulate ourselves that we are the most favored people on the face of the earth. While the people of other countries are struggling to establish free institutions, under which man may govern himself, we are in the actual enjoyment of them—a rich inheritance from our fathers. While enlightened nations of Europe are convulsed and distracted by civil war or intestine strife, we settle all our political controversies by the peaceful exercise of the rights of freemen at the ballot box. . . .

"Within less than four years the annexation of Texas to the Union has been consummated; all conflicting title to the Oregon Territory south of the forty-ninth degree of north latitude, being all that was insisted on by any of my predecessors, has been adjusted, and New Mexico and Upper California have been acquired by treaty . . . the territories recently acquired, and over which our exclusive jurisdiction and dominion have been extended, constitute a country more than half as large as all that which was held by the United States before their acquisition, and, including Oregon, nearly as great an extent of territory as the whole of Europe, Russia only excepted. The Mississippi, so lately the frontier of our country, is now only its center. . . ."

After the inauguration of Zachary Taylor, Polk returned to Tennessee, a man made old before his time by the cares of office. Three months later he was stricken with cholera and died in Nashville on June 15, 1849. James Buchanan, his Secretary of State, said of him:

"He was the most laborious man I have ever known; and in a brief period of four years had assumed the appearance of an old man."

Zachary Taylor
The Twelfth President of the United States
1849–50

1784 (November 24) Born in Orange County, Virginia.

1808–48 Served in U. S. Army, rising from lieutenant to major general.

1810 (June 21) Married Margaret Smith.

1847 (February 22–23) Won the battle of Buena Vista.

1849–50 Twelfth President of the United States.

1850 (July 9) Died in Washington, D.C.

Zachary Taylor was the first President elected to office with no previous political experience. As a result, he was ill-prepared for the politics and problems involved. Like William Henry Harrison, Taylor was chosen by the Whigs as their presidential candidate solely because he was a war hero. And, like Harrison, he died in the White House before he really had an opportunity to prove whether or not he might have coped more effectively than his successors with the issues that were carrying the nation toward civil war.

Taylor spent forty years in the army—fighting Indians, commanding frontier posts, and winning glory in the Mexican War by the victory of Buena Vista, where his troops were outnumbered four to one. He was called "Old Rough and Ready" by his men because of his frontier bluntness and his disregard of dress—he preferred civilian clothes to a uniform even in battle. Short and plump, he had none of the appearance of a military hero and had to be given a leg-up by his orderly when he mounted a horse.

A Frontier Soldier

THE YOUNGEST OF THREE SONS in a family of nine children, Zachary Taylor was born on November 24, 1784, on a farm in Orange County, Virginia. When less than a year old, he was taken west by his family to settle near Louisville, Kentucky, on several thousand acres of land that his father, Colonel Richard Taylor, had received as a bonus for his services in the Revolutionary War. Because there were no schools on the Kentucky frontier, the boy grew up with only a rudimentary education provided by tutors that his father hired from time to time.

When Taylor was twenty-three, he received a commission as a first lieutenant in the U. S. Army through the influence of his relative, James Madison, who was then Secretary of State. Two years later, in 1810, he was promoted to captain.

Also in 1810 Taylor married Margaret Smith, who shared the hardships of life in frontier military posts, and who, like Mrs. Andrew Jackson, enjoyed smoking a corncob pipe. The Taylors had six children. Their only son, Richard, later became a lieutenant general in the Confederate Army. In 1835, against her father's wishes one of their daughters, Sarah, married Lieutenant Jefferson Davis, the future President of the Confederacy. Sarah died three months after the marriage. Taylor and Davis were not reconciled until twelve years later at the battle of Buena Vista where Davis, then a colonel, distinguished himself.

In the War of 1812, Taylor was promoted to the temporary rank of major for his skill in the defense of Fort Harrison, Indiana, from attacks by the Shawnee Chief Tecumseh. At the end of the war, when his rank was reduced to captain, he resigned from the army, but resumed his military career a year later when his commission as a major was restored. In 1819, Taylor was advanced to lieutenant colonel, but thirteen years went by before he was made a full colonel in 1832 at the time of the Black Hawk War. Taylor led his regiment, the 1st Infantry, to victory, personally accepting the surrender of Chief Black Hawk. Five years later he was sent to Florida to fight the Seminole Indians, and after defeating them on Christmas Day in 1837, was promoted to brigadier general and given command of all the troops in Florida. In 1841 he was made commander of the southern division of the army; he established a home at Baton Rouge, Louisiana, and acquired a large plantation with many slaves.

After the annexation of Texas in 1845, Taylor was ordered to defend the territory against any efforts by Mexico to reconquer it, and was given command of troops on the Rio Grande when the Mexican War began. Promoted to major general, he invaded and swiftly conquered the northeastern states of Mexico.

As Taylor's popularity increased with his victories, President Polk became jealous, and many of Taylor's troops were withdrawn from his command and sent to join an army being assembled by Major General Winfield Scott for an invasion of central Mexico. Taylor was left with a small force of about 5,000 men. Polk's plan to prevent Taylor from gaining more public acclaim backfired when Taylor and his small army gallantly withstood an attack by about 20,000 troops led by Mexico's President Santa Anna at Buena Vista in February 1847. Shortly thereafter, Taylor, angered by the maneuvers of Polk's administration, took a leave of absence from the army and returned to his home in Louisiana.

When news of Buena Vista reached the United States, the Whig party immediately set the ball rolling to nominate Taylor for President, even though no one, including Taylor, knew how he stood on the issues of the day. The Whig National Convention in Philadelphia in June 1848 nominated him and named Millard Fillmore of New York as its vice-presidential candidate. To oppose Taylor, the Democratic party nominated Lewis Cass, senator from Michigan. Martin Van Buren also made an attempt to regain the presidency by running as the anti-slavery candidate for the Free Soil party.

Despite Taylor's popular appeal as a war hero, the election of 1848 was close. Taylor won by 1,360,967 popular votes to 1,222,342 for Cass, and by 163 electoral votes to 127. It was Van Buren's candidacy, which split New York's Democratic party and threw that state's thirty-six electoral votes to Taylor, that provided "Old Rough and Ready" with his margin of victory.

Taylor's Administration

BECAUSE MARCH 4, 1849, fell on a Sunday, Taylor postponed his inauguration to the next day. In one of the shortest inaugural addresses of any incoming President, Taylor said nothing of his plans for the nation, noting only that he would look to Congress "to adopt such measures of conciliation as may harmonize conflicting interests and tend to perpetuate that Union which should be the paramount object of our hopes and affections." Even if Taylor had had a substantial program in mind, it is unlikely that he could have carried it out, since both houses of Congress were controlled by the Democrats.

A new controversy between North and South erupted during Taylor's administration over whether the new territories acquired from Mexico should be free or slave. The southern states became particularly bitter when Californians late in 1849 adopted a constitution as a free state and asked admission to the Union, threatening to upset the balance in the Senate between free and slave states. Although a Southerner by birth, Taylor urged California's admission. But Congress refused to act.

In an effort to prevent the same thing from happening in New Mexico, the slave state of Texas claimed that territory. Taylor disputed this claim on grounds that the United States had purchased New Mexico and that it therefore should be administered as a federal territory.

In his only State of the Union message to Congress, on December 4, 1849, Taylor reported that the government would end the fiscal year with a debt of about $16 million, largely as a result of the expenses of the Mexican War and the purchase of California and New Mexico. He called on Congress to raise tariffs on imports both to increase revenue and to aid the development of American industry.

"I do not doubt the right or duty of Congress to encourage domestic industry," he said, "which is the great source of national as well as individual wealth and prosperity. I look to the wisdom and patriotism of Congress for the adoption of a system which may place home labor at last on a sure and permanent footing and by the due encouragement of manufactures give a new and increased stimulus to agriculture and promote the development of our vast resources and the extension of our commerce. Believing that the attainment of these ends, as well as the necessary augmentation of the revenue and the prevention of frauds, a system of specific duties is best adapted, I strongly recommend to Congress the adoption of that system, fixing the duties at rates high enough to afford substantial and sufficient encouragement to our own industry and at the same time so adjusted as to insure stability."

He declared that what little aid the government had previously given to agriculture was "totally inadequate," and asked Congress to establish an agricultural bureau in the Department of the Interior to administer a program "to elevate the social condition of the agriculturist, to increase his prosperity, and to extend his means of usefulness to his country, by multiplying his sources of information."

President Taylor also urged help for the development of a transcontinental railroad: "The great mineral wealth of California and the advantages which its ports and harbors and those of Oregon afford to commerce, especially with the islands of the Pacific and Indian oceans and the populous regions of eastern Asia, make it certain that there will arise in a few years large and prosperous communities on our western coast. It therefore becomes important that a line of communication, the best and most expeditious which the nature of the country will admit, should be opened within the territory of the

United States from the navigable waters of the Atlantic or the Gulf of Mexico to the Pacific. Opinion, as elicited and expressed by two large and respectable conventions lately assembled at St. Louis and Memphis, points to a railroad as that which, if practicable, will best meet the wishes and wants of the country. But while this, if in successful operation, would be a work of great national importance and of a value to the country which it would be difficult to estimate, it ought also to be regarded as an undertaking of vast magnitude and expense, and one which must, if it be indeed practicable, encounter many difficulties in its construction and use. Therefore, to avoid failure and disappointment; to enable Congress to judge whether in the condition of the country through which it must pass the work be feasible, and, if it be found so, whether it should be undertaken as a national improvement or left to individual enterprise, and in the latter alternative what aid, if any, ought to be extended to it by the Government, I recommend as a preliminary measure a careful reconnaissance of the several proposed routes by a scientific corps and a report as to the practicability of making such a road, with an estimate of the cost of its construction and support."

In closing the State of the Union message, Taylor gave warning to those who would disrupt the Union: "For more than half a century, during which kingdoms and empires have fallen, this Union has stood unshaken. The patriots who formed it have long since descended to the grave; yet still it remains, the proudest monument to their memory and the object of affection and admiration with everyone worthy to bear the American name. In my judgment its dissolution would be the greatest of calamities, and to avert that should be the study of every American. Upon its preservation must depend our own happiness and that of countless generations to come. Whatever dangers may threaten it, I shall stand by it and maintain it in its integrity to the full extent of the obligations imposed and the powers conferred upon me by the Constitution."

In special messages to both houses of Congress late in January of 1850, the President called on Congress to allow the people of California and New Mexico to determine their own status "upon the principles laid down in our own Declaration of Independence." He asked Congress "to avoid any unnecessary controversy" that could endanger the Union.

When debate in Congress became more acrimonious, southern leaders threatened to drive federal troops out of the disputed territory of New Mexico. With a military bluntness reminiscent of Andrew Jackson, Taylor declared:

"I will command the army in person and hang any man taken in treason."

Senators Clay, Webster, and Calhoun set about constructing the elaborate Compromise of 1850 in an effort to smooth over the problem, but Taylor scorned compromise. If his death had not intervened, he quite likely would have vetoed the compromise measure. Daniel Webster was convinced that Taylor's death prevented the outbreak of civil war in 1850.

On July 4, 1850, at the laying of the cornerstone of the Washington Monument, the sixty-five-year-old Taylor remained out in the hot sun for many hours and became ill from the heat. He had a fever when he returned to the White House, and five days later, on the evening of July 9, he died. In announcing the President's death to Congress, his successor, Millard Fillmore, reported that Taylor's last words were:

"I have always done my duty. I am ready to die. My only regret is for the friends I leave behind me."

Millard Fillmore

The Thirteenth President of the United States
1850–53

1800 (January 7) Born in Cayuga County, New York.

1815–19 Apprenticed to a cloth-maker.

1823 Admitted to the bar to practice law in New York.

1826 (February 5) Married Abigail Powers.

1828–31 Member of New York state legislature.

1833–35; 1837–43 U.S. representative from New York.

1848 Comptroller of the state of New York.

1849–50 Vice President of the United States.

1850–53 Thirteenth President of the United States.

1856 Defeated for election as President as candidate of the American and Whig parties.

1858 (February 10) Married Caroline McIntosh.

1874 (March 8) Died in Buffalo, New York.

Six feet tall, with blue eyes and a handsome face, Millard Fillmore was more impressive in appearance than he was in accomplishment. He came to the presidency by the only road available to a man of his limited ability—by succeeding to the office upon the death of President Zachary Taylor. Although, as President, Fillmore did everything that he was told to do by the leaders of the Whig party, they refused to give him a chance to run for office on his own at the next election.

From Cloth-Maker's Apprentice to White House

MILLARD FILLMORE was born on January 7, 1800, in Cayuga County, New York, the son of a poor frontier farmer. As a small boy he helped his father clear the land and raise the crops. But with nine children in the family, there was hardly enough food to go around, so at fourteen Millard was apprenticed to a cloth-maker.

At nineteen he fell in love with Abigail Powers, a schoolteacher, two years older than himself. Under her inspiration he purchased his freedom from apprenticeship for $30, bought a dictionary, and obtained a job teaching school.

Presently he won the friendship of a county judge who took the boy into his office to study law. By the time he was twenty-three, Fillmore had learned enough to be admitted to the bar and opened a law office in East Aurora, New York. The youthful lawyer had slow going building his practice, but by 1826 he felt sufficiently established to marry Abigail.

Entering politics in 1828, Fillmore won election to the state legislature. Re-elected twice, he made his most important contribution by sponsorship of legislation to end imprisonment of debtors. In 1830 Fillmore moved to the rapidly growing town of Buffalo where he established a profitable law partnership with Nathan K. Hall, who later served as Postmaster General in Fillmore's Cabinet.

The rising young politician next was elected to Congress in 1832 as a member of the newly formed Whig party. Defeated for re-election in 1834, he regained his congressional seat in 1836 and was re-elected three successive times after that. When the Whigs controlled Congress under President Tyler, Fillmore became chairman of the powerful House Ways and Means Committee. In that post he pushed through protective tariff bills that twice were vetoed by Tyler, and authored the tariff bill finally approved in 1842.

After retiring from Congress in 1843, Fillmore unsuccessfully sought the Whig vice-presidential nomination in 1844. He accepted his party's nomination for governor of New York, but was defeated by the Democratic candidate, Silas Wright. After three years devoted to his law practice and to mending his political fences, he returned to public office with his election in 1847 as state comptroller.

At the Whig National Convention in 1848, Fillmore was chosen as the vice-presidential candidate, and aided in winning New York's crucial electoral vote for the Whig ticket. After assuming office as Vice President in 1849,

Fillmore presided over the debates in the Senate that led to the Compromise of 1850.

Fillmore's Administration

THE FIFTY-YEAR-OLD FILLMORE took the oath of office as President on July 10, 1850, the day after Taylor's death. A supporter of the Compromise, despite his own anti-slavery views, he believed the members of Taylor's Cabinet had influenced the late President against it. He accepted the resignations of all the department heads and appointed an entirely new Cabinet—the first and only time that a Vice President succeeding to the presidency has made such a sweeping change upon assuming office.

In September, Fillmore signed into law the group of measures that made up the Compromise of 1850: admission of California as a free state; establishment of territories in Utah and New Mexico with the provision that neither could pass legislation with respect to slavery; annulment of Texas' claim to New Mexico with payment to Texas of an indemnity of $10 million, prohibition of the slave trade, but continuance of slavery, in the District of Columbia; and finally, a new Fugitive Slave Law that made federal officials responsible for recovering runaway slaves.

Not recognizing that he had signed his own and his party's political death warrant with these measures, more a capitulation to southern slave interests than a compromise, Fillmore, in his first annual message to Congress on December 2, 1850, said:

"It was hardly to have been expected that the series of measures passed at your last session with the view of healing the sectional differences which had sprung from the slavery and territorial questions should at once have realized their beneficent purpose. All mutual concession in the nature of compromise must necessarily be unwelcome to men of extreme opinions. And though without such concessions our Constitution could not have been formed, and can not be permanently sustained, yet we have seen them made the subject of bitter controversy in both sections of the Republic. It required many months of discussion and deliberation to secure the concurrence of a majority of Congress in their favor. It would be strange if they had been received with immediate approbation by people and States prejudiced and heated by the exciting controversies of their representatives. I believe those measures to have been required by the circumstances and condition of the country. I believe they were necessary to allay asperities and animosities that were rapidly alienating one section of the country from another and destroying those fraternal sentiments which are the strongest supports of the Constitution.

They were adopted in the spirit of conciliation and for the purpose of conciliation. I believe that a great majority of our fellow-citizens sympathize in that spirit and that purpose, and in the main approve and are prepared in all respects to sustain these enactments. I can not doubt that the American people, bound together by kindred blood and common traditions, still cherish a paramount regard for the Union of their fathers, and that they are ready to rebuke any attempt to violate its integrity, to disturb the compromises on which it is based, or to resist the laws which have been enacted under its authority.

"The series of measures to which I have alluded are regarded by me as a settlement in principle and substance—a final settlement of the dangerous and exciting subjects which they embraced. Most of these subjects, indeed, are beyond your reach, as the legislation which disposed of them was in its character final and irrevocable. It may be presumed from the opposition which they all encountered that none of those measures was free from imperfections, but in their mutual dependence and connection they formed a system of compromise the most conciliatory and best for the entire country that could be obtained from conflicting sectional interests and opinions."

But the new Fugitive Slave Law caused northern abolitionists to become even more militant. The underground railway came into being to help slaves escape from the South. Mobs attacked federal marshals to free runaway slaves from custody. And Harriet Beecher Stowe's *Uncle Tom's Cabin*, inspired by the law, aroused hatred for slavery throughout the North.

Fillmore continued to stand firm in his belief in the Compromise, however, and in his second annual message to Congress in December 1851, he reiterated his belief that the Compromise represented a "final settlement" of the differences between North and South.

One contribution Fillmore made to the presidency was the modernization of the White House. During his tenancy, a newfangled cast-iron cooking stove was installed in the kitchen to replace the open-hearth fireplace that heretofore had been used in preparing meals. Plumbers hooked up the first White House bathtub with running water, and Mrs. Fillmore established the first White House library in the Oval Room.

In June 1852, the Whig party met in national convention at Baltimore. The main contenders for the presidential nomination in order of their strength on the first ballot were Fillmore, General Winfield Scott, and Secretary of State Daniel Webster. Fifty-three ballots later, with the party irretrievably torn by dissension, the Whigs had decided to dump Fillmore and stake their chances on the only kind of candidate who had ever won for them —a war hero—General Scott. But the convention hung a millstone around Scott's neck by adopting a platform that echoed Fillmore's praise of the

Compromise of 1850 and pledged strict enforcement of the Fugitive Slave Law. The deaths of Henry Clay and Daniel Webster within the next few months and the landslide defeat of Scott in the national election in November brought an end to the political effectiveness of the Whig party.

Fillmore's Last Years

FILLMORE TURNED THE GOVERNMENT OVER to his Democratic successor, Franklin Pierce, on a blustery cold day in March 1853. During the ceremony, Mrs. Fillmore caught a cold that later developed into pneumonia. She died less than a month after leaving the White House. The former President retired sadly to Buffalo to resume his law practice.

As the next national election approached, Fillmore accepted the presidential nomination in 1856 of the anti-Catholic, anti-immigrant American party, whose followers were called the Know-Nothings. He also received the nomination of what was left of the Whig party. But Fillmore ran a poor third behind the Democratic candidate James Buchanan and the Republican candidate John Frémont. He carried only the state of Maryland.

Fillmore then receded into obscurity. In 1858 he married a wealthy widow, Mrs. Caroline McIntosh, thirteen years younger than himself. He continued to make his views known on national politics, but few listened. When the seventy-four-year-old Fillmore died in Buffalo on March 8, 1874, President Grant's eulogy was perfunctory:

"The long-continued and useful public service and eminent purity of character of the deceased ex-President will be remembered beyond the days of mourning in which a nation will be thrown by the event which is thus announced."

Franklin Pierce

The Fourteenth President of the United States
1853–57

1804 (November 23) Born in Hillsboro, New Hampshire.

1824 Graduated from Bowdoin College.

1827 Admitted to the bar to practice law.

1829–33 Member of New Hampshire state legislature.

1833–37 U.S. representative from New Hampshire.

1834 (November 10) Married Jane Means Appleton.

1837–42 U.S. senator from New Hampshire.

1846–48 Served as a brigadier general in the Mexican War.

1850 President of state constitutional convention.

1853–57 Fourteenth President of the United States.

1869 (October 8) Died in Concord, New Hampshire.

A northern Democrat who supported the extension of slavery, Franklin Pierce was chosen as a dark horse presidential nominee by his party in order to win both northern and southern votes. He praised the Compromise of 1850 and promised to prevent slavery from again becoming a national issue, and as a result, swept into office with the greatest electoral landslide since Monroe.

A politician's politician, the dark, curly-haired Pierce never lost an election. He was a master at knowing how to get along with people—evidenced by the fact that he is the only President in history who served out a complete term in office without having to make a single change in his Cabinet.

But he misjudged the temper of the times. He regarded the abolitionists as a lunatic fringe who should be ignored. And, when he signed the Kansas-Nebraska Act and the repeal of the Missouri Compromise of 1820, he unwittingly let loose a storm that made slavery a greater national issue than ever before.

Politician and Mexican War General

ONE OF A FAMILY of nine children, Franklin Pierce was born in Hillsboro, New Hampshire, on November 23, 1804. His father, Benjamin Pierce, was a Revolutionary War veteran, a farmer, a tavern-keeper, and a leader of the Democratic-Republican party in New Hampshire. Young Frank was given a good education in private schools, and at fifteen was sent off to Bowdoin College, where his college mates included Henry Wadsworth Longfellow and Nathaniel Hawthorne. At his graduation in 1824, the nineteen-year-old Pierce ranked third in his class.

Pierce next began studying law, and in 1827, the same year his father was elected governor of New Hampshire, he was admitted to the bar and opened a law office in Hillsboro. Two years later when his father successfully ran for re-election, the twenty-four-year-old Frank also was on the ticket, winning a seat in the legislature. He was re-elected three times, and at the age of twenty-six was chosen speaker of the lower house, an office he held for two sessions.

In 1833, when Pierce was twenty-eight, he was elected to Congress as a Jackson Democrat. He voted consistently for administration-supported measures, achieving a reputation as a loyal party man and easily winning re-election in 1835.

On November 10, 1834, just before his thirtieth birthday, Pierce married Jane Means Appleton, daughter of the late president of Bowdoin College. They honeymooned en route to Washington and did not set up housekeeping in Hillsboro until the next spring. His wife, who suffered from tuberculosis and did not like the national capital, did not accompany him on his return to Washington in 1835. Pierce proceeded to live a boisterous life with other bachelor congressmen, often drinking more than he could hold—a problem that he fought for the rest of his life.

Pierce's political fortunes received a new boost in 1836 when the state legislature elected him to the U. S. Senate. As the youngest senator in Washington, the thirty-two-year-old Pierce was overshadowed by such giants as Clay, Calhoun, and Webster, and, although he was a persuasive orator in his own right, he had few opportunities to demonstrate his ability. His wife

George Washington

John Adams

Thomas Jefferson

James Madison

James Monroe

John Quincy Adams

Andrew Jackson

Martin Van Buren

William Henry Harrison

constantly nagged him to give up his political career and return to New Hampshire, which he finally did by resigning from the Senate in 1842.

Pierce left Washington, but he did not give up politics. As state chairman of the Democratic party he became the political boss of New Hampshire. In 1845 he accepted appointment as U.S. district attorney for New Hampshire, but the following year turned down an offer by President Polk to join the Cabinet as Attorney General of the United States.

Although Pierce had had no other military experience than a nominal appointment as a militia colonel, he received a commission from Polk in February 1847 as a colonel in the volunteer army to fight in the Mexican War. Less than a month later he was promoted to brigadier general. Late in June, Pierce and his New England brigade joined Winfield Scott in the invasion of central Mexico, where in the battle of Contreras in August, Pierce was injured when his horse fell, and fainted from the pain. While pursuing the enemy the next day, he again fainted in front of his troops. These fainting incidents later brought political charges that he was a coward.

Back in New Hampshire in 1848, Pierce resumed his position as head of the Democratic party in the state. He declined nomination as governor in 1848, but two years later presided at a convention to revise the state constitution.

When Pierce and his friends began scheming to obtain the Democratic presidential nomination at Baltimore in 1852, they did not let Mrs. Pierce know about it for fear she would squelch the plan. In any case, the choice of the convention seemed to lie entirely between James Buchanan and Lewis Cass. But in ballot after ballot the two main contenders fought each other to a standstill, neither mustering the needed two-thirds majority. On the thirty-fifth ballot Pierce's friends entered his name. By the forty-ninth ballot the entire convention agreed on Pierce as the dark horse who could pull together the warring factions of the party. Pierce's wife collapsed when she heard the news, and Pierce denied to her that he had sought the nomination. Their eleven-year-old son Benjamin added fuel to the flames of family discord when he wrote to his mother: "I hope he won't be elected for I should not like to be at Washington and I know you would not either."

The ensuing campaign was particularly dirty, with unwarranted calumnies thrown both at Pierce and at his Whig opponent, Lieutenant General Winfield Scott. But the Whig party was in a state of disintegration, and Pierce won the election easily. He received a comfortable margin in the popular vote —1,601,117 to Scott's 1,385,453; and a landslide in the electoral vote—254 to 42, carrying all but four states.

Pierce's Administration

PIERCE ENTERED THE WHITE HOUSE bearing the marks of a personal tragedy that historians believe significantly contributed to destroying his confidence in himself. While President-elect, Pierce had been traveling from Boston to Concord by train with his wife and only son (two other Pierce children had died as infants). Suddenly the railroad car in which the Pierces were riding toppled off the tracks. Pierce and his wife were only slightly injured, but eleven-year-old Benjamin was killed before their eyes. In the days that followed, the deeply religious Mrs. Pierce came to the conclusion that it had been God's will that the boy should die so that concern for the boy's welfare could not distract Pierce from his presidential duties. Pierce suffered a sense of guilt for his son's death, and his sorrowing wife did not attend his inaugural or take part in White House social affairs for the next two years.

Using his most practiced courtroom oratory, the forty-eight-year-old Pierce broke precedent by committing to memory his inaugural address and delivering it without notes. He began it with the words:

"It is a relief to feel that no heart but my own can know the personal regret and bitter sorrow over which I have been borne to a position so suitable for others rather than desirable for myself."

Referring to the slavery issue, Pierce said:

"I believe that involuntary servitude, as it exists in different States of this Confederacy, is recognized by the Constitution. I believe that it stands like any other admitted right, and that the States where it exists are entitled to efficient remedies to enforce the constitutional provisions. I hold that the laws of 1850, commonly called the 'compromise measures,' are strictly constitutional and to be unhesitatingly carried into effect. . . . I fervently hope that the question is at rest, and that no sectional or ambitious or fanatical excitement may again threaten the durability of our institutions or obscure the light of our prosperity."

During the first half of Pierce's administration the Democrats controlled both houses of Congress, but they were so divided that it was difficult for Pierce to get legislation enacted. However, he exerted great effort in helping Illinois Senator Stephen A. Douglas push through the pro-slavery Kansas-Nebraska Act in 1854, which repealed the Missouri Compromise of 1820, enabling Kansas to become a slave state if the settlers voted for it. "Border ruffians" promptly infiltrated from the slave state of Missouri and set up a pro-slavery government, with Pierce upholding their right to do so despite the outcries of anti-slavery Kansans and Northerners everywhere.

It was a serious mistake. The outrages being committed in Kansas contributed to the formation of the new Republican party. At the mid-term congressional elections in 1854, several Democratic congressmen lost seats to Republicans and Know-Nothings.

Pierce had hoped to be another Polk, and in his inaugural address had rattled the saber of "manifest destiny," saying:

". . . the policy of my Administration will not be controlled by any timid forebodings of evil from expansion. Indeed, it is not to be disguised that our attitude as a nation and our position on the globe render the acquisition of certain possessions not within our jurisdiction eminently important for our protection, if not in the future essential for the preservation of the rights of commerce and the peace of the world."

Endeavoring to follow through on his promise of expansion, Pierce offered $50 million to Mexico for much of the northern area of that country and for lower California. But these negotiations resulted only in the Gadsden Purchase of 1854, in which $10 million was paid for a strip of land across southern Arizona and New Mexico to be used as the right of way for a new railroad to the Pacific Coast.

Pierce also made unsuccessful efforts to acquire Cuba, largely because the southern states feared that Spain was about to free the black slaves on that island, and that this in turn might lead to black uprisings in the South.

When Hawaii applied for admission to the Union on the condition that it be allowed immediately to become a state, Pierce rejected the proposal.

Following the precedent of previous Democratic Presidents, Pierce disapproved of using federal funds to pay for internal improvements. The resulting economies enabled him to reduce the national debt from $60 million to $11 million during his four years in office.

Pierce endeavored to win popularity in the West and in the North by favoring land grants to railroads being pushed toward the Pacific. He also made available federal funds to begin construction on the Atlantic cable to provide better communication with Europe.

Through negotiation of many trade treaties with other countries, Pierce did much to encourage the expansion of trade. One of the most far-reaching of these treaties was that negotiated by Commodore Matthew Perry, opening the ports of Japan.

During Pierce's tenure in the White House, he installed the first coal-burning furnace and central heating. His predecessors often had complained that the mansion's fireplaces failed to warm the large rooms satisfactorily.

When the Democratic National Convention met in Cincinnati in June 1856, Pierce anticipated renomination. But his close association in northern minds with the Kansas issue damaged his value as a candidate, and to his great disappointment the nomination went to James Buchanan.

In his final State of the Union message to Congress on December 2, 1856, President Pierce excoriated anti-slavery forces of the North for moving the nation toward civil war, saying in part:

"Associations have been formed in some of the States of individuals who, pretending to seek only to prevent the spread of the institution of slavery into the present or future inchoate States of the Union, are really inflamed with desire to change the domestic institutions of existing States. To accomplish their objects they dedicate themselves to the odious task of deprecating the government organization which stands in their way and of calumniating with indiscriminate invective not only the citizens of particular States with whose laws they find fault, but all others of their fellow-citizens throughout the country who do not participate with them in their assaults upon the Constitution, framed and adopted by our fathers, and claiming for the privileges it has secured and the blessings it has conferred the steady support and grateful reverence of their children. They seek an object which they well know to be a revolutionary one. They are perfectly aware that the change in the relative condition of the white and black races in the slaveholding States which they would promote is beyond their lawful authority; that to them it is a foreign object; that it can not be effected by any peaceful instrumentality of theirs; that for them and the States of which they are citizens the only path to its accomplishment is through burning cities, and ravaged fields, and slaughtered populations, and all there is most terrible in foreign complicated with civil and servile war; and that the first step in the attempt is the forcible disruption of a country embracing in its broad bosom a degree of liberty and an amount of individual and public prosperity to which there is no parallel in history, and substituting in its place hostile governments, driven at once and inevitably into mutual devastation and fratricidal carnage, transforming the now peaceful and felicitous brotherhood into a vast permanent camp of armed men like the rival monarchies of Europe and Asia. Well knowing that such, and such only, are the means and the consequences of their plans and purposes, they endeavor to prepare the people of the United States for civil war by doing everything in their power to deprive the Constitution and the laws of moral authority and to undermine the fabric of the Union by appeals to passion and sectional prejudice, by indoctrinating its people with reciprocal hatred, and by educating them to stand face to face as enemies, rather than shoulder to shoulder as friends."

He defended himself for having upheld the pro-slavery forces in Kansas, claiming the Constitution prevented him from acting otherwise:

"In those parts of the United States where, by reason of the inflamed state

of the public mind, false rumors and misrepresentations have the greatest
currency, it has been assumed that it was the duty of the Executive not only
to suppress insurrectionary movements in Kansas, but also to see to the
regularity of local elections. It needs little argument to show that the President has no such power. All government in the United States rests substantially upon popular election. The freedom of elections is liable to be impaired
by the intrusion of unlawful votes or the exclusion of lawful ones, by im-
proper influences, by violence, or by fraud. But the people of the United
States are themselves the all-sufficient guardians of their own rights, and to
suppose that they will not remedy in due season any such incidents of civil
freedom is to suppose them to have ceased to be capable of self-government.
The President of the United States has not power to interpose in elections, to
see to their freedom, to canvass their votes, or to pass upon their legality in
the Territories any more than in the States. If he had such power the Government might be republican in form, but it would be a monarchy in fact;
and if he had undertaken to exercise it in the case of Kansas he would have
been justly subject to the charge of usurpation and of violation of the dearest
rights of the people of the United States."

Bitter Last Years

PIERCE AND HIS WIFE had lived in the White House with New England
frugality, managing to save about half of his $25,000-a-year salary. They were
able to retire comfortably on this and money he had saved from his law
practice, making two long trips abroad before settling down in Concord.

Refusing all suggestions that he again seek the presidential nomination in
1860, he proposed his former Secretary of War, Jefferson Davis, as the best
candidate that the Democrats could choose.

Even with the onset of the Civil War, Pierce maintained his unpopular
stand, privately and publicly opposing the use of force by the North and
denouncing the Emancipation Proclamation as unconstitutional. He came to
be regarded as a traitor of sorts and was shunned by former friends. Following
the death of his wife in 1863, he began to drink more heavily. Feelings
remained so bitter toward him in his native state that more than half a
century went by after his death in 1869 before a statue was erected in his
honor.

His close friend Nathaniel Hawthorne sought to explain Pierce in these
words:

". . . it would ruin a noble character (though one of limited scope) for
him to admit any ideas that were not entertained by the fathers of the

Constitution and the Republic. . . . There is a certain steadfastness and integrity with regard to a man's own nature (when it is such a peculiar nature as that of Pierce) which seems to me more sacred and valuable than the faculty of adapting one's self to new ideas, however true they may turn out to be."

James Buchanan
The Fifteenth President of the United States
1857–61

1791 (April 23) Born near Mercersburg, Pennsylvania.

1809 Graduated from Dickinson College.

1812 Began to practice law in Lancaster, Pennsylvania.

1814–16 Member of the Pennsylvania legislature.

1821–31 U.S. representative from Pennsylvania.

1832–33 U.S. minister to Russia.

1834–45 U.S. senator from Pennsylvania.

1845–49 Secretary of State under President Polk.

1853–56 U.S. minister to England.

1857–61 Fifteenth President of the United States.

1868 (June 1) Died at his home, Wheatland, near Lancaster, Pennsylvania.

L ast of the weak, compromising Presidents elected by a divided country in the years before the Civil War, James Buchanan was, like Pierce, a northern Democrat, more sympathetic to southern slave-owners than to northern abolitionists. When Buchanan unsuccessfully tried to push through the admission of Kansas as a slave state, he infuriated the North and shattered the Democratic party. As the southern states seceded from the Union one by one in the last months of his administration, Buchanan helplessly stood by, unable to take resolute action.

The only President who never married, Buchanan devoted his life to public service as congressman, senator, diplomat, and Secretary of State before coming to the White House. A friend facetiously said of Buchanan that ever since he had been old enough to marry he had been "wedded to the Constitution."

Legislator, Diplomat, and Cabinet Member

THE ELDEST SON in a family of eleven children, James Buchanan was born in a tiny one-room log cabin in the Blue Mountain country near Mercersburg, Pennsylvania, on April 23, 1791. His father was an Irish immigrant who developed a small frontier trading post into a thriving business. Working in his father's store, young Jimmie learned arithmetic and bookkeeping, which he used to keep meticulous personal accounts throughout his life.

As a youth, he showed a rebellious streak, being expelled from Dickinson College in Carlisle, Pennsylvania, at the end of his first year because of insubordination to his teachers. He was reinstated at the college when he pledged to settle down and work hard. Keeping his promise, he was graduated the next year at the age of eighteen. After studying law for the next three years, he began practice in 1812 in Lancaster, Pennsylvania, where he also bought a part-interest in a tavern.

Volunteering for the War of 1812, he helped defend Baltimore from British attack, then returned to Lancaster and won election to the state legislature in 1814 as a member of the Federalist party. After two terms in the legislature, Buchanan left politics to build a law practice. He proved an able attorney, winning case after case, until at twenty-seven, his income was $8,000 a year—a substantial amount in those days. He lived frugally, slowly accumulating a sizable fortune.

In 1818 Buchanan fell in love. The object of his affections was Ann Coleman, daughter of an extremely wealthy iron-mill owner of Lancaster. This was reaching high. The girl's parents evidently disapproved, believing that Buchanan was a fortune hunter. Ann broke the engagement, writing to Buchanan that she believed he loved her money more than he did her. Shortly thereafter she died under mysterious circumstances, rumors saying that she had committed suicide from grief. The Colemans refused to let Buchanan attend the funeral. He wrote, "I feel that happiness has fled from me forever," and never again became engaged, although he carried on many flirtations.

Resuming his interest in politics, Buchanan won election to Congress in 1820 as a candidate of the Federalist party, but did not take office until December 1821. Buchanan became a supporter of Andrew Jackson in 1824, and personally tried to swing Henry Clay to Jackson's side in the disputed presidential election of that year. Four years later he switched to the new Democratic party, winning election to the House of Representatives for the fifth time.

For his services to Jackson, Buchanan was appointed U.S. minister to Russia. Well-received at the Russian court in 1832, he succeeded in negotiating the first trade treaty between the United States and Russia. But the politically ambitious Buchanan did not wish to remain away from the United States for too long for fear he would be forgotten, and returned home in 1833.

He was elected by the state legislature to the U.S. Senate in 1834, and served in that body for the next eleven years under Presidents Jackson, Van Buren, Harrison, and Tyler. He became a leading member of the conservative wing of the Democratic party, holding the important chairmanship of the Senate Foreign Relations Committee. A northern supporter of the slave interests, Buchanan backed legislation curbing the activities of abolitionists. During this period he declined offers of appointment by Van Buren as Attorney General and by Tyler as an associate justice of the Supreme Court.

After campaigning for Polk in the presidential election of 1844, Buchanan received appointment as Secretary of State. Much of the credit for Polk's successful territorial expansion program was due to Buchanan's effort, but the two men often fought, as Polk feared the Pennsylvanian was using his Cabinet post as a stepping-stone to the presidency. Buchanan complained to a friend: "My life is that of a galley slave."

When he failed to win the Democratic presidential nomination in 1848, Buchanan retired to Wheatland, an estate near Lancaster, Pennsylvania. The "Sage of Wheatland," as he became known, narrowly missed the Democratic nomination in 1852, and at the age of sixty-two was once more given a diplomatic mission abroad, this time as U.S. minister to Great Britain. There he gained unexpected notoriety by joining with his ministerial colleagues to France and Spain, both militant pro-slavery Southerners, in writing the "Ostend Manifesto." Pushing "manifest destiny" to its rashest limits, the three diplomats advocated purchase of Cuba from Spain and asserted that if Spain refused to sell "we shall be justified in wresting" the island from its owners. Widely denounced by anti-slavery Northerners, the Ostend Manifesto was cheered in the South.

At the Democratic National Convention in Cincinnati in June 1856, both the Ostend Manifesto and Buchanan's recent absence from the country stood him in good stead. His two chief rivals, President Pierce and Senator Stephen A. Douglas, were tainted by their espousal of the pro-slavery cause in Kansas, where a bitter little civil war had broken out. Possessing the indispensable attributes of being unconnected with "bleeding Kansas" and yet fully acceptable to the South, Buchanan won the nomination.

Against him in the election were arrayed two new parties, fragments of the now defunct Whigs. The anti-slavery Republican party nominated John C. Frémont, while the more conservative Whigs, calling themselves "Know-Nothings," picked former President Millard Fillmore. Buchanan won easily, though outpolled by the combined totals of his opponents, in an election which clearly showed the depth of division within the nation:

Buchanan	1,832,955 popular votes	174 electoral votes
Frémont	1,339,932	114
Fillmore	871,731	8

Frémont carried eleven free states, Buchanan only five. Buchanan carried every slave state except Maryland, which went to Fillmore.

Buchanan's Administration

SIXTY-FIVE YEARS OLD, Buchanan had finally achieved his lifelong ambition. In his inaugural address he sought to place himself above party conflict by announcing that he would not be a candidate for re-election in 1860, but in so doing only succeeded in sacrificing the leadership of his own party, which passed to Stephen A. Douglas. Discussing the bitter Kansas dispute, Buchanan called upon the nation to regard it as a judicial question to be settled by the Supreme Court, saying, "To their decision, in common with all good citizens, I shall cheerfully submit, whatever this may be . . ." Actually Chief Justice Roger Taney had already informed the President-elect that the Court was about to hand down a pro-slavery decision in the Dred Scott case, holding that Congress did not have power to prohibit slavery in the territories and thereby nullifying the Missouri Compromise of 1820. When the Court's decision was announced, angry Northerners accused Buchanan of double-dealing in trying to make the country accept in advance a decision that could so decisively extend slavery.

Buchanan also announced his intention to try to purchase both Cuba and Alaska, but negotiations with Spain and Russia to these ends did not succeed.

In his inaugural he also boasted that "Our present financial condition is without parallel in history," thanks to the large surplus in the federal treasury. Within a few months Buchanan was embarrassed by the Panic of 1857 and the depression following it, which drove many businessmen into bankruptcy, threw thousands out of work, and swiftly converted the surplus in the treasury into a deficit of $27 million.

Although later in 1860–61 Buchanan would claim he did not have the constitutional power to use force against the seceding states of the Confederacy, he had no such scruples during the first year of his administration in dealing with what he perceived as a rebellion by the territorial government of Utah. Brigham Young, leader of the Mormons, had been governor of the Utah territory since it was formed in 1851. When Young defied federal officials sent to Utah, the President declared in 1857 that Utah was in a state of rebellion, appointed a new territorial governor, and dispatched an army of federal troops to Utah to enforce his orders. In the short-lived "Utah war," Mormons burned two federal forts and attacked wagon trains carrying supplies to the federal army. But by December 1858 Buchanan was able to report in his State of the Union message to Congress: "Our little army behaved admirably . . . I am happy to inform you that the governor and other civil officers of Utah are now performing their appropriate functions without resistance. The authority of the Constitution and the laws has been fully restored and peace prevails throughout the Territory."

With the Democrats holding a majority in both houses, Buchanan decided to try to put an end to the Kansas agitation by obtaining the territory's admission as a slave state. But when he submitted the pro-slavery Lecompton Constitution to Congress, northern Democrats revolted, joining Republicans in the House of Representatives to defeat the bill. Buchanan forces revived the bill with an additional feature, amounting to a bribe of several million acres to finance the new state government. But Kansans voted down the Lecompton Constitution, and in the elections of 1858 anti-Lecompton candidates won victories throughout the North. Stephen A. Douglas, who had led the fight against Lecompton in the Senate, triumphed over a Buchanan-backed candidate and over the Republican candidate, Abraham Lincoln. The memorable Lincoln-Douglas debates, filled with attacks on the Buchanan administration's program, helped solidify northern opinion against the President.

During his remaining two years in office Buchanan slipped more and more into the role of figurehead. John Brown's raid on Harpers Ferry, in an attempt to stir up a slave insurrection, convinced many Southerners that secession from the Union was their only means of protecting themselves from northern abolitionists. Secession was openly discussed throughout the South, and several southern legislatures passed resolutions pledging secession and cooperation in case of the election of a "Black Republican" in 1860. In South Carolina, Mississippi, and a few other states, appropriations for military preparedness were passed.

Buchanan believed secession was unconstitutional, but he also believed that it was unconstitutional for the federal government to use force against secession. He was unwilling to stretch the Constitution by taking into his own hands powers that might have halted the spreading conflagration, and he did little but wait in vain for Congress to act. Meantime the fatal split in the Democratic party, in good part the result of Buchanan's inept handling of the Kansas issue, assured the election of Lincoln, the "Black Republican" the southern firebrands had warned against. South Carolina at once set in motion steps to secede. Buchanan warned of an impending "open war by the North to abolish slavery in the South," and called futilely for amendments to the Constitution to compromise the issues. His one firm resolve was to postpone fighting until he was out of office, so that the onus of civil war would fall on the Republicans.

South Carolina officially seceded from the Union on December 20, 1860. Two weeks later, in a special message to Congress on January 8, 1861, Buchanan pleaded that it still was not too late for adoption of a compromise:

"A common ground on which conciliation and harmony can be produced is surely not unattainable. The proposition to compromise by letting the North have exclusive control of the territory above a certain line and to give Southern institutions protection below that line ought to receive universal approbation. In itself, indeed, it may not be entirely satisfactory, but when the alternative is between a reasonable concession on both sides and a destruction of the Union it is an imputation upon the patriotism of Congress to assert that its members will hesitate for a moment. . . .

"At the beginning of these unhappy troubles I determined that no act of mine should increase the excitement in either section of the country. If the political conflict were to end in a civil war, it was my determined purpose not to commence it nor even to furnish an excuse for it by any act of this government. My opinion remains unchanged that justice as well as sound policy requires us still to seek a peaceful solution of the questions at issue between the North and the South. . . .

"In conclusion it may be permitted to me to remark that I have often warned my countrymen of the dangers which now surround us. This may be the last time I shall refer to the subject officially. I feel that my duty has been faithfully, though it may be imperfectly, performed, and, whatever the result may be, I shall carry to my grave the consciousness that I at least meant well for my country."

Before Buchanan left office, six more Southern states joined South Carolina in withdrawing from the Union: Mississippi on January 9, Florida on January 10, Alabama on January 11, Georgia on January 19, Louisiana on January 26, and Texas on February 23.

Buchanan's Last Years

BREATHING A SIGH OF RELIEF when March 4, 1861, finally arrived, Buchanan turned the government over to Lincoln with the comment: "If you are as happy in entering the White House as I shall feel on returning to Wheatland, you are a happy man indeed."

But Buchanan's remaining years were not as happy as he had anticipated. Though he supported the Union during the war, he spent much of his time defending himself from accusations that his unwillingness to act had helped cause the war.

Shortly before his death in 1868, at the age of seventy-seven, he asserted: "I have always felt and still feel that I discharged every public duty imposed on me conscientiously. I have no regret for any public act of my life, and history will vindicate my memory."

Abraham Lincoln
The Sixteenth President of the United States
1861–65

1809 (February 12) Born near Hodgenville, Kentucky.

1816 Moved with parents to Indiana.

1830 Moved to Illinois.

1832 Served as volunteer in Black Hawk War, but saw no fighting.

1834–42 Member of the Illinois legislature.

1836 Licensed to practice law.

1842 (November 4) Married Mary Todd.

1847–49 U.S. representative from Illinois.

1856 Unsuccessful candidate for Republican vice-presidential nomination.

1858 Won national prominence debating slavery issue with Stephen A. Douglas in unsuccessful campaign for U.S. senator.

1861–65 Sixteenth President of the United States.

1865 (April 14) Wounded by assassin John Wilkes Booth.

1865 (April 15) Died in Washington, D.C.

G iven his lack of education and scant public service, Abraham Lincoln seemed less likely to succeed as President than most of his predecessors. Yet his innate wisdom and humanity made him one of the greatest of the nation's Chief Executives.

Entering the White House at a time when many of the southern states already had seceded from the Union, Lincoln offered them the hand of friendship in his inaugural address. "We must not be enemies," he said, after assuring them that he had no intention of interfering with the institution of slavery and that he would uphold the rights of slave-owners to recover fugitive slaves from other states. But he also firmly warned that "the Union of these States is perpetual."

After hotheaded southern leaders disregarded Lincoln's inaugural plea for peace, he resolutely mobilized for war. The death and destruction of the ensuing fight between North and South made Lincoln's heart bleed, yet his sorrowing bearded face and gaunt black-garbed figure became a symbol of the North's determination to preserve the Union. His Emancipation Proclamation ordering freedom for slaves in the rebelling states crystallized the central issue of the conflict and moved the nation a great step forward toward realizing Jefferson's dream of equality for all men. And finally his assassination in the moment of victory struck the conscience of both North and South and epitomized the hatreds that must be quelled if the nation were once again to be welded together.

The four years and six weeks that Lincoln served as President were more critical than any faced by a previous President. In many ways the events of the time controlled Lincoln's actions and by their results made him a great figure. As he himself said in 1864:

"I claim not to have controlled events but confess plainly that events have controlled me. Now at the end of three years' struggle, the nation's condition is not what either party or any man devised or expected. God alone can claim it."

Lincoln's Brief Autobiography

LINCOLN'S NATURAL HUMILITY and lack of pretension are strikingly revealed in a short autobiography that he wrote in 1859 when he was a candidate for the Republican presidential nomination:

"I was born Feb. 12, 1809, in Hardin County, Kentucky. My parents were both born in Virginia of undistinguished families—second families perhaps I should say. My mother, who died in my tenth year, was of a family of the name of Hanks, some of whom now reside in Adams, some others in Macon counties, Illinois. My paternal grandfather, Abraham Lincoln, emigrated from Rockingham County, Virginia, to Kentucky, about 1781 or 2, where, a year or two later, he was killed by Indians . . .

"My father . . . grew up literally without education. He removed from Kentucky to what is now Spencer County, Indiana, in my eighth year. It was a wild region, with many bears and other wild animals. There were some schools, so called, but no qualification was ever required of a teacher beyond 'reading, writing, and ciphering' to the Rule of Three. The little advance I now have upon this store of education, I have picked up from time to time under the pressure of necessity.

"I was raised to farm work, which I continued till I was twenty-two. At twenty-one I came to Illinois, and passed the first year in Macon County. Then I got to New Salem, at that time in Sangamon, now in Menard County, where I remained a year as a sort of clerk in a store. Then came the Black Hawk war and I was elected a Captain of Volunteers—a success which gave me more pleasure than any I have had since. I went the campaign, was elected, ran for the Legislature the same year (1832), and was beaten—the only time I ever have been beaten by the people. The next, and three succeeding biennial elections, I was elected to the Legislature. I was not a candidate afterwards. During this Legislative period I had studied law, and removed to Springfield to practice it. In 1846 I was elected to the lower House of Congress. Was not a candidate for reelection. From 1849 to 1854, both inclusive, practiced law more assiduously than ever before . . . I was losing interest in politics, when the repeal of the Missouri Compromise aroused me again. What I have accomplished since then is pretty well known.

"If any personal description of me is thought desirable, it may be said, I am, in height, six feet, four inches, nearly; lean in flesh, weighing, on an average, one hundred and eighty pounds; dark complexion, with coarse black hair, and grey eyes—no other marks or brands recollected—"

On the Frontier

LINCOLN'S PARENTS WERE TYPICAL of thousands of American frontier families of the nineteenth century who spent their lives in an endless struggle against poverty and the wilderness. They were barely able to keep a roof over their heads, barely able to keep warm in winter, and barely able to keep fed from one day to the next. Both his father, Thomas Lincoln, and his mother, Nancy Hanks, had come from Virginia—genealogists since have traced the origin of the family in America to a Samuel Lincoln who came to Massachusetts from England in 1637.

Born in a crude log cabin near Hodgenville, Kentucky, on February 12, 1809, young Abe knew few of the comforts of civilization before he was a man. He had a sister, Sarah, who was about two years older, and a younger brother, Thomas, who died as a baby, before the family moved to Indiana.

When Abe was eight his father moved the family west to Indiana where he took possession of 160 acres of forest land in Spencer County. The new Lincoln home was a three-sided lean-to with only a fire to keep out the winter cold. The next year Lincoln's mother died of what was called "the milk sickness."

In 1819 Lincoln's father married Sarah Bush Johnston, a Kentucky widow with three children of her own. The new Mrs. Lincoln improved the family's standard of living with a wagonload of furniture from her previous marriage. More important, she brought Abe affection and instilled in him a desire to better himself.

Although Lincoln went to school no more than a year in all the time he was growing up, he developed a love of books. Since his family was too poor to buy any other books than the Bible, he sometimes walked several miles to borrow one from a neighbor. In later years he recalled that he was particularly impressed with one of these borrowed books, Parson Weems' *Life of Washington*, that gave him insight into the struggles of the Founding Fathers who established the United States.

Tall and strong by the time he was sixteen, Abe began hiring out as a laborer at twenty-five cents a day. He worked as a grocery-store clerk, as a farmhand, as a ferryboat rower on the Ohio River, and in countless other odd jobs that called for a strong back. He also won local renown as a wrestler and for his humorous imitations of some of the eccentric members of the community.

When he was nineteen, Abe had his first look at a city—New Orleans. He floated down the Ohio and Mississippi as a deck hand on a flatboat loaded with farm produce. He made a similar flatboat journey to New Orleans three years later, and it was on this second trip that he is reputed to have acquired his hatred of slavery. One of his companions on the journey, John Hanks, said:

"We saw Negroes chained, maltreated, whipped, and scourged. Lincoln saw it; his heart bled, said nothing much, was silent from feeling, was sad, looked bad, felt bad, was thoughtful and abstracted. I can say, knowing it, that it was on this trip that he formed his opinions of slavery. It run its iron in him then and there—May, 1831. I have heard him say so often and often."

In 1830, after Lincoln had turned twenty-one, his father again decided to seek his elusive fortune by moving west—this time to Illinois. Abe helped move the family to a new farm west of Decatur, put in the first crop, then decided to leave home for good and strike out on his own.

Life in New Salem

IN THE SPRING OF 1831 young Lincoln settled down in the tiny frontier village of New Salem in Illinois. He became a clerk in a store, and won instant popularity with the backwoods people of the community. He proved he could out-wrestle the biggest bullies, could tell funnier stories than anyone, and could be depended on to help out whenever a strong worker was needed.

When a militia company was organized in 1832 to fight Chief Black Hawk, Lincoln volunteered. The men of the company elected him captain, giving him his first taste of winning an election. After a month's service the company was discharged, but Lincoln re-enlisted as a private. In the three months that he served he took part in no battles, "but I had a good many bloody struggles with the mosquitoes; and . . . I was often very hungry."

Before joining the militia, the twenty-three-year-old Lincoln had made an important decision—to run for the state legislature. His military service prevented his doing any campaigning, and by the time he returned to New Salem the election was only a few days away. He was not surprised when he was defeated, and counted the experience a valuable one.

With politics temporarily out of the way, Lincoln went into partnership in a general store in New Salem, but being a better storyteller than businessman, he went broke in a few months. It took him seventeen years to pay off his debts.

After his disastrous experience as a merchant, Lincoln decided to improve himself by studying law, walking twenty miles back and forth to Springfield to borrow books, as there were no law books in New Salem. To support himself, he worked as an assistant surveyor, and then from 1833 to 1836 he served as postmaster of New Salem. Because there was no post office, Lincoln carried the mail "in his hat," which was not too difficult since mail arrived only once a week.

In 1834 the twenty-five-year-old Lincoln again ran for the legislature as a member of the new Whig party. This time he won handily, leading the ticket in his legislative district. He promptly went further in debt by borrowing two hundred dollars to purchase a new outfit so as not to disgrace his constituents with his appearance at the state capital.

The story is told that about this time Lincoln fell deeply in love with Ann Rutledge, the blond, blue-eyed daughter of a New Salem tavern-keeper, and he was so grief-stricken when she died in 1835 that his friends feared he might do away with himself. Modern historians discount the story somewhat because there is no evidence of it in Lincoln's writings, but many people who knew him well declared that Lincoln still spoke fondly and sadly of Ann Rutledge nearly thirty years after her death. One quoted Lincoln as saying, "I loved the woman dearly. She was a handsome girl; would have made a good, loving wife; was natural and quite intellectual, though not highly educated. I did honestly and truly love the girl, and think often, often, of her now."

A year after Ann Rutledge's death, Lincoln agreed sight unseen to marry Mary Owens, a well-to-do Kentucky spinster who was the sister of one of his New Salem friends. He later described his consternation upon seeing her, "I knew she was oversize, but she now appeared a fair match for Falstaff. I knew she was called an 'old maid,' and I felt no doubt of the truth of at least half of the appellation; but now, when I beheld her, I could not for my life avoid thinking of my mother; and this, not from withered features, for her skin was too full of fat to permit of its contracting into wrinkles, but from her want of teeth, weather-beaten appearance in general, and from a kind of notion that ran in my head that *nothing* could have commenced at the size of infancy and reached her present bulk in less than thirty-five or forty years; and, in short, I was not at all pleased with her. But what could I do? I had told her sister that I would take her for better or for worse; and I made a point of honor and conscience in all things to stick to my word, especially if others had been induced to act on it, which in this case I had no doubt they had; for I was now fairly convinced that no other man on earth would have her, and hence the conclusion that they were bent on holding me to my bargain."

But over a period of a year and a half, Lincoln worked at convincing Miss Owens that life with him would not be easy. He finally was overjoyed when she decided in 1838 not to marry him.

Marriage and Politics

LINCOLN WAS RE-ELECTED to the state legislature in 1836, and that same year received his license to practice law. He and the other representatives from Sangamon County had their greatest legislative triumph in the session of 1836–37 when they succeeded in having a bill passed to move the state capital from Vandalia to Springfield. When the move was finally carried out in 1839, Lincoln decided to move his permanent residence there. He became a law partner with John T. Stuart, who had loaned him the law books that he walked from New Salem to borrow.

In 1839 Lincoln met twenty-year-old Mary Todd, a Lexington, Kentucky, girl who was living in Springfield at the home of a married sister. They became engaged and arranged to be married in 1840. But suddenly Lincoln decided that he had fallen in love with another girl who lived at the same house, a Matilda Edwards. His friends were convinced that Lincoln had become "as crazy as a loon." They took him to Kentucky to recover, and he stayed there, missing the 1841–42 session of the state legislature.

After Lincoln returned to Springfield in 1842, he resumed seeing Mary Todd. In the fall of 1842 Mary wrote some politically satirical newspaper articles about a prominent Democratic politician, James Shields. Thinking that Lincoln was the author of the articles, Shields challenged him to a duel. Lincoln accepted the challenge, and they were about to settle the issue with broadswords when Shields backed down. Shortly thereafter, on November 4, 1842, Lincoln married Mary Todd. Their first home was at the Globe Tavern in Springfield. A year and a half later they moved into the frame house that remained their home until Lincoln became President. The Lincolns had four sons, but one died in 1850, another in 1861, and a third a few years after Lincoln's death. The surviving son, Robert Todd Lincoln, later served as Secretary of War under Presidents Garfield and Arthur.

Lincoln unsuccessfully sought the Whig nomination for Congress in 1843, but three years later, in 1846, won both nomination and election, becoming the only Whig in the Illinois delegation to Congress.

Lincoln was thirty-eight when he took his seat in the U. S. House of Representatives. As a congressman he denounced President Polk for having started the Mexican War, but supported bills to supply the army and applauded the generals for winning battles. As a delegate to the Whig National Convention in 1848, he voted for the nomination of Mexican War hero Zachary Taylor for President. But Lincoln's outspoken criticism of the war had lost him support in Illinois, and Whig leaders decided not to renominate him for Congress.

No longer an office-holder, Lincoln settled down in Springfield to improve his law practice and provide for his growing family. His reputation as a lawyer continued to grow. Judge David Davis, who presided over the circuit court where Lincoln most often appeared, had this to say of Lincoln's legal abilities:

"He seized the strong points of a cause, and presented them with clearness and great compactness. His mind was logical and direct, and he did not indulge in extraneous discussion. Generalities and platitudes had no charms for him. An unfailing vein of humor never deserted him; and he was always able to chain the attention of court and jury, when the cause was the most uninteresting, by the appropriateness of his anecdotes.

"His power of comparison was large, and he rarely failed in a legal discussion to use that mode of reasoning. The framework of his mental and moral being was honesty, and a wrong cause was poorly defended by him. The ability which some eminent lawyers possess, of explaining away the bad points of a cause by ingenious sophistry, was denied him. In order to bring into full activity his great powers, it was necessary that he should be convinced of the right and justice of the matter which he advocated. When so convinced, whether the cause was great or small, he was usually successful . . .

"He hated wrong and oppression everywhere; and many a man whose fraudulent conduct was undergoing review in a court of justice has writhed under his terrific indignation and rebukes. He was the most simple and unostentatious of men in his habits, having few wants, and those easily supplied. To his honor be it said, that he never took from a client, even when the cause was gained, more than he thought the service was worth and the client could reasonably afford to pay. The people where he practised law were not rich, and his charges were always small."

In 1844 Lincoln had gone into law partnership with William H. Herndon, who was nine years his junior. Herndon was an ardent abolitionist, and he continually sought to persuade Lincoln to adopt a more vigorous attitude against slavery. As early as 1837, while a state legislator, Lincoln had made his position clear: he did not believe the federal government had any right to interfere with slavery within any of the states, and he equally felt that the abolitionists were causing more harm than good with their agitation to free the slaves. As a congressman, Lincoln had introduced a bill to free the slaves in the District of Columbia, but the bill had not been brought to a vote.

Lincoln vs. Douglas

AT THE AGE OF FORTY-FIVE, Lincoln was almost unknown nationally and had lost much of his political influence in Illinois. But the passage of the Kansas-Nebraska Act in 1854, sponsored by Illinois Democratic Senator Stephen A. Douglas, roused Lincoln to action and gave him his golden opportunity. Lincoln believed that the Act's repeal of the Missouri Compromise would permit the introduction of slavery into northern territories, and he blamed

Douglas for trying to win the Democratic presidential nomination with southern votes by promoting the measure.

In the fall of 1854 Douglas attempted to explain to his Illinois constituents in a speech at the state fair at Springfield that he had sponsored the Kansas-Nebraska Act only to further the cause of democracy by allowing "popular sovereignty" to decide the slavery issue in the territories. Lincoln, chosen to reply to Douglas, made such an effective speech denouncing the "humbuggery" of the legislation that he at once became a leader of the state's anti-Nebraska-Act forces. When Douglas again spoke in defense of the Act in Peoria a few days later, Lincoln followed him there and again debated him. Douglas tacitly conceded defeat on the issue by making no more speeches on the subject in Illinois.

Lincoln was once more elected to the legislature in 1854, but resigned shortly after to become a candidate for the U. S. Senate. Senators, of course, were elected not by the people but by the state legislature. To obtain the support of abolitionist legislators, Lincoln pledged to try to bar slavery from all the western territories. But the legislature was too firmly in control of the Democratic party to permit the combination of Whigs and abolitionists to win Lincoln the senatorial seat.

Meantime the new, anti-slavery Republican party had come into being. Lincoln embraced the principles of the new party, and helped organize it in Illinois. When the first national Republican Convention was held in Philadelphia in June 1856, the Illinois delegation supported Lincoln for the vice-presidential nomination, which, however, went to William L. Dayton. Lincoln, who did not attend the convention, was amazed when he received news that his name had been put in nomination for the nation's second highest office, and exclaimed: "No, it couldn't be: it must have been the *great* Lincoln from Massachusetts." (He was referring to Levi Lincoln, who had been governor of Massachusetts.)

When the Illinois Republican Convention in June 1858 nominated Lincoln to run for the U. S. Senate against Douglas, Lincoln won national attention with his acceptance speech. In it he declared:

". . . 'A house divided against itself cannot stand.' I believe this Government cannot endure permanently half slave and half free. I do not expect the Union to be dissolved,—I do not expect the house to fall; but I do expect it will cease to be divided. It will become all one thing, or all the other. Either the opponents of slavery will arrest the further spread of it, and place it where the public mind shall rest in the belief that it is in course of ultimate extinction, or its advocates will push it forward till it shall became alike lawful in all the States,—old as well as new, North as well as South."

Lincoln's friends and supporters were dismayed by this forthright declaration of a position much stronger than that advocated by conservative members of the Republican party. They feared the speech would be a millstone around Lincoln's neck and would sink him into political oblivion. Informed of these apprehensions, Lincoln said:

"If I had to draw a pen across, and erase my whole life from existence, and I had one poor gift or choice left, as to what I should save from the wreck, I should choose that speech, and leave it to the world unerased."

The famous Lincoln-Douglas debates then ensued, with the two candidates battling all around Illinois. Douglas portrayed Lincoln as an out-and-out abolitionist, while Lincoln accused Douglas, as the author of the Kansas-Nebraska Act, of re-opening the slavery issue and threatening the country with disunion. So important were these debates that they drew national attention, and members of the legislature ran largely on their support of Lincoln or Douglas.

In the election, candidates who favored Lincoln received a majority of votes over Douglas' supporters. But because of inequitable districting of the state more Democratic candidates were elected, and so the legislature chose Douglas for senator.

Winning the Presidency

IN THE WINTER OF 1858–59 more and more people began to discuss the possibility of running Lincoln for President, but in the spring of 1859, Lincoln still was replying to inquirers that he was "not fit to be President." Nevertheless, in October he went on a speaking tour of Ohio and in December he traveled to Kansas.

Early in 1860 he journeyed east, New York making Lincoln's acquaintance in February 1860. In his speech there he contended that only one thing would satisfy the South: "This, and this only: cease to call slavery *wrong*, and join them in calling it *right.*" The day after the speech, the influential New York *Tribune* reported: "No man ever before made such an impression on his first appeal to a New York audience." After leaving New York, Lincoln went to visit his son Robert at Harvard, and made a series of speeches before Republican clubs in Connecticut, Rhode Island, and New Hampshire.

When the Republican state convention met in Decatur, Illinois, on May 9 and 10, 1860, Lincoln's followers tagged him with the nickname of "The Rail-splitter"—bringing to the convention two rails that he supposedly had made with his ax many years before.

The Republican National Convention opened in Chicago later the same month with New York Senator William H. Seward having the largest following among the delegates. On the first ballot Seward received 173½ votes to Lincoln's 102, with several other candidates trailing. To win Lincoln the nomination, Lincoln's friends promised Cabinet posts to the leaders of the Pennsylvania, Indiana, and Ohio delegations. Although Lincoln, who was home in Springfield, had told his managers, "I authorize no bargains and will be bound by none," the promises were made, and as a result Lincoln passed Seward on the third ballot, after which the delegates nominated him by acclamation. Hannibal Hamlin of Maine was chosen as the vice-presidential nominee.

Meanwhile, the Buchanan-Douglas split within the Democratic party deepened into a northern-southern break. The northern Democrats nominated Douglas for President, while the southern Democrats nominated Vice President John C. Breckinridge. The remnants of the Whigs and Know-Nothings formed a new "Constitutional Union" party, nominating John Bell of Tennessee for the presidency.

Confident that the split among the Democrats would assure him of victory, Lincoln remained in Springfield throughout most of the campaign. When the votes were counted, Lincoln received more popular votes than any other candidate, although far from a majority. The election figures were as follows:

	Popular votes	Electoral votes
Lincoln	1,865,593	180
Douglas	1,382,713	12
Breckinridge	848,356	72
Bell	592,906	39

Shortly after his election Lincoln had a disturbing vision. He described the experience to his secretary, young John Hay:

"It was just after my election . . . I was well tired out, and went home to rest, throwing myself upon a lounge in my chamber. Opposite to where I lay was a bureau with a swinging glass upon it; and, in looking in that glass, I saw myself reflected nearly at full length; but my face, I noticed, had two separate and distinct images, the tip of the nose of one being about three inches from the tip of the other. I got up and looked in the glass; but the illusion vanished. On lying down again, I saw it a second time,—plainer, if possible, than before; and then I noticed that one of the faces was paler than the other. I got up, and the thing melted away; and I went off, and in the excitement of the hour forgot all about it,—nearly, but not quite, for the thing would once in a while come up, and give me a little pang, as though something uncomfortable had happened. When I went home, I told my wife about it; and a few days after I tried the experiment again, when, sure enough, the thing came back again; but I never succeeded in bringing the ghost back after that, though I once tried very industriously to show it to my wife, who was worried about it somewhat. She thought it was a 'sign' that I was to be elected to a second term of office, and that the paleness of one of the faces was an omen that I should not see life through the last term."

In the interval before assuming the office of President, Lincoln appointed his Cabinet. He made good on the political promises of his campaign managers by appointing the Republican leaders of Pennsylvania, Indiana, and Ohio, despite warnings by many persons that these men were not statesmen enough to help him meet the problems of the federal government.

A letter that he received from a little girl in New York caused him to change his appearance. She wrote that she thought he should grow a beard. The hitherto clean-shaven Lincoln decided to honor her request, perhaps feeling that the beard would add dignity. On his way to Washington, Lincoln invited the little girl to visit his train, showed her his beard, and gave her a kiss.

The political aspects of Lincoln's Cabinet appointments and the incident with the beard and the little girl made many persons feel that the President-elect was too much a small-town politician to cope with the growing national crisis. In talks that he made in the various towns his train passed through en route to Washington, Lincoln called the crisis an "artificial" one that did not call for a warlike solution. Warned of a supposed plot against his life in Baltimore, Lincoln left his special train in Philadelphia and with one companion slipped through Baltimore at night to arrive unannounced in Washington on February 23, 1861.

By the time Lincoln reached the nation's capital, seven southern states already had left the Union, forming the Confederate States of America with Jefferson Davis as president. Others were preparing to secede. And President Buchanan was avoiding any action which prevented the dissolution of the United States.

Lincoln's Inauguration

STANDING ON A RAISED PLATFORM on the steps of the U. S. Capitol, Lincoln took the oath of office as the sixteenth President of the United States on March 4, 1861. In an attempt to allay southern fears that his accession to office signaled a Republican determination to abolish slavery, he quoted from a previous speech he had made:

"I have no purpose, directly or indirectly, to interfere with the institution of slavery in the States where it exists. I believe I have no lawful right to do so, and I have no inclination to do so.

"I now reiterate these sentiments," he continued, "and in doing so I only press upon the public attention the most conclusive evidence of which the case is susceptible that the property, peace, and security of no section are to be in any wise endangered by the now incoming Administration."

He then warned that he did not recognize the secession from the Union of the southern states:

". . . no State upon its own mere motion can lawfully get out of the Union . . . resolves and ordinances to that effect are legally void . . . acts of violence within any State or States against the authority of the United States are insurrectionary or revolutionary . . .

"I therefore consider that in view of the Constitution and the laws, the Union is unbroken, and to the extent of my ability I shall take care, as the Constitution itself expressly enjoins upon me, that the laws of the Union be faithfully executed in all the States. Doing this I deem to be only a simple duty on my part, and I shall perform it so far as practicable unless my rightful masters, the American people, shall withhold the requisite means or in some authoritative manner direct the contrary. I trust this will not be regarded as a menace, but only as the declared purpose of the Union that it *will* constitutionally defend and maintain itself.

"In doing this there needs to be no bloodshed or violence, and there shall be none unless it be forced upon the national authority. . . .

"In *your* hands, my dissatisfied fellow-countrymen, and not in *mine*, is the momentous issue of civil war. . . .

"We are not enemies, but friends. We must not be enemies. Though passion may have strained it must not break our bonds of affection. . . .'"

The Moment of Decision

LINCOLN DECIDED TO TEST the intentions of the Confederate States to determine whether they wanted peace or war. Most federal forts in the secessionist states already had been taken over by the Confederates without firing a shot. But one important federal fort had held out for the Union—Fort Sumter in the harbor of Charleston, South Carolina. Lincoln ordered supplies to be taken to the fort and notified South Carolina authorities of his intention to deliver them. On April 12, Confederate artillery began a bombardment of the fort, and two days later the defenders of Fort Sumter surrendered. The following day, April 15, 1861, President Lincoln called up 75,000 militia troops to join the regular army "to repossess the forts, places, and property which have been seized from the Union."

Hundreds of thousands of volunteers answered Lincoln's call to arms, and Northerners hoped for an early end to the struggle. This optimism was extinguished in July by the disastrous battle of Bull Run.

By the summer of 1862, as Lincoln later explained, "Things had gone from bad to worse, until I felt that we had reached the end of our rope on the plan we had been pursuing; that we had about played our last card, and must change our tactics or lose the game."

The change of tactics that Lincoln devised was the Emancipation Proclamation. On September 22, 1862, Lincoln signed a proclamation warning that unless the rebelling states returned to the Union by January 1, 1863, he would issue an order freeing their slaves. When that day came and the war continued, Lincoln issued the Emancipation Proclamation.

In July 1863, Union troops turned back Confederate General Robert E. Lee's invasion of Pennsylvania in the battle of Gettysburg, during which more than 7,000 Union and Confederate soldiers died. Four months later Lincoln made his most famous address dedicating a battlefield cemetery at Gettysburg:

"Fourscore and seven years ago our fathers brought forth on this continent, a new nation, conceived in Liberty, and dedicated to the proposition that all men are created equal.

"Now we are engaged in a great civil war, testing whether that nation, or any nation so conceived and so dedicated, can long endure. We are met on a great battlefield of that war. We have come to dedicate a portion of that field, as a final resting place for those who here gave their lives that that nation might live. It is altogether fitting and proper that we should do this.

"But, in a larger sense, we can not dedicate—we can not consecrate—we can not hallow—this ground. The brave men, living and dead, who struggled here, have consecrated it, far above our poor power to add or detract. The world will little note, nor long remember what we say here, but it can never forget what they did here. It is for us the living, rather, to be dedicated here to the unfinished work which they who fought here have thus far so nobly advanced. It is rather for us to be here dedicated to the great task remaining before us—that from these honored dead we take increased devotion to that cause for which they gave the last full measure of devotion—that we here highly resolve that these dead shall not have died in vain—that this nation, under God, shall have a new birth of freedom—and that government of the people, by the people, for the people, shall not perish from the earth."

Throughout the early years of the war Lincoln had searched in vain for a commanding general who could seize the initiative and crush the South.

Early in 1864 he found the right man in Ulysses S. Grant, who had been winning battles in the West. With Grant in command and with northern superiority in troops and supplies it became only a matter of time until the war would be ended.

Second Term and Assassination

IN THE ELECTION OF 1864 the Democrats put up as their candidate for President one of Lincoln's former generals, George B. McClellan. As the election neared, one Union victory after another reinforced the people's faith in Lincoln, and he was re-elected with the huge majority of 212 electoral votes to McClellan's 21. In the popular vote Lincoln received 2,206,938 to his opponent's 1,803,787.

In his second inaugural address Lincoln again spoke with unforgettable eloquence, this time on the theme of reconciliation:

"With malice toward none, with charity for all, with firmness in the right as God gives us to see the right, let us strive on to finish the work we are in, to bind up the nation's wounds, to care for him who shall have borne the battle and for his widow and his orphan, to do all which may achieve and cherish a just and lasting peace among ourselves and with all nations."

Final victory came a little over a month later when Lee surrendered to Grant at Appomattox Court House on April 9, 1865. But five days later the North's exultation was cut short. A brooding southern sympathizer, actor John Wilkes Booth, had long meditated an assassination conspiracy. Even though the Confederacy was beyond all help by the time Booth got his plot to the active stage, he pushed it through with the determination of a fanatic. Extraordinary bad luck and careless guards permitted the assassin to penetrate the presidential box at Ford's Theatre and fatally wound Lincoln with a pistol shot from behind. Booth temporarily escaped by a theatrical flourish, leaping from the box to the stage and fleeing through the wings to a waiting horse. Within a few days Booth was overtaken and slain. But Lincoln had died on April 15, 1865—a tragic loss, as events proved, to the South as well as the North.

His body lay in state at the White House and Capitol, and was borne across the country to Springfield in a train draped in black. Millions of mourners lined the route of the 1,700-mile journey, their sorrow finding an echo in Walt Whitman's lines:

Oh Captain! my Captain! our fearful trip is done,
The ship has weather'd every rack, the prize we sought is won,

The port is near, the bells I hear, the people all exulting,
While follow eyes the steady keel, the vessel grim and daring;
   But O heart! heart! heart!
      O the bleeding drops of red,
         Where on the deck my Captain lies,
         Fallen cold and dead.

Andrew Johnson
The Seventeenth President of the United States
1865–69

1808 (December 29) Born in Raleigh, North Carolina.

1822–24 Worked as a tailor's apprentice.

1827 (May 17) Married Eliza McCardle.

1828–30 Alderman of Greeneville, Tennessee.

1830–33 Mayor of Greeneville, Tennessee.

1835–37; 1839–41 Member of Tennessee house of representatives.

1841–43 Member of Tennessee senate.

1843–53 U.S. representative from Tennessee.

1853–57 Governor of Tennessee.

1857–62 U.S. senator from Tennessee.

1862–64 Military governor of Tennessee.

1865 Vice President of the United States.

1865–69 Seventeenth President of the United States.

1874–75 U.S. senator from Tennessee.

1875 (July 31) Died at Carter Station, Tennessee.

I mpeached because he refused to let Congress usurp presidential rights, Andrew Johnson missed conviction and removal from office by one senatorial vote. His fortitude in the face of overwhelming congressional pressure strengthened the presidency and helped preserve the separation of powers among the legislative, executive, and judicial branches of the government.

A former tailor, who had never been to school a day in his life, Johnson forged his way upward in politics by supporting the common man and by speaking his mind even when it was unpopular to do so. As a Tennessee Democrat, he was the only southern senator who refused to follow his seceding state. Elected Vice President on the National Union ticket in 1864, and thrust into the White House by Lincoln's assassination, he won the enmity of the Republicans because he believed the South should be treated more as a wayward friend than as a conquered enemy. Leaving the presidency a disgraced man in 1869, he triumphantly returned to Washington six years later as the only former President ever elected to the Senate.

From Tailor's Apprentice to Vice President

ANDREW JOHNSON was born in poverty in Raleigh, North Carolina, on December 29, 1808. His father, Jacob Johnson, a laborer, died when Andrew was three. His mother, Mary McDonough Johnson, worked as a seamstress and washerwoman to support Andrew, his three brothers, and herself; but she was unable to afford to send the boys to school.

When he was nearly fourteen, Andrew was apprenticed to a tailor. As he sat cross-legged sewing, one of his fellow-workers taught him to read, but he still did not know how to write. After a boyhood prank for which he feared his master would punish him, he ran away to Laurens Court-House, South Carolina, where he worked as a journeyman tailor.

Although still wanted by his master as a fugitive, Johnson returned briefly to Raleigh when he was seventeen. He talked his mother and stepfather—his mother having remarried—into going west with him to start a new life. They traveled across North Carolina in a two-wheeled cart drawn by a blind pony and settled in Greeneville, Tennessee, just across the border. There Johnson opened his own tailor shop.

A year after coming to Greeneville, Johnson married sixteen-year-old Eliza McCardle, the daughter of a shoemaker. Because she had more education than Johnson, she was able to teach the future President how to write and how to do simple arithmetic. They had five children, including one son who was later killed serving as a Union soldier in the Civil War.

The hard-working young tailor impressed the townspeople with his seriousness, and in 1828, at the age of nineteen, he was elected to the village council. After serving as an alderman for two years, the twenty-one-year-old Johnson received the highest honor his fellow townsmen could bestow, by being elected mayor. A naturally gifted public speaker, Johnson polished his oratory during his three years as mayor by taking an active part in a debating society at Greeneville College.

A follower of Andrew Jackson, Johnson became known as a defender of the rights of the laboring man. In 1835 he was elected to the legislature, was defeated when he ran for re-election in the depression year of 1837, but was returned as a state representative in 1839. Two years later the fast-rising young politician was elected to the state senate where he made a name for himself as an enemy of the state's slave-holding aristocracy.

Johnson was thirty-four when he was first elected to Congress in 1843. Re-elected as a U.S. representative four times, he helped President Polk press the Mexican War, voted for the Compromise of 1850, and tried to win passage of a homestead law to make it easier for poor farmers to obtain western land.

When a redistricting of the state by the Whigs made it impossible for Johnson to be re-elected to Congress, he returned to Tennessee and won election as governor in 1853. Known as the "Mechanic Governor," Johnson still tailored his own clothes and made a suit for the governor of Kentucky as a gesture of friendship. Denouncing the anti-Catholic Know-Nothing movement, he won a second term as governor by a large majority in 1855.

"I have reached the summit of my ambition," Johnson said when the Tennessee legislature elected him to the U. S. Senate in 1857. He again took up the cudgels for a homestead law that eventually was passed in 1862.

In the Democratic National Convention of 1860, Johnson was proposed for the presidential nomination by Tennessee, but he withdrew his name and campaigned for the election of John Breckinridge. Many assumed he was a secessionist. But after Lincoln was elected, Johnson forthrightly denounced the secessionist movement and declared his intention to remain loyal to the Union. Of the secessionists he said:

"I would have them arrested and tried for treason, and, if convicted, by the eternal God, they should suffer the penalty of the law at the hands of the executioner."

When Tennessee joined the Confederacy, Johnson made good on his word, remaining in Washington to be hailed as a patriot in the North and reviled as a traitor in the South.

After northern troops had seized western and central Tennessee in 1862, Lincoln appointed Johnson military governor of the state. He proved a fair-minded, able administrator, granting amnesty to former Confederate sympathizers but also pushing for an amendment to the state constitution to outlaw slavery in the state. Tennessee, specifically exempted from the Emancipation Proclamation, was the only seceding state to end slavery by its own action.

At the National Union Convention in Baltimore in June 1864, the delegates chose Johnson as the vice-presidential running mate of President Lincoln. The presence of a Jackson Democrat on the Union ticket helped Lincoln run up a large majority over his Democratic opponent, General George McClellan. But at the inauguration on March 4, 1865, Johnson embarrassed himself and his friends by appearing drunk. When some persons suggested to Lincoln that he should ask for the Vice President's resignation, the President good-humoredly silenced them with the remark: "I've known Andy a great many years, and he ain't no drunkard."

Johnson's Administration

ON THE NIGHT LINCOLN WAS SHOT, the conspirators had also planned to kill Vice President Johnson, but their plans went awry. Awakened by a friend with the news of the assassination, Johnson hastened to his stricken chief's bedside. After the agonizing night-long vigil, Johnson was sworn in as Chief Executive by Chief Justice Salmon P. Chase. The members of the Cabinet assembled in the parlor of his hotel.

". . . I feel incompetent to perform duties so important and responsible as those which have been so unexpectedly thrown upon me, . . ." Johnson told them. "The course which I have taken in the past in connection with this rebellion must be regarded as a guaranty of the future. . . . The best energies of my life have been spent in endeavoring to establish and perpetuate the principles of free government, and I believe that the Government in passing through its present perils will settle down upon principles consonant with popular rights more permanent and enduring than heretofore. . . . I have long labored to ameliorate and elevate the condition of the great mass of the American people. Toil and an honest advocacy of the great principles of free government have been my lot. Duties have been mine; consequences are God's. This has been the foundation of my political creed, and I feel that in the end the Government will triumph and that these great principles will be permanently established. . . ."

However, despite Johnson's humble tone, he was a fearless, even reckless fighter for what he believed in. As a result he became embroiled in the bitterest intragovernmental conflict this nation has ever seen. The problem was the "reconstruction" of the ex-Confederate states. Johnson, like Lincoln, favored a "mild" reconstruction, in effect turning the state governments over to the white citizens, with only the main leaders of the Confederacy disfranchised. But the Republican congressional leaders favored a "radical" reconstruction, enfranchising the former black slaves and barring most of the former Confederates from government. This solution had special appeal to the Republicans because it promised to permit a continued hold on the federal government for their party, which even in 1860 had been a minority.

At first the Radical Republicans were pleased with the prospect of Johnson's presidency. They mistakenly regarded him as a weak man who would be easier to control than Lincoln. Moreover, they counted on his past antagonism to leaders of the southern aristocracy as assurance that he would be congenial to their plans for severe treatment of the defeated South.

"By the gods! there will be no trouble now in running the government!" This was the sentiment expressed by Republican Senator Benjamin F. Wade of Ohio. But two years later this same Wade, as President of the Senate, had become so confident that he could evict Johnson from the White House and succeed him that he was said to have written an inauguration speech and to have chosen his Cabinet in preparation for the event.

But the new President soon made it clear that he intended to carry out Lincoln's plan to grant a soft peace to the South. He ended the blockade of southern ports and declared a general amnesty except for officials and high officers of the Confederacy and the wealthy southern aristocrats. By the middle of June, Johnson had issued a series of proclamations enabling the southern states to begin setting up civil governments. And by the time Congress met in December 1865, the former states of the Confederacy had elected governors, legislatures, and congressmen. Though they had given formal approval to the Thirteenth Amendment outlawing slavery, they had passed "Black Codes" binding the ex-slaves to the land.

". . . It has been my steadfast object," Johnson said in his first annual message to Congress, "to escape from the sway of momentary passions and to derive a healing policy from the fundamental and unchanging principles of the Constitution. . . . I know very well that this policy is attended with some risk; that for its success it requires at least the acquiescence of the States which it concerns; that it implies an invitation to those States, by renewing their allegiance to the United States, to resume their functions as States of the Union. But it is a risk that must be taken."

But the northern Republicans had no intention of welcoming back the Democratic congressmen and senators from the seceding states. Instead, Congress passed legislation to re-institute military government throughout the South and establish a powerful Freedmen's Bureau to assist the four million freed slaves. Through this means the most radical congressional leaders hoped to revolutionize the southern way of life. Johnson promptly vetoed the measure.

"It is plain that an indefinite or permanent exclusion of any part of the country from representation must be attended by a spirit of disquiet and complaint. It is unwise and dangerous to pursue a course of measures which will unite a very large section of the country against another section of the country, however much the latter may preponderate."

For the time being the Radical Republicans were not strong enough to override Johnson's veto. But by April 1866, they had gained sufficient strength to pass over his veto a civil rights law granting citizenship to the former slaves, a measure Johnson considered unnecessary.

In an effort to rally the people behind his mild reconstruction policies, Johnson went on a national speaking tour in the summer and fall of 1866. But the subsequent elections went against him, and the Radical Republicans increased their majority in Congress.

Now able to ignore Johnson's vetoes, the Radicals pushed into law in the spring of 1867 a series of harsh Reconstruction Acts. Military governments replaced the civil governments set up by southern Democrats. "Carpetbaggers"—immigrant Northerners—and "scalawags"—renegade white Southerners—joined forces with freed blacks to seize control of southern state legislatures. Some of the laws passed by these Reconstruction legislatures were enlightened, such as those providing free public education. But corruption and waste of public funds were common.

Johnson warned that the course upon which Congress had embarked "would engender a feeling of opposition and hatred between the two races, which, becoming deep rooted and ineradicable, would prevent them from living together in a state of mutual friendliness." He termed the Reconstruction Acts "legislation which, looking solely to the attainment of political ends, fails to consider the rights it transgresses, the law which it violates, or the institutions which it imperils."

The Radical Republicans slashed back at Johnson by passing over his veto in the spring of 1867 the Tenure of Office Act, which forbade the President to remove from office any federal official who had been appointed with the advice and consent of the Senate. Sure that the act was unconstitutional (and the Supreme Court ultimately so ruled fifty-nine years later), Johnson removed from office in August 1867 his Secretary of War, Edwin M. Stanton, a Radical Republican who had been an obstructionist in his Cabinet. In Stanton's place he appointed General Ulysses S. Grant. In defiance of the President, Grant turned the office back to Stanton in February 1868. Enraged, Johnson again removed Stanton on February 21 and in his place appointed Major General Lorenzo Thomas. Three days later the House of Representatives voted to impeach Johnson on eleven counts, the most important of which was violation of the Tenure of Office Act.

The trial of the President began in the Senate on March 13 and lasted more than two months. It soon became apparent that the Radical Republican leaders were seeking to get rid of the President's opposition to their political plans. Suspense built as the public speculated whether the Republican leadership could hold in line the necessary thirty-six votes to provide a two-thirds majority needed to convict and remove Johnson from office. If seven Republicans decided to vote with the Democrats, Johnson would be adjudged not guilty. By the time a vote was taken on May 16, six Republicans had indicated they would switch, and one, Senator Edmund Ross of Kansas, had refused to say how he would cast his vote. When it came time for him to vote, Ross cast his ballot as "not guilty." The final tally was thirty-five guilty and nineteen not guilty, one short of conviction. On May 26 the roll was called on two more charges, and again Johnson was saved by a single vote.

After the trial, the deadlock between the President and Congress resumed. Johnson, who had been elected Vice President on the Republican or "National Union" ticket in 1864, entertained some hopes of receiving a presidential nomination from the Democrats in 1868, but he was disappointed. In his last annual message to Congress in December 1868, he bitterly denounced the legislator's repeated violations of the Constitution:

"Our own history, although embracing a period of less than a century, affords abundant proof that most, if not all, of our domestic troubles are directly traceable to violations of the organic law and excessive legislation. The most striking illustrations of this fact are furnished by the enactments of the past three years upon the question of reconstruction. After a fair trial they have substantially failed and proved pernicious in their results, and there seems to be no good reason why they should longer remain on the statute book."

Perhaps the most valuable achievement of the Johnson administration was the acquisition of Alaska. Scoffed at as "Seward's Folly" and "Seward's Icebox," the vast northern territory proved worth far more than its purchase price of $7.2 million.

Return to Washington

FULL OF FIRE, FIGHT, AND DETERMINATION to prove he was right in his actions as President, Johnson returned to Tennessee and ran for Congress in 1869. Beaten in this attempt, he tried and lost again in 1872. Finally, in 1874, the Tennessee legislature elected him to his old office as U.S. senator.

When Johnson took his seat in the Forty-fourth Congress in March 1875, the Democrats had won control of the House for the first time since the Civil War and had greatly increased their strength in the Senate. Johnson made only one speech in the Senate, reaffirming his belief in the milder reconstruction policies he had attempted to institute and denouncing the punitive policies that had been forced on the nation by the Radical Republicans. He felt vindicated by the applause that broke out in the very chamber that had tried to convict him seven years earlier.

Johnson did not have long to enjoy his revitalized reputation. On July 31, 1875, while visiting his daughter at Carter Station, Tennessee, the sixty-six-year-old former President died of a stroke.

Ulysses S. Grant

The Eighteenth President of the United States
1869–77

1822 (April 27) Born in Point Pleasant, Ohio.

1839–43 Attended West Point.

1843–53 Served as officer in U. S. Army, rising to captain.

1848 (August 22) Married Julia Dent.

1854–58 Farmed near St. Louis, Missouri.

1860–61 Clerked in store at Galena, Illinois.

1861–65 Rose to command all Union Armies in Civil War.

1867–68 Secretary of War *ad interim* under President Johnson.

1869–77 Eighteenth President of the United States.

1880 Unsuccessful candidate for Republican presidential nomination.

1885 (July 23) Died at Mount McGregor, New York.

There are but few important events in the affairs of men brought about by their own choice," Ulysses S. Grant observed philosophically in his memoirs. In his own life he seemed marked for quiet obscurity when the outbreak of the Civil War suddenly flung the door open to his talents. As a result of his victorious leadership of the Union Armies, he inherited the presidency almost as a right.

But his military background was not enough to equip him for the complexities of governing a large and swiftly growing nation, and historians have judged him a failure as a President. The common-sense approach that worked so well on the battlefield proved naive in the world of sharpers and intriguers who frequented the White House during his administration.

In his later years, when he waged a courageous struggle against cancer and bankruptcy, Grant won new sympathy and affection from his countrymen.

Farmboy to Career Officer to Storeclerk

"IN JUNE, 1821, MY FATHER, JESSE R. GRANT, married Hannah Simpson," Grant says in his *Personal Memoirs*. "I was born on the 27th of April, 1822 at Point Pleasant, Clermont County, Ohio. In the fall of 1823 we moved to Georgetown. This place remained my home, until at the age of seventeen, in 1839, I went to West Point.

"The schools were very indifferent. . . . They were all supported by subscription, and a single teacher—who was often a man or woman incapable of teaching much, even if they imparted all they knew—would have thirty or forty scholars, male and female, from the infant learning the ABC's up to the young lady of eighteen and the boy of twenty, studying the highest branches taught—the three R's, 'Reading, 'Riting, 'Rithmetic.' I never saw an algebra, or other mathematical work higher than the arithmetic, in Georgetown, until after I was appointed to West Point. I then bought a work on algebra in Cincinnati; but having no teacher it was Greek to me."

Grant's father operated both a tannery and a farm, though young 'Lyss, as he was nicknamed, preferred farm chores to working in the tannery. From the time he was eleven he did most of the plowing. Yet despite the shortcomings of the local education system, he won an appointment to West Point, where a clerical error resulted in a change in his name. Named Hiram Ulysses at birth, he found at the military academy that he had been misregistered as Ulysses Simpson Grant. He did not call the mistake to anyone's attention, preferring the new name because the initials of his old one lent themselves to the nickname "Hug." Instead, his fellow-cadets began calling him "Uncle Sam" and later "Sam."

At West Point, Grant numbered among his friends and acquaintances fifty cadets who later served as generals in the Civil War. He later remarked that knowing the weaknesses and strengths of these men, both friend and foe, helped him in battle. An average student, Grant graduated twenty-first in his class of thirty-nine. Because he particularly liked mathematics, he hoped eventually for assignment as a math instructor at West Point, but meanwhile was sent to join an infantry company in St. Louis.

The Mexican War began while Grant was serving as a second lieutenant with his regiment in Texas in 1846. He fought first under Zachary Taylor and later under Winfield Scott, rising to first lieutenant and winning a brevet—temporary promotion—to captain for gallantry at the capture of Mexico City. The war over, Grant obtained a leave of absence and returned to St. Louis, where on August 22, 1848, he married Julia Dent, the sister of one of his West Point classmates. Grant and his wife had three sons and a daughter.

During the early 1850s Grant was assigned to military posts on the West Coast. He left his wife and children in St. Louis, feeling he could not afford to take them West on his low army pay. Grant received his commission as captain, but living the life of a bachelor on a dull army post he began drinking heavily. Finally, in 1854, he was forced to resign his commission.

He was only thirty-two, but his career seemed finished. Returning to St. Louis, Grant moved his family to a small piece of land given to his wife by her father as a wedding present. He built a log cabin for them to live in, and named the farm "Hard Scrabble." Continued drinking and illness combined to bring failure to the venture, and in 1858 he sold the farm at auction. He tried to sell real estate in partnership with a cousin of Mrs. Grant, but this, too, proved a failure. In hopes of straightening out his problems his younger brothers offered him a job as clerk in a store they were operating in Galena, Illinois, and he moved there in May 1860.

Recall to Arms

WHEN LINCOLN'S CALL FOR VOLUNTEERS to defend the Union came in April 1861, the thirty-nine-year-old Grant saw his opportunity. Quitting his job as a storekeeper, and donning his shabby old army overcoat, he helped raise a company of volunteers in Galena, but he declined election as their captain because he hoped for something better. He wrote a modest letter to the governor, mentioning his military experience, and went to Springfield, where he worked for several weeks as a $3-a-day clerk helping organize Illinois' volunteer regiments. When one of these proved unruly, the governor turned it over to Grant. Demonstrating an immediate aptitude for command, he whipped his regiment into shape and took it into successful combat in a diversionary action. In August he received a commission as brigadier general.

With the aid of America's first ironclad gunboats, he captured Forts Henry and Donelson in Tennessee, taking prisoner more than 20,000 Confederate troops. When the Confederate general in command of Fort Donelson (a former fellow-cadet at West Point) asked Grant's terms for the surrender, Grant replied: "No terms except an unconditional and immediate surrender can be accepted." This won Grant a nickname—"Unconditional Surrender" Grant. He also was promptly promoted to major general.

Two months later Grant was in command at Shiloh in southern Tennessee. Although surprised by a massive Confederate attack—some said he was off on a drinking bout—he hung on grimly and finally beat off the enemy in what was the bloodiest battle fought on the American continent up to that time. Temporarily Grant fell under a cloud as the home front gasped at the casualty figures, but failure of his superiors to achieve progress brought a restoration of his position in October, when he was given command of all Union forces in Tennessee.

He set about at once to capture the powerful Confederate stronghold of Vicksburg, protected by nearly insuperable geographic barriers in the form of bayous, swamps, and its own towering Mississippi River bluffs. The campaign was arduous and frustrating, but in it Grant demonstrated a skill and daring to match his stubbornness. When Vicksburg surrendered unconditionally on July 4, 1863, Grant was hailed throughout the North. Given command of all the western armies, he organized a counter-offensive against a major Confederate thrust into central Tennessee, decisively defeating Confederate General Bragg at the battle of Chattanooga and opening the way for an invasion of Georgia.

Summoned to Washington by President Lincoln in March 1864, Grant was given the highest rank in the army, lieutenant general, and placed in command of all the armies in the field. He at once planned the final campaign against the Confederacy, assigning William T. Sherman to the western armies and establishing his own headquarters with the Army of the Potomac. Sherman's mission was to invade the heart of the Confederacy, capture Atlanta, and bring devastation to the South's "store-house" of Georgia. While Sherman was carrying out his orders to the letter, Grant turned his personal attention to the South's main army, commanded by the renowned Robert E. Lee.

Ignoring criticisms for heavy losses, Grant boldly attacked Lee and pushed him rapidly back into the fortifications of Richmond. Through the winter of 1864–65 Grant applied unremitting pressure. On April 2, 1865, Lee was forced to abandon Richmond and retreat west. One week later the end came at Appomattox Court House. In the moment of triumph Grant proved unassuming and magnanimous, appearing in a mud-spattered uniform to accord generous terms of surrender.

Grant was a national hero. His home town of Galena, Illinois, built him a house, Philadelphia presented him with a mansion, and New York made him a cash gift, raised by popular subscription, of $105,000. Congress honored him with the creation of the new rank of general of the armies.

Not surprisingly, the leaders of the Republican party soon fixed their eyes on Grant as a presidential possibility. Though at first he seemed to side with President Johnson in his feud with Congress, he acted with the Radicals in turning the post of Secretary of War, to which Johnson had appointed him, back to Stanton. When the Republican Convention met in May 1868, Grant was unanimously nominated on the first roll call. His acceptance message that contained the sentence, "Let us have peace," led many persons to believe he favored milder Reconstruction policies for the South. He easily swept to victory in the November election over the Democratic candidate, former Governor of New York Horatio Seymour. Grant received 214 electoral votes to Seymour's 80, although the popular vote was much closer—3,013,421 to 2,706,829.

Grant's Administration

WHEN THE FORTY-SIX-YEAR-OLD GRANT took the oath of office on March 4, 1869, he was the youngest man so far to become President. Vigorous and at the height of his popularity, he seemed to be just what the troubled country needed. In his inaugural address, he declared:

"The responsibilities of the position I feel, but accept them without fear. The office has come to me unsought; I commence its duties untrammeled. I bring to it a conscious desire and determination to fill it to the best of my ability to the satisfaction of the people. . . .

"I shall on all subjects have a policy to recommend, but none to enforce against the will of the people. Laws are to govern all alike—those opposed as well as those who favor them. I know no method to secure the repeal of bad or obnoxious laws so effective as their stringent execution."

Unfortunately, the "bad or obnoxious laws" to which Grant gave the most "stringent execution" were the Reconstruction Acts that had been passed over Johnson's veto. The Southerners against whom they were enforced had no legal power to repeal them, but in retaliation had formed the Ku Klux Klan, a secret terror society that undertook to restore white rule by killings, burnings, and floggings. In the end Radical Reconstruction proved a failure and left a bitter legacy to future generations.

Grant revealed his political ineptitude with his initial Cabinet appointments. He chose two old friends from Galena as Secretaries of State and War —one of whom resigned and the other of whom died during the first year of the administration. He appointed as his Secretary of the Treasury a millionaire war contractor who was forced out of office within a few days because of conflict of interest with government business. And as his Secretary of the

Navy he named a millionaire banker who resigned within three months because the Cabinet position took too much of his time.

The Radical Republicans in Congress who had helped bring Grant into the White House treated him as a puppet. They ignored his mild recommendations to repeal the Tenure of Office Act and to reform the civil service. His rather naive proposal to annex Santo Domingo as a haven for former black slaves was summarily rebuffed.

In 1872 "Liberal"—anti-Radical—Republicans nominated New York newspaper editor Horace Greeley for the presidency, and the Democrats joined them with an endorsement of Greeley in an all-out effort to unseat Grant. But the regular Republicans pressed Grant's campaign for a second term, and he won by 3,596,745 votes to Greeley's 2,843,446, a substantial increase in his margin. The electoral vote was 286 to 66.

Scandal had touched Grant's administration during his first term when his brother-in-law's connivance had helped the financier Jay Gould use inside government information in attempting a spectacular Wall Street coup—"cornering the gold market." By Grant's second term, corruption seethed and boiled throughout the government. Many congressmen, senators, and other officials were involved in illegal dealing in stock connected with the building of the Union Pacific Railroad, which received enormous federal subsidies. Two members of the Cabinet resigned to avoid impeachment for bribery and fraud, as did five federal judges. Grant's secretary was tried as a member of the Whisky Ring that defrauded the government of millions of dollars in excise taxes, and was saved from conviction only by the President's testimony in his behalf.

The voters reacted strongly to these scandals and to the depression which followed the financial panic of 1873. In the congressional elections of 1874, the Democrats won a majority in the House for the first time since the Civil War. Despite pressure from his supporters, Grant decided he should not run for a third time in 1876. In his last annual message to Congress he frankly accepted a share of blame for the disasters of his administration.

"It was my fortune, or misfortune, to be called to the office of Chief Executive without any previous political training. . . .

"Under such circumstances it is but reasonable to suppose that errors of judgment must have occurred. . . . Mistakes have been made, as all can see and I admit, but it seems to me oftener in the selections made of the assistants appointed to aid in carrying out the various duties of administering the Government—in nearly every case selected without a personal acquaintance with the appointee, but upon recommendations of the representatives chosen directly by the people."

A Triumph Abroad

AFTER LEAVING THE PRESIDENCY, Grant went abroad for nearly three years on a tour of Europe and Asia. Everywhere he was greeted with honor, respect, and huge crowds, as the hero of the war for freedom. Newspaper reports of his triumphant trip helped regain some popularity at home, and a faction of the Republican party pushed for his nomination for President in 1880. The effort ended in a convention deadlock between Grant and James G. Blaine, and the ultimate selection of a dark-horse candidate, James Garfield.

Grant and his wife lived quietly for a few years at the house that had been given to them in Galena, and then moved to New York. He invested all his savings, about $100,000 in a banking firm in which one of his sons was a partner. But the head of the firm, Ferdinand Ward, turned out to be a swindler. The firm went bankrupt in 1884, Grant lost all his money, and Ward was sent to prison.

"I have made it a rule of my life to trust a man long after other people gave him up," the sixty-two-year-old Grant commented bleakly, "but I don't see how I can ever trust any human being again."

Not only was Grant left destitute, but he was suffering from a fatal cancer. His courage, however, had not abandoned him. To provide for his family, he undertook to write his memoirs for magazine serialization. From the start the accounts he wrote of his campaigns—clear, simple, straightforward—were a popular success, and remain to this day one of the classics of military literature.

Sticking to his task with all his old-time tenacity, he managed to complete it only weeks before his death at his home in Mount McGregor, New York, on July 23, 1885. Mark Twain had the memoirs published in book form and turned over a half million dollars' profit to the Grant family.

In the concluding chapter, Grant commented on the war that had brought him fame and the presidency:

"It is probably well that we had the war when we did. We are better off now than we would have been without it, and have made more rapid progress than we otherwise should have made."

Rutherford B. Hayes
The Nineteenth President of the United States
1877–81

1822 (October 4) Born in Delaware, Ohio.

1842 Graduated from Kenyon College.

1843–45 Studied law at Harvard University.

1845 Began the practice of law in Ohio.

1852 (December 30) Married Lucy Ware Webb.

1858–61 City solicitor of Cincinnati, Ohio.

1861–65 Served as an officer in the Union Army in the Civil War, rising to the rank of brevet major general.

1865–67 U.S. representative from Ohio.

1868–72; 1876–77 Governor of Ohio.

1877–81 Nineteenth President of the United States.

1893 (January 17) Died in Fremont, Ohio.

The people elected Democrat Samuel J. Tilden of New York President in 1876, but in perhaps the most flagrant misuse of power in the nation's history, the politicians agreed to give the office to Ohio Republican Rutherford B. Hayes. Paradoxically enough, the beneficiary of this political bargain was one of the most high-minded and deeply religious men to occupy the White House. He and his wife—called "Lemonade Lucy" because she forbade the serving of alcohol in the Executive Mansion—began each day by kneeling at morning prayers and closed each day by singing hymns.

As part of the deal that gave him the presidency, Hayes ended the Reconstruction of the South by withdrawing federal troops. As a congressman ten years earlier, Hayes had helped vote the Reconstruction Acts into law over President Johnson's veto and had also voted for Johnson's impeachment.

From the standpoint of background, the red-haired, blue-eyed Hayes had the makings of a great President. He was the only Chief Executive to have been both a dashing military-hero general and an elected state governor. Moreover, he was a well-educated lawyer. But, as in the case of John Quincy Adams, the circumstances under which Hayes came to the presidency made it impossible for him to obtain wide support.

Although little was accomplished politically during Hayes' administration, technological advances moved the nation forward. Alexander Graham Bell installed the first telephone in the White House; Thomas Edison perfected the electric light and at Hayes' invitation came to the Executive Mansion to demonstrate the newly invented phonograph.

Lawyer, Soldier, and Politician

RUTHERFORD BIRCHARD HAYES was born in Delaware, Ohio, October 4, 1822. His merchant father died nearly three months before his birth, but left a large estate which permitted his widow to give a good education to the future President and his brothers and sisters.

Young "Rud," as the boy was called, was regarded by his acquaintances as a rather stuffy fellow who "never had any wild oats to sow." He attended schools in Ohio and Connecticut before enrolling at Kenyon College, from which he graduated at the age of twenty. He studied law under the tutelage of a family friend in Ohio, and rounded out his education with three years of law school at Harvard.

Hayes practiced law for several years in Lower Sandusky (now Fremont), Ohio, then moved to Cincinnati in 1849. Within a few years he gained a reputation as a defender of fugitive slaves. He became a friend of various abolitionists who later helped form the Republican party in Ohio.

When Hayes was thirty, he married twenty-one-year-old Lucy Ware Webb, the daughter of a doctor. As a graduate of Cincinnati's Wesleyan Female College, she later became the first college-educated mistress of the White House and a symbol for such militant women's organizations as the Woman's Christian Temperance Union. The Hayeses had eight children, of whom four sons and a daughter grew to adulthood.

Hayes entered public life for the first time in 1858, when the city council of Cincinnati elected him city solicitor to fill a vacancy. The next year he ran for the office in the regular election and won, but was defeated for re-election in 1861.

With the outbreak of war, Hayes was elected captain of a drilling organization formed by a literary club to which he belonged. He then helped organize the 23d Ohio Volunteers and was commissioned major. His regiment soon moved into action in West Virginia, and by November he had been promoted to lieutenant colonel.

The war brought out qualities that Hayes had never before discovered in himself. He repeatedly distinguished himself, leading charges and joining in hand-to-hand combat. At the battle of South Mountain, in Maryland, he continued leading his men up the mountain in the face of enemy fire even after his arm had been shattered by a bullet and nearly a third of his force had been killed or wounded. Shortly thereafter he was promoted to colonel.

In the campaigns of 1864 and 1865 in Virginia, Hayes was wounded four times and had four horses shot out from under him. He received a battlefield promotion to brigadier general in October 1864, and to brevet major general in March 1865.

While Hayes was busy fighting, his admirers at home nominated him for Congress in 1864. When one wrote to him urging that he come home to campaign for votes, he answered tersely: "Thanks. I have other business just now. Any man who would leave the army at this time to electioneer for Congress ought to be scalped." This patriotic sentiment very likely won him more votes than if he had gone home. Elected, he finally took his seat in Congress in December 1865. Re-elected in 1866, he voted as a party regular with the Radical Republicans in their determination to punish the South and squelch President Johnson's efforts toward a soft peace.

When Ohio Republicans nominated Hayes for governor in August 1867, he resigned from Congress and conducted a vigorous campaign that carried him to victory with a majority of about 3,000. After demonstrating his capabilities as a successful state administrator, he was re-elected to a second term in 1869.

Upon leaving the governorship, he ran unsuccessfully for Congress in 1872, and then retired to his estate, Spiegel Grove, near Fremont, Ohio, believing that he was through with public life. However, three years later, in 1875, the Republicans again nominated him for governor, and he became the first man in the state's history to win a third gubernatorial term.

The Most Controversial Presidential Election

WHEN OHIO REPUBLICANS PUT HAYES FORWARD as their favorite son at the party's National Convention in Cincinnati in 1876, the national leaders paid little attention. James G. Blaine of Maine, who had been Speaker of the House throughout most of Grant's administration seemed to have the nomination sewed up. But Blaine's reputation had been compromised by corruption, and on the seventh ballot the convention gave the presidential nomination to Hayes—an upright teetotaler about whom there never had been and never would be a breath of scandal.

The Democrats chose as their presidential candidate Governor Samuel Jones Tilden of New York, who had won a national reputation as a reformer through his work in overthrowing the notorious Tweed Ring.

The campaign was a bitter one with each party freely accusing its opponents of corruption. Doubting that he could win, Hayes was not surprised by the headlines on the morning after the election that announced Tilden's victory. The popular votes showed 4,284,020 for Tilden and 4,036,572 for Hayes, while the electoral votes stood 203 for Tilden to 166 for Hayes.

But the newspaper headline writers had not reckoned with the determination of the Republican party leaders to hold onto their power. Claiming that blacks had been prevented from going to the polls in South Carolina, Florida, and Louisiana, the Republicans challenged the returns from these states, and those from Oregon as well. By claiming the electoral votes of all four states, the Republicans could muster enough electoral votes to give Hayes a 185 to 184 margin of victory. But who was to decide the issue? If it were left to Congress, the prospect was for a deadlock between the Democratic House and the Republican Senate.

While the country seethed for more than three months over the issue, the leaders of the two parties met in secret. They decided to put special legislation through Congress appointing an Electoral Commission of fifteen men to arbitrate the problem—five from the House, five from the Senate, and five from the Supreme Court. On the surface this seemed nonpartisan, with five Democrats, five Republicans, and five impartial justices. In actuality, three of the justices were Republicans, so the Commission's findings were a foregone conclusion. Nevertheless, the Democratic leadership agreed to House approval of the plan—upon assurance that Hayes would withdraw troops from the South, leaving local government in the hands of southern whites, and perhaps paving the way to future Democratic election victories. The deal was made. And the House formally approved Hayes as the winner just fifty-six hours before the inauguration was scheduled to take place.

Hayes' Administration

THE FIFTY-FOUR-YEAR-OLD HAYES had left Ohio for Washington on March 1 not knowing whether he really would become President. Upon leaving Columbus he remarked that he might be back as governor within a week. But, on Inauguration Day, March 5, 1876, he happily took the oath of office and attempted to soothe the country in his address:

"The President of the United States of necessity owes his election to office to the suffrage and zealous labors of a political party, the members of which cherish with ardor and regard as of essential importance the principles of their party organization; but he should strive to be always mindful of the fact that he serves his party best who serves the country best. . . .

"The fact that two great political parties have in this way settled a dispute in regard to which good men differ as to the facts and the law no less than as to the proper course to be pursued in solving the question in controversy is an occasion for general rejoicing.

"Upon one point there is entire unanimity in public sentiment—that conflicting claims to the Presidency must be amicably and peaceably adjusted, and that when so adjusted the general acquiescence of the nation ought surely to follow.

"It has been reserved for a government of the people, where the right of suffrage is universal, to give to the world the first example in history of a great nation, in the midst of the struggle of opposing parties for power, hushing its party tumults to yield the issue of the contest to adjustment according to the forms of law."

Hayes tried hard to be a good President, but was unable to overcome the stigma of the political bargain that had seated him in the White House. He made good on the bargain by withdrawing troops from the South, leaving southern blacks effectively disfranchised for a long time to come.

The Democrats controlled the House during the first two years of Hayes' administration, and they also captured the Senate during his last two years in office. So Hayes had little chance to obtain passage of any legislation that he wanted.

The continuing economic depression helped bring on the first great national strike—that of railroad workers in 1877. Riots broke out along the railroads and Hayes forcefully responded to calls from the state governors by ordering federal troops to help restore order in West Virginia, Maryland, Pennsylvania, and Illinois.

When Congress attempted to ease the depression by passing legislation to issue "cheap" silver dollars, Hayes vetoed the law in the belief that sound money was the basis of the American economic system. Congress passed the measure over his veto, but relatively few of the new silver dollars were issued. Nevertheless, the economy began to improve, though Hayes had to call a special session of Congress in 1877 to get enough money to pay the soldiers and sailors in the armed forces.

Both Democrats and Republicans turned a deaf ear to Hayes' repeated pleas for a reform of the civil service. He proceeded to infuriate members of his own party by trying to free many jobs from partisan control, especially those having to do with tax collection. He raised a particular storm when he authorized the firing of the Collector of the Port of New York, never dreaming that this man, Chester A. Arthur, would within a few years be presiding in the White House.

Although railroads now ran from coast to coast, Indian fighting still continued in the West. A major war came in 1877 when Chief Joseph tried to lead the Nez Percé tribe to freedom in Canada, but was stopped by federal troops. In an effort to quell further uprisings, Hayes issued an executive order banning the sale of firearms to Indians.

In his inaugural address, Hayes had recommended a constitutional amendment expanding the presidential term to six years and barring re-election. The proposal attracted little support, but when it became apparent in 1880 that he had no chance of obtaining a second-term nomination, Hayes could at least say that he had never wanted it.

When Hayes sent his last annual message to Congress in December 1880, he enumerated a long catalogue of forward-looking legislation that he knew had little likelihood of passage. He called for Congress to appropriate money to supplement the educational budgets of the states "to promote free popular education." He again asked for a reform of the civil service to eliminate patronage. He called for a reorganization of the Territory of Utah, warning that the Mormons were becoming too powerful and were spreading polygamy. And he called for a host of improvements that ranged from a building for the Library of Congress to the completion of the Washington Monument.

He especially called attention to the oppression of freed slaves in the South:

"Continued opposition to the full and free enjoyment of the rights of citizenship conferred upon the colored people by the recent amendments to the Constitution still prevails in several of the late slaveholding States. It has, perhaps, not been manifested in the recent election to any large extent in acts of violence or intimidation. It has, however, by fraudulent practices in connection with the ballots, with the regulations as to the places and manner of voting, and with counting, returning, and canvassing the votes cast, been successful in defeating the exercise of the right preservative of all rights—the right of suffrage—which the Constitution expressly confers upon our enfranchised citizens.

"It is the desire of the good people of the whole country that sectionalism as a factor in our politics should disappear. They prefer that no section of the country should be united in solid opposition to any other section. The disposition to refuse a prompt and hearty obedience to the equal-rights amendments to the Constitution is all that now stands in the way of a complete obliteration of sectional lines in our political contests. As long as either of these amendments is flagrantly violated or disregarded, it is safe to assume that the people who placed them in the Constitution, as embodying the legitimate results of the war for the Union, and who believe them to be wise and necessary, will continue to act together and to insist that they shall be obeyed. The paramount question still is as to the enjoyment of the right by every American citizen who has the requisite qualifications to freely cast his vote and to have it honestly counted. With this question rightly settled, the country will be relieved of the contentions of the past; bygones will indeed be bygones, and political and party issues, with respect to economy and efficiency of administration, internal improvements, the tariff, domestic taxation, education, finance, and other important subjects, will then receive their full share of attention; but resistance to and nullification of the results of the war will unite together in resolute purpose for their support all who maintain the authority of the Government and the perpetuity of the Union, and who adequately appreciate the value of the victory achieved. . . .

"It will be the duty of the Executive, with sufficient appropriations for the purpose, to prosecute unsparingly all who have been engaged in depriving citizens of the rights guaranteed to them by the Constitution."

Perhaps to please his wife, Hayes' last executive order, on February 22, 1881, banned the sale of intoxicating liquor at army camps and forts.

After leaving the White House, Hayes lived in quiet retirement, spending most of his time working on charitable enterprises. His wife preceded him in death by four years, and the seventy-year-old former President's last words before dying in his home in Fremont on January 17, 1893, were: "I know I am going where Lucy is."

James A. Garfield

The Twentieth President of the United States
1881

1831 (November 19) Born at Orange, Ohio.

1856 Graduated from Williams College.

1857–61 President of Hiram Eclectic Institute (now Hiram College).

1858 (November 11) Married Lucretia Rudolph.

1859–61 Member of Ohio state senate.

1861–63 Rose from lieutenant colonel to major general in Union Army in Civil War.

1863–80 U.S. representative from Ohio.

1880 Elected to U. S. Senate.

1881 Twentieth President of the United States.

1881 (July 2) Wounded by assassin in Washington, D.C.

1881 (September 19) Died of wounds at Elberon, New Jersey.

The second President to be killed by an assassin, James A. Garfield served only two hundred days as Chief Executive, and for eighty of those days he lay near death with a bullet through his spine. The six-foot, blue-eyed Garfield brought unquestioned talents to the White House, but he had little opportunity to demonstrate whether they would be used more for the benefit of his country or for the benefit of his party.

The last President to be born in a log cabin, he was a self-made man in the tradition of Horatio Alger (who was then at the height of his popularity).

Garfield worked as a canalboat tow boy at seventeen, became a college president at twenty-six, was the youngest general in the Union Army at thirty, and in seventeen years in Congress became leader of the Republican party in the House and one of the finest orators of his day.

President Hayes, who felt that the nomination of his friend and fellow-Ohioan was a vindication of his own administration, wrote glowingly of Garfield in his diary:

"The truth is no man ever started so low that accomplished so much in all our history. Not Franklin or Lincoln even. . . . He is the ideal candidate because he is the ideal self-made man."

A Log-Cabin Boyhood

THE YOUNGEST OF FIVE CHILDREN, James Abram Garfield was born in a crude one-room log cabin on his father's frontier farm in Orange township, Ohio, on November 19, 1831. The boy was only a year and a half old when his father, Abram, died of a throat infection coupled with exhaustion from fighting a forest fire. Although left deeply in debt, his mother, Eliza Ballou Garfield, was determined to keep her small family together. She sold fifty acres of the farm, paid the debts, and with her children's help worked the remaining thirty acres, barely eking out a living.

From the time he was three years old, Garfield attended local schools, developing a great love for reading and an ambition to go to college. At seventeen he decided to become a sailor, but soon found that life aboard a Great Lakes freighter was not as romantic as he had thought. He next got a job as a "tow boy," driving horses and mules pulling boats on the Ohio Canal. He fell off the narrow tow path many times, and, as he later said, "had fourteen almost miraculous escapes from drowning."

Early in 1848 his mother gave him $17 that she had managed to save, and he and two cousins set out to attend Geauga Seminary in Chester, Ohio. Discovering that he could not afford the $1.50-a-week for room and board at the academy, he and his cousins rented a room in a farmhouse and cooked their own meals while attending school. He earned extra money on Saturdays as a carpenter's helper.

At eighteen he dropped out of the Geauga Seminary for a semester to earn $48 teaching at a country school. He proved he was qualified for the job in true Horatio Alger style, by thrashing the local bully who had driven away the last schoolteacher. He then returned to Chester to complete his preparation for college.

In August 1851, he entered Hiram Eclectic Institute (later Hiram College), a school founded by the Disciples of Christ, to which Garfield and his family belonged. In his three years at Hiram, Garfield became especially proficient in the Greek and Latin languages and paid his expenses by tutoring other students—including his future wife.

A benefactor loaned him money to attend Williams College in Williamstown, Massachusetts, which he entered as a junior in 1854. While there, he taught school one winter at North Pownal, Vermont, where, by a curious coincidence, the previous teacher had been Chester A. Arthur, his future successor as President. While at Williams, Garfield received the special attention of its president, the famous educator Mark Hopkins. This led to Garfield's later description of what he regarded as a perfect school: ". . . a simple bench, Mark Hopkins on one end and I on the other . . ."

After graduating from Williams with honors in 1856, Garfield returned to Hiram, where he was appointed professor of Latin and Greek. During the following year, at the age of twenty-six, he was made president of the school.

In 1858 he married Lucretia Rudolph, a farmer's daughter who had been a fellow student both in Chester and in Hiram. He and his wife "Crete," as he called her, had seven children, one of whom, James Rudolph Garfield, became Secretary of the Interior under President Theodore Roosevelt.

The energetic Garfield, not content with being merely the president of a small college, devoted considerable time to acting as a lay preacher for the Disciples of Christ—an activity that polished his oratory. He also diligently studied to become a lawyer. Entering politics in 1859, he was elected a Republican member of the state senate.

Civil War General and Politician

AT THE OUTBREAK OF THE CIVIL WAR the students of Hiram College formed a company that was attached to the 42d Ohio Infantry Volunteers. The men elected Garfield lieutenant colonel, and he soon was promoted to colonel in command of the regiment. Early in 1862 he led a brigade that drove Confederate forces out of eastern Kentucky, and was rewarded at the age of thirty with the commission of brigadier general. After taking part in the battles of Shiloh and Corinth, he was assigned as a member of the court-martial that found Major General Fitz John Porter guilty of disobeying orders at the second battle of Bull Run.

Returning to battlefront duty, Garfield became chief of staff to Major General William Rosecrans. He distinguished himself at the battle of Chickamauga in September 1863, when, even though his horse was shot from under him, he safely delivered a message that saved the Army of the Cumberland from disaster. For his bravery, he was given a battlefield promotion to major general.

While on active duty in 1862, Garfield was elected to Congress, and in December of 1863, yielding to an urgent request by President Lincoln, resigned his commission and took his seat in the House of Representatives. This began an unbroken period of seventeen years in Congress—a record for any President-to-be, and testimony to his popularity, for during this time many fellow Republicans went down to defeat in Ohio elections, including his friend Rutherford B. Hayes.

In Congress, Garfield sided with the Radical Republicans in pressing for the Reconstruction Acts and the impeachment of President Johnson. His feelings against the South remained strong to the end of his life—at the Chicago convention that nominated him for President, he declared there was only one condition for restoring friendship with the South, "that it shall be admitted, forever and forever more, that in the war for the Union, we were right and they were wrong."

During Grant's administration, Garfield became chairman of such important House committees as Military Affairs, Banking and Currency, and Appropriations. He was also one of the congressmen accused of taking bribes for political favors, but the charges against him were never conclusively proved. In 1877 he was a member of the Electoral Commission named to decide the disputed Hayes-Tilden election, and helped arrange the bargain that brought Hayes to the presidency. While the Democrats held a majority in the House under Hayes, Garfield served as minority leader of the Republicans. In January 1880, the Ohio legislature elected him to the U. S. Senate, but he never served in that office.

At the Republican National Convention in Chicago in June 1880, the party was split into two factions—the "Stalwarts," headed by New York Senator Roscoe Conkling, and the "Half-Breeds," led by Maine Senator James G. Blaine. The Stalwarts were determined to win the nomination for former President Grant, while the Half-Breeds were equally determined to win it for Blaine. As head of the Ohio delegation, Garfield avoided taking either side and placed in nomination his fellow Ohioan, Secretary of the Treasury John Sherman. For thirty-three ballots the Stalwarts and Half-Breeds stalemated each other. On the thirty-fourth ballot Wisconsin swung its votes to Garfield. Blaine gave his support to Garfield, and on the thirty-sixth ballot the presidential nomination was accorded the former canalboat tow boy—the first time a President-to-be was present at his own nomination. To reconcile the Stalwarts, the convention chose for its vice-presidential candidate Chester A. Arthur, the political hack who had been ousted by President Hayes as Collector for the Port of New York.

Upon returning to Washington, Garfield, a superstitious man, told President Hayes of two omens bearing on his nomination, which Hayes noted in his diary of June 15: "As he entered the Convention the day of his nomination a man distributing leaves of the New Testament handed him a leaf which he (Garfield) put in his pocket. Long after the nomination, emptying his pockets the leaf was found. The verse that was uppermost as it was folded read 'The Stone which the builders reject etc. etc.' At one o'clock p.m., the hour of the nomination, an Eagle lit on Garfield's house in Washington and sat there several minutes and was seen by many persons."

Garfield conducted a front-porch campaign from his home at Mentor, Ohio. The Democrats, who had given their presidential nomination to Major General Winfield Scott Hancock, a hero of the battle of Gettysburg and a man with no political experience, revived the charges of bribery that had been hurled at Garfield during the Grant administration. Perhaps the most important issue of the campaign was the protective tariff, supported by the Republicans and opposed by the Democrats. Times were prosperous, President Hayes had helped dispel the shadow of corruption that had fallen on the Republican party, and Garfield narrowly won the election. The popular votes were almost a tie, with 4,453,295 for Garfield and 4,414,082 for Hancock, but Garfield received 214 electoral votes to Hancock's 155.

Garfield's Administration and Assassination

AFTER BEING SWORN IN on the Capitol steps on March 4, 1881, the forty-nine-year-old Garfield's first act was to turn and kiss his aged mother—the first time a President's mother had been present at an inauguration. In his address, Garfield placed particular emphasis on the need for civil service reform:

"The civil service can never be placed on a satisfactory basis until it is regulated by law. For the good of the service itself, for the protection of those who are intrusted with the appointing power against the waste of time and obstruction to the public business caused by the inordinate pressure for place, and for the protection of incumbents against intrigue and wrong, I shall at the proper time ask Congress to fix the tenure of the minor offices of the several Executive Departments and prescribe the grounds upon which removal shall be made during the terms for which incumbents have been appointed."

To pay off his political debt to the Half-Breeds, Garfield appointed Blaine Secretary of State and replaced the politically important Collector of the Port of New York. These moves stirred considerable resentment among the Stalwarts, but no one was prepared for the tragedy that suddenly struck.

On the morning of July 2, 1881, Garfield and Blaine were entering the Baltimore and Potomac railroad station where the President was to board a train to attend the twenty-fifth reunion of his class at Williams College, when a mentally disturbed and disaffected office seeker named Charles J. Guiteau fired two shots. One struck the President in the arm and the other in the back. Guiteau shouted: "I am a Stalwart! Arthur is now President!"

The wounded Garfield was carried to the White House where he lingered near death week after week, the physicians unable to locate and remove the bullet (the X ray was fourteen years in the future). In September the President asked to be removed from the heat of Washington, so he was taken to a seaside cottage at Elberon, New Jersey, where he died on September 19, 1881. After a trial, at which it was shown that the assassin was not acting as part of a conspiracy by the Stalwarts, Guiteau was hanged on June 30, 1882.

Chester A. Arthur
The Twenty-first President of the United States
1881–85

1829 (October 5) Born in Fairfield, Vermont.

1848 Graduated from Union College.

1853 Admitted to bar to practice law in New York City.

1859 (October 29) Married Ellen Lewis Herndon.

1861–62 Served on New York governor's staff with rank of brigadier general helping supply troops for Civil War.

1871–79 Collector of the Port of New York.

1881 Vice President of the United States.

1881–85 Twenty-first President of the United States.

1886 (November 18) Died in New York City.

Chester A. Arthur never in his entire life won election to a public office on his own (unless one counts his tag-along election to the vice presidency). Even the professional military men who became President had the experience of earning election to that office. But Arthur, known as "The Gentleman Boss" of the Republican party in New York City, was always a behind-the-scenes politician, building the party organization and managing the election campaigns of others.

The nation was shocked when Arthur succeeded to the presidency upon the death of Garfield. The word "politician" had become synonymous with "corrupt." Only two years earlier President Hayes had made Arthur the very symbol of the evils of patronage by dismissing him as Collector of the Port of

New York—an action hailed as a triumph of reform. No wonder that even a leading Republican exclaimed:

"Chet Arthur President of the United States! Good God!"

But the nation was agreeably surprised when Arthur turned out to be an honest, conscientious Chief Executive. In fact, he was so honest and conscientious that his party refused to give him a chance to run for the office on his own when his term was up.

The Rise of a Boss

THE SON OF A BAPTIST CLERGYMAN, Chester Alan Arthur was born in Fairfield, Vermont, on October 5, 1829. Later, some of his political enemies claimed he was disqualified from becoming President because he actually had been born in Canada, where his Irish-immigrant father had lived a few years earlier, and that he had adopted the birthplace and birthdate of a younger brother who had died as a baby—but this rather frivolous charge was never proved.

Young Chet attended local schools in various towns in New York where his father preached. At the age of fifteen he entered Union College in Schenectady and joined one of the early college social fraternities, Psi Upsilon. An excellent student, he was one of six in his class of one hundred admitted to the national honor fraternity, Phi Beta Kappa. He graduated in 1848 at the age of eighteen.

For a time Arthur interspersed semesters of law school at Ballston Spa, New York, with periods of teaching school. In 1853 he became a student in the law office of Erastus D. Culver in New York City and later the same year was admitted to the bar to practice law, becoming a member of Culver's firm.

The son of an ardent abolitionist, Arthur often undertook the defense of fugitive slaves and other persecuted blacks. In one famous case, he helped six slaves obtain their freedom from their Virginia owner who had made the mistake of thinking that he could transport them through the free state of New York. In another case that caused much publicity, he obtained $500 damages from a transit company for a black woman named Lizzie Jennings, who had been thrown off a New York City horse-car because of her color.

The young abolitionist lawyer attended the first Republican state convention at Saratoga, New York, and campaigned for Frémont for President in 1856.

In 1859 the twenty-nine-year-old Arthur, who for the rest of his life claimed he was one year younger than he actually was, married Ellen Lewis

Herndon, the twenty-two-year-old daughter of a U. S. Navy officer. They had two sons and a daughter, although the eldest boy died in infancy. After twenty years of marriage, Mrs. Arthur died—the year before her husband became President.

Arthur worked hard to help Republican Governor Edwin D. Morgan win re-election in 1860. As a reward, Morgan appointed Arthur to the honorary post of state engineer-in-chief, with the rank and uniform of a brigadier general. When the Civil War began, the governor appointed him acting quartermaster general to help supply the volunteer troops being organized in the state. The following year, the governor gave Arthur the title of state inspector general of militia, again with the rank of brigadier general. When Morgan was succeeded as governor by Democrat Horatio Seymour in 1863, Arthur returned to his law practice, but continued to use the title "General" for the rest of his life.

Persevering at his work in the Republican party organization, Arthur rose to be recognized as the No. 2 man in the state Republican machine of Senator Roscoe Conkling. He furthered his political fortunes as chairman of the New York club that worked for General Grant's nomination and election in 1868.

Grant rewarded Arthur in 1871 with appointment as Collector of the Port of New York. This was considered the most important federal job in that city because the collector controlled the appointment of more than 1,000 employees of the New York Custom House. In his first year as collector, Arthur was said to have received a personal income of more than $40,000. Holding the position for eight years, he used it to build a loyal political machine. President Hayes incurred the eternal wrath of Conkling and Arthur when he removed the "General" from the post in 1879 as part of his reform effort to eliminate politics from the civil service.

At the Republican National Convention in Chicago in 1880, Arthur was a member of the New York delegation of Stalwarts, supporting the nomination of Grant for a third term. When James G. Blaine's Half-Breeds switched the convention to nominate Garfield for President, Arthur was given the vice-presidential nomination in order to insure Stalwart support for the national ticket.

After taking office as Vice President in 1881, Arthur found himself in an unusually influential position because the Democrats and Republicans in the Senate were evenly divided, thirty-seven to thirty-seven. As presiding officer he was often called upon to cast a deciding vote. He and Garfield openly broke when the President appointed one of Blaine's friends to Arthur's old job of Collector of the Port of New York without consulting either Arthur or Conkling.

After Garfield was shot, Arthur made no effort to assume the duties of the presidency in the eighty-day period while the President hovered near death. He particularly hesitated to make any such move in light of the assassin's declaration that the motive for the crime was to make Arthur President and put the Stalwarts in control of patronage.

Arthur's Administration

WHEN ARTHUR RECEIVED WORD of Garfield's death, he took the oath of office as President on September 20, at his home in New York City, before a New York Supreme Court judge. Two days later the oath was administered to him again in the Vice President's room in the Capitol by Chief Justice Morrison R. Waite. In his inaugural address, Arthur said:

"For the fourth time in the history of the Republic its Chief Magistrate has been removed by death. All hearts are filled with grief and horror at the hideous crime which has darkened our land, and the memory of the murdered President, his protracted sufferings, his unyielding fortitude, the example and achievements of his life, and the pathos of his death will forever illumine the pages of our history.

"For the fourth time the officer elected by the people and ordained by the Constitution to fill a vacancy so created is called to assume the Executive chair. . . . Men may die, but the fabrics of our free institutions remain unshaken. No higher or more assuring proof could exist of the strength and permanence of popular government than the fact that though the chosen of the people be struck down his constitutional successor is peacefully installed without shock or strain except the sorrow which mourns the bereavement."

The wealthy new President felt the White House was too shabby for his tastes. So he employed designer Louis Tiffany of New York to renovate it completely in art nouveau style. He also added an elevator for convenience.

As President, Arthur encouraged American participation in international, political, cultural, and scientific conferences. He called an international conference that helped resolve the chaos in communities depending on local sun time, by establishing standard time zones. He called a meeting of all the countries of the Western Hemisphere to seek ways to prevent war. He suggested that all the countries of North and South America agree to use the same currency system in order to facilitate trade. And he negotiated a treaty, turned down by the Senate, to build an inter-ocean canal through Nicaragua.

More striking than any of these proposals was one Arthur put forward in his first annual message to Congress in December 1881—reform of the civil service system. His own well-known patronage background notwithstanding, he pledged himself to approve any reasonable merit system Congress thought practical. And he made good his word by signing into law, on January 16, 1883, the Pendleton Civil Service Act.

Arthur never had the full co-operation of Congress during his administration, particularly after the Democrats again won control of the House in the mid-term elections of 1882. He used his veto power sparingly. The two most important measures that he vetoed were passed over his veto—a measure excluding Chinese immigration and a nineteen-million-dollar rivers-and-harbors bill that Arthur felt had too many special-interest ramifications.

Many suggestions made by Arthur in his annual messages to Congress were never acted upon. He appealed for federal aid to education, suggesting that the government distribute money to the states on a ratio based on the amount of illiteracy in each state. He suggested that since the country was so prosperous, that all internal revenue taxes be abolished except those on tobacco and alcoholic beverages. He also asked Congress to draw up legislation to clarify the conditions of "inability" under which a Vice President should assume the powers of the presidency.

Arthur had hopes of winning the presidency on his own merits in the election of 1884, but though his good record pleased the country it did not entirely please the politicians of his party. In the Republican National Convention, his political enemy James G. Blaine captured the nomination. Arthur was not too unhappy to see Blaine defeated in the November election by Democrat Grover Cleveland.

One of the last public ceremonies in which Arthur took part before leaving the White House was the dedication of the Washington Monument on February 21, 1885. And on the day before leaving office he sent a note to the Senate asking that impoverished former President Grant be restored to the retired list of the army with full pay as a general.

After Cleveland's inauguration, Arthur returned to New York and resumed his law practice, but soon was forced to retire because of illness. He died of kidney disease in his New York townhouse on November 18, 1886.

Sixty years later, when the Arthur family Bible was given to the New York Public Library, historians learned he actually was fifty-seven at the time of his death, instead of the fifty-six that was generally reported. Whether Arthur concealed his actual age out of vanity or through an honest error is unknown.

"I am but one in fifty-five million," author Mark Twain said, "still in the opinion of this one-fifty-five-millionth of the country's population, it would be hard to better President Arthur's administration."

Grover Cleveland

The Twenty-second President of the United States
The Twenty-fourth President of the United States
1885–89; 1893–97

1837 (March 18) Born in Caldwell, New Jersey.

1851–52 Grocery clerk in Fayetteville, New York.

1853–55 Worked in New York Institution for the Blind in New York City.

1855–62 Studied law and worked as a law clerk in Buffalo, New York.

1859 Admitted to the bar to practice law.

1863–65 Assistant district attorney of Erie County, New York.

1871–73 Sheriff of Erie County.

1882 Mayor of Buffalo, New York.

1883–84 Governor of New York.

1885–89 Twenty-second President of the United States.

1886 (June 2) Married Frances Folsom.

1893–97 Twenty-fourth President of the United States.

1908 (June 24) Died in Princeton, New Jersey.

He is the kind of man who would rather do something badly for himself than have somebody else do it well."

That description of Grover Cleveland by his friend Samuel J. Tilden went far toward explaining how Cleveland achieved the distinction of being the only President to serve one term, lose an election, and then make a comeback for a second term.

A short, jolly, blue-eyed fat man, who was descriptively called "Uncle Jumbo" by young relatives, he was the first Democrat to be elected President after the Civil War. Among other unusual claims to fame, he was the only President who had ever hanged a man—while serving as sheriff in Buffalo, New York. And he was the only President to be married in the White House.

As Chief Executive, Cleveland brought the country no unusual theories of government; but he did restore to the presidency much of the prestige eroded by Congress during the Reconstruction Era. Above all, he exemplified honesty, even when it lost him the support of powerful interests in his party. He fought the corruption of New York City's Democratic Tammany organization. He argued for a low tariff against the eastern industrialists' pleas for protection, but fought the western free silver interests and defended "sound money" as strenuously as his Republican predecessors. He supported government controls on the railroad robber barons, but he also clamped down hard on the rising labor movement. Essentially he was a conservative. In his battles with Congress, he exercised the veto power more times than had all previous Presidents combined. He fittingly summed up his life on his deathbed with these words:

"I have tried so hard to do right."

A Minister's Son

ONE OF A FAMILY OF NINE CHILDREN of a Presbyterian minister, Stephen Grover Cleveland was born in Caldwell, New Jersey, on March 18, 1837. He attended schools in Fayetteville and Clinton, New York, as his father moved from pastorate to pastorate, and ended his formal education at the age of fourteen to help support the family. Young Grover ran errands and clerked in a grocery store in Fayetteville for one dollar a week.

When he was sixteen, his father died. Joining his eldest brother, William, a teacher at the New York Institution for the Blind, Grover worked as an assistant and odd-job helper for two years, regularly sending his meager pay home to his mother.

At eighteen, in the spring of 1855, Grover decided to head West to make his fortune. When he paused in Buffalo, New York, to visit relatives, he was offered a job helping on his uncle's farm and decided to stay. Before the year was up, Cleveland's uncle obtained the boy a clerkship in a local law firm where he could study law while earning his keep at five dollars a week.

Four years later, in 1859, Cleveland was admitted to the bar, and promoted to chief clerk in the same law firm at a wage of $600 a year, with the promise of a $100 raise each year. He needed the steady income to help support his younger brothers and sisters.

The young lawyer began to take an interest in the Democratic party, and he worked especially hard in the successful gubernatorial campaign of Horatio Seymour in 1862. As a political reward, Cleveland was appointed assistant district attorney of Erie County, an office he held throughout the Civil War. Partly because he was an anti-war Democrat and partly because his family depended on him, Cleveland hired a substitute for $300 when his name came up in the draft.

In 1865 Cleveland lost his first election. He ran for district attorney of Erie County, but was defeated by his roommate, Lyman K. Bass, the Republican candidate. After this he established himself in private law practice in Buffalo.

Cleveland tried for public office again in 1870, this time running for sheriff and winning. The thirty-three-year-old sheriff soon made a name for himself as an honest public official, exposing crooked contractors who had been delivering short measures of food and fuel to the county jail. When it came time to hang two convicted murderers, Cleveland sprang the trap himself, explaining that he could not ask his deputies to do a job just because he didn't want to do it himself. By the time his term was up in 1873, Cleveland had saved $20,000 from his salary and fees, and for the first time in his life was out of debt.

For nine years he prospered as a lawyer, while continuing to be active in the local Democratic party inner circle. As a bachelor, he led a happy-go-lucky life, frequenting the local saloons and enjoying extended hunting and fishing trips with his cronies.

In 1881 Cleveland accepted the nomination to run as a reform candidate for mayor, to clean up corruption in the city government of Buffalo. He won by 15,000 votes to his opponent's 11,500, and soon became known as the "veto mayor," turning down one crooked measure after another that had been voted by his corrupt city council.

When the Democratic state convention met in the fall of 1882 to choose a candidate for governor, Cleveland's name was on the lips of many western delegates who wanted to overturn the power of the eastern bloc of the party. Cleveland's friends captured the nomination for him with the aid of New York's Tammany machine, but he made no promises to the New York City politicians. The Republican candidate for governor, Charles J. Folger, was serving as President Arthur's Secretary of the Treasury, and was known as the favored candidate of the corrupt millionaire Jay Gould. Consequently, reform-minded Republicans joined the Democrats in voting for Cleveland in the November election, and he received the largest plurality of any governor up to that time—with 535,000 votes to Folger's 342,000.

To their chagrin, the leaders of the Tammany machine learned that Cleveland meant what he said about reform. In his two years as governor, Cleveland refused to go along with measures designed to feather the nests of Tammany's friends. Cleveland read every word of every law passed by the legislature before he would sign or veto it—even if it meant he had to stay up all night to get the job done.

As the national election of 1884 approached, the Republican party chose as its presidential candidate James G. Blaine, who as Speaker of the House under President Grant had been deeply involved in the railroad scandals. Many prominent members of the GOP angrily declared they would not support such a candidate, and they urged the Democrats to choose a reform candidate.

When the Democratic National Convention met in July 1884, Cleveland's reputation for honesty made him the favorite. The New York City bosses made a last-ditch effort to derail Cleveland's nomination by spreading the story that he was anti-labor, anti-Catholic, and anti-Irish. It was easy for Cleveland's friends to disprove these charges, and on the second ballot the delegates nominated "Grover the Good," as he was somewhat fatuously dubbed, with Governor Thomas A. Hendricks of Indiana as his running mate.

Just ten days later the most sensational bombshell in campaign history exploded. Under the headline "A Terrible Tale," a Buffalo newspaper revealed that eleven years earlier Cleveland had fathered a son by a woman he did not marry. The charge was true and Cleveland refused to deny it. His partisans, without his consent, hit back with a story that Blaine's first son had been born less than three months after he had married his wife. They also made free use of charges of corruption, the evidence for which appeared strong despite Blaine's denials. Republican torchlight parades marched to the chant:

> Blaine! Blaine! James G. Blaine!
> Plum-ed Knight from the State of Maine!

To which the Democrats retorted:

> Blaine! Blaine! James G. Blaine!
> Continental liar from the State of Maine!

The Republicans converted their own favorite theme, Cleveland's illicit paternity, into a memorable chant:

> Ma, ma, where's my Pa?
> Gone to the White House, ha ha ha!

As the most scurrilous campaign in U.S. history drew to a close, Blaine appeared to have the edge. His home state of Maine, voting early as was its custom, gave him the largest victory the Republicans had ever achieved in the state. Blaine was favored to capture the crucial New York electoral vote because of the Tammany disaffection with Cleveland and the effect of the paternity scandal on Irish Catholic voters. But six days before the election a delegation of Protestant clergymen made a courtesy call on Blaine at his New York hotel, and their spokesman referred to the Democrats as the party of "rum, Romanism and rebellion." Blaine neglected to disavow the remark, which was instantly seized on by the Democrats, printed, and distributed outside Catholic churches Sunday morning. Cleveland carried New York by 1,149 votes out of a million cast, and with it the election. Blaine himself attributed his defeat to the unhappy phrase of his supporter. Nationally, Cleveland received 4,879,507 votes to Blaine's 4,850,293.

The victorious Democrats came up with a last triumphant jingle:

> Hurrah for Maria,
> Hurrah for the kid,
> We voted for Grover
> And we're damn glad we did.

Cleveland's First Administration

THE FORTY-SEVEN-YEAR-OLD CLEVELAND stood confidently with one hand behind his back and delivered his inaugural address without notes on the spring-like March 4, 1885. A huge crowd listened as the first Democrat to be elected President in a quarter of a century spoke:

"The people demand reform in the administration of the Government and the application of business principles to public affairs. As a means of this end, civil-service reform should be in good faith enforced. Our citizens have the right to protection from the incompetency of public employees who hold their places solely as the reward of partisan service, and from the corrupting influence of those who promise and the vicious methods of those who expect such rewards; and those who worthily seek public employment have the right to insist that merit and competency shall be recognized instead of party subserviency or the surrender of honest political belief."

Nevertheless, Democrats from all parts of the country descended on Washington expecting to be rewarded with the more than 100,000 jobs that Cleveland had it in his power to fill. In letters to friends, Cleveland called the problem "a nightmare." He wrote, "This dreadful, frightful, damnable office seeking hangs over me and surrounds me . . ." He refused to remove Republicans from office just because they were Republicans, and insisted that for anyone to be removed from office it was necessary to bring charges of incompetence or corruption. Throughout the nation Republican newspapers attacked Cleveland for the charges that were being brought against Republican office holders, while Democratic papers attacked him for not putting good Democrats in office. These attacks brought from the President one of the most sweeping denunciations ever made against the press:

"I don't think there ever was a time when newspaper lying was so general and mean as the present, and there never was a country under the sun where it flourished as it does in this. The falsehoods daily spread before the people in our newspapers, while they are proofs of the mental ingenuity of those engaged in newspaper work, are insults to the American love for decency and fair play of which we boast . . ."

In one of his last acts as President, Arthur had provided for the opening of the Indian Territory (now Oklahoma) for settlement. This would have robbed the Indians of thousands of acres of land they had been promised. So within a week after taking office, Cleveland issued a proclamation canceling the opening of the lands and warning all intruders that they would be removed by troops if necessary.

Throughout his first administration, Cleveland ruthlessly vetoed special-interest legislation, running up a total of more than 300 vetoes during his four years in office, compared to a total of 132 vetoes by the previous twenty-one Presidents.

In his first annual message to Congress, Cleveland called for a reduction in tariffs, pointing out that the federal revenues were "in excess of the actual needs of an economical administration of the Government." He said that the $70 million surplus of revenues over expenses would merely tempt Congress to pass money-wasting laws. He also asked for an end to the coinage of silver dollars, warning that gold was being hoarded and that the country's fiscal system was in danger.

Early in 1886 there were hundreds of railroad strikes throughout the country as the new Knights of Labor union demanded higher wages and an eight-hour workday. Recognizing the importance of the growing labor movement, Cleveland sent a special message to Congress in April—the first by any

President devoted exclusively to the problems of labor. In it he asked for the creation of a three-member commission to settle labor-management disputes. The critical nature of the labor situation was emphasized two weeks later by the Haymarket riot in Chicago, in which seven persons were killed and more than fifty injured in a battle between strikers and police. Two years later Congress passed and Cleveland signed legislation creating the Department of Labor.

Cleveland brought a unique social event to the White House on June 2, 1886, by marrying twenty-one-year-old Frances Folsom, the daughter of one of his former law partners. It remains the only marriage of a President in the White House. The Clevelands had five children. Their second daughter, Esther, born during his second administration, was the first child of a President born in the White House.

The first federal controls on business were enacted in 1887, when Congress passed, with Cleveland's approval, the Interstate Commerce Act. For years the powerful railroads had thwarted attempts by the states to regulate them in such matters as the setting of discriminatory freight rates that could make or break a company or a local community. Largely by executive order, Cleveland also recovered more than eighty million acres of public land grants from the railroads and from the cattle ranchers.

Several of Cleveland's actions antagonized the powerful GAR (Grand Army of the Republic)—the organization of Civil War veterans. He vetoed a pension measure that would have given $12 a month to unemployed veterans, calling it a fraud and a raid on the public treasury. Then in an effort to further heal remaining wounds between the North and South, he ordered the captured southern battle flags to be returned to the southern states. This raised such a hue and cry by veteran groups that even Cleveland had to back down and rescind the order.

Despite the antagonism of the many special interest groups, the Democratic National Convention in June 1888 nominated him by acclamation for a second term, with Allen G. Thurman, a former senator from Ohio, as his running mate. To oppose Cleveland, the Republicans nominated Benjamin Harrison, a grandson of President William H. Harrison, who had served as a general in the Civil War and as a senator from Indiana.

Cleveland knew that the Tammany machine of New York City was determined to beat him this time, and without the electoral votes of New York he knew he would lose. When the votes were counted in November, Cleveland received nearly 100,000 more votes than Harrison; but, as he had anticipated, he lost New York by 13,000 votes, and thus lost the election with only 168 electoral votes to Harrison's 233. When his term ended on March 4, 1889, Cleveland commented that there was "no happier man in the United States" than himself, but young Frances Cleveland cautioned the White House staff to take good care of the furnishings because they would be back in four years.

Preparing for a Comeback

THE CLEVELANDS SETTLED DOWN in New York City where he joined the law firm of Bangs, Stetson, Tracy, and McVeagh. They lived in a four-story house at 816 Madison Avenue, and the former President rode to work each day on a streetcar.

Under President Harrison the Republican-controlled Congress imposed new higher tariffs, increased veterans' pensions, stepped up the coinage of silver, and passed so many appropriations measures that it became known as the "Billion-Dollar Congress." Cleveland attacked the spending program, the new McKinley high tariff, and inflationary silver coinage, getting his views known to the public by having them printed and distributed to the newspapers. In the congressional elections of 1890, the Democrats won a landslide victory with nearly half the Republican members of the House losing their seats.

The Republican National Convention met in Minneapolis in June 1892 and renominated Harrison to run for a second term. As his running mate the Republicans chose Whitelaw Reid, the publisher of the New York *Tribune.*

Cleveland's Tammany enemies, who had lost him the election in 1888, were determined to prevent him from being nominated in 1892. When the Democratic Convention met in Chicago late in June, Tammany controlled the entire New York delegation, and actively fought Cleveland. But despite the fact that he did not receive a single vote from his home state, Cleveland won the nomination on the first ballot. The Democrats chose as their vice-presidential candidate Adlai E. Stevenson, a former congressman from Illinois.

The campaign of 1892 was one of the quietest in the history of American politics with neither Cleveland nor Harrison actively campaigning. Most interest was stirred by the left-wing Populist party, which nominated General James B. Weaver of Iowa for President and campaigned for the free coinage of silver, a graduated income tax, and the establishment of postal savings banks. The Populists were so strong in the West that the Democrats did not even enter a slate in Colorado, Idaho, Kansas, North Dakota, and Wyoming. And no one was more surprised than Cleveland when he won with the huge electoral vote margin of 277 to Harrison's 145 and Weaver's 22. The Populists had drawn more than a million votes, and many of them obviously had been taken from the Republicans. Cleveland received 5,555,426 popular votes to Harrison's 5,182,690 and Weaver's 1,029,846.

Cleveland's Second Administration

CLEVELAND'S FIRST ADMINISTRATION had seen four of the most prosperous years in the nation's history and this prosperity had continued throughout the Harrison administration. But by the time Cleveland took office on a snowy March 4, 1893, there were many signs that the country was in for some serious economic trouble. Gold had been draining out of the country at the rate of about $50 million a year, farm prices were falling, and only a few days before the inauguration the large Philadelphia & Reading Railroad had gone bankrupt with debts of about $125 million. The fifty-five-year-old Cleveland warned in his inaugural address:

"It can not be doubted that our stupendous achievements as a people and our country's robust strength have given rise to heedlessness of those laws governing our national health which we can no more evade than human life can escape the laws of God and nature.

"Manifestly nothing is more vital to our supremacy as a nation and to the beneficent purposes of our Government than a sound and stable currency. Its exposure to degradation should at once arouse to activity the most enlightened statesmanship, and the danger of depreciation in the purchasing power of the wages paid to toil should furnish the strongest incentive to prompt and conservative precaution."

By May, the Panic of 1893 gripped the nation. The stock market collapsed, large companies went bankrupt, silver became a drug on the market. In June, Cleveland called Congress to meet in special session in August "to the end that the people may be relieved through legislation from present and impending danger and distress."

On the same day that he issued the call for the special congressional session, the President hurried to New York and boarded a yacht for a secret operation. It had been discovered that he had a cancer on the roof of his mouth that must be removed immediately, and the President, fearing that the news would heighten the economic panic, decided to have the operation aboard the yacht so that the public would not know about it. On July 1 the operation was successfully performed with the removal of most of his upper jaw. An artificial upper jaw of rubber was made for him, and since there were no external scars the facts of the operation remained a secret until long after Cleveland left office.

When the special session of Congress met, it received a message from

Cleveland asking for the repeal of the Sherman Silver Purchase Act of 1890 which required the Treasury to buy 4,500,000 ounces of silver each month and pay for them with notes redeemable in either gold or silver. A bill repealing the measure was the subject of bitter debate, the Democratic senators from the West and South resisting. In the end Cleveland achieved passage only with the support of Republican senators.

In the field of foreign affairs, Cleveland managed to antagonize public opinion by thwarting the annexation of Hawaii. During Harrison's administration, the U.S. minister in Hawaii had taken part in a bloodless revolution that had overthrown the government of Queen Liliuokalani with the aid of U. S. Marines. A treaty of annexation to the United States had been hastily prepared and sent to the Senate for ratification. Since the Senate had not yet acted when Cleveland took office, he withdrew the treaty and after an investigation concluded that the actions of the U.S. minister had not been honorable. In a special message to Congress in December 1893, he asked for congressional help in finding some way to restore the queen to power in a manner "consistent with American honor, integrity, and morality." Although he was denounced by many newspapers for not expanding the United States possessions into the Pacific, Cleveland stood firm on what he believed was right.

In 1894 economic conditions continued to grow worse. In May about 400 unemployed arrived in Washington, a part of the "army" marching from Massillon, Ohio, under the leadership of "General" Jacob S. Coxey. They asked for Congress to pass a bill establishing a $500 million road-building program to create jobs. For trespassing on White House grounds, Coxey was arrested and sent to jail for twenty days. Even more serious labor troubles erupted in Illinois that same month when the Pullman Company fired about 5,000 workers for protesting a wage cut.

In June the American Railway Union, the most powerful labor union in the United States at that time, called a sympathy strike for the Pullman workers by refusing to handle any train hauling Pullman cars. Because this interfered with the movement of mail, the federal government obtained an injunction against the strike on July 2. In retaliation a mob derailed a mail train outside of Chicago the next day. On July 3, Cleveland ordered federal troops to preserve order in Illinois, even though the governor of Illinois insisted this was not necessary. On July 6, a mob stoned a train, killing the engineer and injuring many passengers. Cleveland then issued an order on July 8 that all persons in Illinois engaged in mob activity must return to their homes. The next day he extended the order to nine other western states. Eugene Debs, the Socialist leader of the American Railway Union, was arrested for conspiracy and for violating the federal injunction. He later was sentenced to six months in jail. Most strikers had returned to work by the second week in July, and federal troops were withdrawn on July 19.

While Cleveland was battling with the unruly labor unions, he also was engaged in combat with Congress over the keystone of his economic plans—the reduction of tariffs. In January 1894, the House had passed a tariff act to his liking, greatly reducing most import duties and in addition calling for the levy of a 2 percent income tax on all incomes over $4,000. But the tariff bill received rough treatment in the Senate. It was amended more than six hundred times before the upper house finally passed it by a vote of thirty-nine to thirty-three in August 1894. Cleveland was disgusted with the measure because the tariff reductions were now so small as to be almost meaningless. He considered vetoing it, but finally allowed the bill to become law without his signature because he was persuaded it was better than nothing. The failure was made even more complete the next year when the Supreme Court ruled that the provision for an income tax was unconstitutional.

Economic conditions continued to grow worse during 1894—farm prices fell and unemployment rose. In the congressional elections of 1894, the Republicans achieved a landslide of even greater proportions than the Democrats had four years earlier.

By January of 1895 only about $40 million in gold remained in the United States Treasury. If something could not be done to replenish the supply it seemed likely that the nation would have to abandon the gold standard, with damaging effect on the government's credit and possibly far-reaching economic effects. To save the situation Cleveland arranged with a syndicate of New York bankers headed by J. P. Morgan to purchase a new issue of bonds for gold and reverse the flow of gold out of the country. The bankers, with a serious stake in keeping money "sound," made good on their promise and delivered more than $65 million in gold to the U. S. Treasury.

In 1895 Cleveland regained some of his waning public support by a vigorous application of the Monroe Doctrine against Great Britain. The British had been engaged in a dispute with Venezuela over the boundary of British Guiana. Cleveland sent a strongly worded message to Congress calling for the appointment of a commission to determine the boundary. He asserted that the United States should "resist by every means in its power, as a willful aggression upon its rights and interests" any attempt by Britain to take any more than the land awarded by the American commission. Congress appropriated money for the commission and war fever spread. Luckily the British reacted reasonably and the dispute was settled.

But jingoism could not solve the country's economic problems, and the Democrats of the West were losing patience with Cleveland's cautious gold-standard conservatism. When the Democratic National Convention met in

Chicago in July 1896, the delegates by a two to one vote adopted a platform repudiating Cleveland's policies and accepting a free silver plank written by Nebraskan William Jennings Bryan. Bryan electrified the convention with his famous "cross of gold" speech in which he said: "Having behind us the producing masses of the nation and the world, the laboring interests and the toilers everywhere, we will answer their demand for a gold standard by saying to them: 'You shall not press down upon the brow of labor this crown of thorns—you shall not crucify mankind upon a cross of gold!' " The convention proceeded to nominate Bryan as its candidate for President—a greater humiliation for Cleveland than even the platform.

Cleveland refused to support Bryan in the ensuing campaign, but he also refused nomination for a third term by the Gold-Democrats, or the National Democratic party as the conservatives called themselves. He rejoiced when the Republican nominee, William McKinley, a "sound money" man, defeated Bryan in the November election.

In his last State of the Union message on December 7, 1896, Cleveland reported that the government had sustained a $25 million deficit between revenues and spending, blaming it on the "great and increasing apprehension and timidity in business circles and the depression in all activities."

"We can not reasonably hope that our recuperation from this business depression will be sudden," he said, "but it has already set in with a promise of acceleration and continuance.

"I believe our present tariff law, if allowed a fair opportunity, will in the near future yield a revenue which, with reasonably economical expenditures, will overcome all deficiencies. In the meantime no deficit that has occurred or may occur need excite or disturb us. To meet any such deficit we have in the Treasury in addition to a gold reserve of $100 millions a surplus of more than $128 millions applicable to the payment of the expenses of the Government, and which must, unless expended for that purpose, remain a useless hoard, or, if not extravagantly wasted, must in any event be perverted from the purpose of its exaction from our people. The payment, therefore, of any deficiency in the revenue from this fund is nothing more than its proper and legitimate use. The Government thus applying a surplus fortunately in its Treasury to the payment of expenses not met by its current revenues is not at all to be likened to a man living beyond his income and thus incurring debt or encroaching on his principal. . . .

"It is not one of the functions of our Government to accumulate and make additions to a fund not needed for immediate expenditure. With individuals it is the chief object of struggle and effort. . . .

"It is immeasurably better to appropriate our surplus to the payment of justifiable expenses than to allow it to become an invitation to reckless appropriations and extravagant expenditures.

"I suppose it will not be denied that under the present law our people obtain the necessaries of a comfortable existence at a cheaper rate than formerly. This is a matter of supreme importance, since it is the palpable duty of every just government to make the burdens of taxation as light as possible. The people should not be required to relinquish this privilege of cheaper living except under the stress of their Government's necessity made plainly manifest. . . .

"In concluding this communication its last words shall be an appeal to the Congress for the most rigid economy in the expenditure of the money it holds in trust for the people. The way to perplexing extravagance is easy, but a return to frugality is difficult. When, however, it is considered that those who bear the burdens of taxation have no guaranty of honest care save in the fidelity of their public servants, the duty of all possible retrenchment is plainly manifest."

Following McKinley's inauguration in March 1897, Cleveland commented:

"I envy him today only one thing and that was the presence of his own mother at the inauguration. I would have given anything in the world if my mother could have been at my inauguration."

The Sage of Princeton

AFTER LEAVING THE PRESIDENCY for the second time, Cleveland settled with his family in Princeton, New Jersey. He had saved about a third of a million dollars and this was sufficient to live in retirement without further income. He took a close interest in Princeton University and became a trustee in 1901. He also gave lectures from time to time to the students.

As the years passed and the free silver movement died, Cleveland came to be regarded with greater and greater respect. In 1905 when the huge Equitable Life Assurance Society came under investigation, Cleveland accepted appointment as one of a board of trustees to reorganize the company. In 1907 he became head of the Association of Presidents of Life Insurance Companies, an organization to lobby against restrictive government regulation of insurance companies.

In his last years, he suffered with heart and kidney ailments as well as gout. Finally, on June 24, 1908, the seventy-one-year-old former President died in his bed at his home in Princeton.

A verse written about Cleveland by James Russell Lowell in 1889 perhaps states most clearly the reason he has been more honored for his efforts than for his accomplishments:

> Let who has felt compute the strain
> Of struggle with abuses strong,
> The doubtful course, the helpless pain
> Of seeing best intents go wrong;
> We, who look on with critic eyes
> Exempt from action's crucial test,
> Human ourselves, at least are wise
> In honoring one who did his best.

Benjamin Harrison
The Twenty-third President of the United States
1889–93

1833 (August 20) Born at North Bend, Ohio.

1852 Graduated from Miami University, Oxford, Ohio.

1853 (October 20) Married Caroline Lavinia Scott.

1854 Began practicing law in Indianapolis, Indiana.

1860 Elected reporter of the Supreme Court of Indiana.

1862–65 Commanded the 70th Indiana Regiment of Volunteers during the Civil War.

1876 Defeated as Republican candidate for governor of Indiana.

1881–87 U.S. senator from Indiana.

1889–93 Twenty-third president of the United States.

1893–94 Lectured on law at Leland Stanford Jr. University.

1896 (April 6) Married Mary Scott Lord Dimmick.

1899 Counsel for Venezuela in boundary dispute with British Guiana.

1901 (March 13) Died in Indianapolis.

Every successful Republican presidential candidate, from the end of the Civil War to 1900, served as an officer in the Union Army and was born in Ohio. Benjamin Harrison had these two qualifications for the presidency, if few others. Before being elected President he had won a popular election to only one other office—that of reporter to the Supreme Court of Indiana. He had been defeated as Republican candidate for governor of Indiana in 1876, and he had served an undistinguished term as U.S. senator from Indiana (elected by the state legislature) under Presidents Garfield, Arthur, and Cleveland.

A cold, austere little man whose hair was prematurely white, he was known as "Little Ben" by his troops in the Civil War, and was nicknamed "Kid Gloves" Harrison by the Democrats of Indiana. Because his grandfather, William Henry Harrison, had also been President, the Republicans campaigned in 1888 with a song, "Grandfather's Hat Fits Ben." But the Democrats countered with cartoons showing that it took a microscope to find Ben under his grandfather's hat.

As President he did not endeavor to exert personal leadership, and allowed Congress to dictate policies. When Congress pushed tariffs to new highs and lavishly appropriated money for special-interest projects, the public turned against "Little Ben" and he lost in his bid for re-election.

Lawyer, Soldier, and Politician

BORN AT NORTH BEND, Ohio, on August 20, 1833, Benjamin Harrison was named for his great-grandfather, who had been a signer of the Declaration of Independence and a governor of Virginia. Young Ben was one of nine children of John Scott Harrison, whose farm was five miles down the Ohio River from that of Ben's grandfather, the hero of Tippecanoe. The boy was seven years old when his grandfather was elected President.

Because the Harrisons lived too far from any town to send their children to regular schools, John Scott Harrison built a one-room log schoolhouse on his farm and hired a teacher each winter to drill his children in reading, writing, and arithmetic. When Ben was fourteen, he was sent to a college preparatory school called Farmer's College, near Cincinnati. After two years there, he transferred to Miami University at Oxford, Ohio, where he studied hard and took a particular interest in debate. When he graduated at the age of eighteen, in 1852, he ranked fourth in his class of sixteen boys.

From school he went directly into a law office in Cincinnati, where he studied for his future profession. Before completing his law studies, he married his college sweetheart, Caroline Lavinia Scott, the daughter of the president of a girls' school in Oxford, Ohio. They were married October 20, 1853, when Harrison was nineteen and his wife was twenty. They had two children.

After completing his law studies, Harrison decided to set up his law practice in Indianapolis, Indiana. He and his wife moved there in March 1854, taking a room in a boardinghouse while Ben got his first job, as crier of the federal court at a salary of $2.50 a day. He quickly became acquainted with most of the lawyers in town, and they began to give him small legal errands. The next year one of them, William Wallace, invited the young man to go into partnership with him.

Harrison entered politics at the age of twenty-seven, when he became the Republican candidate for the office of reporter to the Supreme Court of Indiana. He proved an able speaker, and won handily with a majority of more than 9,000.

In 1862 Governor Oliver Morton offered Harrison command of a regiment of Indiana volunteers, to be recruited by Harrison. The young lawyer set to work energetically, raised the necessary complement of men, and received his commission as colonel. His regiment, the 70th Indiana Volunteers, saw heavy fighting, especially in Georgia in 1864, where "Little Ben" several times led infantry charges against Confederate positions. General Hooker recommended him for promotion to brigadier general, an advancement he received in March 1865.

At the end of the war, young General Harrison returned to Indianapolis and resumed his office as clerk of the state supreme court, having been re-elected while still at the front in 1864. He declined renomination at the next election in order to return to private law practice, forming a new law firm with former Governor Porter as a partner. Aided by his natural gifts, his war record, and his political contacts he became one of the leading figures of the state in law and politics.

In 1876 Harrison reluctantly accepted the Republican nomination for governor. His opponent, a tall gangling farmer who resembled Abraham Lincoln, was known as Jimmy "Blue Jeans" Williams because of the overalls he wore for all occasions. In contrast, the dapper five-foot-six-inch Harrison received the nickname "Kid Gloves." When the votes were tabulated, Harrison had lost by 5,000 votes out of more than 434,000 cast.

Harrison led the Republican delegation of Indiana to the National Convention in 1880 where, after supporting Blaine through thirty ballots, his switch to Garfield helped decide the nomination. After Garfield's election he was offered a Cabinet post, but declined because the Indiana legislature had elected him to the office of U.S. senator.

In the Senate from 1881 to 1887, Harrison played an unobtrusive role, siding with the leaders of his party on most questions. He supported increases in tariff duties, voted for civil service reform, opposed President Cleveland's vetoes of pension bills, and urged increasing the size of the U. S. Navy.

When the Republican National Convention met in Chicago in June 1888, another deadlock developed, this time between John Sherman of Ohio and

Walter Q. Gresham of Indiana. James Blaine cabled from Scotland: "Take Harrison." So on the eighth ballot Harrison was given the nomination, largely because he was "safe" and would be easy to control. His later appointment of Blaine as Secretary of State indicated that his nomination was achieved as the result of a familiar type of political deal.

In the campaign against President Cleveland, Harrison remained in Indianapolis addressing influential groups who called on him. Cleveland had antagonized so many people during his first term that the Republicans figured that they could win with a soft-pedal campaign. Actually Harrison received fewer votes than Cleveland—5,447,129 to Cleveland's 5,537,857; but the distribution of the votes—above all Harrison's narrow victory in New York—gave Harrison an Electoral College victory with 233 votes to Cleveland's 168.

Harrison's Administration

IN A LENGTHY INAUGURAL ADDRESS on a rainy March 4, 1889, Harrison spoke largely in generalities, but he also called for the traditional Republican high protective tariff, the revision of the naturalization laws to restrict Oriental immigration, and the liberalization of veterans' pensions. He opened the door to an increase in federal spending:

". . . There is nothing in the condition of our country or of our people to suggest that anything presently necessary to the public prosperity, security, or honor should be unduly postponed. It will be the duty of Congress wisely to forecast and estimate these extraordinary demands, and, having added them to our ordinary expenditures, to so adjust our revenue laws that no considerable annual surplus will remain. . . ."

The Republicans were firmly in control of both houses of Congress with a 47 to 37 majority in the Senate and 173 to 156 in the House. To please western farmers and mine owners, the Sherman Silver Purchase Act substantially increased the amount of silver the Treasury was required to purchase each month. Since this silver was paid for with notes that could be redeemed for gold, a drain on the government's gold supply resulted; this contributed directly to the Panic of 1893. Also to please western farm organizations, the Sherman Anti-trust Act was passed, outlawing trusts or business combines that interfered with commerce. Congress voted pensions to any Civil War veteran who could not work, even if his disability was not service-connected, nearly doubling the amount of money paid for pensions. And the McKinley Tariff Act, sponsored by the congressman from Ohio who later was to become President, raised duties on imports to new highs. When the Democrats dubbed it the "Billion-Dollar Congress," Speaker of the House Thomas B. Reed retorted that "This is a billion-dollar country!"

But when merchants began marking up prices following passage of the McKinley Tariff Act in 1890, hard-pressed laboring people and farmers went to the polls in the mid-term congressional elections with blood in their eyes. They "threw the rascals out," giving the Democrats a majority in the House of 235 to 88 Republicans.

Harrison pursued a vigorous foreign policy. His Secretary of State was James G. Blaine, the smooth politician who had put both Garfield and Harrison in the White House but missed in his own bid. Harrison and Blaine pushed American claims to Samoa, for a time almost causing naval hostilities with Germany. In 1889 the first Pan-American conference met in Washington, presaging better relations among the nations of the Western Hemisphere.

The most important development of Harrison's administration was the continuing growth of the United States. Six new states were admitted— Washington, Idaho, Montana, Wyoming, North Dakota, and South Dakota —bringing the total number to forty-four. The country's population reached nearly 63 million in 1890, an increase of more than 25 percent in a single decade. And the Bureau of the Census reported in 1890 that the western frontier no longer existed—the country was settled from coast to coast.

Scientific and technical progress was equally impressive. Electric lights were installed in the White House, although the Harrisons continued to use gaslight much of the time.

In 1892, despite a bid by Blaine, Harrison won renomination on the first ballot. But he lost the election to former President Cleveland, partly because the people were dissatisfied with the high prices brought on by the McKinley Tariff Act, and partly because the new Populist party drew many western votes away from the Republican ticket.

In his last State of the Union address on December 6, 1892, President Harrison spoke glowingly of the prosperity attained under the McKinley Tariff Act and of the impending doom that would ensue under its prospective repeal by the Democrats:

"The general conditions affecting the commercial and industrial interests of the United States are in the highest degree favorable. A comparison of the existing conditions with those of the most favored period in the history of the country will, I believe, show that so high a degree of prosperity and so general a diffusion of the comforts of life were never before enjoyed by our people. . . .

"I believe that the protective system, which has now for something more than thirty years continuously prevailed in our legislation, has been a mighty instrument for the development of our national wealth and a most powerful agency in protecting the homes of our workingmen from the invasion of want. . . . We must assume that the present tariff, constructed upon the lines of protection, is to be repealed and that there is to be substituted for it a tariff law constructed solely with reference to revenue. . . .

"The strained and too often disturbed relations existing between the employees and the employers in our great manufacturing establishments have not been favorable to a calm consideration by the wage earner of the effect upon wages of the protective system. The facts that his wages were the highest paid in like callings in the world and that a maintenance of this rate of wages in the absence of protective duties upon the product of his labor was impossible were obscured by the passion evoked by these contests. He may now be able to review the question in the light of his personal experience under the operation of a tariff for revenue only. . . . It may be, indeed I believe is, possible for the American manufacturer to compete successfully with his foreign rival in many branches of production without the defense of protective duties if the pay rolls are equalized; but the conflict that stands between the producer and that result and the distress of our working people when it is attained are not pleasant to contemplate. The Society of the Unemployed, now holding its frequent and threatening parades in the streets of foreign cities, should not be allowed to acquire an American domicile."

Deploring the frequent lynchings of blacks, Harrison called on Congress for legislation giving him power to stop them:

"Lawlessness is not less such, but more, where it usurps the functions of the peace officer and of the courts. The frequent lynching of colored people accused of crime is without the excuse, which has sometimes been urged by mobs for a failure to pursue the appointed methods for the punishment of crime, that the accused have an undue influence over courts and juries. Such acts are a reproach to the community where they occur, and so far as they can be made the subject of Federal jurisdiction the strongest repressive legislation is demanded. A public sentiment that will sustain the officers of the law in resisting mobs and in protecting accused persons in their custody should be promoted by every possible means. The officer who gives his life in the brave discharge of this duty is worthy of special honor. No lesson needs to be so urgently impressed upon our people as this, that no worthy end or cause can be promoted by lawlessness."

Less than three weeks before leaving office, Harrison sent to the Senate a treaty for the annexation of Hawaii. "I do not deem it necessary to discuss at any length the conditions which have resulted in this decisive action," Harrison told the Senate. "Prompt action upon this treaty is very desirable." However, the Senate delayed, and after Cleveland entered office the new

President withdrew the treaty on grounds the U.S. representative had not acted honorably in aiding the overthrow of the Hawaiian government in order to achieve annexation.

A Second Marriage

FIFTY-NINE YEARS OLD when he left the White House, Harrison accepted an invitation to deliver a series of law lectures at Stanford University in 1893–94. Then he returned to Indianapolis to practice law.

He had lost his first wife a few days before the election of 1892, and in 1896, at the age of sixty-two, married her niece, thirty-seven-year-old Mrs. Mary Scott Lord Dimmick. They had one child, a daughter.

In 1897 Harrison wrote a book on the government of the United States titled *This Country of Ours.* He was employed as counsel for the government of Venezuela in the boundary dispute with Great Britain and in 1899 ably upheld the Venezuelan case before an international arbitration tribunal.

On March 13, 1901, at the age of sixty-seven, Harrison died in his home in Indianapolis. In announcing the death of his predecessor, President McKinley said of Harrison:

"The country has been deprived of one of its greatest citizens. A brilliant soldier in his young manhood . . . a leader of the bar . . . an orator and legislator . . . he displayed extraordinary gifts as administrator and statesman. In public and in private life he set a shining example for his countrymen."

William McKinley
The Twenty-fifth President of the United States
1897–1901

1843 (January 29) Born in Niles, Ohio.

1859 Attended Allegheny College in Meadville, Pennsylvania.

1860 Taught in a country school and clerked in the post office.

1861–65 Served in the Union Army in the Civil War, rising from private to major.

1867 Admitted to the bar to practice law.

1869–71 Prosecuting attorney of Stark County, Ohio.

1871 (January 25) Married Ida Saxton.

1877–91 U.S. representative from Ohio.

1892–96 Governor of Ohio.

1897–1901 Twenty-fifth President of the United States.

1901 (September 6) Shot by an assassin in Buffalo, New York.

1901 (September 14) Died of wounds in Buffalo.

A kind gentle man, William McKinley loved everyone and wanted everyone to love him. Most did. He was re-elected to a second term as President with a larger plurality of popular votes than Lincoln or any other previous Chief Executive. When he was struck down by an assassin's bullet, his first thought was of others, crying out to protect his assailant, "Don't let them hurt him!" The third President to be killed by an assassin, he was as deeply and elaborately mourned as were Lincoln and Garfield. A biography issued immediately after his death described the mood of the country: "An universal spasm of grief passed from end to end of the land. . . . Never was there a crime more without purpose, more without possible good effect."

Yet history has not been kind to McKinley's memory. Today his name is used as a symbol for nineteenth-century backward-looking conservatism. He is recalled for his sponsorship of high tariffs and for weakly letting the country be pushed into the Spanish-American War. It is generally forgotten that he led the nation onto the world stage and made the historic declaration: "Isolation is no longer possible or desirable."

From Mess Sergeant to President

THE SEVENTH IN A FAMILY of nine children, William McKinley was born in Niles, Ohio, on January 29, 1843. When he was nine his family moved to nearby Poland, Ohio, where he and his brothers and sisters attended a small private school called Union Seminary. He took an early interest in oratory and became president of the local debating society. He also became a member of the Methodist church, giving his mother hope that he might become a minister. When he was seventeen, McKinley attended Allegheny College in Meadville, Pennsylvania, for a year, but was forced to drop out because of illness.

The eighteen-year-old McKinley was clerking in the Poland post office when the Civil War began. In the tradition of his great-grandfather who fought in the Revolutionary War and his grandfather who fought in the War of 1812, he enlisted in the 23d Ohio Volunteer Infantry in June 1861. A major of the regiment was Rutherford B. Hayes, who also was to become President. Young McKinley was made commissary (mess) sergeant, and in the battle of Antietam, distinguished himself by serving a hot meal to troops under fire. Given a battlefield commission as second lieutenant, he shortly became brigade quartermaster on Hayes' staff. In 1864 the young officer's gallantry in battle advanced him to captain. He was successively transferred to the staffs of Generals George Crook and Winfield S. Hancock. In March 1865, he was promoted to major for his bravery in the battles of Opequan, Cedar Creek, and Fishers Hill.

When the war was over, Major McKinley was only twenty-two. His years of hard life in the field had changed him from the pale sickly boy who had volunteered for army duty into a healthy, robust young man. After turning down an invitation to remain in the army, he decided to begin studying law. Following two years in the office of a prominent attorney in Youngstown,

Ohio, he entered law school in Albany, New York, and was admitted to the bar the next year.

In 1867 he settled in Canton, Ohio, to practice, largely because his elder sister, Anna, was teaching school there. He at once began to take part in Republican party affairs and was welcomed by the politicians for his forensic ability. When McKinley was nominated for prosecuting attorney of Stark County in 1869, even his friends did not think he had a chance because the Democrats regularly won all the county elections. But his vigorous campaigning brought him victory, though two years later the opposition mustered its forces and beat him by forty-five votes.

While still prosecuting attorney, McKinley had married Ida Saxton, the blue-eyed daughter of Canton's leading banker, on January 25, 1871. The marriage was a tragic one, for both their daughters died, one as an infant, the other at the age of four, while Mrs. McKinley became a lifelong invalid. The sincere affection that McKinley showered on his wife won him sympathy in his subsequent political career.

In 1876, when his old commanding officer Hayes ran for President, the thirty-three-year-old McKinley was elected to Congress. He was repeatedly re-elected, serving almost continuously for fifteen years. In the House of Representatives, McKinley was sometimes compared to Napoleon because of his short stature and general appearance, including his habit of putting one hand inside his coat while speaking.

In the first Congress in which he sat, McKinley surprisingly voted with the Democratic majority to pass free silver legislation for "cheap" money over the veto of President Hayes.

But the issue on which McKinley won his principal reputation as a congressman was his support of high protective tariffs. He came by his convictions naturally because his father had been a small iron manufacturer, and McKinley had been imbued from childhood with the importance of protective tariffs for American industry. As author of the McKinley Tariff Act in 1890, he forced tariffs to new highs. But the high retail prices that the legislation caused brought a backlash at the polls, and Republican congressmen, including McKinley, lost their seats.

In 1891 the Ohio Republicans nominated McKinley for governor. For three months he campaigned harder than he ever had in his life, making several speeches a day—130 in all—and appearing in almost every one of the state's eighty-eight counties. He was elected with a narrow plurality of 21,000 votes. Two years later he was re-elected with a plurality of nearly 81,000 votes, indicating a successful administration. In the hard times brought by the depression of 1893, McKinley sent carloads of provisions for the relief of the unemployed in Ohio. His own modest fortune of $20,000 was wiped out by the business failure of a financial partner, leaving him with more than $100,000 in debts. But wealthy friends contributed to a fund that paid his debts and returned him the money he had lost.

While governor, McKinley became famous for his devotion to his invalid wife. Every afternoon at exactly three o'clock he would interrupt whatever business he was engaged in to step to the window of his office and wave his handkerchief to his wife, who awaited this greeting from their hotel suite across the street. And each morning after leaving the hotel he would pause outside, remove his hat, and bow to her window, before proceeding to his office.

McKinley had received 182 votes in the 1892 Republican National Convention that renominated Harrison. The former's industrialist friends, led by Cleveland millionaire Mark Hanna, were determined to help him win the presidency in 1896. To achieve national support, his friends financed a 10,000-mile trip through seventeen states in which he made nearly four hundred speeches in eight weeks. The McKinley boom was so successful that by the time the Republican National Convention met in St. Louis in June 1896, McKinley was nominated on the first ballot. Garret A. Hobart of New Jersey was chosen as the vice-presidential candidate.

Although McKinley was prepared to campaign on the issue of tariffs, the nomination by the Democrats of thirty-six-year-old William Jennings Bryan of Nebraska, an ardent free-silver advocate, changed the central issue. McKinley dropped his advocacy of silver coinage and came out strongly for the gold standard and "sound" money. In doing so he won the support of President Cleveland and many other conservative Democrats. Mark Hanna and his friends raised the largest campaign fund up to that time in American politics, more than $3 million, by frightening bankers and businessmen with the specter of inflation and federal controls on business. Workmen were told that factories would be closed if Bryan won, and banks informed farmers that their payments would be extended at lower rates of interest if McKinley were elected. In the November election, McKinley received 7,102,246 votes to Bryan's 6,492,559, and 271 to 176 electoral votes.

McKinley made a partial payment of his political debt to Hanna by appointing the feeble seventy-three-year-old Senator John Sherman of Ohio as Secretary of State. This created an opening in the Senate to which the Ohio legislature elected Hanna, a maneuver which drew some caustic criticism.

McKinley's Administration

WHILE HIS AGED MOTHER and invalid wife looked on, the fifty-four-year-old McKinley was inaugurated President on a mild, spring-like March 4, 1897. In a long, wordy inaugural address he reviewed the problems of the depression that still gripped the country, but noted the need to "make haste slowly" in grappling with the situation. He called for higher tariffs to increase revenues and stop the climb of the national debt. "Legislation helpful to producers is beneficial to all," he said.

McKinley's long experience in Congress aided him in knowing how to bring pressure to bear in getting the legislation he wanted. He often called recalcitrant members of Congress to the White House and reasoned with them to prevent the introduction of legislation he opposed or to win their support. As a result he was forced to use the veto only fourteen times during his administration. Illinois Senator Shelby Cullom commented, "We have never had a President who had more influence with Congress than Mr. McKinley."

The special session of Congress that McKinley called in March 1897 completed its work by July, passing the higher tariffs that he had requested. Whether as a result of this legislation or the natural course of economic events, an upturn followed.

As recovery set in, the nation's attention turned in a new direction—Cuba. A revolution had begun against Spanish rule of the island in 1895, but President Cleveland had skillfully avoided any American involvement. Popular sympathy was with the Cuban rebels, but McKinley's approach was cautious. In May 1897, he asked Congress to appropriate $50,000 for the relief of Americans stranded on the island. Two rival New York newspaper publishers, William Randolph Hearst and Joseph Pulitzer, began using the Cuban revolution to build circulation. They sent reporters to the scene, and played up lurid stories of atrocities by the Spaniards. At the same time influential men revived the expansionist fever of Polk's administration, repeating that it was the "manifest destiny" of the United States to expand beyond its existing borders. McKinley hoped that he could intervene and act as a mediator between the Cubans and the Spanish.

Two events in February 1898 moved the United States closer to intervention in Cuba. On February 9, Hearst's *Journal* printed the contents of a private letter sent by the Spanish minister in Washington to a friend. In it the Spaniard expressed an insulting opinion of the American President, saying that "McKinley is weak and a bidder for the admiration of the crowd, besides being a would-be politician who tries to leave a door open behind himself while keeping on good terms with the jingoes of his party." Less than a week later, on February 15, the U.S. battleship *Maine* was mysteriously blown up and sunk in Havana Harbor, killing most of the crew and setting off a storm of popular reaction across the United States. While an American commission investigated the explosion, McKinley quietly asked Congress to pass a fifty-million-dollar national defense appropriation. The bill was hurried through and by March 9 had become law.

The nation rushed headlong toward war, and the force of events swept McKinley along with it. Even though on April 10 the American ambassador in Spain cabled word that Spain was ready to suspend hostilities in Cuba and grant the Cubans self-government, McKinley did not feel that he could any longer withstand American demands for war. On April 11 he sent a message to Congress asking that he be empowered to use the army and navy to intervene in Cuba. Nine days later Congress granted the power, but with an amendment forbidding the annexation of Cuba. On April 25, McKinley asked Congress for a declaration of war against Spain. It was approved the same day.

The Spanish-American War itself lasted less than four months. On May 1, Commodore George Dewey destroyed a Spanish fleet in Manila Harbor; on June 10, U. S. Marines landed in force at Guantánamo Bay, Cuba; on July 3, the Spanish Caribbean fleet was destroyed at Santiago, Cuba. American troops landed in Puerto Rico on July 25, and the war ended with the unconditional surrender of the Philippines on August 15. In the entire war, the U. S. Army and Navy reported a total of 1,941 combat casualties, with 298 killed. Some 5,000 others died of disease.

By the time McKinley made his second annual address to Congress in December 1898, he was able to report that most of the troops mustered for the war had already been released from service, and that the American flag was flying over Cuba, Puerto Rico, and the Philippines. Also during the short war, on July 7, 1898, McKinley had signed the congressional resolution approving the annexation of Hawaii. But the new empire was not to be as easily controlled as it had been won. The Filipinos revolted against American rule and a prolonged struggle ensued.

Now a confirmed "sound money" man, McKinley repeatedly urged Congress to settle the issue of gold-vs.-silver by making gold the basis of the country's monetary system. Congress acceded to his wishes in 1900 by passing the Gold Standard Act.

When a secret revolutionary society called the Boxers started a rebellion in China in 1900, with the intent of driving all foreigners out of the country, McKinley ordered U. S. Marines to join an international relief expedition with seven other nations. These troops captured the Chinese capital in August 1900, and the Chinese government was later forced to pay indemnities to each of the foreign powers. The United States returned its share to China, which used the money to educate Chinese students at American universities.

McKinley received the unanimous nomination for a second term as President from the Republican National Convention in Philadelphia in June 1900. Governor Theodore Roosevelt of New York was nominated for Vice President. The Democrats again chose Bryan as their standard bearer, and as his running mate nominated Adlai E. Stevenson, who had served as Vice President during Cleveland's second administration.

The Democrats sought new campaign issues to add to the tariff and free silver. They accused the McKinley administration of being the tool of big business and demanded legislation to control the trusts. They also accused McKinley of a new imperialism, pointing to the use of American troops in the Philippines to quell the uprising of the Filipinos. McKinley spent most of the campaign at his home in Canton, confident of victory. His confidence was justified, for in the election he rolled up the impressive total of 7,218,491 votes to Bryan's 6,356,734 and an electoral vote of 292 to 155.

The first months of his second term of office were pleasantly uneventful. McKinley left Washington on April 29, 1901, for a transcontinental tour that was supposed to last six weeks. However, his wife became ill in California, and after she recovered he decided to spend the rest of the summer in Canton. He left from there to make a promised address on September 5, at the Pan-American Exposition in Buffalo, New York.

McKinley had spent many days preparing what proved to be his last speech. In it he looked forward, forecasting the growing importance of the United States in the world. He said:

"Isolation is no longer possible or desirable. . . . Our capacity to produce has developed so enormously, and our products have so multiplied, that the problem of more markets requires our urgent and immediate attention. Only a broad and enlightened policy will keep what we have. . . . The period of exclusiveness is past. . . . A policy of good will and friendly trade relations will prevent reprisals. Reciprocity treaties are in harmony with the spirit of the times; measures of retaliation are not. If, perchance, some of our tariffs are no longer needed for revenue or to encourage and protect our industries at home, why should they not be employed to extend and promote our markets abroad? . . ."

Thus, in his last public address, McKinley turned away from the ever-higher protectionist tariffs that had first made him a national figure.

On September 6, 1901, the day after his address, the President stood in the Exposition's Temple of Music shaking hands with a long line of well-wishers, when a man approached with his right hand wrapped in a handkerchief. As McKinley extended his hand, two shots were fired from a pistol concealed under the handkerchief. As the wounded McKinley was helped to a chair, he gasped to his secretary: "Be careful about my wife. Do not tell her." Then he cautioned that his assassin should not be hurt.

McKinley was removed to a private residence, and after several days seemed to be recovering. Then he took a turn for the worse. Shortly before his death early on the morning of September 14, he whispered to his wife: "Good-by all, good-by. It is God's way. His will be done."

The assassin, a neurotic young anarchist by the name of Leon F. Czolgosz, who explained that he had shot the President because he wanted to kill a "ruler," was tried and electrocuted.

The nation went into deepest mourning. Millions lined the railroad tracks as the funeral train bore the coffin from Buffalo to Washington for a state funeral and then to Canton for burial.

Former President Grover Cleveland said of McKinley:

"All our people loved their dead President. His kindly nature and lovable traits of character, and his amiable consideration for all about him will long live in the minds and hearts of his countrymen."

Theodore Roosevelt
The Twenty-sixth President of the United States
1901–9

1858 (October 27) Born in New York City.

1880 Graduated from Harvard College.

1880 (October 27) Married Alice Hathaway Lee.

1882–84 Representative in the New York state legislature.

1886 Unsuccessful candidate for mayor of New York City.

1886 (December 2) Married Edith Kermit Carow.

1889–95 Member of U. S. Civil Service Commission.

1895–97 President of board of police commissioners of New York City.

1897–98 Assistant Secretary of the Navy.

1898 Colonel of the "Rough Riders" volunteer cavalry regiment in the Spanish-American War.

1899–1900 Governor of New York.

1901 Vice President of the United States.

1901–9 Twenty-sixth President of the United States.

1912 Defeated in presidential election as candidate of the "Bull Moose" party, or Progressive party.

1913–14 Explored the River of Doubt in Brazil.

1919 (January 6) Died in Oyster Bay, New York.

T he first new President of the twentieth century and the youngest man to hold the office, Theodore Roosevelt brought a vim, vigor, and vitality to the White House that swept away the cobwebs of the nineteenth century. He did not wait for history to make him great, but plunged ahead doing what he felt was best for the nation and the world. With his slogan of "Speak softly and carry a big stick," he carried forward McKinley's ambitions to make the United States a world power—winning for himself the first Nobel Peace Prize awarded to an American while doing so. But he did not speak so softly in tilting against the "invisible government" of business and finance that had dominated the federal government since the days of the Civil War. He skillfully played upon the power of public opinion to help force an unwilling Congress to give the people a "Square Deal" by curbing the power of the barons of Wall Street.

An apostle of "The Strenuous Life," Roosevelt climbed the Matterhorn, hunted in Africa, explored Brazil, led cavalry charges in the Spanish-American War, and worked as a cowboy in the Dakotas. While in the White House, he practiced boxing and judo as well as taking his weary Cabinet on long hikes. After leaving the White House he became the first President, or former President, to ride in an airplane. He also found time to write more than thirty books and tens of thousands of letters.

While many of the Presidents found the chores of office a burden and expressed relief when they had completed their terms, Roosevelt loved every minute of it. He said:

"No President has ever enjoyed himself as much as I have enjoyed myself, and for the matter of that I do not know any man of my age who has had as good a time . . ."

A Born New Yorker

THE SECOND OF FOUR CHILDREN of a wealthy New York City banker, Theodore Roosevelt was born on October 27, 1858—the only President ever born in New York City. A pale, sickly boy, "Teedie," as he was called, was given to fits of asthmatic coughing. He led the pampered life of a rich man's son with private tutors, several trips to Europe with his family, and whatever books and presents he asked for.

When "Teedie" was thirteen, he was given his first gun. And it was when he could not hit the bullseye with it that his parents discovered he was nearsighted and needed glasses. About this same time he had an unhappy experience of being teased by four other boys throughout a stagecoach ride to Maine and was unable to fight them because he was so puny. With his father's encouragement, young Roosevelt determined to improve his body. He began a vigorous program of exercise in a gymnasium his father built on the second floor of their New York City home. For the rest of his life Roosevelt seemed to try to outdo everyone else with his energy and strength.

When Roosevelt was eighteen he entered Harvard College, but was not particularly popular with his classmates because he was trying to learn, while most of them were merely trying to get by. He continued boxing at Harvard, as a lightweight, but he was not very successful because he found it difficult to see his opponents without his glasses. While he was a small boy Roosevelt had developed an intense interest in natural science, and he continued this at Harvard with many science courses. His excellent grades won him election to Phi Beta Kappa. He was graduated in 1880 at the age of twenty-one.

After spending the summer on an extended hunting trip in Iowa and Minnesota with his brother Elliott, Roosevelt returned to Boston to marry Alice Hathaway Lee, the daughter of a socially prominent Boston family, whom he had ardently courted in college. The marriage took place on Roosevelt's twenty-second birthday. The blue-eyed, brown-haired bride was nineteen.

During the winter of 1880–81, Roosevelt attended Columbia Law School, but found legal studies dull. Being a man of means in his own right, his father having died three years earlier, Roosevelt decided to take his bride on a tour of Europe in the summer of 1881. While there, he collected information for his first book, *The Naval War of 1812*, which he had begun while a senior at Harvard. He also climbed the Matterhorn in Switzerland during this trip.

When Roosevelt returned from Europe in the fall of 1881 he found himself suddenly propelled into a political campaign. He had joined a local Republican club that had met over a saloon the previous year, and now a rebellious group within the club asked him to become their nominee for the state legislature. He was given the nomination on October 28, and twelve days later at the age of twenty-three was elected to the New York assembly.

Roosevelt took his seat in the legislature in Albany in 1882, and that same year his book on the War of 1812 was published with favorable reviews in the New York newspapers. At first Roosevelt's fellow legislators treated him as a joke, because of his Harvard accent and the fact that he dressed like a "dude," wearing his eyeglasses at the end of a long silk cord. Roosevelt soon made a name for himself as a fearless legislator by calling for an investigation of corruption involving railroad magnate Jay Gould and a state supreme court justice. He was re-elected by a large majority in 1882—a year in which the Democrats, headed by Grover Cleveland running for governor, drove many Republicans out of Albany. With the Democrats holding a majority of assembly seats in 1883, the Republicans put up the twenty-four-year-old Roosevelt for the office of Speaker—knowing he would lose. The following year when the Republicans won back control of the assembly the party leaders refused to let him have the office. Although a reformer, Roosevelt was generally conservative in outlook and was particularly opposed to labor legislation. He voted against a bill to reduce the working day of streetcar employees to twelve hours, and opposed raising the pay of New York City firemen to $1,200 a year.

Tragedy hit Roosevelt a double blow on February 14, 1884, when both his wife and his mother died on the same day from unrelated diseases. His mother died of typhoid fever, his wife of Bright's disease following the birth of their only child. "When my heart's dearest died," Roosevelt wrote, "the light went from my life for ever."

To try to overcome his grief, Roosevelt plunged even harder into work. He completed his term at Albany, attended the Republican National Convention that nominated James Blaine to oppose Grover Cleveland for President, and campaigned for Blaine in the election, although he had opposed Blaine's nomination.

After the election, still suffering from his personal tragedy, Roosevelt went West to make a new life for himself as a cattle rancher in the Bad Lands of Dakota. For three years he shuttled back and forth from East to West. In the Dakotas he lived the life of a cowboy, became a deputy sheriff, captured some thieves, and was challenged to a duel. He also found time to write many magazine articles. After most of his cattle were lost in blizzards in the winter of 1886–87, he gave up the experiment and returned to the East.

Political Defeat and Remarriage

IN OCTOBER 1886, Roosevelt agreed to run for mayor of New York City as the Republican candidate. Although the Republicans regularly lost this office, Roosevelt had some hope of winning because this time it was a three-cornered race, in which he was opposed by Henry George, the Socialist philosopher, who was running as an independent, and by Abram S. Hewitt, a wealthy Democrat. When Hewitt easily won the contest with the help of Tammany Hall and Roosevelt came in third behind George, everyone agreed that Roosevelt's political future looked black. The humor magazine *Puck* commented in a mocking letter: "You are not the timber of which Presidents are made."

A month after his election defeat, Roosevelt married again; this time to Edith Kermit Carow, three years younger than himself, who had been a childhood playmate in New York. The ceremony took place in London on December 2, 1886. The young couple remained in Europe until the spring of 1887.

Roosevelt campaigned for the election of Benjamin Harrison as President in 1888, and was rewarded the next year by his appointment to the U. S. Civil Service Commission. He served in this office for six years, being reappointed by President Cleveland in 1893.

When a reform mayor, William Strong, was elected in New York City on a fusion ticket, Roosevelt was invited to become commissioner of the corruption-ridden police force. He accepted with alacrity, resigning his civil service post. He forced the resignation of the chief of the uniformed police, a man who explained that his $300,000 fortune had been made in stock speculation with the aid of Jay Gould. Roosevelt adopted the practice of prowling the streets at night in a black cape, on the lookout for policemen not doing their duty. These nocturnal strolls made good newspaper copy, and there was even talk that the energetic police commissioner would be a good man to run for President. But his popularity dimmed with many of the citizens of New York City when he insisted on enforcing the Sunday bluc laws closing saloons. New Yorkers were glad to see him go in 1897, when he accepted President McKinley's appointment as Assistant Secretary of the Navy.

The thirty-seven-year-old Roosevelt soon began to overshadow the Secretary of the Navy, John D. Long. A forceful orator, Roosevelt was in frequent demand as a speaker. He used the opportunities to call for a more powerful navy and to hint that the United States should intervene in the Cuban revolution against Spain. He made such jingoistic comments as, "No triumph of peace is quite so great as the supreme triumphs of war." When the *Maine* was sunk in Havana Harbor, Roosevelt denounced it as "an act of dirty treachery" on the part of the Spaniards, even though no proof of Spanish complicity appeared. Privately he told friends that McKinley had "no more backbone than a chocolate eclair" in not going to war at once.

The Rough Riders in Cuba

WITHIN TWO WEEKS after Congress declared war against Spain in April 1898, Roosevelt had resigned from the Navy Department to accept a commission as lieutenant colonel, second in command to Leonard Wood, in the Volunteer 1st Cavalry. The outfit quickly became known as Roosevelt's Rough Riders, as cowboys from the West and polo players from the East joined up to train at the unit's camp in San Antonio, Texas.

Roosevelt's regiment finally reached Cuba at the end of June, but without its horses, which were left in the United States. A few days after arriving, Roosevelt was promoted to colonel and Wood was advanced to commander of the brigade. On July 1 Roosevelt achieved glory when he led the Rough Riders in a charge up San Juan Hill in the face of intense enemy fire, losing a quarter of his men. Two days later the U. S. Navy destroyed the Spanish fleet at Santiago, and two weeks after that the fighting in Cuba was over. When American troops began to fall ill of yellow fever, Roosevelt pulled strings to get his Rough Riders shipped back to the United States as quickly as possible and by mid-August they were home. "San Juan was the great day of my life," Roosevelt still said twenty years later.

Certainly San Juan made his political career. On the strength of it, Roosevelt immediately won the Republican nomination for governor of New York. In November he beat the Tammany-supported Democratic candidate by the slim plurality of 17,800 votes. After taking office in 1899, he alienated the leaders of the Republican party by forcing the legislature to pass a tax on corporation franchises. It was in his dealings with the Republican state machine that Roosevelt commented: "I have always been fond of the West African proverb: 'Speak softly and carry a big stick, you will go far.' "

By early 1900 it had become apparent that the Republicans of New York would like to get rid of this young governor that they could not control. They began to talk of pushing him upstairs into the vice presidency. Promptly, in February 1900, Roosevelt issued a statement: ". . . under no circumstances could I or would I accept the nomination for the Vice-Presidency."

At the Republican National Convention in Philadelphia in June, Roosevelt was a sensation in his Rough Rider campaign hat. When he made one of the seconding speeches for the renomination of McKinley, the convention went wild and nominated him as McKinley's running mate by acclamation, although Mark Hanna, the Republican national chairman, was not pleased. "Don't any of you realize that there's only one life between this madman and the White House?" he warned.

Roosevelt did the lion's share of the campaigning against Democratic candidate William Jennings Bryan, while McKinley stayed quietly at home. The energetic vice-presidential nominee toured the country making hundreds of speeches, and in November, McKinley and Roosevelt were elected by a huge majority.

After Roosevelt was inaugurated as Vice President on March 4, 1901, he presided over the Senate for five days in a special session called to approve presidential appointments. This completed his official duties as Vice President until Congress convened in December. He busied himself with plans to resume his law studies, and spent a good deal of time at his summer home, Sagamore Hill, in Oyster Bay, Long Island, romping with his six children.

Roosevelt was on a hunting and fishing excursion in Vermont when he received word that President McKinley had been seriously wounded by an assassin at Buffalo, New York. He hurried to McKinley's bedside, but assured that the President would recover, he left to join his family on a vacation in the Adirondacks.

Roosevelt's Administration

ON SEPTEMBER 13, 1901, Roosevelt was coming down from a mountain-climbing expedition when he was met by a messenger carrying word that the President was dying. By the time Roosevelt could reach a railroad the next day, he learned that McKinley was dead. He hurried on to Buffalo, and, in the house where McKinley's body lay, the forty-three-year-old Roosevelt was sworn in as the youngest President in the history of the United States to that time.

The stock-manipulators and trust-builders of Wall Street worried about what this hotheaded young upstart would do in the White House. Roosevelt's friends cautioned him to behave conservatively or he might start a financial panic that would plunge the country into a new depression. So for several months Roosevelt repeatedly said he intended to carry out McKinley's policies. He retained all the members of McKinley's Cabinet, even though he did not respect them. And he even made friends with Senator Mark Hanna, who had once called him a "madman."

But Wall Street learned its fears had been justified when Roosevelt sent his first message to Congress in December. He warned:

"There is a widespread conviction in the minds of the American people that the great corporations known as trusts are in certain of their features and tendencies hurtful to the general welfare. . . . Corporations engaged in interstate commerce should be regulated if they are found to exercise a license working to the public injury. It should be as much the aim of those who seek for social betterment to rid the business world of crimes of cunning as to rid the entire body politic of crimes of violence."

He went on to call for a new Cabinet post of Secretary of Commerce and Industries, and for the right of the government to inspect the books and records of corporations engaged in interstate commerce. "What further remedies are needed in the way of governmental regulation, or taxation, can only be determined after publicity has been obtained . . ."

The lengthy message called for important new efforts toward improving the conservation of natural resources. He asked for a stronger navy, and urged that a canal be built at once to connect the Atlantic and Pacific oceans.

The warm-hearted Roosevelt unwittingly created southern antagonism early in his administration when he invited the distinguished black educator Booker T. Washington to have dinner with him at the White House. When it was learned that for the first time in history a President had sat down to dinner with a black, southern newspapers fulminated, one calling the dinner "the most damnable outrage ever."

Meanwhile, Roosevelt moved quietly to carry out some of the threats to Wall Street that he had hinted at in his message to Congress. Without even letting his Cabinet know that he was doing so, he had Attorney General Philander Knox prepare an anti-trust suit against the Northern Securities Company, a giant railroad trust organized by J. P. Morgan. No anti-trust suits had been successful under the McKinley administration, but Roosevelt was determined to get the Supreme Court to uphold the law. After two years of litigation, the Supreme Court reversed its previous opinions and upheld the Sherman Anti-trust Act, deciding on March 14, 1904, that the Northern Securities Company should be dissolved.

In May 1902, 140,000 members of the United Mine Workers union went on strike for higher wages and better working conditions in the anthracite mines of Pennsylvania. These miners were earning an average yearly wage of less than $600 a year, and most of that went to pay grocery bills to company-owned stores and rent for company-owned houses. Coal-mine owners refused to negotiate with the union, and the strike dragged on into the fall with coal prices rising and stocks of coal disappearing. By October many schools and hospitals had been forced to close because of lack of fuel. Determined to get the mines back into operation before winter, Roosevelt privately threatened the owners that he would take over the mines if they would not agree to arbitration—even though he had no legal power to do so. In the face of this threat, the owners agreed to let Roosevelt appoint an arbitration commission, which ended the strike with the miners eventually winning a 10 percent wage increase.

Roosevelt always regarded the building of the Panama Canal as his most important contribution as President, and six months after he urged the project in his first message to Congress, he had signed the Spooner Act authorizing the government to negotiate for construction of the canal. At that time Panama was a province of Colombia, and in the subsequent negotiations the government of Colombia resisted giving up some of its sovereign rights in

Panama unless the United States was willing to pay more than Roosevelt was willing to offer. With encouragement from Roosevelt, a revolt was organized in Panama on November 3, 1903, the rebels declaring Panama's independence from Colombia. Roosevelt immediately recognized the new government, and U.S. warships stood off both coasts of Panama. Soon a treaty was concluded with the upstart government, and the construction of the canal got underway. "I took Panama without consulting the Cabinet," Roosevelt candidly wrote later in his *Autobiography*.

In June 1904, the Republican National Convention nominated Roosevelt for President by acclamation and gave the vice-presidential nomination to Senator Charles W. Fairbanks of Indiana. The Democrats named Judge Alton B. Parker of New York for President and Henry G. Davis of West Virginia for Vice President. Roosevelt won by an even greater margin than McKinley had achieved in 1900—7,628,461 to 5,084,223 popular votes and 336 to 140 electoral votes.

Elected President in his own right, Roosevelt began to act with an even bolder hand than before. In his annual message to Congress in December 1904, he announced an expansion of the concept of the Monroe Doctrine that became known as the Roosevelt Corollary. He said: ". . . in the Western Hemisphere the adherence of the United States to the Monroe Doctrine may force the United States, however reluctantly, in flagrant cases of such wrongdoing or impotence, to the exercise of an international police power." Shortly after announcing it, Roosevelt used this new power to intervene in the island country of Santo Domingo (now the Dominican Republic). Because this small Latin American country was not making good on its payment of foreign debts, Roosevelt had American officials seize the customs office of the Dominican government to collect taxes and make payments on the debts. This arrangement continued for more than two years until the country's foreign finances were straightened out.

The Russo-Japanese War had been going on for more than a year when Roosevelt began efforts in 1905 to act as a mediator. He succeeded in bringing representatives of the two nations together in August in Portsmouth, New Hampshire, where agreement was reached on terms for peace. His role as peacemaker won recognition the next year when he was awarded the Nobel Peace Prize.

A temporary coolness developed between Japan and the United States as a result of Portsmouth. Japan had been pressured by Roosevelt to forego a demand for a large indemnity from Russia; relations between the two countries were made worse when the San Francisco school board barred Japanese children from public schools. Roosevelt put pressure on the school board to reverse its decision, and when the U.S. "Great White Fleet" visited Japan on a round-the-world cruise, American sailors were greeted with friendship.

Roosevelt put on a determined fight to obtain federal regulation of the railroads. The Interstate Commerce Act of 1887 had proven ineffective in controlling the abuses of the railroads in rate-fixing and rebates to favored customers. By March 1906, Roosevelt had put enough pressure on Congress to obtain passage of the Hepburn Act that gave the Interstate Commerce Commission increased powers over transportation.

Although Roosevelt had obtained congressional approval to establish a Department of Commerce and Labor in 1903, he did not press too vigorously to break up the large trusts. A brilliant group of journalists—Lincoln Steffens, Ida Tarbell, Upton Sinclair, and others—were directing attention to the evils of politics and business. Roosevelt coined the epithet *muckraker* to describe them, but nevertheless was influenced by them. In 1906 he was inspired by Sinclair's *The Jungle,* an exposé of sordid conditions in the packing industry, to force the passage of legislation requiring federal inspection of packing houses. That same year Roosevelt obtained the Pure Food Act, providing regulation of the food industry.

Roosevelt was away from Washington on a bear hunt in October 1907, when a financial panic hit Wall Street, sending stock prices tumbling and forcing the collapse of some large investment companies. Depression followed. In a special message to Congress in January 1908, he made his strongest speech denouncing "gambling in the stock market" and dishonesty in the business world. He also criticized the use of injunctions to stop strikes, and boldly proclaimed: ". . . if it were true that to cut out rottenness from the body politic meant a momentary check to an unhealthy seeming prosperity, I should not for one moment hesitate to put the knife to the corruption."

When the Roosevelts and their six lively children moved into the White House, it quickly became apparent that there was insufficient room for both family life and governmental offices. Roosevelt undertook a complete remodeling, the first in nearly a hundred years. The nation's leading architects, McKim, Mead, and White, designed a new west wing of executive offices that was joined to the main building by an open colonnade. The second floor of the main building had its offices ripped out and replaced by private bedrooms, sitting rooms, and playrooms for the presidential family. Mrs. Roosevelt redecorated the mansion to get rid of what she called the "dowdy" Victorian décor, including the art nouveau stained glass that had been installed by Chester Arthur. The President's hunting-trophy heads of big game were hung in the State Dining Room.

During his last two years in office Roosevelt had little success in obtaining the passage of legislation. There was a large Republican majority in both houses of Congress, but the representatives and senators knew that Roosevelt was not going to run for office again, so they paid little attention to his recommendations.

Roosevelt used what remaining power he had to obtain the Republican nomination for President in 1908 for William Howard Taft, believing that Taft would carry on his policies. He worked hard to achieve Taft's nomination, which came on the first ballot. And he continued to labor in the campaign that followed, offering advice at every step of the way until Taft had been elected.

The Bull Moose

ONLY FIFTY YEARS OLD when he left the White House for the last time, Roosevelt was determined to continue to lead the strenuous life that he loved. Within three weeks after turning the presidency over to Taft, he sailed for Africa with his twenty-year-old son Kermit to hunt big game, one of the first Americans to do so. At the end of the year-long adventure he listed nearly three hundred animals that he had bagged, including nine lions, five elephants, thirteen rhinoceroses, and seven hippopotamuses. He and his wife then went on a triumphal tour of Europe, where he was wined and dined by kings and queens and cheered by the masses.

When Roosevelt returned home to New York in June 1910, he was soon made aware of the fact that Taft was not carrying forward progressive policies but had succumbed to the influence of the business forces that Roosevelt had fought. In the summer of 1910 he made a political speaking tour to the West and Southwest, where he was greeted by crowds as large as those that had gathered while he was still President. When he stopped at St. Louis he took a ride in an airplane piloted by Arch Hoxsey. But such dramatic incidents to exhibit his fearlessness were subordinate to his theme of the New Nationalism in which "every man holds his property subject to the general right of the community to regulate its use to whatever degree the public welfare may require it." He made another speaking tour into the South in October, campaigned for the Republican candidate for New York, and helped edit the political-opinion magazine *Outlook*.

Early in 1912 Roosevelt declared in a talk in Cleveland that "My hat is in the ring" to win the Republican presidential nomination. But at the National Convention that met in Chicago in June, the party's National Committee was ruled by Taft-supporters who refused to seat many delegates pledged to Roosevelt. Consequently, Taft was nominated to run for a second term, but 344 delegates refused to vote. That night these and other Roosevelt supporters met with Roosevelt and pledged him their support for an independent campaign. He told them: "If you wish me to make the fight, I will make it."

In July the Democratic National Convention nominated Woodrow Wilson and some of Roosevelt's followers deserted him to join Wilson.

A meeting of 10,000 Roosevelt boosters in Chicago in August formed the Progressive party and nominated Roosevelt for President. Hiram Johnson of California was the new party's candidate for Vice President. The platform called for the enactment of a wide range of political and social reforms, including woman suffrage.

In the midst of the campaign, on October 14, just before a speech in Milwaukee, a deranged assassin fired a bullet into Roosevelt's chest. Although the bullet had actually entered his lung and Roosevelt did not know whether or not he was dying, he insisted on going ahead with his speech, saying: "I have a message to deliver and will deliver it as long as there is life in my body." After completing the address he was rushed to a hospital. Wilson and Taft called a halt to the campaign until Roosevelt recovered, but within two weeks the robust ex-Rough Rider was well enough to address a crowd of 12,000 in Madison Square Garden in New York City.

Roosevelt had not expected to win, so he was well pleased with the results in which he came in second to Wilson with Taft trailing as a poor third.

During the winter of 1913–14 Roosevelt went to South America on an even more strenuous expedition than his earlier African big-game hunt. He and his son Kermit explored a Brazilian waterway called the River of Doubt, later renamed the Roosevelt. He seriously injured his leg on this trip and also came down with a tropical fever, but his brimming good health pulled him through.

A Progressive party convention again nominated Roosevelt as its candidate for President in 1916, but this time he declined to run, throwing his support to the Republican candidate, Charles Evans Hughes. Roosevelt campaigned bitterly against Wilson, whom he denounced for not doing enough to protect American lives and ships in the World War then raging in Europe.

Final Years

IMMEDIATELY AFTER THE UNITED STATES declared war on Germany in April 1917, Roosevelt hurried to Washington to plead with Wilson to let him form a "Roosevelt Division" and lead it to France. But Wilson rejected the offer. A year later the former President aged visibly after his youngest son, Quentin, was killed while flying in battle in France.

Roosevelt's own death came unexpectedly at Sagamore Hill, his home near

Oyster Bay on Long Island, New York. On the evening of January 5, 1919, he dictated an article for the Kansas City *Star,* and then retired. Early on the morning of January 6, he succumbed to an arterial blood clot.

Roosevelt himself provided perhaps the best description of his effect upon the presidency:

"While President I have *been* President, emphatically; I have used every ounce of power there was in the office and I have not cared a rap for the criticisms of those who spoke of my 'usurpation of power'; for I knew that the talk was all nonsense and that there was no usurpation. I believe that the efficiency of this Government depends upon its possessing a strong central executive, and wherever I could establish a precedent for strength in the executive . . . I have felt not merely that my action was right in itself, but that in showing the strength of, or in giving strength to, the executive, I was establishing a precedent of value. I believe in a strong executive; I believe in power; but I believe that responsibility should go with power, and that it is not well that the strong executive should be a perpetual executive. Above all and beyond all I believe as I have said before that the salvation of this country depends upon Washington and Lincoln representing the type of leader to which we are true."

William Howard Taft

The Twenty-seventh President of the United States
1909–13

1857 (September 15) Born in Cincinnati, Ohio.

1878 Graduated from Yale University.

1880 Received law degree from Cincinnati College and admitted to the bar to practice law.

1882–83 Tax collector, appointed by President Arthur.

1886 (June 19) Married Helen Herron.

1887–90 Judge of the superior court of Cincinnati.

1890–92 Solicitor General of the United States, appointed by President Harrison.

1892–1900 U. S. Circuit Judge, appointed by President Harrison.

1896–1900 Professor and dean of the law department of the University of Cincinnati.

1900 President of the U. S. Philippine Commission.

1901–4 First civil governor of the Philippine Islands, appointed by President McKinley.

1904–8 Secretary of War, appointed by President Roosevelt.

1909–13 Twenty-seventh President of the United States.

1913 Appointed professor of law at Yale University.

1918–19 Joint chairman of the National War Labor Board, appointed by President Wilson.

1921–30 Chief Justice of the United States, appointed by President Harding.

1930 (March 8) Died in Washington, D.C.

Anyone who followed Teddy Roosevelt as President was bound to seem dull, but the six-foot two-inch William Howard Taft with his walrus mustache and 300-pound girth was so ponderous and slow-moving that he appeared to be the very antithesis of his active predecessor. Prodded into the presidency by his ambitious wife, he said he found it "the lonesomest place in the world." A judge both by profession and temperament, Taft achieved his greatest distinction as the only former President to be appointed Chief Justice of the United States.

Before becoming President, Taft had occupied a succession of appointive positions, such as Governor of the Philippines and Secretary of War. Like most other men who became Chief Executive without working their way along the elective stepping-stones of politics, he was ill-equipped to cope with political bosses, patronage, and pleasing the public. Worse, he committed the error of angering Roosevelt—the man who had single-handedly put him in the White House. And T.R. wrecked the Republican party to prevent "Big Bill" Taft from having a second term.

"I was a man of straw," Taft said of himself, during his last year in the White House.

A Scholar-Athlete

BORN ON SEPTEMBER 15, 1857, in Cincinnati, Ohio, William Howard Taft, or "Willie" as he was called as a boy, was the son of a prominent attorney, Alphonso Taft. Although Willie came close to being killed at the age of nine when a horse ran away with the carriage in which he was riding, his comfortable childhood was relatively uneventful.

By the time he entered high school he had reached his full height, and his powerful physique had won him a reputation as a wrestler and fighter to be feared. His father even boasted to heavyweight champion John L. Sullivan that he believed "My Will is a better man." And young Taft took as easily to books as he did to sports, usually ranking first in his class.

In 1874 he enrolled at Yale University, where he continued to distinguish himself in his studies. During his college years his father served in President Grant's Cabinet, first as Secretary of War and then as Attorney General. When Will graduated in 1878 at the age of twenty, his parents were somewhat disappointed that he ranked only second in his class of 191.

Returning home he studied for two years at the Cincinnati Law School and received his law degree and admission to the bar in 1880. His father's political connections won him appointment as assistant prosecuting attorney of Hamilton County in 1881, and the following year he was appointed by President Arthur as tax collector for the first district. At about the same time Arthur appointed the elder Taft ambassador to Austria-Hungary. In 1883, Will Taft resigned as tax collector, spent a few months in Europe visiting his parents at the court of the Hapsburgs in Vienna, and then joined his father's law firm.

After several years of courtship, the twenty-eight-year-old Taft married twenty-five-year-old Helen "Nellie" Herron on June 19, 1886. He was deeply in love with her, but it also was an advantageous marriage because she was the daughter of a law partner of former President Rutherford B. Hayes. They had two sons and a daughter. Their oldest son, Robert Alphonso Taft, became a leading U.S. senator, and their youngest, Charles Phelps Taft II, mayor of Cincinnati.

In 1887 the Republican governor of Ohio appointed Taft a judge of the superior court, and the following year he was elected to the court for a five-year term. To accept an appointment by President Harrison as U. S. Solicitor General, he resigned from the judgeship in 1890. He established a good record during his two years in court, winning a high percentage of the cases he handled, including an important anti-trust suit. This brief sojourn in Washington also gave him the opportunity to become acquainted with Theodore Roosevelt, then serving on the Civil Service Commission.

At the age of thirty-four, Taft was appointed by President Harrison as judge of the U. S. Sixth Circuit Court of Appeals, over which he presided from 1892 to 1900, establishing a reputation as a strict interpreter of the law. During most of this time he served as a professor of law and dean of the law department at the University of Cincinnati.

His fellow Ohioan President McKinley appointed him President of the U. S. Philippine Commission in 1900.

Upon arriving in Manila with his wife and children, he and his fellow commissioners set about establishing the basis for a civil government while U.S. troops still were putting down the revolution that had broken out in opposition to American occupation. When Taft remarked that the Filipinos were his "little brown brothers," American soldiers who were fighting them composed the verse:

"He may be a brother of Big Bill Taft,
But he ain't no friend of mine."

Taft soon came to the conclusion that the Filipinos were not well enough educated to the idea of democracy to be able to administer their own government, so in 1901 he accepted an appointment by McKinley as the island's first civil governor.

In 1902 Taft became seriously ill with an internal abscess that necessitated three operations over a period of several months. He was called back briefly to Washington for Senate hearings on the Philippines, and while there became better acquainted with Roosevelt, now President, concerning whom he wrote privately: "I wish he would not think out loud so much." He returned to the Philippines by way of Europe, where he stopped in Rome as a special envoy from Roosevelt to Pope Leo XIII to request that the Roman Catholic Church give up the hundreds of thousands of acres of farm land it owned in the islands.

When Roosevelt offered to appoint him to the Supreme Court—an office for which he had expressed repeated longing—Taft turned down the opportunity, feeling that there remained too much important work to be done in the Philippines. But his wife and brothers also advised against his taking the judicial position because they felt it would block any possibility of his becoming President.

Washington Bound

In 1904 Taft accepted appointment by Roosevelt as Secretary of War, but not until he had obtained the approval of his well-to-do brothers along with their assurance that they would give him a special allowance to help him meet the high cost of entertaining in Washington. Because the administration of the Philippines came under the War Department, Taft continued to have a strong influence on efforts to improve conditions in the islands.

As Secretary of War, Taft became the most widely-traveled American of the times. He repeatedly made trips to Panama to supervise the work on the Panama Canal, and in 1905 he was sent to Japan to encourage that nation to accept American mediation in the Russo-Japanese War. In 1906 he went to Cuba to intervene in a threatened revolution against the weak government of the former Spanish colony. Roosevelt sent him the next year on a 24,000-mile trip around the world that included a stop in Japan to allay fears of war with that country.

All his life Taft's vice was overeating. But even he became alarmed when his weight reached 314 pounds in 1905. He went on a rigid diet for a few months that dropped him to 255, but in later years his weight and his girth continued to expand.

From 1906 on, it became clear that Roosevelt had chosen Taft as his successor. Taft's mother gave him no encouragement, writing: "I do not want my son to be President. His is a judicial mind and he loves the law." But his wife urged him on toward the White House.

At the Republican Convention in Chicago in 1908 Taft won the presidential nomination by acclamation on the first ballot. James S. Sherman, a New York congressman, was chosen as the vice-presidential nominee. For Taft's opponent the Democrats again chose William Jennings Bryan, who had previously been defeated by McKinley in 1896 and 1900. With Roosevelt urging him, "Hit them hard, old man!" Taft campaigned throughout the country. Issues were few and relatively unimportant. When the voters went to the polls they elected Taft with 7,675,320 popular votes to Bryan's 6,412,294, and with an electoral vote of 321 to 162.

Taft's Administration

"I ALWAYS SAID it would be a cold day when I got to be President of the United States," Taft joked to Roosevelt when a winter storm descended on Washington on Inauguration Day in 1909. Taft's inaugural address covered many subjects. He gave special emphasis to the need for a revision of tariffs and announced that he was calling a special session of Congress for March 15 to reduce the tariff rates. He also said he planned to submit proposals for amendments to the Constitution to regulate trusts and interstate commerce.

In June he sent a special message to Congress urging an amendment to the Constitution that would authorize an income tax. He said such a measure was needed to overcome the deficit in government spending. This measure ultimately became law in 1913.

Taft suffered a major legislative defeat by the Republican Congress in August 1909, when it passed the Payne-Aldrich Tariff Act that kept tariff rates high. Although he disliked the measure, Taft did not veto it. As a consequence he, more than Congress, was blamed by the public for the continuing high prices. He publicly declared: "I am bound to say that I think the Payne tariff bill is the best tariff bill that the Republican party ever passed," which might be construed as faint praise.

Taft's administration had many positive accomplishments. Postal savings and parcel post services were established. Arizona and New Mexico were admitted to the Union, bringing the total number of states to forty-eight. And about twice as many anti-trust suits were prosecuted by the federal government under Taft as had been under Roosevelt.

Improving working conditions both for himself and future Presidents, Taft in 1909 added the White House Oval Office next to the executive office wing that had been built by Roosevelt.

Liberal Republicans turned against Taft, feeling he had fallen under the influence of millionaires and corporation lawyers. They rallied around Roosevelt, who called for a "New Nationalism" and actively campaigned to win delegates for the 1912 presidential nomination. Taft was bewildered that Roosevelt had turned on him, and then became bitter, writing to his aunt: "I have a sense of wrong in the attitude of Theodore Roosevelt toward me which I doubt if I can ever get over. But I have an abiding confidence . . . in the eventual justice of the American people, and I am quite sure that in the end the hypocrisy, the insincerity, the selfishness, the monumental egotism . . . that possesses Theodore Roosevelt will make themselves known to the American people in such a way that his place in history will be accurately defined."

The regulars in the Republican party stuck with Taft and helped him win the presidential nomination in 1912, but Taft was dismayed when Roosevelt organized the Progressive party and became its candidate for President. The Democrats nominated Woodrow Wilson, then governor of New Jersey. Taft made campaign speeches in nearly five hundred towns and cities, but he knew he could not win the three-cornered race. He wrote: "If I cannot win I hope Wilson will." When the election came in November, Taft ran behind Wilson and Roosevelt—the worst defeat ever suffered by a President running for re-election.

Taft's final State of the Union message sent to Congress in December 1912 was so long that he divided it into three separate parts delivered over a period of more than two weeks.

The first part of the message sent on December 3, 1912, dealt with foreign relations, and in it he gave no hint of the forces at work in Europe that within less than a year and a half would plunge Europe into World War I. He declared, "The relations of the United States with all foreign powers remains upon a sound basis of peace, harmony, and friendship," but later described U.S. intervention during the year in Cuba, the Dominican Republic, and Nicaragua.

Fiscal affairs were discussed in the second part of Taft's State of the Union message sent to Congress on December 6, 1912. Of the general economy, he said:

"The condition of the country with reference to business could hardly be better. While the four years of the administration now drawing to a close have not developed great speculative expansion or a wide field of new investment, the recovery and progress made from the depressing conditions following the panic of 1907 have been steady and the improvement has been clear and easily traced in the statistics."

During 1912 the government had operated with a deficit of $22 million, and the national debt had climbed to $1.1 billion, he reported. Taft said the "most crying need" of the country was for a "proper banking and currency system." He also urged Congress to pass a workman's compensation act to apply to railroads and interstate transportation.

The President put forth "needed reforms" in the third State of the Union message delivered on December 19, 1912. He called for legislation that would give each Cabinet member a nonvoting seat in each house of Congress, so that they could be present in discussions bearing on their departments. He also asked Congress to appropriate money to build a Lincoln Memorial in Washington as well as new buildings for most of the executive departments.

Chief Justice

Upon leaving the White House, the fifty-five-year-old Taft accepted an appointment as a law professor at Yale. He became immensely popular with the students and found fun in the campus activities for eight years. During World War I he served on the War Labor Board.

Taft supported Warren G. Harding's campaign for the presidency—Harding had made Taft's nomination speech at the Republican Convention in 1912—and was pleased when his friend won, partly because he was hopeful that he might finally achieve his lifelong ambition of an appointment to the Supreme Court. When Chief Justice Edward D. White died shortly after Harding's inauguration, Taft was swiftly appointed to fill the vacancy.

His last nine years were the happiest of his life. His geniality brought a spirit of harmony to the Supreme Court. He avoided writing any dissenting opinions, noting: "I would not think of opposing the views of my brethren if there is a majority against my own."

In February 1930, at the age of seventy-two, Taft resigned as Chief Justice because of heart trouble. A month later, on March 8, 1930, he died in Washington and was buried in Arlington National Cemetery.

Woodrow Wilson

The Twenty-eighth President of the United States
1913–21

1856 (December 29) Born in Staunton, Virginia.

1879 Graduated from Princeton University.

1879–81 Attended University of Virginia law school.

1882–83 Practiced law in Atlanta, Georgia.

1883–85 Attended Johns Hopkins University, earning Ph.D.

1885 (June 24) Married Ellen Louise Axson.

1885–88 Associate professor of history at Bryn Mawr College.

1888–90 Professor of history and politics at Wesleyan University.

1890–1902 Professor of jurisprudence and politics at Princeton University.

1902–10 President of Princeton University.

1911–13 Governor of New Jersey.

1913–21 Twenty-eighth President of the United States.

1915 (December 18) Married Edith Bolling Galt.

1924 (February 3) Died in Washington, D.C.

Many parallels can be found between Woodrow Wilson and Abraham Lincoln. Like Lincoln, Wilson was elected President with less than a majority of the popular vote because of a split in the opposition party. Like Lincoln, he had the ability to speak in simple meaningful words that inspired the people of the nation and of the world to a deeper belief in democracy. And, like Lincoln, he became a great wartime President, directing America's effort in World War I.

But he also was the opposite of Lincoln in many ways. He was the most highly educated man ever to become President, having received more than a dozen college degrees and having written many scholarly books before entering the White House. He had a cold, austere appearance, lacking the personal magnetism or "common touch" of most successful politicians. And, unlike Lincoln, he did not die at the height of his popularity. At the end of his administration he suffered as the Senate revolted against his leadership, rejecting his plea for participation in the League of Nations—just as Lincoln, if he had lived, likely would have experienced a congressional revolt against his liberal plans for Reconstruction of the South.

As a university graduate student in his twenties, Wilson wrote: "The President is at liberty, both in law and conscience, to be as big a man as he can." A quarter of a century later, when he himself filled the office, President Wilson successfully followed his own earlier advice.

A Southern Boy in the Reconstruction Period

THE ELDEST SON of a Presbyterian minister, Thomas Woodrow Wilson was born on December 29, 1856, in Staunton, Virginia. He later dropped his first name, but throughout his boyhood he was called "Tommie." He had two older sisters, and a younger brother born in 1866. When Tommie was two, his family moved to Augusta, Georgia, where his father, Joseph Ruggles Wilson, became pastor of the First Presbyterian Church.

In later years, Wilson said that his earliest recollection as a child was of a man standing at the gate to his father's house and shouting: "Mr. Lincoln's elected. There'll be war!" He had a few other scattered memories of the war years—of having once stood and looked up to General Robert E. Lee, of staring at the wounded Confederate soldiers brought to his father's church when it was used as a temporary hospital, and at the end of the war of seeing Confederate President Jefferson Davis as a prisoner of Union soldiers.

Southern schools had been disrupted by the war, so Tommie was nine before he started school, and was eleven before he could read very well. When the boy was thirteen, Joseph Wilson moved his family to Columbia, South Carolina, where he became a professor in a theological seminary, as well as minister of the local Presbyterian church. In 1873, when he was sixteen, the bespectacled young Wilson was sent to Davidson College near Charlotte, North Carolina, to prepare himself for the ministry. He withdrew from the school the next spring because of poor health. Later that year, 1874, the Wilsons moved again, this time to Wilmington, N.C., where the elder Wilson again had a new pastorate.

A Rising Young Scholar

AFTER A YEAR AND A HALF spent nursing his health and reading, the eighteen-year-old Wilson went north in 1875 to attend the Presbyterian College of New Jersey at Princeton, where he took part in many student activities and was managing editor of the campus newspaper in his senior year. He helped found the Liberal Debating Club, but refused to compete for a prize when he drew the affirmative for a debate defending the protective tariff, in which he did not believe. Most important in his time at Princeton, he decided not to follow his parents' wishes that he become a minister.

Young Wilson, who had made up his mind to become a statesman, decided first to take up law, entering the best law school in the South—the University of Virginia at Charlottesville in the fall of 1879. He soon found that studying law was "as monotonous as . . . Hash," but he enjoyed taking part in debates and polished his writing style with essays for the campus magazine. Early in 1881 illness again forced him to drop out of school. He returned to his family home in Wilmington, and while recovering his health continued with his studies. In 1882 he received a law degree *in absentia* from the University of Virginia and was admitted to the bar.

Wilson formed a law partnership with a friend in Atlanta, Georgia, and from 1882 to 1883 tried to make a living as a lawyer. However, the Georgia capital was filled with lawyers who had better family and political connections, so he decided to return to school to prepare himself to teach.

The twenty-six-year-old Wilson entered the graduate school of Johns Hopkins University at Baltimore in the fall of 1883, and soon after began work on his first book, a study of how Congress rules the American government when a weak President holds office. Under the title *Congressional Government*, it received favorable attention among students of government.

When he completed his studies at Johns Hopkins, he accepted a $1,500-a-year position as associate professor at the opening session of a new women's college, Bryn Mawr, in Pennsylvania. As soon as he had accepted the position, he married twenty-five-year-old Ellen Louise Axson, a Presbyterian minister's daughter whom he had wooed for two years. While teaching at Bryn Mawr in 1886 he persuaded the Johns Hopkins faculty to grant him his Ph.D. degree without having to take the oral examinations. From 1888 to 1890 he served as professor of history and politics at Wesleyan University at

Middletown, Connecticut, also coaching the Wesleyan football team in a victorious season.

In 1890 Wilson received an appointment as professor of jurisprudence and history at Princeton University, an achievement that he regarded as "a crowning success." By this time the Wilsons had three daughters, and they needed the added income from the Princeton professorship as much as the honor. He was a popular lecturer and indefatigable researcher, a familiar campus sight riding a bicycle to class while working in every spare minute on a tremendous five-volume *History of the American People,* for which he received $12,000 from its publisher.

His remarkable personal qualities are evident in the fact that when the president of Princeton University resigned in 1902 in a dispute with the trustees, the forty-five-year-old Wilson was unanimously chosen as the new president. Among the trustees voting for him was former President Grover Cleveland. As swiftly as possible Wilson forced new standards of scholarship on the university, temporarily causing a drop in enrollment as students who did not want to work turned elsewhere. In 1905 he introduced what was called the preceptoral plan, which provided for adding fifty bright young teachers to the staff to live in the student dormitories and act as tutors.

Although Wilson's educational reforms had been widely hailed as lending a new vigor to Princeton, he met defeat from the alumni in 1907 when he proposed to abolish the students' private eating clubs and substitute college dining halls. But although the plan was voted down, Wilson's stock rose with the public because the newspapers played him up as a fighter for democracy against the privileges of the rich.

In the spring of 1910 Wilson made a speech to Princeton alumni in Pittsburgh that made headlines throughout the nation. In it he denounced private universities for neglecting "opportunities to serve the people," and said that Lincoln would never have been as important a President if he had attended a private university. He accused the Protestant churches of "serving the classes and not the masses," and said they had "more regard for pew rents than for men's souls." And as a crescendo he predicted a revolution with "fields of blood" if the United States could not find "the leadership of men who know her needs."

The Pittsburgh speech did not sit well with the conservative elements of the Princeton alumni. Moreover, Wilson had lost face in a squabble with the dean of the graduate college of the university. There was open speculation that Wilson would leave Princeton for political office if the right opportunity presented itself.

College President Turns Politician

SHORTLY AFTER THE SPRING graduation exercises at Princeton in 1910, Wilson was called to a meeting with George Harvey, the New York publisher of Wilson's books; James "Sugar Jim" Smith, the Democratic political boss of New Jersey; and Colonel Henry Watterson, the Louisville, Kentucky, editor who was a power in the national Democratic party. These men confided to Wilson that they wanted to make him President, and that as the first step Smith would arrange to get him the party's nomination for governor of New Jersey. After receiving assurances that if he won the governorship he would not be interfered with by the Democratic machine, Wilson accepted the invitation.

Wilson was playing golf when word came to him in September that the Democratic state convention had nominated him for governor on the first ballot. He hurried to the convention still wearing his golf clothes and accepted the nomination with a speech that he had prepared well in advance. At the request of the Princeton trustees he resigned as president of the university in October.

The Republicans who had controlled the state government for fourteen years attacked Wilson as a man who pretended to be progressive but was in reality a stooge of the Democratic boss system. To this Wilson replied: "If elected I shall not, either in the matter of appointments to office or assent to legislation, or in shaping any part of the policy of my administration, submit to the dictation of any person or persons, special interest or organization." The voters listened, because on election day he won by a majority of more than 50,000.

Even before he was inaugurated, Wilson was put to the test. Smith announced that he wished to be elected U.S. senator by the Democratic legislature that had come into office on Wilson's coat-tails. Wilson remonstrated with Smith privately, and when the boss refused to withdraw, the governor-elect stumped the state in support of an opposing candidate. When the legislature voted down Smith's candidacy in January, the newspapers reported that the "long-haired bookworm of a professor" had "licked the gang to a frazzle."

As governor, Wilson guided, cajoled, and forced the legislature to pass one reform measure after another. These included the substitution of direct primaries to prevent behind-the-scenes selection of party candidates, electoral reforms to prevent ballot-box stuffing, regulation of public utilities to fix rates and set service standards, a workmen's compensation law, a pure food law, a regulation of the laboring conditions of women and children, and local option to adopt the commission form of government in cities. The Republicans won control of both houses of the legislature in 1912, and after that Wilson was unable to obtain passage of further reform legislation. In the 1912 session of the legislature he vetoed about 10 percent of all the bills that were passed.

From 1911 on, Wilson openly sought the Democratic presidential nomination, but the machine politicians felt that the more conservative Champ Clark of Missouri, Speaker of the House of Representatives, would be a safer candidate. When the Democratic Convention opened in Baltimore in June 1912, a week after the Republicans had rejected Teddy Roosevelt and renominated Taft, Clark had won pledges from almost twice as many delegates as had Wilson, although he still did not have the necessary 726 votes needed to secure the nomination. The convention was deadlocked between these two leading candidates, neither of whom would withdraw. Up to the thirtieth ballot Clark consistently led, but from the fourteenth ballot, on which William Jennings Bryan switched from Clark to Wilson, the New Jersey governor steadily gained support, finally going ahead of Clark on the thirtieth roll call. At last on the forty-sixth ballot, Wilson won the nomination. Throughout the nerve-racking days and nights of the voting from June 27 until the final ballot on July 2, Wilson firmly refused to let his managers make any political deals or promise any political offices, saying, "not a single vote can be or will be obtained by means of a promise."

When former President Roosevelt accepted the presidential nomination of the new Progressive party early in August, this split the Republican party and nearly assured Wilson's election. Wilson and Roosevelt each campaigned strenuously for the progressive vote, while Taft, convinced that he would be defeated, did almost no campaigning. Both Wilson's "New Freedom" and Roosevelt's "New Nationalism" were principally attacks on Big Business, along two divergent lines: Roosevelt emphasized the necessity for regulation, while Wilson advocated breaking up monopolies to the advantage of small business. The count of the popular vote gave Wilson 6,296,547, Roosevelt 4,118,571, and Taft 3,486,720; in the electoral votes Wilson had 435, Roosevelt 88, and Taft 8. To Princeton students who came to cheer him on election night Wilson said: "I myself have no feeling of triumph tonight. I have a feeling of solemn responsibility."

Wilson's Inauguration

As WILSON TOOK THE OATH of office on a bright, spring-like March 4, 1913, no one had any premonition of the coming war in Europe, destined to overshadow all other questions in the next several years. Wilson delivered a memorable inaugural address, full of idealism and reform, couched in language not heard since Lincoln's day, and meriting citation at some length:

"No one can mistake the purpose for which the Nation now seeks to use the Democratic party. It seeks to use it to interpret a change in its own plans and point of view. Some old things with which we had grown familiar, and which had begun to creep into the very habit of our thought and of our lives, have altered their aspect. . . . Some new things, as we look frankly upon them . . . have come to assume the aspect of things long believed in and familiar, stuff of our own convictions. We have been refreshed by a new insight into our own life.

"We see that in many things . . . life is very great. It is incomparably great in its material aspects, in its body of wealth, in the diversity and sweep of its energy, in the industries which have been conceived and built up by the genius of individual men and the limitless enterprise of groups of men. It is great, also, very great, in its moral force. Nowhere else in the world have noble men and women exhibited in more striking forms the beauty and energy of sympathy and helpfulness and counsel in their efforts to rectify wrong, alleviate suffering, and set the weak in the way of strength and hope. We have built up, moreover, a great system of government, which has stood through a long age as in many respects a model for those who seek to set liberty upon foundations that will endure against fortuitous change, against storm and accident. Our life contains every great thing, and contains it in rich abundance.

"But the evil has come with the good, and much fine gold has been corroded. With riches has come inexcusable waste. We have squandered a great part of what we might have used, and have not stopped to conserve the exceeding bounty of nature, without which our genius for enterprise would have been worthless and impotent, scorning to be careful, shamefully prodigal as well as admirably efficient. We have been proud of our industrial achievements, but we have not hitherto stopped thoughtfully enough to count the human cost, the cost of lives snuffed out, of energies overtaxed and broken, the fearful physical and spiritual cost to the men and women and children upon whom the dead weight and burden of it all has fallen pitilessly the years through. The groans and agony of it all had not yet reached our ears, the solemn, moving undertone of our life, coming up out of the mines and factories and out of every home where the struggle had its intimate and familiar seat. With the great Government went many deep secret things which we too long delayed to look into and scrutinize with candid, fearless eyes. The great Government we loved has too often been made use of for private and selfish purposes, and those who used it had forgotten the people.

"At last a vision has been vouchsafed us of our life as a whole. We see the bad with the good, the debased and decadent with the sound and vital. With this vision we approach new affairs. Our duty is to cleanse, to reconsider, to restore, to correct the evil without impairing the good, to purify and humanize every process of our common life without weakening or sentimentalizing it. There has been something crude and heartless and unfeeling in our haste to succeed and be great. Our thought has been 'Let every man look out for himself, let every generation look out for itself,' while we reared giant machinery which made it impossible that any but those who stood at the levers of control should have a chance to look out for themselves. We had not forgotten our morals. We remembered well enough that we had set up a policy which was meant to serve the humblest as well as the most powerful, with an eye single to the standards of justice and fair play, and remembered it with pride. But we were very heedless and in a hurry to be great.

"We have come now to the sober second thought. The scales of heedlessness have fallen from our eyes. We have made up our minds to square every process of our national life again with the standards we so proudly set up at the beginning and have always carried at our hearts. Our work is a work of restoration.

"We have itemized with some degree of particularity the things that ought to be altered and here are some of the chief items: A tariff which cuts us off from our proper part in the commerce of the world, violates the just principles of taxation, and makes the Government a facile instrument in the hands of private interests; a banking and currency system based upon the necessity of the Government to sell its bonds fifty years ago and perfectly adapted to concentrating cash and restricting credits; an industrial system which, take it on all its sides, financial as well as administrative, holds capital in leading strings, restricts the liberties and limits the opportunities of labor, and exploits without renewing or conserving the natural resources of the country; a body of agricultural activities never yet given the efficiency of great business undertakings or served as it should be through the instrumentality of science taken directly to the farm, or afforded the facilities of credit best suited to its practical needs; watercourses undeveloped, waste places unreclaimed, forests untended, fast disappearing without plan or prospect of renewal, unregarded waste heaps at every mine. We have studied as perhaps no other nation has the most effective means of production, but we have not studied cost or economy as we should either as organizers of industry, as statesmen, or as individuals.

"Nor have we studied and perfected the means by which government may be put at the service of humanity, in safeguarding the health of the Nation, the health of its men and its women and its children, as well as their rights in the struggle for existence. This is no sentimental duty. The firm basis of government is justice, not pity. These are matters of justice. There can be no equality or opportunity, the first essential of justice in the body politic, if men and women and children be not shielded in their lives, their very vitality, from the consequences of great industrial and social processes which they can not alter, control, or singly cope with. Society must see to it that it does not itself crush or weaken or damage its own constituent parts. The first duty of law is to keep sound the society it serves. Sanitary laws, pure food laws, and laws determining conditions of labor which individuals are powerless to determine for themselves are intimate parts of the very business of justice and legal efficiency.

"These are some of the things we ought to do, and not leave the others undone, the old-fashioned, never-to-be-neglected, fundamental safeguarding of property and of individual right. This is the high enterprise of the new day: To lift everything that concerns our life as a Nation to the light that shines from the hearthfire of every man's conscience and vision of the right. It is inconceivable that we should do this as partisans; it is inconceivable we should do it in ignorance of the facts as they are or in blind haste. We shall restore, not destroy. We shall deal with our economic system as it is and as it may be modified, not as it might be if we had a clean sheet of paper to write upon; and step by step we shall make it what it should be, in the spirit of those who question their own wisdom and seek counsel and knowledge, not shallow self-satisfaction or the excitement of excursions whither they can not tell. Justice, and only justice, shall always be our motto.

"And yet it will be no cool process of mere science. The Nation has been deeply stirred, stirred by a solemn passion, stirred by the knowledge of wrong, of ideals lost, of government too often debauched and made an instrument of evil. The feelings with which we face this new age of right and opportunity sweep across our heartstrings like some air out of God's own presence, where justice and mercy are reconciled and the judge and the brother are one. We know our task to be no mere task of politics but a task which shall search us through and through, whether we be able to understand our time and the need of our people, whether we be indeed their spokesmen and interpreters, whether we have the pure heart to comprehend and the rectified will to choose our high course of action.

"This is not a day of triumph; it is a day of dedication. Here muster, not the forces of party, but the forces of humanity. Men's hearts wait upon us; men's lives hang in the balance; men's hopes call upon us to say what we will do. Who shall live up to the great trust? Who dares fail to try? I summon all honest men, all patriotic, all forward-looking men, to my side. God helping me, I will not fail them, if they will but counsel and sustain me!"

Wilson's First Term

LESS THAN TWO WEEKS after his inauguration, Wilson called the first regularly scheduled press conference because he believed the people had a right to know regularly from the President the state of affairs of the nation. Because all his life Wilson had been an admirer of liberal British prime ministers and felt that the British parliamentary system in which the head of the government led the legislature brought cohesiveness to national government, he seized the opportunity of a special session of Congress in April 1913 to address a joint session of the two houses—a precedent-shattering event that had not occurred since the administration of John Adams. In all the more than a hundred intervening years Presidents had sent their messages to be read to Congress. But Wilson was determined to lead, not follow. He told the joint session: "I am very glad indeed to have this opportunity . . . to verify for myself the impression that the President of the United States is a person, not a mere department of the Government hailing Congress from some island of jealous power, sending messages, not speaking naturally and with his own voice—that he is a human being trying to cooperate with other human beings in a common service."

Wilson had called Congress into special session to enact a tariff reform law. The tariff bill was quickly passed by the House, not bogged down in the Senate, where so many tariff reform bills of the past had died or been emasculated. Wilson appealed directly to the people to help defeat the business lobbies working against the measure. He declared that never before had there been "so insidious a lobby." He said "money without limit is being used to sustain this lobby . . . Only public opinion can check and destroy it." Senators were deluged by letters, and on October 3, 1913, the measure was signed into law by Wilson, removing tariffs on wool, sugar, iron, food, and generally reducing tariffs by about 25 percent. The law also provided for the first income tax under the Sixteenth Amendment to the Constitution.

Wilson went before Congress a second time, on June 23, 1913, to ask for legislation to reform the nation's banking and currency laws. "We must have a currency, not rigid as now, but readily, elastically responsive to sound credit . . . Our banking laws must mobilize reserves . . . And the control of the system of banking and of issue . . . must be vested in the Government itself, so that the banks may be the instruments, not the masters, of business and of individual enterprise and initiative." The result, despite the opposition of the banking interests, was the Federal Reserve Act of 1913—regarded by many as the most important piece of domestic legislation of Wilson's administration.

He helped push through Congress the most far-reaching series of laws concerned with social justice of any President to that time. This legislation included the establishment of the Federal Trade Commission to regulate business, the Clayton Anti-trust Law to strengthen the government's power to prevent monopolies, and the Seamen's Act to provide greater safety for sailors and greater freedom for them in their relations with ship owners. Later in his administration he helped forward child labor legislation and government loans to farmers.

Perhaps Wilson's greatest failure in the area of social justice was his unwillingness to aid blacks to achieve equality. Booker T. Washington and other black leaders were distressed and angered that Wilson did nothing to prevent the imposition of segregation rules in federal departments and agencies as southern Democrats came to power.

Wilson was dismayed in the congressional elections of 1914 when the Democrats lost forty-eight seats in the House of Representatives, retaining their majority by only twenty-five seats. But after consideration he determined to proceed with his program for the New Freedom as strongly as ever.

But foreign affairs soon demanded his attention. Trouble loomed first in Mexico, where civil war broke out and forced Wilson to order the navy to occupy Vera Cruz. The Mexican bandit-patriot Francisco Villa briefly invaded New Mexico in 1916, and American troops fruitlessly pursued him across the Rio Grande. Wilson was momentarily on the verge of asking for a declaration of war with Mexico in 1916, but decided to withdraw the troops.

Far more important, though seeming more remote, was the war that broke out in Europe in July 1914. On August 4, Wilson issued a Neutrality Proclamation spelling out in detail the means by which the United States would avoid participation. In succeeding months his patience wore thin as both Germany and the Allies repeatedly ignored American neutrality. Wilson tried hard to keep the United States out of the conflict while trying to protect American lives and property. But Germany's violation of the neutrality of Belgium and the attacks by German submarines on passenger ships created a strong pro-Allied public opinion in the United States.

Meantime personal tragedy struck with the death of Mrs. Wilson in August 1914. For a time Wilson was a sad and lonely man, then, in 1915, he met Mrs. Edith Bolling Galt, an attractive Washington widow. Nine months after their first meeting Wilson married the forty-three-year-old Mrs. Galt in a quiet ceremony at her Washington home.

When the Republican National Convention met in June 1916, the delegates rejected the candidacy of former President Roosevelt and nominated

Charles Evans Hughes, an associate justice of the Supreme Court and a former governor of New York.

In the summer of 1916 the railroad unions threatened a nationwide strike unless the railroads granted an eight-hour working day. Wilson intervened and got the unions to accept arbitration, but the presidents of the railroad companies arrogantly refused. A week before the strike deadline Wilson called a joint session of Congress and pleaded for legislation for an eight-hour day. Congress acted swiftly and Wilson signed the measure into law.

The Republican presidential candidate, Hughes, denounced Wilson's action as a surrender to the unions, "the most shameful proceeding that has come to my attention since I have observed public life." But Wilson won new support from progressive and labor circles.

Yet the overriding issue of 1916 was war. The Democrats campaigned with the slogan, "He kept us out of war," and they cited Theodore Roosevelt's demands for intervention as proof that if the Republicans won office the nation would be drawn into the European conflict.

Election returns on the evening of November 7 showed that Hughes had won almost every eastern state, and the Democratic New York *World* conceded Hughes' victory. Wilson went to bed in the White House believing he had been defeated, but the next day returns from the West showed that Wilson had done better there than had been expected. He carried California by about 4,000 votes, winning that state's critical thirteen votes—enough to give him victory. The final count of popular votes gave Wilson 9,127,695 and Hughes 8,533,507. In the electoral votes it was Wilson 277 and Hughes 254.

For the remainder of his first term Wilson busied himself with efforts to bring about a settlement of the war in Europe. In January 1917, he addressed the Senate, calling on the European nations to accept "peace without victory." But a few days later the German government, having decided that war with the United States was inevitable, announced that starting February 1, 1917, its submarines would sink without warning any ship, including any American ship, engaged in trade with the Allies. On February 3, Wilson spoke to a joint session of Congress, announcing the breaking off of diplomatic relations with Germany, but expressing his continuing hope for peace. These hopes were further blasted when at the end of February a message between Germany and Mexico was intercepted in which Mexico was promised the recovery of Texas, Arizona, and New Mexico if it joined in war on the United States. Wilson kept this note secret, but immediately went before Congress again to ask for power to arm American merchant ships. When Congress appeared loath to grant this authority, Wilson revealed the Germany-Mexico note on March 1. Although the House passed a bill giving the authority the same day, action was blocked in the Senate until the Sixty-fourth Congress expired on March 4.

Wilson's Second Term

PROMPTLY AFTER HIS SECOND INAUGURATION, Wilson announced that even without special congressional approval he intended on his own authority to arm American merchant ships. When German submarines sank without warning three U.S. merchantmen on March 18, influential persons throughout the country joined former President Roosevelt in calling for an immediate declaration of war. Two days later Wilson called for a special session of Congress to meet on April 2, and he began drafting a war message.

Addressing Congress on April 2, Wilson asked for a declaration of war: "There are, it may be, many months of fiery trial and sacrifice ahead of us. It is a fearful thing to lead this great peaceful people into war . . . but the right is more precious than peace, and we shall fight for the things which we have always carried nearest our hearts,—for democracy, for the right of those who submit to authority to have a voice in their own Government, for the rights and liberties of small nations, for a universal dominion of right by . . . a concert of free peoples . . ." After action by the Senate and House, Wilson signed the declaration of war on Germany.

Wilson showed the same strength of leadership in war as he had in peace. He directed the mobilization of America's economic and manpower resources, and perhaps most important, he voiced the moral ideals and objectives that the peoples of the world might hope for. When the Bolshevik Revolution broke out in Russia in 1917, the new government published secret treaties among Britain, France, and Czarist Russia which cast a dubious light on Allied war aims. The American President was the logical man to counter these disclosures by stating public war aims to which liberals and idealists could give their adherence, and for which America's power furnished a guarantee. Accordingly, Wilson delivered a major address to Congress on January 8, 1918, setting forth "Fourteen Points" as "the only possible program" for peace from the American viewpoint. The Fourteen Points included open instead of secret treaties; freedom of the seas; removal of tariff barriers; disarmament; colonial adjustments; evacuation of Russian, Belgian, French, and Balkan territory by the Germans; return of Alsace-Lorraine to France; self-determination for the subject peoples of Austria-Hungary and Turkey; an independent Poland; and finally, as the Fourteenth Point, "a general association of nations must be formed under specific covenants for the purpose of affording mutual guarantees of political independence and territorial integrity to great and small states alike."

American troops and supplies poured into Europe, turning the tide of war against Germany. Eleven months later Germany asked for an armistice. The fighting ended on November 11, 1918.

In an effort to insure that his Fourteen Points would truly be the basis of settlement in Europe, Wilson decided to head the American peace delegation—the first trip to Europe by an American President while holding office. He arrived in France in December 1918 and was received triumphantly everywhere. But at the peace conference Wilson found himself forced to give up on one point after another in order to preserve his idea of a League of Nations.

When Wilson brought the Treaty of Versailles back to the United States in July 1919, he found that great opposition had built up to it. He had made the tactical mistake of not including a representative of the U. S. Senate or a representative of the Republican party in his peace delegation. The Republicans had won control of Congress in the 1918 election, and now they were determined to embarrass Wilson.

Trying to rally public opinion to his side, Wilson went on an 8,000-mile speaking tour throughout the Midwest and to the Pacific Coast. On the night of September 25, 1919, after speaking at Pueblo, Colorado, he collapsed from exhaustion. Canceling the rest of his engagements, he returned to Washington, where on October 2 he had a stroke that paralyzed his left side. Suddenly he was an invalid, hardly able to quit his bed or wheel chair.

Wilson refused to accept reservations that Republican senators insisted on adding to the Treaty of Versailles, and instructed Democratic senators to vote against the treaty unless the Republicans withdrew their amendments. As a result the treaty was voted down twice in the Senate, in November 1919, and in March 1920. Confident that the public still would come to the support of the League of Nations, Wilson insisted that this should be the central issue of the presidential campaign of 1920. His hopes were crushed when Republican Warren G. Harding was elected President overwhelmingly in the race with Democratic candidate James M. Cox. But international faith in his leadership was reaffirmed when Wilson was awarded the Nobel Peace Prize in December 1920 for his efforts in seeking a just peace and in supporting the idea of the League of Nations.

Three important amendments to the United States Constitution were proclaimed during Wilson's presidency. The Seventeenth, in 1913, provided for the direct election of senators by the people instead of by the state legislatures. The Eighteenth, in 1919, prohibited the manufacture, sale, or transportation of intoxicating beverages. And the Nineteenth, in 1920, gave women the right to vote.

A Prophecy

BROKEN IN HEALTH, though not in spirit, Wilson retired with his wife to a small house on S Street in Washington. He joined in a law partnership with Bainbridge Colby, his last Secretary of State, but did not take an active part in the affairs of the firm. To the end he was confident that his belief in the League of Nations as the salvation of the world would be vindicated. At the age of sixty-seven he died in his sleep on February 3, 1924, and his body was buried in the National Cathedral in Washington.

Less than two decades later the world would remember his prophecy made during the national tour that led to his collapse:

"There will come sometime . . . another struggle in which, not a few hundred thousand fine men from America will have to die, but many millions . . . to accomplish the final freedom of the peoples of the world."

Warren Gamaliel Harding
The Twenty-ninth President of the United States
1921–23

1865 (November 2) Born on a farm in Morrow County, Ohio.

1882 Graduated from Ohio Central College.

1884 Became editor and publisher of the daily *Marion Star.*

1891 (July 8) Married Florence Kling DeWolfe.

1900–4 State senator in Ohio legislature.

1904–6 Lieutenant governor of Ohio.

1909 Defeated as Republican candidate for governor.

1915–20 U.S. senator from Ohio.

1921–23 Twenty-ninth President of the United States.

1923 (August 2) Died in San Francisco.

The brief, scandal-ridden presidential administration of Warren G. Harding stands as a black mark in American history. The road to the nation's highest office was opened for Harding when politicians meeting in a Chicago hotel room chose him as a compromise candidate to break a deadlock in the 1920 Republican National Convention. The Ohio senator's handsome face and genial personality won him wide support from a war-weary electorate seeking a return to "normalcy." But his death three years later came opportunely, some believed *too* opportunely, saving him from extreme embarrassment in the governmental crime and corruption that soon was revealed.

The first man to move directly from the U. S. Senate to the presidency,

Harding received over 16 million votes, nearly twice as many as any previous presidential candidate. Many of these votes came from women, voting nationally for the first time under the woman suffrage amendment to the Constitution. Under Harding the nation plunged into the Jazz Age with its mixed morals that brought public support for prohibition while bootleg whisky continued to flow freely, even in the White House. The nation also entered the Radio Age as station KDKA in Pittsburgh made the first broadcasts of election returns on the Harding victory.

Harding's Boyhood

THE FIRST OF EIGHT CHILDREN of George and Phoebe Harding, the future President was born on November 2, 1865, on a farm in Morrow County in north-central Ohio. His early years were like those of most farm boys of the time, filled with day-to-day chores that he did not particularly enjoy. When Harding was eight, his father completed a quick course in homeopathic medicine in Cleveland, and after that the boy sometimes accompanied him on horse-and-buggy calls.

But young Harding's interests soon fixed on newspaper work. His father had become part-owner of an intermittently published weekly, the *Caledonia Argus*, where Harding became a printer's devil, learning to set type, run the press, and clean ink from press rollers. At fourteen, his family sent him to little Ohio Central College, where he played the alto horn, edited the school yearbook, and was graduated in 1882. The seventeen-year-old Harding took up teaching in a country school, but quit the $30-a-month job after one term because he found trying to educate big farm boys a difficult process.

Harding's never-successful father had moved to Marion, Ohio, in 1882, hoping to improve the family's fortunes, and the boy followed the family there after he quit teaching. He tried studying law and selling insurance, but preferred shooting pool and playing poker with the town sports. His greatest early success came with helping organize the Citizen's Cornet Band of Marion, which won third place in a state band festival.

Newspaperman and Politician

ALMOST NINETEEN, Harding became a $1-a-week reporter for the weekly *Marion Democratic Mirror*, but this job lasted only a few weeks. Harding was an enthusiastic supporter of Republican presidential candidate James G. Blaine in the 1884 national election, and this did not sit well with the Democratic owner of the *Mirror*, who fired him.

John Tyler

James Knox Polk

Zachary Taylor

Millard Fillmore

Franklin Pierce

James Buchanan

Abraham Lincoln

Andrew Johnson

Ulysses S. Grant

Rutherford B. Hayes

James A. Garfield

Chester A. Arthur

Grover Cleveland

His love for newspaperwork undampened, Harding persuaded two unemployed friends, John Sickel and Jack Warwick, to join him in scraping up $300 to take over a bankrupt daily newspaper, the *Marion Star*. The first edition of the revived newspaper rolled off the press on November 26, 1884, with an offer of a weekly subscription to readers for ten cents. First Sickel, then Warwick, dropped out of the enterprise, but Harding stuck to the job and kept the paper in business.

Although Harding proclaimed that the daily *Star* was independent politically, he cleverly started a separate *Weekly Star* that openly supported Republican candidates, to obtain a share of politically dispensed county government advertising. Battling with two other local papers for the advertising dollars, the tobacco-chewing Harding joined in the rough-and-tumble journalism of the times that disregarded laws of libel in mudslinging at rivals. In one of these printer's-ink engagements a competing newspaper hinted that Harding was part-black—an unproved rumor that cropped up in subsequent political campaigns.

When Harding was twenty-five, he married Florence Kling DeWolfe, a thirty-year-old divorcée who was the daughter of the richest man in Marion. Flossie, as she was called by her friends, had been deserted by her husband and disowned by her father. At the time of her marriage to Harding, she was struggling to support herself and her child by giving piano lessons. She soon took over the business side of running the *Marion Star* and became a driving force behind Harding's business and political career. Because of her domineering manner, Harding jokingly called her "Duchess."

Harding's first attempt to win public office ended in defeat, when in 1892 he lost overwhelmingly in the race for county auditor. After the election, he commented wryly in the *Star* that the opposition Democrat won because he "had an easy mark for an opponent."

By the end of the 1890s, the *Star* had become a financial success and an influential voice in Republican party affairs. Its editor made regular appearances as a speaker in political campaigns. His oratory and handsome appearance made politicians think of him as a likely candidate for office, and at the 1899 state Republican convention, Harding was awarded nomination for the state senate. This time he won the election.

In his first term in the legislature, Harding proved himself a loyal supporter of the party leaders. He sought and won personal popularity with his fellow-lawmakers, also working to compromise differences between the two main factions of the state party led by Joseph Benson Foraker of Cincinnati and Mark Hanna of Cleveland.

Because of Harding's services to the party, the Republicans suspended a long-standing rule against renominating a state senator for re-election in his district, and Harding easily won a second term. In 1903, with the backing of the Cincinnati political machine, he won the nomination for lieutenant governor and went on to win the election.

At the end of his term as lieutenant governor, Harding temporarily abandoned elective office to return to his newspaper career in Marion. Perhaps he foresaw the defeat that came to the state Republican ticket in the next election, or perhaps he decided he should wait for a chance at a higher office.

In 1909 Harding won the Republican nomination for governor. His campaign was managed by Harry M. Daugherty, a small-town lawyer who was to figure importantly in Harding's later career. Although Harding worked hard to win the governorship, he was badly beaten in the election, largely because of a split in the Republican party between reform and machine factions that even Harding's skill could not reconcile.

National honor first came to Harding in 1912 when he was chosen to place President William Howard Taft's name in nomination for a second term at the Republican National Convention. Harding's eloquent oratory brought favorable comment from his fellow politicians, but he was gravely disappointed when Taft went down to election defeat with the national party torn apart by Theodore Roosevelt's Bull Moosers.

Senator from Ohio

DISCOURAGED BY THE EBB in his political fortunes, Harding at first refused to consider a proposal by Harry Daugherty that he run for the United States Senate in 1914. But Daugherty's persuasiveness and the ambition of Mrs. Harding overcame his doubts. He won the Republican nomination in Ohio's first direct primary, then went on to soundly beat the Democratic candidate, although the Cleveland *Plain Dealer* labeled him a "spokesman of the past."

Harding thoroughly enjoyed his term as a U.S. senator, entering enthusiastically into the club-like spirit of the Senate. He continued to seek popularity, never openly criticizing his colleagues of either party, not even when they occasionally made him the butt of their ill-humor.

As in the state legislature, Harding's record as a lawmaker was undistinguished. Almost half the time he failed to answer roll calls. He introduced no measures of great significance, and displayed few convictions other than those established by his party. On the two great domestic issues of the period on which no legislator could avoid taking a stand, he voted for Prohibition, although he personally liked to drink, and he voted for woman suffrage, although he doubted the wisdom of letting women vote. In both cases he voted against his own beliefs to curry favor with important voting blocs.

During World War I, he loyally supported President Woodrow Wilson's efforts to win the war. But when the fighting was over, he joined with Henry Cabot Lodge to thwart Wilson's plan for American participation in the League of Nations.

It was during Harding's term as senator that he established a liaison with Nan Britton, a Marion, Ohio, blonde who was thirty years his junior. Her book about the affair, *The President's Daughter*, created a sensation when it was published in 1927. It describes how Harding obtained a job for her in New York, how they met frequently in New York and Washington, and how she accompanied him on trips as his "niece." After Harding's death, Miss Britton unsuccessfully sued for a share of his estate for herself and her child who she claimed was Harding's daughter. More than forty years after Harding's death love letters were discovered that detailed another illicit romance between the President and a Marion matron.

Meanwhile, Harding's political career continued to move forward under the management of Daugherty. The tireless Ohio politician engineered the selection of Harding as keynote speaker of the 1916 Republican National Convention that nominated Charles Evans Hughes. Although the keynote address did not rouse huge enthusiasm in the lethargic delegates, it did help win Harding the permanent chairmanship of the convention. His noble appearance and lofty words impressed the delegates—they remembered him in 1920.

The Smoke-filled Room

BECAUSE HE LIKED THE LIFE of a senator and because he recognized his own limitations, Harding was not enthusiastic about Daugherty's urgings that he run for President. He did not think he could win either the nomination or the election, and refused to act until Daugherty told him that by not announcing his presidential candidacy he was jeopardizing his chances of returning to the Senate for a second term. Finally, in December 1919, in a letter to a Republican committee in Ohio that had urged his candidacy, he agreed to seek the presidential nomination.

Daugherty entered his candidate in three preferential primaries: Ohio, Indiana, and Montana. Harding won the Ohio primary over General Leonard Wood by a slim majority, but he lost the Indiana primary by a landslide and received only a handful of votes in the Montana primary. Harding believed he should quit the race, but his wife and Daugherty urged him to continue, hoping that a deadlock would develop at the convention between the two favorites, General Wood and Governor Frank Lowden of Illinois. It did. With Wood and Lowden each more than 200 votes short of a winning majority, the Chicago convention adjourned till morning.

The night was filled with politics. Messengers came and went among the busy candidates and their managers. Strings were pulled. Offers were made. But the most important meeting took place in a room at the Blackstone Hotel, attended by a group of influential Republican senators who wanted neither Wood nor Lowden. After canvassing all possibilities, they decided to offer to swing their support to Harding. Apparently there was some suspicion of the prospective dark horse's private life, because he was called to the hotel and asked bluntly if he had anything in his life or background that might embarrass the party. He was left alone to consider the question, and after a few minutes' communion with himself, Harding assured the group that his past was an open record. In turn, the group assured him of the nomination.

Next day, Wood and Lowden continued to hold first and second place through eight ballots, but Harding's voting strength slowly climbed. On the ninth ballot he moved into the lead, and on the tenth ballot he won the nomination with 692½ of the convention's 984 votes. Harding's comment as quoted by the *Literary Digest* was typical: "I feel like a man who goes in on a pair of eights and comes out with aces full."

As Harding's running mate, the convention chose Governor Calvin Coolidge of Massachusetts. Coolidge had enthusiastic support in the Republican party because of his firm stand in the Boston police strike of the previous year.

To oppose Harding, the Democratic Convention nominated James M. Cox, governor of Ohio. As their vice-presidential candidate, the Democrats chose Franklin D. Roosevelt, Assistant Secretary of the Navy under President Wilson.

The campaign was dull. For most of the time, Harding remained in Marion conducting a "front porch" campaign. He greeted thousands of well-wishers and spoke informally to them, sticking to bland expressions of his love of humanity, his patriotism, and his belief in the Republican party. In the fall, he climbed aboard a campaign train and made a series of speeches filled with generalities that could be interpreted by his listeners as they wished. The Democrats endeavored to make American participation in the League of Nations an issue, but Harding's position was obscure largely because he had no strong feelings on the matter, other than a determination to preserve the Senate's constitutional right to pass on foreign treaties.

When the voters went to the polls in November, the politicians learned that the campaign had not mattered. The people were so tired of the government restrictions and hardships imposed by the war that they wanted a complete change in administrations to bring back the old days when America did not have to look beyond its own borders. Harding received 16,143,407 popular votes to 9,130,328 for Cox. In the Electoral College he won 404 votes to 127. It is interesting, if futile, to speculate on what might have happened if the two other women in Harding's life had been discovered during the campaign.

Harding's Administration

BETWEEN THE ELECTION and the inauguration Harding chose his Cabinet, carefully balancing its membership. Some were close political friends; others represented various leading factions in the Republican party. It had a surprising number of distinguished men, including Secretary of State Charles Evans Hughes, a former governor of New York, Supreme Court justice, and candidate for President in 1916; Secretary of Agriculture Henry C. Wallace of Iowa, editor of a leading farm journal; and Secretary of Commerce Herbert Hoover, an eminent engineer and war-relief administrator. Secretary of the Treasury Andrew W. Mellon was a multimillionaire Pittsburgh banker, who was chosen at the behest of the Republican political machine of Pennsylvania. Secretary of War John W. Weeks of Massachusetts had served in the U. S. Senate with Harding. Postmaster General Will H. Hays of Indiana had been chairman of the Republican National Committee during the Harding presidential campaign.

Secretary of the Navy Edwin Denby was a Detroit, Michigan, lawyer who had made a fortune in the automobile business and had served as a congressman from Michigan.

Secretary of the Interior Albert B. Fall of New Mexico, another ex-senatorial colleague, was a friend of western oilmen who had contributed heavily to the presidential campaign fund.

Secretary of Labor James J. Davis of Pennsylvania had been a steelworker and director of the Loyal Order of Moose.

Finally, Harry Daugherty, the man who had masterminded Harding's rise to the White House, was Attorney General.

This was the formal Cabinet. But much of the real business of Harding's administration took place at the evening poker and drinking parties in the White House. These were regularly attended by Daugherty and Fall, by Jesse Smith, a Harding friend of dubious repute, and various other cronies and hangers-on.

Friends and acquaintances of Harding and Daugherty flocked from Ohio to Washington for jobs. Headquarters of the "Ohio Gang" as they were soon called, was the "Little Green House" at 1625 K Street. Government favors and appointments were bought and sold at this headquarters, but there never has been any evidence to show that Harding himself knew of these transactions. His friends merely knew that he would agree with their suggestions in order to please them.

On the international stage, Harding won the respect of other nations by calling the Washington Conference for the Limitation of Armament in 1921. At this conference the United States urged the end of the arms race between nations and the actual destruction of existing machines of war. Although the treaties designed by this conference were not ratified by the Senate until after Harding's death, the President's reputation as a man of peace was assured in foreign capitals.

Because the Senate disapproved of the Versailles Peace Treaty ending World War I, separate treaties with Germany and its allies were arranged in 1921 that excluded United States participation in the League of Nations.

Perhaps the most lasting contribution of Harding's administration was his establishment of the system of preparing a national budget. For the job of director of the budget, he made one of his best appointments, Charles G. Dawes of Chicago, who proceeded to place the fiscal affairs of the government on a businesslike basis.

In the field of labor, Harding appealed to the steel industry to abolish the twelve-hour working day, which was then the standard in the industry. Although he was rebuffed several times on the matter, he persisted in his efforts. Shortly after his death, the steel firms agreed to shorten the workday.

With Harding's approval, Congress increased protective tariffs to new highs with the Fordney-McCumber Act of 1922. But when Congress passed a huge soldier's bonus bill for the veterans of World War I, the President courageously vetoed it, pointing out that the bill did not provide for necessary additional revenues to pay the bonus.

In the elections of 1922, the Republican majority was reduced in both houses of Congress. This may have been partly caused by a depression in the economy, but Harding worried that the election results showed a loss in confidence in his administration. He resolved to go on a nationwide speaking tour in 1923 to strengthen his popularity.

Death and Scandals

LATE IN 1922, Harding began to learn of irregularities in the Veterans' Bureau. Huge amounts of war surplus materials had been disposed of far below their value to favored purchasers without competitive bidding. In turn new supplies had been purchased above their normal cost. Harding was shocked, because the head of the Veterans' Bureau, Charles R. Forbes, a Medal of Honor war hero, was one of his poker-playing intimates. In January 1923, Forbes was allowed to leave on a trip to Europe. Then Harding announced Forbes' resignation and the appointment of Brigadier General Frank T. Hines to replace him. Harding received a second shock in March 1923 with the suicide of Charles F. Cramer, the attorney for the Veterans' Bureau, who had purchased the Washington house where Harding had lived as a senator.

Apparently Harding was aware that further scandals were in the offing, because he ordered another close friend, Jesse Smith, to leave Washington. Smith had shared a Washington apartment with Attorney General Daugherty, and had been one of the most powerful members of the Ohio Gang in dispensing jobs and favors. But on the night of May 29, Smith returned to Washington and shot himself to death in Daugherty's apartment.

Harding was a badly worried man when he set out from Washington in a special train on June 20, 1923, on what he called a "voyage of understanding." The trip was to take him across the continent and to Alaska. When Harding reached Kansas City, he was visited in his hotel suite by Mrs. Albert B. Fall, whose husband had resigned as Secretary of the Interior a few months earlier. Harding was visibly shaken by the secret conversation, in which he almost surely learned something of Fall's dealings with oil companies over navy-reserved oil fields. When he reached Alaska in July, Harding received a long code message that had been flown to him from Washington. It, too, must have revealed more about the impending scandals, because he repeatedly muttered comments about friends who had betrayed him.

After returning to the United States from Alaska, Harding was stricken on July 27 in Seattle with what his physician, Surgeon General Charles E. Sawyer, at first diagnosed as indigestion caused by crab meat. It later was believed this may have been a heart attack. Although further public appearances were canceled, the President seemed to be recovering when he arrived in San Francisco on July 29. Then pneumonia struck. Distinguished physicians were called in, including Ray Lyman Wilbur, president of Stanford University. Again the President passed the crisis and seemed to be recovering. Then, at 7:35 p.m., on August 2, Harding died in bed while being read to by Mrs. Harding. The doctors, believing that a blood clot had been carried to the President's brain, asked for permission to perform an autopsy, but Mrs. Harding refused to allow it. Because the exact cause of the President's death remained in doubt, there later was much speculation that the President might have been poisoned to prevent his testifying against friends.

The public, not yet aware of anything wrong with Harding's administration, crowded the tracks by the thousands to watch the presidential funeral train pass by on its journey back to Washington. Services were held in Washington on August 8, attended by the new President, Calvin Coolidge, and by former Presidents Wilson and Taft. Then Harding's body was escorted back to his hometown of Marion for burial. Eight years later a memorial tomb was dedicated in Marion and there were laid to final rest the bodies of Harding and his wife, who died in 1924.

Even before Harding's death, Senator Thomas J. Walsh of Montana had been growing suspicious of manipulations by Secretary of the Interior Fall that had opened up to private oil companies two huge oil fields that had been held in reserve for future naval needs. Control of the fields, Elk Hills in California and Teapot Dome in Wyoming, had been transferred from the Navy Department to the Department of the Interior in 1921 with Harding's approval. Suspicions of bribery were aroused by the fact that Fall had made lavish improvements on his New Mexico ranch with no sufficient visible source of income.

As Walsh's investigation progressed, it became clear that Fall had received bribes of more than $400,000 from oil millionaires E. L. Doheny and Harry F. Sinclair. After many hearings and court cases, the oil leases of the reserves were canceled in 1927 by the United States Supreme Court. In 1929 Fall was convicted of bribery and sent to prison. Doheny and Sinclair both were brought to trial, but were freed of charges of conspiracy or bribery, although Sinclair was sentenced to jail for six months for contempt of court.

Meanwhile, a Senate investigation of the Veterans' Bureau was launched. Evidence was turned up that hundreds of millions of dollars had been spent for overpriced materials, land sites, and construction. Harding's friend, former director of the Veterans' Bureau Charles R. Forbes, was brought to trial in 1924 for bribery and conspiracy, along with John W. Thompson, an official of one of the firms with which he had been doing business. Both were convicted, fined $10,000 apiece, and sentenced to two years in prison.

Next, the Senate began an investigation of Attorney General Daugherty to determine why he had not prosecuted the central figures in the oil and Veterans' Bureau scandals. Senator Burton K. Wheeler of Montana served as counsel for the committee and dug up masses of testimony about Daugherty's associations with the late Jesse Smith and other members of the Ohio Gang. When Daugherty refused to appear before the Senate committee and would not deliver records to it, President Coolidge asked for his resignation from the Cabinet.

Daugherty and Alien Property Custodian Thomas W. Miller were brought to trial in 1924 on charges of conspiracy growing out of a transaction in which the federal government had turned over nearly $7 million as payment of a claim for a German-owned company that had been confiscated during the war. There was evidence indicating that more than $400,000 had been used to bribe government officials to grease the way for the settlement. Daugherty refused to testify in his own defense on grounds that he might tend to incriminate himself. He and his attorney also implied that his testimony might incriminate the dead President. Miller was convicted and sentenced to prison, but a hung jury could not agree on Daugherty's innocence or guilt. Daugherty was retried and again there was a hung jury. Then the case was dropped.

How much President Harding knew of the corruption among his friends and associates will never be known. After his death, Mrs. Harding burned his papers and correspondence, making a diligent effort to recover and destroy even personal letters that he had written to others. As a result, historians have been thwarted in their search for facts about Harding.

At the dedication of the Harding tomb in Marion in 1931, President Herbert Hoover epitomized the tragedy of the man in whose Cabinet he had served:

"Here was a man whose soul was seared by a great disillusionment. We saw him gradually weaken, not only from physical exhaustion, but also from mental anxiety. Warren Harding had a dim realization that he had been betrayed by a few of the men whom he had believed were his devoted friends. That was the tragedy of the life of Warren Harding."

Calvin Coolidge
The Thirtieth President of the United States
1923–29

1872 (July 4) Born in Plymouth Notch, Vermont.

1884–90 Attended Black River Academy in Ludlow, Vermont.

1891–95 Attended Amherst College, graduating *cum laude.*

1897 Admitted to the bar to practice law in Massachusetts.

1899–1900 Member of city council of Northampton, Mass.

1900–2 City solicitor of Northampton.

1905 (October 4) Married Grace Anna Goodhue.

1907–8 Member of Massachusetts house of representatives.

1910–11 Mayor of Northampton.

1912–15 Member of Massachusetts state senate, president 1914–15.

1916–18 Lieutenant governor of Massachusetts.

1919–20 Governor of Massachusetts.

1921–23 Vice President of the United States.

1923–29 Thirtieth President of the United States.

1933 (January 5) Died in Northampton, Massachusetts.

A Puritan in Babylon," as Calvin Coolidge was aptly described in the title of William Allen White's biography, presided over the White House during the Roaring Twenties. The red-haired, freckle-faced Coolidge with his sharp nose and Vermont twang somehow represented the almost-forgotten moral conscience of a nation preoccupied with bootleg booze, sex, and getting-rich-quick.

The first New Englander elected since Franklin Pierce, Coolidge had less aptitude for the presidency than Pierce, but he made more of a success of the job—largely because he had fewer important decisions to make than did Pierce.

As President, Coolidge assiduously followed the maxim that the government that governs least governs best. He made political capital of two traits uncommon for a President—he was naturally tight-lipped as well as tight-fisted. After reporters and comedians told exaggerated stories about these characteristics of an otherwise colorless man, Coolidge joined the game with witty, brief, and unsmiling repartee. He enjoyed the jokes about himself and relished the nickname "Silent Cal." Shortly before leaving the White House in 1929, he gave President-elect Herbert Hoover his best advice on how to get rid of the visitors who would call upon him:

"If you keep dead still they will run down in three or four minutes."

Vermont Farm Boy

THE ONLY PRESIDENT to be born on Independence Day, John Calvin Coolidge entered the world on July 4, 1872, in the crossroads village of Plymouth Notch, Vermont. His father ran the local general store, which was attached to the house where Coolidge was born. Young Cal—he dropped the name "John" while still a boy—received a forty-acre farm as a present from his grandfather when he was only six. His grandfather taught him all he knew about farming, and the boy learned early the importance of hard work and saving ways.

His mother, an invalid, died when he was twelve. "The greatest grief that can come to a boy came to me," he said later. For the rest of his life, Coolidge carried his mother's picture in the back of his watch.

From the time he was thirteen until he was seventeen, young Coolidge attended Black River Academy at Ludlow, Vermont, twelve miles from his home. His lonely father drove the distance in a horse-drawn wagon almost every weekend to be with him.

When he failed to pass the entrance examinations for Amherst College in 1890, he went to St. Johnsbury Academy for a term, then gained admittance to Amherst. In his scholastic work in college he was an average student, making mostly B's and a few C's, but was graduated in 1895 *cum laude*. More important to him than his studies, he had learned to debate and make speeches, and a humorous oration that he delivered as part of the closing festivities of his college days was a highlight of his years at Amherst.

The next fall, after spending the summer in Plymouth Notch, Coolidge went off on his own to Northampton, Massachusetts, a few miles from Amherst, and with a friend's help got a job as a law clerk so that he could become a lawyer. Two years later, in 1897, he was admitted to the bar.

He set up his own law office in Northampton and began to take an active part in Republican politics. His willingness to work hard for the party was rewarded. At twenty-six he was elected to the city council, became city solicitor two years later, was re-elected once, and then was defeated for re-election in 1902.

In 1905 the shy young lawyer-politician surprised Northampton by winning for his wife one of the most attractive girls in town, Grace Anna Goodhue, a teacher at a school for the deaf. She was twenty-six and he was thirty-three. They had two sons.

The year after his marriage, Coolidge was elected to the state legislature, serving two years in the lower house. At the age of thirty-nine, he was elected mayor of Northampton for two years, following this with election to the state senate in 1912, to which he was returned three times. He established a reputation as a party regular and won enough friends to be elected president of the senate in 1914. Another small boost up the political ladder came in 1915 when he was elected lieutenant governor. He was re-elected to this office twice.

Finally, Coolidge's long persistence in sticking doggedly to the task of taking only one rung at a time in his climb to political power paid off when he captured the Republican nomination for governor of Massachusetts in 1918. That fall he was elected by a majority of less than 17,000 votes.

A strike by the police of Boston in 1919 brought Coolidge national fame. The police had struck because they were not allowed to form an American Federation of Labor union. Rioting and looting broke out when the police failed to report for duty, and the mayor was unable to control the situation. Coolidge called out the state militia to restore order, then, when the head of the AFL, Samuel Gompers, protested that the police were being treated unfairly, Coolidge fired off this reply to him: "There is no right to strike against the public safety by anybody, anywhere, any time!" In a period when there were widespread labor troubles throughout the country, Coolidge's remark caught the fancy of many people because it made him seem to be more fearless and forthright than he actually was.

During his first term as governor, Coolidge undertook a task that he considered required more courage than his actions during the police strike. This was a reorganization of the state government necessitated by an amendment to the state constitution that had been passed during the previous administration. In this reorganization, Coolidge had to reduce the number of departments in the state government from 144 to 20—in effect demoting 122 important job holders.

Coolidge was re-elected governor in 1919 by a large majority. Although he was always a conservative, he sponsored some legislation during his second term that was praised by progressives. He was particularly interested in housing and helped put through laws preventing rent increases of more than 25 percent a year and prohibiting a landlord from evicting a tenant with less than thirty days' notice.

When the Republican National Convention met in Chicago in 1920, Coolidge was the favorite son of the Massachusetts delegation, receiving thirty-four votes on the first ballot. The Senate leaders who had decided that Harding would be a "safe" man for the presidency had chosen as his running mate Senator Irvine L. Lenroot of Wisconsin. The Republican leaders sent out the word to the delegates, and Lenroot's vice-presidential nomination was supposed to be unchallenged. But when a delegate from Oregon nominated Coolidge, the convention suddenly revolted against the dictates of their leaders and nominated Coolidge as the Republican vice-presidential candidate with 674 votes to Lenroot's 146.

At the age of forty-eight, Coolidge became Vice President of the United States.

He did a good job of presiding over the Senate, having a knowledge of parliamentary procedure from his years of experience in the Massachusetts legislature. He also was the first Vice President to be invited to sit regularly at Cabinet meetings.

Coolidge's Administration

COOLIDGE WAS AT HIS BIRTHPLACE in Vermont, where he and his family had been spending the summer, when he was awakened shortly after midnight on August 3, 1923, by a telegraph messenger bringing word that President Harding had died in San Francisco. After dressing, he had his storekeeper father, who was a notary public, swear him in—the only President ever to take the oath of office from his own father. Then with characteristic calm he went back to bed—he gained the reputation in succeeding years of getting more rest than any other President because of his ability to go to sleep quickly whenever he wanted a nap.

Immediately upon moving into the White House, Coolidge restored some of the dignity it had lost under Harding. There were no more drinking and card parties, but he retained Harding's Cabinet and made few changes in offices. He made his philosophy clear in a talk he gave during the first year in office in which he said "the business of America is business."

The scandals of the Harding administration began to rock the country shortly after Coolidge took office, but they did not touch Coolidge himself. Early in 1924 he accepted the resignation of Secretary of the Navy Denby and forced the resignation of Attorney General Daugherty. To deal with the scandals he appointed two future Supreme Court Justices: Owen J. Roberts as special prosecutor and Harlan F. Stone as Attorney General. In a press conference, he summed up, "Let the guilty be punished."

In the spring of 1924 Coolidge vetoed a bonus bill for veterans of World War I, but Congress passed the measure over his veto. Next, he vetoed a measure granting a general increase to the pensions of veterans of all wars, and this veto was upheld.

Although Coolidge and the Republican leaders of Congress were not in complete harmony, by the time the Republican National Convention met in Cleveland in June 1924, Coolidge firmly controlled the machinery of the party. This convention, the first nationally broadcast by radio, was dull in comparison to previous conventions, as Coolidge received the presidential nomination on the first ballot with only token opposition. The President had indicated he wanted Senator William Borah of Idaho as his running mate, but Borah refused. The convention then nominated former governor Frank Lowden of Illinois for Vice President, but Lowden also refused to accept the office. Finally, the convention again balloted for the vice-presidential nomination, and this time gave it to budget director Charles G. Dawes.

Coolidge was assured of winning the election when the Democratic party became bitterly divided in its convention in New York City. The two leading Democratic contenders were Governor Al Smith of New York and former Secretary of the Treasury William G. McAdoo. Southerners backing McAdoo included members of the Ku Klux Klan, and they were determined that the Roman Catholic Smith should not be nominated. More than one hundred ballots were taken before a compromise candidate, John W. Davis of Virginia, a former ambassador to Great Britain, was given the nomination. Liberals who were dissatisfied with the conservatism of the candidates of both national parties revived Teddy Roosevelt's Progressive party and nominated for President Robert La Follette of Wisconsin.

In November, Coolidge won election to a full term in his own right, though not by as large a majority as Harding had received four years earlier. The results gave him 15,718,211 popular votes to Davis' 8,385,283 and La Follette's 4,031,289. Coolidge won 382 electoral votes to 136 for Davis and 13 for La Follette.

Coolidge's victory was clouded by the death of his youngest son, sixteen-year-old Calvin, Jr., who had developed blood poisoning from a blister while playing tennis on the White House lawn. Later, in his *Autobiography,* Coolidge wrote: "When he went, the power and glory of the Presidency went with him. . . . I don't know why such a price was exacted for occupying the White House."

In his inaugural address on March 4, 1925, Coolidge dealt largely in generalities, concluding on a high religious-patriotic note: "America seeks no earthly empire built on blood and force. No ambition, no temptation, lures her to thought of foreign dominions. The Legions which she sends forth are armed, not with the sword, but with the cross. The higher state to which she seeks the allegiance of all mankind is not of human, but of divine origin. She cherishes no purpose save to merit the favor of Almighty God."

Soon after his inauguration Coolidge learned that he was faced with a coalition of Progressive Republicans and Democrats that had enough power in Congress to make his life difficult. In March 1925, this coalition blocked Coolidge's appointment of a conservative Michigan attorney, Charles Warren, as Attorney General. The defeat was made more irritating to Coolidge in that the Senate was evenly divided on the nomination, but Vice President Dawes was at his hotel taking a nap at the time of the vote and was not present to cast the deciding vote in favor of the appointment.

Domestically, the Coolidge administration practiced economy in government, substantially reducing the national debt. In the field of foreign affairs, Coolidge's Secretary of State, Frank B. Kellogg, won the 1929 Nobel Peace Prize for negotiating the Kellogg-Briand Pact outlawing war. It is significant that where Theodore Roosevelt and Woodrow Wilson, both strong Presidents, won Nobel prizes in their own right for their work in international affairs, Coolidge left such matters to his Secretary of State.

While Coolidge had regular visits from the financiers of Wall Street and gave encouraging words to the continuing industrial boom, he turned a deaf ear to the problems of the American farmer, who was not sharing in the general prosperity of the 1920s. Coolidge twice vetoed measures intended to bring relief to the farmers by permitting the government to buy surplus crops and send them abroad.

Because he had served only one full term, the Republican machine of Massachusetts prepared to press Coolidge's renomination. But in August 1927, while vacationing in the Black Hills, the President dropped a bombshell. He handed out to reporters a ten-word statement: "I do not choose to run for President in 1928." He refused to amplify the statement in any way. Its ambiguity worried the politicians because it could be interpreted to mean that he would be willing to run if he were forced to do so by a draft at the next convention.

Coolidge had a reputation for contributing to the stock-market boom by issuing optimistic statements that buoyed up the confidence of investors, and later it was said, though never proved, that he took himself out of the 1928 campaign because he foresaw a depression.

With Coolidge apparently withdrawing, Herbert Hoover, the Secretary of Commerce, became the front runner for the Republican nomination. Coolidge's friends hoped that the convention in Kansas City would deadlock and that the President would be drafted. Coolidge himself seemed to hope that this would happen. But Hoover, whom Coolidge sarcastically called the "wonduh boy," received the nomination on the first ballot.

Coolidge did little to help Hoover's campaign and did not evidence any particular pleasure when the latter won. Shortly before the inauguration he told a friend: "The best thing I can do for the Hoover administration is to keep my mouth shut." Coolidge and his wife left by train for their home in Massachusetts on the evening of Inauguration Day.

Retirement to Northampton

ALTHOUGH COOLIDGE regularly went to his law office in Northampton, he did not resume practicing law. With the proceeds from the sales of his *Autobiography* he bought a large mansion called "The Beeches" near Northampton, where he and his wife lived in seclusion. He also accepted appointment as a member of the board of directors of the New York Life Insurance Company, and began writing a syndicated newspaper column of political observations.

With the stock market crash of 1929 and the deepening depression of the early 1930s, Coolidge seemed to become even more withdrawn than usual. If he blamed himself for the economic disaster that had overtaken the country, he did not say so. When Hoover ran for re-election in 1932, Coolidge gave some help to the campaign with a speech in Madison Square Garden in New York. After Hoover's defeat, a friend asked Coolidge if he would consider running for the presidency again in 1936. He answered: "Nothing would induce me to take office again."

On January 5, 1933, the sixty-year-old Coolidge unexpectedly died of a heart attack while shaving in the bathroom of his Northampton home. He was buried in the graveyard of his birthplace in Vermont. Years later, Herbert Hoover wrote:

"Mr. Coolidge was a real conservative, probably the equal of Benjamin Harrison. The country was prosperous and I suspect that he enjoyed the phrase 'Coolidge prosperity' more than any other tag which the newspapers and the public pinned on him. . . . Any summation of Mr. Coolidge's services to the country must conclude that America is a better place for his having lived in it."

Herbert Clark Hoover
The Thirty-first President of the United States
1929–33

1874 (August 10) Born in West Branch, Iowa.

1884 Moved to Oregon to live with relatives after the death of his father (1880) and mother (1883).

1891–95 Attended Stanford University, graduating with an A.B. degree in engineering.

1897–98 Managed gold mining operations in Australia.

1899 (February 10) Married Lou Henry in Monterey, California.

1899–1900 Chief engineer of China's bureau of mines.

1901 General manager of the Chinese Engineering and Mining Company.

1901–8 Partner in a British engineering firm, traveling throughout the world.

1908–14 Headed own engineering firm supervising projects in many countries.

1914–17 Chairman of the Commission for Relief in Belgium.

1917–19 United States Food Administrator.

1921–28 Secretary of Commerce under Harding and Coolidge.

1929–33 Thirty-first President of the United States.

1946–49 Headed various government commissions appointed by President Truman.

1953–55 Headed a commission on reorganization of the federal government, appointed by President Eisenhower.

1964 (October 20) Died in New York City.

N<small>o</small> other President came to the White House with more dazzling visions of achievements and left with more shattered illusions than did Herbert Hoover. It was his first and last elective office—and therein lies one of the major causes for his failure. As former President Taft commented: "Hoover does not speak the language of the politicians . . ."

Hoover's personal story is one of rags to riches, while the history of the nation during his administration was one of riches to rags. The first President born west of the Mississippi River, Hoover was an orphan who became a highly successful mining engineer, and a millionaire by forty.

During and after World War I, Hoover won a reputation as a great humanitarian by his efficient administration of war relief in Europe.

A liberal Republican, he supported Wilson in the 1918 elections, and both Republicans and Democrats began to talk of him as a possible candidate for the presidency. After serving under both Harding and Coolidge as Secretary of Commerce, he won the 1928 presidential election in a campaign that promised "a chicken in every pot and a car in every garage."

When the stock market crashed seven months after he took office in 1929, Hoover was automatically doomed to the same obloquy—or worse—that Van Buren faced in the first national depression nearly a century earlier. By the time he left office the economic life of the country was nearing a standstill and his limited measures to meet the crisis appeared catastrophically inadequate. Eighteen years later he still believed he had followed the right course, writing:

"I am so immodest as to believe that had we been continued in office we would have quickly overcome the depression and approached economic and social problems from the point of view of correcting marginal abuse and not of inflicting a collectivist economy on the country."

A Self-made Engineer

THE SON OF A BLACKSMITH, Herbert Hoover was born in the middle of the horse-and-buggy age August 10, 1874, in West Branch, Iowa. By the time he was eight his father and mother had both died, leaving him, his brother, and his sister to be parceled out among Quaker relatives.

At ten, Herbert was sent to Newberg, Oregon, to live with an aunt and uncle. His uncle was a country doctor who had helped found a Quaker secondary school called Newberg College. Here Herbert received the initial basis of what was to be one of the best formal educations of any President.

At the age of fifteen, he left Newberg College to become a $15-a-month office boy in a real-estate business founded by his uncle in Salem, Oregon. At night he attended a small business college where he learned algebra and geometry. At the real-estate office he met several engineers and fell in love with the profession. Hearing about plans to open a new engineering school, Stanford University in California, Hoover traveled to Portland, Oregon, to take entrance exams. His mathematical talent so impressed the examiners despite the deficiency of his general background that he was recommended for admission.

At Stanford, Hoover worked his own way via a variety of jobs. In addition he took part in many activities—managing the baseball and football teams and taking an active role in student politics on the side of the independents versus the fraternity men. When he graduated in 1895 he had only his degree, $40, and no visible prospects. Unable to find work as an engineer, he took a $2-a-day job as a gold miner's helper in Nevada City, Nevada. When he had saved $100, he decided to go to San Francisco where his brother was working as a linotype operator to support their younger sister. While there he visited the office of Louis Janin, a leading mining engineer, and, when told there were no engineering jobs available, accepted work as a typist. Soon Janin appointed him as an engineering assistant at $150 a month. From that day, as Hoover later wrote, he "never again had to ask for or look for an engineering job of any kind."

At the age of twenty-three, Hoover was hired by a British engineering firm to manage their Australian gold-mining operations. So successful was he that by the time he left two years later he was earning $10,000 a year and was part owner of a profitable gold mine.

In 1899 the Chinese government offered him an appointment as chief engineer of China's bureau of mines. Before going there he returned to the

United States where he married his college sweetheart, Lou Henry. They spent their honeymoon on a steamship bound for China.

The Hoovers were in Tientsin when the Boxer Rebellion broke out in 1900. Hoover directed construction of barricades and assumed charge of the water and food supply of the beleaguered foreign quarter. When the rebellion ended, they sailed for London, but returned to China in 1901. Later that year he accepted a lucrative offer of a partnership in the British engineering firm for which he was working.

The twenty-seven-year-old Hoover and his wife arrived back in London in November 1901. As a 20 percent owner of the reorganized British firm, Hoover was well on his way to becoming wealthy only five years after leaving college. For the next dozen years he traveled to every continent except Antarctica, planning and supervising major engineering projects, making them profitable, and often sharing in their profits. As a hobby during this period, he turned to writing, preparing a textbook called *Principles of Mining*. In addition, he and his wife spent five years producing the first English translation from the Latin of the sixteenth-century classic work on mining, Agricola's *De Re Metallica*.

A Practical Humanitarian

THE GUNS OF WORLD WAR I abruptly ended Hoover's career as an engineer by opening a new one for him as a humanitarian and public servant. In London he organized a committee that helped more than a hundred thousand stranded Americans get back to the United States. That done, he took on an even bigger job—chairman of the Commission for Relief in Belgium. Through this agency he conveyed food and supplies to German-occupied Belgium.

Shortly after the United States declared war on Germany in 1917, President Wilson appointed Hoover as United States Food Administrator. In this job he was responsible for stabilizing food prices and insuring that food be distributed to those who needed it. One of the measures he recommended to hold prices down was the first excess-profits tax. Hoover himself recommended the title "administrator" for the job—creating an important new organizational title in the federal government; previously, boards or commissions had been appointed to handle the work of such independent agencies, but Hoover insisted that he be given power as an individual rather than as chairman of a committee.

When the war was nearing its conclusion in 1918, Hoover became chairman of the Allied Food Council, handling millions of tons of food for civilians in war-ravaged areas. He directed not only relief but reconstruction, and by the time he returned to the United States in 1919 he was hailed as "the great humanitarian" and was regarded as one of the most important living Americans.

Hoover made a number of statesmanlike speeches supporting the League of Nations, and unsuccessfully tried to persuade Wilson that it would be better to accept certain reservations demanded by various senators than to have American participation in the League rejected altogether.

Democrats and Republicans alike began to talk of Hoover as a possible presidential candidate in 1920. However, he quickly made clear that he was a Republican of long standing, although he had supported Theodore Roosevelt in 1912 and had called for the election of a pro-Wilson Congress in 1918. He did not campaign actively for the 1920 Republican presidential nomination, although his name was entered in several primaries as a representative of the progressive wing of the party. After Harding was nominated, Hoover supported him in the belief that Harding would favor American membership in the League of Nations.

Harding first offered Hoover the post of Secretary of the Interior in his Cabinet, but Hoover said he would prefer to be Secretary of Commerce. Although the conservative wing of the party opposed Hoover's appointment, Harding pushed it through, telling Hoover that he had informed the conservatives that they must accept Hoover if they wanted Andrew Mellon named as Secretary of the Treasury.

Hoover was unscathed by the subsequent scandals in the Harding administration and continued to serve as Secretary of Commerce throughout most of Coolidge's administration, even though Coolidge had little regard for him. During his seven and a half years in the Harding and Coolidge Cabinets, Hoover reorganized the Department of Commerce, worked to improve child health and eliminate child labor, helped reduce the working day from twelve to eight hours, and in general supported the cause of social welfare. He also did a great deal to develop dams, flood control, and hydroelectric projects on the river systems of the nation.

After Coolidge issued his equivocal "I do not choose to run" statement in the summer of 1927, hundreds of Hoover's friends urged him to seek the Republican presidential nomination in 1928. When he asked Coolidge if it would be all right to enter some of the Republican primaries, Coolidge replied, "Why not?" By the time the convention met in Kansas City in June, Hoover had more than 400 of the 1,084 delegates pledged to him. Despite a "Stop Hoover" campaign launched by the old guard members of the party, Hoover was nominated on the first ballot with 837 votes. Senator Charles

Curtis of Kansas was given the vice-presidential nomination to mollify the senators and machine politicians who had opposed Hoover.

In the 1928 campaign against Democratic nominee Governor Al Smith of New York, Hoover made only a few speeches, leaving most of the grass-roots campaigning to his supporters. Some of his remarks in these speeches later were to come back to haunt him. For example, of America's economic system he said: "We in America are nearer to the final triumph over poverty than ever before in the history of any land. . . . We have not yet reached the goal, but, given a chance to go forward with the policies of the last eight years, we shall with the help of God be in sight of the day when poverty will be banished from the nation . . ."

The Democrats made the repeal of Prohibition a major issue of the campaign, denouncing it as a law that had not worked. Hoover supported Prohibition and called it "a great social and economic experiment, noble in motive and far-reaching in purpose."

Because Smith was a Catholic, the forces of bigotry, particularly in the South, introduced the issue of religion in the campaign. Hoover denounced the use of religious intolerance by his supporters.

The election results gave Hoover the White House by a landslide. In the popular vote he received 21,391,993 to Smith's 15,016,169, and in the electoral vote he won 444 to 87—the largest electoral vote margin since the election of Grant.

Hoover's Administration

HOOVER'S INAUGURAL ADDRESS reflected the rosy optimism in which America was then bathed. He proposed to pursue the goals of ". . . the preservation of self-government and its full foundations in local government; the perfection of justice whether in economic or in social fields; the maintenance of ordered liberty; the denial of domination by any group or class; the building up and preservation of equality of opportunity; the stimulation of initiative and individuality; absolute integrity in public affairs; the choice of officials for fitness to office; the direction of economic progress toward prosperity and the further lessening of poverty; the freedom of public opinion; the sustaining of education and of the advancement of knowledge; the growth of religious spirit and the tolerance of all faiths; the strengthening of the home; the advancement of peace. . . ." It was a program to put the final finishing touches on a near-perfect society.

Yet, as Hoover wrote later, he recognized that "there was urgent need for reform in our social and business life. . . . Little had been done by the federal government in the fields of reform or progress during the fourteen years before my time. After 1914 the Wilson administration had been absorbed mostly in problems of war. The Harding and Coolidge administrations had been concerned with economic reconstruction after the war. Mr. Coolidge was reluctant to undertake much that either was new or cost money. And by 1929 many things were already fourteen years overdue. . . ." Thus Hoover intended his administration to be a progressive, reform regime.

Totally unforeseen, seven months later the stock market crash of October 1929 turned this dream into a nightmare. At first neither Hoover nor anyone else had any notion of how bad the Great Depression was to be. Very soon more than twelve million Americans were out of work and businesses were going bankrupt by the thousand.

Hoover tried hard to do something about the Depression. Unfortunately, neither he nor his advisers, nor the orthodox economists of the country knew what to do. He launched new public works programs, hoping that the building industry could absorb the unemployed. He also asked for and received from Congress a substantial reduction in income tax rates, hoping this would stimulate the economy. Both were small steps in the right direction. But he opposed direct federal relief to the mass of unemployed, and his Republican Congress in February 1931 had to pass over his veto the Bonus Act giving almost a billion dollars to veterans.

The temper of the country had already been shown in the congressional elections of 1930, the Democrats winning control of the House of Representatives and reducing the Republican majority in the Senate to one vote. But owing to the archaic "lame duck" congressional organization, this Seventy-second Congress did not meet until December 1931. In his message to Congress, Hoover called for the establishment of a Reconstruction Finance Corporation with a "reasonable capital" to aid businesses and home owners with loans. When Congress capitalized the RFC with $2 billion, Hoover vetoed the measure saying that it would make the RFC a "gigantic banking and pawnbroking business." But by July 1932, he signed a new measure enlarging the loan power of the RFC to $3.3 billion.

In the spring of 1932 thousands of World War I veterans marched on Washington as a "Bonus army," and they and their families camped in ramshackle huts on the outskirts of Washington in what was called "Hooverville." When Congress adjourned in July without giving the veterans all that they had asked in bonus payments, they continued to live on in their huts. Late in July, Hoover ordered the army to move the veterans out of Washington, and troops under General Douglas MacArthur herded the veterans and their families out of Washington while the huts were burned.

No one was surprised at the results of the national election in 1932 in which Hoover was defeated for re-election by the Democratic presidential nominee, Franklin Delano Roosevelt, in a landslide of equal proportions to the one by which Hoover had come into office. The country had completely reversed its view of Hoover and was impatient that it had to wait four months until his successor could be inaugurated. This impatience helped bring about the "Lame Duck" Twentieth Amendment to the Constitution that advanced the President's inauguration to January 20 and the opening of the new Congress to January 3. But this amendment did not go into effect until December 1933.

In the months between the election and the inauguration of the new President, Hoover endeavored to obtain the co-operation of the President-elect. But Roosevelt was as cautious as Lincoln had been in a similar situation when Buchanan had urged him to help solve the nation's problems before taking office. The Depression continued to worsen.

Busy Later Years

AFTER LEAVING THE WHITE HOUSE in March 1933, Hoover and his wife retired to their home in Palo Alto, California, near the Stanford University campus. For a while he devoted considerable time to the Hoover Library that he had founded at the university, then he began to take a more active role in national politics again as a critic of President Roosevelt's New Deal programs.

A year after retiring, Hoover published *The Challenge to Liberty* in which he denounced the expansion of government under Roosevelt, saying:

"We cannot extend the mastery of government over the daily life of a people without somewhere making it master of people's souls and thoughts. That is going on today. It is part of all regimentation.

"Even if the government's conduct of business could give us the maximum of efficiency instead of least efficiency, it would be purchased at the cost of freedom. It would increase rather than decrease abuse and corruption, stifle initiative and invention, undermine the development of leadership, cripple the mental and spiritual energies of our people, extinguish equality of opportunity, and dry up the spirit of liberty and the forces which make progress.

"It is a false Liberalism that interprets itself into government dictation, or operation of commerce, industry, and agriculture. Every move in that direction poisons the very springs of true Liberalism. It poisons political equality, free thought, free press, and equality of opportunity. It is the road not to liberty but to less liberty. True Liberalism is found not in striving to spread bureaucracy, but in striving to set bounds to it. Liberalism is a force proceeding from the deep realization that economic freedom cannot be sacrificed if political freedom is to be preserved. True Liberalism seeks all legitimate freedom first in the confident belief that without such freedom the pursuit of other blessings is in vain.

"The nation seeks for solution of its many difficulties. These solutions can come alone through the constructive forces from the system built on Liberty. They cannot be achieved by the destructive forces of Regimentation. The purification of Liberty from abuses, the restoration of confidence in the rights of men, the release of the dynamic forces of initiative and enterprise are alone the methods by which these solutions can be found and the purpose of American life assured."

After his wife's death in 1944, Hoover lived much of his time in an apartment in New York City.

Hoover wrote many books including his own three-volume memoirs. In 1938 he published *The Ordeal of Woodrow Wilson*—the first book by a former President about a President.

President Truman recalled Hoover to public life after World War II. He first served as chairman of the Famine Emergency Commission, an organization to prevent starvation of Europeans in the wake of the war, and in 1947, accepted Truman's appointment as chairman of the Commission on Organization of the Executive Branch of the Government. This group became known as the "Hoover Commission" and recommended many important structural changes in the federal government. President Eisenhower in 1953 appointed Hoover as head of another such commission that recommended further changes in the federal structure.

The ninety-year-old former President died in New York City on October 20, 1964. After funeral ceremonies in New York City and in Washington, D.C., he was buried near his birthplace in West Branch, Iowa. In his memoirs Hoover had summed up his attitude toward the presidency:

"I had felt deeply that no President should undermine the independence of legislative and judicial branches by seeking to discredit them. The constitutional division of powers is the bastion of our liberties and was not designed as a battleground to display the prowess of Presidents. They just have to work with the material that God—and the voters—have given them."

Franklin Delano Roosevelt
The Thirty-second President of the United States
1933–45

1882 (January 30) Born in Hyde Park, New York.

1896–1900 Attended Groton School in Massachusetts.

1900–4 Attended Harvard University, graduating in 1903.

1904–7 Attended Columbia University Law School.

1905 (March 17) Married Eleanor Roosevelt.

1907 Admitted to the bar to practice law.

1911–12 Senator in the state legislature of New York.

1913–20 Assistant Secretary of the Navy under President Wilson.

1920 Ran unsuccessfully as the Democratic nominee for Vice President.

1921 Crippled by an attack of polio.

1929–32 Governor of New York.

1933–45 Thirty-second President of the United States.

1945 (April 12) Died at Warm Springs, Georgia.

With a jaunty smile, a soothing voice, and supreme self-confidence, Franklin D. Roosevelt rallied a fear-ridden nation to overcome the Great Depression, and then mustered the mightiest military host the world had ever seen to free the enslaved people of three continents. Singing his campaign song, "Happy Days Are Here Again," the people of the

United States elected him President four times—a greater honor and trust than ever given any other man.

With his New Deal—a program of social justice more sweeping than ever dreamed of by Theodore Roosevelt or Woodrow Wilson—he brought security to the aged, relief to the unemployed, and shorter hours and higher wages to workingmen. He remade the federal government, adding scores of new agencies and services. And he reshaped the principles of his Democratic party, casting aside the long-standing commitment to states' rights and forcing acceptance of Hamilton's belief in a strong central government.

No obstacle short of death could stop him. At thirty-nine an attack of polio crippled both his legs for life, but this did not deter him from becoming governor of New York and then President. To put through his New Deal he put down conservative businessmen, reactionary senators, and even recalcitrant Supreme Court justices. Foreseeing the inevitable clash of America with the power-mad dictators of Germany, Italy, and Japan, he armed the nation despite the opposition of die-hard isolationists. And, after Japan's sneak attack at Pearl Harbor had shattered the U.S. fleet, he guided the strategy that ultimately brought victory in World War II.

As President, his creed was a simple one. He said he believed that the role of any President was ". . . to preserve under the changing conditions of each generation a people's government for the people's good."

A Wealthy Background

THE ONLY SON OF A RAILROAD EXECUTIVE, Franklin Delano Roosevelt was born on his father's estate in Hyde Park, New York, on January 30, 1882. His mother Sara, who was twenty-six years younger than his father, played a dominant role in his life—still treating him as a small boy even after he had become President.

He never attended an American public school as he was growing up, receiving most of his early education from governesses and tutors. But his education was a broad one, for his family took him on trips to Europe almost every year.

When he was fourteen, young Roosevelt was enrolled at Groton, a private preparatory school in Massachusetts, where he spent four years. Like his cousin Theodore Roosevelt, he attended Harvard University, where he majored in history and received his degree in three years. He then took an additional year of graduate study. But at Harvard he was at least as interested in extra-curricular activities as he was in studies. He led an active social life and felt that one of his greatest accomplishments was becoming editor of the *Harvard Crimson,* the campus newspaper.

While still at Harvard, Roosevelt became engaged to a distant cousin, Eleanor Roosevelt, who was two years younger than himself. Despite mild opposition by his mother, they were married on March 17, 1905. They had six children, one of whom died as a baby. Later, after Roosevelt became President, Eleanor became the most active first lady to that time, making countless trips as her husband's representative, and working to assist the poor and members of minority groups.

Meanwhile, Roosevelt began attending classes at Columbia University Law School. He found the study of law dull, just as Theodore Roosevelt had, and did not graduate, but he learned sufficient law to pass a bar examination in 1907.

When Roosevelt was twenty-eight, he entered politics. Though the famous name he bore was associated with the GOP, his own branch of the family was Democratic. He made a substantial contribution to the Democratic campaign fund in 1910 and was pleasantly surprised when the state convention nominated him as the Democratic candidate for the state senate from Dutchess County. This may have been considered a joke by the machine politicians, because no Democrat had been elected in Dutchess County in half a century. But Roosevelt took it seriously, used an automobile to travel to every rural by-way, and so impressed the farmers with his integrity that he was elected with a majority of more than a thousand votes.

Again emulating his cousin Theodore, Roosevelt led a revolt against the political bosses that dominated the state government. He received some national notice when he and his friends forced the party leaders to dump their choice for U.S. senator and substitute a man with better qualifications. Reelected to the state senate in 1912, he shortly thereafter received an appointment by President Wilson as Assistant Secretary of the Navy. In 1914 he made an unsuccessful attempt to win the Democratic nomination for U.S. senator in New York, but lost to a Tammany-supported candidate. He continued his work in the Navy Department, writing at the height of World War I:

"When the United States entered the war, I found that I would have to decide between doing my bit in keeping the Navy at the highest point of efficiency, and neglecting important work to keep run of matters political. . . . I have literally not given the slightest thought or attention to anything but the work immediately before me since."

Later, after he had become President, Roosevelt recalled an incident from this period of his life in an address he made to midshipmen at Annapolis:

"The only time I disgraced myself was, I think, during the World War. Because of the strenuous work in the Navy Department I was a bit arrears on sleep. On that occasion the temperature in Bancroft Hall was in the neighborhood of a little over a hundred. There I was sitting on the right hand of the Superintendent of the Naval Academy. The speaker of the occasion began his address. My eyes slowly but firmly closed. I think, indeed, that my mouth fell open. I slept ungracefully but soundly, directly in front of the eyes of the entire graduating class. Could anything be more unmilitary, more humiliating, and, at the same time, more completely satisfactory?"

In 1920 the Democratic National Convention met in San Francisco in June and nominated James Cox of Ohio for President and Roosevelt for Vice President. Roosevelt campaigned strenuously, making speeches in almost every state in support of the major campaign issue—the League of Nations. But the Republican ticket of Harding and Coolidge won by a landslide. "I am not really much surprised at the result," Roosevelt wrote, "because I have felt all along that we are in the middle of a kind of tidal flow of discontent and destructive criticism, as a result of the tremendous efforts of the war."

Overcoming a Handicap

In August 1921, the thirty-nine-year-old Roosevelt was vacationing at the family's summer home on Campobello Island, in Canada, when he suffered an attack of poliomyelitis that crippled both his legs. He never again was to regain the use of his legs, but in the following months he learned to get about by the use of crutches, leg braces, and a wheelchair, greatly strengthening his arms and shoulders.

Roosevelt discovered that swimming gave him an opportunity to exercise his legs, and began vacationing at Warm Springs, Georgia, where he could swim in a pool of warm spring water. In 1927 he founded the Georgia Warm Springs Foundation to provide inexpensive treatment for polio victims.

Meanwhile, Roosevelt continued his interest in national politics. He made a dramatic entrance at the Democratic National Convention in New York City's Madison Square Garden in June 1924, where from a wheelchair he rose and walked to the speaker's rostrum on crutches to deliver a nomination speech for Al Smith, whom he called "the 'Happy Warrior' of the political battlefield." Smith did not win the nomination, but the delegates remembered Roosevelt's courage.

Four years later at the 1928 Democratic National Convention in Houston, Texas, Roosevelt again nominated Smith, and this time Smith received the nomination to run against Herbert Hoover. In October the Democratic New York state convention selected Roosevelt to run for governor. Roosevelt campaigned vigorously throughout the state speaking out against the "vile thing" of religious intoleration that had been introduced because of Smith's Roman Catholicism. In the November vote Roosevelt carried the state by a small margin, although Smith lost.

The new governor pushed the legislature to grant tax relief to farm communities in economic difficulty. He also promoted a plan for "old age secured against want," declaring "the first duty of a State, and by that I mean Government, is to promote the welfare of the citizens of that state." Thus Roosevelt already had something of a reputation for social reform when the stock market crashed. Though he had no more inkling than anyone else of the magnitude of the economic disaster, when he was re-elected in the Democratic landslide of 1930 he called the legislature into special session to provide $20 million in relief to the unemployed—the first direct unemployment aid by any state.

When the Democratic National Convention nominated Roosevelt for President in 1932, he dramatically flew to Chicago to become the first nominee ever to deliver his acceptance speech in person. He said, in part, "Never before in modern history have the essential differences between the two major American parties stood out in such striking contrast . . . I pledge you, I pledge myself, to a *new deal* for the American people."

President Hoover, campaigning for re-election, warned that if Roosevelt were elected "the grass will grow in the streets" and "weeds will overrun the fields of millions of farms." But the people blamed the Great Depression on the Republican party and on Hoover, and reacted by electing Roosevelt by a landslide, giving him 22,809,638 popular votes to Hoover's 15,758,901, and 472 electoral votes to 59.

In the interval before taking office, Roosevelt narrowly escaped death when a mentally deranged man fired shots at him in Miami, Florida. His automobile companion, Mayor Anton Cermak of Chicago, was killed.

Roosevelt's First Term

WHEN THE FIFTY-ONE-YEAR-OLD ROOSEVELT took office on March 4, 1933, the nation had never before been in such desperate economic plight. There were millions of unemployed, thousands of farmers with mortgages foreclosed. Thousands of banks had gone bankrupt, and virtually all those still operating were closed by state governors to head off further failures. The nation listened via radio as Roosevelt, a fine speaker, brought an accent of hope to the stricken country.

"This is preeminently the time to speak the truth, the whole truth, frankly and boldly . . .

"First of all, let me assert my firm belief that the only thing we have to fear is fear itself—nameless, unreasoning, unjustified terror which paralyzes needed efforts to convert retreat into advance. In every dark hour of our national life a leadership of frankness and vigor has met with that understanding and support of the people themselves which is essential to victory. I am convinced that you will again give that support to leadership in these critical days. . . .

"The money changers have fled from their high seats in the temple of civilization. We may now restore that temple to the ancient truths. . . . The measure of the restoration lies in the extent to which we apply social values more noble than mere monetary profits. . . .

"Our greatest primary task is to put people to work . . . Finally, in our progress toward a resumption of work we require two safeguards against a return of the evils of the old order; there must be a strict supervision of all banking and credits and investments, so that there will be an end to speculation with other people's money; and there must be provision for an adequate but sound currency. . . .

"I am prepared under my constitutional duty to recommend the measures that a stricken Nation in the midst of a stricken world may require. These measures, or such other measures as the Congress may build out of its experience and wisdom, I shall seek, within my constitutional authority, to bring to speedy adoption. . . .

"But in the event that Congress shall fail to take one of these two courses, and in the event that the national emergency is still critical, I shall not evade the clear course of duty that will then confront me. I shall ask the Congress for the one remaining instrument to meet the crisis—broad Executive power to wage a war against the emergency, as great as the power that would be given to me if we were in fact invaded by a foreign foe. . . .

"We do not distrust the future of essential democracy. The people of the United States have not failed. In their need they have registered a mandate that they want direct, vigorous action. They have asked for discipline and direction under leadership. They have made me the present instrument of their wishes. In the spirit of the gift I take it."

In the next hundred days Roosevelt put the federal government through the greatest upheaval it had ever known in peacetime. He called a special session of Congress to meet on March 9. Meanwhile, on March 6 he declared a national "bank holiday" that closed all the banks in the United States until they could be inspected to insure their soundness. He called a conference of state governors on March 6 and warned them that the federal government would step in to prevent starvation if the local and state governments failed to act. On March 12 he gave the first of his "fireside chat" radio addresses, in which he reassured the nation about the reasons for the bank holiday. On March 13 the banks that were sound were permitted to reopen. The Agricultural Adjustment Act (AAA) was passed to bring the farmers more purchasing power and limit their production of agricultural surpluses. The National Industrial Recovery Act (NIRA) was an ambitious attempt to regulate business. The Tennessee Valley Authority (TVA) was created to develop the hydroelectric resources of the destitute Tennessee valley. Home Owners Loan Corporation (HOLC) provided assistance to home owners threatened with foreclosures. By executive order Roosevelt took the country off the gold standard to preserve its gold reserves. A Federal Emergency Relief Administration was set up with Harry Hopkins as administrator to make direct grants to states for relief to the unemployed. The Civilian Conservation Corps (CCC) was organized to provide work for unemployed youth. At the conclusion of the congressional session in June, Roosevelt wrote:

"I am certain that this Special Session of Congress will go down in the history of our country as one which, more than any other, boldly seized the opportunity to right great wrongs, to restore clearer thinking and more honest practices, to carry through its business with practical celerity and to set our feet on the upward path."

In the field of foreign relations, Roosevelt restored diplomatic relations with Russia that had been broken off since the Russian Revolution.

In the succeeding years of his first term Roosevelt led Congress in developing many other new agencies of the federal government, including the Federal Communications Commission, the Securities Exchange Commission, the Federal Housing Administration, a National Resources Board, and the Rural Electrification Administration. In 1935, at Roosevelt's urging, Congress passed social security measures to provide old age pensions, unemployment insurance, aid to dependent children, and health services.

The proliferation of government agencies during Roosevelt's administration caused him greatly to expand the White House office space, largely by the expedient of building offices underground. In addition, a White House swimming pool was constructed so that the polio-crippled President could exercise by swimming.

Roosevelt relished the discomfiture that his programs for the poor were causing the wealthy and privileged, and in a letter to a friend told of an incident that supposedly had occurred in the Rittenhouse Club in Philadelphia while he was making a radio address in Atlanta in 1935:

"Four gentlemen sipping their drinks in comfortable armchairs in the Rittenhouse Club were going through the usual motions of damning Roosevelt and all his works—the vice president of the Pennsylvania Railroad, the president of a trust company, a retired millionaire art collector, and the head of a great oil company. The knocking party went on for some time when one of the four finished his drink, rose, walked over to the mahogany encased radio, and turned it on. Out came that well-known voice—the voice that Wall Street uses to inculcate fear in the breasts of their little grandchildren—and the voice said, 'I am thinking in connection with the care of our poor and hungry. I wonder what is being said by my rich friends in their over-stuffed armchairs in their well-stocked clubs.' All four in the Rittenhouse recoiled—and one of them, finding his voice, exclaimed: 'My God, do you suppose that blankety blank could have overheard us?' "

In 1936 Roosevelt was re-elected to a second term, defeating the Republican candidate, Governor Alfred M. Landon of Kansas, in a landslide giving him a higher percentage of the popular and electoral votes than he had received four years earlier. The popular vote gave him 27,752,869 to Landon's 16,674,665. The electoral vote was 523 to 8, Landon carrying only Maine and Vermont.

Roosevelt's Second Term

In his second inaugural address, on January 20, 1937, Roosevelt frankly admitted that the nation had not yet reached the "happy valley" that he envisioned at the beginning of his first term. But he pledged himself to continue to work to relieve the poverty of "one third of a nation ill-housed, ill-clad, ill-nourished."

Starting in 1935 the Supreme Court of the United States had been causing trouble for Roosevelt's New Deal by declaring such important pieces of legislation as the NIRA and the AAA unconstitutional. Most of the justices of the Supreme Court were conservatives who had been appointed by Presidents Taft, Harding, Coolidge, and Hoover—six of the nine justices were over seventy years old. Roosevelt proposed legislation to require retirement by justices at the age of seventy, declaring that he wanted "a modernized judiciary that would look at modern problems through modern glasses." When Congress balked at Roosevelt's plan, calling it an effort to "pack the Supreme Court," Roosevelt made a new "fireside chat" defending the need for changing the personnel of the Court.

Suddenly, without any court reform legislation having been passed, the Supreme Court took on a more liberal tone, upholding the right of states to fix a minimum wage, and reporting that the federal social security laws were constitutional under the "general welfare" clause. As time wore on and death intervened among the members of the Court, Roosevelt had the opportunity to appoint a new Chief Justice and eight associate justices, all of a more liberal background.

But meantime the historical focus was shifting to the war clouds in Europe. The Axis powers of Germany, Italy, and Japan grew stronger and more aggressive during the late 1930s, attacking and conquering one weak neighbor after another. Roosevelt warned Hitler and Mussolini that if they started a general war, history would "hold them accountable." At Roosevelt's urging, Congress revised the nation's neutrality laws in 1939 to make it possible for the United States to sell supplies to friendly nations fighting the Axis powers.

When Hitler's army marched into Poland in September 1939, starting World War II, Roosevelt addressed the nation in a fireside chat: ". . . I have said not once, but many times, that I have seen war and that I hate war. I say that again and again. I *hope* that the United States will keep out of this war. I *believe* that it will. And I give you assurance and reassurance that every effort of your Government will be directed toward that end." Nevertheless, it was at Roosevelt's request that Congress revised neutrality laws to permit sale of arms to the Western Allies.

The following year the Democratic Convention met at the moment of France's fall, with Britain standing alone and beleaguered, and the Nazi peril at its flood height. Despite a formal disclaimer of third-term ambitions, Roosevelt was renominated unanimously. The Republicans nominated a political newcomer, Wendell L. Willkie of Indiana.

The campaign was carried on before the darkening backdrop of the war in Europe. In September, Roosevelt negotiated a deal with Britain whereby fifty old U.S. destroyers were lent to the British in return for naval bases on British West Indies islands. He lashed out strongly at the Republican party, which he said had obstructed his attempts to strengthen the military defense of the United States. In the election he again won by a large majority, though not as large as before: 27,307,819 votes to Willkie's 22,321,018, and 449 electoral votes to 82.

In his State of the Union message to Congress in January 1941, Roosevelt said:

"In the future days, which we seek to make secure, we look forward to a world founded upon four essential human freedoms.

"The first is freedom of speech and expression—everywhere in the world.

"The second is freedom of every person to worship God in his own way—everywhere in the world.

"The third is freedom from want—which, translated into world terms, means economic understanding which will secure to every nation a healthy peacetime life for its inhabitants—everywhere in the world.

"The fourth is freedom from fear—which, translated into world terms, means a world-wide reduction of armaments to such a point and in such a thorough fashion that no nation will be in a position to commit an act of physical aggression against any neighbor—anywhere in the world."

Roosevelt's Third and Fourth Terms

IN AUGUST 1941, Roosevelt met with Prime Minister Winston Churchill aboard a cruiser in the North Atlantic to draft a document subsequently called the "Atlantic Charter," which set forth an eight-point agreement on the common principles which they believed should be part of any future peace.

The United States had cut off trade with Japan because of repeated Japanese aggression in Southeast Asia. Relations soon became tense. In December 1941, a special Japanese envoy had arrived in Washington to confer with the American government. On December 7, without warning, the Japanese bombed Pearl Harbor, the U. S. Navy base in Hawaii, and launched an attack on the Philippines. Calling this "a date which will live in infamy," Roosevelt asked Congress for a declaration of war against Japan. A few days later war was declared between the United States and Germany and Italy.

Under Roosevelt's leadership the country went all out for victory, with rigid controls on prices and wages, hundreds of billions in appropriations, massive conscription of manpower. Censorship was imposed. All strikes and lockouts were forbidden. One major effort was successfully concealed from the general public and the enemy: the development of the atomic bomb.

On New Year's Day, 1942, twenty-six countries subscribed to the principles of the Atlantic Charter and agreed to fight until victory could be won over the Axis powers. At Roosevelt's suggestion the Allies called themselves the "United Nations." This formed the basis for the UN organization created at the end of the war.

During the course of the war Roosevelt conferred several times with Churchill and other allied leaders, planning the grand strategy of the war. After such a conference in Casablanca, Morocco, in 1943, he and Churchill announced that the war would be waged until the Axis had been forced to an unconditional surrender.

By 1943 more than ten million Americans had been inducted into the armed forces, and the Allies had begun to push back the Axis powers. At a press conference late in the year Roosevelt acknowledged that the New Deal had been ended by the war. But he hastened to add, ". . . it seems pretty clear that we must plan for, and help bring about, an expanded economy which will result in more security, more employment, more recreation, for our citizens so that the conditions of 1932 and the beginning of 1933 won't come back."

Allied troops under General Dwight Eisenhower invaded France in June 1944. That same month the Republican National Convention met and nominated Thomas E. Dewey as its candidate for President. In July, Roosevelt announced, "If the Convention should . . . nominate me for the Presidency, I shall accept. If the people elect me, I will serve." Again Roosevelt, this time with Harry S Truman, senator from Missouri, as his running mate, won by a large majority, although by a smaller margin than in his three previous elections. He received 25,606,585 votes to Dewey's 22,014,745, and 432 electoral votes to 99.

In his fourth inaugural address in January 1945, Roosevelt declared, "We can gain no lasting peace if we approach it with suspicion and mistrust—or with fear. We can gain it only if we proceed with the understanding and the confidence and courage which flow from conviction."

In February 1945, Roosevelt traveled to Yalta in southwestern Russia to discuss plans for peace with Churchill and Joseph Stalin, the dictator of Russia. He reported to Congress that plans had been agreed to for an organizational meeting of the United Nations on April 25, 1945. He said, "There, we all hope, and confidently expect, to execute a definite charter of organization under which the peace of the world will be preserved and the forces of aggression permanently outlawed. . . . No one can say exactly how long any plan will last. Peace can endure only so long as humanity really insists upon it, and is willing to work for it—and sacrifice for it."

Upon his return from Yalta, Roosevelt looked tired and older than his sixty-three years. Late in March he went to Warm Springs, Georgia, for a rest. On April 12, 1945, he was working at his desk while an artist painted his portrait when he suddenly complained of "a terrific headache." A few hours later, at 4:45 P.M., he died of a cerebral hemorrhage. After services in Washington, his body was buried at his birthplace in Hyde Park. The last words that he had written on the day of his death were:

"The only limit to our realization of tomorrow will be our doubts of today. Let us move forward with strong and active faith."

Harry S Truman
The Thirty-third President of the United States
1945–53

1884 (May 8) Born in Lamar, Missouri.

1890–1901 Attended public school in Independence, Missouri.

1906–17 Farmed near Grandview, Missouri.

1917–19 Commanded an artillery battery in World War I, rising to rank of major.

1919 (June 28) Married Elizabeth "Bess" Wallace.

1919–22 Partner in men's clothing store in Kansas City.

1923–24 County judge of Jackson County, Missouri.

1927–34 Presiding judge of Jackson County.

1935–45 U.S. senator from Missouri.

1945 Vice President of the United States.

1945–53 Thirty-third President of the United States.

1972 (December 26) Died in Kansas City, Missouri.

The first President to take office in the midst of a war, Harry S Truman said at the time that he felt "like the moon, the stars and all the planets had fallen on me." The nation and the world wondered if he was a big enough man to fill Roosevelt's shoes. His background and even his appearance were unpromising. He was the first President in fifty years without a college education. He spoke the language of a Missouri dirt farmer and World War I artilleryman—both of which he had been. Instead of looking like a statesman, he looked like a bank clerk or haberdasher—both of which he also had been. And, worst of all, everyone knew that for more than twenty years he had been a lieutenant of Tom Pendergast, one of the most corrupt political bosses in the country.

What most people didn't know was that he was an unswervingly honest man who knew his own mind and one of the most knowledgeable students of history ever to enter the White House. He understood the powers of the President, and he knew why some men had been strong Chief Executives and others had been weak ones.

He ordered the atomic bomb dropped because he was sure it would save American lives and end World War II quickly. It did not bother him in later years that intellectuals questioned whether one man should have made such an awesome decision. He knew he had been right.

When World War II had been won, Truman helped shift the nation smoothly from a war footing to a peacetime economy—the first time in its history that the United States did not suffer a depression as an aftermath of war. When the former New Dealers in his Cabinet sneered at him, Truman fired them, so the liberals decided he was too conservative. When he called for extended social welfare and sweeping civil rights measures in his domestic Fair Deal program, southern Democrats and conservative Republicans fought him because he was too liberal.

Despite opposition by isolationists who felt the United States should bring home all its troops and forget the problems of the war-torn countries, Truman upheld America's newly won responsibilities as the world's most powerful nation. He brought to fruition Wilson's dream of bringing the United States into a world peace-keeping organization—the United Nations. He helped rebuild Europe. And he launched a gigantic foreign-aid program in which the United States underwrote the cost of helping underprivileged nations improve themselves.

When communist Russia and communist China challenged America in the Cold War, Truman held them back with the stubbornness of a Missouri mule. To prevent the Russians from overrunning Europe, he helped organize the North Atlantic Treaty Organization with troops of the United States and Western Europe under a unified command. On the other side of the world, when communist troops invaded South Korea, Truman instantly dispatched American armed forces to repel the aggressors.

Despite his accomplishments on the world scene, Truman had made so many enemies at home among New Dealers, southern Democrats, conservative Republicans, and liberal intellectuals, that when he ran for a second term in 1948 everyone expected him to be defeated. But the common people trusted Truman, ignored the political prophets, and gave him a substantial victory.

"I wasn't one of the great Presidents," Truman said after leaving the White House, "but I had a good time trying to be one, I can tell you that." Winston Churchill went much further, declaring to Truman:

"You, more than any other man, have saved Western civilization."

Farmer, Soldier, and Storekeeper

THE SON OF A MULE-TRADER, Harry S Truman was born in a small house in Lamar, Missouri, on May 8, 1884. Because his family could not agree on a middle name for him, his middle initial "S" does not stand for a name. Mule-trading was not a particularly prosperous business, so the Trumans moved about to various Missouri towns until settling down in Independence when Harry was six.

Before he started school at eight, Harry had been outfitted with thick-lensed glasses because of an eye condition called hyperopia. Because of his glasses, the boy was excluded from much of the rough-and-tumble play of his friends and spent a good deal of his time reading the Bible, biographies, and history. He also took piano lessons.

At sixteen he had his first experience with politics when he obtained a job as a page at the Democratic National Convention held in Kansas City in 1900. He was particularly impressed at hearing William Jennings Bryan speak. The next year he was graduated from high school in a ceremony in which his friend Charlie Ross was the class valedictorian.

Because his father had had business reverses, Harry had to go to work to help support his younger brother and sister. He worked for about a year as a timekeeper with a railroad work gang, then obtained a $7-a-week job in the mailroom of the Kansas City *Star*. Next, he became a bank clerk, then a bookkeeper. For a time he roomed in a boardinghouse with a fellow bank clerk named Arthur Eisenhower who had a younger brother named Dwight.

In 1906, when Truman was twenty-two, his father asked him to come to Grandview, Missouri, and run his grandmother's 600-acre farm. For the next eleven years he lived the life of a dirt farmer, raising corn, hogs, and cattle— which he did with success.

His father died in 1914, and Harry was named to succeed him in a minor political job, that of road overseer in Jackson County. The next year he was appointed postmaster of Grandview, and began going into Kansas City regularly to attend meetings of a Democratic political club that was part of the party machine of the city's boss, T. J. Pendergast.

Shortly after the United States entered World War I in 1917, Truman joined a National Guard artillery company as a lieutenant. In August it was taken into the Regular Army as the 129th Field Artillery of the 35th Division. While the troops trained at Fort Sill, Oklahoma, Truman acted as canteen officer. Under his management the post store earned a profit of $15,000 in six months.

Truman landed in France in April 1918. A few weeks later he was promoted to captain, and in July was given command of Battery D of the Second Battalion of the 129th. He first saw action in September when his battery laid down a barrage of gas shells on the German lines in the Vosges Mountains. Later in the same month he and his men took part in the heavy fighting in the Argonne Forest. In October, Truman and his artillery battery advanced with the 35th Division on Verdun—he was firing on the German-held city of Metz when the war ended in November. Truman arrived back in the United States in the spring of 1919, and after being promoted to the rank of major was mustered out of the army in May.

The thirty-five-year-old Truman gave up bachelorhood on June 28, 1919, when he married Elizabeth "Bess" Wallace, an Independence, Missouri, girl who had gone through school with him from fifth grade and to whom he had become engaged shortly before joining the army. He and his wife lived at his mother-in-law's home in Independence, while he and an army friend opened a men's clothing store in Kansas City. At first the store prospered, but as farm prices fell during the Harding administration business slacked off. He and his partner finally had to close the store in 1922, Truman losing about $30,000. It took him more than fifteen years to pay off his debts, but he refused to declare himself bankrupt.

Local Politician, Senator, and Vice President

TRUMAN DECIDED IN 1922 to make politics his career. With the help of his wartime buddies and the Pendergast political machine, he was elected one of the three "judges" of Jackson County—the county that includes Kansas City and Independence. Despite its title, the position was nonjudicial and was largely concerned with road and bridge building and maintenance. During the two years he was in this office, Truman decided to improve his education and attended night classes at the Kansas City Law School, but did not attain a law degree.

Two major events took place in 1924. His only child, a daughter named Mary Margaret, was born. And he was defeated for re-election, largely because of the opposition of the Ku Klux Klan, which mistakenly believed he was part-Jewish because one of his grandfathers was named Solomon Young. For the next two years he earned a living in a variety of jobs, from selling auto-club memberships to being a partner in a small bank that failed.

In 1926 Truman was elected presiding judge of Jackson County—a position that controlled hundreds of patronage jobs important to the Pendergast machine. He held this office for eight years, winning re-election in 1930, and during this time controlled public works projects totaling more than $50 million—which involved a sizable amount of concrete bought from Tom Pendergast's Ready Mixed Concrete Company. But despite the well-merited reputation of the Pendergast machine, no suspicion of dishonesty ever fell on Truman.

In 1934 Pendergast was having trouble with his own machine as well as with rival factions in the Missouri Democratic party. Desperate for a candidate for the U. S. Senate, he finally hit on the obscure Truman, who surprisingly won a three-cornered race for the Democratic nomination in August, and went on to capture the Senate seat in November with a plurality of more than 260,000 votes. With astounding suddenness, fifty-year-old Harry Truman was launched in big-time politics.

One of thirteen new Democratic senators who took office in January 1935, he soon became a good friend of Vice President John Nance Garner and frequently was chosen by Garner to stand in for him in presiding over the Senate. Truman voted consistently for Roosevelt's New Deal program and made a bit of a name for himself by conducting subcommittee hearings of the Senate Interstate Commerce Committee, looking into dubious practices in railroad financing. Truman was genuinely shocked in 1939 when political boss Tom Pendergast was indicted for bribery, pleaded guilty, and was sent to prison, leaving the machine in the hands of his nephew Jim Pendergast.

When Truman ran for re-election for senator in 1940, the feeling was that with the Pendergast power broken he stood little chance. Once more he proved a skillful and indefatigable campaigner, battling two strong rivals in the primary: Lloyd Stark, the governor, and Maurice Milligan, the U.S. attorney who had prosecuted Pendergast. Truman won the primary by the narrow plurality of 8,000 votes. In the fall election he defeated his Republican opponent with a plurality of nearly 45,000 votes, even though the Republicans captured the governorship.

During his second term as senator, Truman became nationally prominent as chairman of a committee that investigated war profiteering. By the end of the war Truman estimated that the work of this committee had saved the government about $15 billion. In the spring of 1944 a survey of Washington newspapermen showed that they regarded Truman second only to Roosevelt as the man in government who had contributed most to the successful prosecution of the war.

As the Democratic National Convention of 1944 approached, Truman's name was repeatedly mentioned as a possible running mate for Roosevelt in place of Henry Wallace, who had alienated party leaders by his too exuberant liberalism. Democratic National Committee Chairman Robert Hannegan, a St. Louis political leader, persuaded Roosevelt to designate Truman as his choice. Truman, heading the Missouri delegation to the convention, believed that Senator James F. Byrnes of South Carolina was the President's choice and had even agreed to make the nomination speech for Byrnes. Hannegan persuaded Byrnes to withdraw and convinced Truman that Roosevelt really wanted him. When the convention began to vote for its vice-presidential choice, Henry Wallace led Truman on the first ballot by more than a hundred votes. On the second ballot Truman was nominated.

After Roosevelt's fourth-term victory over Thomas E. Dewey, the sixty-year-old Truman was sworn in as Vice President on January 20, 1945. During the subsequent eighty-two days that Truman was Vice President, he met with the Cabinet a few times and had a half dozen conversations with the President, but he was not filled in on many details of Roosevelt's problems largely because the President was not in Washington most of the period.

Truman's First Term

TRUMAN HAD JUST FINISHED presiding over a session of the Senate on April 12, 1945, when he received a phone call from the White House asking him to come at once. When he reached there at 5:25 P.M., Mrs. Roosevelt greeted him with the words, "Harry, the President is dead." By shortly after seven o'clock most of the members of the Cabinet had been assembled, and Truman was sworn in as President by Chief Justice Harlan Stone.

The swearing-in ceremony had hardly been completed when he was asked to make his first presidential decision. Would the organizational meeting of the United Nations still be held in San Francisco as planned on April 25? Yes, came the answer. "I did not hesitate a second," he explained later. "It was of supreme importance that we build an organization to help keep the future peace of the world."

Truman had been President only twenty-five days when Germany surrendered, and he was able to proclaim his sixty-first birthday, May 8, as Victory-in-Europe Day. In June the United Nations Charter was agreed to and Truman flew to San Francisco to give the delegates his personal congratulations.

Early in July he sailed for Europe aboard the cruiser U.S.S. *Augusta* to meet with Churchill and Stalin at Potsdam, Germany.

At the Potsdam conference, the five-foot-ten-inch Truman was surprised to find that both Churchill and Stalin were shorter than he was, and that they preferred to stand a step higher when having their pictures taken with him. The conference lasted from the middle of July into early August. Terms for the occupation of Germany were agreed upon and an ultimatum was sent to Japan calling for that country's unconditional surrender. During the meeting, Churchill's conservative party was defeated in a general election in Great Britain, and he was replaced by Prime Minister Clement Attlee.

While at Potsdam, Truman had received word of the first successful atomic bomb test and had authorized its use against Japan to hasten the end of the war. On his way home across the Atlantic, he was informed that the first A-bomb had been dropped on Hiroshima with devastating results on August 6. Three days later a second A-bomb was dropped on Nagasaki. On August 14 Japan surrendered.

With the end of World War II, Truman now turned his attention to the problems of converting the American economy to a peacetime status. On September 6, he sent Congress a twenty-one-point message outlining his Fair Deal program. He said later this date "symbolizes for me my assumption of the office of President in my own right." The heart of the message was the request for legislation to ensure full employment for all Americans regardless of race, religion, or color. In December, the President called for an extension of his powers to regulate prices and rents in peacetime to prevent a runaway inflation. Truman vetoed the first legislation passed by Congress to extend these controls, declaring that it was worse than no bill at all. On June 30, 1946, price controls expired, and in the next two weeks prices zoomed upward 25 percent. Congress finally acted and on July 25, 1946, Truman signed new price controls into law. Meanwhile, Congress had passed in February 1946 the full-employment act that Truman had requested.

Although Truman intended to carry out Roosevelt's policies, he was determined to be President in his own right. He had replaced most of Roosevelt's Cabinet with men of his own choosing by the end of 1945. Then in 1946 he fired both Harold Ickes and Henry Wallace from their Cabinet posts.

The labor unions demanded that government controls on wages be lifted, and an epidemic of strikes broke out across the country in late 1945 and 1946. When railroad unions called a strike in May 1946, Truman seized the railroads in the name of the government. Then he went before Congress and asked for legislation to draft the workers into the army so they could be made to go back to work. Just as he was concluding his address, the unions capitulated and returned to their jobs. When coal miners called a national strike,

Truman took over the mines and operated them under the Department of the Interior.

In the congressional elections in November 1946, the Republicans won control of both houses of Congress. This Eightieth Congress devoted much of its time to harassing and trying to embarrass Truman. Its investigative subcommittees sought "scandals" to prove that the President's appointees were corrupt, and it passed scores of conservative laws that Truman vetoed. Over Truman's veto, Congress passed a tax reduction bill for persons with incomes over $5,000, and followed this with the Taft-Hartley Labor Act, also passed over his veto, which placed stringent curbs on the rights of labor unions.

In the area of foreign policy, the Soviet Union had repeatedly gone back on its agreements made at Yalta and Potsdam, making it clear that the communists intended to try to rule the world. To combat Russia, the President announced the "Truman Doctrine" in a speech to Congress in March 1947. He said: "I believe that it must be the policy of the United States to support free peoples who are resisting attempted subjugation by armed minorities or by outside pressures." Congress responded to his call and voted money that was used to save Greece and Turkey from being taken over by the Communists.

In June 1947, Secretary of State George Marshall in a speech at Harvard announced plans to extend the Truman Doctrine to reconstruct war-torn Europe. The following March, Congress approved the multi-billion-dollar Marshall Plan.

Truman brought consternation to the ranks of southern Democrats when, in February 1948, he sent a message to Congress calling for a ten-point civil rights program to end religious and racial discrimination.

When the British ended their World War I mandate over Palestine in May 1948, Truman immediately recognized the sovereignty of the new Israeli government over the objections of Secretary of State Marshall, who feared the action would cause Arab enmity.

Just before the 1948 national political conventions, Truman went on a cross-country speaking tour in which he made dozens of off-the-cuff speeches denouncing the Republican Congress. Shortly after he returned to Washington late in June, he was faced with a major international crisis. The Russians had cut off all ground transportation to Berlin and seemed to be on the point of trying to push American forces out of the former German capital. Truman was determined to resist the Russian intimidation, ordering the Air Force to break the blockade with the "Berlin Airlift." This round-the-clock air supply continued for the next eleven months, until the Russians backed down.

In the spring of 1948 Truman's domestic political fortunes appeared to be at a low ebb. The polls showed his popular support to be so poor that many Democrats talked of drafting General Eisenhower as their party's candidate. Southern Democrats threatened to bolt the party over civil rights, and former Vice President Wallace's ultra-liberal following planned a third-party ticket. Despite the formidable odds, Truman resolved to run for re-election. He picked Senator Alben Barkley of Kentucky, veteran majority leader of the Senate, as his running mate and roused the delegates at Philadelphia with a fighting speech.

The Republicans, confident of victory though harmed somewhat by their own intra-party conflicts, united behind Governor Thomas E. Dewey of New York, who had run vigorously against Roosevelt in 1944. The threatened defections on both the right and left of the Democratic party materialized in the form of the "Dixiecrat" candidacy of Governor Strom Thurmond of South Carolina and the "Progressive" candidacy of Henry Wallace.

In an ingenious piece of campaign strategy, Truman outraged the Republicans by calling a special session of Congress on July 26, immediately after the conventions, challenging the GOP to carry out its platform promises to pass expanded social legislation. When the session adjourned after eleven days without passing any of the legislation, Truman could effectively claim that the Republicans were not serious about their platform promises.

Public opinion polls, newspapers, and magazines almost unanimously predicted Truman's defeat. Undaunted, Truman set out on a "whistle-stop" campaign that ran from Labor Day to Election Day, traveling thousands of miles by train and making hundreds of speeches before large and small crowds. He addressed himself to the common people, tirelessly denouncing the "do-nothing" Republican Eightieth Congress. His homey appearance— Bess and Margaret accompanied him—and his sincerity and seriousness won the crowds. "Give 'em hell, Harry!" the crowds shouted.

Yet so certain were the experts of the outcome that when the first count of returns showed Truman leading, political commentators shrugged it off, and maintained that Dewey was bound to win. But the pattern of the astounding upset continued throughout the night, and Dewey finally conceded defeat at eleven o'clock the next morning. The jubilant Truman returned to Washington from his Independence home happily waving to crowds a copy of the Republican Chicago *Tribune* that carried the banner: DEWEY DEFEATS TRUMAN. The final count gave Truman 303 electoral votes and 24,105,812 popular votes to Dewey's 189 and 21,970,065; Thurmond's 39 and 1,169,063; and Wallace's 0 and 1,157,172.

Truman's Second Term

IN HIS INAUGURAL ADDRESS on January 20, 1949, Truman announced a significant new concept in foreign relations. This was "Point Four" in his listing of foreign policy aims, which he described as "a bold new program for making the benefits of our scientific advances and industrial progress available for the improvement and growth of underdeveloped areas." A year later Congress approved $25 million to start this program.

Of perhaps greater immediate importance was the signing of the treaty for the North Atlantic Treaty Organization (NATO) that took place in Washington on April 4, 1949. The Russians still were blockading Berlin, and the threat of war hung over Europe. NATO joined the United States with Great Britain, France, Canada, and eight other nations in a mutual defense agreement with a single commander in charge of military units of all twelve nations. General Eisenhower was named as the first NATO commander.

Although the Democrats had won control of Congress in the 1948 election, Truman soon discovered that he still could not get his Fair Deal legislation past the coalition of conservative southern Democrats and Republicans. Only one major part of his program was approved in 1949, a public housing act.

President Truman in 1947 added a balcony on the south portico of the White House to shade the windows of the Blue Room. But he had little time to enjoy it. When a leg of Margaret Truman's piano forced the floor beneath it to give way, an inspection revealed that rotted wooden timbers throughout the building left it in imminent danger of collapse. The Trumans moved across the street to Blair House, and a massive renovation of the Executive Mansion was undertaken. In the three-year project, the entire interior was torn out and replaced by a concrete and steel framework. New basements and sub-basements were dug to provide additional office space.

During this time an attempt on Truman's life was made. On November 1, 1950, two fanatical Puerto Rican nationalists tried to shoot their way into Blair House. One of the assassins and a Secret Service agent were killed. The President was not harmed.

Truman's enormous energy enabled him to work harder than had many earlier Presidents. He retained the early rising habits of a dirt farmer, usually getting up at 5:30 A.M. and going for a walk of a mile or two, followed by a short swim before breakfast. Newspaper reporters often joined him in these early morning walks and had to trot to keep up with his fast pace.

Although Truman pushed for international control of atomic energy, the

Russians thwarted any effective agreement. After Russia exploded its first A-bomb in September 1949, Truman authorized the development of the larger and more awesome hydrogen bomb—the first of which was tested late in his administration in November 1952.

Truman's worst set-back in foreign relations was the loss of China to communism. Missions headed by General Marshall and General Wedemeyer failed to prevent a civil war in which the Nationalist side, headed by Generalissimo Chiang Kai-shek, and backed by the United States, was defeated. Late in 1949, Chiang fled to Formosa (now called Taiwan), and the Communists triumphantly held all the Chinese mainland.

Fear of communist subversion in the United States was whipped to a hysterical pitch by congressional investigations throughout Truman's administration. Two of the most prominent figures in these investigations were Representative Richard Nixon of California and Senator Joseph McCarthy of Wisconsin. In 1950, Alger Hiss, a former State Department official under Roosevelt and Truman, was convicted of perjury for denying that he had been part of a communist spy ring in the 1930s. In the 1950s McCarthy claimed that there were more than two hundred communists working in the State Department and that Secretary of State Dean Acheson was "soft on Communism." In the general hysteria of the period persons merely suspected of having once attended a communist meeting were fired by their employers and blacklisted to prevent their obtaining new jobs. Congressional committees jailed witnesses who refused to testify against their friends. Truman denounced McCarthyism, but it remained an important issue.

In June 1950, Truman was faced with what he later said was the most difficult decision of his presidency. On June 25, communist North Korean troops invaded American-supported South Korea. After the United Nations Security Council—with Russia absent—denounced the North Koreans as aggressors and called on UN members to send aid to South Korea, Truman on June 28 ordered U.S. armed forces into action. The fighting was to last more than three years, and more than 54,000 American servicemen were to die in the struggle. When UN forces under the command of General Douglas MacArthur were on the point of winning the war in October 1950, powerful Chinese communist forces entered the conflict on the side of the North Koreans and inflicted a serious defeat on the UN Army. In the succeeding months MacArthur repeatedly disagreed with the Truman administration's policy of not widening the war to include fighting in China. His patience worn thin, Truman finally relieved MacArthur of his command on April 11, 1951.

On the home front, the Korean War caused a fresh burst of inflation before Congress voted powers to reinstitute price and wage controls. In April

1952, after wage negotiations between steelworkers and steel mill owners had broken down, Truman seized the steel industry. In June the Supreme Court ruled that the seizure was unconstitutional. A seven-week strike resulted before settlement was reached.

In the spring of 1952 Truman announced that he would not run for re-election. The Republican Congress had approved the Twenty-second Constitutional Amendment limiting the President to two full terms, but this amendment, which had been written largely in vindictiveness against Roosevelt's four terms, did not apply to Truman, who had less than two full terms. The President chose as his successor Governor Adlai Stevenson of Illinois. He helped Stevenson obtain the nomination, but was disappointed when Stevenson seemed deliberately to refuse to defend Truman's record in the campaign.

The Republicans nominated General Eisenhower and campaigned on issues that included the Korean War, the graft scandals in which some Truman subordinates had been involved, and accusations that the Truman administration was "soft on communists in government." When Eisenhower won by a large majority, Truman expressed some personal regrets that he had decided not to run for re-election.

Home in Independence

AFTER EISENHOWER'S INAUGURATION, Truman returned to his home in Independence. For the next several years he devoted considerable time to writing the two-volume memoirs of his presidency, *Year of Decisions*, published in 1955, and *Years of Trial and Hope*, published in 1956. The Harry S Truman Library, dedicated in Independence in 1957, was built by contributions of his friends to house his presidential papers and provide office space for the former President.

In 1960 the seventy-six-year-old Truman gave a series of lectures to Columbia University students, elucidating the problems of his presidency. These lectures were later published under the title *Truman Speaks*. In them he especially denounced the Twenty-second Amendment, which he said "made a lame duck" out of every President serving a second term. He recalled that the amendment could not apply to him, and jokingly announced that: "I'm going to run again when I'm ninety."

He was pleased when the Democrats returned to power under President John F. Kennedy in 1961, and were continued in power with President Lyndon Johnson's election in 1964. He was particularly honored when President Johnson flew to Independence to sign into law the Medicare Act providing medical assistance for the aged—legislation that first had been proposed as part of Truman's Fair Deal.

At the age of eighty-eight Truman died, on December 26, 1972, at the Research Hospital and Medical Center in Kansas City, Missouri, where for twenty-two days he had been fighting for his life against a respiratory infection and failing body systems. After a simple funeral attended mostly by family and old friends, the former President's body was buried in the courtyard of the Truman Library in Independence, Missouri.

Former President Lyndon B. Johnson, who himself was to die less than a month later, said at Truman's death: "A twentieth-century giant is gone. Few men of any times ever shaped the world as did the man from Independence." President Nixon said: "Our hopes today for a generation of peace rest in large measure on the firm foundation that he laid."

Truman himself had this to say of the presidency in his *Memoirs:*

"The presidency of the United States carries with it a responsibility so personal as to be without parallel.

"Very few are ever authorized to speak for the President. No one can make decisions for him. No one can know all the processes and stages of his thinking in making important decisions. Even those closest to him, even members of his immediate family, never know all the reasons why he does certain things and why he comes to certain conclusions. To be President of the United States is to be lonely, very lonely at times of great decisions."

Dwight David Eisenhower
The Thirty-fourth President of the United States
1953–61

1890 (October 14) Born in Denison, Texas.

1892 Moved with family to Abilene, Kansas.

1909 Graduated from Abilene High School.

1911–15 Attended U. S. Military Academy at West Point, graduating with commission as second lieutenant.

1916 (July 1) Married Mamie Geneva Doud; promoted to first lieutenant.

1917–18 Commander of tank training school at Camp Colt, Gettsyburg, Pennsylvania, advanced to lieutenant colonel (temporary rank).

1932–35 Senior aide to General Douglas MacArthur, chief of staff of the U. S. Army.

1935–39 Senior military assistant to General MacArthur as military adviser to the Philippine government.

1941 Chief of staff of the Third Army, headquartered in San Antonio, Texas; advanced to brigadier general.

1942 Appointed commanding general of U.S. forces in Europe.

1943–45 Supreme Commander of Allied Expeditionary Forces in Europe.

1945–48 Chief of staff of the U. S. Army.

1948–50 President of Columbia University.

1951–52 Supreme commander of NATO forces in Europe.

1953–61 Thirty-fourth President of the United States.

1969 (March 28) Died in Washington, D.C.

O f all the previous Presidents, Dwight D. Eisenhower had the most in common with Ulysses S. Grant. He and Grant were the only two West Point graduates to become President. Both had been commanding generals of victorious armies, and neither had had any political experience or ever been elected to a lesser public office. Perhaps most surprising, they were the only two Republican Presidents to serve out two complete four-year terms.

Hero-worshiped as the commander of the Allied armies that defeated Germany in World War II, Eisenhower was elected and re-elected by huge majorities in 1952 and 1956. But although the people were happy to chant "We Like Ike," they did not like his party, so he had to work with a Congress controlled by the opposition through six of his eight years in office.

The Space Age began during Eisenhower's administration with the launching of earth-circling satellites by Russia and the United States. Atomic energy plants were first used to produce electricity, and an International Atomic Energy Agency was organized at Eisenhower's suggestion to control the peaceful uses of atomic energy. The United States grew to fifty states with the admission of Alaska and Hawaii.

As in the Truman administration, the Cold War between the communist nations and the western democracies dominated the time. Communism gained its first foothold in the Western Hemisphere when Fidel Castro overthrew the government of Cuba.

Eisenhower sought to organize the presidency in the style of a commanding general. He tried to have a staff which would keep him informed and provide him with alternate courses of action, although the ultimate responsibility remained his. He did not see himself as the leader of a political party, in the old-fashioned sense, as evidenced by a note written in his diary a few days before his first inauguration in which he commented that he hoped "that I will be compelled to have a little to do, during the next four years, with the distribution of Federal patronage."

A Career Soldier

DWIGHT DAVID EISENHOWER was born in Denison, Texas, October 14, 1890, the third of seven brothers, one of whom died as a baby. The Eisenhowers lived only briefly in Texas, having gone there following the failure of a general store the elder Eisenhower had managed in Hope, Kansas. Before Dwight was two, they had moved back to Kansas and settled in Abilene, where the father worked in a creamery.

With many mouths to feed and little income, the Eisenhowers had to struggle to make ends meet. As soon as each boy became old enough he worked in the family garden to help grow vegetables for the table, and when he became a little older usually began working at odd jobs. Dwight worked in the creamery after school and on vacations.

Eisenhower's parents, members of a Protestant sect called the River Brethren, brought up their children in an old-fashioned atmosphere of puritanical morals. Prayer and Bible reading were a daily part of their lives. Violence was forbidden, though in a family of six boys the edict was a bit hard to enforce.

As he was growing up, Dwight had a narrow escape. When he developed blood poisoning in his leg from a scratch, the family doctor advised amputation. Dwight and his older brothers resisted the doctor, and the leg healed.

In school Dwight, whose favorite subject was history, particularly enjoyed reading about military heroes of the past. When he graduated from Abilene High School in 1909, the class prophecy predicted that he would "wind up as a professor of history at Yale."

But the Eisenhowers could not afford to send Dwight to college. Temporarily he took a full-time job at the creamery, but he was determined to go to college and a year later applied for admittance to the U. S. Naval Academy at Annapolis. When he went to Topeka to take the examination, he found the same exam was being given for both Annapolis and West Point. He passed with flying colors, and was jubilant when he was appointed to West Point.

Five feet, ten and a half inches tall, the twenty-year-old Eisenhower was bigger and older than most of the others in his class at the Point in 1911. For a time it looked as though Ike would become one of Army's great football stars, but he injured his knee in the 1912 season and after that became a member of the cheerleading squad. An average student, Eisenhower ranked sixty-first in his class of 168 when he graduated in 1915.

As a second lieutenant, Eisenhower's first duty post was with the 19th Infantry at Fort Sam Houston in San Antonio, Texas. While there he met and became engaged to Mamie Geneva Doud, the nineteen-year-old daughter of a well-to-do Denver businessman. They were married on July 1, 1916, the day he received his promotion to first lieutenant. They had two sons, one of whom died as a baby. The other, John Eisenhower, followed his father's career as an officer in the U. S. Army.

During World War I, Eisenhower was kept in the United States as an instructor at various military camps. In the spring of 1918 he was given command of the Tank Training Center at Camp Colt, near Gettysburg,

Pennsylvania. Although he did not have any tanks until after the war had ended, he trained his troops in the theory of operating tanks, and rose to the temporary rank of lieutenant colonel.

After the war Ike was reduced to his permanent rank of captain. For two years he was assigned to duty in the Panama Canal Zone, and then after several routine assignments was sent to the Army General Staff School in Leavenworth, Kansas, in 1926. He knew that if he did well in this school it would mark him for eventual command, so with hard work he managed to graduate first in his class of 275 officers. As a result, Ike was picked to attend the War College in Washington, D.C.

In the early years of the Depression, Major Eisenhower served on the staff of the Assistant Secretary of War. In 1932 he was appointed aide to General Douglas MacArthur, at that time chief of staff of the U. S. Army. Two years later, when MacArthur was assigned to help the Filipinos build an army, Eisenhower went along to the Philippines as his assistant. In the four years he spent in the islands, Eisenhower was advanced to the permanent rank of lieutenant colonel. He also learned to fly while helping train the Philippine Air Force.

When Eisenhower returned to duty in the United States in 1940, there were fewer than 50,000 foot soldiers in the U. S. Army. During the peaceful years since World War I the army had dwindled to a point where regulars like Eisenhower were beginning to wonder if there was going to be anything left. But in the spring of 1940 Hitler's troops swept through Europe, causing the United States to begin a hasty build-up of its armed forces with the first draft of civilians since World War I.

By the spring of 1941 Eisenhower had been promoted to colonel and assigned as chief of staff of the Third Army in San Antonio, Texas. That summer Eisenhower distinguished himself in the big maneuvers held in Louisiana by the Second and Third Armies and won promotion to brigadier general.

Crusader in Europe

FIVE DAYS AFTER THE JAPANESE ATTACK on Pearl Harbor, Eisenhower received orders from Chief of Staff General George Marshall to report for duty with the War Department in Washington, D.C. Ike's long experience in the Philippines was needed to help plan American strategy in the Pacific. In March 1942, Eisenhower was appointed by Marshall as chief of the Operations Division of the War Department General Staff with the temporary rank of major general. In his new position Eisenhower and his staff developed the strategy for opening a "second front" with the invasion of German-occupied France. When Eisenhower reported to Marshall in June 1942 that the plans were ready for execution, Marshall asked, "When can you leave?"

The dizzying rise from lieutenant colonel to commanding general of the European Theater of Operations in a little more than two years had advanced Eisenhower over more than 350 senior general officers. During the next two years he won an increasing reputation as an organizer, a planner, and a man who could bring into agreement diverse leaders with conflicting views. He commanded the successful Allied invasions of French North Africa in November 1942, and of Sicily and Italy in the late summer of 1943. Then, in December 1943, President Roosevelt appointed Eisenhower Supreme Commander of all Allied forces in Europe, with the particular task of directing nearly three million troops in the invasion of France.

On Eisenhower's order the D-Day cross-channel assault on Normandy—the greatest amphibian invasion in history—was launched on June 6, 1944. He then directed the triumphant series of battles that freed Europe from Hitler's control, culminating in the German surrender in May 1945.

With victory achieved in Europe, Eisenhower was hailed as America's No. 1 hero, and in December 1945, President Truman called him to Washington as Chief of Staff of the U. S. Army. In this post, which he held for more than two years, Eisenhower supervised the demobilization of the army. He also worked with President Truman in an effort to unify the armed forces under a single command, resulting in the organization of the Department of Defense in 1947. He wrote *Crusade in Europe*, an account of his World War II service, which was published in 1948 and instantly became a best seller.

In May 1948, Eisenhower retired from active duty to become President of Columbia University. Besieged by both Democrats and Republicans to run for President, he repeatedly rejected all offers, and did not even disclose his political identity as a Democrat or a Republican.

In 1950, at President Truman's invitation, he returned to active military duty as Supreme Commander of NATO. Going to Europe in the spring of 1951, he welded together a powerful unified military force.

As the presidential election of 1952 approached, politicians of both parties again began to make overtures to Eisenhower. Then, Governor Thomas E. Dewey of New York, the Republican presidential nominee in 1944 and 1948, publicly threw his support to Eisenhower. Dewey represented the liberal wing of the Republican party and was determined to prevent the nomination of Senator Robert Taft of Ohio, leader of the conservative elements. In January 1952, Eisenhower disclosed that he was a Republican. He was nominated on the first ballot at the Republican National Convention. Senator

Richard M. Nixon of California was chosen as his vice-presidential running mate.

The Democrats nominated Governor Adlai E. Stevenson of Illinois, and as his running mate picked Senator John J. Sparkman of Alabama.

The contest was an unequal one because Stevenson was little known outside his own state, while Eisenhower was the hero who had brought victory in World War II. At the climax of the campaign, Eisenhower said he would personally go to Korea to bring the war there to an end—a pledge that won him wide support. Eisenhower won by a tremendous margin with 33,936,234 votes to Stevenson's 27,314,992, and with 442 electoral votes to 89.

In the interval before assuming office Eisenhower made good on his promise to fly to Korea and take a firsthand look at conditions there. A truce agreement ending the Korean War was signed several months later—on July 27, 1953.

Eisenhower's Administration

EISENHOWER HAD JOINED the Presbyterian church after his election, and on the morning of Inauguration Day he and his family attended an early morning communion service. Afterward he wrote a short prayer with which he began his inaugural address:

"Almighty God, as we stand here at this moment my future associates in the Executive branch of government join me in beseeching that Thou will make full and complete our dedication to the service of the people in this throng, and their fellow citizens everywhere.

"Give us, we pray, the power to discern clearly right from wrong, and allow all our words and actions to be governed thereby, and by the laws of this land. Especially we pray that our concern shall be for all the people regardless of station, race or calling.

"May cooperation be permitted and be the mutual aim of those who, under the concepts of our Constitution, hold to differing political faiths; so that all may work for the good of our beloved country and Thy glory. Amen."

In the heart of his address he called for the removal of "the causes of mutual fear and distrust among nations," and he declared that "we must be ready to dare all for our country. For history does not long entrust the care of freedom to the weak or timid . . ."

In closing, he said: "The peace we seek, then, is nothing less than the practice and fulfillment of our whole faith. . . . It signifies much more than the stilling of guns, easing the sorrow of war. More than an escape from death, it is a way of life. More than a haven for the weary, it is a hope for the brave."

In the field of domestic policy Eisenhower established himself as a "middle of the roader," calling his program "Modern Republicanism" or "Dynamic Conservatism." He supported a huge highway-building program including the far-sighted Interstate Highway System. He approved expansion of social security and the increase of the national minimum wage to one dollar an hour.

The domestic revolution that was to bring increased civil rights to blacks had its beginning during the Eisenhower administration, when in 1954 the Supreme Court, headed by Eisenhower appointee Earl Warren, ruled that compulsory segregation in public schools was unconstitutional. Later, Eisenhower sent federal troops to Arkansas to protect black students when a high school in Little Rock was integrated for the first time in 1957.

In the area of foreign relations, the death of Premier Stalin of Russia raised hopes that some new working accord might be reached with the new leaders of the Soviet Union. In 1955 Eisenhower attended a "summit meeting" with the leaders of Russia, France, and Great Britain in Geneva, but was unable to reach agreement on means to reduce Cold War tensions.

During his first year in office, Eisenhower made a dramatic appearance before the United Nations General Assembly in which he called on the world organization to plan for peaceful uses of atomic energy. This resulted in 1957 in the formation of the International Atomic Energy Agency.

Senator Joseph McCarthy of Wisconsin continued to fan hysteria against communists and communist sympathizers in the government during Eisenhower's first two years in office. After McCarthy accused the State Department of carrying communist and pro-communist books in overseas libraries, a number of books from these libraries were burned by U.S. officials. Eisenhower spoke out against these book burnings, but seemed unable to exert sufficient leadership to enforce his views. Finally, when McCarthy attacked the U. S. Army as being infiltrated by communists, pro-administration senators succeeded in passing a resolution censuring McCarthy for his activities.

Although the country experienced a continued high level of prosperity and public-opinion polls showed that Eisenhower retained his popularity with the people, the Republican party lost control of Congress in the elections of 1954. For the next six years Eisenhower exercised his skill of conciliation, working with the leaders of the opposition party in order to keep the business of the government going. In this he was particularly aided by Senator Lyndon Johnson of Texas, the Democratic majority leader of the Senate.

Eisenhower had three serious attacks of illness while President. In September 1955, he had a heart attack while vacationing in Colorado, but returned to duty in Washington three months later. In June 1956, an inflammation of his small intestine required an emergency operation from which he recovered rapidly. Then in November 1957, he had a mild stroke that for a time affected his speech.

In the 1956 election, Eisenhower again faced Adlai E. Stevenson as his Democratic opponent, and won, but by an even larger majority than in 1952. He received 35,590,472 popular votes to Stevenson's 26,022,752, and 457 electoral votes to 73. Amazingly, the Republicans failed to win either house of Congress—the first time this had occurred in a presidential election since that of Zachary Taylor in 1848. Obviously, the victory was a personal one for Ike.

Two crises in foreign affairs took place shortly before the 1956 election. On October 23, the people of Hungary revolted against their Communist rulers, appealing to the United States for help. A few days later France, Great Britain, and Israel invaded Egypt, apparently in an effort to recover the Suez Canal, which Egypt had nationalized. The United States joined Russia in condemning the action, and aided the United Nations in arranging a cease-fire. Meantime, Russian tanks crushed the Hungarian rising. In both cases, the United States was accused in some circles of failing to back its friends.

A year later, on October 4, 1957, Russia startled the world by launching *Sputnik*, the first man-made space satellite. The Space Age had begun. American prestige suffered throughout the world from this unexpected Soviet technological triumph, and the American press and public began a long-term debate as to whether something was wrong with the country's educational system if Soviet scientists had been able to forge ahead so spectacularly. But the first successful American earth satellite, *Explorer I*, was put in orbit in January 1958, and though Russia held its initial lead, the "space race" between the two countries became a reality.

At the request of the President, Congress in 1957 had approved a new foreign-policy posture which came to be called the "Eisenhower Doctrine." This authorized the President to use armed force to aid any nation or group of nations "requesting assistance against armed aggression from any country controlled by international communism." When the government of Lebanon requested such assistance in 1958, Eisenhower sent the U. S. Marines to protect that tiny Middle Eastern country.

When communist China threatened to invade Formosa in September 1958, and began shelling islands between Formosa and the Chinese mainland, Eisenhower ordered the U. S. Navy to provide protection for Chinese nationalist ships supplying military outposts on the islands. In the face of this strong stand, the Chinese communists backed down.

After the death of Secretary of State John Foster Dulles in 1959, President

Eisenhower became visibly more active in directing American foreign policy, hopeful that he could ease the tensions between the United States and communist Russia. In 1959, Eisenhower entertained Russian Premier Khrushchev on a visit to the United States. In turn, Khrushchev invited Eisenhower to visit Russia and a second "summit conference" was scheduled in Paris.

However, world hopes for accord were dashed in May 1960, just before the planned meeting in Paris, when Russia shot down an American U-2 high-altitude reconnaissance plane and Eisenhower admitted that "spy" flights over Russia had been going on for four years. Khrushchev broke up the Paris summit meeting with a demand that Eisenhower personally apologize for the spy flights. When the President refused, Khrushchev withdrew the invitation for Eisenhower to visit Russia.

The continued expansion of the federal government during Eisenhower's administration brought a need for additional office space for his staff. Instead of increasing the size of the White House itself, President Eisenhower had a new Executive Office Building constructed across the street, connecting it to the Executive Mansion by an underground tunnel.

Prevented from consideration of a third term by the Twenty-second Amendment, Eisenhower gave his support for the Republican presidential nomination in 1960 to Vice President Richard M. Nixon. Though Eisenhower did not campaign vigorously for Nixon, he was disappointed by the narrow election defeat to Democratic Senator John F. Kennedy of Massachusetts. "I felt as though I had been hit in the solar plexus with a ball bat—as though eight years of work had been for naught. It was a low moment . . ."

The United States suffered one further setback in foreign affairs in the closing days of Eisenhower's administration. In 1959, in Cuba, Fidel Castro overthrew the dictatorship of Fulgencio Batista and moved steadily leftward, finally revealing himself openly as a Communist. Early in January 1961, the Eisenhower administration broke off diplomatic relations with Cuba.

Eisenhower's Farewell Address

BY THE TIME HE LEFT OFFICE Eisenhower was seventy—the oldest man ever to be President. He made an unusual farewell address by radio and television to the American people, warning them of the dangers that lay ahead and of the necessity for moderation:

". . . threats, new in kind or degree, constantly arise. I mention two only. . . . we have been compelled to create a permanent armaments industry of vast proportions. Added to this, three and a half million men and women are directly engaged in the defense establishment. We annually spend on military security more than the net income of all United States corporations.

"This conjunction of an immense military establishment and a large arms industry is new in American experience. The total influence—economic, political, even spiritual—is felt in every city, every state house, every office of the federal government. We recognize the imperative need for this development. Yet we must not fail to comprehend its grave implications. . . .

"In the councils of government, we must guard against the acquisition of unwarranted influence, whether sought or unsought, by the military-industrial complex. The potential for the disastrous rise of misplaced power exists and will persist.

"We must never let the weight of this combination endanger our liberties or democratic processes. . . .

"Akin to, and largely responsible for the sweeping changes in our industrial-military posture, has been the technological revolution during recent decades.

"In this revolution, research has become central; it also becomes more formalized, complex, and costly. A steadily increasing share is conducted for, by, or at the direction of, the federal government. . . .

"The prospect of domination of the nation's scholars by federal employment, project allocations, and the power of money is ever present and is gravely to be regarded.

"Yet, in holding scientific research and discovery in respect, as we should, we must also be alert to the equal and opposite danger that public policy could itself become the captive of a scientific-technological elite. . . .

"Down the long lane of the history yet to be written America knows that this world of ours, ever growing smaller, must avoid becoming a community of dreadful fear and hate, and be, instead, a proud confederation of mutual trust and respect.

"Such a confederation must be one of equals. The weakest must come to the conference table with the same confidence as do we, protected as we are by our moral, economic, and military strength. That table, though scarred by many past frustrations, cannot be abandoned for the certain agony of the battlefield.

"Disarmament, with mutual honor and confidence, is a continuing imperative. Together we must learn how to compose differences, not with arms, but with intellect and decent purpose. Because this need is so sharp and apparent I confess that I lay down my official responsibilities in this field with a definite sense of disappointment. As one who has witnessed the horror and the lingering sadness of war—as one who knows that another war could utterly destroy this civilization which has been so slowly and painfully built over thousands of years—I wish I could say tonight that a lasting peace is in sight.

"Happily, I can say that war has been avoided. Steady progress toward our ultimate goal has been made. But, so much remains to be done. As a private citizen, I shall never cease to do what little I can to help the world advance along that road. . . .

"To all the peoples of the world, I once more give expression to America's prayerful and continuing aspiration:

"We pray that peoples of all faiths, all races, all nations may have their great human needs satisfied; that those now denied opportunity shall come to enjoy it to the full; that all who yearn for freedom may experience its spiritual blessings; that those who have freedom will understand, also, its heavy responsibilities; that all who are insensitive to the needs of others will learn charity; that the scourges of poverty, disease, and ignorance will be made to disappear from the earth, and that, in the goodness of time, all peoples will come to live together in a peace guaranteed by the binding force of mutual respect and love. . . ."

Eisenhower's Final Years

AFTER LEAVING THE PRESIDENCY, Eisenhower retired to his farm near Gettysburg, Pennsylvania. There he wrote two volumes of memoirs of his two terms as President.

At the age of seventy-eight he died of congestive heart failure, on March 28, 1969, at Walter Reed General Hospital in Washington, D.C. He was buried at his boyhood home in Abilene, Kansas.

Though in general he had expressed satisfaction with his eight years in office, he also had voiced his greatest disappointment:

"One of my major regrets is that as we left the White House I had to admit to little success in making progress in global disarmament or in reducing the bitterness of the East-West struggle. . . . I think no one can justifiably charge the bleak record to any lack of striving on our part. . . . But though, in this, I suffered my greatest disappointment, it has not destroyed my faith that in the next generation, the next century, the next millennium these things will come to pass."

John Fitzgerald Kennedy
The Thirty-fifth President of the United States
1961–63

1917 (May 29) Born in Brookline, Massachusetts.

1935 Attended Princeton University.

1936–40 Attended Harvard University, graduating *cum laude*.

1940 Published his first book, *Why England Slept*, which became a best seller.

1940–41 Attended Stanford University graduate business school.

1941–45 Served in World War II in the U. S. Navy, rising from seaman to lieutenant (senior grade).

1945 Worked as a newspaper reporter.

1947–52 U.S. representative from Massachusetts.

1953–60 U.S. senator from Massachusetts.

1953 (September 12) Married Jacqueline Lee Bouvier.

1956 Published *Profiles in Courage*, a best-selling book that won Kennedy a Pulitzer Prize.

1961–63 Thirty-fifth President of the United States.

1963 (November 22) Assassinated in Dallas, Texas.

The first President born in the twentieth century, John Fitzgerald Kennedy captured the imagination of the nation's youth with his vigorous and idealistic "New Frontier" program. At forty-three he was the youngest man ever elected President—symbolizing, in his own words, "renewal as well as change" in taking over the White House from the oldest President who had ever served. In his inaugural address Kennedy prophetically warned that his far-reaching program would not be completed "in the life of this Administration, nor even perhaps in our lifetime on this planet." And to the grief and horror of the nation these words came true when an assassin killed him after he had served in office only two years and ten months.

As the first Roman Catholic to become President, Kennedy won out over the religious bigotry that had helped defeat Al Smith thirty years earlier. His election victory over Republican Vice President Richard M. Nixon also was hailed as a triumph for the modern communication marvel of television, because he overshadowed his better-known opponent in a series of TV debates during the political campaign. But Kennedy's plurality was the smallest in history—only .2 percent of the popular vote. This narrow victory margin made it difficult for him to lead Congress during his short administration.

The focus of attention throughout most of Kennedy's presidency was on foreign affairs. Both Russia and the United States increased the pace of their nuclear arms race, stockpiling hydrogen bombs, building more and more sophisticated long-range guided missiles, and increasing the sizes of their armies. The Cold War reached a climax in October 1962, when Russia secretly began arming Cuba with atomic missiles. Kennedy coolly ordered a naval blockade of the island. For several days Russia and the United States stood "eyeball to eyeball," in the words of Secretary of State Dean Rusk, and then Russia backed down, removing the missiles from Cuba. Tension was further eased in August 1963, when the United States, Great Britain, and Russia signed a treaty ending the testing of atomic weapons in the earth's atmosphere.

In the speech which he had prepared for delivery on the day that he was killed, Kennedy had written:

"We in this country, in this generation, are, by destiny rather than choice, the watchmen on the walls of world freedom. We ask, therefore, that we may be worthy of our power and responsibility, that we may exercise our strength with wisdom and restraint, and that we may achieve in our time and for all time the ancient vision of 'peace on earth, good will toward men.' That must always be our goal—and the righteousness of our cause must always underlie our strength. For as was written long ago: 'Except the Lord keep the city, the watchman waketh but in vain.' "

Student, Author, and War Hero

LIKE THEODORE ROOSEVELT and Franklin D. Roosevelt, John Kennedy was the son of wealthy parents. Born on May 29, 1917, in Brookline, Massachusetts, he was the second of nine children of Joseph and Rose Kennedy. His father, one of the wealthiest men in the United States, served in various important government posts in Franklin Roosevelt's administration. His mother was the daughter of a former mayor of Boston.

While Jack was in elementary school, his father moved the family to New York, where they lived first in Riverdale, and then in Bronxville, an exclusive suburb north of New York City. After completing sixth grade in the Bronxville public schools, the thirteen-year-old Jack Kennedy was sent first to Canterbury School in New Milford, Connecticut, a Roman Catholic private school, then to Choate, a non-sectarian private school, in Wallingford, Connecticut. Although an average student, with a scholastic rank barely in the upper half of his class, he was recognized by his classmates as "most likely to succeed."

As they grew up, Jack and his brothers and sisters led an active life in vacation periods when they were all together. In winter they vacationed in Palm Beach, Florida, and in summers lived at Hyannis Port, Massachusetts, on Cape Cod. There was much swimming, tennis, boating, touch football, and other sports and games.

The summer after graduating from Choate, eighteen-year-old Jack went to England to study under socialist professor Harold Laski at the London School of Economics, but an attack of jaundice caused him to drop out of this school. Returning to the United States, he matriculated at Princeton, but after two months a recurrence of jaundice again forced him to drop his studies.

After recovering his health, Jack entered Harvard, his father's alma mater. For the first three years his grades were mostly "C's," but in his senior year he blossomed as he concentrated on courses in economics and political science. A thesis that he wrote discussing the British and French appeasement of Hitler at Munich won such faculty praise that he was graduated with honors in 1940.

Encouraged by the praise he had received for his thesis, the twenty-three-year-old Kennedy decided to expand it and try to get it published as a book. Under the title *Why England Slept*, the book became a best seller soon after it was published in the summer of 1940.

In the winter of 1940–41, while his father had a falling out with President

Roosevelt and was forced to resign as ambassador to England because of anti-British statements, Jack Kennedy attended graduate business school at Stanford University. In the spring of 1941 he signed up for an enlistment in the army, but was turned down because of a back injury he had received playing football. After taking a strenuous course of exercises, he passed a navy physical and was accepted as a seaman in September 1941.

For more than a year, even after the Japanese attack on Pearl Harbor, Kennedy's military duties were routine desk jobs. Finally, he asked his father to use his influence to get him sea duty. He soon was assigned to PT-boat training, received a commission as a lieutenant (j.g.), and in March 1943, was given command of his own torpedo boat in the South Pacific.

In the early morning darkness of August 2, 1943, a Japanese destroyer sliced through Kennedy's PT 109 west of New Georgia island. Two of the crew were killed, but Kennedy and ten others clung to the wreckage. After fifteen hours in the water they reached a tiny island. Kennedy kept up the men's courage and for four days they swam from island to island until they found some natives who took a message carved on a coconut to the nearest navy base. When rescued, Kennedy discovered he and his crew had been given up as lost and their families had been notified of their deaths.

Sick with malaria and a recurrence of his old back injury, Kennedy was returned to the United States. He was in a navy hospital near Boston when word came that his older brother, Joe, had been killed while flying a bomber in Europe. Discharged from the navy early in 1945 because of his physical condition, Kennedy covered the United Nations organizational meeting in San Francisco as a reporter for the Hearst newspapers. Later that year he reported the British elections for Hearst, and then dropped newspaper work to try his hand at politics.

Winning the Presidency

KENNEDY LATER EXPLAINED that he entered politics "because Joe died"—his elder brother having been counted on as the member of the family most likely to go far in politics. At twenty-eight, gray-eyed, curly-headed John Kennedy took up residence in Boston and began a campaign to win the Democratic nomination for Congress in the Eleventh District. Most of the members of the Kennedy family plunged in to help the campaign, hundreds of house parties were held for voters, and when the primary election was held in June 1946, "the poor little rich kid"—as one opponent called him—beat out the nine other candidates for the nomination. In November he easily overcame his Republican opponent in the normally Democratic district. He repeated his congressional election victory twice, in 1948 and in 1950.

During his six years as a U.S. representative from Massachusetts, Kennedy lived the carefree life of a bachelor. He supported most of President Truman's "Fair Deal" program against the combination of conservative Republicans and southern Democrats that opposed it. When the leaders of the American Legion opposed a bill he had introduced for federal funds for slum clearance and low-cost housing, Kennedy denounced them as having "not had a constructive thought for the benefit of this country since 1918." As a congressman he insisted that federal aid to education must be for both parochial and public schools, contributing to the defeat of federal aid to education at that time. From time to time he attacked President Truman's foreign policy, particularly the loss of China to the Communists, the reduction of U.S. forces in Europe during the Korean War, and the huge expenditures of money in foreign aid to other parts of the world.

In the spring of 1952 the thirty-five-year-old Kennedy began a campaign for U.S. senator from Massachusetts against Republican Henry Cabot Lodge, Jr., who had held the office since 1936 except for a period of military service in World War II. As his campaign manager, Kennedy chose his twenty-seven-year-old brother, Robert, who directed the spending of about $500,000 on the contest. Again, all the Kennedys pitched in to help, holding receptions and coffee parties for voters, knocking on doors, and asking everyone to vote for Jack. On election day he beat Lodge with a plurality of 70,000 votes, although the Republicans won the state governorship and Eisenhower carried the state by more than 200,000. This made Kennedy the leading Democrat in Massachusetts, and an important figure nationally.

Two years earlier Kennedy had met Jacqueline Lee Bouvier, an attractive co-ed at George Washington University. Kennedy was thirty-six and Jackie, an inquiring photographer for the Washington *Times-Herald*, was twenty-four when they were married on September 12, 1953. They had three children, one of whom died shortly after birth.

The freshman senator from Massachusetts was first assigned to two committees, the Labor and Public Welfare Committee, and the Government Operations Committee, the chairman of which was Senator Joseph McCarthy of Wisconsin. John's younger brother Robert worked for the McCarthy committee as an attorney. By 1954 McCarthyism—the charges of communism and pro-communism against public officials—had become one of the central issues of American politics. John Kennedy attempted to sit on the fence between those who admired and those who loathed the McCarthy investigations, and when the Senate voted to censure McCarthy, was in a hospital recovering from surgery to correct his old back ailment.

While there he filled in his time writing *Profiles in Courage,* a series of biographies of senators who had taken courageous stands throughout American history. Published in 1956 the book became a best seller, and won Kennedy the Pulitzer Prize for biography. It also won him considerable popularity among literary liberals.

After returning to the Senate in 1955, Kennedy took the leadership in a fight to prevent a constitutional amendment to change the Electoral College system. This amendment, sponsored by conservatives, would have made it possible for losing candidates to receive a proportion of a state's electoral vote —in effect it would have reduced the political effectiveness of minority groups that sometimes swing an entire state's vote to one candidate. Kennedy again picked up liberal support by helping defeat the amendment.

With the approach of the 1956 presidential campaign, Kennedy made an effort to win the vice-presidential nomination on the ticket with Adlai Stevenson. At the Chicago convention, Kennedy was chosen to place Adlai Stevenson in nomination for President. After Stevenson won the presidential nomination on the first ballot, a fight for the vice-presidential nomination developed between Kennedy and Senator Estes Kefauver of Tennessee. On the first ballot Kefauver led, on the second ballot Kennedy jumped into the lead, but on the third ballot Kefauver won. Kennedy went on to help campaign for the Stevenson-Kefauver ticket, making speeches in twenty-six states.

When Kennedy was appointed to the Senate Foreign Relations Committee in 1957, he began to be listened to more and more on foreign affairs. He created a particular furor when he recommended that the United States support Algerian nationalists to obtain freedom from France. He also began to speak about the "missile gap" between the United States and Russia— warning that President Eisenhower had weakened national defense so much that Russia was moving ahead in the production of intercontinental ballistic missiles with which to wage an atomic war.

With an eye to the Democratic presidential nomination in 1960, Kennedy's voting record in the Senate became increasingly liberal. He supported the compromise civil rights legislation in 1957—the first such measure since Reconstruction days, spoke widely throughout the country, and wrote many articles for magazines. Public opinion polls showed him as the leading contender for the next presidential nomination by his party. In his re-election for senator in 1958 he proved his power as a vote getter, receiving the largest plurality ever given a candidate in Massachusetts to that time—a record 875,000 votes more than his Republican opponent.

The efforts of all the Kennedy family concentrated for the next two years on winning Jack the presidential nomination. Robert Kennedy managed the campaign, as he had his brother's previous successes. To show his political strength, Kennedy went into presidential preference primaries in seven states and won them all. After defeating Senator Hubert Humphrey of Minnesota in the hotly contested West Virginia primary, Humphrey withdrew from the race. This left as Kennedy's main opponents Senator Lyndon Johnson of Texas, the majority leader of the Senate; Senator Stuart Symington of Missouri, formerly Secretary of the Air Force under President Truman; and Adlai Stevenson.

By the time the delegates met at the Democratic Convention in Los Angeles in July, Kennedy had the nomination all but wrapped up. He won on the first ballot with 806 votes to Johnson's 409, Symington's 86, and Stevenson's 79½, and topped off his triumph by persuading Johnson to accept the vice-presidential nomination.

The Republicans met at Chicago shortly thereafter to nominate Vice President Richard M. Nixon. As their vice-presidential nominee they chose Henry Cabot Lodge, Jr., U.S. delegate to the United Nations.

The highlight of the political campaign was the series of four televised debates between Kennedy and Nixon—the first time in history that most of the American people were able to see and hear both major party candidates state their views and question each other face-to-face. The Democratic platform on which Kennedy and Johnson ran was the most liberal ever presented up to that time by a political party. It promised greatly expanded civil rights for minorities and an enlarged social security program. Nixon and Lodge ran largely on the record of the Eisenhower administration.

In the election the vote was so close that the result was in doubt until the next day. Kennedy received 34,227,096 votes to Nixon's 34,108,546, and 303 electoral votes to Nixon's 219.

Kennedy's Administration

A BLIZZARD HAD FILLED the streets of Washington with snow on January 20, 1961, when the forty-three-year-old Kennedy was sworn in as President. His inspirational inaugural address was aimed primarily at the youth of the country. In it he said:

". . . Let the word go forth from this time and place, to friend and foe alike, that the torch has been passed to a new generation of Americans, born in this century, tempered by war, disciplined by a hard and bitter peace, proud of our ancient heritage, and unwilling to witness or permit the slow undoing of those human rights to which this nation has always been committed, and to which we are committed today at home and around the world.

"Let every nation know, whether it wishes us well or ill, that we shall pay any price, bear any burden, meet any hardship, support any friend, oppose any foe to assure the survival and the success of liberty.

". . . In the long history of the world, only a few generations have been granted the role of defending freedom in its hour of maximum danger. I do not shrink from this responsibility; I welcome it. I do not believe that any of us would exchange places with any other people or any other generation. The energy, the faith, the devotion which we bring to this endeavor will light our country and all who serve it, and the glow from that fire can truly light the world.

"And so, my fellow Americans, ask not what your country can do for you; ask what you can do for your country. . . ."

In his State of the Union address less than two weeks later, Kennedy told a joint session of Congress:

". . . No man entering upon this office, regardless of his party, regardless of his previous service in Washington, could fail to be staggered upon learning, even in this brief ten-day period, the harsh enormity of the trials through which we must pass in the next four years. Each day the crises multiply. Each day their solution grows more difficult. Each day we draw nearer the hour of maximum danger, as weapons spread and hostile forces grow stronger."

Breaking precedent, President Kennedy appointed his younger brother Robert, to his Cabinet as Attorney General. He relied heavily on "Bobby" as an adviser on all critical policy decisions. In 1962 his youngest brother, Edward, was elected U.S. senator from Massachusetts. This was the first time that three members of the same family ever had held such high positions at the same time in the federal government. Naturally, there was considerable discussion of the Kennedy family influence by the President's opponents, but he shrugged off all criticism.

During his first several months in office Kennedy sent many messages to Congress outlining in detail the legislation that he wanted to carry out his "New Frontier" program. However, the Eighty-seventh Congress was slow to act, and a coalition of conservative Democrats and Republicans blocked the passage of many of his proposals.

In the political campaign and in his State of the Union message Kennedy had called for the establishment of a peace corps "enlisting the services of all those with the desire and capacity to help foreign lands meet their urgent needs for trained personnel." This program, which appealed especially to college students, was passed by Congress in March 1961. Kennedy appointed one of his brothers-in-law, Sargent Shriver, to direct the Peace Corps, which became one of the Kennedy administration's most successful achievements. The next month Kennedy suffered his greatest defeat in foreign relations.

On April 17 an army of Cuban exiles attempted to invade Cuba to overthrow the government of dictator Fidel Castro. The exiles had been trained by the CIA, the U.S. government's top intelligence agency, but the invasion of the Bay of Pigs failed miserably with more than 1,000 of the exiles taken prisoner. Kennedy took personal responsibility for the failure, although the project had been started under the Eisenhower administration.

A new Kennedy-sponsored foreign-aid program to Latin America was launched in 1961 under the name Alliance for Progress. The program called for a ten-year plan to develop the resources of Latin American countries.

In Europe, relations with Russia continued to deteriorate. Kennedy flew to Vienna in June 1961 to confer for two days with Soviet Premier Khrushchev about Russian threats that communist East Germany would be given control of supply routes to West Berlin. No agreements were reached at the meeting. In August the Communists built a high wall to seal off West Berlin from East Berlin in order to prevent the escape of East Berliners to the West. Kennedy later said of it: ". . . the wall is the most obvious and vivid demonstration of the failures of the Communist system . . ."

When Kennedy became President the economy had been undergoing a mild recession for several months, but by the end of his first year in office he was able to report that the country was "on the highroad of recovery and growth." The minimum hourly wage had been raised to $1.25. In the Trade Expansion Act, Congress had given Kennedy new powers to reduce tariffs. Defense spending had been increased, and the number of nuclear submarines and intercontinental ballistic missiles had been expanded. But Congress failed to act on Kennedy's requests for improved civil rights measures, medical care for the aged financed by social security, or broad federal aid to education. Even after the Democrats won the mid-term congressional elections of 1962, Kennedy continued to have difficulty getting Congress to go along with his proposals for major domestic legislation.

Kennedy won great praise for his handling of the crisis over Cuba in 1962 that came close to starting World War III. Dictator Fidel Castro of Cuba had revealed in December 1961 that he was a communist and that he was aligning Cuba with Russia and China. Russia began supplying military aid to Cuba. Then, in October 1962, U.S. aerial photos of Cuba showed that missiles were being installed that could launch atomic warheads at the United States or Latin America. Kennedy ordered a blockade of Cuba and insisted that Russia dismantle the missile bases and remove the missiles. Although he did not directly say so, Kennedy implied that the United States would bomb the bases if U.S. demands were not met. When Soviet Premier Khrushchev ordered the missiles withdrawn, the threat of war was averted.

Under President Eisenhower, the Soviet Union and the United States had reached an unofficial understanding ending the testing of atomic weapons because of the danger of contaminating the earth's atmosphere with radiation. But in September 1961, Russia resumed such testing, and Kennedy ordered the resumption of U.S. atomic tests shortly after. Kennedy then initiated discussions with Russia that led to the signing of a treaty on August 5, 1963, banning nuclear tests in the earth's atmosphere. The United States, Russia, and Great Britain originally signed the treaty and other nations subscribed to it later.

Many persons saw the nuclear test ban treaty as the basis for hope that further agreements might be reached with Russia to reduce the possibility of nuclear war. To such persons, Kennedy said, "Let us always make clear our willingness to talk, if talk will help, and our readiness to fight, if fight we must. Let us resolve to be the masters, not the victims, of our history, controlling our own destiny without giving way to blind suspicion and emotion. . . ."

The revolutionary drive for black civil rights continued under President Kennedy, who sent federal marshals to Montgomery, Alabama, in 1961, when riots grew out of a black boycott of a bus line. Federal troops had to intervene in riots at the University of Mississippi in 1962 when black student James Meredith insisted on his right to enroll at that previously all white school. In 1963 Kennedy twice had to call the National Guard into federal service in Alabama to protect blacks seeking to integrate schools. In August 1963, about 200,000 black and white civil rights demonstrators came to Washington on a "Freedom March," demanding action on civil rights legislation Kennedy had sent to Congress. In a television address to the American people, he said, "One hundred years of delay have passed since President Lincoln freed the slaves, yet their heirs, their grandsons, are not fully free. They are not yet freed from the bonds of injustice. They are not yet freed from social and economic oppression, and this nation, for all its hopes and all its boasts, will not be fully free until all its citizens are free. . . ."

Throughout his administration Kennedy pressed the nation's scientists to step up the race with the Soviet Union for the mastery of outer space. In April 1961, the Russians had sent the first man into space, and the next month the United States had sent up its first astronaut. Kennedy promised that the United States would be the first to land a man on the moon. He said, "We choose to go to the moon in this decade, and do the other things, not because they are easy but because they are hard; because that goal will serve to organize and measure the best of our energies and skills; because that challenge is one that we are willing to accept, one we are unwilling to postpone, and one which we intend to win . . ."

The Assassination

IN NOVEMBER 1963, Kennedy went on a speaking trip to Texas. He dedicated a new Aero-Space Medical Health Center at Brooks Air Force Base, spoke at a dinner in Houston, and next day at a breakfast in Fort Worth. At noon on November 22 he was scheduled to speak at a luncheon in Dallas.

While driving in a motorcade through the streets of Dallas, Kennedy was struck in the head and neck by rifle bullets fired by an assassin and died a few minutes later. The governor of Texas, John B. Connally, who was riding with him also was seriously wounded, but later recovered. Lee Harvey Oswald, an emotionally unbalanced former U. S. Marine who believed in communism and had once renounced his U.S. citizenship to live in Russia, was arrested as the assassin after he killed a Dallas policeman while trying to evade arrest. Two days later, as millions of Americans watched in shocked horror on television, Oswald himself was shot dead by a Dallas nightclub owner, Jack Ruby. Ten months later a commission headed by Chief Justice Earl Warren certified Oswald's guilt, but without being able to establish a motive other than his "deep-rooted resentment of all authority." In succeeding years many persons claimed Oswald was part of a larger conspiracy against Kennedy.

The body of forty-six-year-old President Kennedy was flown to Washington on the evening of the day of assassination. His wife, who had been riding with him, escorted his body back to the White House still wearing a dress stained with his blood. Lyndon Johnson, who had been in the motorcade, was sworn in as President aboard the airplane before it took off. On Monday, November 25, millions of grieving Americans watched the presidential funeral on TV. Kennedy was buried in Arlington National Cemetery and an eternal flame was lighted over his grave. Two days later President Johnson addressed a joint session of Congress, emphasizing the need to carry out President Kennedy's program:

"All I have I would have given gladly not to be standing here today.

"The greatest leader of our time has been struck down by the foulest deed of our time. Today John Fitzgerald Kennedy lives on in the immortal words and works that he left behind. He lives on in the mind and memories of mankind. He lives on in the hearts of his countrymen.

"No words are sad enough to express our sense of loss. No words are strong enough to express our determination to continue the forward thrust of America that he began.

"The dream of conquering the vastness of space—the dream of partnership across the Atlantic—and across the Pacific as well—the dream of a

Peace Corps in less-developed nations—the dream of education for all of our children—the dream of jobs for all who seek them and need them—the dream of care for our elderly—the dream of an all-out attack on mental illness—and above all, the dream of equal rights for all Americans, whatever their race or color—these and other American dreams have been vitalized by his drive and by his dedication.

"And now the ideas and ideals which he so nobly represented must and will be translated into effective action. . . ."

Lyndon Baines Johnson
The Thirty-sixth President of the United States
1963–69

1908 (August 27) Born near Stonewall, Texas.

1924 Graduated from Johnson City, Texas, high school.

1927–30 Attended Southwest Texas State Teachers College, graduating with a bachelor of science degree.

1930–31 Taught public speaking and debate in Sam Houston High School in Houston, Texas.

1932–35 Secretary to U.S. Representative Richard M. Kleberg of Texas.

1934 (November 17) Married Claudia "Lady Bird" Taylor.

1935–37 Director of the National Youth Administration in Texas.

1937–48 U.S. representative from Texas.

1941–42 Served on active duty during World War II as a lieutenant commander in the U. S. Navy.

1949–60 U.S. senator from Texas; majority leader of the Senate, 1955–60.

1961–63 Vice President of the United States.

1963–69 Thirty-sixth President of the United States.

1973 (January 22) Died at his ranch near Johnson City, Texas.

The eighth Vice President to succeed to the nation's highest office on the death of a President, Lyndon Baines Johnson was far better prepared to do so than any of his seven predecessors. Under President Kennedy he had been given greater responsibility and had been kept better informed of the inner workings of the government than had any previous Vice President. Moreover, he was a master politician in his own right, having served in Congress for twenty-four years—twelve years as a representative and twelve as a senator, the last several as majority leader.

Upon Kennedy's death, Johnson pledged to press forward the New Frontier program that had become bogged down in legislative inaction. He did so. Then in the election of 1964 he won the presidency in his own right, topping all previous records by receiving over 43 million popular votes. Calling his own program the "Great Society," Johnson obtained passage of sweeping new civil rights laws, tax reductions to stimulate the economy, a multi-billion-dollar anti-poverty program, federal aid for all aspects of education, and increased social security benefits that included medical care for the aged.

Johnson met with much less success in foreign affairs. When he sent American troops into the Dominican Republic to prevent communists from taking over the government, he aroused Latin American fears of a new United States interventionist policy. When the American troops later were made part of an inter-American force commanded by a Brazilian general, the Latin American fears eased. However, Johnson's greatest disaster was the Vietnam War, in which he escalated American participation in an effort to prevent a communist take-over of South Vietnam, but succeeded only in making it America's costliest war and in severely dividing the American people. Ultimately, the Vietnam situation and unrest at home forced him to withdraw from seeking a second elected term as President.

The six-foot-three-inch Texan made it clear that he regarded himself as a Southwesterner rather than a Southerner. He often spoke in a more folksy manner than his Harvard-educated predecessor. In describing his vision of a "Great Society" in his inaugural address in 1965 he said:

"I do not believe that the Great Society is the ordered, changeless and sterile battalion of the ants. It is the excitement of becoming—always becoming, trying, probing, falling, resting and trying again—but always trying and always gaining. In each generation—with toil and tears—we have had to earn our heritage again."

From Texas Ranch to New Deal Washington

LYNDON BAINES JOHNSON was born on a ranch in the bleak hill country near Stonewall, Texas, on August 27, 1908. He was the first of five children of Samuel and Rebekah Johnson. Both his mother and father had been teachers, so they helped him learn to read even before he started to school. As his father and both his grandfathers had been members of the Texas legislature, Lyndon grew up hearing the inside story of politics.

At the age of five, Lyndon moved with his family to Johnson City, Texas—named for his grandfather—and started to public school the same year. Like most families in the small town, the Johnsons had barely enough money to live on, so as he grew older Lyndon earned spending money for movies and other entertainment by such odd jobs as shining shoes and picking cotton. At the age of fifteen, he was graduated from high school.

Tired of study and books, Lyndon decided to make his own way in the world with no further education. He and some friends bummed their way to California, where he lived the life of a hobo, picking oranges, washing dishes for meals, and finding out how hard it was to earn money in the period of farm depression then underway.

After nearly a year he returned to Johnson City where he got a job on a road gang. It was hard manual labor, but he stubbornly stuck to it for about a year despite the urging by both his parents that he continue his education. When he was eighteen, he finally changed his mind, borrowed $75 from the Johnson City bank, and enrolled in Southwest State Teachers College, in San Marcos, Texas.

Johnson earned his way through college. He worked as a janitor and then as an office helper for the college president. He dropped out of school one year to earn extra money by teaching Mexican children in a tiny school in the town of Cotulla—where he spent a good part of his small salary buying playground equipment for his poverty-stricken students. Then he went back to college, graduating in 1930 at the age of twenty-one.

After teaching debate and public speaking for a year in a Houston high school, the opportunity came that drew Johnson into politics. U.S. Representative Richard Kleberg, one of the owners of the million-acre King ranch, invited Johnson to come to Washington with him as his secretary at $3,000 a year. From 1932 to 1935—in the last months of the Hoover administration and in the exciting first years of the Roosevelt administration—Johnson learned just how Congress worked.

On a trip home to Texas in 1934 Johnson met twenty-year-old Claudia

Alta Taylor, called Lady Bird by her family and friends. The twenty-six year-old Johnson conducted a whirlwind courtship, and they were married on November 17, 1934—just two months after they had first been introduced. Several years later, using money she had inherited from her mother, Mrs. Johnson bought a small radio station in Austin and with great business skill pyramided her investment into a multimillion-dollar fortune. The Johnsons had two daughters.

When President Roosevelt established the National Youth Administration (NYA) in 1935 as a program to help unemployed young people earn money and go to school, Johnson applied for a job with the new organization. At twenty-six he was appointed NYA administrator for Texas—the youngest of the state directors. He swiftly organized projects that employed tens of thousands of youths.

Congressman, Senator, and Vice President

IN 1937, REPRESENTATIVE JAMES P. BUCHANAN of Johnson's Texas congressional district, died, and a special election was called to fill the vacancy. Johnson was one of ten candidates, but the only one who forthrightly supported the policies of President Roosevelt. In the election he received almost twice as many votes as the next nearest candidate.

President Roosevelt heard of this young man who had run and won as his supporter. He invited Johnson to ride on his special train, and offered him his help in obtaining assignment to important congressional committees. Johnson also had another influential friend in Washington—Sam Rayburn, the majority leader of the House of Representatives, who had once been a fellow state legislator with Johnson's father in Texas.

In his early years in Congress, Johnson devoted much of his effort to pushing the building of federally-supported electrical services for farmers. He also was a supporter of public housing to clean up city slums and was an active member of the Naval Affairs Committee. He did such a good job for his home congressional district that he was not opposed for re-election in 1938, 1940, and 1942.

When one of the senators from Texas, Morris Sheppard, died in April 1941, Johnson ran as a candidate to fill the remainder of the term. Although he campaigned hard throughout Texas, he lost to conservative Governor W. Lee O'Daniel by the narrow margin of 1,311 votes out of nearly 600,000 cast. Disappointed but not discouraged, he returned to Washington to resume his duties in the House of Representatives.

A few months later the Japanese bombed Pearl Harbor. As soon as he heard the news, Johnson asked for active duty as a member of the Naval Reserve, in which he had the rank of lieutenant commander. He was the first member of Congress to go on active military duty in World War II. In May 1942, President Roosevelt sent Johnson on a special fact-finding mission in the South Pacific. During this tour one bomber in which he was flying was shot up by Japanese fighter planes. Another time he was aboard a plane that crash-landed in Australia. General Douglas MacArthur decorated him with the Silver Star for gallantry under enemy fire. In July, President Roosevelt ordered Johnson and all other members of Congress to return to their legislative posts in Washington.

In 1948 the thirty-nine-year-old Johnson decided to try again to win a seat in the U. S. Senate. He was one of eleven candidates to enter the Democratic primary. Using a helicopter, a kind of flying machine few people in Texas had seen at that time, Johnson hopped about the state campaigning. In the July vote he came in second to Governor Coke Stevenson with 405,617 votes to Stevenson's 477,077. The nine other candidates combined received 320,000. Since neither Johnson nor Stevenson had a clear majority, a runoff election was required. After another hard-fought campaign the vote was taken. This time Johnson won by an eyelash—with 494,191 to Stevenson's 494,104—a difference of only eighty-seven votes. Stevenson contested the election, but the courts and the state Democratic party's executive committee upheld Johnson. (In 1977, four years after Johnson's death, a former Texas voting official told newsmen he had stolen the 1948 runoff election for Johnson by counting fictitious votes. Authorities discounted the story because earlier challenges to the election had been so thoroughly investigated.) In the November 1948 general election Stevenson supported the Republican candidate against Johnson, but Johnson won the Senate seat by a two-to-one vote.

As a senator, Johnson began to win national attention in the 1950s as chairman of the Preparedness Investigating Subcommittee. This was a successor to the investigating committee that had been headed by Harry S Truman during World War II. It was estimated that during the Korean War Johnson's committee saved the nation more than $5 billion by exposure of wasteful practices.

In 1951 Johnson took an important step toward party leadership when his fellow Democratic senators elected him party whip—or assistant leader of the Senate Democrats. In this post he was responsible for seeing to it that Democratic members were on the floor of the Senate whenever a crucial vote was taken.

In the presidential election of 1952 many Texas Democrats, including the then governor, Allan Shivers, supported the Republican candidacy of Dwight Eisenhower against Democrat Adlai Stevenson. But Johnson backed Stevenson and campaigned with him throughout Texas. Johnson's efforts were not enough to stem the Eisenhower tide, and Texas placed its electoral votes in the Republican column. But his party loyalty stood Johnson in good stead. The Democratic leader of the Senate, Ernest McFarland of Arizona, lost his seat in the Eisenhower sweep, and when the new Congress met in January 1953, the Democratic senators elected Johnson their leader. This made him, at forty-four, the youngest man ever elected Senate floor leader by either the Democrats or the Republicans.

As minority leader of the Senate, Johnson was determined that the Democrats should not indulge in obstruction of Republican measures for the mere sake of obstruction. He said, "When we are forced by our convictions to oppose Administration proposals, our opposition will be based on principle and will be expressed in a principled manner." To strengthen his influence with new Democratic senators who had just been elected, he persuaded the more senior members of his party to relax seniority rules to the extent that each freshman senator received at least one important committee assignment. One of these freshmen senators who was to remember with gratitude this action was John F. Kennedy, newly elected senator from Massachusetts.

Following what he called "politics of responsibility," Johnson saw to it that Senate Democrats accumulated a record of supporting the President on many issues in which the majority of conservative Republican senators opposed him. Johnson was up for re-election in 1954, but he did not leave Washington to campaign in the Democratic primary in Texas. Nevertheless, he defeated his one opponent by a vote of nearly three to one.

In the congressional election campaign of 1954 Johnson made speeches throughout the western states, hitting hard at the theme that a Democratic Congress would help Eisenhower more than would a Republican Congress. The theme paid off, for the Democrats again won control of both houses—a majority control they would continue to hold through the remainder of Eisenhower's administration.

When the Eighty-fourth Congress met in January 1955, the forty-six-year-old Johnson was the youngest man ever to have served as majority leader of the Senate. An astute politician, he now wielded great power of persuasion to bring together senators of divergent viewpoints. He became known for his expression, "Let us reason together." Senator Hubert Humphrey of Minnesota, who years later was to be Johnson's Vice President, said of him at the time that Johnson was "a genius in the art of the legislative process."

Although the tall, thin Johnson seemed easy-going and calm as he directed the Senate, he was working harder than he ever had. He paid the consequences when he was struck down by a heart attack on the Fourth of July weekend in 1955. "It was as bad an attack as a man could have and still live,"

Johnson said later. His doctors made him give up cigarette smoking—he had been a chain smoker—and he was forced to rest for six months. But in January 1956, he resumed his work as majority leader of the Senate.

Johnson's greatest accomplishments during his remaining time in the Senate was the passage of civil rights acts in 1957 and 1960. These measures, designed to help blacks achieve equal voting rights with whites, were the first pieces of civil rights legislation to be approved by Congress since the period of Reconstruction. Johnson also gave personal leadership in Congress to efforts to vitalize the American space program after Russia surprised the world by beating the United States to the launching of the first successful man-made satellite in 1957.

Election as Vice President

As THE 1960 PRESIDENTIAL ELECTION APPROACHED, Johnson hoped he would be chosen as the Democratic nominee. But he did not enter the presidential preferential primaries to compete with John F. Kennedy, and he did not announce his candidacy for the nomination until shortly before the National Convention met in Los Angeles in July. By that time Kennedy had the nomination sewed up. On the first ballot Kennedy won with 806 votes to Johnson's 409. When Kennedy asked Johnson to become his running mate, the Texas senator accepted and the convention delegates nominated him for Vice President by acclamation.

In the election campaign Johnson concentrated his efforts on the southern and western states, helping bring back into the Democratic column the electoral votes of Texas, Louisiana, New Mexico, and Nevada. In the close-fought election the combined vote of these states was enough to provide the margin of victory.

After taking office as Vice President in January 1961, Johnson continued to work hard. President Kennedy gave him greater responsibilities than ever before had been given a Vice President. Johnson was a regular member of the Cabinet and the National Security Council. He also served as chairman of the National Aeronautics and Space Council, the President's Committee on Equal Employment Opportunities, and the Peace Corps Advisory Council. He traveled widely throughout the world as the President's good-will ambassador—going to Africa, South Asia, the Far East, the Middle East, Europe, and Latin America.

Johnson's Administration

ON NOVEMBER 22, 1963, in the fatal cavalcade at Dallas, Vice President Johnson rode in a car a short distance back of President Kennedy's. When the shots rang out, the Secret Service man assigned to Johnson threw him to the floor of the car and flung himself on top to protect the Vice President. Johnson's car then followed the President's at high speed to a hospital where the President was pronounced dead.

At 2:39 P.M., less than two hours after the assassination, the fifty-five-year-old Johnson was sworn in as President aboard the presidential plane. The oath was administered by Federal Judge Sarah T. Hughes, the first time a woman had ever sworn in a President. Then Johnson issued his first presidential order, "Now, let's get airborne."

A few hours later, while millions of Americans watched on television, the presidential jet landed in Washington. With Mrs. Johnson at his side, President Johnson stepped to a microphone at the airport and addressed his first words to reassure the people of the United States: "I will do my best. That is all I can do. I ask your help, and God's."

Johnson purposely stayed in the background as the people expended their grief in the funeral ceremonies for Kennedy. Then five days after the assassination—on the day before Thanksgiving—Johnson addressed a special joint session of Congress. He called on the senators and representatives to honor Kennedy's memory by carrying forward the dead President's New Frontier program, saying, "Let us continue."

He asked for early passage of a new civil rights bill "to eliminate from this nation every trace of discrimination and oppression that is based upon race or color." He asked for passage of Kennedy's tax revision measure "to provide insurance against recession." And he appealed, "Let us here highly resolve that John Fitzgerald Kennedy did not live—or die—in vain."

Johnson knew and respected the members of Kennedy's Cabinet, so he retained them, including the late President's brother, Attorney General Robert Kennedy. The next year Kennedy became the first to leave the Cabinet when he resigned in order to run successfully for the U. S. Senate in New York.

In his first State of the Union address to Congress on January 8, 1964, Johnson repeated his call for action to fulfill Kennedy's program, saying:

"Let this session of Congress be known as the session which did more for civil rights than the last hundred sessions combined; as the session which enacted the most far-reaching tax cut of our time; as the session which declared all-out war on human poverty and unemployment in these United States; as the session which finally recognized the health needs of all of our older citizens; as the session which reformed our tangled transportation and transit policies; as the session which achieved the most effective, efficient foreign aid program ever; and as the session which helped to build more homes and more schools and more libraries and more hospitals than any single session of Congress in the history of our Republic."

Congress responded to Johnson's appeal by passing all of the laws which he asked for except medical care for the aged. To head his new "war on poverty" program, Johnson appointed Sargent Shriver, Kennedy's brother-in-law who had successfully directed the Peace Corps.

In July 1964, the Republican National Convention named Senator Barry Goldwater of Arizona as its candidate for President. He was leader of the conservative wing of the party, and his nomination represented the first time in forty years—since the days of Calvin Coolidge—that conservatives had controlled the Republican Convention. Goldwater had voted against the Civil Rights Act of 1964, and in his acceptance speech he appealed to ultra-rightist organizations with the phrases "extremism in the defense of liberty is no vice" and "moderation in the pursuit of justice is no virtue." His vice-presidential running mate was Representative William E. Miller of New York.

The Democratic National Convention that met in Atlantic City, New Jersey, in August adopted a platform plank that denounced "extremism" and named such organizations as the Communist party, the Ku Klux Klan, and the John Birch Society as examples of extremist groups. By acclamation the delegates nominated Johnson as their choice for President. Johnson flew to the convention while his nomination was underway, and minutes after it had been accomplished asked the delegates to nominate for Vice President liberal Senator Hubert Humphrey of Minnesota as the man most fitted to succeed him. The delegates approved Humphrey without opposition.

In November the Johnson-Humphrey ticket won by one of the greatest landslides in American history, receiving 61.1 percent of the popular vote. Johnson won 43,129,484 votes to Goldwater's 27,178,188, and 486 electoral votes to Goldwater's 52. Johnson lost only in Alabama, Georgia, Louisiana, Mississippi, South Carolina, and Arizona. In addition the Democrats won increased majorities in both houses of Congress.

In his inaugural address on January 20, 1965, Johnson expressed his ideals and his hopes for the future:

"On this occasion, the oath I have taken before you—and before God—is not mine alone, but ours together. We are one nation and one people. Our fate as a nation and our future as a people rests not upon one citizen but upon all citizens. That is the majesty and the meaning of this moment. For every generation, there is a destiny. For some, history decides. For this generation, the choice must be our own. Even now, a rocket moves toward Mars. It reminds us that the world will not be the same for our children, or even for ourselves in a short span of years. The next man to stand here will look out on a scene that is different from our own, because ours is a time of change—rapid and fantastic change, baring the secrets of nature, multiplying the nations, placing in uncertain hands new weapons for mastery and destruction, shaking old values and uprooting old ways.

"Our destiny in the midst of change will rest on the unchanged character of our people—and on their faith. They came here—the exile and the stranger, brave but frightened—to find a place where a man could be his own man. They made a covenant with this land. Conceived in justice, written in liberty, bound in union, it was meant one day to inspire the hopes of all mankind. And it binds us still. If we keep its terms, we shall flourish. . . ."

As President in his own right, Johnson met continued success in dealing with Congress for implementation of his Great Society domestic program. The Eighty-ninth Congress approved a multi-billion-dollar federal-aid-to-education program to improve schools and libraries at all grade levels. The social security system was expanded to provide medical care for persons over sixty-five. The anti-poverty program was expanded. A new civil rights bill was approved to insure the rights of blacks to register to vote. A new Cabinet-level Department of Housing and Urban Development was created in 1966 to aid cities in attacking their problems of housing and planning. And in 1967 a new Department of Transportation was established.

Johnson received sharp criticism in 1965 for reviving U.S. imperialism in Latin America when he sent 28,000 U. S. Marines into the Dominican Republic to put down a revolt against that nation's government. He explained he was preventing communists from taking over the nation as had occurred in Cuba. He later placed the American troops under supervision of the Organization of American States, and withdrew them in 1966.

Vietnam War and National Unrest

JOHNSON'S MISCALCULATIONS in handling another foreign affairs crisis—Vietnam—far overshadowed the good he had accomplished in his domestic policies, dooming him to low esteem in history. Under Presidents Eisenhower and Kennedy military supplies and advisers had been sent to help South Vietnam preserve its sovereignty in a guerrilla war with communist North Vietnam that had been intensifying since 1955.

When U.S. destroyers were reported to have been attacked on August 2–4, 1964, by North Vietnamese torpedo boats in the Gulf of Tonkin, Johnson pushed through Congress on August 7 the "Tonkin resolution" that gave him the authority "to prevent further aggression." Johnson launched a retaliatory attack on North Vietnam with U.S. aircraft and stepped up aid to South Vietnam. When communist guerrillas attacked U.S. bases in Vietnam in February 1965, Johnson ordered all-out bombing of North Vietnam below the 20th parallel.

Because U.S. air power proved ineffective in halting the guerrilla attacks, Johnson ordered U.S. ground troops into action in Vietnam on June 28, 1965, believing American military might could quickly end the war. But he and his military advisers had seriously overestimated three things: the ability of U.S. soldiers to fight a guerrilla war, the capability of South Vietnamese armed forces, and the willingness of the American people to support a war in Asia with the lives of their sons.

The Vietnam War seriously divided the United States. Critics of the war demanded that Johnson unconditionally end the bombing of North Vietnam and were supported in this demand by Secretary General U Thant of the United Nations. But President Johnson insisted that the United States should not stop the bombing unless North Vietnam also reduced its war effort. Critics of the administration urged young men of draft age to refuse to fight in Vietnam. Tens of thousands evaded the draft, many fleeing to Canada and Europe to avoid arrest. But other groups called on Johnson to step up the war and win a clear-cut victory over North Vietnam.

In the congressional elections of 1966, the Democratic party retained control of both the Senate and the House of Representatives, but with greatly reduced majorities. Public opinion polls showed that Johnson had lost much of his popularity with the voters, largely because of the growing anti-war sentiment.

Johnson repeatedly sent messages to North Vietnam asking for negotiations to end the fighting. But the North Vietnamese rejected these messages, insisting that the United States end its bombing of North Vietnam and withdraw its forces from South Vietnam.

Although the United States had half a million troops fighting in Vietnam by 1968, North Vietnam demonstrated the ineffectiveness of the American forces by launching the biggest offensive of the war on January 30 with large-scale attacks on thirty South Vietnamese cities, including Saigon, the capital. American casualties mounted, as did protests against the war.

Desperate to find a way out of the morass in which he had become entangled, Johnson announced, in a dramatic television address to the American people on March 31, 1968, that he was calling a partial halt to the bombing of North Vietnam in an effort to show America's seriousness in seeking peace negotiations. At the same time, to remove all possibility that his move might be interpreted as promoting his own political fortunes, Johnson announced he would not be a candidate for another term as President. North Vietnam responded favorably, and in May face-to-face negotiations began between American and North Vietnamese emissaries in Paris.

In deciding not to run for another term, Johnson followed the historical precedent that no "accidental" President ever had been twice elected to the presidency. All those before him had either not tried or had failed if they did try, including John Tyler, Millard Fillmore, Andrew Johnson, Chester Arthur, Theodore Roosevelt, Calvin Coolidge, and Harry S Truman. And, in fact, only two former Vice Presidents ever have been twice elected President —Thomas Jefferson, who had served as Vice President under John Adams, and later Richard Nixon (in 1968 and 1972).

Meanwhile, domestic violence was growing in the United States, partly as a result of protests against the Vietnam War and partly because poor blacks in the nation's cities believed that funds they should be receiving were being diverted to the war effort. Riots broke out in the black ghettos in scores of cities in 1966 and 1967. The worst took place in Detroit on July 23–30, 1967, when forty-three persons were killed and more than 2,000 injured before federal troops and National Guardsmen brought the fighting and looting under control. When black civil rights leader Reverend Martin Luther King, Jr., was assassinated on April 4, 1968, in Memphis, Tennessee, racial riots exploded in more than 100 cities. Johnson even had to call out federal troops to put down rioting in the nation's capital.

After Johnson's withdrawal from the 1968 presidential race, New York Senator Robert F. Kennedy, who had served as Attorney General both under his brother, John F. Kennedy, and under Johnson, became one of the leading contenders for the Democratic nomination. Kennedy strongly opposed the Vietnam War and supported greater efforts to help blacks and the poor. He had just won the important California Democratic primary when, like his brother, he was shot down by an assassin on June 5, 1968, and died the next day.

Kennedy's death markedly changed the political picture for the Democrats. In August Johnson flew to Chicago to unite the party and to help Vice President Humphrey win the Democratic presidential nomination. Protest against the Vietnam War had by then reached a fever pitch, dividing the nation. While the convention proceeded in orderly fashion indoors, outside the convention hall thousands of youthful anti-war demonstrators staged demonstrations, loudly vocalizing their opposition to the war. When the demonstrators organized a protest march, police and National Guardsmen attacked with clubs, injuring hundreds as TV cameras broadcast the violence into millions of homes across the nation.

The Vietnam peace talks dragged on through the summer and fall of 1968 with no positive results, because the North Vietnamese continued to insist that all bombing of North Vietnam must be halted before any agreements could be reached. Then on October 31, 1968, President Johnson announced that he was ordering an end to all bombing of North Vietnam and that the Paris peace talks would be expanded to include representatives of the South Vietnamese government and the Viet Cong, the communist rebels of South Vietnam. But subsequent resistance by the South Vietnamese to sitting down with their communist enemies continued to delay resumption of the talks despite the bombing halt.

Johnson had hoped that ending the bombing in North Vietnam would give a boost to Humphrey's chances in the November presidential election. He was disappointed when Humphrey was narrowly defeated by the Republican candidate, former Vice President Richard Nixon. But Johnson received some satisfaction from the inability of the Republicans to win a majority in either house of Congress.

An ardent supporter of the nation's space program from its advent when he was a senator, Johnson was pleased with a major American breakthrough in the last month of his administration. During Christmas week in 1968, three American astronauts in the Apollo 8 spacecraft successfully made man's first deep flight into space, spectacularly orbiting the moon ten times before returning safely to earth.

Johnson's Final Years

AFTER LEAVING THE PRESIDENCY, Johnson lived quietly at his LBJ Ranch near Johnson City, Texas, making few public appearances. There, he wrote his autobiography published in 1971, *The Vantage Point: Perspectives of the Presidency, 1963–1969.*

On January 22, 1973, less than a month after the death of former President Truman, the sixty-four-year-old Johnson died of a heart attack at his ranch. Ironically, his death came just one day before an agreement was initialed in Paris to end the fighting in the Vietnam War, for which he had sacrificed his political career. However, it was disclosed that shortly before his death, he had been informed by phone by President Nixon of the impending truce agreement.

Johnson's body was flown to Washington for memorial services in the same plane aboard which he had been sworn in as President nine years earlier.

After services in the nation's capital, his body was flown back to Texas and buried in a family graveyard a few hundred feet from his birthplace in Stonewall, Texas.

It had seemed when Johnson won the presidency by a landslide in 1964 and as he ramrodded through Congress his liberal legislative program in 1965 and 1966 that he might go down in history as one of the nation's great Presidents. But his failure to bring the Vietnam War to a successful conclusion and the domestic violence and spirit of discontent that developed in American life turned his administration into a disaster.

Johnson blamed his failure on the inability of the public to understand the importance of what he had been trying to achieve in South Vietnam:

". . . a President must do what he thinks is right. He must think in terms of the national interest and the Nation's security—even if this means stirring up some segments of public opinion, no matter how vociferous. I confess that on the homefront it is easier for the public to understand what an administration is planning to do. They see that some of our schools are overcrowded, that we must do something to help our Negro citizens, that we are rapidly outgrowing our cities, and they are responsive to programs that seek remedies. But when the President takes an extremely serious step in foreign matters, then it is really a more difficult proposition for people to grasp."

Richard Milhous Nixon
The Thirty-seventh President of the United States
1969–74

1913 (January 9) Born in Yorba Linda, California.

1934 Graduated from Whittier (California) College.

1937 Received law degree from Duke University in Durham, North Carolina.

1937–41 Practiced law in Whittier, California.

1940 (June 21) Married Thelma Catherine "Pat" Ryan.

1942 Attorney in the Office of Price Administration in Washington, D.C.

1942–46 Served in U. S. Navy during World War II.

1947–50 U.S. representative from California.

1950–53 U.S. senator from California.

1953–61 Vice President of the United States.

1960 Republican nominee for President, defeated by John F. Kennedy.

1962 Republican candidate for governor of California, defeated by Governor Edmund G. "Pat" Brown.

1963–68 Practiced law in New York City.

1969–74 Thirty-seventh President of the United States.

1974 (August 9) Resigned as President to avoid impeachment.

The first President to resign to avoid impeachment and conviction by Congress for misuse of power, Richard Milhous Nixon left a stain on the office of the presidency. His first term as Chief Executive from 1969 to 1973 was marked by foreign policy achievements that brought improved relations with the Soviet Union and communist China and ended United States participation in the unpopular Vietnam War—the longest and one of the costliest in U.S. history. But his second term was wrecked and aborted by the Watergate scandals that ultimately forced him to leave the White House.

After a fourteen-year career as a Republican congressman, U.S. senator, and Vice President, Nixon lost his first bid for the presidency to John F. Kennedy in a close election in 1960. Eight years later he made a surprising political comeback by winning the 1968 presidential election over Vice President Hubert H. Humphrey. He followed this with a triumphant re-election landslide in 1972 over Senator George S. McGovern of South Dakota. However, illegal actions, many stemming from his 1972 election campaign, led to Nixon's downfall and the conviction of his Vice President, three Cabinet officers, his top White House aides, and many other administration officials and campaign supporters.

Throughout the five years and six-and-a-half months of his administration, Nixon faced a politically hostile Congress. For the first time a President twice won election for himself while being unable to lead his party to a victory in either house of Congress. As a result, Nixon's administration was marked by constant conflict with Congress. The President found it difficult to get his legislative proposals enacted and he repeatedly impounded and refused to spend money on projects for which Congress had appropriated funds.

Nixon had promised during his campaign for the presidency in 1968 that he had a plan for ending the Vietnam War, which had severely divided the nation. As President he gradually brought home most of the half-million American fighting men from South Vietnam while strengthening the army of that country so it could defend itself from the forces of communist North Vietnam. The President's chief foreign policy adviser, Henry A. Kissinger, worked tirelessly to negotiate a settlement of the war. Finally, a week after President Nixon was inaugurated for his second term, a cease-fire was signed. American prisoners of war were released by the communists, and remaining American servicemen in Vietnam came home.

President Nixon also made progress in creating what he called "a new structure of peace" in the world. When he first took office, the world still was split by the Cold War between communist and anti-communist nations, causing many to fear that an atomic war between the two sides might blaze forth at any moment. Although throughout his previous political career Nixon had built a reputation as a hard-line anti-communist, he reversed the twenty-year-old official policy of the United States that had refused to recognize the communist rule of China. He helped communist China gain membership in the United Nations and then flew to Peking to dramatize America's new friendship. Next, he traveled to Moscow, where he signed agreements with the Soviet Union providing for the first limitations on the production and deployment of atomic weapons. This was followed by later summit meetings in the United States and the Soviet Union that officially brought an end to the Cold War.

Student, Lawyer, and Navy Officer

RICHARD MILHOUS NIXON was born January 9, 1913, on a farm in Yorba Linda, California, where his father raised lemons. His mother was, as he later described her, "a gentle, Quaker mother, with a passionate concern for peace," who reared her five sons as Quakers and imbued them with peaceful ideals. When Dick was nine years old, the family moved to Whittier, California. There his father opened a combination gasoline station and general store, where the brothers worked when they were not in school.

During his school years Dick Nixon took part in many activities and attained excellent grades as well. He was a leading member of the debate teams both in high school and college, winning prizes for public speaking. He acted in plays, performed on the organ at the Quaker meeting house and the piano at parties. He was elected to various school offices, including president of the college student body. And, when he graduated from Whittier College in 1934, he stood second in his class.

Nixon continued his education at the Duke University Law School in Durham, North Carolina. He had been awarded a tuition scholarship and helped pay the rest of his expenses by doing research for the dean for thirty-five cents an hour. When he graduated from Duke in 1937, he was third in his class.

Years later Nixon attributed his scholastic drive to efforts to please his father, who had been forced to leave school after the sixth grade in order to earn his living. "Never a day went by when he did not tell me and my four brothers how fortunate we were to be able to go to school. I was determined not to let him down. My biggest thrill in those years was to see the light in his eyes when I brought home a good report card. . . ."

Upon graduation from law school, Nixon returned to California, passed the state bar examination, and joined a law firm in Whittier. One of his special interests was acting in an amateur theater group. There he was introduced to Thelma Catherine "Pat" Ryan, a red-haired high school typing teacher. He proposed to her the night they met, but she refused him for two years. They finally married on June 21, 1940, when they were both twenty-seven years old, and later had two daughters, Patricia (Tricia) and Julie. After Nixon had been elected President, in 1968, his daughter Julie married David Eisenhower, the grandson of President Eisenhower. In 1971 Tricia married E. F. Cox in a White House rose-garden wedding.

After the Japanese attack on Pearl Harbor in December 1941, Nixon left his law practice to take part in the war effort. He went to Washington and obtained a $61-a-week job doing legal work in the Office of Price Administration. But after a few months he decided that despite his Quaker background he should help more directly to fight the war.

He applied for and received a navy commission as a lieutenant (j.g.) in September 1942. The following year he was sent to the South Pacific as operations officer for a navy air transport unit. After fifteen months on islands and coral atolls, he returned to shore duty in the United States, advancing to the rank of lieutenant commander by the time the war was over.

Congressman and Senator

WHILE NIXON WAS AWAITING RELEASE from the navy in November 1945, a banker friend suggested that he enter politics. He pointed out that a committee of California Republicans had unsuccessfully advertised for a congressional candidate, and would Nixon be interested. He was. The committee agreed to back him in the campaign against Jerry Voorhis, the Democratic representative from California's Twelfth District for ten years.

During the 1946 campaign the politically unknown Nixon established a reputation in a series of face-to-face debates with Voorhis. Nixon attacked Voorhis as a left-wing socialist and ridiculed his record in Congress. Because Nixon had no previous political record to attack, Voorhis was forced on the defensive. In the November election the thirty-three-year-old Nixon rode to victory as part of a nationwide Republican landslide.

Nixon became one of the youngest members of the Republican-controlled Eightieth Congress, which President Truman came to label the "Do-Nothing Congress." He was assigned to the Education and Labor Committee, where he became acquainted with another freshman congressman, John F. Kennedy. The main effort of this committee was directed toward writing the Taft-Hartley bill, called the "slave labor law" by unions. Long before they or anyone else suspected that someday they might run against each other for President, Nixon and Kennedy were called upon to debate the Taft-Hartley bill before a public meeting in McKeesport, Pennsylvania. Nixon said later of this debate: "I was for the bill. Kennedy was against it. And we both presented our points of view as vigorously as we could. As far as the audience was concerned, I probably had the better of the argument because most of those present, as employers, tended to be on my side in the first place." Nixon helped pass the Taft-Hartley Act over President Truman's veto.

The Cold War between the United States and the Soviet Union was developing in intensity in 1947 and 1948 with the United States becoming increasingly aware that Russia did not intend to free the countries of Eastern Europe that it had "liberated" during World War II. It was against this background that Nixon received two other committee appointments that were to shape his future career.

Nixon was named a member of the congressional Herter Committee to investigate the need for the Marshall Plan. He traveled to Europe with the other members of the committee and came back convinced that economic aid was necessary to prevent the war-torn countries of Western Europe from falling to communism. He became an ardent supporter of foreign aid, a stance that in later years conservative members of his party criticized as being too liberal.

It was Nixon's assignment to the House Committee on Un-American Activities that brought him to national prominence and set the stage for his becoming Vice President and ultimately President. The committee was holding many hearings trying to determine the extent of Communist infiltration into the government, the motion picture industry, and other areas of American life. Nixon put his skills as a lawyer and a debater to work in questioning witnesses called before the committee. He seemed to have a sixth sense as to when a witness was telling less than the full truth.

Early in August 1948, a witness before the committee, Elizabeth Bentley, testified that thirty-two government officials had delivered information to her to pass on to a communist spy ring. A few days later Whittaker Chambers, a senior editor for *Time* magazine, named seven more officials and former officials as members of the Communist party or fellow travelers. Among those named was Alger Hiss, a former State Department officer who had organized the UN charter meeting in San Francisco. Two days later Hiss appeared before the committee and denied he had ever been a communist or had even known anyone named Whittaker Chambers. Hiss made such a convincing appearance that newspapers and prominent persons attacked the committee for besmirching the name of Hiss, who was then president of the Carnegie Endowment and had taken that job at the request of its board chairman, John Foster Dulles.

The majority of members of the committee were ready at this point to drop the entire Hiss-Chambers affair, but Nixon was not. He persuaded the committee to carry on the investigation in the face of public criticism, and Nixon was appointed head of a subcommittee to pursue the matter. At a press conference in Washington, President Truman dismissed the case against Hiss as a "red herring."

Throughout August 1948, Nixon, Hiss, and Chambers made newspaper headlines. Nixon brought the two together at a closed subcommittee meeting on August 17. Hiss was quite shaken because on the same day newspapers reported the death by a heart attack of Harry Dexter White, a former assistant secretary of the treasury and associate of his who had been named by Chambers as a "fellow traveler." After much hesitation, Hiss admitted he had known Chambers thirteen years earlier under the name "George Crosley," but continued to deny he had ever been a Communist. The confrontation between Hiss and Chambers was repeated in a televised public hearing on August 25. When Chambers again stated his charges on a TV show, Hiss sued for libel.

The national election campaign was in progress during this period, so for the next several weeks Nixon devoted himself to politics. He easily won re-election to Congress, although the Democrats took control and President Truman defeated his Republican opponent, Thomas E. Dewey. Nixon felt Dewey had not hit hard enough at the "communists-in-government" issue.

In November, Chambers produced secret documents that he claimed had been given to him by Hiss and by White as part of a Communist spy ring. These papers became known as the "pumpkin papers," because some were on microfilm that Chambers had hidden in a hollowed-out pumpkin on his farm.

In December, Nixon made new headlines by charging that the Democratic administration intended to diminish the impact of the Hiss-Chambers affair by prosecuting Chambers for perjury instead of Hiss. A few days later a New York grand jury indicted Hiss for perjury. Hiss' first trial ended in a hung jury in July 1949. In a second trial that ended in January 1950, he was found guilty and sentenced to five years in prison. Nixon and the House Committee on Un-American Activities had been vindicated.

Nixon's drive to expose communist infiltration in the government received a new boost in the spring of 1950 when the FBI revealed that communist agents had stolen the secret of the atomic bomb. Several Americans were arrested and convicted as part of the communist A-bomb spy ring. Two of the American spies for Russia, Julius and Ethel Rosenberg, were executed in 1953.

Riding high on the crest of his fame as a communist-hunter, Nixon ran for the United States Senate in 1950 against Democratic Congresswoman Helen Gahagan Douglas. His campaign attacked Mrs. Douglas' reputation, claiming she had supported communist policy against the best interests of the United States. Earl Warren, who was at that time the popular Republican governor of California, refused to campaign with Nixon. But in the November election Nixon won by a plurality of nearly 700,000 votes.

At thirty-seven, Nixon became the youngest Republican U.S. senator. But, as a freshman Republican senator in a Senate controlled by Democrats, he had little opportunity for significant assignments. Yet his popularity continued to grow, and during 1951 he appeared as a speaker at many Republican meetings across the country. On a trip to Europe he met with General Dwight Eisenhower and joined the Eisenhower campaign for the Republican presidential nomination.

Vice President of the United States

AT THE REPUBLICAN NATIONAL CONVENTION in July 1952, in Chicago, Eisenhower received the nomination with little difficulty. He then invited Nixon to be his vice-presidential running mate. "No one has done more to put the fear of God into those who would betray their country," said one of the speakers who supported Nixon's candidacy.

But in September it looked as though Nixon would be forced to drop out of the race. The New York *Post* ran a front-page story accusing Nixon of using a secret $18,000 fund collected by a "millionaires' club" for personal expenses. Demands flooded in to Eisenhower asking him to remove Nixon from the ticket. Eisenhower replied that to remain a candidate Nixon would have to prove he was "as clean as a hound's tooth." On September 23, five days after the story had broken, Nixon, with his wife at his side, appeared on a nationwide TV show to clarify the issue. The largest television audience to that time—some sixty million persons—watched and listened as Nixon explained that the fund had been used solely to aid his political campaign and had not been used for personal expenses. He listed all of his assets. And he told viewers that although someone had given his children a small dog called Checkers, he did not believe he should take the dog away from them simply because he was a public figure. "I don't believe I ought to quit because I am not a quitter," he said. He appealed to the audience to send in their views as to what he should do. Millions of letters and phone calls poured in during the next several days with a response that was overwhelmingly pro-Nixon. It was one of his greatest triumphs over his detractors.

As the campaign proceeded, Nixon ruthlessly attacked Adlai Stevenson, the Democratic nominee for President. He particularly denounced Stevenson for once having given testimony upholding Alger Hiss' character, and for failing to recognize the threat of communist subversion in the United States. The Eisenhower-Nixon ticket won by a landslide, as it did again in the election of 1956.

During his eight years as Vice President, from 1953 to 1961, Nixon took a more active role in the government than had any previous holder of the office. However, he later described the vice presidency as ". . . a hollow shell—the most ill-conceived, poorly defined position in the American political system." During Eisenhower's absences from Washington, Nixon presided over nineteen meetings of the President's Cabinet and twenty-six meetings of the National Security Council. The United States Senate was evenly divided between Republicans and Democrats in 1953 to 1954, but Nixon as presiding officer was called upon to decide only eight tie votes.

Nixon was one of the first to provoke public controversy over Vietnam. In 1954, when it became apparent that the French were about to pull their forces out of that Communist-torn country, Nixon openly advocated sending American troops to Vietnam if necessary to prevent the entire country from falling to communism.

In the early years of the Eisenhower presidency, Senator Joseph McCarthy was in his heyday, claiming that all communists still had not been rooted out of government jobs. At first Nixon acted as an intermediary between Eisenhower and McCarthy, warding off a direct fight. But Nixon broke with McCarthy in 1954 when the senator openly attacked the Eisenhower administration and held a long series of hearings probing the U. S. Army's handling of security risks. During the congressional election of 1954, Nixon crisscrossed the country assuring voters that the administration had "fired the communists and fellow travelers and security risks by the thousands." But the Democrats won control of Congress and held it for the last six years of the Eisenhower-Nixon administration.

When President Eisenhower was incapacitated by a heart attack in 1955, by an intestinal disorder in 1956, and by a stroke in 1957, Nixon kept the executive branch of the government running smoothly. As he later explained: "My role was to absorb some of the more routine duties of the President, relieving the burden on him, and yet not to appear to be stepping into his shoes."

Eisenhower frequently called upon Nixon to make good-will trips to foreign countries, and in the course of these assignments he visited fifty-four nations. On a tour of South America in 1958, communist-led mobs jeered Nixon, spat on him, and tried to overturn his car and kill him. He showed great courage in the face of these attacks, increasing his popularity in the United States because of his cool-headed actions. On a visit to Russia in 1959, Nixon engaged in a series of informal public debates with the Russian leader, Nikita Khrushchev, on the merits of democracy versus communism. Most Americans felt that Nixon came out ahead.

Losing Two Big Elections

BY LATE 1959 it was generally accepted that Nixon and Kennedy were likely to be the opposing candidates in the next presidential election. Nixon was heartened as public opinion polls showed him leading Kennedy in popularity by a margin of 53 percent to 47 percent. Nixon entered and won all the state Republican preferential primaries unopposed. Kennedy also won in the primaries, overcoming his strongest opponent, Senator Hubert Humphrey of Minnesota. By the time the primaries came to an end, Kennedy led Nixon in the public opinion polls by a percentage of fifty-two to forty-eight.

Nixon's main opponent for the Republican presidential nomination in 1960 was Nelson Rockefeller, who had won the governorship of New York in 1958 despite Republican losses all across the nation. Rockefeller was critical of the Eisenhower administration and demanded a more liberal GOP party platform. Nixon went to New York and in a meeting with Rockefeller reached agreement on the wording of the platform.

With the backing of President Eisenhower, Nixon won by acclamation the Republican presidential nomination at the Chicago convention in July. He chose as his running mate Henry Cabot Lodge, Jr., the U.S. ambassador to the UN. "I believe in the American dream," Nixon told the convention in his acceptance speech, "because I have seen it come true in my own life." In the weeks that followed he campaigned tirelessly in every one of the fifty states.

Nixon reluctantly agreed to a series of four public debates with Kennedy on TV. "I knew from long experience," Nixon said, "that in debate the man who can attack has a built-in advantage that is very hard to overcome." On the other hand, he felt obligated to take part in the debates. "Had I refused the challenge, I would have opened myself to the charge that I was afraid to defend the Administration's and my own record."

Political commentators have generally agreed that the Nixon-Kennedy debates were an important factor in Nixon's losing the election. Nixon later believed he made a serious mistake in not using TV makeup to improve his appearance before the cameras. He realized it when his mother phoned him from California after the first debate to ask if he was "feeling all right." She was one of an estimated eighty million viewers.

The results of the November election were very close. There were indications of fraud in the vote count in Illinois and Texas, both of which went to Kennedy by small margins. But Nixon did not fight for a recount, feeling that it would do "incalculable and lasting damage throughout the country." He conceded the election and sent Kennedy his best wishes.

After his term as Vice President was completed, Nixon returned to California where he joined the law firm of Adams, Duque & Hazeltine of Los Angeles. During the next year he wrote the book *Six Crises*, which detailed the highlights of his career to date. It was published in March 1962. In it he indicated why he would not give up politics:

". . . probably the greatest magnet of all is that those who have known great crisis—its challenge and tension, its victory and defeat—can never become adjusted to a more leisurely and orderly pace. They have drunk too deeply of the stuff which really makes life exciting and worth living to be satisfied with froth."

Eleven months following his defeat in the presidential election, Nixon announced he would run for governor of California in 1962. He fought a hard campaign against Democratic Governor Edmund G. "Pat" Brown. But Brown easily won with 53.6 percent of the vote. At a news conference soon after the election, Nixon lost his temper, blaming his defeat on what he considered was biased coverage of the campaign by newsmen. After that, almost everyone believed Nixon's political career was over.

Historic Comeback to Win the Presidency

As NIXON HAD TOLD 60 MILLION TV viewers in 1952 at the time of the "fund scandal," he was not a quitter. He changed his base of operations in 1963 by moving to New York City, where he became a partner in the law firm of Nixon, Mudge, Rose, Guthrie, Alexander & Mitchell. Although he made no effort to win the Republican presidential nomination in 1964, he hit the campaign trail to support the party's nominee, Senator Barry Goldwater. After Goldwater's disastrous loss to Lyndon Johnson, Nixon helped rebuild the shattered forces of the Republican party. He campaigned vigorously to aid local candidates throughout the nation in the elections of 1965 and 1966. By 1967 he was again a leading contender for the presidency, and public opinion polls in November of that year showed he was more popular than President Johnson.

The Democratic party was bitterly divided in 1968 over President Johnson's policy of massive U.S. intervention in the Vietnam War. Senator Eugene McCarthy of Minnesota launched a campaign for the Democratic presidential nomination as a peace candidate. He won a surprisingly strong showing in the first presidential preferential primary of 1968 in New Hampshire. Shortly after, Senator Robert Kennedy of New York, the late President's brother, announced his candidacy in opposition to Johnson. Then on March 31 Johnson declared a halt to the bombing of much of North Vietnam and at the same time said he would not be a candidate for re-election in order to devote his full time to trying to obtain a peace in Vietnam. Vice President Humphrey then entered the race with Johnson's backing.

Calling for the country to "move in a different direction," Kennedy seemed to be gaining the most popular support for the nomination. But shortly past midnight on June 5, just as he had finished a victory speech upon winning the crucial California primary, an assassin's bullet struck him down. His sorrowing followers refused to join McCarthy in a stop-Humphrey drive.

At the Democratic National Convention in Chicago, a further pall was thrown over the party by violence that broke out in the streets between police and peace demonstrators, many of whom were McCarthy supporters. The proceedings of the convention were disrupted for a short time, but the delegates went on to nominate Humphrey as the Democratic candidate for the presidency. He chose as his running mate Senator Edmund Muskie of Maine.

Nixon had proved his ability to attract the voters in the Republican primaries. In March he captured the New Hampshire primary from Governor George Romney of Michigan. And in May he triumphed over Governor Nelson Rockefeller of New York in the Oregon primary. At the Republican National Convention in Miami, he received the presidential nomination on the first ballot, naming Governor Spiro Agnew of Maryland as his choice for Vice President.

The election campaign was complicated by the entrance of a third party—the American Independent party. It was formed by George C. Wallace, a former governor of Alabama who was a symbol of the Deep South's antagonism toward the liberalization of civil rights for blacks. Wallace and his running mate, retired Air Force General Curtis LeMay, sought the vote of those who felt that both Humphrey and Nixon were too liberal. LeMay advocated use of the atomic bomb if necessary to end the Vietnam War. Wallace hoped to garner enough electoral votes to prevent either major party candidate from winning a clear-cut victory and thus throw the choice of the next President to the House of Representatives. There, Wallace believed, he could force one or the other of the two leading candidates to accept his policies in return for enough votes to be elected.

At the start of the campaign, public opinion polls indicated that Nixon would be the winner. Nixon campaigned in a more relaxed manner than ever before. His posters used the bland slogan, "Nixon's the One." He refrained from making the Vietnam War an issue. And he avoided any TV debates with Humphrey.

Five days before the election, President Johnson announced that he was ordering a halt to all bombing of North Vietnam. Peace advocates, such as McCarthy, had been calling for this action for months. McCarthy, who had first refused to support Humphrey's campaign, now endorsed him as the Democratic nominee. Public opinion polls indicated that Humphrey was rapidly overtaking Nixon's lead and might even win.

On election night, November 5, it appeared for some time that Nixon was about to lose again. Humphrey took an early lead in the East, winning such states as Connecticut and New York by large majorities. Then Nixon began to pick up strength, winning many southern states, most of the states of the Midwest, and all the western states except Washington and Hawaii. In the final count Nixon won in thirty-two states with 301 electoral votes, Humphrey won thirteen states with 191 electoral votes, and Wallace took five states with 46 electoral votes. The popular vote was much closer, with Nixon leading Humphrey by only seven-tenths of one percent of more than seventy-two million votes cast.

The Uniqueness of Nixon's Victory

NIXON'S TRIUMPH WAS UNIQUE in several ways. Four other men had made similar presidential comebacks—Thomas Jefferson, Andrew Jackson, William Henry Harrison, and Grover Cleveland. But, on their successful second tries, each of these men had waited only four years to run again. Nixon was the first to wait eight years before making good on a second try. He was the first to overcome a fresh opponent rather than a man he already had run against. And he was the first Republican to achieve such a comeback.

Nixon was the twelfth President to have once been a Vice President. But he was the first former Vice President in 132 years to enter the presidency by winning it. Before him, only Vice Presidents John Adams (1796), Thomas Jefferson (1800), and Martin Van Buren (1836) had done so. The other eight succeeded to the presidency upon the deaths of their predecessors.

The 1968 election between Nixon and Humphrey was only the second time in history that a former Vice President and an incumbent Vice President had run against each other. The only other such race took place 168 years earlier in 1800, when Adams was defeated by Jefferson. And Nixon's win over Vice President Humphrey was only the second time that anyone had defeated an incumbent Vice President seeking the White House. The first time was in 1960 when Nixon himself was defeated by Kennedy.

Nixon was unable to carry enough Republican congressmen and senators to victory, and the Democrats retained control of both houses of Congress. It was the first time in 120 years—since the election of Zachary Taylor—that the party of a new man being elected President had failed to win either house of Congress. Thus from the outset of his term of office, Nixon was faced with the necessity of compromising with the opposition party in order to get any legislation passed.

The fifty-six-year-old Nixon was sworn into office as the thirty-seventh President less than a month after American astronauts had accomplished man's first triumphal flight around the moon. Referring to this in his inaugural address, Nixon drew an ironic parallel: "We find ourselves rich in goods, but ragged in spirit; reaching with magnificent precision for the moon, but falling into raucous discord on earth." He called for unity and an end to the strife that had divided America on the issues of the Vietnam War and expanded civil rights for blacks, saying, "To go forward at all is to go forward together."

Above all else, Nixon dedicated his administration to seek world peace:

"I have taken an oath today in the presence of God and my conscience: To uphold and defend the Constitution of the United States. And to that oath, I now add this sacred commitment: I shall consecrate my office, my energies and all the wisdom I can summon, to the cause of peace among nations."

Nixon became the highest-paid President to take office to that time. Less than a week before his inauguration, Congress, acting on a recommendation from President Johnson, doubled the presidential salary from $100,000 to $200,000.

Early Years of the Nixon Administration

IN THE FIRST SEVERAL MONTHS of Nixon's administration, the country adopted a wait-and-see attitude. Vietnam peace talks had begun in Paris in January 1969 among the United States, North Vietnam, South Vietnam, and the Viet Cong. For some time public hope remained high that a breakthrough for peace might take place at the conference table, but as fighting in the war went on in the spring of 1969 new anti-war protests broke out among draft-age students at many college campuses. In answer Nixon announced in June that, although there had been no progress in the Paris talks or in secret negotiations, he planned to begin the gradual withdrawal of American forces from the war zone with the first 25,000 troops due home by September. He made continued withdrawal contingent (1) upon what he termed the "Vietnamization" of the war—the increased capability of South Vietnamese soldiers to take over the defense of their country, and (2) upon the exercise of restraint by the North Vietnamese in not increasing their attacks on the remaining U.S. forces in Vietnam.

A temporary lift to American spirits took place in July 1969 when American astronauts Neil A. Armstrong and Edwin E. Aldrin of the Apollo 11 flight became the first men to land on the moon. Uncounted millions of people watched as television cameras sent back pictures to earth of the historic feat.

President Nixon talked by radio-telephone to the astronauts from 200,000 miles away, saying, "For one priceless moment in the whole history of man all the people on this earth are truly one—one in their pride in what you have done and one in our prayers that you will return safely to earth."

Subsequently, the flight of Apollo 12 in November 1969 gave two more astronauts, Charles Conrad, Jr., and Alan L. Bean, an opportunity to explore the moon's surface.

Both flights brought back rocks that indicated the moon was over four billion years old, but the astronauts found no signs of life, past or present, on the moon.

Another moon flight, Apollo 13 in April 1970, nearly ended in disaster when the spacecraft experienced a power failure deep in space near the moon, but emergency procedures brought the crew safely back to earth. Four more successful moon trips took place—two in 1971 and two in 1972.

Although the space flights to the moon clearly showed America's technological advancement to the rest of the world, many persons raised questions as to why such complicated scientific achievements could be accomplished while seemingly simpler problems, such as poverty, hunger, inadequate education, and other social ills, remained unsolved. Partly in response to such criticism, President Nixon reduced the budget for future space explorations, although he pledged that the program would continue in the 1970s with a "grand tour" of all the planets in the solar system by unmanned spacecraft and with the development of an atomic-powered spaceship.

Difficulty Filling Supreme Court Vacancies

THE SUPREME COURT became embroiled in greater political controversy than at any time since Franklin D. Roosevelt's attempt to "pack" the Court with liberals in the late 1930s. In the waning months of President Johnson's administration, seventy-seven-year-old Chief Justice Earl Warren had announced his desire to retire. Johnson attempted to fill the position by nominating Associate Justice Abe Fortas. But opposition to the appointment developed in the Senate when doubt was cast on Fortas' ethics, for accepting a teaching fee and for jeopardizing Constitutional separation of powers by acting as an adviser to Johnson while sitting on the Supreme Court. Consequently, Fortas withdrew his name and Warren continued as Chief Justice into the early months of the Nixon administration.

Controversy continued to swirl about Fortas as it was revealed he had accepted a $20,000 fee from the family foundation of a financier who had been convicted of stock swindling. Although Fortas declared he had returned the money and had not been guilty of misconduct, he resigned in May 1969 —the first Associate Justice ever to quit the Court under fire.

Shortly after Fortas' resignation, Nixon named a new Chief Justice, Warren E. Burger, a conservative federal judge from Minnesota. The nomination was quickly confirmed.

Then new controversy broke as Nixon, in an effort to repay debts to southern political leaders who had helped him win the presidency, attempted to fill Fortas' chair with a southern conservative. He first nominated Federal Judge Clement F. Haynsworth, Jr., of South Carolina. But a Senate investigation revealed that Haynsworth had dealt in the stock of companies whose cases he had heard as a federal judge, and the Senate rejected his nomination. Then Nixon named another southern conservative, Federal Judge G. Harrold Carswell of Florida. This time evidence was turned up that Carswell had run for the Georgia legislature many years earlier as a white supremacy racist. Again the Senate rejected the nomination.

Angered by these rebuffs to his judgment, Nixon declared that it was obvious that the Senate would never approve a Southerner to the Court. He then nominated Federal Judge Harry A. Blackmun of Minnesota, a childhood friend of Chief Justice Burger. The Senate confirmed this nomination unanimously in May 1970, and Fortas' seat finally was filled after having remained vacant for more than a year.

In 1971 the retirement of two Associate Justices of the Supreme Court enabled Nixon to appoint two additional conservatives: Lewis F. Powell, Jr., a

Virginian, and William H. Rehnquist of Arizona. The appointments gave the Supreme Court a conservative majority for the first time in more than three decades.

Vietnam War Protests

NATIONWIDE ANTI-WAR PROTESTS calling for an immediate end to the Vietnam War were organized by students who had been supporters of Senator Eugene McCarthy's presidential candidacy. Many prominent officials spoke at rallies on Vietnam Moratorium Day, October 15, 1969. But Nixon maintained silence after observing that he would "under no circumstances whatever" be affected by the protests.

Vice President Spiro Agnew answered for the administration four days later by saying, "A spirit of national masochism prevails, encouraged by an effete corps of impudent snobs who characterize themselves as intellectuals." Agnew later criticized TV and newspaper coverage of administration policies as biased against the President.

Nixon broke his self-imposed silence on November 3 with an appeal on television for support from "the great silent majority." Public opinion polls substantiated that some 60 percent of the country supported his efforts to end the war.

Protests reached a new climax when more than 300,000 demonstrators gathered in Washington, D.C., on November 15–16. They participated in a "March Against Death," carrying the names of the more than 40,000 American servicemen who had died in the war. Police and U. S. Army troops guarded the White House as the march took place, while the President remained inside watching a televised football game to indicate he would not be influenced by the protestors.

Anti-war sentiment heightened with the revelation in November that U.S. troops had massacred hundreds of Vietnamese civilians in the village of My Lai on March 16, 1968. In March 1971, after a court-martial that lasted four months, Lieutenant William Calley was found guilty of premeditated murder in the massacre. Many persons charged that the army had made Calley a scapegoat while higher officers were only given reprimands. President Nixon intervened personally in the case to save Calley from going to prison pending his appeal of the court-martial finding. Later, in 1974, Calley was freed when a federal court overturned his conviction.

Environmental Concerns and Race Relations

IN AN EFFORT TO DIVERT NATIONAL ATTENTION to a noncontroversial issue that might bring greater unity, Nixon made the theme of his first State of the Union address in January 1970 the need to rescue the natural environment from pollution, which he said "may well become the major concern of the American people in the decade of the seventies."

He proposed a ten-billion-dollar program over the next ten years to clean the nation's rivers and lakes.

"Restoring nature to its natural state," the President said, "is a cause beyond party and beyond factions. It has become a common cause of all the people of this country. It is the cause of particular concern to young Americans because they, more than we, will reap the grim consequences of our failure to act on the programs which are needed now, if we are to prevent disaster later—clean air, clean water, open spaces. These should once again be the birthright of every American. If we act now they can be. . . . Through our years of past carelessness we incurred a debt to nature and now that debt is being called."

Nixon enraged white liberals and black leaders by pursuing a policy of "benign neglect" on the issue of race relations. This policy had been recommended to him by one of his close advisers, Daniel P. Moynihan, who wrote in a confidential memo to the President:

"The time may have come when the issue of race could benefit from a period of 'benign neglect.' The subject has been too much talked about. The forum has been too much taken over by hysterics, paranoids and boodlers on all sides. We may need a period in which Negro progress continues and racial rhetoric fades."

As it became apparent in 1970 that the administration had slowed down the drive to integrate whites and blacks in previously segregated public schools, unrest developed within the administration, with many protests and resignations in the Department of Health, Education and Welfare. This culminated in the shifting of HEW Secretary Robert H. Finch from the Cabinet to a position as a White House adviser and the firing of U. S. Commissioner of Education James E. Allen, Jr., a strong advocate of school integration.

Invasion of Cambodia and New Student Unrest

THE VIETNAM WAR took a new turn in the spring of 1970, after military leaders overthrew the pro-communist chief of state of Cambodia, Prince Norodom Sihanouk. The new Cambodian government appealed for military supplies and assistance as North Vietnamese communist troops began moving toward the Cambodian capital.

After Secretary of State William Rogers had assured congressional leaders that the United States had no intention of sending U.S. troops to the aid of Cambodia, President Nixon surprised the nation on April 30 by announcing that U.S. and South Vietnamese troops were marching into Cambodia in an effort to capture North Vietnamese troops and supplies. He promised that the action would be of short duration and that all American troops would be withdrawn by June 30.

Senators and congressmen of both major political parties protested Nixon's move, pointing out that under the Constitution only Congress has the power to declare war on another country. On June 30, the day on which all American ground forces were removed from Cambodia, the Senate, in a major rebuff to Nixon's war policies, voted fifty-eight to thirty-seven for the Cooper-Church amendment, which would cut off all funds for the support of any further American military operations in Cambodia. Three years later, in 1973, a Senate investigation revealed that the U. S. Air Force had been bombing communist forces in Cambodia since 1969, while concealing the bombing from Congress and the American public.

The nation was thrown into new turmoil in May 1970, when National Guard troops fired into a crowd of student protesters on the campus of Kent State University in Ohio, killing four students.

Again, thousands of students and anti-war protesters descended on Washington, D.C., to demonstrate against the Cambodian operation and the Kent State killings. This time President Nixon indicated his concern by making a predawn visit to students camped near the Lincoln Memorial, but he gave no evidence of changing his mind about his policies on the Vietnam War.

Early in June the President again took to television to defend his sending American troops into Cambodia, terming it "the most successful operation of this long and very difficult war." He showed movies of captured enemy arms and supplies, reminded his listeners that 110,000 American troops already had been brought home from the fighting, reiterated a previous pledge that 150,000 more American troops would be withdrawn from Vietnam in the ensuing twelve months, and reaffirmed that all American troops would be removed from Cambodia by June 30.

Congress passed and President Nixon signed into law in June 1970 an act lowering the voting age from twenty-one to eighteen, although he expressed doubt that the measure was constitutional. A year later, in June 1971, constitutional doubts were erased when the Twenty-sixth Amendment to the Constitution was ratified by the states, lowering the voting age to eighteen in all elections, both federal and local.

Congressional Elections and the Pentagon Papers

IN THE CONGRESSIONAL ELECTIONS OF 1970, Nixon and Agnew personally campaigned throughout the nation in an effort to purge representatives and senators that they called "radical-liberals" and replace them with conservatives who would support administration-backed legislation. The Vietnam War did not play a significant role in the mid-term campaign issues.

Nixon, Agnew, and the Republican candidates largely emphasized their qualifications to deal with student violence and preserve law and order. On the other hand, Democratic candidates for Congress pointed to rising unemployment and worsening economic conditions under the Nixon administration.

When the votes were counted in November, Republicans made some slight gains in the Senate, lost a handful of seats in the House of Representatives, and again failed to gain a majority in either house of Congress. Nixon was left in the position of having to continue to try to work with a Democrat-controlled Congress to achieve his legislative aims.

When thousands of anti-war demonstrators staged a huge protest in Washington, D.C., on May 3–5, 1971, police at the instigation of Attorney General John N. Mitchell made the largest mass arrests in the nation's history, jailing 13,400 youths. President Nixon praised the police, but nearly four years later in January 1975 a federal court awarded $12 million damages to those arrested for violation of their civil rights.

In June 1971 the Senate passed, as an amendment to a bill extending the military draft, a measure calling for all American troops to be withdrawn from Vietnam within nine months. Shortly after, the Viet Cong proposed at the peace talks in Paris that if the United States would withdraw all forces from Vietnam by the end of 1971, the Communists would release all their war prisoners simultaneously. They further proposed that as soon as a withdrawal date had been set, a cease-fire could be agreed upon.

Opponents of President Nixon accused him of trying to prolong the Vietnam War so that he could bring it to an end in 1972—a presidential election year—and thus help himself win re-election.

Attempts by the Nixon administration to restrict the freedom of the press reached a climax in June 1971 when, for the first time in the nation's history, the federal government obtained injunctions to prevent the *New York Times* and other newspapers from publishing documents about the Vietnam War that the government contended would endanger the national security.

The Supreme Court by a six to three vote upheld the newspapers' right to publish the so-called "Pentagon Papers," which were part of a history of the Vietnam War compiled by the Department of Defense and classified as "top secret." The documents, which had been provided to the newspapers by Daniel Ellsberg, a former government employee who opposed the war, showed that the government had concealed much vital information from the public during the course of the American build-up in Vietnam.

Ellsberg and an associate, Anthony J. Russo, were indicted on charges of espionage for taking the Pentagon Papers, but their trial was dismissed two years later in 1973 as the result of disclosures during the investigation of the Watergate scandals, including the wire-tapping of Ellsberg's phone and the illegal break-in at the office of Ellsberg's psychiatrist. The break-in had been carried out by a secret White House group called the "plumbers" because they were supposed to stop "leaks" of government information to the press. Nixon's No. 2 aide, John D. Ehrlichman, was convicted and sentenced to prison with several others in 1974 for conspiracy in the "plumbers" break-in case.

Recession and Inflation

DURING THE EARLY YEARS of Nixon's administration the nation's economy slid into a recession. Prices of consumer products rose at a rate of 10 percent or more a year while labor unions continued to win large wage increases. At the same time the production of goods declined and unemployment increased to 6 percent.

For more than two years President Nixon relied on high interest rates on bank loans and reduced levels of government spending to try to adjust the economy. He repeatedly refused to insitute wage and price controls to halt inflation or to increase government spending in order to reduce unemployment.

Then, on August 15, 1971, President Nixon dramatically reversed himself, announcing in a twenty-minute nationwide telecast a "new economic policy" which called for controls on prices and wages to halt inflation, a new 10 percent tax on most imported goods, a reduction in the number of federal employees, reduced spending on foreign aid, and devaluation of the dollar by suspending its convertibility into gold.

After Nixon ended wage and price controls in 1973, inflation resumed unchecked for the remainder of his administration.

Opening the Door to China

As PART OF HIS PLAN to bring about a "generation of peace," President Nixon culminated a period of careful diplomatic preparation by flying to communist China in February 1972 for an eight-day visit to open the way toward normalization of relations, cultural exchanges, and trade with the world's largest nation.

For more than two decades, the United States had refused official recognition to the communist government of China.

As senator, Vice President, and presidential candidate, Nixon himself had been one of the foremost advocates of containing communist China. Therefore, the policy reversal had almost as many personal overtones as it did international implications and warranted the President's own assessment that "This was the week that changed the world."

The stage for the China trip had begun to be set nearly two years earlier. In 1970, the journalist Edgar Snow reported that, in a conversation he had had with Communist party Chairman Mao Tse-tung (Mao Zedong), the Chinese leader had expressed interest in a visit by the American President. Next, the "Bamboo Curtain" that had separated China from the Western world throughout the period of the Cold War parted widely enough to permit an American table tennis team to visit mainland China, where it was treated with friendliness. Then, in July 1971, Dr. Henry Kissinger, assistant to the President for national security affairs, flew to China for secret meetings with China's Premier Chou En-lai (Zhou Enlai), ensuring that a summit meeting between the leaders of the two nations would have positive results. Shortly after, President Nixon was able to surprise the world with a television announcement of the impending China trip. In October, the U.S. withdrew its opposition to China's membership in the UN, and communist China promptly was admitted to the UN while nationalist China (Taiwan) was expelled.

To make sure that all the drama of the first journey in history of an American President to China would be brought into the homes of the American public, a special TV communications satellite was launched to hover 23,000 miles over the mid-Pacific. An American advance party set up a portable TV station in China to beam instant coverage to the United States. An estimated sixty million Americans watched the pomp and ceremony of the visit, most getting their first look behind the Bamboo Curtain.

Upon his return to the U.S., the President could state with conviction that the trip had been a success: "We entered into agreements to expand cultural, educational, and journalistic contacts between the Chinese and the American people. We agreed to work to begin and broaden trade between our two countries. We have agreed that the communications that have now been established between our Governments will be strengthened and expanded. Most important, we have agreed on some rules of international conduct which will reduce the risk of confrontation and war in Asia and in the Pacific.

"We agreed that we are opposed to domination of the Pacific area by any one power. We agreed that international disputes be settled without the use of the threat of force, and we agreed that we are prepared to apply this principle to our mutual relations. . . . We've agreed that we will not negotiate the fate of other nations behind their back and we did not do so in Peking. There were no secret deals of any kind."

Ending the Cold War with the Soviet Union

PLANS FOR A U.S.-SOVIET UNION summit meeting in Moscow—the first state visit by an American President to the Russian capital—had been made public in the fall of 1971, when progress in the Strategic Arms Limitation Talks (SALT) had convinced both sides that solid achievements would be possible at a meeting of the top leaders. Trip preparations proceeded through the spring of 1972, despite a sharp escalation of fighting in Vietnam when Hanoi committed most of its main-force army to a full-scale invasion of South Vietnam.

But early in May 1972, following North Vietnam's rejection of renewed American initiatives for a negotiated settlement, the President decided new measures were needed to counter the threat to the remaining U.S. forces in Vietnam. North Vietnamese ports would be mined, he announced May 8 in a TV address to the nation, and air bombing of other supply routes would be stepped up.

Would the result be a military confrontation with the Soviet Union—main supplier of war materials to North Vietnam—or a cancellation of the forthcoming Moscow visit? President Nixon made clear that the action was not directed at the Soviet Union and that he was looking forward to better relationships with the Moscow leaders. Moscow agreed. Plans for the trip went forward.

The President and his official party arrived in Moscow on May 22. During the next eight days' ceaseless round of talks and ceremonies, a new spirit of good will formed between the leaders of the world's two most powerful nations. On Sunday, May 28, President Nixon was invited to make the first direct address on TV to the Russian people by an American chief of state. The President keynoted his message with these words: "As great powers, we shall sometimes be competitors, but we need never be enemies."

In all, nine agreements and treaties were signed during the summit meeting, the most important of which were those restricting atomic weapons. Other agreements were concerned with environmental protection, medicine, space, science and technology, the prevention of incidents at sea between military ships and planes, the creation of a joint trade commission, and a twelve-point declaration of guidelines to provide "peaceful co-existence" between the two nations.

Soviet leader Leonid I. Brezhnev flew to the United States in June 1973 for more summit meetings that were hailed as bringing an official end to the quarter century of Cold War between the world's two superpowers. Brezhnev, in a TV address to the American people, praised the new spirit of cooperation and world peace. Nine more agreements were signed for U.S.-Soviet co-operation in agriculture, transportation, and other areas.

A final summit meeting between Brezhnev and Nixon in Moscow in June 1974 failed to make substantive progress on further limitations on atomic armament, but was hailed by both leaders as having been successful as an expression of continuing friendly relations.

The 1972 Presidential Election

PRESIDENT NIXON'S 1972 diplomatic triumphs with China and the Soviet Union were accomplished while Democratic presidential aspirants battled each other in preferential primaries. In July Democrats chose Senator George S. McGovern of South Dakota as their presidential candidate and Senator Thomas F. Eagleton of Missouri as his running mate. When newspapers disclosed that Eagleton had a record of hospitalization for "nervous exhaustion," McGovern asked him to withdraw and chose R. Sargent Shriver, Jr., brother-in-law of the late President Kennedy, as the Democratic vice-presidential candidate.

Republicans meeting at Miami Beach in August nominated Nixon and Agnew for a second term by acclamation. Nixon called on Democrats and new eighteen-to-twenty-one-year-old voters to join in forming a "new majority."

To ensure his re-election, Nixon set up a campaign organization called the Committee to Re-elect the President, nicknamed CREEP by his opponents. This group collected a record-breaking $60.2 million for use in the campaign. During the later Watergate investigations, it was disclosed that much of this money had been donated illegally and had been used for illegal purposes.

The CREEP organization was responsible for the break-in and illegal wiretapping of the Democratic National Headquarters in the Watergate office building in June 1972 that ultimately led to Nixon's downfall.

Although newspapers, especially the *Washington Post,* carried stories during the 1972 campaign that tied the Watergate break-in to the White House and to the CREEP organization, Nixon and his associates were so vehement and convincing in their denials of any connection with the Watergate affair and in their attacks on the press as "irresponsible" that the public was lulled by what later became known as the "Watergate cover-up." Voter attention remained focused on the administration's efforts to end the Vietnam War.

On October 26, twelve days before the election, presidential adviser Kissinger announced in a White House press conference that "peace is at hand" in the Vietnam War. He explained that he had reached substantial agreement in secret negotiations with North Vietnamese diplomats in Paris, even though a cease-fire had not yet been signed.

In the ensuing election a record 77,718,554 voters went to the polls and gave the Nixon-Agnew ticket a landslide victory. They captured 60.7 percent of the votes to 37.5 percent for McGovern-Shriver. However, the Republicans again failed to win either house of Congress.

End of U.S. Participation in the Vietnam War

AFTER THE ELECTION, Kissinger resumed negotiations in Paris with North Vietnam's chief negotiator, Le Duc Tho. The talks went poorly. In mid-December Kissinger announced the talks had been suspended because Tho had tried to change previously agreed-upon matters.

Two days later, on December 18, President Nixon ordered the beginning of the heaviest bombing attacks of the war against North Vietnam. The intense bombing continued for nearly two weeks, despite protests about their severity from many of America's allies, including Canada. Then, on December 30, the White House announced that peace negotiations would resume in Paris and that bombing of North Vietnam's capital and main seaport would be halted. As the renewed peace talks showed progress, the President halted all bombing of North Vietnam on January 15, 1973.

In his second inauguration address, on January 20, the President said: "We stand on the threshold of a new era of peace in the world." Three days later he announced that an agreement had been reached "to end the war and bring peace with honor in Vietnam and Southeast Asia."

The formal signing of the agreements took place in Paris on January 27, and the next day the cease-fire began in Vietnam. As provided in the agreement, the remaining 25,000 American troops were withdrawn from South Vietnam during the next sixty days, and during the same period the communists released the 590 American prisoners of war they were holding. But, after a brief respite, fighting resumed between South Vietnamese and North Vietnamese forces.

Unknown to the public or to Congress, Nixon secretly had promised North Vietnam's leaders $4.75 billion in American aid to rebuild their country if they ended the war. The secret promise went unfulfilled and was not disclosed to the public until four years later, after North Vietnam had conquered South Vietnam.

The American people breathed a universal sigh of relief at the end of U.S. participation in the Vietnam War. They eagerly anticipated the "era of peace" promised by Nixon. It would take time to heal the deep wounds caused by the alienation of a substantial proportion of the nation's youth who had protested the war. More than two hundred thousand young men had refused to answer draft calls and more than half a million had deserted after being drafted. The nation's traditions of patriotism and respect for government had been seriously damaged.

But before the public could enjoy the fruits of peace, a new crisis—the Watergate scandals—erupted, bringing new divisiveness and the most serious challenge to the United States Constitution in this century.

Watergate Scandals and "White House Horrors"

THE WATERGATE SCANDALS began to transcend all other domestic concerns soon after President Nixon began his second term. The affair had its origin in the 1972 presidential election campaign in which the Republicans collected a record sum of more than $60 million and ended with a surplus of more than $4 million. But as investigations of the scandals developed and expanded during 1973–74, many "White House horrors" extending back into the President's first term were exposed. The term "White House horrors" itself was coined by Nixon's former law partner, campaign manager, and Attorney General of the United States, John N. Mitchell, who was among those subsequently convicted in the scandals and who used the term in describing those

Benjamin Harrison

William McKinley

Theodore Roosevelt

William Howard Taft

Woodrow Wilson

Warren Gamaliel Harding

Calvin Coolidge

Herbert Clark Hoover

Franklin Delano Roosevelt

Harry S Truman

Dwight David Eisenhower

actions by the administration that he conspired to keep secret to ensure Nixon's re-election.

The scandals got their name from the Watergate office-hotel buildings in Washington, D.C. There, on the night of June 17, 1972, five burglars were captured in the offices of the Democratic National Committee, carrying with them telephone wiretapping equipment and spy cameras. One of the burglars turned out to be James W. McCord, Jr., a former CIA agent and security chief of the Committee to Re-elect the President (CREEP). Mitchell, then chairman of CREEP, immediately denied that his committee had anything to do with the burglary. A White House press spokesman called it a "third-rate burglary attempt." And, five days after the burglary, President Nixon told a press conference, "There is no involvement by the White House."

In the face of these denials, the Democrats were unable to stir public opinion to regard the burglary as much more than a minor political escapade. Public apathy continued even after Washington newspapers exposed in August that $114,000 in Nixon campaign checks had been deposited to the bank account of one of the burglars, especially when the President declared on August 29, 1972:

"I can say categorically that . . . investigation indicates that no one in the White House staff, no one in this Administration, presently employed, was involved in this very bizarre incident."

Two weeks later the five burglars were indicted along with two other men: G. Gordon Liddy, an attorney for Nixon's campaign finance committee, who was said to have been fired because he refused to answer FBI questions, and E. Howard Hunt, a former White House consultant and former CIA secret agent.

All seven indicted men remained silent. But an eighth member of the bugging-burglary team, Alfred C. Baldwin III, a former FBI agent, agreed to be a government witness against the others in return for immunity from prosecution.

On October 4 the *Los Angeles Times* published Baldwin's story in which he said CREEP officials were involved and that he had transcribed wiretapped conversations of Democratic party officials, delivering them to CREEP headquarters. On October 10 the *Washington Post* reported the Republicans were sabotaging the campaigns of Democratic candidates and named Donald H. Segretti as head of the operation. On October 23 *Time* magazine reported that Segretti had been employed for the political sabotage work by Dwight L. Chapin, the President's appointments secretary, and had been paid by Herbert W. Kalmbach, the President's personal lawyer. (All three later were sent to prison.) On October 25 the *Washington Post* named H. R. "Bob" Haldeman, one of President Nixon's top two assistants in the White House, as being one of a group controlling a special White House fund of half a million dollars used for political espionage.

There were other similar stories. But, largely because the Nixon administration had for years hammered at the press, usually through speeches by Vice President Agnew claiming that the press was anti-Nixon, the public generally seemed to feel the news stories were politically inspired. By their overwhelming vote for President Nixon on November 7 the American people clearly indicated thier disbelief in the statement by Senator George McGovern that Nixon's administration was "the most corrupt in history."

The trial of the seven-man Watergate bugging-burglary team began on January 8, 1973. Hunt and four others pleaded guilty. Liddy and McCord stood trial and were found guilty on January 30. All the men refused to tell what they knew about the Watergate affair. The judge postponed sentencing until March 23 in hopes one of the convicted men might talk in order to get a reduced sentence.

During the presidential election campaign, the Justice Department had urged Congress not to conduct an investigation of Watergate so as not to impede the trial of the burglars. The House Banking and Currency Committee had voted on October 3, 1972, not to probe the Nixon campaign finances, even though the government's General Accounting Office had discovered several violations of the Federal Election Campaign Act of 1971. The GAO investigation had led to an indictment of the Nixon re-election finance committee, and a fine of $8,000 had been levied by a federal district court against the committee on January 26, 1973, after the committee did not contest the charges.

Public interest in these matters had not been great, because they had been overshadowed by the events leading to the end of American involvement in the Vietnam War and by the ceremonies surrounding the President's inauguration for his second term. But now, with all these events in the past, the Senate voted unanimously, 70–0, on February 7, 1973, to establish a seven-member select committee chaired by Democratic Senator Sam J. Ervin of North Carolina, to conduct a year-long investigation of the Watergate incident and the 1972 presidential election campaign. Other investigations of Watergate also were proceeding: a Washington grand jury was continuing to hear testimony on the Watergate burglary, a New York grand jury was exploring the campaign financing, and depositions were being taken in several civil damage suits in connection with the campaign and the Watergate incident.

While promising to co-operate with the Senate investigating committee, the White House said that the constitutional doctrine of separation of powers or executive privilege would prevent members of the administration from testifying before the committee under oath but that they might give informal testimony. Senator Ervin declared: "That is not executive privilege. That is executive poppycock."

New and startling disclosures began to be revealed almost daily. A court deposition in New York on February 27 disclosed that a $200,000 cash contribution by a financier under investigation by the Securities and Exchange Commission (SEC) had been made to CREEP. Nixon campaign officials had concealed the contribution that had been made in April 1972 and said they had given it back to the financier, Robert L. Vesco, in January 1973. Later, on May 10, a New York grand jury indicted Mitchell and former Secretary of Commerce Maurice H. Stans, on charges of perjury and conspiracy in the Vesco case. (In April 1974, after a ten-week trial, a New York jury ruled that neither was guilty. But on March 12, 1975, Stans pled guilty to five counts of election law violations during the 1972 campaign.)

On February 28, 1973, the Senate Judiciary Committee began hearings on President Nixon's nomination of L. Patrick Gray III to become director of the FBI. Gray confirmed earlier newspaper stories about the political sabotage activities of Kalmbach, Chapin, and Segretti. Gray revealed that he had been ordered not to discuss the Watergate scandals by Attorney General Richard G. Kleindienst, but on March 22 he told the committee that President Nixon's chief legal counsel, John W. Dean III, "probably" had lied in answering FBI questions during the agency's investigation of the Watergate incident.

On March 23, when the Watergate burglars were brought up for sentencing, McCord told the judge he was ready to tell who was behind the affair. Five days later, in a closed session of the Senate Watergate investigating committee, McCord named Mitchell as the "over-all boss."

President Nixon withdrew Gray's nomination as FBI director on April 5. Then, on April 17, Nixon announced he had uncovered "major developments" in the Watergate case and was reversing his stand on executive privilege, ordering his staff members to testify before the Senate inquiry. The White House withdrew previous statements about having "full confidence" in Dean, and on April 19 Dean issued a statement that no one would succeed in making him a "scapegoat" in the Watergate scandals. That same day Attorney General Kleindienst announced his withdrawal from the Watergate investigation because of "personal and professional relationships." On April 26 newspapers reported that acting FBI director Gray had admitted to friends he destroyed secret Watergate files. The next day Gray resigned.

On April 27 the *Washington Post* reported that Dean had told federal prosecutors that the President's two top assistants, Haldeman and Ehrlichman, were involved in the Watergate scandals. That same day the judge in the trial in Los Angeles of Daniel Ellsberg, who was being tried for having disclosed the Pentagon Papers to newspapers, revealed that two of the convicted Watergate burglars, Liddy and Hunt, had in 1971 broken into the office of Ellsberg's psychiatrist seeking evidence.

President Nixon, in an emotional TV address on April 30, announced the resignations of his top aides Ehrlichman, Haldeman, Dean, and Kleindienst. He named Secretary of Defense Elliot L. Richardson to succeed Kleindienst as Attorney General, giving him power to appoint a special prosecutor in the Watergate case—a step the Democrats had been urging since the previous summer. The President asked his audience "for your prayers to help me in everything that I do," saying that facts about the unfolding scandal had been concealed from him as well as from the public.

In the days immediately following the President's address, newspapers disclosed that Liddy and Hunt had been part of what was called the "plumbers" unit in the White House, using illegal methods to discover "leaks" of information that the administration wanted kept secret. On May 7 it was disclosed that the President's former White House counsel Charles W. Colson had used the "plumbers" to forge cables to show to newsmen to make them believe President Kennedy had ordered the assassination of South Vietnamese President Ngo Dinh Diem in November 1963. (In 1974 Colson pleaded guilty to charges in relation to activities of the "plumbers" and began serving a one- to three-year prison sentence.)

On May 11, 1973, the judge dismissed the Pentagon Papers trial in Los Angeles because secret wiretaps of telephone conversations of Ellsberg could not be found by the FBI. Three days later the missing wiretap documents were found in a safe in Ehrlichman's White House office along with other secret wiretaps the "plumbers" had made on the phones of newsmen and government officials. The same day, May 14, the Senate Armed Services Committee heard testimony that the White House had tried to enlist the CIA in illegal domestic spy activity, and two days later heard the deputy CIA director tell of White House attempts to use the CIA to cover up the Watergate scandal.

The Senate Watergate Investigation

THE SENATE WATERGATE investigating committee began televised public hearings on May 17, 1973—hearings that for the next several months were to bring home to millions of Americans a real-life soap opera with the names, faces, places, and events of the unfolding scandals. On May 18 McCord told the senators that he had been offered executive clemency in the name of President Nixon if he would refuse to talk. That same day the White House announced that President Nixon had no intention of resigning as had been suggested by defeated Democratic vice-presidential candidate Sargent Shriver. The next day, Mrs. Martha Mitchell, wife of the former Attorney General, told newsmen that her husband had been protecting President Nixon and that the President should resign rather than wait to be impeached.

On June 15 Jeb Stuart Magruder, former deputy director of the CREEP group, spent five hours before the televised Senate hearings detailing how he and other high administration officials financed the Watergate break-in and then conspired to cover up the scandal with perjury and payments to the accused burglars. His testimony implicated Ehrlichman, Haldeman, Mitchell, Dean, and others. (Magruder later became the first to plead guilty in the Watergate cover-up and in 1974 began serving a prison sentence of ten months to four years.)

During the week of June 17–23 the Senate investigators suspended their hearings while Soviet leader Leonid I. Brezhnev attended a summit meeting in the United States.

The Senate hearings resumed on June 25 with a full week of testimony by former White House counsel Dean, who shocked listeners with charges that President Nixon had misled the nation by denying involvement in the Watergate cover-up. He accused the President of telling him that raising a million dollars to pay "hush money" to the Watergate defendants was no problem. Dean also revealed a White House list of "political enemies" and told of efforts to get the Internal Revenue Service and other government departments to harass these people. (Dean began serving a prison sentence of one to four years in 1974 after pleading guilty in the conspiracy.)

The President refused on July 7, 1973, a request by the Senate investigators to turn over presidential papers to the committee and said that he would refuse on constitutional grounds to appear before the committee.

Mitchell, testifying before the senators in July, denied authorizing the Watergate burglary, but admitted being present at meetings where it was discussed. He claimed that his central role in the conspiracy was one of trying to protect the President from finding out about the scandals, fearing that if the President learned the details he would have destroyed his chances for reelection by disclosing them to the public.

On July 16 the Senate investigators heard testimony, and the White House confirmed, that all conversations and phone calls in the President's offices had been automatically taped since 1971.

Revelation of the existence of the White House tapes came during routine questioning of a former White House aide, Alexander H. Butterfield, who was not involved in the Watergate affair.

Sure that these tapes would provide important evidence in the investigation, both the Senate committee and the Justice Department's Watergate prosecutors served subpoenas on the White House to obtain the recordings. On July 26 the President announced he would refuse to honor the subpoenas. However, a few days later Haldeman, while testifying before the Senate investigators, revealed that the President had allowed him to take several of the tapes home. Haldeman said that what he remembered from listening to the recordings indicated the President was not involved in the cover-up of the Watergate scandals. Not satisfied with this, the senators moved ahead with efforts to get the courts to force the President to release the taped conversations.

A Vice-Presidential Resignation and Appointment

THE PROBLEMS OF THE NIXON ADMINISTRATION were further compounded in August 1973 when newspapers revealed that U.S. attorneys in Baltimore were investigating charges that Vice President Agnew had accepted bribes from contractors both before and after he became Vice President. Agnew held a televised press conference at which he admitted he was under investigation for a possible criminal indictment, but denounced the charges as "damned lies" and said that news reports that he had taken bribes were "false, scurrilous, and malicious."

Late in September a Baltimore grand jury began hearing testimony from former associates of the Vice President. Agnew filed suit to try to stop the investigation.

Suddenly Agnew announced on October 10, 1973, at what had been expected to be a routine court appearance in Baltimore, that he had resigned as Vice President. He pleaded no contest to one charge of evading federal income taxes and was sentenced to three years' probation and a fine of $10,000. The government made public evidence supporting charges that Agnew had accepted bribes of more than $100,000 as governor of Maryland and as Vice President. The bribes were paid by construction firms to obtain Maryland state contracts. Agnew continued to deny that he was guilty of any wrongdoing, claiming he resigned only to save the Nixon administration the embarrassment of a public trial.

Two days after Agnew's resignation, President Nixon used the Twenty-fifth Amendment to the Constitution for the first time, to nominate a new Vice President: Gerald R. Ford, a Republican congressman from Michigan who had been minority leader of the House of Representatives since 1965. Both houses of Congress held lengthy televised hearings dealing with Ford's background before confirming the nomination. Finally, Ford was sworn in as the nation's fortieth Vice President on December 6, 1973.

Confrontations with Congress

THROUGHOUT PRESIDENT NIXON'S ADMINISTRATION he repeatedly vetoed measures passed by Congress that would have expanded U.S. funding of education and social programs. Although both houses of Congress were controlled by Democrats, the President usually had sufficient support to uphold his vetoes. He also impounded, or refused to spend, funds voted by Congress for programs he did not support. But by 1973 opposition to any further U.S. military action in Indochina was so widespread and the President's authority had sunk so low because of the Watergate scandals that Congress began to override his vetoes.

After the Vietnam cease-fire in January 1973, the U.S. continued to bomb communist forces in Cambodia in order to make them join in the cease-fire. In May Congress voted to cut off all funds for the Cambodian bombing. Nixon vetoed the measure and the House upheld his veto.

However, Congress passed new legislation in June 1973 to halt all funds for military action in Indochina, including the Cambodian bombing. In an effort to force the President to accept it, Congress attached the measure to a bill needed to fund all federal activities beyond July 1. For a time a complete breakdown of U.S. government operations appeared imminent when Nixon vetoed the legislation on June 27 and the House again upheld his veto. Two days later the crisis was averted after Republican congressional leaders prevailed on the President to accept new legislation to end all U.S. military action in Indochina on August 15, 1973.

Fears of U.S. future involvement in another prolonged conflict like the Vietnam War caused Congress to approve legislation limiting the President's war-making powers. When Nixon vetoed the measure in November 1973, both houses of Congress overrode his veto. The law requires the President to consult with Congress before committing U.S. armed forces in hostilities and requires termination of such military activities within sixty days unless Congress declares war or otherwise approves continuation of U.S. participation.

When the fourth Arab-Israeli War in three decades broke out in October 1973, the U.S. rushed military supplies to aid Israel. In retaliation, Arab nations placed a six-month embargo on oil shipments to the U.S. and other nations friendly to Israel. The embargo brought a shortage of gasoline and fuel oil in the winter months of 1973–74. President Nixon ordered restrictions on the use of fuel, but resisted demands for gasoline rationing. He called on Congress to support his plans for Project Independence, to make the U.S. self-sufficient in energy by the 1980s. In March 1974 President Nixon vetoed an emergency energy bill passed by Congress because it called for a roll-back of rising oil prices.

Impeachment Proceedings and New Revelations

THE WATERGATE SCANDALS reached a new crescendo in what was called the "Saturday Night Massacre," on October 20, 1973. In an effort to prevent the disclosure of damaging evidence in the scandals, the President had ordered special Watergate prosecutor Archibald Cox to drop his efforts to subpoena White House tapes of presidential conversations relating to Watergate. When Cox refused, the President ordered Attorney General Richardson to fire Cox. Richardson and Deputy Attorney General William D. Ruckelshaus immediately resigned rather than carry out the order. Cox then was fired by the new Acting Attorney General, Robert H. Bork.

These highhanded actions by the President brought a public outcry and new demands for his resignation or impeachment. The House of Representatives instituted impeachment proceedings, with the House Judiciary Committee collecting evidence and holding closed hearings to determine whether impeachment was warranted. The President refused to co-operate with the committee and would not honor committee subpoenas for White House tapes and documents.

In the winter of 1973–74 new events and revelations steadily worsened the President's position. He made unsuccessful efforts to regain public confidence by such measures as a TV address on November 17, 1973, in which he declared, "I'm not a crook."

After newspaper articles accused the President of improprieties in the handling of his personal income taxes, the White House revealed in December 1973 that he had become a millionaire since taking office but admitted that he had paid only $1,670.84 in income taxes for the years 1970 and 1971. After a congressional investigation of the matter, the President announced in April 1974 that he would pay $432,787.13 in back income taxes for 1969–72.

During 1973 and 1974 there were many reports of large sums having been spent by the government as "security measures" to improve estates owned by President Nixon in California and Florida. A House subcommittee in March 1974 reported that these government improvements had totaled $17 million. The White House claimed the report was distorted.

A new special Watergate prosecutor, Leon Jaworski, had been appointed in November 1973. He continued Cox's efforts to secure White House tapes and documents as evidence, receiving some but being denied others. On March 1, 1974, Jaworski obtained grand jury indictments of Nixon's former two top assistants, Haldeman and Ehrlichman, of former Attorney General Mitchell, and of several others on charges of involvement in a conspiracy to cover up the Watergate affair. (On January 1, 1975, after a three-month trial, Haldeman, Ehrlichman, and Mitchell were found guilty by a jury on all counts, and were sentenced to two-and-a-half to eight years in prison. The Supreme Court rejected their appeals in 1977 and they were jailed.)

In a further futile effort to defend himself, President Nixon on April 30, 1974, made public edited transcripts of some of the White House tapes of conversations that had previously been made available to the Watergate grand jury. The President claimed in vain these White House-edited tapes would prove his non-involvement in the Watergate cover-up. Published in paperback editions for newsstand sale, the Watergate tape transcripts became instant best sellers, and they were widely interpreted as proving the President *had* approved the payment of "hush money" to Watergate burglars to ensure their silence.

The Watergate grand jury, on June 6, 1974, was revealed to have named the President as an unindicted co-conspirator in the Watergate cover-up. The grand jury forwarded its evidence to the House Judiciary Committee considering the President's impeachment. Another blow at the integrity of President Nixon's administration was delivered the next day when former Attorney General Kleindienst, who had pleaded guilty to having misled a Senate committee, received a suspended sentence, the first Cabinet officer convicted of a crime since the days of the Harding administration's Teapot Dome scandal in the 1920s.

The President's position further eroded in July 1974. A staff report of the Senate Watergate investigating committee indicated Nixon had used campaign funds to buy his wife diamond earrings and pay for improvements to his Florida estate. His former chief domestic adviser, John Ehrlichman, was convicted with three others of conspiracy in the "plumbers' " break-in of Daniel Ellsberg's psychiatrist's office to obtain evidence for the Pentagon Papers trial. Ehrlichman was sentenced to twenty months to five years in prison. Former Secretary of the Treasury John B. Connally, who had been repeatedly mentioned as a contender for the 1976 Republican presidential nomination, was indicted by the Watergate grand jury on charges of accepting a $10,000 bribe from a dairy co-operative to influence an increase in milk prices.

Before a huge nationwide television audience, the House Judiciary Committee began public debate on articles of impeachment of the President on July 24, 1974. Six Republicans joined twenty-one Democrats on the committee on July 27 to vote for impeachment of President Nixon for obstructing justice in the Watergate cover-up, with the final vote twenty-seven to eleven. By an even larger bipartisan vote of twenty-eight to ten, the committee on July 29 approved a second article of impeachment charging the President with abuse of power and violating the Presidential Oath of Office. A third article of impeachment for contempt of Congress was approved twenty-one to seventeen on July 30, because of the President's defiance of committee subpoenas.

Nixon's Resignation and Pardon

CLAIMING "EXECUTIVE PRIVILEGE," President Nixon had for months fought to prevent release to the special Watergate prosecutor of an additional sixty-four White House tapes and other documents. However, on July 24, 1974, the Supreme Court had ruled unanimously by an eight to zero vote that the President must comply with the special prosecutor's subpoenas.

Admitting that his impeachment by the House was "virtually a foregone conclusion," President Nixon on August 5 made public parts of the additional tapes he now was required to turn over to the courts. They revealed that less than a week after the Watergate break-in in 1972 the President had instructed his then chief of staff, H. R. Haldeman, to obstruct the FBI investigation of the affair.

Almost all support for the President now collapsed. Republican congressional leaders reported to the President that not only would he be impeached by the House but that the Senate was sure to convict him.

On August 9, 1974, Richard Milhous Nixon became the first President ever to resign. In a televised speech to the nation the night before he did so, the sixty-one-year-old Nixon announced he had decided to resign because "it has become evident to me that I no longer have a strong enough political base in the Congress" to justify continued efforts to remain in office. He did not mention his impending impeachment, nor did he admit being guilty of any of the charges leveled against him. Nixon's resignation became effective shortly before noon on August 9, while he was flying west to retirement at his home in San Clemente, California.

A month after Nixon's resignation, his successor, President Gerald R. Ford, on September 8, 1974, surprised and shocked the nation by granting the former President a "full, free, and absolute pardon" for all offenses committed during his administration. By this action Ford saved Nixon from the possibility of criminal indictment and trial. In accepting the pardon, Nixon again made no admission of guilt. He said:

"Looking back on what is still in my mind a complex and confusing maze of events, decisions, pressures, and personalities, one thing I can see clearly now is that I was wrong in not acting more decisively and more forthrightly in dealing with Watergate, particularly when it reached the stage of judicial proceedings and grew from a political scandal into a national tragedy.

"No words can describe the depths of my regret and pain at the anguish my mistakes over Watergate have caused the nation and the Presidency, a nation I so deeply love and an institution I so greatly respect.

"I know that many fair-minded people believe that my motivation and actions in the Watergate affair were intentionally self-serving and illegal. I now understand how my own mistakes and misjudgments have contributed to that belief and seemed to support it. This burden is the heaviest one of all to bear.

"That the way I tried to deal with Watergate was the wrong way is a burden I shall bear for every day of the life that is left to me."

Four years later, in 1978, he published his autobiographical *RN: The Memoirs of Richard Nixon*. In the book he admitted involvement in the efforts to cover up White House participation in the Watergate affair. He disclosed that he preserved the tapes that were ultimately his undoing because he believed they would protect him from charges by aides who might testify against him.

Gerald Rudolph Ford
The Thirty-eighth President of the United States
1974–77

1913 (July 14) Born in Omaha, Nebraska.

1915 Moved with mother to Grand Rapids, Michigan, where he grew up.

1935 Graduated from the University of Michigan; named to college all-stars football team.

1935–41 Assistant football coach at Yale University.

1941 Received law degree from Yale University.

1941–42 Practiced law in Grand Rapids, Michigan, in partnership with Philip Buchen.

1942–46 Served in U. S. Navy during World War II, rising from ensign to lieutenant commander.

1946–48 Practiced law in Grand Rapids, Michigan.

1948 (October 15) Married Elizabeth Bloomer Warren.

1949–73 U.S. representative from Michigan; minority leader of the House, 1965–73.

1973 (December 6) Sworn in as the fortieth Vice President of the United States under President Nixon, the first person ever appointed to the office under the Twenty-fifth Amendment.

1974–77 Thirty-eighth President of the United States.

T he first Chief Executive to reach the White House by the route of a vice-presidential appointment rather than election, sixty-one-year-old Gerald R. Ford became President at the climax of a constitutional crisis in 1974 over the Watergate scandals that had caused his predecessor, Richard Nixon, to resign in disgrace. A determinedly honest and deeply religious Episcopalian, Ford promised upon being sworn in that "our long national nightmare is over."

The people of the United States, weary and disillusioned by the almost daily revelations of misdeeds by government officials, welcomed Ford's accession. As the first Eagle Scout to become President, he seemed sure to restore honesty and integrity to the nation's highest office. For the first time since Franklin D. Roosevelt had moved into the White House in 1933 during the Great Depression, Americans were almost unanimous in their support of a Chief Executive. But the honeymoon was short-lived.

Without prior consultation with congressional leaders or with the special Watergate prosecutor, and without giving any previous hint of his intentions, Ford made a surprise announcement only a month after taking office that he had granted Nixon a "full, free, and absolute pardon for all offenses" committed during his administration. At the same time he revealed that Nixon eventually would be allowed to destroy the tapes of conversations that played an important part in his downfall, but this agreement was later nullified by Congress.

Outraged that Nixon would be allowed to escape indictment and trial while his associates went to prison, the news media recalled a sarcastic comment attributed to President Lyndon Johnson: "Jerry Ford is a nice guy, but he played too much football with his helmet off." More seriously, congressional leaders called the pardon a "misuse of power"—an impeachable offense. Questions were raised as to the constitutionality of granting a pardon prior to conviction in a court of law, and speculation was widely voiced that the pardon was part of a political "deal" by which Ford had attained the presidency.

Defending his action, Ford declared: "There was no understanding, no deal between me and the former President . . . I am absolutely convinced, when dealing with the reality in this very, very difficult situation that I made the right decision in an effort, an honest conscientious effort, to end the discussions and turmoil in the United States."

Throughout most of Ford's twenty-nine-month administration the nation suffered a severe economic recession. Inflation pushed consumer prices to record highs. Unemployment hit the largest number of Americans since the 1930s. As a Republican, Ford was unable to develop a comprehensive program for his administration that was acceptable to the Democratic-controlled Congress. He exercised his veto sixty-six times to kill legislation. In turn, Congress overrode his veto twelve times—more overrides than for any President since Andrew Johnson deadlocked with Congress over a century earlier. In the presidential election of 1976 Ford was defeated in his effort to win a full term in his own right.

Boyhood in Michigan

THE FUTURE PRESIDENT was born on July 14, 1913, in a basement apartment in Omaha, Nebraska. Named Leslie Lynch King at birth, he was the son of Dorothy Gardner King and Leslie King, a wool trader. When his parents were divorced in 1915, he and his mother returned to her home town, Grand Rapids, Michigan. There his mother met and soon married a young paint salesman, Gerald Rudolf Ford. His new stepfather formally adopted the boy, renaming him Gerald Rudolph Ford, Jr.

Growing up in Grand Rapids, the boy was called "Junie," short for Junior. The elder Ford had dropped out of high school and had little interest in reading, so there were few books in the Fords' comfortable middle-class home. Unlike some other Presidents who were avid readers in boyhood, young Ford was more interested in outdoor activities and competitive sports. As soon as he was old enough, he joined the Boy Scouts and doggedly accumulated merit badges until he finally attained the coveted honor of Eagle Scout. By the time he was fourteen, he had three younger half brothers: Thomas, Richard, and James.

In the 1920s the Ford paint selling business prospered. The family made vacation trips to Florida in their open touring car and in 1929 the elder Ford formed a paint manufacturing corporation. The family moved to a more fashionable neighborhood in East Grand Rapids. Young Ford was able to buy his own car—a $75 seven-year-old Model T.

But, like millions of other Americans, the Fords were hard hit by the stock market crash of 1929 and the ensuing Depression. Unable to meet the mortgage payments on their new home, the Fords were forced to move to a more modest house. A more personal disaster struck sixteen-year-old Jerry, then a high school junior, when his cherished Model T burned up because he had carelessly covered the hood with a blanket on a cold night when the engine still was hot.

At seventeen Jerry Ford had an even more traumatic experience. He had not known he was an adopted child, his mother and stepfather having concealed the information because child guidance experts of the 1920s told them it would be harmful for a child to be told. So it was a shock one day, while he was working to earn pocket money in the sandwich shop across from his high school, when a stranger approached and said, "Leslie, I'm your father." Disbelieving, young Ford heard for the first time the story of his parents' divorce. He confirmed it later that day when he confronted his mother and stepfather. Loyal to them, the boy directed his resentment at his obviously well-to-do real father for failing to offer financial help to the hard-pressed Fords.

As a student at Grand Rapids' South High School, Jerry Ford became a football star. Big for his age, he played center, a bruising position that called for great strength and stamina, especially in those days when a center played throughout a full game on both offense and defense. Determined to do his best, Ford helped lead his team to a state championship in his senior year. He was chosen center on Grand Rapids' "All-City" team three years in a row. Contrary to the stereotype of football players, Ford was a conscientious student, earning mostly B grades with a few As.

College Athlete, Law Student, and Assistant Coach

WHEN FORD GRADUATED from high school in 1931, the country was sliding deeper into the Great Depression. His family had no money to spare for a college education. But the boy's athletic ability won him a scholarship to the University of Michigan, where he helped work his way with jobs as a dishwasher, janitor, and waiter. As a sophomore he joined the Delta Kappa Epsilon fraternity. Two fraternity brothers later were to play major roles in his life. Jack Stiles would manage his first successful campaign for Congress. Philip Buchen would become his law partner and much later his chief legal counsel when he was President.

Although during his sophomore and junior years in 1932 and 1933 the University of Michigan won honors for having the best college football team in the country, Ford's athletic career languished somewhat. He was second best to Michigan's all-American center, Chuck Bernard. After Bernard's graduation, Ford became the first-string center in his senior year. But 1934 was a disastrous season for Michigan. The team defeated only Georgia Tech in its eight-game schedule.

Ford, however, received recognition for his football skill, being chosen to play in the East-West game in San Francisco on January 1, 1935, and in the College All-Stars game in Chicago the following August. His performance in these games won him professional football offers, but they had slight appeal because in those days there was little glamour and less money for the pros.

While football was his first love, Ford had not neglected his studies. He graduated from Michigan in 1935 with a B average, having received four As during his four years—in American government, organized labor, European history, and in an economics course on money and credit.

Jobs were hard to come by in 1935. Ford counted himself lucky when Yale's football coach, Raymond "Ducky" Pond, offered him a $2,400-a-year position as assistant football line coach and boxing coach. Even though he knew next to nothing about boxing, Ford accepted the job, which was to begin in September. That summer he worked at the family paint factory and in his spare time went to the YMCA three times a week to take boxing lessons from a former amateur boxing champion, Stanley Levandoski. For the next six years Ford coached at Yale.

While at Yale Ford made frequent weekend trips to New York City. There he dated a beautiful model, Phyllis Brown, of whom he later said, "I almost married that girl." She persuaded Ford to put up $1,000 to go into partnership with a friend of hers, Harry Conover, to form a model agency. Blond and handsome, Ford himself posed with Phyllis for pictures that appeared in *Look* magazine and on the cover of *Cosmopolitan.* After a financial disagreement, Ford withdrew from the agency partnership.

Meanwhile, Ford applied for entrance to the Yale law school. The faculty tried to discourage him, pointing to his undistinguished academic record at Michigan and warning him that a majority of the Yale law students were Phi Beta Kappas. In 1938 the law professors relented and let Ford take two courses as a trial. When he completed them satisfactorily, he was allowed to begin a full-time law schedule the following semester. While continuing to work as a coach, he studied at night and on weekends, determined to succeed. He finally received his law degree from Yale in 1941, graduating in the upper third of his class. Significantly, his highest grade—an A plus—was for a course in legal ethics.

War Years and Entrance into Politics

RETURNING TO GRAND RAPIDS in 1941, Ford was admitted to the Michigan bar and began law practice in partnership with his college friend Philip Buchen.

After the Japanese attack on Pearl Harbor, the twenty-eight-year-old Ford volunteered for service in the U. S. Navy, receiving a direct commission as ensign on April 20, 1942. He was assigned as a physical education instructor in the naval air cadet training program and spent his first year of war at Chapel Hill, North Carolina. Chafing for a more active role in the war, Ford applied for sea duty. He was then assigned to the U.S.S. *Monterey*, a new light aircraft carrier being readied for sea at Camden, New Jersey, following gunnery training at Norfolk, Virginia.

The *Monterey* joined the Pacific fleet in 1943, taking part in the island-hopping campaign to Japan. One of the worst moments of the war for Ford and his ship came during the typhoon that struck the fleet in December 1944, sinking three destroyers and severely damaging many other ships. At the height of the storm the *Monterey*'s planes caught fire and the ship's engine rooms had to be abandoned. As 100-mile-an-hour winds battered the ship, Ford lost his footing on the flight deck and narrowly escaped being blown overboard. In all, he took part in ten battles and rose to the rank of lieutenant commander.

Ford came home on terminal leave from the navy to Grand Rapids in December 1945. He resumed his law practice and interest in politics, aided by his stepfather, who had won election as Kent County Republican chairman with the backing of the Home Front reform group. Jerry Ford's first efforts were concentrated in helping organize a veterans' committee to pressure local officials into facilitating construction of low-cost housing for returning GIs.

Counting on assistance from the reform Home Front group, Jerry Ford decided to run for Congress in 1948 in Michigan's Fifth District. The district had been represented since 1940 by sixty-four-year-old Bartel J. Jonkman, who was backed by McKay's regular Republican organization. The reactionary Jonkman had alienated many of the district's young veterans of World War II. As a senior member of the House Foreign Affairs Committee he had repeatedly attacked President Truman's foreign policy, especially the multibillion-dollar Marshall Plan for aid to Europe. To win a congressional seat, Ford's first task was to defeat Jonkman in the Republican primary.

With his college fraternity brother Jack Stiles as his campaign manager, Jerry Ford worked hard in the summer of 1948 to make himself better known to the voters. One of his problems as a candidate was that, while many remembered him as a high school and college football star, questions were raised as to whether he was smart enough to be a congressman. But when voters asked his stand on issues with which he was unfamiliar, the handsome young candidate disarmed them by candidly admitting he did not know the answers but would find out. To woo the large number of farmers in the district, Ford went out into their fields and helped with the chores while asking for their support. Jonkman, who was counting on the help of the regular Republican organization, made few appearances in Grand Rapids during the campaign and refused to debate Ford on the issues. In the primary election on September 14, 1948, Ford won with a 62.2 percent majority, garnering 23,632 votes to 14,341. Ford's victory almost assured him of a seat in Congress because the district had not sent a Democrat to Washington since 1910.

Now confident that he would become a congressman, Ford went ahead with plans to marry Betty Bloomer Warren, a thirty-year-old former Martha Graham dancer, who in 1947 had divorced her husband, William C. Warren, a furniture salesman, on grounds of incompatibility. But because the district had a large number of Dutch Calvinists who opposed divorce, Ford kept his October 15, 1948, marriage secret during the remainder of the election campaign. The marriage was a happy one, with four children born in following years: Michael Gerald in 1950, John Gardner in 1952, Steven Meigs in 1956, and Susan Elizabeth in 1957.

In the November election Ford defeated the Democratic candidate, Fred J. Barr, Jr., by 74,191 to 46,972—a majority of 61 percent. Many of Ford's fellow Republicans were not so lucky—in that election President Truman upset Republican Thomas E. Dewey and the Democrats took control of Congress.

Quarter of a Century as a Congressman

DURING THE NEXT TWENTY-FIVE YEARS, Ford won re-election a dozen times, never with less than 60 percent of the vote.

Ford took his seat in Congress in 1949 as a junior member of the minority party, a situation that was not conducive to the building of a brilliant legislative reputation. However, Ford had no inclination in that direction. He was satisfied with honestly and conscientiously representing his constituents in Grand Rapids. This meant keeping a low profile, promptly answering requests from back home, maintaining a good record of attendance, and voting as the Republican leadership decided.

During his first term Ford became acquainted with another young navy veteran, Richard M. Nixon, then a U.S. representative from California. But Ford made no effort to emulate his new friend's publicity-garnering tactics as a Communist hunter.

In his second term Ford became a member of the powerful House Appropriations Committee, which controls all bills for expenditures by the federal government. He became a specialist on defense budgets, winning friends among the generals and admirals for his consistent support of increased armed forces spending. As part of this assignment Ford made many trips abroad on military planes, receiving appropriately friendly receptions at the facilities he visited.

In 1952 Ford turned down an offer to run for the Senate. He felt that he was well on his way toward building the seniority necessary to eventually become Speaker of the House—his long-term goal. Like other Republicans, Ford achieved improved status when Dwight D. Eisenhower won the presidential election in 1952, helping the GOP regain control of Congress. However, Ford still did not have sufficient seniority to chair a committee. After the Republicans lost their majority in the House two years later, he had no further opportunities to become a congressional committee chairman.

In 1963, after fourteen years in Congress, Ford began to win national attention when the "young Turks" of the GOP elected him chairman of the House Republican caucus, replacing long-term conservative Iowa Representative Charles B. Hoeven.

Ford was appointed by President Johnson in December 1963 as a member of the seven-man Warren Commission to investigate the assassination of President Kennedy. In turn Ford named to the commission staff his old college friend and manager of his first election campaign, Jack Stiles. After the commission reported its findings, Stiles and Ford in 1965 co-authored a book on the subject, *Portrait of the Assassin.*

The fifty-one-year-old Ford achieved the next-to-last rung on his climb toward Speaker of the House in 1965 when he was elected Republican minority leader of the House, defeating Representative Charles A. Halleck of Indiana. In this internal party fight Ford was aided by three close friends: Representatives Robert Griffin of Michigan, Melvin R. Laird of Wisconsin, and Charles E. Goodell of New York. With Senate Minority Leader Everett M. Dirksen of Illinois, Ford began appearing on a GOP television series, called "The Ev and Jerry Show," which presented the Republican congressional views on current issues.

Although Ford preferred to describe himself a "moderate on domestic issues," his voting record was that of a conservative on most of the major domestic legislation proposed by President Johnson. He opposed increased aid to education, establishment of a "war on poverty," and Medicare for social security recipients.

In 1967 Ford made one of his rare speeches from the floor of the House to attack President Johnson's handling of the Vietnam War. He urged increased U. S. Air Force bombing of communist forces and a blockade of North Vietnam. "Why are we pulling our best punches in Vietnam?" he asked.

As Republican minority leader of the House throughout President Nixon's first term, Ford was noted for his loyal support of White House measures. He often arranged behind-the-scenes coalitions with southern Democrats to pass administration proposals.

Ford raised the hackles of liberals in 1970 when he called on the House to impeach Associate Justice of the Supreme Court William O. Douglas. He charged Douglas among other things with defending the civil disobedience of youthful anti-Vietnam War protesters, of supporting the publication of pornography, and of accepting money from a private foundation. In his speech in the House, Ford made a statement that was to be much quoted at the time of the Nixon impeachment hearings: "An impeachable offense is whatever the House of Representatives considers it to be at a given moment in history."

When President Nixon won re-election in 1972 by one of the greatest landslides in U.S. history but was unable to lead Republicans to majority control of Congress, Ford saw his chances of becoming Speaker of the House go glimmering. He began to think of retiring from politics while there was still time left to resume a private career as a lawyer. Neither he nor anyone else could predict the onrush of events that within less than two years would propel him into the highest office in the land.

Fortieth Vice President of the United States

WHEN VICE PRESIDENT SPIRO AGNEW resigned in 1973, accepting conviction for income tax violations in lieu of facing trial on bribery charges, the door to high office suddenly swung open for Ford. The Twenty-fifth Amendment to the United States Constitution, which had been ratified in 1967, came into use for the first time. It provided that a vacancy in the office of Vice President could be filled by nomination by the President and confirmation by both houses of Congress.

President Nixon, suffering from the twin blows of the Watergate scandals and the Agnew bribery charges, began a frantic scramble to find someone to fill the vacancy. This someone had to exude honesty to be acceptable to the public. He had to have unquestioned loyalty to the President. And he had to be someone whom Congress would quickly approve. Who could fit this bill of particulars better than Jerry Ford?

Democratic Speaker of the House Carl Albert of Oklahoma took credit for being the first to suggest to Nixon that Ford be nominated. Albert, who stood next in succession to the presidency after Agnew's resignation, had no desire to become President himself, and he was afraid that just might happen if the vice presidency remained vacant very long.

In the glare of TV lights, Ford's nomination as Vice President was announced by President Nixon on October 12, 1973, to the enthusiastic applause of congressional leaders of both parties. In accepting, Ford promised to "do my utmost to the best of my ability to serve this country well and to perform those duties that will be my new assignment as effectively and efficiently and with as much accomplishment as possible."

In the next two months Ford underwent a searching investigation to determine his fitness for the office. The critical nature of his nomination was heightened late in October when the House Judiciary Committee formally began proceedings to determine whether President Nixon should be impeached. About the worst thing the confirmation hearings turned up on Jerry Ford was that he had associated with lobbyists, and the members of Congress knew that was unavoidable. His net assets were disclosed as $256,378, mostly in the value of three homes, in Grand Rapids, Alexandria, Virginia, and Vail, Colorado. Even his handful of political enemies were unable to find any evidence he ever had even considered committing an illegal act. During the hearings he made a statement that would later prove truer than he apparently believed. In reply to a question about whether he would have the power to pardon President Nixon should he resign, Ford replied: "I do not think the public would stand for it." The Senate approved his nomination 92 to 3 on November 27, and the House voted approval by 387 to 35 on December 6. An hour after the House vote, Ford was sworn in as the fortieth Vice President.

In the eight months Ford occupied the nation's second highest office he was a man swaying on a tightrope. He had to continue to exhibit loyalty to President Nixon, even while public confidence in the President rapidly eroded with each new revelation in the Watergate scandals. At the same time Ford had to maintain his own credibility with the public as a leader who could be trusted.

Vice President Ford stumped the country, traveling about 100,000 miles to forty states, speaking to conventions, to university convocations, and to almost any other large group that would invite him. His success was demonstrated by public opinion polls that showed his popularity steadily rising.

Thirty-eighth President of the United States

FORD BECAME PRESIDENT in a moment of high drama at noon on August 9, 1974. Shortly before, the nation had watched on TV as Richard Nixon, the first President in history to resign, had bade a tearful farewell to his staff and departed the White House in disgrace. A few minutes later, the TV cameras turned to Gerald Ford, the first Vice President to have come to the presidency by appointment. As his wife held the Bible on which Ford rested his left hand, Chief Justice Warren E. Burger administered the oath of office. Ford then made a moving address that said in part:

"I am acutely aware that you have not elected me as your President by your ballots, and so I ask you to confirm me as your President with your prayers. And I hope that such prayers will also be the first of many.

"If you have not chosen me by secret ballot, neither have I gained office by any secret promises. I have not campaigned either for the Presidency or the Vice Presidency. I have not subscribed to any partisan platform. I am indebted to no man, and only to one woman—my dear wife—as I begin this very difficult job. . . .

"In all my public and private acts as your President, I expect to follow my instincts of openness and candor with full confidence that honesty is always the best policy in the end.

"My fellow Americans, our long national nightmare is over.

"Our Constitution works; our great Republic is a Government of laws and not of men. Here the people rule. But there is a higher power, by whatever name we honor Him, who ordains not only righteousness but love, not only justice but mercy.

"As we bind up the internal wounds of Watergate, more painful and more poisonous than those of foreign wars, let us restore the golden rule to our political process, and let brotherly love purge our hearts of suspicion and of hate. . . .

"God helping me, I will not let you down."

The new President asked all members of the Cabinet and the heads of government agencies to remain indefinitely in his administration. But in the following two years he replaced all the heads of the executive departments except for Secretary of State Henry Kissinger and Secretary of the Treasury William E. Simon.

Ford announced on August 20, 1974, his nomination for Vice President: sixty-six-year-old Nelson Aldrich Rockefeller, one of the world's wealthiest men, who had served four terms as governor of New York from 1958 to 1973, and had been expected to be a contender for the Republican nomination for President in 1976. After months of congressional hearings, Rockefeller was finally confirmed and sworn in as Vice President on December 19, 1974.

During Ford's first month in office, public opinion polls showed that only 3 percent of the people disapproved of the job he was doing as President—as close to universal approval as any President is ever likely to get. However, this was to be the peak of his popularity.

Nixon Pardon and Vietnam Conditional Amnesty

ON A QUIET SUNDAY MORNING in Washington, on September 8, 1974, when the President returned to the White House from attending church services, he called in the handful of newsmen then on duty. He proceeded to drop a bombshell—the announcement of unconditional pardon of former President Nixon—a decision he reached without consulting party leaders, members of Congress, the special Watergate prosecutor, or the public. Ford's press secretary, J. H. terHorst, expressed the disapproval felt by millions of Americans by immediately resigning. TerHorst, a Michigan newsman who had supported Ford since his first campaign for Congress, felt his word had been undermined because he previously had assured newsmen that Ford would stand by his 1973 statement regarding a possible Nixon pardon. At that time Ford had said: "I do not think the public would stand for it."

Ford, who at his swearing-in speech a month earlier had promised "openness and candor," was deluged by phone calls, telegrams, and letters denouncing his action. Members of Congress of both parties were angered both by the pardon and at not having been consulted in advance. A few days later, when the White House indicated Ford was considering pardons for everyone connected with the Watergate scandals, the Senate quickly voted fifty-five to twenty-four for a resolution that the President should not pardon anyone prior to conviction. The White House then announced that Ford would not consider pardoning anyone else in the Watergate scandals before they had been convicted.

Eight days after the Nixon pardon, Ford announced an offer of conditional amnesty for the thousands of young men who had opposed the Vietnam War by evading the draft or by deserting the armed forces. The amnesty was conditional on a youth agreeing to up to two years of service in a low-paying public service job. Ford's new action did little to revive his popularity. Those who had supported the Vietnam War thought his action too generous; those who had opposed the war believed the amnesty should have been unconditional. In ensuing months relatively few resisters turned themselves in to accept the amnesty.

Bewildered that he should have become the center of a storm of controversy for actions that he regarded as humanitarian, Ford could only repeat to his critics that the pardon and the conditional amnesty both were "my honest and conscientious effort to heal the wounds."

To allay suspicions that he had made some kind of a "deal" with Nixon—for example, promising the pardon in order to obtain the presidency—Ford took the unprecedented step of appearing before a congressional subcommittee and answering the members' questions about the pardon. His formal testimony before the House Judiciary Subcommittee on October 17, 1974, was the first time a sitting President ever had given up claims of executive privilege and appeared in person to submit to a congressional inquiry. As TV carried the proceedings into home living rooms across the nation, Ford answered every question put to him with confidence and candor.

"I want to assure you," he said, "members of this subcommittee, members of Congress, and the American people, there was no deal."

Political analysts unanimously predicted a Democratic landslide in the November 1974 congressional elections, with voters punishing the Republicans for the Watergate affair and the Nixon pardon. In the weeks before the election, President Ford did his best to try to stem the tide, barnstorming by plane from coast to coast and warning the voters not to give the Democrats such a substantial majority that they would create a "veto-proof" Congress. When the election results were tabulated, the Democrats had increased their majority control of both houses of the Ninety-fourth Congress, winning forty-seven additional seats in the House and six more in the Senate. Republicans took some comfort in pointing out that the landslide was not as great as that achieved by the Democrats in the 1964 presidential election of Lyndon Johnson.

Inflation, Unemployment, and Economic Recession

WHEN FORD took office a raging inflation was pushing up prices at a higher rate than at any time since the immediate post-World War II period. In his first address to a joint session of Congress on August 12, 1974, Ford named inflation as "domestic enemy No. 1." After calling a "summit conference" of economists and representatives of various segments of the economy in September to discuss ways of combating inflation, he again addressed a joint session of Congress on October 8, calling for enactment of higher taxes and other measures to hold down prices.

At the same time he asked Americans to join in a mobilization of volunteers, to be called "WIN," to "whip inflation now." He urged consumers to buy less and save more. "Only two of my predecessors have come in person to call upon Congress for a declaration of war," Ford said, "and I shall not do that. But I say to you with all sincerity, that our inflation, our public enemy No. 1, will, unless whipped, destroy our country, our homes, our liberties, our property, and finally our national pride, as surely as any well-armed wartime enemy."

Responding to Ford's urging to buy less, many consumers stopped purchasing new cars, TV sets, and appliances. During the next year the inflation rate dropped from 12 to 7.8 percent. But the cost to the economy was steep. By November 1974 the hard-hit automobile manufacturing companies were closing down plants and laying off workers. By December more than a million additional workers had joined the ranks of the unemployed since Ford made his speech. At the same time Wall Street stock values had plummeted by nearly 50 percent from the year's high.

By 1975 the United States was in a full-scale recession with the economy sliding toward depression. Industrial production fell 3.6 percent in January for the worst monthly showing since 1937. In May unemployment climbed to 8.9 percent with over 8.2 million persons out of work—the highest rate of unemployment since 1941 when it had reached 9.9 percent.

Addressing a joint session of the new Ninety-fourth Congress on January 15, 1975, President Ford summed up bluntly:

"I must say to you that the state of the Union is not good. Millions of Americans are out of work. Recession and inflation are eroding the money of millions more. Prices are too high, and sales are too slow."

Reversing the appeal he had made for tax increases only three months earlier, the President now asked Congress for an immediate tax reduction with rebates to taxpayers on their 1974 payments. Congress responded quickly with a $22.8 billion tax reduction that was signed by Ford on March 29, 1975. Earlier he had signed emergency $4.5 billion legislation to extend unemployment benefits and provide additional public service jobs.

President Ford presented Congress with a record $349.9 billion federal budget for fiscal 1976, providing for the largest deficit spending since World War II in an effort to stimulate the economy.

Blaming the economic disruptions of the world and of the United States on the quadrupling of the world price of petroleum in 1974, President Ford proposed a program in 1975 to make the United States independent of foreign energy imports, setting the following goals:

"—First, we must reduce oil imports by 1 million barrels per day by the end of this year and by 2 million barrels per day by the end of 1977.

"—Second, we must end vulnerability to economic disruption by foreign suppliers by 1985.

"—Third, we must develop our energy technology and resources so that the United States has the ability to supply a significant share of the energy needs of the free world by the end of this century."

Worsening Relations with Congress

THROUGHOUT HIS ADMINISTRATION Ford experienced a continually worsening relationship with Congress. In 1974 Congress overrode four of his fifteen vetoes, the highest percentage since five out of nine of Franklin Pierce's vetoes were overridden in 1853–57. During 1975 Ford exercised his veto repeatedly in an effort to prevent Congress from extending price controls on oil and gas because he believed higher prices would force a reduction in fuel consumption. Finally, a compromise was reached and Ford signed a measure on December 22, 1975, that provided for an end to price controls on oil by 1979. The new law also required automobile manufacturers to improve the fuel economy of new cars.

The President used his veto to try to keep Congress from passing appropriations for health, education, and social services that exceeded his budget. Overriding Ford's veto when necessary on such measures, Congress increased the federal spending during fiscal 1976 to $373.5 billion, ending the year with a deficit of more than $66 billion—the highest to date in the nation's history. The federal spending programs caused unemployment to drop by more than 1 million persons by mid-1976, but about 7 million persons remained without jobs.

Ford repeatedly vetoed legislation supported by environmentalists seeking to curb the operations of strip mines and force strip mine owners to restore the environment.

Foreign Relations

TURNING TO FOREIGN AFFAIRS in an effort to revive his flagging leadership, President Ford went on a week-long trip to the Far East in late November 1974. He made the first visit of an American President to Japan, emphasizing the friendship that has developed since Japan's defeat in World War II. He then traveled to South Korea, where he reaffirmed continued American support to preserve that nation's independence.

As the main objective of his Far Eastern tour, President Ford flew to the Soviet Union on November 23 for his first summit meeting with communist leader Leonid Brezhnev. In talks held at Vladivostok, Ford and Brezhnev reached agreement on the basic terms for a new treaty that would limit the production and deployment of atomic weapons for the period 1977 to 1986. In a report to the American people on December 2, 1974, Ford declared that the agreement "put a firm ceiling on the strategic arms race which has heretofore eluded us since the nuclear age began."

However, in the months that followed, as it became more and more apparent that Ford was unlikely to win another term as President, the Soviet leadership stalled on negotiating the new strategic arms limitation treaty. And Ford's administration ended without achieving a "firm ceiling" on the arms race.

American prestige in international affairs sank to a low ebb in 1975 when a final humiliating chapter closed the Vietnam War that had cost the United States billions of dollars and the lives of more than 56,000 American soldiers. When communist North Vietnam launched an offensive that broke the truce of 1973, Ford called on Congress to provide emergency funds to help South Vietnam stem the onslaught. But Congress refused the request, not wishing to reopen the old wounds that had divided the nation for so many years under Presidents Johnson and Nixon. Without American support the governments of South Vietnam, Cambodia, and Laos collapsed. Remaining American diplomats and military personnel fled by helicopter to waiting warships in April as Communist troops closed in on Saigon and Phnom Penh. Hundreds of thousands of refugees found their way to neighboring countries or were picked up by U. S. Navy ships. Congress and the President acted quickly to provide funds for the refugees and by the end of the year some 130,000 had been admitted to the United States to find new homes.

Two weeks after the fall of South Vietnam, President Ford seized an opportunity to demonstrate that the United States still would use its military might if provoked too far. Cambodian communists had captured an American freighter, the *Mayaguez*, on May 12, 1975, and had taken as prisoners the thirty-nine American crewmen. President Ford ordered the U. S. Navy to rescue them. Operating from U.S. bases in Thailand, U. S. Marines landed by helicopter on May 15, attacking an island where the crewmen were believed to be held, and boarded the *Mayaguez*. The incident ended later that day when Cambodia freed the freighter's crewmen. Forty-one American servicemen were killed during the action and fifty were wounded. Secretary of State Kissinger summed up the *Mayaguez* incident by declaring: "The impact ought to be to make clear that there are limits beyond which the United States cannot be pushed."

However, the *Mayaguez* incident had an unlooked-for consequence of more lasting importance. The government of Thailand, angered because it had not been consulted by Ford as to the use of American bases there during the action, insisted that the United States withdraw all its planes and military personnel from Thai soil. Forced to comply, Ford removed the last of about 50,000 U.S. servicemen in 1976, leaving behind some ninety-three military installations built during the Vietnam War. The evacuation ended the U.S. military presence on the mainland of Southeast Asia.

In the wake of the communist successes in Southeast Asia, President Ford made several trips abroad in 1975, traveling to Europe and to Asia to assure allied leaders that the United States remained strong, and to tell communist leaders that he intended to continue President Nixon's policy of détente with the Soviet Union and other communist nations.

Ford had additional meetings with Brezhnev in Helsinki, Finland, where they and the leaders of thirty-three other nations signed the Helsinki Agreement on August 1, 1975. The treaty guaranteed the boundaries of European nations that had been established after World War II. It also promised basic human rights for citizens of all the signatory nations, which included not only the democracies but also all the totalitarian countries of Europe (except for Albania).

Attacked by conservative members of his own party for having signed a treaty that recognized the Soviet Union's World War II conquests of territory from its neighbors, Ford defended his action as one that would help stabilize peace in Europe. But, he admitted, "Peace is not a piece of paper."

Emulating his predecessor's historic journey to China, Ford flew to Peking in December 1975, where he had a friendly meeting with Communist leader Mao Tse-tung (Mao Zedong) but achieved no substantive agreements. During his 27,000-mile Asian trip, Ford also stopped in Japan, Indonesia, and the Philippines. Upon returning home, he announced a "Pacific Doctrine" of "peace with all—and hostility toward none."

Unsuccessful Campaign for a Full Term

PUBLIC OPINION polls in 1975 showed that Ford was unlikely to win the Republican nomination for President in 1976 because he trailed in popularity behind the main competitor in his own party, conservative former California governor and ex-movie star Ronald Reagan. But with the determination that once won him all-star honors as a football center, Ford plunged into the campaign early.

On two political sorties into California in 1975 his life was endangered by assassination attempts, each time by a woman. As the President made his way through a crowd in Sacramento on September 5, twenty-seven-year-old Lynette Fromme, a cult-follower of convicted mass murderer Charles Manson, pulled out a loaded Colt .45-caliber pistol and pointed it at the President when he was about two feet away. Secret Service agents grabbed the gun before it could be fired. Less than three weeks later, as Ford left a San

Francisco hotel on September 22, forty-five-year-old Sara Jane Moore, a civil rights activist, fired a .38-caliber revolver at him, but an alert bystander deflected the shot. Both women were convicted of attempted assassination and sentenced to life in prison.

During the first half of 1976 the President campaigned throughout the nation in a nip-and-tuck race with Reagan for Republican convention delegates. In an effort to win support from anti-Communist Reagan followers, the President became more conservative, ordering his staff members to cease using the word détente in discussions of international relations. At the GOP convention in Kansas City, Missouri, Ford narrowly won the nomination on August 19 with a first-ballot victory of 1,187 votes to 1,070 for Reagan. Ford then chose Senator Robert J. Dole of Kansas as his vice-presidential nominee.

When public opinion polls showed that the President was far less popular than his Democratic opponent Jimmy Carter in the 1976 election campaign, Ford challenged Carter to a series of televised debates—the first such debates in history between a President and an opponent. Ford campaigned hard and nearly overtook Carter, but in the November election he became the first President turned out of office by the voters since Hoover's defeat by Roosevelt in 1932. Ford graciously assisted Carter in the transition of power before leaving office in January 1977. Then Ford and his wife retired to Palm Springs, California, where they built a new home.

Despite urging by his friends, Ford decided not to seek the Republican nomination for the presidency actively in 1980. After Ronald Reagan won the party's presidential nomination, excitement at the GOP national convention reached a climax when word was leaked from Reagan headquarters that Ford would join the ticket as candidate for the vice-presidency. Ford confirmed in TV interviews that he was available for the nomination. Some newspapers went to press announcing the Reagan–Ford ticket as an accomplished fact. But at the last minute the two leaders were unable to agree on a mutually acceptable plan to share the powers of the presidency. So George Bush emerged as Reagan's choice for his running mate.

In the spring of 1981 the $4.3 million Gerald R. Ford Library was dedicated to house Ford's presidential papers on the Ann Arbor campus of the University of Michigan, his alma mater. Later, in September 1981, Ford was honored at the dedication of the $12 million Ford Presidential Museum in his boyhood hometown, Grand Rapids. Among the dignitaries attending were President Reagan, Prime Minister Pierre Trudeau of Canada, and President José López Portillo of Mexico.

"I am proud of the part I have had in rebuilding confidence in the presidency, confidence in our free system, and confidence in our future," Ford said in his final State of the Union address to Congress on January 12, 1977. "Once again Americans believe in themselves, in their leaders, and in the promise that tomorrow holds for their children."

Jimmy Carter

The Thirty-ninth President of the United States
1977–1981

1924 (October 1) Born in Plains, Georgia.

1946 Graduated from the U. S. Naval Academy.

1946 (July 7) Married Rosalynn Smith.

1946–53 Served as officer in the U. S. Navy, advancing to the rank of senior-grade lieutenant.

1963–67 State senator in Georgia legislature.

1966 Defeated in Democratic primary election as a candidate for the gubernatorial nomination.

1971–75 Governor of Georgia.

1977–81 Thirty-ninth President of the United States.

A southern Democrat who vigorously supported the widening of U.S. civil rights for blacks and women and the extension of basic human rights to the downtrodden in other countries, Jimmy Carter brought to the White House an honest grin, a disarming candor, and lots of inexperience.

At first the people wanted it that way. Disenchanted by "Washington insiders" because of the scandals of the Watergate years, the voters turned to Carter, a man most of them had never heard of before he began his campaign for the presidency. They chose him largely for the very reason that he never had held office in the nation's capital. Moreover, the majority of voters were impressed by his accomplishments as a self-made peanut farmer-businessman, as an honest governor of Georgia who had brought efficiency to state government through reorganization and "zero-base budgeting," as a humanitarian who had won the respect of black civil rights leaders, and as a former naval officer in the submarine service who could speak authoritatively on nuclear physics and atomic power.

Only two men—Grover Cleveland and Woodrow Wilson—previously had become President without ever having held civilian office in the nation's capital or having been a commanding general. Like Carter, each had won election because of a reputation for honesty and reform as a state governor. And, like Carter, they had difficulties getting everything they wanted from Congress because of their lack of national legislative experience.

During his first year in office, President Carter smilingly admitted he had a great deal to learn about his job and about Congress. "I spend about half the time being a student," he cheerfully told a questioner on television. "I put in an enormous amount of time, and it's pleasant—I am not complaining—learning about security matters and defense matters and studying the Congress and how it operates and learning about foreign affairs."

In his autobiography, *Why Not the Best,* published early in his campaign for the Democratic presidential nomination, Jimmy Carter said the two questions he believed most concerned the American people were: "Can our government be honest, decent, open, fair, and compassionate?" and "Can our government be competent?" He declared both could be answered, "Yes."

As President, Carter devoted himself to trying to make the answer come true. But although his Democratic party held large majorities in both houses of Congress, Carter and his staff were unable to provide the leadership needed to get many of his most important legislative proposals enacted into law. As a result, his popularity steadily fell as shown by public opinion polls.

He won his greatest triumph and suffered his severest blow in the field of international affairs. As a peacemaker he brought together the leaders of Egypt and Israel, winning their agreement to a treaty in 1979 that ended their long-standing belligerency. However, his leadership suffered irreparable damage during the last two years of his administration when the revolutionary government of Iran punished him for showing friendship to the overthrown Shah by seizing the American Embassy and holding its staff hostage for more than fourteen months in defiance of all Carter's efforts to free them.

On the domestic front, the President was criticized for his administration's management of the economy as the nation slid into a recession in 1980 with high inflation and increasing unemployment.

After overcoming a strong challenge from within the Democratic party and winning nomination for a second term, he was defeated in an electoral landslide by Republican candidate Ronald Reagan in the 1980 presidential election. As the ninth incumbent President to lose a bid for another term,

Carter received only forty-nine electoral votes—fewer than any other except President Taft in 1912.

Farm Boy and Navy Officer

BORN ON OCTOBER 1, 1924, in the small town of Plains, Georgia, James Earl Carter, Jr., preferred his nickname "Jimmy" to his more formal given name, later using it officially both as governor of Georgia and as President of the United States. He was the first President born in a hospital instead of at home. As the fifth generation of his family to live in Plains, Carter counted among his ancestors some of the earliest settlers in the region. His father, James Earl Carter, Sr., a storekeeper and farmer, was a conservative traditionalist who believed in the old southern ways of segregation. His mother, Lillian Gordy Carter, a registered nurse, worked at the local hospital and provided her poor rural neighbors with health care. A liberal who was always willing to adopt new ways, she served as a model of unselfish community service to her children, even joining the Peace Corps at the age of sixty-eight in 1966 and serving overseas as a nurse in a village in India until she was seventy. The eldest of four children, Jimmy had two sisters and a brother: Mrs. Gloria Carter Spann (born in 1926), an art teacher; Mrs. Ruth Carter Stapleton (born in 1929), an evangelist; and Billy Carter (born in 1937), who became a partner with his brother in the peanut wholesale business.

When Jimmy was four, the Carters moved to a farm three miles west of Plains near a railroad flag stop called Archery. The wooden clapboard farmhouse in which the boy grew up had no indoor toilet and was without electricity until after he was thirteen. Water was obtained from a well by a hand pump on the back porch, and water for bathing was heated on the wood-burning kitchen stove.

Like other farm boys, Jimmy learned to work hard, helping his father and the field hands with the chores. From the time he was five, he was learning to be a businessman, selling boiled peanuts at a nickel a bag on the streets of Plains. Saving his money, he was able to buy five bales of cotton at the age of nine, which he stored until the price tripled several years later, giving him a handsome return on his investment.

As a child, Jimmy's playmates were the children of the black farm workers who lived nearby. But, like other white children of the rural South, Jimmy rode a school bus to Plains to attend the all-white public school there, while his black playmates walked to their own one-room school. Later Carter said that it was not until he was an adult that he became conscious of this racial discrimination and began to work to change it.

Encouraged by his mother and his teacher, Jimmy became an avid reader, soon enjoying works in advance of his grade level. One of his favorite books became Tolstoy's *War and Peace*, which he first read when he was twelve.

U. S. Naval Officer

THE CARTER FAMILY was too poor to finance a four-year college education for Jimmy, so he decided at an early age that he wanted to attend the U. S. Naval Academy, where his education would be assured by the government. He was influenced in choosing the U. S. Navy over the U. S. Army because a favorite uncle was a navy enlisted man who occasionally wrote to him and sent him souvenirs from far-off places. After graduating from high school at the age of sixteen, and while awaiting his hoped-for naval academy appointment, Carter attended Georgia Southwestern College at Americus, Georgia. When he received word in 1942 that he had been accepted at the academy for the following year, he enrolled at Georgia Tech in Atlanta to take the courses in mathematics recommended by the navy.

He entered the U. S. Naval Academy at Annapolis, Maryland, in 1943, and received his commission as an ensign three years later with a rank of fifty-ninth in his class of 820. At the academy he participated in cross country track and played intramural football on an under-140 pound team. He also learned to fly.

On July 7, 1946, a month after his graduation, the twenty-one-year-old Carter was married in the Methodist Church in Plains to eighteen-year-old Rosalynn Smith, the best friend of his sister Ruth. They had four children: John William in 1947, James Earl III ("Chip") in 1950, Donnel Jeffrey in 1952, and Amy Lynn in 1967. A tireless worker, Rosalynn Carter later helped her husband by keeping the accounts of the family business, campaigned for him in his elections, accomplished diplomatic missions for him as President, and played a major role as an adviser.

Carter's first naval assignment for two years was as a gunnery and electronics instructor for enlisted men on the old battleships *Wyoming* and *Mississippi*, operating out of Norfolk, Virginia.

Accepted for submarine duty in 1948, he received six months of training at the officers' school in New London, Connecticut, and then was assigned to duty in the Pacific aboard the U.S.S. *Pomfret*. After Carter joined the submarine in Hawaii, it set out for the Far East on a journey in which the future President nearly lost his life. When the ship was running on the surface at night to recharge the batteries, it was struck by a huge storm. A giant wave swept Carter off the bridge and carried him thirty feet back along the deck.

Fortunately, he was able to grab the barrel of a cannon, saving himself from being carried into the sea, from which he could not have been rescued in the storm and darkness.

After two-and-a-half years aboard the U.S.S. *Pomfret*, Carter was assigned in 1950 as the senior officer for the pre-commissioning assembly of a new experimental submarine, the U.S.S. *K-1*, being built in New London, Connecticut. When it was completed, Carter became one of the officers of the ship's crew. While serving aboard the *K-1* he passed his qualifications to command a ship, but because there were so many officers senior to him in the submarine service he never actually received his own ship to command.

When the navy began building atomic-powered submarines, Carter applied to become part of the program. In 1952 he was assigned as engineering officer of the U.S.S. *Sea Wolf*, then under construction. As part of his assignment he took graduate courses in nuclear physics at Union College in Schenectady, New York. When an experimental nuclear reactor went out of control at Chalk River, Canada, Carter was one of a team sent to undertake the dangerous task of disassembling it. Because of the high-intensity radiation, each person could spend only one-and-a-half minutes working on the damaged reactor, because during that time, despite protective clothing, the body received the maximum radiation that could be safely absorbed in a year. During his work with atomic submarines, Carter was under the command of Admiral Hyman Rickover, who had almost singlehandedly convinced the navy of the necessity of using nuclear power. Carter later wrote that the hard-working Rickover "had a profound effect on my life—perhaps more than anyone except my own parents" because of his insistence on perfection.

In 1953 Carter received emergency leave to return to Plains to visit his father who was dying of cancer. In hours of conversation at his father's bedside and in observing the warmth of community spirit exhibited by his parents' friends, Carter came to the conclusion that life in Plains was more meaningful than his naval career. Although his wife Rosalynn opposed the idea, Carter resigned from the navy and moved his family to Plains after his father died.

Businessman, Farmer, and Burgeoning Politician

THE TWENTY-NINE-YEAR-OLD CARTER obtained an apartment in a public housing project for his family, which now included three young children. He and Rosalynn had managed to buy a $75 savings bond each month out of his income as a naval officer, saving several thousand dollars during the seven years that Carter was in the navy. They used this money to form a partnership with Carter's mother for operating the family farm and peanut warehouse. During the first year they made a profit of only $200, but Carter worked diligently, took courses to learn new farming techniques, and reestablished friendships with his father's old customers. Soon the business prospered.

The Supreme Court decision in 1954 outlawing segregation in the public schools and the black civil rights crusade launched in 1955 by the Reverend Martin Luther King, Jr., brought apprehension to many Southerners. White Citizens Councils to fight desegregation formed in communities throughout the South. When a local chapter was organized in Plains, Carter refused to join, but a boycott by members of the council only temporarily hurt the Carter business.

Appointed to the Sumter County Board of Education in 1955, Carter served for seven years, the last two as chairman. He received his first political setback during this period when he campaigned throughout the county in favor of a referendum to consolidate small rural schools and saw the proposal fail by eighty-eight votes.

In 1962 Carter decided to run for a seat in the Georgia senate. His opponent was supported by the established political machine, while Carter was largely helped by war veterans and other newcomers to politics. On the day of the primary election Carter visited each of the major towns in the senatorial district. At Georgetown he discovered the ballot box being stuffed by a supporter of his opponent. His protests were ignored, and when the votes were counted, the results showed that Carter would have won by seventy votes except for the count from Georgetown. Carter challenged the results, and after many hearings was declared the Democratic nominee for the senate seat just three days before the general election. In the election, Carter won by about fifteen hundred votes. He was re-elected two years later more easily. During his four years in the state legislature, Carter was appalled by the influence of lobbyists and special interest groups that obtained legislation to fit their desires while the interests of the general public went by the board.

Realizing that only by obtaining a more influential position could he bring about reforms in government, Carter announced his candidacy for the Democratic nomination for governor in 1966. During the next three months he campaigned throughout the state, but lost by about twenty thousand votes out of the million that were cast. Segregationist restaurant owner Lester Maddox became governor.

For the next four years Carter campaigned for the governorship. Hardly a day went by that he did not attend a meeting in some part of the state to make a speech, often leaving the family business to be managed by his younger brother Billy.

From the time he was a child Jimmy Carter had regularly attended church, and after he had returned to Plains from his naval career he had become a Sunday-school teacher and a deacon of the Baptist Church. But his religious beliefs became stronger after his loss in the Democratic gubernatorial primary of 1966. He made many evangelistic trips throughout Georgia and to other states calling on more people to change their lives by renewed belief in Christianity.

In the last few months before the Democratic primary of 1970, he and Rosalynn usually campaigned separately so that they could cover more ground. He later said they had personally shaken hands with more than half the voters in Georgia—over 600,000 handshakes. Rated as the underdog in his campaign against the liberal former governor, Carl E. Sanders, Carter surprised political forecasters by winning the Democratic nomination. He then went on to defeat Republican candidate Hal Suit in the general election.

Reform Governor of Georgia

THE NATION'S NEWS MEDIA turned the spotlight on Carter at his inauguration in January 1971 when he took over the governorship from the highly publicized segregationist Maddox. In his eight-minute address, Carter said:

"Our people are our most precious possession. We cannot afford to waste the talents and abilities given by God to one single person. . . . Every adult illiterate, every school drop-out, and every untrained retarded child is an indictment of us all. Our state pays a terrible and continuing human and financial price for these failures. It is time to end this waste. . . .

"At the end of a long campaign, I believe I know the people of this state as well as anyone. Based on this knowledge of Georgians north and south, rural and urban, liberal and conservative, I say to you quite frankly that the time for racial discrimination is over. Our people have already made this major and difficult decision, but we cannot underestimate the challenge of hundreds of minor decisions yet to be made. Our inherent human charity and our religious beliefs will be taxed to the limit. No poor, rural, weak, or black person should ever have to bear the additional burden of being deprived of the opportunity of an education, a job, or simple justice."

The first southern governor to take such a bold stand, Carter became regarded as a leader of the "New South," in which the people were ready to turn their backs on long-standing racial prejudices and move forward to new harmonious relationships with blacks treated as equals. Symbolically, he placed a portrait of Martin Luther King, Jr., in the state capitol where only pictures of white Georgians had hung before. More practically, he reduced racial tensions. During Maddox's term as governor the amount of time spent by state police in shows of force at civil disturbances had grown to 45,910 hours a year. Under Carter, by 1973, only 177 hours of state patrol time was spent on civil disorders.

When Carter became governor only three blacks held appointive state jobs in agencies and on boards. The new governor increased the number to fifty-three. Overall the number of black state employees rose by about 40 percent.

A major campaign promise Carter made during his gubernatorial campaign was to reorganize the state government to make it more efficient. His analysis showed there were three hundred separate state departments and agencies at the beginning of his administration. By the end of his four-year term, he had abolished all but twenty-two by consolidating functions and services.

He discovered that state government budgets expanded because no one bothered to analyze the need for previously budgeted items, being concerned only with new items. He switched to what he called "zero base budgeting," in which each person responsible for a certain government function had to prepare a budget to perform that function. Each department or agency then had to arrange these separate budget requests in order of priority. This enabled functions with the lowest priority to be analyzed and reduced or deleted. The substantial savings that resulted provided the Georgia state treasury with a $200 million surplus during Carter's administration.

With an eye already on the White House, Carter began participating in national election campaigns. In 1972 he chaired the Democratic Governors' Campaign Committee, aiding the party's gubernatorial candidates throughout the nation. In 1974 he was chairman of the National Democratic Party Campaign Committee helping all the party's major candidates and in addition personally taking part in sixty key campaigns. The election, coming only three months after President Nixon's resignation to avoid impeachment, brought a Democratic landslide victory.

Campaign for the Presidency

CARTER could not run for a second term to succeed himself as governor of Georgia because of a state law in effect at that time. So he decided that the 1976 election would be the ideal time to run for President. He would be free of the responsibilities of public office and be able to devote full time to his campaign. Moreover, the recently approved election campaign reform law signed by President Ford on October 15, 1974, provided public financing for presidential candidates for the first time, making it possible for someone to run for President without having tens of millions of dollars raised from wealthy backers and special interests. So on December 12, 1974, a month before leaving the Georgia governorship, Carter became the first person officially to announce his candidacy for the 1976 Democratic presidential nomination.

The reaction throughout most of the country to the announcement was, "Jimmy Who?" He seldom had been mentioned by the news media in other states since his inauguration speech nearly four years earlier. The political pundits of TV and the newspapers laughed off his announcement as a publicity stunt—after all, no southern governor had been elected President since James K. Polk's victory in 1844. And, in the succeeding months, a dozen or so better-known Democrats announced their candidacies or indicated their willingness to accept the nomination if chosen.

Familiar with the role of underdog, Carter grinned and went to work. He campaigned steadily throughout 1975 while most of the other contenders sat at home pondering their possibilities. He and Rosalynn traveled back and forth across the nation, staying overnight at the homes of supporters to conserve finances, meeting as many people as they could, and shaking as many hands as possible. "My name is Jimmy Carter and I'm running for President," he said in beginning every speech and in meeting every stranger. But in December 1975 most people still discounted his candidacy, and the Gallup Poll reported that Senator Hubert H. Humphrey of Minnesota, the Democratic presidential candidate in 1968, was the front runner for the nomination.

The first sign that a political miracle might be in the making came on January 19, 1976, when Carter won more votes than any other candidate in Iowa's precinct caucuses. Carter captured twice as many votes as his nearest rival, Senator Birch Bayh of Indiana, and far outdistanced the other contenders: former Senator Fred R. Harris of Oklahoma; Representative Morris K. Udall of Arizona; the 1972 vice-presidential candidate, Sargent Shriver; and Senator Henry M. Jackson of Washington.

In the first state primary of the campaign, on February 24, 1976, in New Hampshire, Carter did it again, winning a plurality of the votes over five rivals. It proved, the soft-spoken Carter said, that "a progressive Southerner can win in the North."

Hundreds of thousands of handshakes and twenty-six primaries later the fifty-one-year-old Georgian had the nomination in hand with 1,117 convention delegate votes. His closest competitor, Udall, had 329 1/2. On July 15, 1976, at the Democratic National Convention in New York City Jimmy Carter was nominated on the first ballot with 2,238 1/2 votes. Other candidates split the remaining 769 1/2 votes. He named Senator Walter F. Mondale of Minnesota as his running mate, and the convention ratified his choice. "My name is Jimmy Carter and I'm running for President," Carter began his acceptance speech to the convention, bringing down the house with this allusion to the concept that there still might be some Democrat who did not know who he was and what he could do.

The election campaign began in earnest after President Ford narrowly edged out Ronald Reagan for the Republican presidential nomination at the GOP convention in Kansas City, Missouri, on August 19, 1976. A Gallup Poll taken immediately after Ford's nomination showed Carter leading with 49 percent of the vote, Ford with 39 percent, and the remaining 12 percent undecided. In an effort to overtake the Georgian, the President took the unusual expedient of challenging him to a series of face-to-face TV debates. Carter accepted, but lost ground in the first debate, giving an appearance of being nervous and hesitant in his replies to questions while the President projected himself forcibly. The tables were turned in the second debate as Ford made a glaring error in categorically denying that the Soviet Union dominated Poland and the other communist countries of eastern Europe. The final debate on October 15 generally was regarded as a standoff. Carter also made some serious errors during the campaign, most notably an interview in the sex-oriented *Playboy* magazine in which he said that, although he had "loved no other woman" than his wife, he had "committed adultery in my heart many times." Even though Carter apologized to his supporters for having given the interview, it did not assuage many of his fundamentalist followers. By November some public opinion polls showed Ford slightly ahead of Carter, while others had Carter leading Ford by a narrow margin.

The election on November 2, 1976, was so close that even with computers tabulating votes and projecting the outcome, voters had to wait into the early morning hours of November 3 to learn that the Carter-Mondale ticket had won. A switch from Carter to Ford of 3,700 votes in Hawaii and 4,700 in Ohio would have been enough to have given the electoral victory to Ford even though Carter still would have led Ford in the popular vote. A third party candidate, liberal Democrat Eugene J. McCarthy, a former senator from Minnesota, won less than 1 percent of the vote, but took enough from Carter to throw several states to Ford. Carter captured all the southern states and most of the northeastern states, while Ford won all the western and southwestern states except for Texas and Hawaii. Carter's winning margin in the popular vote was 50.02 percent to Ford's 47.97 percent.

Carter's Presidential Inauguration

MORE THAN FOR ANY PREVIOUS PRESIDENT since Andrew Jackson, the inauguration of Jimmy Carter emphasized informality and lack of pomposity. As he was sworn in at noon on a cold but sunny January 20, 1977, the fifty-two-year-old Georgian wore a business suit instead of the formal cutaway attire favored by his predecessors since the nineteenth century. And in taking the oath he gave his name as "Jimmy Carter" instead of the more formal James Earl Carter, Jr.

Unlike previous Presidents who ignored as nearly as possible their predecessors, Carter opened his seventeen-minute inaugural address with an accolade to President Ford that brought applause and cheers from the crowd as he said: "For myself and for our nation, I want to thank my predecessor for all he has done to heal our land." Tears welled in Ford's eyes as he acknowledged the crowd's approval.

Carter continued: "Ours was the first society openly to define itself in terms of both spirituality and human liberty. It is that unique self-definition which has given us an exceptional appeal—but it also imposes on us a special obligation, to take on those moral duties which, when assumed, seem invariably to be in our own best interests.

"You have given me a great responsibility—to stay close to you, to be worthy of you and to exemplify what you are. Let us create together a new national spirit of unity and trust. Your strength can compensate for my weakness, and your wisdom can help to minimize my mistakes.

"Let us learn together and laugh together and work together and pray together, confident that in the end we will triumph together in the right."

He concluded the address by saying that he hoped when his administration ended people might say this about the nation:

"That we had remembered the words of Micah and renewed our search for humility, mercy, and justice;

"That we had torn down the barriers that separated those of different race and region and religion, and where there had been mistrust, built unity, with a respect for diversity;

"That we had found productive work for those able to perform it;

"That we had strengthened the American family, which is the basis of our society;

"That we had insured respect for the law, and equal treatment under the law, for the weak and the powerful, for the rich and the poor;

"And that we had enabled our people to be proud of their own government once again.

"I would hope that the nations of the world might say that we had built a lasting peace, based not on weapons of war but on international policies which reflect our own most precious values.

"These are not just my goals. And they will not be my accomplishments, but the affirmation of our nation's continuing moral strength and our belief in an undiminished, ever-expanding American dream."

The new President even more forcibly emphasized his closeness to the people when he left his bullet-proof limousine to walk the mile-and-a-half inaugural parade route from the Capitol to the White House—the first President ever to do so. He waved and smiled as his nine-year-old daughter Amy skipped along at his side, her hands clasped in those of her father on her right and her mother on her left. Behind them walked other members of the Carter family with the President's fifteen-month-old grandson, Jason, perched on the shoulders of his father, Jack Carter.

On his first full day in office, Carter acted to carry out one of his campaign promises by issuing a pardon to the approximately ten thousand young men who evaded the draft during the Vietnam War. Later in the year he made it possible for the 433,000 veterans who had been given less than honorable discharges to have their cases reviewed and more than 29,000 took advantage of the offer.

In a "fireside chat" two weeks after coming to the presidency, Carter made his first televised address to the American people since his inauguration. Wearing a sweater and seated in the White House library, he reviewed his campaign promises and reaffirmed his intention to carry them out. That same day he had signed emergency legislation requesting Congress to ease the natural gas shortage in the northeastern states, where the worst winter of the century had brought about gas shortages that closed many factories and schools.

Carter took an unprecedented step to bring the presidency closer to the people when he spent two hours on radio on March 5, 1977, answering the questions of citizens who dialed a toll-free number. In all he answered the questions of forty-two callers selected at random. Their questions ranged from requests for information on how to get a federal job to wondering whether he liked being President.

The Bert Lance Affair

DURING CARTER'S FIRST YEAR in office, what was called the "Bert Lance Affair" did more to hurt the President's popularity and tarnish his image of high ethical standards than any other problem. One of the first appointments announced by Carter after his election was that of Bertram Lance as director of the Office of Management and Budget (OMB). Lance, a forty-five-year-old Georgia banker, was a close personal friend and also had helped Carter in reorganizing the Georgia state government. Carter had backed Lance's unsuccessful 1974 campaign to become Georgia's governor.

Even before President Carter took office, it was reported that the Justice Department had investigated Lance for possible prosecution for illegal banking practices, but had dropped the investigation for lack of evidence.

When the Senate confirmed Lance's appointment, it stipulated that he should sell his 207,000 shares of Georgia bank stock by the end of 1977 to avoid any conflict of interest. In July President Carter asked the Senate Governmental Affairs Committee to free Lance from the stock sale deadline because the OMB director stood to lose more than a million dollars as a result of the stock's drop in value. As the committee prepared to hold hearings, the news media began carrying stories alleging that Lance had improperly obtained a $3.4 million loan to buy the stock. Other news stories said Lance was being investigated by various governmental agencies for his past activities as a banker.

In mid-August U. S. Comptroller of the Currency John G. Heimann issued a report that seemed to clear Lance of wrongdoing. But three weeks later, testifying before the Senate committee, Heimann accused Lance of abusing his position as a bank president by writing large overdrafts on his personal checking account.

In early September, U.S. Senators Abraham A. Ribicoff of Connecticut and Charles Percy of Illinois, the chairman and vice chairman of the committee investigating Lance, went to the White House to ask for Lance's resignation, saying they had received new evidence of illegalities.

Lance refused to resign, demanding a public hearing of the charges. Carter continued to back him, even though more and more leading Democrats were calling for the resignation.

Additional embarrassment for Carter came when Chicago newspapers revealed that White House press secretary Jody Powell had tried to get them to carry news stories smearing Percy in retaliation for charges Percy had made against Lance. Powell apologized to Percy and admitted his action had been "inappropriate, regrettable, and dumb."

In three days of televised testimony before the Senate committee September 15–17, 1977, Lance denied he had done anything illegal, accused the senators of violating his rights with unfounded charges, and claimed he was being "drummed out of government by a series of false charges, half truths, misrepresentations, innuendos, and the like."

Temporarily, Lance seemed to have won public opinion to his side, but almost immediately new charges began appearing in the news media.

Four days after the TV hearings, Carter called in White House newsmen. With tears in his eyes, the President announced that his friend had resigned even though he had "exonerated himself completely" of the charges. In his letter of resignation, Lance said he had decided to quit "because of the amount of the controversy and the continuing nature of it," but he reiterated that "my conscience is clear."

More than two and a half years later, on April 30, 1980, a federal jury in Atlanta acquitted Lance on six charges of bank fraud. At the same time the jury was unable to agree on his guilt or innocence on three other charges. Two months later the Justice Department dropped the remaining charges on the grounds that further prosecution was not worth the expense.

Domestic Policies

THROUGHOUT CARTER'S ADMINISTRATION the Democratic party held control of both houses of Congress. However, Congress had grown used to battling with the White House during the Nixon and Ford administrations and continued to do so despite the fact that Carter was the nominal leader of the majority party. The President found it increasingly difficult to get his legislative proposals adopted without drastic change. Carter's own lack of experience—he had never served in either house of Congress—led to some of the difficulties. Perhaps of greater importance in obstructing close relations between the Capitol and the White House was Carter's belief that he had no political debts to pay to members of Congress because he had won the office without their help. Likewise, the senators and congressmen felt they owed no debt to the President, being sure that his campaign had little effect on their having won their own elections. Carter had an especially hard time exerting leadership over the Senate, many of whose members had competed against him for the Democratic presidential nomination. During his last year in office relations deteriorated to the extent that Congress twice overrode his vetoes with overwhelming majorities—the first time in twenty-eight years that a Democratic Congress had expressed so little regard for the leadership of a Democratic President. Later, looking back on his presidency, Carter said his "biggest misjudgment" was the lack of coordination between his administration and Congress and his "overoptimism about the speed with which Congress could act on controversial matters."

Congress gave Carter a nearly free hand to reorganize the government to make it more responsive to the people. Legislation signed by the President in April 1977 reserved to Congress the right to veto his reorganization plans only for a period of sixty days after they were submitted by him. As the first step in reorganization, the President cut his own White House staff by 28 percent, abolished several agencies directly responsible to him, and transferred the functions of other White House agencies to the executive departments.

The President included many women, civil rights activists, and consumer advocates among the five hundred appointments he made to key positions in government during his first year. But their presence was far overshadowed by the more than 2.7 million federal employees who continued in their jobs from previous administrations.

Upon Carter's urging, Congress approved the first major Civil Service reform since the days of President Arthur. The measure ended automatic job promotions based on length of service, making promotions and salary increases for federal employees dependent upon job performance. The measure also made it easier for supervisors to fire incompetent employees. In signing the Civil Service reform into law on October 13, 1978, Carter called it the "centerpiece" of his efforts to bring greater efficiency to the federal government.

Two new Cabinet-level departments were added to the federal government. The Department of Energy came into being on October 1, 1977. James R. Schlesinger, who had served as Secretary of Defense under Presidents Nixon and Ford, was named as the first Secretary of Energy to supervise the department's more than 21,000 employees and an annual budget of more than $7 billion. A separate Department of Education was created in 1979 with more than 7,000 employees to administer an annual budget of about $30 billion. Carter appointed a federal judge, Shirley M. Hufstedler, as the first Secretary of Education. With Education thus assigned to a separate department the old Department of Health, Education, and Welfare was renamed, becoming the Department of Health and Human Services.

In an effort to carry out his campaign pledges of reducing government interference in private business, Carter sponsored measures that were passed by Congress to cut back the powers of agencies regulating the airlines, trucking, and railroad industries.

As part of a program to stimulate the economy and reduce unemployment, the President asked Congress for a cut in income taxes that was approved in May 1977. The legislation reduced income taxes by about $35 billion over a three-year period, largely for low-income families. When the economy continued to falter in 1978, Carter asked Congress for another income tax cut of $25 billion. But this measure bogged down because Congress wanted to encourage capital spending by reducing capital gains taxes, while the President believed most of the tax relief should go to middle and lower income families. Finally, Congress approved an $18.7 billion tax reduction measure that Carter signed on November 6, 1978. The tax reductions proved illusory, however, as double-digit inflation pushed most taxpayers into higher brackets, increasing the percentage of their income collected for taxes. Fueled by inflation, the nation's gross national product passed the $2 trillion mark in 1978. The rate of unemployment fell to its lowest level in five years by 1979, but in the recession in the following year it rose again as the number of unemployed topped 7.8 million.

Throughout most of his four years in the White House, Carter's difficulties with Congress were focused on his inability to obtain legislative approval for a comprehensive program to deal with the nation's energy problems. Three months after taking office, the President made a TV address to the nation on April 18, 1977, declaring that the United States faced the likelihood of a "national catastrophe" unless its people gave up their wasteful use of energy and adopted a program that would be the "moral equivalent of war." In presenting his program to Congress two days later, he called for a wide range of measures that included a fifty-cent-per-gallon tax on gasoline to reduce consumption, a "windfall profits" tax on oil companies, the development of synthetic fuels, and the creation of a Department of Energy. Although Congress moved relatively quickly to create the new Energy Department in 1977, the legislators dragged their feet on the other proposals. They especially disliked the idea of an additional tax on gasoline, believing it would be highly unpopular with voters. When Carter endeavored to use his executive powers to impose a fee on imported oil that would have resulted in a surcharge to users of ten cents per gallon of gasoline, Congress humiliated the President by forbidding him to do so, overriding his veto on June 6, 1980. However, three weeks later Congress finally approved an energy bill that contained watered-down versions of many of his other proposals. In signing the legislation on June 30, 1980, Carter declared: "The Energy Security Act will launch this decade with the greatest outpouring of capital investment, technology, manpower, and resources since the space program. Its scope, in fact, is so great that it will dwarf the combined efforts expended to put

Americans on the Moon and to build the entire Interstate Highway System of our country."

The President and Congress also fell into dispute over what new weapons were needed to preserve the nation's military defense. Despite Carter's opposition, Congress approved spending nearly $2 billion to add a fifth huge nuclear aircraft carrier to the U. S. Navy fleet. Reacting with anger, President Carter vetoed the entire $37 billion defense appropriation measure, asking Congress to reallocate the money that would be spent for the carrier to other defense items that he regarded as more urgent. His veto was upheld by the House of Representatives in September 1978. A new measure excluding the carrier was soon passed and approved by the President. In the following year, the President reversed himself and began calling on Congress to increase military spending. He also approved plans in 1979 for a $33 billion project to build a new MX intercontinental missile system that would be hidden underground in a network of two thousand miles of tunnels. In 1980 Carter won congressional approval to revive Selective Service registration of young men as a preparatory measure for a national emergency. However, Congress rejected his proposal that young women also be registered for a military draft.

In the waning months of Carter's administration the Congress approved two major environmental conservation measures that had been put forward by the President. On December 2, 1980, he signed a measure that doubled the size of the nation's national park and wildlife refuge system, adding 104 million acres of Alaska's wilderness areas. Nine days later he signed legislation creating a $1.6 billion dollar "superfund" to pay for the cleanup of dangerous chemicals that had been spilled or dumped in the environment.

Despite campaign promises that he would balance the federal budget, Carter was unable to hold down government spending. Federal expenditures rose from $402.7 billion in 1977 to a record $579 billion in 1980. Large deficits each year pushed up the national debt from $709 billion in 1977 to $914 billion in 1980, an increase of $205 billion.

Foreign Affairs

EARLY IN HIS ADMINISTRATION President Carter began a drive to obtain greater respect for human rights in other countries. "We can't expect overnight success," he told his first news conference. "I'm not looking for magic answers, but my determination is very deep." Military regimes in Argentina, Brazil, and Uruguay refused to accept further U.S. military aid because of criticism regarding their treatment of their citizens. A chill developed in Soviet-American relations as Soviet leaders felt the human rights campaign was directed at them. Later, in a speech to the United Nations General Assembly, Carter pointed out that the policy was meant to embrace all nations.

"All the signatories of the United Nations Charter have pledged themselves to observe and to respect basic human rights," he said. "Thus, no member of the United Nations can claim that mistreatment of its citizens is solely its own business. Equally, no member can avoid its responsibilities to review and to speak when torture or unwarranted deprivation occurs in any part of the world."

To emphasize his continuing determination to help the people of other countries win their rights, he issued a warning to other nations at a news conference on December 15, 1977, declaring, "Our foreign assistance programs will now reflect more clearly our concern for human rights."

Demonstrating disdain for Carter's pleas on human rights, Soviet leaders ordered public trials in 1978 of dissidents who complained of government interference with civil liberties, sentencing them to serve long terms in prison.

Although the President's campaign for human rights seemed to have some success as various military governments released political prisoners and announced plans to reestablish civilian governments, Carter's efforts were not universally applauded even by close allies. Chancellor Helmut Schmidt of West Germany characterized Carter as an evangelist who developed foreign policy "from a pulpit."

Following a policy that the United States should have diplomatic relations with all countries, regardless of their ideologies, American emissaries carried on talks with Vietnam, and in May 1977 withdrew U.S. objections to that nation's application for membership in the United Nations. But after Vietnamese troops invaded Cambodia to set up a puppet government in 1978–79, U.S.-Vietnam relations cooled.

Steps were also taken to restore relations with Cuba, which had been broken off in 1961. In March 1977 the Carter administration lifted restrictions on American tourism in Cuba. In the following month American and Cuban diplomats held their first formal discussions in sixteen years, reaching agreement on the rights of fishermen in the overlapping fishing zones of the United States and Cuba. Then on September 1, 1977, the U.S. and Cuba exchanged diplomatic representatives below the rank of ambassador. When the Cuban government announced in April 1980 that Cubans wishing to leave for the U.S. were free to do so, President Carter declared the United States would welcome them with "an open heart and open arms." But as tens of thousands of Cuban refugees began flooding into Florida by boat, Carter tried to stem the tide by having the Coast Guard seize the boats that were being used. By the time Cuba's President Fidel Castro ended the exodus in September, some 125,000 had made their way to the United States. Among the refugees were several thousand criminals who had been released from prison so that they could leave the country.

President Carter established full diplomatic relations with China on January 1, 1979, completing the process that had begun during the Nixon administration in 1971. At the same time, acceding to China's demands, Carter severed formal diplomatic relations with Taiwan and abrogated the mutual defense treaty with that country. Conservative opponents of the President criticized his action as a "cowardly act" and questioned its legality. However, his power to end the treaty later was upheld in the courts. After leaving the presidency, Carter visited China in 1981.

For the first time in the history of the United States, a black was appointed to a Cabinet-level post when Carter made Andrew Young U. S. Ambassador to the United Nations. Both through his daily contacts at the UN and in his many trips abroad, Young managed to win a new cordiality between the United States and the black leaders of Africa. Young helped draft a British-American plan for white-ruled Rhodesia (now Zimbabwe) to turn over its government to black majority rule. After white-ruled South Africa imposed harsh measures on black activist groups, jailing more than fifty black leaders, Young cast the U.S. vote in the UN Security Council on November 4, 1977, when it was unanimously agreed to declare a mandatory arms embargo on South Africa—the first time the UN ever had taken such action against a member nation.

Young also gained a reputation as the most outspoken member of the Carter administration, often making statements to the press that disagreed with the official position of the State Department or the White House. At the height of the U.S.-Soviet dispute over human rights in 1978, Young declared his belief that there were many political prisoners in American jails just as there were in Soviet prisons. He was severely reprimanded by Carter for the statement, but was allowed to continue in office. However, in August 1979, after admitting that contrary to the government's policy he had held secret talks with the Palestine Liberation Organization (PLO), he resigned. Carter appointed another black diplomat, Donald F. McHenry, to replace him.

For most of the twentieth century U.S. control of the Panama Canal had been viewed by many Latin-American leaders as a flagrant symbol of Yankee imperialism dividing the otherwise sovereign nation of Panama with a zone of American military occupation. Since Lyndon Johnson's administration in 1964, American and Panamanian diplomats had been wrestling with the wording of a new treaty to replace that which had been imposed on Panama in 1903 by President Theodore Roosevelt. Carter brought the drawn-out negotiations to an end in 1977, signing new Panama Canal treaties on September 7 that would turn over control of the Canal and the Panama Canal Zone to Panama at noon on December 31, 1999. Former President Ford endorsed the new treaties, but more conservative Republicans denounced them and called for the Senate to reject their ratification. To overcome the objections and obtain ratification, Carter approved amending the treaties to affirm the right of the United States to intervene with military force to protect the Canal if necessary in the interests of national security. Carter narrowly won Senate ratification of the treaties in 1978 in votes of sixty-eight to thirty-two with only one vote more than the necessary two-thirds majority.

President Carter made several trips abroad, largely as get-acquainted meetings with leaders of other nations. In 1978 he made the first state visit of a U.S. President to black-ruled nations of Africa south of the Sahara, traveling to Nigeria and Liberia on a trip that also included stops in Venezuela and Brazil.

Believing that one of the greatest threats to world peace lay in the spread of atomic weapons to additional nations, Carter obtained the agreement of fourteen other countries including the Soviet Union in January 1978 to a code that would prevent the export of materials and equipment that could be used to make atomic weapons. In furtherance of his policy to reduce the proliferation of atomic weapons, he decided in April 1978 to defer production of the neutron bomb, a tactical nuclear weapon designed to kill people with minimum damage to buildings or other structures.

Triumphant Camp David Summit Conference

WHEN PRESIDENT CARTER took office the greatest immediate threat to world peace lay in the Middle East, where Israel and its Arab neighbors had fought four wars since 1948. Although a truce had existed since 1974, both sides continued to arm for future conflicts, and the Arab nations refused to recognize Israel's right to exist as a sovereign nation or to negotiate with Israeli diplomats to work out a lasting peace.

When President Anwar al-Sadat of Egypt, the largest of Israel's Arab neighbors, came to Washington, D.C., in April 1977 to visit Carter, the two found the basis for mutual respect and friendship in their private discussions. In the months that followed, Carter and Sadat kept in touch with each other with personal letters that Sadat later credited with influencing a dramatic turnaround in his thinking. Sadat announced in November that he would be willing to go to Israel itself if it would help bring peace. Israel's Prime Minister Menachem Begin quickly issued a formal invitation. On November 19–21 Sadat visited Israel, addressing the Israeli parliament and meeting privately with Begin in the first face-to-face talks between Arab and Israeli leaders since the Jewish state first declared its independence three decades earlier.

At Sadat's invitation a formal peace conference began in Cairo on December 14, 1977, with Israeli, Egyptian, and American representatives in attendance. Other Arab nations refused to send their diplomats, denouncing Sadat as a traitor to the Arab world for even talking with the Israelis. Begin flew to the United States in mid-December to discuss his bargaining position with Carter, and then flew to Egypt on Christmas Day 1977 for another meeting with Sadat. But the talks bore no fruit.

To break the deadlock, Carter invited Sadat and Begin to join him in September 1978 at the Presidential retreat, Camp David, in Maryland. Sealed off from the rest of the world by a wall of secrecy for thirteen days, the three leaders bargained with each other while the world anxiously awaited the outcome.

Then, on September 17, 1978, the three leaders emerged from seclusion at Camp David to announce the successful conclusion of their negotiations. Sadat had been persuaded to give up his adamant demand for an independent Palestinian Arab nation as a prerequisite for a peace agreement. And Begin had agreed to return to Egypt the Sinai Peninsula, which Israel had captured in the Third Arab-Israeli War of 1967. After flying by helicopter to the White House, Carter, Sadat, and Begin appeared on television to sign two agreements that established frameworks for conclusion of a peace treaty between Egypt and Israel and principles for a general peace in the Middle East.

During the next several months, however, final agreement between Israel and Egypt became elusive as both sides objected to the specific wording of sections of the treaty being drafted with the aid of American diplomats. Upon his arrival in the United States for further talks with President Carter at the beginning of March 1979, Israel's Prime Minister Begin cantankerously called the draft treaty a "sham document." After conversations with Begin, Carter announced that he personally would endeavor to bring the treaty to a conclusion by flying to the Middle East for talks with both sides. From March 8 to March 13 President Carter shuttled back and forth between Egypt and Israel, winning concessions and compromises from both sides. His skill in personal diplomacy was rewarded on March 14 as the Israeli Cabinet voted to accept the revised treaty. Less than two weeks later Sadat and Begin flew to the United States, where on March 26 the treaty was ceremonially signed in the White House. After being ratified, the treaty formally went into effect a month later, on April 25, ending the state of war between Egypt and Israel. The treaty called for Israel to return to Egypt the Sinai area in a three-year staged withdrawal, which began in May 1979. In achieving the agreement on the treaty, President Carter had pledged about $5 billion in aid to Egypt and Israel over the ensuing three years. Other Arab countries ostracized Egypt for having signed the treaty, which left to later discussion the demand by Palestinian Arabs for an independent nation of their own to be created from areas that continued to be held by Israel.

SALT II and the Afghanistan Invasion

AFTER SEVEN YEARS of negotiations that had begun under President Nixon, Soviet and American diplomats reached agreement on a new strategic arms limitation treaty called SALT II. At a summit meeting in Vienna, Austria, with Soviet President Brezhnev, Carter signed the treaty on June 18, 1979. That same day he flew back to Washington and, to emphasize the importance of the treaty, addressed a joint meeting of Congress that night. The President called for Senate ratification of the treaty, explaining:

"The SALT II treaty reduces the danger of nuclear war. For the first time —for the first time—it places equal ceilings on the strategic arsenals of both sides, ending a previous numerical imbalance in favor of the Soviet Union. SALT II preserves our options to build the forces we need to maintain that strategic balance. The treaty enhances our own ability to monitor what the Soviet Union is doing and it leads directly to the next step in more effectively controlling nuclear weapons. . . .

"The Soviet Union will have to destroy or dismantle some 250 strategic missile systems. . . . By contrast, no operational United States forces will have to be reduced."

The President was unable to expedite Senate approval of the treaty. For more than four months the Senate Foreign Relations committee considered testimony on its provisions, hearing both those who attacked it for placing too severe limits on U.S. strength and those who believed it was not strict enough in limiting armament. Finally, the committee approved the treaty on November 9, 1979, by a vote of nine to six. A vote by the full Senate was deferred to 1980, giving the Carter administration time to try to gather enough support to ensure the necessary two-thirds majority. But the fate of the SALT II treaty was sealed by Soviet actions in the following month.

On Christmas Day 1979 the Soviet Union began an invasion of Afghanistan with about 85,000 troops. The Afghan president was executed and replaced with a pro-Soviet puppet ruler. The Soviet Union attempted to justify its invasion by claiming that the United States had been financing guerrilla forces attempting to overthrow Afghanistan's communist government. The former president of Afghanistan was described as an agent "of United States imperialism."

On January 2, 1980, President Carter announced that he was asking the U. S. Senate to defer indefinitely further consideration of the SALT II treaty. Two days later he addressed the nation on TV, announcing that in retaliation for the Soviet action he was embargoing the shipment of 17 million metric tons of grain that the Soviet Union had purchased in the United States. He also suspended the sale of high technology equipment to the Soviet Union and curtailed Soviet fishing in American waters. The President further announced that he would lead a boycott of the 1980 Summer Olympic Games, scheduled to be held in Moscow. Later, when the Soviet Union still refused to withdraw its troops from Afghanistan, about 57 other nations followed the lead of the United States in absenting themselves from the sports event. The Soviet Union called Carter's measures "a revival of the Cold War."

In his annual State of the Union address on January 23, 1980, President Carter issued a warning to the Soviet Union that the United States would not hesitate to go to war if necessary to protect the oil supply routes of the Persian Gulf. In what became known as the Carter Doctrine, he said: "An attempt by any outside force to gain control of the Persian Gulf region will be regarded as an assault on the vital interests of the United States of America. And such an assault will be repelled by any means necessary, including military force."

The Disastrous Hostage Crisis with Iran

PRESIDENT CARTER'S HANDLING of the hostage crisis with Iran has generally come to be regarded as the single most important issue leading to his defeat for a second term. During 1978 a rising number of riots, demonstrations, and strikes had been directed against the regime of Iran's Shah Mohammed Reza Pahlevi. Ever since American CIA agents had helped the Shah regain his throne in 1953, he had been an important ally of the United States, purchasing billions of dollars' worth of American arms and supplying much of the nation's oil imports. However, in light of the Carter administration's campaign for worldwide human rights, the Shah was something of an embarrassment because of his use of secret police, torture, and harsh punishment to quell opposition. The revolutionary campaign to overthrow the Shah was orchestrated from France by the exiled Iranian Islamic leader Ayatollah Khomeini, who regarded the United States as an enemy and had openly vowed to cut off oil exports to the U.S. if he gained control of the Iranian government. However, in secret talks with members of Khomeini's staff, the Carter administration had come to believe that an accommodation could be reached with him if he was successful. Therefore, as the uprising reached a crescendo early in January 1979, the Carter administration advised the Shah not to call out his army against the street demonstrators, but to leave the country. On January 16, 1979, the Shah flew into exile, first to Egypt and later to Mexico. He was dissuaded by the Carter administration from coming to the United States, for fear that such an action would give Khomeini a pretext for cutting off oil shipments to the United States. Khomeini returned to Iran in February and seized control of the government. Hundreds of the Shah's officials and military officers were executed. The thousands of Americans who had been working in Iran were permitted to leave, many in hastily arranged airlifts. On February 14, 1979, Iranian militants attacked the U. S. Embassy in Teheran, holding it under siege for several hours until the U.S. ambassador and about 100 other Americans were rescued by the intervention of Khomeini's troops. However, Iran continued to ship about 700,000 barrels of oil to the United States each day, meeting about 4 percent of the nation's imported oil needs.

After calling the U.S. ambassador home from Iran for consultation, Carter was preparing to send a new ambassador when the Senate passed a resolution condemning the many executions by the Khomeini government. On May 20 the Iranian government angrily told the United States not to dispatch the new ambassador. However, the Carter administration continued diplomatic relations, maintaining the U. S. Embassy in Teheran with lower-level personnel. Although U.S. diplomats in Teheran advised Carter that if the deposed Shah was allowed to enter the United States the Khomeini regime was sure to make severe reprisals, the President decided in October to let the Shah come to New York for medical treatment, reportedly persuaded to do so by such friends of the Shah as former Secretary of State Kissinger and billionaire banker David Rockefeller.

Immediately after the Shah's arrival in the United States on October 23, thousands of Iranians filled the streets around the U. S. Embassy in Teheran chanting such slogans as "Death to Carter" and "Death for the Shah." Then, on November 4, Iranian militants rushed the embassy, overcoming the U. S. Marine Corps guards and capturing most of the embassy personnel and visitors. They paraded the blindfolded American prisoners before the chanting crowds and threatened to execute them as spies unless Carter returned the Shah and his wealth to Iran. Carter dispatched U.S. envoys to Iran to negotiate release of the hostages, but Khomeini forbade their admittance.

Pressed by outraged members of Congress to take some action, President Carter on November 12 banned any further purchase of oil from Iran, rejecting Khomeini's demand that the Shah be returned to Iran in exchange for the hostages. After reports were received that Iran was about to withdraw some $6 billion in funds from American banks, Carter on November 14 froze most Iranian assets within the United States. However, because Carter continued to hope for a negotiated release of the captives, diplomatic relations with Iran were not broken and bank accounts of the Iranian embassy and Iranian consulates in the United States were not frozen.

In an effort to win support in the United States from minority activists, Iran on November 19–20 released a group of the American hostages that included eight blacks and five women, who were allowed to fly out of the country.

Meanwhile, Khomeini stirred the hatred of radical Muslims throughout the world against the United States. In one of the worst incidents, mobs in Pakistan attacked and severely damaged the U. S. Embassy in Islamabad on November 21 before being driven off by Pakistani troops. Six persons died in the incident, including two American servicemen. U.S. embassies in several other Muslim countries were damaged.

Trying to appease Iran, the Carter administration persuaded the Shah to leave the United States on December 15, 1979. He flew to exile in Panama. Later, when Iran tried to extradite him from that country, the Shah left Panama on March 23, 1980, for asylum in Egypt. He died there of lymphatic cancer four months later on July 27. The only prominent American to attend his funeral was former President Nixon, who described the Carter administration's treatment of the Shah as "shameful."

Six American embassy employees escaped from Iran on January 2, 1980, having been hidden and aided by Canadian diplomats. One of the American hostages was permitted to leave Iran on July 11, 1980, for health reasons. But fifty-two other Americans continued to be held prisoner by the Iranians for the duration of the crisis.

In the months immediately following the seizure of the U. S. Embassy in Teheran, American public opinion united behind Carter in his efforts to negotiate their release. But as the months dragged by with no success, Americans felt increasingly humiliated that the most powerful country in the world was unable to free the hostages. Finally Carter ordered a secret military operation to be carried out to rescue the hostages. But the nation was shocked on April 25 when Carter, in an early morning TV broadcast, announced the failure of the military mission. The operation had been aborted by the President after three out of eight helicopters failed during the mission. In the withdrawal of the military force, a helicopter and a transport plane collided, killing eight servicemen and injuring others. Secretary of State Cyrus R. Vance resigned three days later because the President had ordered the military mission against his advice. He was replaced as Secretary of State by Senator Edmund S. Muskie of Maine.

It later became apparent that Khomeini was perhaps even more interested in punishing Carter than in humbling the United States. Only two days before the national presidential election of 1980, Iran announced stiff terms for release of the hostages—timing the announcement so it would have the maximum effect on American voters going to the polls on November 4, which by coincidence marked one full year of captivity for the hostages. Serious negotiations, with Algerian diplomats acting as intermediaries, did not begin until after Carter's electoral defeat. In the weeks of negotiation that followed, although Carter readily agreed to most of Iran's demands, the Iranians procrastinated over minor points. The delaying tactics persisted to the end of Carter's administration, so that the hostages were not actually allowed to fly out of Iran to freedom until after President Reagan was sworn into office on Inauguration Day.

Defeated in Bid for Second Term

DURING THE CAMPAIGN for the Democratic presidential nomination in the first half of 1980, President Carter remained largely at the White House on the grounds that his presence there was needed for important decisions regarding the efforts to free the hostages in Iran. He left campaign speechmaking appearances to Vice President Mondale, his wife, and other supporters. Carter's major opponent for the Democratic nomination, Senator Edward M. Kennedy, the youngest brother of President Kennedy, called for Carter to meet him in face-to-face debates on the issues, but Carter refused to do so. Kennedy denounced Carter's conservative policies, appealing to liberals and to ethnic minority voters. In the early primaries of the campaign, Carter benefited from the feeling by voters that they should support the President in the nation's confrontation with Iran. But after the botched attempt at a military rescue of the hostages, Carter's popularity plummeted. Kennedy won primary elections in states with the largest numbers of delegates, including California, New York, Pennsylvania, New Jersey, and Massachusetts.

When the Democratic national convention convened in August in New York City, the President had accumulated enough pledged delegates early in the campaign to control the outcome. Although many Democratic leaders were convinced that Carter could not win a second term in November, he refused to withdraw and would not free his delegates from their pledges so they could vote for anyone else. Kennedy's supporters brought the "open convention" issue to a vote, but were able to muster only 1,390.58 votes to the President's 1,936.42, after which Kennedy formally withdrew his candidacy. In the ballot for the presidential nomination on August 13, Carter received 2,123 votes, while 1,150.5 still went to Kennedy. Mondale was endorsed by the convention as Carter's running mate.

Carter set the tone for the ensuing presidential election campaign in his acceptance speech to the convention in which he attacked his Republican opponent, Ronald Reagan, as the proponent of "radical and irresponsible" policies that "could put the whole world in peril."

During the campaign, Carter feared that Representative John B. Anderson of Illinois, who was running as an Independent candidate, would draw off enough liberal Democratic votes to defeat him. So he repeatedly refused to participate in a three-way televised debate that would include both Reagan and Anderson. Finally, just one week before the election, he and Reagan faced each other in a ninety-minute TV debate. Carter continued to attack Reagan as "dangerous and belligerent," charges that Reagan largely overcame by his warm and friendly demeanor, asking the voters to choose between them on the basis of the question, "Are you better off than you were four years ago?"

Irresponsible activities by Carter's younger brother, Billy, helped contribute to the President's declining popularity. The younger Carter, who relished his role as a red-neck and beer drinker, admitted to a Senate investigating committee in August that he had received $220,000 as an agent for the government of Libya. He denied that he had attempted to influence the President. But in its report issued in October, the Senate committee denounced his actions as "contrary to the interest of the President and the United States."

After Carter's overwhelming defeat in the presidential election in November, he devoted much of his time in the remaining months of his presidency to the negotiations with Iran for release of the hostages. On January 14, 1981, a few days before leaving the presidency for retirement at his home in Plains, Georgia, Carter made a televised farewell address. In it he repeated the words of the Declaration of Independence and then related them to the contemporary world situation, saying, "For this generation, life is nuclear survival, liberty is human rights; the pursuit of happiness is a planet whose resources are devoted to the physical and spiritual nourishment of its inhabitants." He then added, "As I return home to the South where I was born and raised, I am looking forward to the opportunity to reflect and further to assess —I hope with accuracy—the circumstances of our times." In conclusion, he pledged support to President Reagan.

Ronald Reagan
The Fortieth President of the United States
1981–89

1911 (February 6) Born in Tampico, Illinois.

1932 Graduated from Eureka College in Illinois.

1937 Appeared as actor in first motion picture, *Love Is on the Air.*

1940 (January 25) Married actress Jane Wyman.

1942–45 Served in U. S. Army Air Forces with rank of captain.

1948 Divorced from Jane Wyman.

1952 (March 4) Married Nancy Davis.

1967–75 Governor of California.

1981 (January 20) Inaugurated as fortieth President of the United States.

1981 (March 30) Wounded in attempted assassination.

1981–1989 Fortieth President of the United States.

At the age of sixty-nine, Ronald Reagan was the oldest person ever elected President of the United States. He then beat his own record by winning reelection at age seventy-three. But as the nation's Chief Executive he displayed a vigor and youthful appearance that belied the fact he was well beyond the age at which most Americans retired.

Well known to most Americans as an actor who had performed in more than fifty movies and appeared as host in two television series, Reagan had turned to politics in the 1960s as a conservative Republican. After winning the governorship of California, he twice tried unsuccessfully to obtain his party's presidential nomination, in 1968 and 1976. When he finally achieved the nomination in 1980, he easily defeated incumbent President Jimmy Carter by promising to restore the nation's diminished prestige abroad and to solve its economic problems at home. Reflecting the more permissive morality of the times, Reagan was the first person to win the presidency despite having been divorced. He also was the first former leader of a labor union to become President, having twice headed the Screen Actors Guild and having led its members in a long strike against the movie industry.

In the midst of his Inauguration Day ceremonies in 1981, Reagan was able to give a lift to the nation's spirit by announcing that the long ordeal of captivity by fifty-two American hostages in Iran had ended with their flight to freedom. Two months later, when he narrowly missed death from an assassin's bullet, his self-deprecating humorous quips and his speedy recovery from the near fatal wound caused his popularity to soar.

With the Congress divided between a Republican-controlled Senate and a Democratic-controlled House of Representatives, it took every ounce of his self-assured sincerity and persuasive skill to achieve passage of his legislative programs. To do so, he brought public pressure to bear on recalcitrant members of Congress in effective nationwide telecasts to the people.

In his first Inaugural Address, the President gave priority to his conservative economic program, which later was dubbed "Reaganomics." Calling for the beginning of "an era of national renewal," he summarized the hopes for his administration:

"As we renew ourselves here in our own land we will be seen as having greater strength throughout the world. We will again be the exemplar of freedom and a beacon of hope for those who do not now have freedom."

By the end of President Reagan's second term, the management of the economy was successful in holding down inflation and creating millions of new jobs. One of the President's most ambitious goals, tax reform and simplification, had been achieved. A historic arms reduction treaty had been signed with the Soviets as well, and seemed to offer much hope for a securer peace between the two superpowers.

In his farewell address to the Republican National Convention, the President reviewed the achievements of his administration and in speaking of his term in office said, "Having temporary custody of this office has been for me a sacred trust and an honor beyond words or measure."

Small-town Boy to Radio Sportscaster

RONALD WILSON REAGAN was born on February 6, 1911, in Tampico, Illinois, a town with a population of about one thousand. His birthplace was a second-floor apartment over a store. His father, John Edward Reagan, earned his living as a shoe clerk. His mother, Nellie Wilson Reagan, from time to time also helped augment the family's meager income by working as a store clerk. His brother, John Neil Reagan, nicknamed "Moon," was three years older. The father was addicted to alcohol, later termed "the Irish disease" by his youngest son. As a consequence, the elder Reagan from time to time had to move his family to another town to find a new employer. When Ronald Reagan was nine, the family settled in Dixon, Illinois, about eighty miles west of Chicago, where his father borrowed enough money to become part owner of a store.

"Dutch," as the youngest Reagan had been nicknamed by his father, grew up in Dixon in the 1920s. He later called these years "the happiest times of my life." In high school he played football and other sports. His popularity won him the presidency of the student council. In the summers he earned money as a lifeguard at a nearby rustic resort, where over a period of seven years he rescued seventy-eight people from drowning.

During the Great Depression, Reagan attended Eureka College, a small Disciples of Christ school near Peoria, Illinois. Playing football as a running guard, acting in college plays, and taking part in campus politics were more important to him than academic studies.

After graduation in 1932, he spent one final summer as a lifeguard. Having decided to become a radio sports announcer, he set out to find a job, hitchhiking from station to station until the program director of station WOC in Davenport, Iowa, decided to give him a chance. After a short stint there, he moved to a larger station, WHO in Des Moines, Iowa, where he gained a wide following with his play-by-play descriptions of football, baseball, and other sports.

Movie Actor and Labor Leader

TAKING advantage of a spring training trip to California with the Chicago Cubs in 1937, Reagan visited Hollywood, where a friend arranged for him to have a screen test. Upon viewing the test, Warner Brothers offered him a seven-year $200-a-week contract that he instantly accepted. In his first movie,

Love Is on the Air, he was cast in a role he already knew—that of a radio announcer.

His first leading role in an "A" film came in 1938 in *Brother Rat,* which also featured Jane Wyman, whom he married two years later, on January 25, 1940. In their marriage, which was broken by divorce in 1948, they had two children: Maureen, who was born in 1941, and Michael, an adopted son who was born in 1945. Reagan's acting career received a boost when in 1940 he played the role of the dying football player George Gipp in *Knute Rockne—All-American.* Movie critics also acclaimed Reagan's acting in 1941 in *King's Row,* in which he played a young man whose legs were amputated by a sadistic surgeon. His most famous line in that film was, "Where's the rest of me?" He later used this question as the title of his autobiography, written in 1965.

World War II interrupted Reagan's acting career. While still a sportscaster in Iowa, he had joined the U.S. Army Reserve, training with the cavalry at Fort Des Moines, where he held a commission as a second lieutenant. However, his nearsightedness caused him to be placed on a "limited service" status. After the Japanese attack on Pearl Harbor, he was called up for active duty. Because of his poor sight he was not assigned to combat, but instead was transferred to an army motion picture unit. He spent the remainder of the war helping make films for the military, rising to the rank of captain and refusing a promotion to major.

After the war Reagan returned to the acting profession. In the following years he made an additional twenty-two feature films, the last in 1964, but none was as notable as his earlier successes.

Like many of his generation, Reagan came out of the war filled with idealism and a sense of public duty. He began taking an active part in the Screen Actors Guild, a labor union of movie performers. He was president of the union for five years, from 1947 to 1952. He devoted much time to union activities because this was a troubled time in Hollywood in which communists sought to penetrate the movie industry to use it for propaganda. Reagan later wrote, ". . . we met for so many long hours each day to try and keep the studios open in the face of the communist-inspired attempt through labor troubles to dominate the industry." In those years, Reagan was a liberal Democrat. In 1948 he aided Harry S Truman's presidential campaign, and in 1950 supported Helen Gahagan Douglas in her race against Richard Nixon for the U.S. Senate. He again served as president of the union in 1959–60, during which time he led a performers' strike that won actors a share of the profits from the sale of their old movies to the television networks.

While Reagan was president of the Screen Actors Guild, a young actress by the name of Nancy Davis asked him for help because she was receiving communist propaganda in the mail that she did not want. His help developed into a romance, and they were married on March 4, 1952, in a ceremony in which actor William Holden was best man. They had two children: Patricia, who was born in 1953, and Ronald Prescott, who was born in 1958. Reagan and his wife appeared in their only movie together, *Hellcats of the Navy,* in 1957. It was her eleventh and last movie. After that Nancy Reagan gave up her own career to devote herself to her husband and her family. As she said in her autobiography, *Nancy,* "Having one husband for all of your life just seems to me how things should be."

As his career as a motion picture actor waned, Reagan turned to television. From 1954 to 1962 he served as host of the *General Electric Theater* television series, sometimes starring in the dramatic offerings. And from 1962 to 1965 he was master of ceremonies for *Death Valley Days,* a TV Western series in which he sometimes performed. While acting as host for the General Electric TV shows, Reagan also became a public relations representative for the firm, making many personal appearances throughout the country and mastering the art of after-dinner speaking.

Governor of California

BEGINNING in the 1950s, Reagan became increasingly more conservative in his political views. While ostensibly remaining a Democrat, he supported the Republican presidential candidacies of Eisenhower in 1952 and 1956 and of Nixon in 1960. As a spokesman for the General Electric Company, he emphasized conservative principles. He changed his voter registration in 1962 from Democrat to Republican.

"If there is a weakness in our two-party system," he later wrote, "it is that we accept a party label as ours and then vote the label without questioning whether the party continues to represent our own philosophical beliefs.

"I was a Democrat when the Democratic party stood for states rights, local autonomy, economy in government, and individual freedom. Today it is a party that has changed, openly declaring for centralized federal power and government-sponsored redistribution of the individual's earnings."

The date October 27, 1964, marked a watershed in Reagan's life. On that day the fifty-three-year-old converted Republican made his first nationally televised political speech, supporting the party's presidential candidate, Barry Goldwater. Hundreds of thousands of dollars in contributions for Goldwater's campaign poured in from conservatives who were impressed by Reagan's good-humored, anecdotal style in attacking big government and high taxes.

Of greater consequence for Reagan, the speech convinced wealthy California conservatives that he had potential as a political candidate.

When first approached with the idea that he should run for governor of California, Reagan laughed and brushed the suggestions aside. But by the autumn of 1965 he had become convinced he had a chance to win. He easily won the Republican nomination for governor with a primary victory over George Christopher, former mayor of San Francisco.

Democratic Governor Edmund G. (Pat) Brown was seeking a third term in office in 1966. Having overwhelmingly defeated former Vice President Richard Nixon to win his second term in 1962, Brown did not regard Reagan as an especially formidable opponent. Brown and his supporters believed the voters could not possibly choose a former actor who was totally inexperienced in government. One political advertisement even reminded voters that it was an actor who had assassinated Abraham Lincoln.

Reagan, sensing that the voters were tired of professional politicians, turned his inexperience to advantage, describing himself as a "citizen-politician." Instead of playing down his background as an actor, he welcomed at his campaign appearances such fellow performers as Andy Devine and Edgar Bergen. And when the ballots were tabulated on election day, Reagan had defeated Brown by nearly a million votes.

After taking office as governor on January 2, 1967, Reagan managed the government in a manner resembling that of a chairman of the board of a large corporation, holding semiweekly cabinet meetings of the top officials of the state government. On the basis of the reports and discussions at these cabinet meetings, the governor made his decisions.

More than a decade later, Reagan brought to Washington several of his earlier associates. Among them was his former gubernatorial cabinet secretary Edwin Meese III, who became Reagan's closest White House adviser and later Attorney General.

The state legislature was controlled by the Democratic party during Governor Reagan's administration. Compromises were necessary to obtain passage of any part of his legislative proposals. Consequently, it is difficult to assess whether Reagan or the legislature was responsible for successes and failures. Although he had campaigned to reduce the cost of government, Reagan discovered after taking office that the previous administration had run up debts of $194 million because there was no withholding provision in the state income tax. He called for new taxes and the legislature obliged. Because of inflation, revenues soared higher than anticipated. Substantial amounts of the revenue surplus were rebated to taxpayers. But by the time Reagan left office the state treasury was in sound shape, with a surplus of more than half a billion dollars. The governor's welfare reforms cut thousands from the state's relief rolls. Despite Reagan's campaign promises to reduce the number of state employees, their number grew by more than forty thousand.

Voter satisfaction with Reagan's administration was registered in 1970 when he won a second term, receiving a majority of nearly 53 percent in defeating Democratic candidate Jesse M. Unruh, who had been Democratic majority leader of the lower house of the legislature.

Winning the Presidency

ALMOST IMMEDIATELY after becoming governor, Reagan began to be urged by his supporters to seek the Republican presidential nomination in 1968. Having pledged in his campaign that he did not regard the governorship as a stepping-stone and would serve a full term if elected, Reagan was loath to go back on his word even to attain the presidency. He refused to announce his candidacy officially, even though his name was entered in the Oregon presidential primary, which was won by former Vice President Nixon, the leading candidate for the nomination. However, Nixon's losses in the 1960 presidential election and in the 1962 California gubernatorial election had convinced many politicians that he was a "loser." Reagan's supporters believed a deadlock could develop in the balloting at the national convention and that then the California governor might become the delegates' choice. Reagan waited until the Republican National Convention was in session in August before officially announcing his availability for the nomination. By then it was too late. Nixon won handily on the first ballot and went on to capture the White House. Reagan and his supporters reconciled themselves to waiting until the 1976 presidential election for another chance.

Reagan did not run for a third term as governor in 1974. The Republican candidate, Houston I. Flournoy, lost to Democrat Jerry Brown (Edmund G. Brown, Jr.), son of the former governor whom Reagan had defeated eight years earlier.

Nearly sixty-three when he turned the governorship of California over to Brown early in 1975, Reagan was now independently wealthy, having wisely invested his movie earnings in real estate in the early 1950s. He looked forward to spending more time at his ranch near Santa Barbara, where he enjoyed horseback riding and other outdoor activities. But he had no intention of retiring. He still had his eye on the presidency, although he felt reluctant about trying to wrest the nomination from an incumbent Republican President—the last time this had been accomplished was in 1884 when the party rejected President Chester A. Arthur in favor of James G. Blaine. However, Reagan's supporters overcame whatever qualms he may have had, and on November 20, 1975, he formally announced his candidacy. In the following month a Gallup public opinion poll showed Reagan leading President Ford in popularity.

In the nation's first 1976 presidential primary in New Hampshire on February 24, Ford narrowly edged out Reagan, winning slightly more than 50 percent of the vote. In March the President defeated Reagan with ever larger margins in Florida and Illinois. Up to this point Reagan had observed the tradition that one Republican candidate should not speak ill of another. But when some of his supporters suggested he should consider withdrawing, Reagan decided to pull off the gloves and begin attacking President Ford. The tactic worked, for on March 23 he won an upset victory over Ford in the North Carolina primary—the first time an incumbent President had lost a primary since Lyndon Johnson was defeated in the New Hampshire primary by Senator Eugene McCarthy in 1968. Reagan next won the Texas, Georgia, Alabama, and Indiana primaries, while Ford won in Michigan and Ohio.

With the date for the Republican national convention less than three weeks away and with Ford holding a slight lead in delegate strength, Reagan decided to adopt an unusual tactic suggested by his campaign manager. On July 26 he named a liberal Republican, Senator Richard S. Schweiker of Pennsylvania, as his choice for Vice President. It was the first time in history a major candidate had made such a preconvention announcement, and the tactic failed. Conservatives denounced Reagan for abandoning his principles while liberal delegates made no move to join the Reagan camp.

A switch of only fifty-nine votes by the delegates would have given the nomination to Reagan, but it was not to be. When the GOP national convention voted in Kansas City, Missouri, on August 19, Ford received a majority of 1,187 to Reagan's 1,070. The former California governor would have to wait four more years for another chance.

During the administration of President Carter, Reagan lived a comfortable life in California on his yearly income of more than a quarter of a million dollars, earned largely from investments and lecture fees. He spent considerable time planning and raising funds for the 1980 presidential campaign.

Formally announcing his candidacy at a fund-raising dinner in New York City on November 13, 1979, Reagan used Franklin D. Roosevelt's "rendezvous with destiny" phrase in describing his goals, saying:

"A troubled and afflicted mankind looks to us, pleading for us to keep our rendezvous with destiny: that we will uphold the principles of self-reliance, self-discipline, morality, and, above all, responsible liberty for every individual."

At the outset Reagan faced an uphill battle. Polls showed him trailing President Carter, Senator Edward Kennedy, and former President Ford, and to further complicate his troubles, nine other Republicans, not including Ford, had announced their candidacy for the GOP nomination.

In the first real test of political appeal, in January 1980, Reagan's confidence was shaken when former CIA director George Bush defeated him in Iowa Republican caucuses. However, Reagan snapped back the following month in the New Hampshire primary, winning as many votes as all of his other opponents combined. In the following months he developed a commanding lead, winning twenty-eight out of thirty-four primaries as the other candidates dropped out one by one.

The most liberal of the Republican candidates, Representative John B. Anderson of Illinois, announced on April 24 that because he no longer had any chance of winning the Republican nomination he would run as an Independent in the November election. His independent candidacy seemed more likely to hurt the election chances of President Carter than those of Reagan.

At the Republican convention in Detroit on July 16, Reagan received 1,939 votes with only fifty-five going to other candidates or abstaining. Suspense developed only over the selection of the vice-presidential candidate. After former President Ford confirmed in interviews that he was available for the vice-presidential nomination, delegates and newsmen anticipated a "dream ticket" of Reagan and Ford. After several conferences with Ford, Reagan addressed the convention in the early morning hours of July 17, announcing that Ford had decided he would be of more value as a campaigner than as a member of the ticket. Reagan then proposed Bush for the vice-presidential candidacy and the convention ratified the decision. Authoritative sources said Ford had demanded greater powers as Vice President than Reagan was able or willing to grant.

In his acceptance speech to the convention, Reagan said:

"More than anything else, I want my candidacy to unify our country; to renew the American spirit and sense of purpose. . . . Never before in our history have Americans been called upon to face three grave threats to our very existence, any one of which could destroy us. We face a disintegrating economy, a weakened defense, and an energy policy based on the sharing of scarcity.

"The major issue of this campaign is the direct political, personal, and moral responsibility of Democratic party leadership—in the White House and in the Congress—for this unprecedented calamity which has befallen us."

After President Carter won the Democratic presidential nomination in August, the Gallup public opinion poll showed a close race—with Reagan receiving 39 percent of the vote, Carter 38 percent, and Anderson 14 percent. It seemed possible that the presidential electoral vote might be so divided that the House of Representatives would have to decide the election for the first time since the election of John Quincy Adams in 1825.

The League of Women Voters sought to arrange a debate among the three candidates in September, but Carter refused, insisting that Anderson should not be included. Reagan and Anderson accepted the invitation, debating each other on September 21 in Baltimore, Maryland. By mid-October public opinion polls showed Anderson's popularity had declined to the point that he was unlikely to be a significant factor in the election, so the League of Women Voters excluded him in a new invitation to the major candidates for a debate on election issues.

Only one week before the election, Reagan and Carter faced each other in a ninety-minute televised confrontation in Cleveland, Ohio, on October 28. The President emphasized the importance of new nuclear arms controls to limit the risk of war, terming Reagan's views as "extremely dangerous and belligerent." Reagan responded with genial denials of the President's charges. His remarks focused on the problems of the nation's economy, asking voters to decide whom they should vote for by answering the question, "Are you better off than you were four years ago?"

Most public opinion polls indicated that the election was too close to call and that neither major candidate would receive a majority of the vote. Some observers believed it might be weeks or even months before the outcome of the election would be decided.

But on Election Day, November 4, the vote was so lopsided in favor of Reagan that President Carter conceded his defeat about 9 P.M. EST, long before voters had finished going to the polls in Alaska, Hawaii, and the West Coast states. Out of the more than 86 million votes cast, Reagan received 43,904,153 or slightly more than half. Only 35,483,883 votes or 41 percent went to Carter. Anderson's slightly more than 6.6 percent of the vote had no effect on the outcome. Reagan's landslide won 489 electoral votes, carrying forty-two states, while Carter received only 49 from six states and the District of Columbia. Figures released by the Federal Election Commission showed that Reagan and Carter each had spent about $28 million on their campaigns, with Reagan spending only slightly more than Carter.

President Reagan's Inauguration

IN ONE OF THE MOST dramatic inaugurations in the nation's history, Reagan was sworn into office as the nation's fortieth President at noon on January 20, 1981. The drama was heightened far beyond the usual excitement of a change of administrations as the nation waited tensely to find out whether the long hostage crisis with Iran actually was over.

Favored by bright sunshine and balmy temperatures, the ceremony took place for the first time on the West Front of the Capitol, giving the new President a sweeping view of Washington's famous monuments. Reagan and his guests dressed in formal attire, contrasting with the informality emphasized four years earlier in the inauguration of President Carter.

At the outset of his inaugural address, Reagan lauded Carter for his cooperation during the transition period since the national election.

Then, calling for an "era of national renewal," the new President highlighted the importance of improving the national economy.

". . . this administration's objective," he said, "will be a healthy, vigorous, growing economy that provides equal opportunities for all Americans with no barriers born of bigotry or discrimination.

"Putting America back to work means putting all Americans back to work. Ending inflation means freeing all Americans from the terror of runaway living costs.

"It is time to reawaken this industrial giant, to get government back within its means and to lighten our punitive tax burden.

"And these will be our first priorities, and on these principles there will be no compromise."

Shortly after completing his twenty-minute inaugural address, the smiling President Reagan told the millions watching on television the news they had been hoping for—that the 444-day captivity of the fifty-two American hostages had ended and they were flying out of Iran to freedom. Soon after, details of the agreement with Iran were made public, consisting largely of procedures for restoring to Iran the approximately $8 billion in Iranian funds that had been frozen in American banks. In a gesture of gratitude to Carter for his role in settling the hostage crisis, Reagan appointed his predecessor as a special envoy to welcome the hostages to freedom. So immediately after the inauguration Carter flew to West Germany, where the hostages were being taken for rest and health examinations.

Reaganomics and the New Beginning

AT THE FIRST MEETING of his Cabinet on his first full day in office, President Reagan told its members, "We've got to get control of the federal budget. It's out of control." The Carter administration's budget called for the spending of $662.7 billion in 1981 with a deficit of $55.2 billion. A week before Reagan's inauguration Carter had presented a budget for fiscal 1982, beginning October 1, 1981, that envisioned federal spending of $739.3 billion with a deficit of $27.5 billion.

In the presidential election campaign Reagan had pledged himself to achieve a balanced federal budget, a one-third reduction in income taxes, and increased spending for national defense. He was determined to make good on these promises. To do so would require severe pruning of government expenditures.

Less than one month after taking office, Reagan went before a joint meeting of Congress on February 18, 1981, to present his first State of the Union address in which he detailed a four-point economic plan. First, it called for a reduction of $41.4 billion in the 1982 budget, largely in social service programs, but affecting all government departments and agencies except national defense. Second, he asked for an across-the-board 30 percent cut in income taxes to be phased in at 10 percent each year for three years, while at the same time stimulating capital spending by business through more liberal depreciation tax write-offs. Third, he would eliminate and reform "inefficient and burdensome" government regulations. Fourth, he called for a national monetary policy to curb inflation by slowing the growth of the money supply. Although the President called his economic plan "America's New Beginning: A Program for Economic Recovery," it soon was dubbed "Reaganomics."

Reagan's victory in the national election had won the Republican party control of the Senate, but the Democratic party still held a majority in the House. To win passage of his program in Congress, Reagan knew it would be necessary to cajole, threaten, and bargain with members of the Democratic party. Therefore, in closing his address, he said:

". . . The people are watching and waiting. They don't demand miracles. They do expect us to act. Let us act together."

President Reagan narrowly escaped death on March 30, 1981, when he was wounded in the chest in an attempted assassination. The gunman, John W. Hinckley, Jr., who later claimed he had been temporarily insane, also wounded Reagan's press secretary, a Secret Service agent, and a policeman. The incident occurred as the President was leaving a Washington, D.C., hotel. "Honey, I forgot to duck," the seventy-year-old Reagan told his wife when she rushed to the hospital where he was being treated. His rapid recovery and good humor expressed in other quips helped allay whatever fears the public had that his age might be a handicap in dealing with the rigors of his presidential office.

President Reagan repeatedly demonstrated his determination to stand by principles he believed in despite political pressures to modify them. An example of his firmness occurred during his first year in office when about twelve thousand federal air traffic controllers began a strike in August 1981. They had hoped to shut down the nation's major airports in an effort to win higher pay, even though federal law forbade them to strike and they had been warned by Reagan that they would be fired if they did so. Military personnel were called in to help keep the airports open until new air traffic controllers could be trained. Reagan ordered the strikers fired and refused to rehire them despite pleas by labor union leaders who organized a huge protest demonstration in Washington, D.C., in September.

In recognition of the growing role of women in public life, Reagan appointed the first woman associate justice to the United States Supreme Court when a vacancy occurred in 1981. She was Sandra Day O'Connor, an Arizona state appeals court judge.

Late in 1981 the nation's economy slid into its eighth recession since the end of World War II. During the next two years unemployment rose to more than ten million workers—the highest rate of unemployment since the Great Depression.

In the mid-term congressional elections in 1982, Democrats blamed Reaganomics for the economic recession while the President remained firm in declaring that his economic policies soon would turn the economy around. The Republicans managed to hold on to control of the U.S. Senate, but Democrats increased their majority in the U.S. House of Representatives, winning an additional twenty-five seats from the Republicans.

National Defense and Foreign Affairs

WARNING that the Soviet Union was winning the nuclear arms race with the United States, President Reagan on October 2, 1981, called on Congress to approve a $180.3 billion national defense program that included construction of new MX intercontinental ballistic missiles, each equipped with ten nuclear warheads capable of hitting targets 8,000 miles away.

Reagan administration plans to equip NATO forces in Europe with medium range nuclear missiles were protested in massive demonstrations in many European cities in 1981. The President sought to counter the reaction in a major address on November 18, 1981, in which he offered to cancel plans to deploy the weapons if the Soviet Union would dismantle its medium range nuclear missiles aimed at Western Europe. American and Soviet diplomats began discussions on the issue two weeks later.

During his first term President Reagan was unsuccessful in attempting to bring peace to the Middle East. Both Israel and the Arab nations rejected his efforts to mediate agreements. Angered because Lebanon (a nation wracked by civil war since 1975) was being used as a base for terrorist attacks by the

Palestine Liberation Organization (PLO), Israel invaded Lebanon in June 1982, captured its capital Beirut, and expelled some fourteen thousand members of the PLO. The United States joined with Britain, France, and Italy in sending troops to Beirut to supervise the expulsion of the PLO and to act as a peacekeeping force. Arab terrorists who opposed intervention by the Western allies simultaneously bombed the headquarters of United States and French troops in October 1983, killing 241 American Marines and 58 French military personnel. Unable to bring an end to hostilities in Lebanon, the United States and its allies withdrew their forces in 1984.

President Reagan actively sought to prevent the spread of communist power in the Caribbean and Central America. During President Carter's administration, communist revolutionaries supported by the Soviet Union and by Cuba had seized control in 1979 of the Caribbean island nation Grenada and of the Central American nation Nicaragua. President Reagan cut off economic aid to Nicaragua in January 1981, increased military and economic assistance to Nicaragua's neighbors, and helped anticommunist rebels fighting against Nicaragua's government. When in-fighting broke out among the communist leaders of Grenada, President Reagan ordered American troops to land on the island on October 25, 1983, ostensibly to protect American students in Grenada. The United States forces quickly defeated a Cuban military garrison and arrested the communist leaders of the Grenada Government. After Grenadian voters elected a noncommunist government in 1984, American military forces were withdrawn.

As part of his program to strengthen the nation's military defense, President Reagan announced in March 1983 his support for a new strategic military policy to develop futuristic weapons that could destroy enemy nuclear weapons in flight before they could reach their targets. In ordering research undertaken to develop these weapons, he asked scientists "to turn their great talents to the cause of mankind and world peace: to give us the means of rendering these nuclear weapons impotent and obsolete." Opponents of the program sought to ridicule it by terming the proposed armaments "Star Wars" weapons—taking the name from a popular science fiction movie. They claimed development of such weapons would bring the arms race with the Soviet Union to a new crescendo and could bankrupt the nation with a cost of one trillion dollars or more.

Reelection to a Second Term

FROM THE TIME PRESIDENT REAGAN formally announced in January 1984 that he and Vice President Bush would seek a second term, the entire Republican Party was solidly behind the ticket. At the party's national convention in Dallas, Texas, in August, only 2 of the 2,235 delegates indicated some disapproval by withholding their votes for Reagan's nomination. And only 4 delegates chose not to vote for Bush.

On the other hand, the Democratic party was in disarray as it sought a candidate who might win the White House. At the beginning of 1984, eight major candidates competed for the Democratic presidential nomination. However, by March the field had narrowed to three main contenders: former Vice President Walter F. Mondale, backed by labor unions and by most Democratic office holders; Senator Gary Hart of Colorado, supported by younger members of the party and advocates of a "nuclear freeze" in armaments; and civil rights leader Rev. Jesse Jackson, the first black to campaign nationally for a major party presidential nomination. In a series of twenty-nine Democratic presidential primaries from February to June, Hart won the popular vote in sixteen, Mondale in eleven, and Jackson in two. However, because party rules enabled entrenched Democratic officials to appoint many delegates, Mondale captured the presidential nomination at the Democratic National Convention at San Francisco in July. On the first ballot, Mondale received 2,191 votes to Hart's 1,200.5 and Jackson's 465.5. In an effort to gain support from women and from followers of Hart and Jackson, Mondale broke precedent by choosing a woman as his running mate—U.S. Representative Geraldine A. Ferraro of New York.

Many political observers believed Mondale sealed his ultimate defeat with a pessimistic acceptance address to the convention delegates. Calling his program the "new realism," Mondale painted a gloomy picture of the future. He declared that he would raise taxes to reduce the multibillion-dollar deficits in the national budget that had reached record levels during President Reagan's first term, and he accused the President of having a similar "secret" plan to increase taxes.

Contrasting with Mondale's gloomy assessment of the future, President Reagan in an up-beat acceptance speech to the Republican National Convention in August described the nation as being "in the midst of a springtime of hope for America."

When voters went to the polls in November, President Reagan won reelection in a landslide. He carried the popular vote by 58.8 percent to Mondale's 40.6 percent and the electoral vote by 525 to 13. Mondale received the electoral votes only of his home state Minnesota and of the District of Columbia.

The President's insistence that strengthening the military defense of the United States was the only sure way to get the Soviet Union to negotiate realistically on disarmament began to bear fruit after his reelection. At a meeting in Geneva, Switzerland, in January 1985, U.S. Secretary of State George P. Shultz and Soviet Foreign Minister Andrei A. Gromyko agreed to resume nuclear arms talks that had been broken off by the Soviets in 1983. President Reagan declared that the goal of his administration would be "the complete elimination of nuclear weapons," but he cautioned that "it takes two sides to have constructive negotiations."

Because the constitutionally designated day for the presidential inauguration, January 20, fell on Sunday in 1985, President Reagan took the oath of office in a brief televised ceremony at the White House, deferring public ceremonies to the following day. However, these plans were disrupted when a cold wave sent the temperature to near-zero, forcing cancellation of the inaugural parade and outdoor ceremonies for the first time since 1833.

After being sworn in for a second time on January 21 before a standing crowd of several hundred dignitaries in the rotunda of the Capitol, the President made a short, inspirational Inaugural Address.

"Let history say of us," he said, "these were golden years—when the American Revolution was reborn, when freedom gained new life, and America reached for her best. . . ."

Dealing with International Terrorism

THROUGHOUT 1985 THE WESTERN WORLD was plagued by incidents of international terrorism. The President searched for ever more effective ways to deal with terrorists and to protect American citizens abroad. Since his inauguration day in 1981, seven Americans had been captured in Beirut, Lebanon, and were being held by militant groups there. One, William Buckley, an American embassy official, was later brutally tortured to death.

As the President agonized over how to free these hostages, Americans abroad again and again became targets for militant Arab groups, aided and abetted by the leaders of Iran, Libya, and other countries who denounced America's policies in the Middle East.

In June 1985 a TWA airliner was hijacked after leaving Athens and was forced to fly to Beirut, Algiers, back to Beirut, and again to Algiers. The forty Americans on board were targeted for harsh treatment, threats, and beatings. One American sailor was brutally beaten and later murdered. His body was thrown from the plane to the runway. The incident lasted seventeen days and was described as the most frustrating one to confront the Reagan administration to date.

At home, President Reagan underwent major abdominal surgery on July 13. The surgery removed a cancerous polyp and part of the President's intestine. Executive power was officially transferred to Vice President Bush for about eight hours during the operation and recovery time.

In October 1985 an even more spectacular hijacking occurred when an Italian cruise ship, the *Achille Lauro,* was hijacked in Egypt with more than four hundred passengers on board. Again, American citizens were singled out for particularly brutal treatment. An invalid American tourist who was confined to a wheelchair was murdered and his body thrown into the sea. Determined to bring the terrorists to justice, President Reagan ordered Navy planes to intercept the Egyptian airliner that was flying the perpetrators to Tunis after the incident. The hijackers were forced to land in Italy and later stood trial in Germany. A determined President Reagan said in a news conference that the capture was a message to all terrorists that "you can run but you can't hide."

In December 1985 the EL AL (Israel) Airlines ticket counters in both Rome and Vienna were bombed simultaneously, killing thirteen people. Four terrorists were killed and three were captured. Several of the dead were American.

International efforts to trace the financing and training facilities of the increasingly professional terrorists led to evidence that Libya and her fanatical leader Muhamar Qadhafi were promoting these acts.

The Vienna/Rome airport bombings implicated Libya again, and President Reagan, determined to respond, severed all official ties with that country. He ordered Libyan assets in the United States frozen. In a show of force, naval exercises were scheduled for the week of March 23 in the international waters of the Gulf of Sidra, an area claimed by Libya. Qadhafi threatened war with the United States if ships crossed what he called the "line of death" and entered the gulf. During the exercises, Libya fired six missiles at U.S. ships. The U.S. Navy retaliated by firing on land-based missile sites and damaging two Libyan patrol boats. The exercises ended on March 28 and a few days later, on April 5, a bomb blast in a Berlin discotheque frequented by American military personnel killed an American soldier and wounded 155 other people.

This time there was good evidence that the attack was directly ordered by Libya. President Reagan called the Libyan leader the "Mad Dog of the Middle East" and secretly ordered U.S. bombers based in England to bomb Tripoli, the capitol of Libya. In a raid heard live on the evening news in the United States, an affluent section of the city was bombed and Qadhafi's headquarters was hit. Fifteen people were killed, including the fifteen-month-old daughter of the Libyan leader. One U.S. plane was lost.

Gorbachev and Arms Reduction

IN NOVEMBER 1985 PRESIDENT REAGAN flew to Geneva to meet with a new Soviet leader, Mikhael S. Gorbachev, who had come to power in March. Gorbachev, at age 54, represented a vigorous new generation of Soviet leaders. The meeting was the first between a Soviet general secretary and an American president in six years, and marked a turning point in the President's hard-line anticommunist stance of past years when he had referred to communist Russia as the "evil empire." At the summit, the two leaders agreed to increase arms negotiation talks between the two super powers and raised hopes for improved Soviet/American relations.

In October 1986 President Reagan met again with Gorbachev, this time in Reykjavik, Iceland. The meeting ended on a sour note when it was reported that the Soviet leader had agreed to the elimination of major nuclear weapons systems, but President Reagan refused to give up his plans to try to develop a space-based defense shield, the Strategic Defense Initiative, or SDI, which was popularly called "Star Wars."

During 1987 arms reductions talks continued to progress with the Soviet Union. It became increasingly clear that the new Soviet leader was determined to make major changes in the Soviet society and economy, and that he considered the arms race an unwanted obstacle in his path. The negotiations were successful and led to a historic arms reduction treaty. The United States did not have to agree to give up research and development of a space-based defense. The new treaty provided for the elimination of medium- and short-range nuclear missiles and for stringent verification procedures to ensure that no banned missiles were manufactured in the future. In December Gorbachev and his wife, Raisa, made a historic visit to Washington, D.C. He and President Reagan signed the new treaty and agreed to improve relations between the two countries. In early 1988 President and Mrs. Reagan made a reciprocal visit to the Soviet Union. The President spoke to Soviet citizens on television and held the first press conference ever for an American President in the Soviet Union.

In December 1988 Soviet General Secretary Gorbachev, accompanied by his wife, made another visit to the United States, this time to New York. In an unprecedented gesture President Reagan travelled to New York to host a lunch for the Soviet leader. They were joined by President-Elect Bush. It was a triumphant meeting with the three men posing for photographs before the Statue of Liberty. The official reason for the Gorbachev visit was to address the United Nations General Assembly. In his speech he called for a more dynamic Soviet-United States relationship and announced a unilateral reduction of Soviet conventional armed forces.

Domestic Policies

IN JANUARY 1986 the United States looked forward to a historic flight of the space shuttle, *Challenger*. The nation's schoolchildren eagerly awaited the launch because Christa McAuliffe, a school teacher, was the first ordinary citizen to obtain permission to travel into space. The flight ended in disaster when a large fuel tank sprang a leak and exploded into a spectacular fireball a little over one minute into the launch. All seven crew members died and the nation was overcome by horror and disbelief. A shaken President Reagan postponed his annual State of the Union address. All space flights were canceled indefinitely. It was more than two and one half years before the United States was able to successfully launch another satellite with the flight of the shuttle in late 1988.

President Reagan achieved one of the most important objectives of his term when he signed into law the Tax Reform Act of 1986, the most thorough revision of the Federal Income Tax Code in forty years. The historic tax bill lowered tax rates and simplified the tax code. The President had long sought to clean up and make fairer a code he called "a disgrace to the human race." He called the near revolutionary change in the tax laws a "triumph for the American people and the American system."

Despite the President's best personal efforts, the 1986 interim elections gave control of the Senate to the Democrats for the first time in the Reagan presidency. The President had campaigned vigorously in twenty-two states for Republican candidates but was unable to convert his tremendous personal popularity into election victories for his party. The Democrats gained eight seats in the Senate for a majority and five seats in the House. The President promised to "complete the Revolution that we have so well begun," despite the loss of control of the Senate. This loss was to contribute to some very bitter conflicts between the Senate and the White House during the last two Reagan years.

Two of President Reagan's nominees to the Supreme Court failed to be confirmed in 1987. The President's most conservative supporters urged him to make a definitive mark on the Supreme Court by nominating conservative Judge Robert Bork to the position of associate justice. The Senate Judiciary Committee held prolonged televised hearings. The nomination proved very controversial and divisive, polarizing the Senate and the nation. Ultimately the committee recommended that the Senate reject the nomination and

Judge Bork was not confirmed. The administration was further embarrassed when the second nominee, Douglas H. Ginsburg, had to withdraw his nomination. This time even some of the President's most faithful supporters withdrew their approval when the judge revealed that he had at one time experimented with marijuana smoking. Finally the President named a less controversial judge, Anthony M. Kennedy, who was confirmed without dispute.

Many other Reagan appointees came under suspicion of ethical misconduct and some were investigated for criminal activities. Raymond Donovan, Secretary of Labor, stood trial for illegal activities involving his construction company but was not convicted. Attorney General Edwin Meese was investigated for ethical misconduct while in office but was never indicted. He was forced to resign because the investigation raised serious questions about his judgement and truthfulness. Meese was a long time personal friend and associate of the President. Other Reagan friends and appointees were actually convicted and sentenced to prison. More than one hundred Reagan appointees came under suspicion of ethical improprieties and many were forced to resign. This led the President's critics to accuse him of a lack of moral leadership and to complain of corruption and incompetence in his administration.

The Iran-Contra Scandal

In November of 1986 the nation was shocked to learn of a secret trip to Iran by top White House National Security Council staff. The revelation became the biggest scandal of the Reagan administration when it was revealed that the administration had secretly sold arms and military spare parts to Iran and had diverted the proceeds to the Contra forces fighting the communist government in Nicaragua. Congress had passed a law outlawing U.S. government military aid to these forces. Congress was outraged that they had not been informed of the secret operation and ordered a full investigation. The nation was shocked since it appeared that the administration had provided arms to Iranian enemies of the United States in a failed attempt to obtain the release of the American hostages still held in Beirut. The President's national Security Advisor, Admiral John Poindexter, resigned and his deputy, Lieutenant Colonel Oliver North, was dismissed from his post.

The scandal grew even greater when Colonel North revealed that he had destroyed official documents in the White House to cover up the operation. The President appointed a commission to investigate and Congress held televised hearings in the summer of 1987. A special prosecutor was named and by 1988 both North and Poindexter were indicted for illegal activities. Their trials were postponed until after the upcoming presidential elections.

The Deficit and Wall Street

AFTER THE SEVERE RECESSION OF 1981–82 the economy began to expand in late 1982, and the longest peacetime economic expansion in history commenced, continuing throughout the Reagan years despite financial upheaval on Wall Street. The unemployment rate, which had stood at about seven percent for nearly four years, dramatically improved in 1987 and 1988. It dipped below six percent in August 1987 and reached a fourteen-year low in June and again in October 1988 when the nation enjoyed an unemployment rate of 5.2 percent. More than 117 million Americans had jobs—the largest number in history to that time.

But the nation's trade deficit soared during the 1980s, and the United States became the world's largest debtor nation. As the dollar's value rose in relation to other currencies, it hit forty-year highs against many of them in 1985. Foreign trading partners could no longer afford to buy goods from the United States. At the same time foreign goods became very inexpensive in the United States, and American consumers spent unprecedented amounts of dollars for cars, clothes, electronics, and other consumer goods produced abroad. The yearly trade deficit soared to an all-time record of 159.2 billion for fiscal 1987.

In an expanding economy the New York Stock Exchange and other financial markets registered unprecedented gains in the longest bull market in history. In August 1982 the Dow Jones Industrial Average stood in the low 800s and five years later on August 25, 1987, it reached a historic high of 2722.42. The following nineteenth of October the New York Stock Exchange suffered the worst day in its history and the Dow dropped 508 points in panic trading. The decline was far greater than the crash of October 28, 1929, when the market dropped 12.82 percent of its value, and touched off the Great Depression of the 1930s. In 1987 the Dow lost 36 percent of its value in a few days, raising fears of economic recession and financial chaos, before the panic receded. Every financial market around the world fell dramatically. But the American economy proved very resilient and continued its expansion throughout President Reagan's term.

Central America and the Middle East

TROUBLE FLAIRED AGAIN IN CENTRAL AMERICA and the Middle East during 1988. In Panama there was a growing movement against military strongman Manuel Noriega. He was accused of corruption and illegal activities. The State Department began negotiations with him to convince him to leave power. In February a court indicted him on drug charges and the United States stepped up pressure on Noriega to resign and to leave his country. The affair was damaging to the Reagan administration because it seemed they had long ignored strong evidence of his drug trafficking in order to obtain his support for other foreign policy objectives in Central America, especially support for the Contra forces trying to overthrow the communist government in Nicaragua.

The United States halted all economic payments to the Panamanian government in April, causing severe economic hardship in the country, but Noriega resisted all efforts to resign. Even when the United States offered to drop the legal charges against him and allow him to stay in Panama, their efforts were not successful. Noriega remained in power and the situation calmed but was not resolved, raising many questions about the future of American policy and influence in Central America.

In the Middle East, the Iran-Contra scandal had weakened the U.S. position and damaged the trust of America's Arab allies in the region. In an effort to underline U.S. resolve to maintain the safety of international shipping in the vital Persian Gulf despite the Iran-Iraq war, the United States agreed to reflag Kuwaiti tankers and to escort them with U.S. warships through the gulf. This put U.S. military forces in a war zone and exposed them to underwater mines placed by the warring countries. Several incidents occurred, tankers were damaged, an Iranian patrol boat was seized planting mines, and an Iraqi war plane accidentally fired on a ship, causing heavy loss of life and extensive damage. The worst accident occurred on July 3, 1988, when the U.S. Navy in the tense region accidentally shot down an Iranian civilian airliner with more than 290 passengers on board. The tragedy underscored the difficulty of using United States military power to further American policy.

Shortly after the unfortunate incident, on July 19, Iran made a surprise reversal of policy and agreed to accept a United Nations plan for peace in the region. A cease-fire was put into effect and progress for peace in the region continued throughout the year. The war between Iran and Iraq had continued for eight years and had taken more than a million lives.

The chairman of the Palestine Liberation Organization, Yasir Arafat, had been scheduled to address the U.N. General Assembly in December. The United States, however, denied him a visa to enter the country on the grounds that the PLO would not renounce terrorism. International opinion turned against the United States and the United Nations agreed to convene in Geneva, Switzerland to hear Arafat's speech. When he did speak to the General Assembly, the PLO leader made major concessions to longstanding U.S. demands. Once these demands had been met the U.S. agreed to enter into direct talks with the Palestinians regarding peace in the Middle East. President Reagan and his Secretary of State, George Shultz, had managed to change the U.S. relationship with the PLO in an important way. There was hope that the new relationship could help move Israel toward a more permanent and peaceful settlement with its neighbors.

Earlier President Reagan underscored this move toward peace in the world when he gave a rousing farewell address to the Republican convention. He endorsed his Vice President, George Bush, as the man most capable of continuing the Reagan policies into the future. As President Reagan prepared to leave office, he continued to enjoy enormous popularity with the American people. His personal optimism and grace along with his charismatic personality allowed him to use the symbols of his office to capture the imagination of his fellow citizens and to gain their admiration and trust. He had become the first president since Eisenhower to serve two full terms in office. In his farewell address he said, "When our children turn the pages of our lives, I hope they'll see that we had a vision to pass forward a nation as nearly perfect as we could. Where there's decency, tolerance, generosity, honesty, courage, common sense, fairness, and piety."

George Herbert Walker Bush
The Forty-first President of the United States
1989–1993

1924 (June 12) Born in Milton, Massachusetts.

1942–45 Served in the U.S. Navy in World War II receiving the Distinguished Flying Cross.

1945 (January 6) Married Barbara Pierce.

1948 Graduated from Yale College.

1948–64 Moved to Texas and founded an independent oil production company.

1966 Elected to U.S. House of Representatives.

1971–72 Served as U.S. Ambassador to the United Nations.

1973–74 Chairman of the Republican National Committee.

1974–75 Chief, U.S. Liaison Office, Beijing, China.

1976–77 Director, Central Intelligence Agency.

1981–89 Vice President of the United States.

1989–1993 Forty-first President of the United States.

G EORGE BUSH BECAME THE FIRST sitting vice president to make a successful run for the presidency since Martin Van Buren in the election of 1838.

The son of a privileged family, he had attended a prestigious prep school in Massachusetts and Yale College. He had been a successful businessman in Texas and had founded his own oil development company.

His father, Prescott Bush, had been a U.S. Senator from Connecticut from 1952 until 1962. George Bush entered local Republican politics in Texas in 1962. By 1964 his commitment to public life increased when he entered a race for the U.S. Senate. That bid was unsuccessful, but two years later he was elected to the U.S. House of Representatives. After losing a second race for the U.S. Senate in 1970, he began a long career of high-level appointments under Presidents Nixon and Ford. Nixon appointed him U.S. ambassador to the United Nations and chairman of the Republican National Committee. President Ford called on him to lead the U.S. Diplomatic Mission to China and later to become director of the CIA. After unsuccessfully seeking the Republican nomination for President in 1980, George Bush was tapped for the vice-presidential spot.

He was a loyal and supportive Vice President to an extremely popular President Reagan, and as the Reagan presidency drew to a close in 1988, George Bush was able to capitalize on the American electorate's desire to continue the years of peace and prosperity they had enjoyed for the past eight years.

Bush vowed to continue the policies of the Reagan years. During the 1988 election campaign he repeatedly urged voters to "read my lips, no new taxes."

The voters clearly endorsed this continuation of policies and George Bush became president with 54 percent of the popular vote.

At his nominating convention he restated his conservative principles and said that an American president "must see to it that government intrudes as little as possible in the lives of the people, and yet remember that it is right and proper that a nation's leader take an interest in the nation's character. And he must be able to define—and lead—a mission." He also vowed that he would "keep America moving forward, always forward—for a better America, for an endless enduring dream and a thousand points of light."

Navy Flyer

GEORGE HERBERT WALKER BUSH was born on June 12, 1924, in Milton, Massachusetts. He was the second son of Prescott Bush, Sr., and Dorothy Walker. His father was an executive of U.S. Rubber and a graduate of Yale College. When U.S. Rubber moved their headquarters to New York, the young Bush family settled in the exclusive suburb of Greenwich, Connecticut, to raise their five children. Summers were spent at the family compound, Walker Point, in Kennebunkport, Maine. It was named for Bush's grandfather and great-grandfather, who had purchased the site as a vacation home. Prescott Bush later became a partner in Brown Brothers, Harriman and Company, an investment banking firm. The Bush children were sent to exclusive boarding schools for their secondary education. George Bush attended Phillips Academy in Andover, Massachusetts, where he graduated in 1942. His father would later become a U.S. Senator from Connecticut, serving from 1952 to 1962.

A few months after the Japanese attack on Pearl Harbor in 1941, George Bush graduated from high school. On his eighteenth birthday he traveled to Boston to enlist in the Navy. He enrolled in flight school and was sent to Chapel Hill, North Carolina, for preflight training. When he got his wings in early 1943, he became one of the youngest pilots in the Navy. He was assigned to a torpedo squadron flying Grumman Avenger bombers in the Pacific. The Navy awarded the Distinguished Flying Cross to the young pilot after he was shot down during a bombing raid on the island of Chichi Jima. After his plane was hit by anti-aircraft fire during the bombing run, he ordered his crew to bail out, and managed to do so himself. Neither one of the other two crew members survived the crash of their plane into the sea, but Bush was luckier. He found his survival raft and managed to stay afloat until a U.S. submarine in the area picked him up a short time later. He later rejoined his squadron for action in the Philippines and flew fifty-eight combat missions before being sent home for Christmas of 1944.

Two weeks later, on January 6, 1945, he married his high school sweetheart, Barbara Pierce. They had met at a Christmas dance three years before and had become engaged before George left for the Pacific. The Japanese surrendered in August before he was to return to another assignment with the Navy.

Yale and Sports

OUT OF THE MILITARY, the young veteran lost no time enrolling in college. He, like his father, attended Yale. He majored in economics and joined the exclusive campus secret society, Skull and Bones. He and his wife lived off-campus and their first son, George, Jr., was born in the summer of 1946. Sports became an important part of the years at Yale, especially baseball and soccer. George played first base on the college team that won the Eastern Regional Championship two years in a row, 1947 and 1948. They played in the first ever College World Series in 1947 and again the following year, losing both times to California teams. A local newspaper described George's performance on the field as "impressive" and called him a "classy first baseman." He dreamed of receiving an offer to play professional ball, but it never came. Athletics came naturally to George Bush. His maternal grandfather, George Herbert Walker, for whom he had been named, had been amateur heavyweight boxing champion of Missouri and later was very active in golfing, establishing the Walker Cup, an international competition for amateur golfers. George and his brothers also credit their mother for their interest in sports. He once remarked, "Mother was a first-rate athlete. She wasn't big but she was a match for anyone in tennis, golf, basketball, or baseball."

Oil Man in West Texas

AFTER GRADUATING FROM COLLEGE, George Bush made an unusual choice when he took a job as a trainee with a subsidiary of Dresser Industries. The postwar oil boom was just getting under way in Texas and it looked very promising for young men willing to start at the bottom and work their way up. In 1948 Bush drove his Studebaker to Odessa, Texas, to look for living quarters for his young family and to learn about the oil business. After less than one year in Odessa, he transferred to California, where he took a series of jobs with Dresser Industries before moving back to Texas in 1950.

The Bushes had two children by the time they returned to Texas. A daughter, Robin, had been born in 1949. She died tragically three and a half years later of leukemia. The death of this child would mark the future president. In later years he referred to her death as one of the most difficult experiences of his life. In addition to George, Jr., and Robin, the Bushes had four other children, Jeb, Neil, Marvin, and Dorothy.

In 1951 George Bush and his friend John Overbey formed their own independent oil company, Bush-Overbey Oil Development Company, Inc. After three years, the company joined another small company and formed Zapata Petroleum. The following year a subsidiary, Zapata Off Shore, was formed to manage the company's interests in the newest field of technology for oil production, offshore oil wells. In August 1959 Zapata Off-Shore became a separate entity and George Bush became president of his own oil exploration company. The Bush family moved to Houston, where the headquarters of the company would be located. That city would become his home base for many years to come.

Running for Congress

BY 1962 GEORGE BUSH WAS READY to look for new challenges. Zapata Off-Shore was flourishing, most of his investments had been successful, and his family's financial future was secure. He was approached by the local leaders of the Republican party and asked to run for county chairman. He won and chaired the Harris County Republican party for the next two years. He worked to revitalize the party in Texas and to increase its membership.

In the Texas Senate race in 1964 Bush was persuaded to challenge incumbent Democratic Senator Ralph Yarborough. He ran an energetic race but was defeated.

He became more and more intrigued with a career in public service, however. Determined to make a mark in this field, fifteen months after his defeat in the run for the Senate, he resigned as chairman and chief executive officer of Zapata Off-Shore to devote himself full-time to politics.

In the interim elections of 1969 Bush decided to run for Congress from a new district in Houston. He ran a successful race and he and his entire family moved to Washington, D.C., in 1967. He was reelected to his seat in 1968, running unopposed.

By 1970 the Republican Nixon was in the White House, and President Johnson was retired to his Texas ranch. Once again George Bush considered running against the liberal Yarborough for the Senate seat. He decided to take on the challenge when national Republican party leaders urged him to do so, despite the fact it would mean giving up his seat in the U.S. House of Representatives. It seemed that Yarborough's seat was vulnerable in a year when he could not count on the coattails of a strong national candidate. In a surprise development Senator Yarborough's seat was more vulnerable than even the Republicans had predicted. Influential national democratic figures, including former President Johnson, supported a conservative Democrat, Lloyd Bentsen, who ran against Senator Yarborough in the primary. In a surprise upset the incumbent senator was defeated for his party's nomination and George Bush was running against a totally different opponent. In the final election Texans had to choose between two men perceived as conservative, one a Democrat and one a Republican. Given this choice, they stuck to their traditional voting patterns and elected the Democrat, Lloyd Bentsen, to the Senate. This race was to be recalled in 1988 when Lloyd Bentsen, still in the Senate, was tapped by the Democrats to be their vice-presidential candidate against the Bush-Quayle ticket.

After this second attempt to gain a Senate seat failed, George Bush was nominated by President Nixon to be United States Ambassador to the United Nations. Bush remained at the United Nations for two years. They proved very valuable ones for his grounding and experience in foreign affairs and international diplomacy.

In 1972 President Nixon had been reelected to the presidency in a landslide. For his second term he envisioned an in-depth restructuring of the executive branch and proceeded to reshuffle a large number of his appointments and to make many changes. In this period he asked George Bush to become chairman of the Republican National Committee.

Once again the Bush family moved to Washington to immerse themselves in the life of domestic politics. Almost immediately after Bush took up his new post, the problems of the Republican party became more and more dominated by the Watergate investigation into the recent election practices and the break-in of the Democratic National Headquarters. The Republican National Committee had to walk the difficult narrow ground between supporting and defending the Republican President and disassociating themselves from the illegal fund-raising and other activities which had taken place on the President's behalf during the recent election. Bush held the post until Nixon resigned in disgrace in 1974.

When Vice President Gerald Ford assumed the Presidency in 1974, he wanted to offer George Bush an ambassadorship and a chance to serve his country abroad. Once again Bush made an unusual choice and told the President he would like to represent the United States in China. While at the United Nations, Bush had been a very close observer of the revolutionary changes in the U.S.-China relationship. President Nixon had made his historic trip to China in 1972 and had officially recognized the communist government in China for the first time. Communist China had been admitted to the United Nations while Bush was the U.S. ambassador there, and he was eager to participate in forming the new relationship between the two countries. The United States did not yet maintain formal diplomatic relations with China and so there could be no ambassador to that country. The post carried the title of Chief, U.S. Liaison Office in China.

The Bushes were in China only thirteen months when they were recalled to Washington to another difficult post. President Ford asked George Bush to take charge of the Central Intelligence Agency. The CIA had been under intense scrutiny for some time. The nation had been stunned during the Vietnam and then the Watergate years to learn that many topics and issues had not been fully aired with the American public for what were called "national security" reasons. Later it seemed that many of these issues were kept secret mainly for political reasons. It was a difficult time in a demanding job. George Bush made fifty-one appearances before congressional committees in less than one year as the Congress delved into past excesses of the intelligence agency and devised new laws and regulations aimed at curbing excesses in the future.

A *Run for the Presidency*

IN THE 1976 PRESIDENTIAL ELECTION, President Ford lost to the Democratic governor from Georgia, Jimmy Carter. By 1977 George Bush had returned to Houston and settled into private life, out of government for the first time in ten years.

With a Democrat in the White House, the Republican party was looking for a candidate who could lead the party back to the White House in the 1980s. From the beginning, the front runner in the campaign was Ronald Reagan, who had mounted a serious challenge for the nomination against sitting President Ford four years earlier. The challenge for George Bush and the other announced candidates in the 1980 primaries was to turn the contest into a two-man race by proving themselves a viable alternative to Reagan.

George Bush's family had maintained a home in Maine since before his birth, it was a place where he had many ties and considered home. His mother had made her permanent home there since her husband's death in 1972 and the entire family still spent summer holidays there. Bush gave an enthusiastic speech to the delegates at the informal convention the night of a straw poll and managed to come in first. It was an early boost to his campaign and a surprise to the reporters in attendance. The headlines called it an upset victory.

In the Iowa caucuses a little over two months later, Bush won a decisive victory pulling 31.5 percent of the votes to Reagan's 29.4 percent. Bush had managed to establish himself as the strongest alternative to Ronald Reagan in the Republican party.

In the Pennsylvania primary, George Bush first called the economic policies Reagan was proposing "Voodoo Economics," a phrase that he would be reminded of when he eventually became Reagan's running mate and was loyally supporting all the nominee's positions. The Bush campaign was to continue to challenge Reagan through the spring primaries, but even after Bush won some contests, it became clear that Ronald Reagan would be the party's choice. The Bush and Reagan positions were so close on most issues that voters were left to choose between personalities and styles. By the beginning of June, George Bush stopped campaigning and pulled out of the presidential race.

At the 1980 Republican National Convention in Detroit, everyone waited expectantly to learn of Ronald Reagan's choice for his vice-presidential running mate. The Reagan campaign had conducted nationwide polls to determine which vice-presidential candidate would be most popular with the voters. Former President Ford had come in first, and Bush second. At the convention it became clear that Ronald Reagan had yet to choose his running mate. Things seemed to swing in Ford's favor when word came of top-level meetings between members of Ford's administration and the Reagan team. Authoritative sources later reported that Ford had wanted greatly expanded powers as Vice President if he were to agree to join the ticket. Reagan seriously considered this option and only at the last minute decided against it. George Bush received the phone call asking him to join the ticket only minutes before Reagan officially announced it to the convention delegates.

The Reagan-Bush ticket won the 1980 election easily with far greater majorities than were predicted before the voting. The Republican party gained control of the Senate for the first time since the 1952 election, when war hero Dwight Eisenhower was first elected President.

The Vice-presidential Years

GEORGE BUSH BECAME AN EXTREMELY LOYAL and supportive Vice President. President Reagan continued the policies of his recent predecessors of having the Vice President attend cabinet meetings and occupy offices in the White House.

During his eight years as Vice President, Bush took up the usual duties of traveling throughout the world representing the United States. He was named by the President to head an illegal drug interdiction task force. He came under fire, along with the entire administration, when the leader of Panama, General Manuel Noriega, was indicted on drug trafficking charges and the United States suddenly withdrew its support of his government. Critics claimed the Vice President should have known about the illegal activities earlier and done something to prevent the crisis in U.S.-Panama relations.

Bush also came under fire from the press during the Iran-Contra controversy when he refused to reveal what he had counseled the President about selling arms to the Iranians. He also denied that he knew the full details of the scheme despite his presence at several top-level meetings and briefings where it was discussed.

There were two times during the Reagan Presidency where it seemed that George Bush was very close to having to assume the office of President. The first time was when President Reagan was shot in an assassination attempt in 1981. Vice President Bush cut short a trip to Texas and returned to Washington under unusually tight security in the tense hours after the attack while the President was undergoing surgery. Before Bush's plane arrived, however, the President was out of the operating room and reports on his recovery were optimistic.

On another occasion, presidential powers were actually transferred to George Bush for about eight hours. In 1985 the President underwent major surgery for cancer. There were some tense hours before the reports on the probable outcome of the President's disease were released. Presidential powers were transferred to Vice President Bush while the President was feeling the effects of anesthesia. President Reagan recovered rapidly, however, and the doctors reported that there was a good chance he would suffer no lingering effects or recurrence of the disease.

As his years as Vice President came to a close, George Bush noted that he and his wife, Barbara, had lived in the vice-presidential mansion in Washington longer than they had lived in any other single residence since their marriage more than forty years earlier.

Winning the Presidency

As THE 1988 ELECTION APPROACHED, the nation watched the economy warily for any recessionary effects of the 1987 stock market crash. It also seemed possible that the aftermath of the Iran-Contra scandal might tarnish the Vice President's image or that his dealings with Panamanian President Manuel Noriega could lead to charges of lack of leadership in the nation's fight to prevent the entrance of illegal drugs, a cause with which the Vice President had been involved.

The Democratic party searched for a leader who could challenge the Republicans on these issues.

Gary Hart, the Reverend Jesse Jackson, and six other candidates announced their intention to run for the Democratic nomination. Three were senators, one was a congressman, and two were governors.

As the primaries progressed throughout 1988, Michael Dukakis, governor of Massachusetts, emerged as the front runner of the Democratic party, and clinched the nomination of his party in June, not through any ability to dazzle voters but through months of disciplined hard work.

On the Republican side of the ticket, several candidates announced their intention to challenge Bush for the nomination. Of these, Senator Bob Dole of Kansas seemed to have the best challenge. He had served as Republican majority and minority leader in the Senate and was well known nationally. His wife, Elizabeth, served in the Reagan Cabinet. In the early campaigning, Dole won the Iowa caucuses. Iowa, a farm state like Dole's own, had suffered from hard times during the Reagan years and seemed ready to endorse a change in Republican leadership.

Another Republican candidate, the Reverend Pat Robertson, mounted an effective grass roots campaign in Iowa and came in second. He was a conservative who was well known around the country as a popular television preacher who tried to mobilize his religious following to propel himself into national politics. The strategy worked reasonably well in Iowa. Robertson came in second, humbling the Vice President, who came in third.

After a feeble finish in Iowa, Vice President Bush entered the New Hampshire primary with renewed determination and dedication. The race had become crucial to his nomination and he committed extra time, energy, and resources to a successful outcome. His strategy paid off when he defied the polls and soundly defeated Senator Dole. Dole accused the Vice President's last-minute negative television ads of misleading the voters.

From then on, the Vice President's campaign for the nomination was not seriously challenged. His victories in the March primaries in the South were overwhelming, and by the end of the month Senator Dole had withdrawn from the race and endorsed the Vice President.

Michael Dukakis, the Democratic nominee, chose Lloyd Bentsen, a popular and powerful Senator from Texas, as his running mate. Senator Bentsen had defeated George Bush for the Texas Senate race in 1970, and his popularity in Texas seemed to give the Democrats a chance to win in the South and even in Bush's home state of Texas.

During the Republican National Convention in August, speculation mounted over whom George Bush would select as his running mate. He surprised many in his own party and the nation at large by choosing a conservative, little-known senator from Indiana, J. Danforth (Dan) Quayle.

Dan Quayle was young (forty-one), handsome, pleasant, and wealthy. His votes in the Senate had consistently supported conservative causes but he had done little to distinguish himself in that body. By choosing him, the Vice President sought to solidify the future of the conservative movement and to appeal to younger voters who had come of age during the Reagan years. The choice sent a message to the most conservative segment of the Republican party, signaling the Vice President's solidarity with their concerns. Critics of the choice argued that Dan Quayle did not have the stature or experience to qualify for the nation's second highest office. Criticism increased when the press reported that Dan Quayle had chosen to serve in the Indiana National Guard rather than the regular army during the height of the Vietnam War. There were very few vacancies in the

National Guard in those years and influential friends of Quayle's family had made phone calls on his behalf to help secure a place for him.

Although controversy about George Bush's choice of a running mate dominated much of the Republican Convention, the candidate gave an inspirational and rousing acceptance speech, which was received with enthusiasm.

He made an emphatic pledge that he would never raise taxes, saying, "The Congress will push me to raise taxes—and I'll say to them, read my lips, no new taxes."

He celebrated the nation's complexity with a captivating poetic image, calling it "a brilliant diversity spread like stars, like a thousand points of light in a broad and peaceful sky."

He called for a gentler nation and he said the President "must be a shrewd protector of America's interests and he must be an idealist who leads those who move for a freer and more democratic planet."

With his choice of a conservative running mate, Bush moved quickly to further establish his conservative credentials. He emphasized the importance of the pledge of allegiance and prayer in schools, his support for the death penalty and a citizen's right to own firearms, and his opposition to abortion.

After the convention the Republicans dominated the campaign. National polls now showed they had a comfortable lead over the Democrats. Bush criticized Boston Harbor as a polluted disgrace and blamed his opponent. He highlighted the case of a Massachusetts murderer and portrayed Dukakis as soft on crime. And he labeled the governor as a card-carrying member of the American Civil Liberties Union, and a man out of the political mainstream and out of touch with American voters.

The campaign was criticized by many as being the most negative in recent memory with campaign commercials showing convicted murderers and sewer sludge.

During the election year, however, Americans could look to a long list of favorable conditions that they hoped would continue into the 1990s. The Arms Reduction Treaty with the Soviets had gone into effect and tensions had eased between the two superpowers. There seemed to be a chance for positive changes within Soviet society and for a productive dialogue to continue between the two countries. Around the world, tensions had eased in many troublespots. The Soviets were making progress in withdrawing their troops from the ten-year-old war in Afghanistan. Iran and Iraq had agreed to a cease-fire and were moving toward peace in their bloody eight-year-old religious war. The United States agreed to direct talks with the Palestine Liberation Organization raising hopes for movement toward a more peaceful arrangement between Israel and her neighbors. In Central America the difficult peace process seemed to offer at least some small hope for a negotiated settlement in Nicaragua. Americans had good reason to hope for a calmer international climate in many regions.

The economy had performed very well during the Reagan years and continued its expansion even after the 1987 stock crash. Inflation remained under control and unemployment was at a fourteen-year low.

In the elections of 1988, American voters were not convinced that the Democrats could outline a better course for the country and elected George Bush to the presidency with 54 percent of the popular vote. The country sought to build on the promise of President Reagan's policies and philosophy. George Bush was a loyal Vice President with much varied experience in public life and offered the nation the chance to continue in the direction which President Reagan had so compellingly outlined.

Although Americans selected George Bush as their President, they did not give him the mandate that President Reagan and other Presidents had enjoyed. The Democrats increased their majorities in both the Senate and the House of Representatives.

Activist in Foreign Policy

ON THE DAY AFTER THE ELECTION, George Bush announced that his campaign manager, long-time friend and trusted advisor, James Baker, III, would become his Secretary of State. It was a convincing sign that the new President intended to focus his administration on international relations and foreign policy. He centered the formulation of U.S. foreign policy in the White House at daily meetings of the National Security Council. The President became known for hundreds of handwritten notes to leaders, both public and private. He maintained close personal relationships with leaders throughout the world and telephoned them frequently.

China Policy

NOWHERE DID THE PRESIDENT'S PERSONAL INFLUENCE have more effect than in U.S. policy toward China. Early in his presidency a strong student pro-democracy movement took hold in China. Students took to the streets in increasingly large marches and demonstrations. More than 100,000 demonstrators held a vigil in Beijing's central Tiananmen Square demanding democratic reforms and direct discussions with government leaders. They constructed a handmade model of the Statue of Liberty and participated in hunger strikes in defiance of authorities. The Chinese government was humiliated by its inability to control civil unrest in the streets of the capital. Soviet leader Mikhail Gorbachev arrived in Beijing on an historic tour but his visit was overshadowed by the student unrest. It was the first time a Soviet leader had visited China in thirty years. Gorbachev had come to formally announce the normalization of relations between the two important countries.

After Gorbachev's departure, tens of thousands of Chinese troops were ordered to clear Tiananmen Square and secure the streets. More than one million Chinese citizens poured into the streets to physically block the army's movement and protect the students. More than 300 people died. At least eight student leaders were sentenced to death and three were publicly executed. Some escaped and were smuggled to freedom in the West.

Western nations were outraged and shocked at the brutal crackdown. China had been encouraging economic reforms and was enjoying the fruits of promising free market experiments and increased assistance and friendship from the U.S. Many urged the President to use his influence to denounce and punish China for its brutal repression of democratic ideals. He steadfastly refused to break relations with China. He did voice disapproval of the events in China but insisted that the best way to foster change there was to maintain the U.S. relationship with that country. He limited U.S. response to banning arms sales and to forbidding high-level official contacts and government-to-government trade. The House of Representatives voted to strengthen sanctions against China but the President vetoed the move. He later permitted the sale of a Boeing aircraft to China, even though the plane's navigation system was on the list of banned military hardware. The Congress passed a law allowing Chinese students studying in the U.S. to overstay their student visas but the President vetoed the measure. The President steadfastly refused to impose any new sanctions on China.

Later it was revealed that President Bush had sent personal envoys secretly to China on two occasions, even though his own order officially banned high-level contacts with that country. One of these trips took place only one month after the brutal Chinese crackdown on the students. The President was criticized for not standing up for democracy and human rights in China, and for carrying on secret diplomacy with that country, but he never waivered in his conviction that his policy was the best one.

Military Action Abroad

PRESIDENT BUSH ordered American troops into action three times during his presidency. In 1989 he ordered ten thousand American troops into the streets in Panama to take control of that country. Strongman General Manuel Noriega had been in control of Panama since 1981. U.S. courts had indicted him on charges of drug dealing and money laundering. The Reagan administration had tried severe economic and diplomatic moves in attempts to force him from power but had not been successful. In May presidential elections were held in Panama to return the country to civilian rule. An international commission headed by former President Jimmy Carter declared the elections to be rigged and called for international condemnation. Nevertheless, Noriega's opposition won the election by a 3 to 1 margin and Noriega declared the results null and void. President Bush called for Noriega to step down and encouraged the Panamanian people to overthrow the dictator. In December President Bush ordered a surprise night-time airlift of additional American forces to the country and ordered them to take control of the capitol. Noriega was captured a few days later and flown to the U.S. to stand trial on drug charges. Enrique Endara, the winner of the May elections, was installed as President and the country slowly returned to order.

Sending troops into action strengthened Bush politically at home. Increasingly Americans saw him as a strong and decisive leader. Polls showed that the President had a higher approval rating than any President except Kennedy at the end of his first year in office.

Less than one year later American troops were once again on the move far from home in unfamiliar terrain. On August 2, 1990, Saddam Hussein, the ruthless military dictator of Iraq, launched a surprise invasion of Kuwait, a small and tremendously wealthy oil-producing kingdom to its south. Iraq was in desperate need of money to pay its debts and to finance the huge military machine Hussein needed to further his dreams of power in the region. Kuwait had refused to limit oil production to raise prices as Iraq demanded. The invasion was sudden and decisive and within 24 hours the ruling emir of Kuwait had fled to Saudi Arabia and the Iraqi army controlled his kingdom. Hussein immediately began massing his troops on the border between Kuwait and Saudi Arabia and was in a position to threaten the Saudi oil fields on which the West also depended.

President Bush reacted with outrage and indignation. He strongly condemned the invasion and ordered economic sanctions against Baghdad. In the greatest crisis of his presidency, President Bush sought international support and participation. Largely through the sort of personal diplomacy that had become his trademark, he telephoned a broad array of foreign leaders and rallied an unprecedented international alliance. Ultimately twenty-eight countries sent military forces to the Persian Gulf region to confront Iraq. In an unparalleled arrangement, wealthy countries who could not make a significant military contribution agreed to contribute billions of dollars to finance the military action of the others.

The U.N. Security Council, with unusual unanimity, voted to condemn the invasion and to demand the immediate and unconditional withdrawal of Iraqi troops. The Security Council also voted to impose a sweeping trade and financial embargo on Iraq and approved the use of military force to halt marine shipping into and out of Iraq. This was the first time in the history of the U.N. that the council had approved the use of a military force that would not be under the U.N.'s flag or command to enforce its sanctions. Largely at U.S. urging, the U.N. later authorized the use of force against Iraq if it did not withdraw totally from Kuwait before January 15, 1991.

The cooperation and support of the Soviet Union was a key factor in making possible such swift and decisive action at the U.N. In the changing climate of improved East–West relations, the Soviet leader Mikhail Gorbachev joined most of the world's leaders in condemning the invasion.

The invasion of Kuwait became the biggest crisis of the Bush presidency. The President ordered the greatest American overseas military build-up since the Vietnam War. Approximately 500,000 U.S. troops were deployed to Saudi Arabia and the surrounding oceans. For the first time since the 1968 Tet Offensive in the Vietnam War, the military reserves were called up for action overseas. The President made his position emphatically clear when he declared, "This will not stand, this aggression against Kuwait." The U.S. military operation was named Desert Storm.

On September 11, 1990 the President addressed a joint session of Congress on live television. He spoke of the crisis in the Persian Gulf and of America's place in a post Cold War world. "We stand today at a unique and extraordinary moment. The crisis in the Persian Gulf, as grave as it is, also offers a rare opportunity to move toward an historic period of cooperation." He went on to say, "Out of these troubled times, a new world order can emerge: a new era, freer from the threat of terror, stronger in the pursuit of justice and more secure in the quest for peace. An era in which the nations of the world, east and west, north and south, can prosper and live in harmony." In poetic language the President said, "a hundred generations have searched for this elusive path to peace, while a thousand wars raged across the span of human endeavor. Today that new world is struggling to be born. A world quite different from the one we've known. A world where the rule of law supplants the rule of the jungle. A world in which nations recognize the shared responsibility for freedom and justice. A world where the strong respect the rights of the weak."

President Bush emphasized the significance of the new relationship with the Soviet Union when he said, "Clearly no longer can a dictator count on East–West confrontation to stymie concerted U.S. action against aggression. A new partnership of nations has begun." The press called the war the first post Cold War crisis. After an extended and heated debate, on January 12, 1991, Congress voted President Bush the authority to use "all necessary means" to drive Iraq from Kuwait. On January 15 the U.N. Security Council deadline expired and the next day the first wave of war planes was launched against Baghdad and all the military and communications installations in Iraq. In forty-three days of hostilities more than 106,000 military flights were launched—the most intensive air campaign in history.

A massive array of high technology weapons was turned furiously against Iraq. The Iraqi defenses proved hopelessly limited and were powerless to defend the country against such an onslaught. This was the first war to be televised live around the world. As the first bombs fell on Baghdad, an American television crew broadcast the event from their hotel room in the city. Each day of the war television audiences around the world viewed detailed military film of the destruction and the accuracy and effectiveness of an astounding array of computer- and laser-guided bombs and missiles which had never before been used in any military conflict. On February 23 a massive ground attack began that lasted only 100 hours. The Iraqi army put up very little resistance. They did, however, set nearly 600 oil wells on fire as they retreated in an unprecedented act of environmental terrorism which severely damaged the oil fields and poisoned the atmosphere and the waterways. Very quickly coalition troops took control of Kuwait City. Iraq was forced to surrender unconditionally on March 3rd. There were less than 200 American deaths reported in the military action.

In the final days of his presidency, American troops were once again on the move far from home. In Africa, the government of Somalia had fallen in early 1991. Since that time the country had drifted into anarchy and chaos. Armed bands of undisciplined local warlords ruled the streets and highways, destroying the economy and the transportation system. International relief agencies had responded to the emergency with supplies of food and medicine, but the aid could not be unloaded or distributed because of the anarchy. The U.N. sent 500 peacekeeping troops but they were hopelessly outnumbered and could not guarantee safe passage to the convoys of food. Hundreds of thousands of Somalis died of starvation and equal numbers were suffering malnutrition and were in grave danger. President Bush decided that American troops would be committed to the crisis. On December 3rd, 1992, the U.N. voted to authorize the use of force in Somalia and on December 4th the President announced the deployment of U.S. troops to that country. It was the first time American troops had been used in such a purely humanitarian effort in a foreign country where no strategic or national security interests of the U.S. were involved.

End of the Cold War

IN HIS INAUGURAL ADDRESS President Bush called on Americans to "make kinder the face of the nation and gentler the face of the world." He went on to say "A new breeze is blowing, and a world refreshed by freedom seems reborn. The totalitarian era is passing, its old ideas blown away like leaves from an ancient, lifeless tree." No one guessed how quickly the breeze the President mentioned would become a gale. Mikhail Gorbachev, the energetic and reform-minded leader of the Soviet Union, abandoned the Brezhnev Doctrine by which the U.S.S.R. reserved the right to intervene militarily on behalf of marxist regimes around the world. Popular pro-democracy movements began to grow in Eastern European countries and Gorbachev declared that political upheavals there must be allowed to run their course. In a whirlwind of events the Communist governments of Hungary, Poland, Czechoslovakia, East Germany, Romania, Bulgaria, and Yugoslavia gave up their monopolies on power and held popular elections. These astonishing changes came quickly and with remarkably little violence.

Only in Romania did the ouster of a repressive communist government lead to widespread bloodshed. Thousands of demonstrators were killed by government forces before Nicolae Ceaucescu, the brutal communist leader who had been in power for twenty-four years, was forced to flee. Ceaucescu and his wife were detained, interrogated and executed. A provisional government took power and announced plans for free elections. Only in Yugoslavia did the communists win election victories. In Yugoslavia, the republics of Serbia and Montenegro elected their communist leaders to continue in power. In a short time this was to prove disastrous as Serbia, using the arms of the former Yugoslavia, brutally attacked, starved and tortured its neighbors in Croatia and Bosnia-Herzegovina.

In November 1989 reforms in East Germany led to the lifting of travel restrictions. East Berliners began to cross the Berlin Wall by the thousands to view the bright lights and overflowing shops of the previously forbidden western sector of the city. Leaders of East and West Germany met and agreed to reopen the Brandenburg Gate, a famous landmark which had been blocked by the Berlin Wall for nearly three decades. On December 23, the gate was reopened and jubilant citizens from all parts of the city celebrated by chipping away at the wall with hand tools and ropes. In a tumultuous scene that was broadcast to the world on live television, complete with fireworks and speeches, the Berlin Wall crumbled.

Immediately, Germany began to consider reunification. East Germany held its first free elections since 1933 and voted for unification to take place as quickly as possible. The parliaments of both Germanys passed matching measures and set July 1, 1990 as the date for economic and social union. Germany's membership in NATO was still making final unification impossible since the U.S.S.R. was opposed to this arrangement. To ease the way, President Bush proposed sharp new troop reductions in West Germany and in July Gorbachev agreed to drop his opposition to a unified Germany belonging to NATO. In September, representatives of the four Allied Powers who defeated Germany in 1945 met and signed a treaty relinquishing all occupation rights, leaving Germany free to unite. On October 3, 1990, Germany was reunited in jubilant celebration, forty-five years after being carved up in defeat and disgrace. One million people gathered at the Old Reichstag building in Berlin to mark the occasion.

The Conference on Security and Cooperation in Europe met in November 1990 and signed an agreement which significantly reduced conventional weapons and troops in Europe. Called the "Charter of Paris for a New Europe," the document proclaimed an "end to the era of confrontation and division in Europe." French President François Mitterand observed, "This is the first time in history that we witness a profound transformation of the European landscape which is not the result of a war or a bloody revolution." President Bush proclaimed, "The Cold War is over. In signing the Charter of Paris, we have closed a chapter of history."

Soon after, in 1991, the Warsaw Pact military alliance, which had mounted such a formidable threat to the West for more than forty years, was formally disbanded. Earlier Gorbachev was awarded the Nobel Peace Prize for his policies to promote political change in Eastern Europe and his initiatives in ending the Cold War, but peaceful change seemed far from certain in the Soviet Union itself.

Collapse of the Soviet Union

IN 1989 THE SOVIET UNION held its first free election in seventy years and chose a new Congress of Deputies. Boris Yeltsin, a former supporter of Soviet leader Mikhail Gorbachev, had become an outspoken critic of the Soviet central government. Yeltsin was easily elected to represent the Republic of Russia. The electorate rebuked the Communist Party by defeating many prominent leaders. The new Congress elected Mikhail Gorbachev to the newly strengthened post of President of the Soviet Union. A whirlwind of reforms followed, churches were returned to their congregations, and labor unions were given the right to strike. While the West celebrated Gorbachev's reforms, strikes and unrest disrupted industry and transport and brought the Soviet economy to the brink of collapse.

The parliament of the Baltic republic of Lithuania voted to legalize rival parties and abolish the guaranteed monopoly of power of the Communist Party. The central government condemned the action. In 1990 Lithuania overwhelmingly rebuffed the Communist Party in their first multiparty election in 70 years. Lithuania declared its independence from the Soviet Union but Gorbachev could not allow the Soviet Union to break up. He ordered tanks into Vilnius, the capital of Lithuania, in a show of force to demonstrate Moscow's control of the rebellious republic. He ordered oil supplies cut off, closed the principal refinery and halted air traffic. Despite the violent crackdown, the Lithuanian population voted to become independent. In similar votes both Latvia and Estonia also elected to declare independence from Moscow. Gorbachev officially rejected these moves toward independence.

Boris Yeltsin, a popular Russian politician, and thousands of his followers demanded more power for the Soviet Republics and pressured for Gorbachev's resignation. The central government held a referendum on maintaining Soviet unity, but six of the fifteen republics boycotted the vote and the results of the referendum were not clear. Yeltsin easily won an election to become the first popularly elected president in the history of Russia.

On August 19, 1991, the world was stunned by news that the internationally popular Soviet leader, Mikhail Gorbachev, had been forcibly removed from power. Vacationing in the Crimea, Gorbachev had reached an historic agreement with the Soviet Republics that would give them greatly increased powers at the expense of the central Soviet government. The day before he was to return to Moscow to sign the treaty handing over power to the republics, he was forcibly detained at his vacation house. Hard-line communist leaders who did not agree with the plan to weaken the central government, declared a state of emergency and ordered the army into the streets of Moscow.

But the coup leaders did not correctly calculate the power and the popularity of the democratically elected president of Russia, Boris Yeltsin. Hundreds of people immediately surrounded the Russian Parliament to protect Yeltsin from the Soviet army tanks. Yeltsin ordered troops and vehicles of the Russian Republic to surround the parliament building. A few tanks from the regular army defected to defend the parliament. In a heroic gesture Yeltsin himself spoke to the crowd from atop a tank which flew the tricolor Russian flag, and called for a general strike. Yeltsin defied the coup leaders by calling for the resignation and criminal trials for the eight members of the junta who pretended to take control of the country. Russian people took direct action and erected makeshift barricades around the Russian parliament building and held an all-night vigil to protect it from military action.

President Bush, at a hastily called press conference at his summer home in Maine, issued a strongly worded statement calling the coup misguided and illegitimate. In a dramatic move the President said he supported Boris Yeltsin and his call for the restoration of legally elected government. On August 21, President Bush telephoned Yeltsin directly to offer his support. The U.S. President refused to recognize the illegal government of the coup leaders and he urged the Russian people to stand firm for constitutional government.

On August 22, the coup collapsed and Gorbachev returned to Moscow to thank Boris Yeltsin, his long-time opponent, for standing up to the coup leaders.

After the failed coup, Gorbachev was not able to recapture his hold on power. He refused to blame the Communist Party, some of whose leaders had tried to force him from power. Yeltsin and the elected parliament of Russia were outraged and ordered the Communist Party building sealed. On August 25, Gorbachev was forced to resign from the Communist Party and on August 30, the Soviet Parliament voted to suspend all activities of the Communist Party. The once monolithic party, which had ruled the vast land with iron control for seven decades, was no more.

On August 28, the European Community recognized Lithuania as an independent country. The United States was still reluctant to do so. President Bush wanted to strengthen Gorbachev's position and hoped the Soviet Union would not disintegrate into chaos. At a secret meeting, Yeltsin and the leaders of Ukraine and Byelorussia agreed to form a Commonwealth of Independent States and invited the other republics to join. They proposed a common currency and agreed to accept the obligations of foreign treaties signed by the former U.S.S.R., as well as central control of the nuclear arsenal. On December 22, eleven former republics formally agreed to join the Commonwealth of Independent States (CIS). This move effectively disbanded the Soviet Union and stripped Gorbachev of his power. Gorbachev submitted his resignation as president of the now defunct Soviet Union and handed the launching codes for the nuclear arsenal over to Boris Yeltsin. The seventy-four-year history of the Soviet Union had come to an end. On New Year's Eve 1991 the familiar red flag of the Soviet Union with its famous hammer and sickle was lowered from the Kremlin in Red Square in Moscow for the last time.

After the failed coup, President Bush signaled a major shift in American foreign policy and a shift away from central Soviet government when he decided to immediately recognize the independence of Ukraine if their upcoming vote supported independence. Russia also requested diplomatic recognition for their country, forcing the U.S. to choose between Gorbachev and Yeltsin. Bush waited for Gorbachev's resignation speech and then quickly gave formal recognition to Russia and the other republics.

Historic International Agreements

THE BUSH ADMINISTRATION made historic advances in arms control and nuclear disarmament with the Soviet Union. Secretary of State James Baker worked tirelessly to hammer out more and more sweeping agreements and to make the most of the new flexibility in the policies of the Soviet Union. Soviet leadership was convinced that they could no longer afford the luxury of an arms race and pushed the Bush administration to hasten arms reductions and nuclear disarmament. Even before the Bush inauguration the Soviets announced that they would begin the unilateral destruction of chemical weapons, in addition to the ban on production which they already had in effect. They pressed for a peace conference with the U.S. They urged prompt resumption of the START talks aimed at cutting long range nuclear weapons by fifty percent. Again they announced a unilateral plan to reduce their nuclear arsenal in Europe.

In May President Bush made his first major address on U.S. Soviet policy. He stated it was time to "move beyond containment and seek the integration of the Soviet Union into the community of nations."

In June 1989 the President seized the initiative. At the 40th anniversary of NATO, he announced a bold new plan to reduce East–West troop levels in Europe. His plan required the troops be removed from Europe and demobilized. It was the first disarmament plan from a Western power to include troop reductions and it met with widespread approval. At the NATO meeting a plan was also agreed to for East–West talks regarding short range nuclear weapons. The successful meeting was the President's first major policy victory and European leaders applauded his impressive leadership.

The rapid advances in disarmanent agreements continued that autumn at the United Nations. George Bush made his first speech before that body as President and offered an eighty percent reduction in chemical weapons if the U.S.S.R. would also make cuts. The Soviets immediately responded with an even better offer, the immediate and total elimination of the weapons and a ban on production as well.

On December 3, 1989, President Bush and President Gorbachev held their first official summit on shipboard off Malta in the Mediterranean. It was the first superpower summit ever held at sea. No arms agreements were signed, but the two leaders agreed to speed up the negotiations on reducing conventional forces in Europe and long range nuclear arms. Gorbachev was eager to proclaim the end to the Cold War but the President and his advisors preferred to be more cautious until the recent changes in Europe were solidified and made more permanent. Bush offered economic assistance and disarmament proposals if the Soviet Union would liberalize its emigration policies. The two leaders agreed to conclude treaties on long range nuclear weapons and to meet again in June.

With U.S. encouragement NATO began to restructure for new challenges. The two Germanys were swiftly moving toward reunification and the Soviet Union was beginning to withdraw its troops from Eastern Europe. NATO voted to accept a unified Germany as a member of NATO even though Soviet troops were still stationed on East German territory. To encourage the Soviets to accept a reunified Germany and the NATO proposals, President Bush agreed to begin talks regarding short range nuclear weapons as soon as a Conventional Forces in Europe agreement was reached.

On May 31, 1990, Mikhail Gorbachev arrived in Washington for the first full formal summit between the two leaders. They signed over twelve significant accords on strategic arms, chemical weapons, trade, and other issues. They were unable to agree on German reunification or on the Kremlin economic embargo and show of force in Lithuania. Gorbachev remained opposed to German membership in NATO. In a surprise move President Bush signed an agreement to normalize trade between the two countries, despite his previous threat not to because of Soviet treatment of Lithuania and its failure to enact more liberal emigration laws.

In August 1991 President Bush traveled to Moscow to sign an historic and far reaching START agreement by which the stockpiles of nuclear arms were cut by nearly one third. It was the first treaty in which the two superpowers had agreed to reduce, as opposed to limit, long range nuclear arms. Talks toward this long-awaited agreement had begun in 1982. The summit was the fifteenth full-fledged superpower summit that had taken place since 1959. It would also be the last.

The revolutionary realignments between East and West were having unexpected consequences in the Middle East too. Washington and Moscow agreed to work to convene a peace conference to advance the cause of peace between Israel and its Arab neighbors. The Soviet Union had long sought more influence in the Middle East and had promoted the idea of a peace conference. On October 30, 1991, in Madrid, leaders from all the major powers in the Middle East met together for the first time since the founding of Israel. In a major breakthrough, the Palestinians were allowed to send representatives to the peace conference.

In June 1992, President Bush held the first Russian/American summit with President Boris Yeltsin of the Republic of Russia. They signed a surprise agreement which went significantly beyond the 1991 START arms reduction agreement. It included drastic bilateral cuts in long range nuclear missiles. The agreement was a result of five long months of talks between Secretary of State James Baker and Foreign Minister Kozyrev. For the first time the Russians broke the parity which was established in START and agreed to limit nuclear warheads to less than half of those stipulated in the START treaties. Yeltsin vowed to work toward the elimination of land-based missiles, the heart of Russian strategic forces. The U.S. would reduce by fifty percent its submarine launched missiles. By the year 2003 the two countries hoped to reduce the nuclear stockpiles to approximately one third of the current level. Russia was granted Most Favored Nation status for commercial trade with the U.S.

International Trade

ON JANUARY 1, 1989, the U.S. Canada Trade Pact went into effect. It called for the elimination of most trade tariffs between the two countries within the next ten years. Trade between the two countries was already the world's largest and the treaty was expected to increase it even further. The treaty was hailed as a landmark and was expected to stimulate both economies and to have a far-reaching influence on the global trading system.

In October of 1989 President Bush and President Carlos Salinas de

Gotari of Mexico signed a broad economic agreement meant to stimulate trade and investment between the U.S. and Mexico. Mexico was the third largest U.S. market and the stimulation of trade between the two countries could benefit both of them.

In January 1991 international trade agreements were again improved. The U.S., Mexico, and Canada reached an agreement to negotiate together toward a continent wide free trade zone. Congress authorized an accelerated process of negotiation and approval called "fast track." The North American Free Trade Agreement was signed on December 17, 1992, by the presidents of the three countries and would take effect after approval by the legislatures of all three countries. The agreement would eliminate trade barriers between the three countries and promised to usher in a new era of international commerce.

The six-year-old negotiations on the so-called Uruguay Round of the General Agreement on Tariffs and Trade inched its way toward conclusion. It was a very comprehensive agreement encompassing trade among 108 nations of the World. In an attempt to open the doors to world trade for the Soviet Union, President Bush supported observer status for the Soviets in this international body. In November of 1992 the talks deadlocked over the issue of French subsidies to their farmers. In frustration and determined to hammer out a good agreement, the Bush administration imposed punitive tariffs on French wine and other products. While the move threatened to derail the talks, it also forced other countries to pressure the French to compromise. A broad, trans-atlantic compromise was reached and GATT negotiations were set to resume once again as the Bush administration drew to a close. The President was still hopeful that free trade could be expanded throughout the world, ushering in a new era of prosperity.

Earth Summit

In June 1992 an extraordinary international summit sponsored by the U.N. took place in Rio de Janeiro. It was the first full-scale global summit of world leaders since the end of World War II. 178 countries participated and a record number of 117 heads of state attended. This was the largest number of heads of state ever to assemble at one time. Their purpose was to reach global agreement on environmental concerns affecting the entire planet. Seven major pacts and initiatives were signed. The most controversial issue was the biodiversity treaty which aimed to protect the widest possible variety of living things on earth. President Bush was opposed to this treaty, feeling it would put American biotechnology firms at a disadvantage. He reluctantly attended the summit, but he refused to sign the biodiversity treaty. He did agree to sign a global warming agreement even though the U.S. was criticized for taking positions in the negotiations that weakened the treaty. President Bush was faulted for failing to take a leadership role in world environmental issues and was accused of undermining the summit. Nevertheless, the ground-breaking meeting was hailed as a success in a new era of international cooperation.

A Listless Economy and Re-election Defeat

AS SOON AS THE PRESIDENT took office, his administration was forced to face the scandal of the massive failure of government insured Savings and Loans banks. The banks had lost billions of depositor dollars in fraudulent dealings and ill-advised loans and investments. Bush proposed a bailout plan costing 166 billion dollars over 10 years, which Congress approved. It was the largest Federal bailout in U.S. history. By August of 1989 the expected cost of the bailout had ballooned to 300 billion over 10 years.

The U.S. economy had been growing only very slowly in the first 18 months of the Bush administration. The federal budget deficit grew from 155.2 billion dollars in 1988 and was projected to reach 400 billion dollars in fiscal 1992. In 1989 the national debt ceiling had been fixed at 2.8 trillion dollars and grew rapidly. It was expected to exceed 4 trillion dollars sometime in 1992, or 52.5 percent of the gross national product. In addition, stalemate developed in Washington between the President and Congress. A bitter budget compromise in 1990 resulted in gridlock. The President blamed Congress for pushing him to break his campaign pledge for "no new taxes" and Congress, controlled by the Democrats, was content to let the President take the heat for the budget agreement. As the stalemate in Washington worsened, Congress persisted in passing legislation that the President vowed to veto. He used his veto fifteen times in 1990 alone.

Beginning with the threat of war in the Persian Gulf, the price of petroleum shot up, roiling international markets. With market instability and the approach of possible hostilities, the U.S. economy slipped into recession. When the war ended so quickly, with so few casualties for Americans, there was an immediate burst of optimism and the economy slowly began to turn positive in the spring of 1991. By summer, however, the huge national debt, the scandalous mismanagement and failure of the Savings and Loans banks, and the still high rates of interest mandated by the Federal Reserve Board brought the enthusiasm to an end. After nearly a decade of granting risky loans, many banks had gone out of business, causing the U.S. Government to budget and borrow billions of extra dollars to replace the lost money of depositors. In addition, American business and American consumers had built up historic levels of debt in the 1980s and were using profits and earnings to pay it down. Banks were turning very stringent in their requirements for borrowers, and citizens and businesses alike were curbing new purchases. As a result the economy again began to register negative growth and unemployment rose.

As the presidential campaign of 1992 got underway the economy was still very sluggish. It was showing some small measure of growth, but not enough to bring down unemployment. The President had tried to remain optimisitic for more than a year about an economic turnaround that most economists had assured him was just around the corner. Even though the recession was a fairly mild one, the mood in the country was pessimistic. Cuts in the defense budget that had become possible because of the end of the Cold War were putting many people out of work. The government had cancelled many orders for weapons and military equipment, and was cutting back on defense research. The President persisted in his belief that the shallow recession would soon end and that the usual business cycle would put the economy in a growth pattern soon. The voters sensed something more serious at work in the economy.

During the campaign, the President could point to his many triumphant successes. The Cold War was over and the United States was the undisputed single superpower in the world. Communism had collapsed, along with the Warsaw Pact and the military threat it had so long posed to the U.S. and its allies. The President had proven himself to be a powerful and convincing international leader. He had, largely through his own personal efforts, conceived, assembled, and effectively led an unprecedented international military coalition against a strong military dictator who threatened to divide the nations of the Middle East against the United States and to endanger international economic well-being by controlling the supply of oil. He had forged unparalleled international agreements on arms control, nuclear disarmament, and free trade.

Despite all these successes, the American voters insisted on focusing on their own economic insecurities. They could not be convinced that the President was the best candidate to prepare the country for the 21st century. Americans seemed to sense that the "New World Order" which President Bush had proclaimed and which had been born so dramatically during his administration, required changes in the country which the President did not seem to value and could not articulate to their satisfaction. They blamed the President for not keeping his "no new taxes pledge" and for not being "the education President" and a leader for the environment as he had promised. They sensed that the current recession was more than the usual temporary layoffs and that many American jobs in industry, finance, and construction were gone for good. In the months since the end of the Gulf War, the President's popularity in the polls fell from a record high to a level so low that in the 1992 election sixty-two percent of the voters voted against him. Instead, the voters chose to follow Governor Bill Clinton of Arkansas, a little known politician with very little international experience.

After the bitter disappointment of his re-election defeat at the hands of American voters, President Bush lost no time in returning to his activist role in the international arena. He took a strong position in the negotiations on the General Agreement on Tariffs and Trade (GATT), threatening France with punitive tariffs. He signed the North American Free Trade Agreement with Mexico and Canada and he sent American troops on a humanitarian mission to Somalia. On January 2 and 3 President Bush made a sudden trip to Russia to meet once again with President Boris Yeltsin. They met to sign the most sweeping arms control treaty ever, START II. The treaty called for a two-thirds reduction in Russian and American nuclear arsenals. President Bush asserted himself in the Middle East too. When Iraq became more intransigent about allowing U.N. inspection teams access to its defense plants as required by U.N. resolutions agreed to at the end of the Gulf War, President Bush ordered bombing raids and missile attacks on Iraqi military installations. As the country prepared for the inauguration of a new President who promised to focus on domestic issues, the White House was the center of difficult international conflicts. President Bush who had so focused on American foreign policy issues continued to do so throughout the last days of his administration.

William Jefferson Clinton
The Forty-second President of the United States
1993–

1946 (August 19) born in Hope, Arkansas

1968 Graduated from Georgetown University

1968–70 Rhodes Scholar at Oxford University in England

1973 Graduated from Yale Law School

1973–76 Taught Law at Univ. of Arkansas in Fayetteville

1974 Lost an election to become U.S. Representative

1975 (October 11) Married Hillary Rodham

1976 Elected Attorney General of Arkansas

1978 Elected Governor of Arkansas

1980 Defeated in re-election bid

1982 Won election to again serve as Governor of Arkansas

1983–92 Governor of Arkansas

1992 Elected Forty-second President of the United States

In 1993 BILL CLINTON became the first President to be born after the end of World War II and the first Rhodes Scholar to be elected President. He was the first President since Franklin Roosevelt who had never served in the armed forces. He was also the first sitting governor since Franklin Roosevelt to be elected President.

He was born to a single mother of very limited economic means. His father died in an automobile accident three months before his birth. He became a student leader, graduated from Georgetown University in Washington, D.C., traveled to England and Europe, studied at Oxford University and graduated from Yale Law School. Upon graduation from Yale he taught at the Law School at the University of Arkansas at Fayetteville. He began his professional political career in 1976 when he gained his first elective office as Attorney General of Arkansas. Two years later he ran for governor of that state and became the youngest governor in the nation at age thirty-two.

In his presidential campaign he tried to speak to and for, in his words "all those who do the work, pay the taxes, raise the kids and play by the rules . . . the hardworking Americans who make up our forgotten middle class."

A Difficult Beginning

BILL CLINTON was born William Jefferson Blythe, IV, in the small, rural town of Hope, Arkansas. His parents had been separated by World War II while his father served in the military. When the war ended the young soldier re-entered civilian life and looked for a new job. He found promising work in Chicago, and bought a house. He was driving to Arkansas to take his pregnant wife back with him to begin their new life together, when he was killed in an automobile accident. His son was born three months later. Virginia Blythe named her newborn after her recently deceased husband and left the infant in the care of his grandparents while she traveled to Louisiana to continue her studies as a nurse. She later returned to Arkansas with her new diploma and married Roger Clinton. The family moved to Hot Springs, Arkansas, and the couple had another son Roger Clinton, Jr. Bill enrolled in the Catholic school. Two years later he transferred to a public elementary school. He began calling himself Bill Clinton immediately, but did not legally change his name until he was fifteen years old. Roger Clinton, Sr., was a difficult father who frequently drank too much and who sometimes abused his wife and sons. This situation contributed to a difficult childhood for Bill. The older boy tried to keep peace in the family and to protect his mother and younger brother. Despite these difficulties, he excelled in school. He was popular and successful at many activities, including debate and music, and became a student leader at an early age. In 1963, Bill Clinton was seventeen and was elected delegate to Boys Nation, a youth organization which taught young people about the electoral process. The group met in Washington, D.C., where Clinton was awed to meet and shake the hand of President Kennnedy. He returned home to Arkansas determined to become an elected office holder.

When Bill Clinton graduated from Hot Springs High School he enrolled at Georgetown University and chose a course of International Studies. He needed additional money to finance his education and he found a job on the staff of Senator William Fulbright of Arkansas. Fulbright had long distinguished himself as Chairman of the Senate Foreign Relations Committee and was a powerful force on Capitol Hill and around the world.

When he graduated from college in 1968 Clinton submitted an application for a Rhodes Scholarship. Senator Fulbright had himself been a Rhodes Scholar and encouraged young Bill Clinton to become a candidate for the prestigious award. Clinton was thrilled and excited when he was chosen to become a Rhodes Scholar at the world-famous Oxford University in England. He left for Great Britain in the fall of 1968. He enjoyed life at Oxford and threw himself enthusiastically into his studies.

The Vietnam War was at its most violent and was deeply dividing popular opinion in the United States and overseas. Americans of Clinton's age were more and more troubled by the difficult choices the war presented. Many thousands were being drafted for military service. President Johnson had already announced that he would not seek another term as President because of the civil unrest due to the war. Bill Clinton, like most of his generation, felt compelled to take sides in this vital issue dividing the nation. He became one of thousands of students who believed the interests of the United States could best be served by ending the war. He became an opponent of the war in Vietnam and participated in some anti-war demonstrations while in England.

He secured a deferment to the draft, and he never served in the U.S. military. In 1969, while Clinton was still eligible for the military draft, the U.S. instituted a lottery system to determine who would serve. Clinton's number was drawn near the end and he was never inducted. When he became President, he was the first person to hold that office since Franklin Roosevelt who had not served in the U.S. military.

Returning to the United States, Clinton was accepted at Yale Law School, which he entered in the fall of 1970. While at Yale he met and fell in love with a brilliant fellow student from Illinois. Hillary Rodham had grown up in a Chicago suburb and had graduated with honors from prestigious Wellesley College near Boston.

When George McGovern ran for President in 1972 on a peace platform, both Hillary and Bill traveled to Texas during the summer to work on his campaign.

Public Service in Arkansas

UPON GRADUATION FROM YALE, Clinton kept his promise to himself to return to Arkansas. He got a job teaching law at the University of Arkansas at Fayetteville. Hillary went to work in Boston for the legal staff of the Children's Defense Fund. It was 1974 and the Watergate investigation into President Nixon's misuse of presidential power was underway. Bill Clinton was offered a job working on the congressional impeachment staff investigating Nixon. He declined, but recommended Hillary Rodham, who was then offered the job and accepted.

In the summer of 1974 President Nixon suddenly resigned, and Hillary Rodham was unemployed. She decided to take a position teaching law at the University of Arkansas. Bill Clinton had decided to run for Congress. When Hillary arrived in Arkansas his campaign was in full swing and she became an enthusiastic campaign worker and a valuable member of the campaign organization. Clinton's opponent was a powerful and very popular Republican, John Paul Hammerschmidt, who had served three terms in Congress. No one gave Clinton the slightest chance of unseating this powerful incumbent, but he mounted a very energetic grass roots campaign. He got a lot of attention from the press and was recognized as a credible campaigner. He lost the election by a surprisingly small margin, confounding the skeptics and earning the admiration of his party.

In October of 1975 Hillary Rodham and Bill Clinton were married at a private ceremony at a house Bill Clinton had purchased in Fayetteville.

In 1976 Clinton again decided to run for elective office. This time he ran unopposed for Attorney General of Arkansas and was elected. The young couple moved to the capital city of Little Rock and Hillary began to practice law at a private firm. Two years later, in 1978, Clinton mounted a successful campaign to become governor of Arkansas. He won the election by a decisive majority, becoming the youngest governor in the nation. He was thirty-two years old when he took the oath of office.

In his campaign and in his inaugural speech, Clinton made it clear that education reform would be a priority of his administration. He immediately proposed several bills. The Legislature passed a bill that would require new teachers to take competency tests before being certified. Arkansas became one of the last states to adopt this requirement. Another bill called for mandatory testing of students. The third proposal was the most controversial. It called on Arkansas to consolidate its school districts and do away with some small rural districts. In a major failure the governor was forced to withdraw the bill from consideration. Too many legislators represented areas with small school districts and were opposed to consolidation.

Clinton appointed a young, idealistic staff to manage the governor's office. The appointments were a political mistake. The inexperienced staff offended many interest groups and made enemies for the Governor. Another mistake was a very unpopular tax on vehicle registration. The tax was not a large one but it was roundly criticized. In addition, a local newspaper war developed and focused on uncovering waste and inefficiency in government, further embarrassing the Clinton administration.

In Arkansas, governors were elected for terms of only two years, and in 1980 Clinton stood for re-election. His first administration had fought for too many changes on too many issues and did not have many accomplishments to its credit. During the election, the worst controversy of the administration came to a head. The government in Washington was dealing with a heavy influx of refugees from Cuba who had to be housed until their legal status could be clarified and visas granted. 19,000 refugees were sent to Fort Chaffee in northwest Arkansas. The security at the U.S. government facility there was lax and during the campaign 350 refugees left the base and scattered throughout the countryside. Later, a riot occurred and 200 Cubans escaped and had to be forcibly returned, causing anger and concern among nearby residents. In August before the election, to the dismay of Arkansans, the federal government announced that 10,000 more refugees would be sent to their state.

In the national election, voters were becoming very disenchanted with President Carter and, by a wide margin, swung their votes to an increasingly popular Ronald Reagan. In Arkansas, the swing to the Republicans was particularly noticeable, and in a surprising outcome no one had predicted, Bill Clinton lost his re-election bid. A former Democrat, Frank White, who had changed parties so he could challenge the Governor, won the election.

Clinton was shocked and unnerved by his defeat. He entered a period of depression and partial seclusion. Eventually he was to gain valuable insight from his defeat, but some time would have to pass before his disappointment and bitterness would fade.

During his first term as governor, Hillary Clinton gave birth to their daughter, Chelsea. The fact that his own father had died before he was born had always given Clinton a certain sense of urgency about his own life. His daughter's birth was a very important milestone and he felt a special joy and pride.

Bill Clinton joined a private law firm and in 1982 once again campaigned for a chance to return to the governor's mansion. Frank White, his opponent two years earlier, had proved a very ineffective governor. The Clinton campaign focused on what he had learned from previous mistakes and one campaign slogan said it well, "You can't lead without listening." Once again in contact with the people of his state, Clinton seemed to come alive. He was a relentless campaigner and seemed to gain energy and enthusiasm from his contact with the crowds. Campaigning gave him a chance to connect with the people and he seemed to thrive on it. His second campaign for governor, even more than the first, centered on education reform. Clinton proved himself a masterful communicator and his campaign was well organized. He won re-election with 54.7 percent of the vote and became the first governor in the state's history to be defeated and then come back to regain the office. The voters of Arkansas believed that their promising young governor had learned humility, organization, how to choose his legislative priorities, and how to involve the people more effectively in the formulation of his policies. The voters determined to give him a second chance. He had earned his nickname "the Comeback Kid."

Clinton's second term proved to be a turning point in education for the state. Arkansas was hard hit by a deep national recession and extremely high unemployment. But Clinton insisted that "over the long run, education is the key to our economic revival and our perennial quest for prosperity." The Legislature passed a school consolidation bill that included the creation of a fifteen-member commission under the State Board of Education to develop a new set of minimum standards for the schools. Bill Clinton signed the bill and then made a daring political move. He appointed his wife, Hillary, to chair the commission. She was thirty-five years old and the appointment would put her on center stage as the leader of Clinton's most ambitious political undertaking. Bill Clinton said of his wife's appointment, "I don't know if it's a politically wise move, but it's the right thing to do."

The commission became known as the Education Standards Committee and was given nine months to complete its preliminary report. It held public meetings in all 75 counties, gathering comments and ideas on how Arkansas could improve its schools. The Governor decided not to approach the legislature for funds until the committee had time to complete its work. Instead he traveled the state seeking support and consensus for educational reform. He mounted an extensive and costly public relations campaign including newspaper, radio and television advertisements, and a 26,000 piece mailing to gain public support for the program. The State Board of Education enthusiastically endorsed the proposals made by the Educational Standards Committee and one member praised chairperson Hillary Clinton saying she was "the best thing to come along for education in Arkansas in the last 50 years." In October of 1983 Bill Clinton called a special legislative session to raise revenues for his education plan. He proposed to raise the sales tax, corporate income taxes, and taxes on natural gas companies. Big business interests in the state quickly came to oppose taxes on their industries and the sales tax became the only viable way of raising the necessary money. Governor Clinton backed away from a big fight with business interests and chose not to confront both business and the education establishment at once. It was a sign that Clinton was willing to forgo some of his ideals to advance others.

The most controversial part of the reform package came directly from the Governor himself when he decided that teachers should be required to pass standard tests to retain their certification. This requirement met great opposition from teacher's organizations. Clinton insisted on the requirement saying it was a small price for teachers to pay for the biggest tax increase in the state's history to benefit their profession. He linked teacher testing to the tax increase saying there would be no additional money for education without accountability from the teachers. After weeks of debate, the Arkansas Senate approved the Governor's bill and the House was expected to follow suit. When the Arkansas Education Association actively sought to block the Governor's proposals, he fought back, accusing them of caring nothing about teacher raises or more money for education standards or higher education. The Governor won his battle and the so-called "teacher testing" bill was passed. The law was the only one of its kind in the nation. It was followed four days later by passage of the sales tax increase. Bill Clinton had been more politically assertive than ever before, he had chosen his battleground carefully, he had become less idealistic, he had taken the risky and controversial decision of appointing his own wife to a powerful position when he felt it was the right thing to do, and all his difficult choices and battles had paid off.

Bill Clinton won re-election bids in 1984, 1986 (by which time the state had changed the length of the governor's term to four years) and 1990. He became the longest serving governor in Arkansas history. Personal troubles surfaced during his time in office. Bill Clinton learned his younger brother was a serious drug user when in 1984 his brother was arrested on six counts of cocaine distribution. Roger Clinton pleaded guilty and spent more than one year in a federal prison. It was a difficult time for Bill Clinton, but the family crisis never became an issue with the voters. They seemed to sympathize with Bill Clinton and could understand his pain, which was similar to the suffering of many families in the cocaine "epidemic" of the 1980's.

Another time rumors of marital infidelity threatened to become public. A former appointee, who Clinton had fired, filed a lawsuit to be reinstated in his job and accused Clinton of having extramarital affairs with five women. Local news media played down the lawsuit but assigned teams of reporters to investigate the rumors. None of the reporters could find any evidence to substantiate the charges and nothing was written in the local papers. Clinton was also criticized for being evasive about whether he had ever experimented with illegal drugs.

Governor Clinton began to make many public appearances outside Arkansas and some people began to encourage him to run for President. He was active in several national organizations and served as chairman of the National Governor's Association in 1986 and 1987. He headed the Democratic Leadership Council in 1990 and 1991. The council was a coalition of moderate-to-conservative politicians devoted to shifting the Democratic Party toward the political center. During the 1988 presidential campaign he spent many days traveling around the country, speaking, receiving awards, and maintaining a high profile. He was chosen by the Democratic candidate, Michael Dukakis, to make the nominating speech at the Democratic National Convention in Atlanta. It was Clinton's first appearance before a national political audience. The speech was a real disaster. Clinton, who was known as an effective communicator with a masterful television presence, was a failure. The house lights were not dimmed for the speech and the delegates were noisy and disruptive and impatient. Clinton was nervous and seemed uncertain and tense. His performance was a terrible embarrassment and the cause of much criticism and ridicule in the press and on television. Clinton came right back and proved he could overcome a difficult situation with grace and good humor. The people of Arkansas came to his support with an outpouring of letters of encouragement which told him not to lose faith in himself and his promise.

He continued to speak around the country and was given a standing ovation for his views on education presented at the Democratic Leadership Council. Governor Clinton had become a national leader for education issues. In 1989 President Bush asked him to co-chair a national summit of governors to study improvements in education and in 1990 the National Governors Association drafted a set of national education goals, many of which were devised by the Governor of Arkansas. More and more the national media and political leaders pointed to Clinton as a new leader for the Democratic Party and for the country.

Winning the Presidency

On October 3, 1991 forty-five-year-old Bill Clinton announced he would seek his party's nomination for President. The race would become one of the most unpredictable and turbulent in recent history. Though many prominent Democrats declined to run, seven men entered the race. President Bush's high approval rating after the enormous undertaking of the Persian Gulf War made him seem impossible to defeat. Bill Clinton was young, had little name recognition among the general public and Arkansas was a small and weak rural state. Nevertheless, Clinton moved quickly to introduce his program, which he called a "New Covenant." He stressed the need for change, the need to restore the faith of the citizens in their government's ability to effect positive change in their lives. He focused relentlessly on the recession, and the economic pessimism of the population, and offered an immediate plan of government spending in highways, bridges, sewer systems, and other infrastructure projects as a way to quickly create new jobs and to lay the basis for future prosperity. He focused on the need for a national health care policy, improved education and job training, and criticized what he called the failed economic policy of the Republicans. He declared a major shift away from national defense and military might as the basis of foreign policy and instead declared that "national security is largely economic." He declared again that a vibrant economy at home was America's only hope for a solution to domestic problems and for national security as well. He stressed that America must play a dominant role in the world economy. He spoke of "a new economic policy to serve ordinary Americans by launching a new era of global growth."

Clinton campaigned hard in the important, early New Hampshire primary. He was in the state in November already campaigning for the February primary. In an early poll he came in sixth as he struggled to introduce himself to the voters. He relentlessly persued his well-practiced style of hand-to-hand campaigning and person-to-person contact in the state. He conducted town meetings and interacted directly with the voters of the state listening to their concerns.

On January 13th the first of many controversies would threaten to derail the Clinton campaign. A grocery store tabloid published the old charges about Governor Clinton's rumored extramarital affairs. The national press could no longer ignore the story when another tabloid story was published on February 4 claiming that Gennifer Flowers, one of the women involved, confirmed the rumors, and claimed she had carried on a twelve year affair with the Governor. Only one year before she had threatened to sue a local radio station for mentioning her name in connection with the allegations. Checking the Flowers story, many falsehoods were discovered in her accounts and she was further discredited when it was revealed that she had been paid a substantial amount for the interview. Clinton attempted to weather the storm reminding the voters that only they could determine which issues would dominate the campaign. Both he and his wife agreed to appear on the popular TV news show "60 Minutes" to deal directly with the issue. They defended their marriage and pointed to the fact that they were being punished for keeping their marriage together. They admitted that their marriage had survived some troubled times. Clinton also made the case that he would refuse to discuss his personal life further and that even candidates for public office had a right to some degree of personal privacy. Upon returning to New Hampshire, Clinton declared, "I'm not going to talk about it anymore, I'm going on with this campaign." Four years earlier Senator Gary Hart had been forced to withdraw from the primaries when a similar sex scandal was reported in the press. It seemed probable that the same outcome would result from the Clinton controversy. The campaign got more and more difficult for Clinton. His ratings went down in the polls and Gennifer Flowers called a news conference in New York City to personally confirm her version of the story. She played tapes of conversations she had with the Governor discussing how she could handle questions from the press about the allegations. Time and again Bill Clinton acknowledged how difficult and painful the campaign had become, but refused to give up. He said many ordinary citizens were enduring far rougher times, losing their jobs and not being certain they could support their children in the current recession. Clinton's lead in New Hampshire had been lost, but he and his wife had both become household names. At least, for better or worse, he had gained the name recognition he so desperately needed.

Another controversy struck before the New Hampshire vote. On February 6 a news story was published describing how Clinton had managed to avoid the draft more than twenty years earlier. The story revealed new information about Clinton's draft status at the time and was made worse when the candidate did not immediately have a clear, coherent explanation of the events. A late night TV news program obtained a long letter Clinton had written at the time explaining his actions and his views on the controversial Vietnam War then raging. Many more hours of television were again focused on a Clinton controversy. Newspapers and radio programs dedicated much attention to the most recent questions. Many experts and political observers predicted that these controversies, and the muddled way Clinton handled them would doom his campaign. They said so much controversy would make it impossible for Clinton to win the votes he needed. But Clinton refused to give up. He told the voters they were being shortchanged when the focus of the campaign shifted to his personal problems when it should be on issues that affected their lives. He told them "Only you can decide what this election is about."

The night of the New Hampshire vote Clinton was jubilant. He held a victory party and declared that New Hampshire had once again made Bill Clinton the "Comeback Kid." He had finished in second place, and by sheer determination and persistence, and an excellent campaign organization, he was still a contender. In previous campaigns lesser controversies had ended the ambitions of stronger candidates, but Clinton had proved he could continue to win votes.

During the important New York primary, Clinton himself unleashed yet another firestorm. On a New York television debate he admitted he had experimented with marijuana while a student in England. The New York tabloids jumped on the new revelation and played up the story. The rampage of criticism turned to ridicule. Clinton was described as a country bumpkin and "slick Willie" who tried to squirm out of uncomfortable situations rather than explain them forthrightly. He was heckled by the public and grilled by the media but he managed to survive the harsh treatment and continued to work the crowds, even when they jeered. Eventually he won the respect of even New York's most seasoned reporters. One of them, Jimmy Breslin, wrote "Say what you want, but do not say that he quits." He even won an endorsement from the "New York Post," the newspaper that had bashed him hardest and most often. Clinton won the New York primary with 41 percent of the vote.

Clinton was well on his way to collecting the delegates he needed for the nomination, but the public still seemed unenthusiastic. With all of the doubts the press had raised, the voters longed for another choice on the ballot. When billionnaire businessman H. Ross Perot appeared on a television talk show and challenged his fans to mount a grass roots campaign to put his name on the presidential ballot, the response was overwhelming. Volunteer organizations sprang up in every state and were successful in putting his name on the ballot in all 50 states. It was clear that a great many voters were tired of politics as usual. They were receptive to Mr. Perot's message that the enormous national debt could not be overlooked. He took his ideas to the public largely through television interview shows and avoided as much as possible direct contact with the news media. He galvanized his supporters with his folksy wise cracks and focused on government gridlock and the undue influence of special interest groups and lobbyists on the federal government. The Perot volunteer movement became a phenomenon unparalleled in American politics. Ross Perot was still an undeclared candidate with no published program and no official campaign organization. He had pledged to spend 100 million dollars of his own money on television advertising to win the election and he was winning considerable support from disillusioned voters from both parties.

The President had swept all the Republican primaries since New Hampshire where Patrick Buchanan had mounted a bruising challenge with his harsh criticisms of the President. But the President remained largely aloof from the primary process. He seemed content to allow his re-election team to carry the ball and his campaign was in disarray. He shuffled his staff and a few days before the Republican Convention, in a desperate attempt to give a new direction to the campaign, he called on his old friend James Baker, III, who was Secretary of State, to take charge of the re-election effort. The President's team could not make the enormous changes in world affairs, the end of the Cold War, the peaceful overthrow of communism, and the winding down of the dangerous arms race resonate with the public. The enormous popularity the President enjoyed at the end of the Persian Gulf War had evaporated.

The public pessimism focused exclusively on the economic malaise in the country and the President could not seem to undertand or connect to voters' concerns.

In a grueling campaign, Clinton won the delegates he needed to lock up the Democratic nomination. He had started late, defeated six other well-known candidates, survived numerous scandals both personal and political, and damaged his health. He had gained twenty-three pounds and lost his voice. Despite his victories, Clinton still had major challenges ahead. Nationwide surveys showed that he was the third choice of the voters, behind both President Bush and as yet undeclared independent candidate H. Ross Perot.

As Clinton prepared for the Democratic Convention in New York in July, public perception began to change. Clinton made a popular choice when he selected Senator Albert Gore, Jr., of Tennessee to serve as his running mate. The choice went against conventional political wisdom since the two men were unusually similar in regional background and political philosophy. Al Gore was forty-four years old, two years younger than Clinton. Like Clinton, he was from the South and had a similar political following and base. Both were well educated. Al Gore had graduated from Harvard and studied law at Vanderbilt University. They had both come of age during the trying years of the Vietnam War and had spent many years in public life. Gore, unlike Clinton, was a Vietnam veteran and had spent most of his life in Washington, D.C. He had been elected to the House of Representatives in 1976 where he served four terms until he was elected to the U.S. Senate in 1984. He sat on the Senate Armed Services Committee and headed the Commerce subcommittee on science, technology, and space. The young Senator was recognized as one of the nation's foremost experts on nuclear disarmament. In addition, Al Gore had become an active and well-informed expert on the global environment. In 1992 he published a book, "Earth in the Balance" which became a best seller. He led the Senate delegation to the 1992 U.N. Earth Summit in Rio de Janeiro. He himself had run unsuccessfully for his party's presidential nomination in 1988. His selection as Clinton's Vice Presidential running mate met with almost unanimous praise from party leaders, the press, and the public. The Clinton ticket's popularity began to rise.

In New York, in July, the Democrats put together an unusually harmonious and unified national convention. The convention was an effective showcase for the Democratic candidates who were presented as a new generation of political moderates with powerful ideas and prepared to lead.

On the evening he was to formally accept his nomination, candidate Clinton got another unexpected boost. Independent candidate H. Ross Perot announced that he would not formally become a candidate after all. He said the Democratic Party had been "revitalized" and that his candidacy would only be a disruption and potentially weaken the country. His followers were stunned and disappointed. They had risen to Perot's challenge and worked tirelessly to support his candidacy. Already disillusioned by the political process, the withdrawal of their candidate was a crushing blow. Many had defected from the Republican Party and were reluctant to return. Clinton welcomed them to join the Democrats.

Immediately after the convention in New York, Bill Clinton and Al Gore enjoyed a dramatic surge in the national polls, putting them well ahead of the Republicans. Some increase in popularity could be expected by the attention to the convention and they were determined not to lose the momentum gained. They announced a dramatic, imaginative campaign bus tour to the midwest. They met with enthusiastic crowds at every stop; the national press reported daily on their popularity and their growing support with the American public. This tactic was to become one of their most effective. Again and again they campaigned together, frequently with their wives, and traveled by bus to many places not usually visited by presidential candidates. They held rallies at roadside stops, town parks, and city centers. They granted countless interviews to local reporters who normally did not get to meet the candidates and their trips got extensive media coverage on both local and national television and press outlets.

After a devisive Republican Convention in Houston in August, the President finally began to dedicate more time and energy to the election. Time and again he tried to frame the issues to his advantage. He tried to focus the voters on his international successes. He tried to damage Clinton's reputation by questioning his participation in anti-war demonstrations during the Vietnam years. He tried to portray Clinton as uncertain of his positions and less than candid with the American people. The President blamed the Democratically-controlled Congress for his lack of progress on the many domestic concerns of the voters. His historically high approval rating in the spring of 1991 at the conclusion of the Persian Gulf War gradually but steadily declined as voters perceived him as responding passively to the recession. He was never able to articulate a convincing plan for economic revival in the 1990s or to persuade the voters that his domestic policies could adequately address the voters' concerns.

One month before the election the tumultuous campaign of 1992 received yet another jolt when businessman H. Ross Perot announced he would formally enter the race. Once more the election became a three-way race. Many of Perot's followers, however, no longer believed in the seriousness of his commitment and he would never regain the high ratings he had enjoyed in the polls before his withdrawal. The election drew more voter interest than any election in the last twenty years. Despite many distractions the voters insisted on focusing on the economy and domestic issues and turned out to vote in numbers not seen since 1972, with a fifty-five percent voter turnout.

On election day in November 1992, Bill Clinton was elected the forty-second President of the United States. He won 370 electoral votes, 100 more than necessary, but only forty-three percent of the popular vote. He was the fourth post-World War II president to be elected with less than a majority of the popular vote. It was the ninth time in the nation's history that an incumbent had been defeated. Independent candidate Ross Perot received 19 percent of the vote, more than any third party candidate since Theodore Roosevelt's third party candidacy in the election of 1912.

In a jubilant victory scene on the steps of the Old State House in Little Rock where he had begun his campaign 13 months earlier, Bill Clinton emotionally embraced his new Vice President-elect, Al Gore, and as he had done many times during his campaign, referred to his birthplace claiming "I still believe in a place called Hope."

During the transition, as he prepared to appoint the new team who would accompany him to Washington, D.C., he promised to seek new ways to keep open the lines of communication between the public and the top leadership. In December he called a two day Economic Summit where more than 350 leaders from the broadest possible spectrum of American life met to discuss the economy of the nation. President-elect Clinton and Vice President-elect Gore themselves chaired the sessions, directing and commenting on the proceedings. The lengthy sessions were telecast live and Clinton took calls from several citizens around the country who added their questions and comments to the proceedings.

It was clear that American leadership had passed into the hands of a new generation, one born after World War II and eager to lead the country toward a new century where the biggest challenges would be global economics, trade, environment, and a new international order. Though dominated by democracies and free markets, world politics has become much more unstable and unpredictable because of the end of the Cold War and collapse of the balance of military power between two world superpowers.

KEY FACTS ABOUT THE PRESIDENTS

President (Years Served)	Birthplace (Burial Place)	Birth Date (Death Date)	Age Took Office (Age at Death)
1. George Washington (1789–97)	Westmoreland Co., Va. (Mount Vernon, Va.)	Feb. 22, 1732 (Dec. 14, 1799)	57 (67)
2. John Adams (1797–1801)	Braintree, Mass. (Quincy, Mass.)	Oct. 30, 1735 (July 4, 1826)	61 (90)
3. Thomas Jefferson (1801–9)	Albemarle Co., Va. (Monticello, Va.)	Apr. 13, 1743 (July 4, 1826)	57 (83)
4. James Madison (1809–17)	Port Conway, Va. (Montpelier, Va.)	Mar. 16, 1751 (June 28, 1836)	57 (85)
5. James Monroe (1817–25)	Westmoreland Co., Va. (Richmond, Va.)	Apr. 28, 1758 (July 4, 1831)	58 (73)
6. John Quincy Adams (1825–29)	Braintree, Mass. (Quincy, Mass.)	July 11, 1767 (Feb. 23, 1848)	57 (80)
7. Andrew Jackson (1829–37)	Waxhaw, S.C. (Hermitage, Tenn.)	Mar. 15, 1767 (June 8, 1845)	61 (78)
8. Martin Van Buren (1837–41)	Kinderhook, N.Y. (Kinderhook, N.Y.)	Dec. 5, 1782 (July 24, 1862)	54 (79)
9. William H. Harrison (1841)	Berkeley, Va. (North Bend, Ohio)	Feb. 9, 1773 (Apr. 4, 1841)	68 (68)
10. John Tyler (1841–45)	Greenway, Va. (Richmond, Va.)	Mar. 29, 1790 (Jan. 18, 1862)	51 (71)
11. James K. Polk (1845–49)	Pineville, N.C. (Nashville, Tenn.)	Nov. 2, 1795 (June 15, 1849)	49 (53)
12. Zachary Taylor (1849–50)	Orange Co., Va. (Louisville, Ky.)	Nov. 24, 1784 (July 9, 1850)	64 (65)
13. Millard Fillmore (1850–53)	Locke, N.Y. (Buffalo, N.Y.)	Jan. 7, 1800 (Mar. 8, 1874)	50 (74)

President (Years Served)	Birthplace (Burial Place)	Birth Date (Death Date)	Age Took Office (Age at Death)
14. Franklin Pierce (1853–57)	Hillsboro, N.H. (Concord, N.H.)	Nov. 23, 1804 (Oct. 8, 1869)	48 (64)
15. James Buchanan (1857–61)	Mercersburg, Pa. (Lancaster, Pa.)	Apr. 23, 1791 (June 1, 1868)	65 (77)
16. Abraham Lincoln (1861–65)	Hardin Co., Ky. (Springfield, Ill.)	Feb. 12, 1809 (Apr. 15, 1865)	52 (56)
17. Andrew Johnson (1865–69)	Raleigh, N.C. (Greeneville, Tenn.)	Dec. 29, 1808 (July 31, 1875)	56 (66)
18. Ulysses S. Grant (1869–77)	Point Pleasant, Ohio (New York, N.Y.)	Apr. 27, 1822 (July 23, 1885)	46 (63)
19. Rutherford Hayes (1877–81)	Delaware, Ohio (Fremont, Ohio)	Oct. 4, 1822 (Jan. 17, 1893)	54 (70)
20. James Garfield (1881)	Orange, Ohio (Cleveland, Ohio)	Nov. 19, 1831 (Sept. 19, 1881)	49 (49)
21. Chester Arthur (1881–85)	Fairfield, Vt. (Albany, N.Y.)	Oct. 5, 1829 (Nov. 18, 1886)	51 (57)
22. Grover Cleveland (1885–89)	Caldwell, N.J. (Princeton, N.J.)	Mar. 18, 1837 (June 24, 1908)	47 (71)
23. Benjamin Harrison (1889–93)	North Bend, Ohio (Indianapolis, Ind.)	Aug. 20, 1833 (Mar. 13, 1901)	55 (67)
24. Grover Cleveland (1893–97)	Caldwell, N.J. (Princeton, N.J.)	Mar. 18, 1837 (June 24, 1908)	55 (71)
25. William McKinley (1897–1901)	Niles, Ohio (Canton, Ohio)	Jan. 29, 1843 (Sept. 14, 1901)	54 (58)
26. Theodore Roosevelt (1901–9)	New York, N.Y. (Oyster Bay, N.Y.)	Oct. 27, 1858 (Jan. 6, 1919)	42 (60)
27. William H. Taft (1909–13)	Cincinnati, Ohio (Arlington, Va.)	Sept. 15, 1857 (Mar. 8, 1930)	51 (72)
28. Woodrow Wilson (1913–21)	Staunton, Va. (Washington, D.C.)	Dec. 29, 1856 (Feb. 3, 1924)	56 (67)
29. Warren G. Harding (1921–23)	Morrow Co., Ohio (Marion, Ohio)	Nov. 2, 1865 (Aug. 2, 1923)	55 (57)
30. Calvin Coolidge (1923–29)	Plymouth Notch, Vt. (Plymouth, Vt.)	July 4, 1872 (Jan. 5, 1933)	51 (60)

President (Years Served)	Birthplace (Burial Place)	Birth Date (Death Date)	Age Took Office (Age at Death)
31. Herbert Hoover (1929–33)	West Branch, Ia. (West Branch, Ia.)	Aug. 10, 1874 (Oct. 20, 1964)	54 (90)
32. F. D. Roosevelt (1933–45)	Hyde Park, N.Y. (Hyde Park, N.Y.)	Jan. 30, 1882 (Apr. 12, 1945)	51 (63)
33. Harry Truman (1945–53)	Lamar, Mo. (Independence, Mo.)	May 8, 1884 (Dec. 26, 1972)	60 (88)
34. Dwight Eisenhower (1953–61)	Denison, Tex. (Abilene, Kan.)	Oct. 14, 1890 (Mar. 28, 1969)	62 (78)
35. John F. Kennedy (1961–63)	Brookline, Mass. (Arlington, Va.)	May 29, 1917 (Nov. 22, 1963)	43 (46)
36. Lyndon Johnson (1963–69)	Gillespie Co., Tex. (Stonewall, Tex.)	Aug. 27, 1908 (Jan. 22, 1973)	55 (64)
37. Richard Nixon (1969–74)	Yorba Linda, Calif. (——)	Jan. 9, 1913 (——)	56 (—)
38. Gerald R. Ford (1974–77)	Omaha, Nebr. (——)	July 14, 1913 (——)	61 (—)
39. Jimmy Carter (1977–81)	Plains, Ga. (——)	Oct. 1, 1924 (——)	52 (—)
40. Ronald Reagan (1981–89)	Tampico, Ill. (——)	Feb. 11, 1911 (——)	69 (—)
41. George Bush (1989–93)	Milton, Mass. (——)	June 12, 1924 (——)	64 (—)
42. Bill Clinton (1993–)	Hope, Ark. (——)	Aug. 19, 1946 (——)	46 (—)

FIRST LADIES AND WIVES OF THE PRESIDENTS

Name[1] (Dates)	Birthplace	Married	Children[2]
Washington, Martha (Dandridge) Custis (1731–1802)	New Kent Co., Va.	1759	—
Adams, Abigail Smith (1744–1818)	Weymouth, Mass.	1764	5
Jefferson, Martha (Wayles) Skelton (1748–82)	Charles City Co., Va.	1772	6
Madison, Dorothea "Dolley" (Payne) Todd (1768–1849)	Guilford Co., N.C.	1794	—
Monroe, Elizabeth Kortright (1768–1830)	New York, N.Y.	1786	3
Adams, Louisa Catherine Johnson (1775–1852)	London, England	1797	4
Jackson, Rachel (Donelson) Robards (1767–1828)	Halifax Co., Va.	1791	—
Van Buren, Hannah Hoes (1783–1819)	Kinderhook, N.Y.	1807	4
Harrison, Anna Symmes (1775–1864)	Morristown, N.J.	1795	10
Tyler, Letitia Christian (1790–1842)	Cedar Grove, Va.	1813	8
Tyler, Julia Gardiner (1820–89)	Gardiner's Is., N.Y.	1844	7
Polk, Sarah Childress (1803–91)	Murfreesboro, Tenn.	1824	—
Taylor, Margaret Smith (1788–1852)	Calvert Co., Md.	1810	6
Fillmore, Abigail Powers (1798–1853)	Stillwater, N.Y.	1826	2

[1] Names in parentheses are maiden names of previously married women.
[2] Children by previous marriages are not included. Children who died in infancy are included.

Name[1] (Dates)	Birthplace	Married	Children[2]
Fillmore, Caroline (Carmichael) McIntosh (1813–81)	Morristown, N.J.	1858	—
Pierce, Jane Means Appleton (1806–63)	Hampton, N.H.	1834	3
Lincoln, Mary Todd (1818–82)	Lexington, Ky.	1842	4
Johnson, Eliza McCardle (1810–76)	Leesburg, Tenn.	1827	5
Grant, Julia Dent (1826–1902)	St. Louis, Mo.	1848	4
Hayes, Lucy Ware Webb (1831–89)	Chillicothe, Ohio	1852	8
Garfield, Lucretia Rudolph (1832–1918)	Hiram, Ohio	1858	7
Arthur, Ellen Lewis Herndon (1837–80)	Fredericksburg, Va.	1859	3
Cleveland, Frances Folsom (1864–1947)	Buffalo, N.Y.	1886	5
Harrison, Caroline Lavinia Scott (1832–92)	Oxford, Ohio	1853	2
Harrison, Mary Scott (Lord) Dimmick (1858–1948)	Honesdale, Pa.	1896	1
McKinley, Ida Saxton (1847–1907)	Canton, Ohio	1871	2
Roosevelt, Alice Hathaway Lee (1861–84)	Chestnut Hill, Mass.	1880	1
Roosevelt, Edith Kermit Carow (1861–1948)	Norwich, Conn.	1886	5
Taft, Helen Herron (1861–1943)	Cincinnati, Ohio	1886	3
Wilson, Ellen Louise Axson (1860–1914)	Savannah, Ga.	1885	3
Wilson, Edith (Bolling) Galt (1872–1961)	Wytheville, Va.	1915	—
Harding, Florence (Kling) DeWolfe (1860–1924)	Marion, Ohio	1891	—
Coolidge, Grace Anna Goodhue (1879–1957)	Burlington, Vt.	1905	2
Hoover, Lou Henry (1875–1944)	Waterloo, Iowa	1899	2

[1] Names in parentheses are maiden names of previously married women.
[2] Children by previous marriages are not included. Children who died in infancy are included.

Name[1] (Dates)	Birthplace	Married	Children[2]
Roosevelt, Anna Eleanor Roosevelt (1884–1962)	New York, N.Y.	1905	6
Truman, Elizabeth "Bess" Wallace (1885–1982)	Independence, Mo.	1919	1
Eisenhower, Mamie Geneva Doud (1896–1979)	Boone, Iowa	1916	2
Kennedy, Jacqueline Lee Bouvier (1929–)	Southampton, N.Y.	1953	3
Johnson, Claudia Alta "Lady Bird" Taylor (1912–)	Marshall, Texas	1934	2
Nixon, Thelma Catherine Patricia "Pat" Ryan (1912–)	Ely, Nev.	1940	2
Ford, Elizabeth "Betty" (Bloomer) Warren (1918–)	Chicago, Ill.	1948	4
Carter, Rosalynn Smith (1927–)	Plains, Ga.	1946	4
Reagan, Jane Wyman (1914–)	St. Joseph, Mo.	1940	2
Reagan, Nancy Davis (1923–)	New York, N.Y.	1952	2
Bush, Barbara Pierce (1925–)	Rye, N.Y.	1945	6
Clinton, Hillary Rodham (1947–)	Chicago, Ill.	1975	1

[1] Names in parentheses are maiden names of previously married women.

[2] Children by previous marriages are not included. Children who died in infancy are included.

John Fitzgerald Kennedy

— *Lyndon Baines Johnson* —

Richard Milhous Nixon

Gerald Rudolph Ford

Jimmy Carter

Ronald Reagan

George Herbert Walker Bush

William Jefferson Clinton

VICE PRESIDENTS

	Name (Party)	Birthplace	Served Under	Took Office
1.	John Adams (F) (1735–1826)	Braintree, Mass.	Washington	1789
2.	Thomas Jefferson (DR) (1743–1826)	Shadwell, Va.	J. Adams	1797
3.	Aaron Burr (DR) (1756–1836)	Newark, N.J.	Jefferson	1801
4.	George Clinton (R) (1734–1812)	Little Britain, N.Y.	Jefferson Madison	1805
5.	Elbridge Gerry (R) (1744–1814)	Marblehead, Mass.	Madison	1813
6.	Daniel D. Tompkins (R) (1774–1825)	Fox Meadows, N.Y.	Monroe	1817
7.	John C. Calhoun (R) (1782–1850)	Abbeville District, S.C.	J. Q. Adams Jackson	1825
8.	Martin Van Buren (D) (1782–1862)	Kinderhook, N.Y.	Jackson	1833
9.	Richard M. Johnson (D) (1780–1850)	Beargrass, Ky.	Van Buren	1837
10.	John Tyler (W) (1790–1862)	Charles City Co., Va.	W. H. Harrison	1841
11.	George M. Dallas (D) (1792–1864)	Philadelphia, Pa.	Polk	1845
12.	Millard Fillmore (W) (1800–74)	Cayuga Co., N.Y.	Taylor	1849
13.	William R. King (D) (1786–1853)	Sampson Co., N.C.	Pierce	1853
14.	John C. Breckinridge (D) (1821–75)	Lexington, Ky.	Buchanan	1857

Name (Party)	Birthplace	Served Under	Took Office
15. Hannibal Hamlin (R) (1809–91)	Paris, Me.	Lincoln	1861
16. Andrew Johnson (NU)[1] (1808–75)	Raleigh, N.C.	Lincoln	1865
17. Schuyler Colfax (R) (1823–85)	New York, N.Y.	Grant	1869
18. Henry Wilson (R) (1812–75)	Farmington, N.H.	Grant	1873
19. William A. Wheeler (R) (1819–87)	Malone, N.Y.	Hayes	1877
20. Chester A. Arthur (R) (1830–86)	Fairfield, Vt.	Garfield	1881
21. Thomas A. Hendricks (D) (1819–85)	Muskingum Co., Ohio	Cleveland	1885
22. Levi P. Morton (R) (1824–1920)	Shoreham, Vt.	B. Harrison	1889
23. Adlai E. Stevenson (D)[2] (1835–1914)	Christian Co., Ky.	Cleveland	1893
24. Garret A. Hobart (R) (1844–99)	Long Branch, N.J.	McKinley	1897
25. Theodore Roosevelt (R) (1858–1919)	New York, N.Y.	McKinley	1901
26. Charles W. Fairbanks (R) (1852–1918)	Unionville Center, Ohio	T. Roosevelt	1905
27. James S. Sherman (R) (1855–1912)	Utica, N.Y.	Taft	1909
28. Thomas R. Marshall (D) (1854–1925)	N. Manchester, Ind.	Wilson	1913
29. Calvin Coolidge (R) (1872–1933)	Plymouth Notch, Vt.	Harding	1921
30. Charles G. Dawes (R) (1865–1951)	Marietta, Ohio	Coolidge	1925

[1] Andrew Johnson: A Democrat nominated by Republicans and elected with Lincoln on the National Union ticket.

[2] Adlai E. Stevenson: 23rd Vice President. Grandfather of the Democratic candidate for President, 1952 and 1956.

	Name (Party)	Birthplace	Served Under	Took Office
31.	Charles Curtis (R) (1860–1936)	Topeka, Kan.	Hoover	1929
32.	John N. Garner (D) (1868–1967)	Red River Co., Texas	F. Roosevelt	1933
33.	Henry A. Wallace (D) (1888–1966)	Adair Co., Iowa	F. Roosevelt	1941
34.	Harry S Truman (D) (1884–1972)	Lamar, Mo.	F. Roosevelt	1945
35.	Alben W. Barkley (D) (1877–1956)	Graves Co., Ky.	Truman	1949
36.	Richard M. Nixon (R) (1913–)	Yorba Linda, Calif.	Eisenhower	1953
37.	Lyndon B. Johnson (D) (1908–73)	Near Stonewall, Texas	Kennedy	1961
38.	Hubert H. Humphrey (D) (1911–78)	Wallace, S.D.	L. Johnson	1965
39.	Spiro T. Agnew (R) (1918–)	Baltimore, Md.	Nixon	1969
40.	Gerald R. Ford (R) (1913–)	Omaha, Neb.	Nixon	1973
41.	Nelson A. Rockefeller (R) (1908–79)	Bar Harbor, Me.	Ford	1974
42.	Walter F. Mondale (D) (1928–)	Ceylon, Minn.	Carter	1977
43.	George Bush (R) (1924–)	Milton, Mass.	Reagan	1981
44.	J. Danforth Quayle (R) (1947–)	Indianapolis, Ind.	Bush	1989
45.	Albert Gore, Jr. (D) (1948–)	Washington, D.C.	Clinton	1993

PRESIDENTIAL ELECTIONS

THE popular and electoral votes for major candidates in presidential elections are included in the following table. In those years where the percentages do not add up to 100%, votes for minor candidates have not been included in the table. Political party abbreviations: F—Federalist; DR—Democratic-Republican; D—Democratic; NR—National Republican; W—Whig; CU—Constitutional Union; A—American; R—Republican; P—Populist; Pr—Progressive; AI—American Independent; SR—States' Rights; NU—National Union; IND—Independent.

Year	Winner and Loser	Popular Vote and Percentage	Electoral Vote
1789	George Washington (No party) No opposition	Unknown	69
1792	George Washington (F) No opposition	Unknown	132
1796	John Adams (F)	Unknown	71
	Thomas Jefferson (DR)	Unknown	68
1800	Thomas Jefferson (DR)[1]	Unknown	73
	Aaron Burr (DR)	Unknown	73
	John Adams (F)	Unknown	65
	Charles C. Pinckney (F)	Unknown	64
1804	Thomas Jefferson (DR)	Unknown	162
	Charles C. Pinckney (F)	Unknown	14
1808	James Madison (DR)	Unknown	122
	Charles C. Pinckney (F)	Unknown	47
1812	James Madison (DR)	Unknown	128
	De Witt Clinton (F)	Unknown	89
1816	James Monroe (DR)	Unknown	183
	Rufus King (F)	Unknown	34

[1] Elected by the House of Representatives because of a "tie" vote in the Electoral College as a result of a flaw in the Constitution.

Year	Winner and Loser	Popular Vote and Percentage	Electoral Vote
1820	James Monroe (DR)	Unknown	231
	John Quincy Adams (No party)	Unknown	1
1824	John Quincy Adams (No party)[2]	108,740 — 30.6%	84
	Andrew Jackson (No party)	153,544 — 43.1%	99
	William H. Crawford (No party)	46,618 — 13.1%	41
	Henry Clay (No party)	47,136 — 13.2%	37
1828	Andrew Jackson (D)	647,286 — 56.0%	178
	John Quincy Adams (NR)	508,064 — 44.0%	83
1832	Andrew Jackson (D)	687,502 — 56.5%	219
	Henry Clay (NR)	530,189 — 43.5%	49
1836	Martin Van Buren (D)	765,483 — 50.9%	170
	William H. Harrison (W)	549,567 — 41.8%	73
1840	William H. Harrison (W)	1,274,624 — 53.1%	234
	Martin Van Buren (D)	1,127,781 — 46.9%	60
1844	James K. Polk (D)	1,338,464 — 49.6%	170
	Henry Clay (W)	1,300,097 — 48.1%	105
1848	Zachary Taylor (W)	1,360,967 — 47.3%	163
	Lewis Cass (D)	1,222,342 — 42.5%	127
1852	Franklin Pierce (D)	1,601,117 — 50.9%	254
	Winfield Scott (W)	1,385,453 — 44.1%	42
1856	James Buchanan (D)	1,832,955 — 45.3%	174
	John C. Frémont (R)	1,339,932 — 33.1%	114
	Millard Fillmore (A)	871,731 — 21.6%	8
1860	Abraham Lincoln (R)	1,865,593 — 39.8%	180
	Stephen A. Douglas (D)	1,382,713 — 29.5%	12
	John C. Breckinridge (D)	848,356 — 18.1%	72
	John Bell (CU)	592,906 — 12.6%	39
1864	Abraham Lincoln (NU)	2,206,938 — 55.0%	212
	George McClellan (D)	1,803,787 — 45.0%	21
1868	Ulysses S. Grant (R)	3,013,421 — 52.7%	214
	Horatio Seymour (D)	2,706,829 — 47.3%	80
1872	Ulysses S. Grant (R)	3,596,745 — 55.6%	286
	Horace Greeley (D)[3]	2,843,446 — 44.0%	66
1876	Rutherford B. Hayes (R)	4,036,572 — 48.0%	185
	Samuel J. Tilden (D)	4,284,020 — 51.0%	184

[2] Elected by the House of Representatives, no candidate having polled a majority.
[3] Horace Greeley died November 29, 1872. His 66 electoral votes were split as follows: Thomas A. Hendricks, 42; B. Gratz Brown, 18; Charles J. Jenkins, 2; David Davis, 1.

Year	Winner and Loser	Popular Vote and Percentage	Electoral Vote
1880	James A. Garfield (R)	4,453,295 — 48.5%	214
	Winfield S. Hancock (D)	4,414,082 — 48.1%	155
1884	Grover Cleveland (D)	4,879,507 — 48.5%	219
	James G. Blaine (R)	4,850,293 — 48.2%	182
1888	Benjamin Harrison (R)	5,447,129 — 47.9%	233
	Grover Cleveland (D)	5,537,857 — 48.6%	168
1892	Grover Cleveland (D)	5,555,426 — 46.0%	277
	Benjamin Harrison (R)	5,182,690 — 43.0%	145
	James Weaver (P)	1,029,846 — 8.5%	22
1896	William McKinley (R)	7,102,246 — 51.0%	271
	William J. Bryan (D)	6,492,559 — 46.7%	176
1900	William McKinley (R)	7,218,491 — 51.7%	292
	William J. Bryan (D)	6,356,734 — 45.5%	155
1904	Theodore Roosevelt (R)	7,628,461 — 56.4%	336
	Alton B. Parker (D)	5,084,223 — 37.6%	140
1908	William H. Taft (R)	7,675,320 — 51.6%	321
	William J. Bryan (D)	6,412,294 — 43.1%	162
1912	Woodrow Wilson (D)	6,296,547 — 41.9%	435
	Theodore Roosevelt (Pr)	4,118,571 — 27.4%	88
	William H. Taft (R)	3,486,720 — 23.2%	8
1916	Woodrow Wilson (D)	9,127,695 — 49.4%	277
	Charles E. Hughes (R)	8,533,507 — 46.2%	254
1920	Warren G. Harding (R)	16,143,407 — 60.4%	404
	James M. Cox (D)	9,130,328 — 34.2%	127
1924	Calvin Coolidge (R)	15,718,211 — 54.0%	382
	John W. Davis (D)	8,385,283 — 28.8%	136
	Robert M. La Follette (Pr)	4,031,289 — 16.6%	13
1928	Herbert C. Hoover (R)	21,391,993 — 58.2%	444
	Alfred E. Smith (D)	15,016,169 — 40.9%	87
1932	Franklin D. Roosevelt (D)	22,809,638 — 57.4%	472
	Herbert C. Hoover (R)	15,758,901 — 39.7%	59
1936	Franklin D. Roosevelt (D)	27,752,869 — 60.8%	523
	Alfred Landon (R)	16,674,665 — 36.5%	8
1940	Franklin D. Roosevelt (D)	27,307,819 — 54.8%	449
	Wendell Willkie (R)	22,321,018 — 44.8%	82
1944	Franklin D. Roosevelt (D)	25,606,585 — 53.5%	432
	Thomas E. Dewey (R)	22,014,745 — 46.0%	99

Year	Winner and Loser	Popular Vote and Percentage	Electoral Vote
1948	Harry S Truman (D)	24,105,812 — 49.5%	303
	Thomas E. Dewey (R)	21,970,065 — 45.1%	189
	J. Strom Thurmond (SR)	1,169,063 — 2.4%	39
	Henry A. Wallace (Pr)	1,157,172 — 2.4%	0
1952	Dwight D. Eisenhower (R)	33,936,234 — 55.1%	442
	Adlai E. Stevenson (D)	27,314,992 — 44.4%	89
1956	Dwight D. Eisenhower (R)	35,590,472 — 57.4%	457
	Adlai E. Stevenson (D)[4]	26,022,752 — 42.0%	73
1960	John F. Kennedy (D)[5]	34,227,096 — 49.5%	303
	Richard M. Nixon (R)	34,108,546 — 49.4%	219
1964	Lyndon B. Johnson (D)	43,129,484 — 61.1%	486
	Barry M. Goldwater (R)	27,178,188 — 38.5%	52
1968	Richard M. Nixon (R)	31,785,480 — 43.4%	301
	Hubert H. Humphrey (D)	31,275,165 — 42.7%	191
	George C. Wallace (AI)	9,906,473 — 13.5%	46
1972	Richard M. Nixon (R)[6]	47,169,911 — 60.7%	520
	George S. McGovern (D)	29,170,383 — 37.5%	17
	John G. Schmitz (AI)	1,098,482 — 1.4%	0
1976	Jimmy Carter (D)	40,825,839 — 50.0%	297
	Gerald R. Ford (R)[7]	39,147,770 — 47.9%	240
	Eugene J. McCarthy (IND)	680,390 — 0.8%	0
1980	Ronald Reagan (R)	43,904,153 — 50.8%	489
	Jimmy Carter (D)	35,483,883 — 41.0%	49
	John B. Anderson (IND)	5,719,222 — 6.6%	0
1984	Ronald Reagan (R)	54,450,603 — 58.8%	525
	Walter F. Mondale (D)	37,573,671 — 40.6%	13
1988	George Bush (R)	47,917,342 — 54%	426
	Michael Dukakis (D)	41,013,030 — 46%	112
1992	Bill Clinton (D)	43,728,275 — 43%	370
	George Bush (R)	38,167,416 — 38%	168
	H. Ross Perot (none)	19,237,447 — 19%	0

[4] Democrats elected 74 electors but one from Alabama refused to vote for Stevenson and voted for Walter B. Jones. [5] Senator Harry F. Byrd (D-Va) received 15 electoral votes; 6 from unpledged Alabama Democrats, 8 from unpledged Mississippi Democrats, and 1 from a defecting Oklahoma Republican elector. [6] One Virginia Republican elector switched his vote from Nixon to a minor party candidate, reducing Nixon's total from 521 to 520. [7] One of Ford's Washington electors cast his ballot for Ronald Reagan.

CABINETS AND LEADING OFFICIALS

LEADING OFFICIALS during the administrations of each of the Presidents are
listed in the following table, including the Chief Justice, Vice President, and
Cabinet-level department heads.

1st PRESIDENT GEORGE WASHINGTON 1789–1797

Office	Name	Years Served
Chief Justice	John Jay	1790–95
	*John Rutledge	1795
	Oliver Ellsworth	1796–97
Vice President	John Adams	1789–97
Secretary of State	Thomas Jefferson	1789–93
	Edmund Randolph	1794–95
	Timothy Pickering	1795–97
Secretary of the Treasury	Alexander Hamilton	1789–95
	Oliver Wolcott, Jr.	1795–97
Secretary of War	Henry Knox	1789–95
	Timothy Pickering	1795–96
	James McHenry	1796–97
Attorney General	Edmund Randolph	1789–94
	William Bradford	1794–95
	Charles Lee	1795–97
Postmaster General	Samuel Osgood	1789–91
	Timothy Pickering	1791–95
	Joseph Habersham	1795–97

2nd PRESIDENT JOHN ADAMS 1797–1801

Office	Name	Years Served
Chief Justice	Oliver Ellsworth	1797–1800
	John Marshall	1801–35

* Senate refused to confirm appointment.

Office	Name	Years Served
Vice President	Thomas Jefferson	1797–1801
Secretary of State	Timothy Pickering	1797–1800
	John Marshall	1800–1
Secretary of the Treasury	Oliver Wolcott, Jr.	1797–1800
	Samuel Dexter	1801
Secretary of War	James McHenry	1797–1800
	Samuel Dexter	1800
Attorney General	Charles Lee	1797–1801
Postmaster General	Joseph Habersham	1797–1801
Secretary of the Navy	Benjamin Stoddert	1798–1801

3rd PRESIDENT THOMAS JEFFERSON   1801–1809

Office	Name	Years Served
Chief Justice	John Marshall	1801–35
Vice President	Aaron Burr	1801–5
	George Clinton	1805–9
Secretary of State	James Madison	1801–9
Secretary of the Treasury	Samuel Dexter	1801
	Albert Gallatin	1801–9
Secretary of War	Henry Dearborn	1801–9
Attorney General	Levi Lincoln	1801–5
	Robert Smith	1805
	John Breckinridge	1805–7
	Caesar A. Rodney	1807–9
Postmaster General	Joseph Habersham	1801
	Gideon Granger	1801–9
Secretary of the Navy	Robert Smith	1801–9

4th PRESIDENT JAMES MADISON   1809–1817

Office	Name	Years Served
Chief Justice	John Marshall	1801–35
Vice President	George Clinton	1809–12
	Elbridge Gerry	1813–14
Secretary of State	Robert Smith	1809–11
	James Monroe	1811–17

Office	Name	Years Served
Secretary of the Treasury	Albert Gallatin	1809–14
	George W. Campbell	1814
	Alexander J. Dallas	1814–16
	William H. Crawford	1816–17
Secretary of War	William Eustis	1809–13
	John Armstrong	1813–14
	James Monroe	1814–15
	William H. Crawford	1815–17
Attorney General	Caesar A. Rodney	1809–11
	William Pinkney	1811–14
	Richard Rush	1814–17
Postmaster General	Gideon Granger	1809–14
	Return J. Meigs, Jr.	1814–17
Secretary of the Navy	Paul Hamilton	1809–12
	William Jones	1813–14
	Benjamin W. Crowninshield	1815–17

5th President JAMES MONROE 1817–1825

Office	Name	Years Served
Chief Justice	John Marshall	1801–35
Vice President	Daniel D. Tompkins	1817–25
Secretary of State	John Quincy Adams	1817–25
Secretary of the Treasury	William H. Crawford	1817–25
Secretary of War	John C. Calhoun	1817–25
Attorney General	Richard Rush	1817
	William Wirt	1817–25
Postmaster General	Return J. Meigs, Jr.	1817–23
	John McLean	1823–25
Secretary of the Navy	Benjamin W. Crowninshield	1817–18
	Smith Thompson	1819–23
	Samuel L. Southard	1823–25

6th President JOHN QUINCY ADAMS 1825–1829

Office	Name	Years Served
Chief Justice	John Marshall	1801–35
Vice President	John C. Calhoun	1825–29

Office	Name	Years Served
Secretary of State	Henry Clay	1825–29
Secretary of the Treasury	Richard Rush	1825–29
Secretary of War	James Barbour	1825–28
	Peter B. Porter	1828–29
Attorney General	William Wirt	1825–29
Postmaster General	John McLean	1825–29
Secretary of the Navy	Samuel L. Southard	1825–29

7th PRESIDENT ANDREW JACKSON 1829–1837

Office	Name	Years Served
Chief Justice	John Marshall	1801–35
	Roger B. Taney	1836–64
Vice President	John C. Calhoun	1829–32
	Martin Van Buren	1833–37
Secretary of State	Martin Van Buren	1829–31
	Edward Livingston	1831–33
	Louis McLane	1833–34
	John Forsyth	1834–37
Secretary of the Treasury	Samuel D. Ingham	1829–31
	Louis McLane	1831–33
	William J. Duane	1833
	Roger B. Taney	1833–34
	Levi Woodbury	1834–37
Secretary of War	John H. Eaton	1829–31
	Lewis Cass	1831–36
	Benjamin F. Butler	1836–37
Attorney General	John M. Berrien	1829–31
	Roger B. Taney	1831–33
	Benjamin F. Butler	1833–37
Postmaster General	John McLean	1829
	William T. Barry	1829–35
	Amos Kendall	1835–37
Secretary of the Navy	John Branch	1829–31
	Levi Woodbury	1831–34
	Mahlon Dickerson	1834–37

8th PRESIDENT MARTIN VAN BUREN 1837–1841

Office	Name	Years Served
Chief Justice	Roger B. Taney	1836–64
Vice President	Richard M. Johnson	1837–41
Secretary of State	John Forsyth	1837–41
Secretary of the Treasury	Levi Woodbury	1837–41
Secretary of War	Joel R. Poinsett	1837–41
Attorney General	Benjamin F. Butler	1837–38
	Felix Grundy	1838–40
	Henry D. Gilpin	1840–41
Postmaster General	Amos Kendall	1837–40
	John M. Niles	1840–41
Secretary of the Navy	Mahlon Dickerson	1837–38
	James K. Paulding	1838–41

9th PRESIDENT WILLIAM H. HARRISON 1841

Office	Name	Years Served
Chief Justice	Roger B. Taney	1836–64
Vice President	John Tyler	1841
Secretary of State	Daniel Webster	1841
Secretary of the Treasury	Thomas Ewing	1841
Secretary of War	John Bell	1841
Attorney General	John J. Crittenden	1841
Postmaster General	Francis Granger	1841
Secretary of the Navy	George E. Badger	1841

10th PRESIDENT JOHN TYLER 1841–1845

Office	Name	Years Served
Chief Justice	Roger B. Taney	1836–64
Vice President	None	
Secretary of State	Daniel Webster	1841–43
	Abel P. Upshur	1843–44
	John C. Calhoun	1844–45
Secretary of the Treasury	Thomas Ewing	1841
	Walter Forward	1841–43

Office	Name	Years Served
	John C. Spencer	1843–44
	George M. Bibb	1844–45
Secretary of War	John Bell	1841
	John C. Spencer	1841–43
	James M. Porter	1843–44
	William Wilkins	1844–45
Attorney General	John J. Crittenden	1841
	Hugh S. Legaré	1841–43
	John Nelson	1843–45
Postmaster General	Francis Granger	1841
	Charles A. Wickliffe	1841–45
Secretary of the Navy	George E. Badger	1841
	Abel P. Upshur	1841–43
	David Henshaw	1843–44
	Thomas W. Gilmer	1844
	John Y. Mason	1844–45

11th PRESIDENT JAMES K. POLK 1845–1849

Office	Name	Years Served
Chief Justice	Roger B. Taney	1836–64
Vice President	George M. Dallas	1845–49
Secretary of State	James Buchanan	1845–49
Secretary of the Treasury	Robert J. Walker	1845–49
Secretary of War	William L. Marcy	1845–49
Attorney General	John Y. Mason	1845–46
	Nathan Clifford	1846–48
	Isaac Toucey	1848–49
Postmaster General	Cave Johnson	1845–49
Secretary of the Navy	George Bancroft	1845–46
	John Y. Mason	1846–49

12th PRESIDENT ZACHARY TAYLOR 1849–1850

Office	Name	Years Served
Chief Justice	Roger B. Taney	1836–64
Vice President	Millard Fillmore	1849–50
Secretary of State	John M. Clayton	1849–50

Office	Name	Years Served
Secretary of the Treasury	W. M. Meredith	1849–50
Secretary of War	G. W. Crawford	1849–50
Attorney General	Reverdy Johnson	1849–50
Postmaster General	Jacob Collamer	1849–50
Secretary of the Navy	William B. Preston	1849–50
Secretary of the Interior	Thomas Ewing	1849–50

13th PRESIDENT MILLARD FILLMORE   1850–1853

Office	Name	Years Served
Chief Justice	Roger B. Taney	1836–64
Vice President	None	
Secretary of State	Daniel Webster	1850–52
	Edward Everett	1852–53
Secretary of the Treasury	Thomas Corwin	1850–53
Secretary of War	Charles M. Conrad	1850–53
Attorney General	John J. Crittenden	1850–53
Postmaster General	Nathan K. Hall	1850–52
	Samuel D. Hubbard	1852–53
Secretary of the Navy	William A. Graham	1850–52
	John P. Kennedy	1852–53
Secretary of the Interior	T. M. T. McKennan	1850
	A. H. H. Stuart	1850–53

14th PRESIDENT FRANKLIN PIERCE   1853–1857

Office	Name	Years Served
Chief Justice	Roger B. Taney	1836–64
Vice President	William R. D. King	1853
Secretary of State	William L. Marcy	1853–57
Secretary of the Treasury	James Guthrie	1853–57
Secretary of War	Jefferson Davis	1853–57
Attorney General	Caleb Cushing	1853–57
Postmaster General	James Campbell	1853–57
Secretary of the Navy	James C. Dobbin	1853–57
Secretary of the Interior	Robert McClelland	1853–57

15th PRESIDENT JAMES BUCHANAN 1857–1861

Office	Name	Years Served
Chief Justice	Roger B. Taney	1836–64
Vice President	John C. Breckinridge	1857–61
Secretary of State	Lewis Cass	1857–60
	Jeremiah S. Black	1860–61
Secretary of the Treasury	Howell Cobb	1857–60
	Phillip F. Thomas	1860–61
	John A. Dix	1861
Secretary of War	John B. Floyd	1857–61
	Joseph Holt	1861
Attorney General	Jeremiah S. Black	1857–60
	Edwin M. Stanton	1860–61
Postmaster General	Aaron V. Brown	1857–59
	Joseph Holt	1859–61
	Horatio King	1861
Secretary of the Navy	Isaac Toucey	1857–61
Secretary of the Interior	Jacob Thompson	1857–61

16th PRESIDENT ABRAHAM LINCOLN 1861–1865

Office	Name	Years Served
Chief Justice	Roger B. Taney	1836–64
	Salmon P. Chase	1864–73
Vice President	Hannibal Hamlin	1861–65
	Andrew Johnson	1865
Secretary of State	William H. Seward	1861–65
Secretary of the Treasury	Salmon P. Chase	1861–64
	William P. Fessenden	1864–65
	Hugh McCulloch	1865
Secretary of War	Simon Cameron	1861–62
	Edwin M. Stanton	1862–65
Attorney General	Edward Bates	1861–64
	James Speed	1864–65
Postmaster General	Montgomery Blair	1861–64
	William Dennison	1864–65

Office	Name	Years Served
Secretary of the Navy	Gideon Welles	1861–65
Secretary of the Interior	Caleb B. Smith	1861–63
	John P. Usher	1863–65

17th PRESIDENT ANDREW JOHNSON 1865–1869

Office	Name	Years Served
Chief Justice	Salmon P. Chase	1864–73
Vice President	None	
Secretary of State	William H. Seward	1865–69
Secretary of the Treasury	Hugh McCulloch	1865–69
Secretary of War	Edwin M. Stanton	1865–67
	Ulysses S. Grant	1867–68
	Lorenzo Thomas	1868
	John M. Schofield	1868–69
Attorney General	James Speed	1865–66
	Henry Stanbery	1866–68
	William M. Evarts	1868–69
Postmaster General	William Dennison	1865–66
	Alexander W. Randall	1866–69
Secretary of the Navy	Gideon Welles	1865–69
Secretary of the Interior	John P. Usher	1865
	James Harlan	1865–66
	Orville H. Browning	1866–69

18th PRESIDENT ULYSSES S. GRANT 1869–1877

Office	Name	Years Served
Chief Justice	Salmon P. Chase	1864–73
	Morrison R. Waite	1874–88
Vice President	Schuyler Colfax	1869–73
	Henry Wilson	1873–75
Secretary of State	Elihu B. Washburne	1869
	Hamilton Fish	1869–77
Secretary of the Treasury	Alexander T. Stewart	1869
	George S. Boutwell	1869–73
	William A. Richardson	1873–74

Office	Name	Years Served
	Benjamin H. Bristow	1874–76
	Lot M. Morrill	1876–77
Secretary of War	John A. Rawlins	1869
	William T. Sherman	1869
	William W. Belknap	1869–76
	Alphonso Taft	1876
	James D. Cameron	1876–77
Attorney General	Ebenezer Rockwood Hoar	1869–70
	Amos T. Akerman	1870–71
	George H. Williams	1871–75
	Edwards Pierrepont	1875–76
	Alphonso Taft	1876–77
Postmaster General	John A. J. Creswell	1869–74
	James W. Marshall	1874
	Marshall Jewell	1874–76
	James N. Tyner	1876–77
Secretary of the Navy	Adolph E. Borie	1869
	George M. Robeson	1869–77
Secretary of the Interior	Jacob D. Cox	1869–70
	Columbus Delano	1870–75
	Zachariah Chandler	1875–77

19th PRESIDENT RUTHERFORD B. HAYES   1877–1881

Office	Name	Years Served
Chief Justice	Morrison R. Waite	1874–88
Vice President	William A. Wheeler	1877–81
Secretary of State	William M. Evarts	1877–81
Secretary of the Treasury	John Sherman	1877–81
Secretary of War	George W. McCrary	1877–79
	Alexander Ramsey	1879–81
Attorney General	Charles Devens	1877–81
Postmaster General	David M. Key	1877–80
	Horace Maynard	1880–81
Secretary of the Navy	Richard W. Thompson	1877–81
	Nathan Goff, Jr.	1881
Secretary of the Interior	Carl Schurz	1877–81

20th PRESIDENT JAMES A. GARFIELD   1881

Office	Name	Years Served
Chief Justice	Morrison R. Waite	1874–88
Vice President	Chester A. Arthur	1881
Secretary of State	James G. Blaine	1881
Secretary of the Treasury	William Windom	1881
Secretary of War	Robert T. Lincoln	1881
Attorney General	Wayne MacVeagh	1881
Postmaster General	Thomas L. James	1881
Secretary of the Navy	William H. Hunt	1881
Secretary of the Interior	Samuel J. Kirkwood	1881

21st PRESIDENT CHESTER A. ARTHUR   1881–1885

Office	Name	Years Served
Chief Justice	Morrison R. Waite	1874–88
Vice President	*None*	
Secretary of State	James G. Blaine	1881
	Frederick T. Frelinghuysen	1881–85
Secretary of the Treasury	William Windom	1881
	Charles J. Folger	1881–84
	Walter Q. Gresham	1884
	Hugh McCulloch	1884–85
Secretary of War	Robert T. Lincoln	1881–85
Attorney General	Wayne MacVeagh	1881
	Benjamin H. Brewster	1881–85
Postmaster General	Thomas L. James	1881
	Timothy O. Howe	1881–83
	Walter Q. Gresham	1883–84
	Frank Hatton	1884–85
Secretary of the Navy	William H. Hunt	1881–82
	William E. Chandler	1882–85
Secretary of the Interior	Samuel J. Kirkwood	1881–82
	Henry M. Teller	1882–85

22nd PRESIDENT GROVER CLEVELAND   1885–1889

Office	Name	Years Served
Chief Justice	Morrison R. Waite	1874–88
	Melville W. Fuller	1888–1910
Vice President	Thomas A. Hendricks	1885
Secretary of State	Thomas F. Bayard	1885–89
Secretary of the Treasury	Daniel Manning	1885–87
	Charles S. Fairchild	1887–89
Secretary of War	William C. Endicott	1885–89
Attorney General	Augustus H. Garland	1885–89
Postmaster General	William F. Vilas	1885–88
	Don M. Dickinson	1888–89
Secretary of the Navy	William C. Whitney	1885–89
Secretary of the Interior	Lucius Q. C. Lamar	1885–88
	William F. Vilas	1888–89
Secretary of Agriculture	Norman J. Colman	1889

23rd PRESIDENT BENJAMIN HARRISON   1889–1893

Office	Name	Years Served
Chief Justice	Melville W. Fuller	1888–1910
Vice President	Levi P. Morton	1889–93
Secretary of State	James G. Blaine	1889–92
	John W. Foster	1892–93
Secretary of the Treasury	William Windom	1889–91
	Charles Foster	1891–93
Secretary of War	Redfield Proctor	1889–91
	Stephen B. Elkins	1891–93
Attorney General	William H. H. Miller	1889–93
Postmaster General	John Wanamaker	1889–93
Secretary of the Navy	Benjamin F. Tracy	1889–93
Secretary of the Interior	John W. Noble	1889–93
Secretary of Agriculture	Jeremiah M. Rusk	1889–93

24th PRESIDENT GROVER CLEVELAND 1893–1897

Office	Name	Years Served
Chief Justice	Melville W. Fuller	1888–1910
Vice President	Adlai E. Stevenson 1893–97	
Secretary of State	Walter Q. Gresham	1893–95
	Richard Olney	1895–97
Secretary of the Treasury	John G. Carlisle	1893–97
Secretary of War	Daniel S. Lamont	1893–97
Attorney General	Richard Olney	1893–95
	Judson Harmon	1895–97
Postmaster General	Wilson S. Bissel	1893–95
	William L. Wilson	1895–97
Secretary of the Navy	Hilary A. Herbert	1893–97
Secretary of the Interior	Hoke Smith	1893–96
	David R. Francis	1896–97
Secretary of Agriculture	Julius Sterling Morton	1893–97

25th PRESIDENT WILLIAM McKINLEY 1897–1901

Office	Name	Years Served
Chief Justice	Melville W. Fuller	1888–1910
Vice President	Garret A. Hobart	1897–99
	Theodore Roosevelt	1901
Secretary of State	John Sherman	1897–98
	William R. Day	1898
	John Hay	1898–1901
Secretary of the Treasury	Lyman J. Gage	1897–1901
Secretary of War	Russell A. Alger	1897–99
	Elihu Root	1899–1901
Attorney General	Joseph McKenna	1897–98
	John W. Griggs	1898–1901
	Philander C. Knox	1901
Postmaster General	James A. Gary	1897–98
	Charles E. Smith	1898–1901
Secretary of the Navy	John D. Long	1897–1901

Office	Name	Years Served
Secretary of the Interior	Cornelius N. Bliss	1897–99
	Ethan A. Hitchcock	1898–1901
Secretary of Agriculture	James Wilson	1897–1901

26th PRESIDENT THEODORE ROOSEVELT 1901–1909

Office	Name	Years Served
Chief Justice	Melville W. Fuller	1888–1910
Vice President	Charles W. Fairbanks	1905–9
Secretary of State	John Hay	1901–5
	Elihu Root	1905–9
	Robert Bacon	1909
Secretary of the Treasury	Lyman J. Gage	1901–2
	Leslie M. Shaw	1902–7
	George B. Cortelyou	1907–9
Secretary of War	Elihu Root	1901–4
	William H. Taft	1904–8
	Luke E. Wright	1908–9
Attorney General	Philander C. Knox	1901–4
	William H. Moody	1904–6
	Charles J. Bonaparte	1906–9
Postmaster General	Charles E. Smith	1901–2
	Henry C. Payne	1902–4
	Robert J. Wynne	1904–5
	George B. Cortelyou	1905–7
	George von L. Meyer	1907–9
Secretary of the Navy	John D. Long	1901–2
	William H. Moody	1902–4
	Paul Morton	1904–5
	Charles J. Bonaparte	1905–6
	Victor H. Metcalf	1906–8
	Truman H. Newberry	1908–9
Secretary of the Interior	Ethan A. Hitchcock	1901–7
	James R. Garfield	1907–9
Secretary of Agriculture	James Wilson	1901–9
Secretary of Commerce and Labor	George B. Cortelyou	1903–4
	Victor H. Metcalf	1904–6
	Oscar S. Straus	1906–9

27th PRESIDENT WILLIAM H. TAFT 1909–1913

Office	Name	Years Served
Chief Justice	Melville W. Fuller	1888–1910
	Edward D. White	1910–21
Vice President	James Schoolcraft Sherman	1909–12
Secretary of State	Philander C. Knox	1909–13
Secretary of the Treasury	Franklin MacVeagh	1909–13
Secretary of War	Jacob M. Dickinson	1909–11
	Henry L. Stimson	1911–13
Attorney General	George W. Wickersham	1909–13
Postmaster General	Frank H. Hitchcock	1909–13
Secretary of the Navy	George von Lengerke Meyer	1909–13
Secretary of the Interior	Richard A. Ballinger	1909–11
	Walter L. Fisher	1911–13
Secretary of Agriculture	James Wilson	1909–13
Secretary of Commerce and Labor	Charles Nagel	1909–13

28th PRESIDENT WOODROW WILSON 1913–1921

Office	Name	Years Served
Chief Justice	Edward D. White	1910–21
Vice President	Thomas R. Marshall	1913–21
Secretary of State	William Jennings Bryan	1913–15
	Robert Lansing	1915–20
	Bainbridge Colby	1920–21
Secretary of the Treasury	William G. McAdoo	1913–18
	Carter Glass	1918–20
	David F. Houston	1920–21
Secretary of War	Lindley M. Garrison	1913–16
	Newton D. Baker	1916–21
Attorney General	James C. McReynolds	1913–14
	Thomas W. Gregory	1914–19
	A. Mitchell Palmer	1919–21
Postmaster General	Albert S. Burleson	1913–21
Secretary of the Navy	Josephus Daniels	1913–21

Office	Name	Years Served
Secretary of the Interior	Franklin K. Lane	1913–20
	John B. Payne	1920–21
Secretary of Agriculture	David F. Houston	1913–20
	Edwin T. Meredith	1920–21
Secretary of Commerce	William C. Redfield	1913–19
	Joshua W. Alexander	1919–21
Secretary of Labor	William B. Wilson	1913–21

29th PRESIDENT WARREN G. HARDING   1921–1923

Office	Name	Years Served
Chief Justice	Edward D. White	1910–21
	William Howard Taft	1921–30
Vice President	Calvin Coolidge	1921–23
Secretary of State	Charles Evans Hughes	1921–23
Secretary of the Treasury	Andrew W. Mellon	1921–23
Secretary of War	John W. Weeks	1921–23
Attorney General	Harry M. Daugherty	1921–23
Postmaster General	Will H. Hays	1921–22
	Hubert Work	1922–23
	Harry S. New	1923
Secretary of the Navy	Edwin Denby	1921–23
Secretary of the Interior	Albert B. Fall	1921–23
	Hubert Work	1923
Secretary of Agriculture	Henry C. Wallace	1921–23
Secretary of Commerce	Herbert Hoover	1921–23
Secretary of Labor	James J. Davis	1921–23

30th PRESIDENT CALVIN COOLIDGE   1923–1929

Office	Name	Years Served
Chief Justice	William Howard Taft	1921–30
Vice President	Charles G. Dawes	1925–29
Secretary of State	Charles Evans Hughes	1923–25
	Frank B. Kellogg	1925–29
Secretary of the Treasury	Andrew W. Mellon	1923–29

Office	Name	Years Served
Secretary of War	John W. Weeks	1923–25
	Dwight F. Davis	1925–29
Attorney General	Harry M. Daugherty	1923–24
	Harlan F. Stone	1924–25
	John G. Sargent	1925–29
Postmaster General	Harry S. New	1923–29
Secretary of the Navy	Edwin Denby	1923–24
	Curtis D. Wilbur	1924–29
Secretary of the Interior	Hubert Work	1923–28
	Roy O. West	1928–29
Secretary of Agriculture	Henry C. Wallace	1923–24
	Howard M. Gore	1924–25
	William M. Jardine	1925–29
Secretary of Commerce	Herbert Hoover	1923–28
	William F. Whiting	1928–29
Secretary of Labor	James J. Davis	1923–29

31st PRESIDENT HERBERT C. HOOVER 1929–1933

Office	Name	Years Served
Chief Justice	William Howard Taft	1921–30
	Charles Evans Hughes	1930–41
Vice President	Charles Curtis	1929–33
Secretary of State	Frank B. Kellogg	1929
	Henry L. Stimson	1929–33
Secretary of the Treasury	Andrew W. Mellon	1929–32
	Ogden L. Mills	1932–33
Secretary of War	James W. Good	1929
	Patrick J. Hurley	1929–33
Attorney General	William D. Mitchell	1929–33
Postmaster General	Walter F. Brown	1929–33
Secretary of the Navy	Charles Francis Adams	1929–33
Secretary of the Interior	Ray Lyman Wilbur	1929–33
Secretary of Agriculture	Arthur M. Hyde	1929–33
Secretary of Commerce	Robert P. Lamont	1929–32
	Roy D. Chapin	1932–33

Office	Name	Years Served
Secretary of Labor	James J. Davis	1929–30
	William N. Doak	1930–33

32nd PRESIDENT FRANKLIN D. ROOSEVELT 1933–1945

Office	Name	Years Served
Chief Justice	Charles Evans Hughes	1930–41
	Harlan Fiske Stone	1941–46
Vice President	John Nance Garner	1933–41
	Henry A. Wallace	1941–45
	Harry S Truman	1945
Secretary of State	Cordell Hull	1933–44
	Edward R. Stettinius, Jr.	1944–45
Secretary of the Treasury	W. H. Woodin	1933–34
	Henry Morgenthau, Jr.	1934–45
Secretary of War	George H. Dern	1933–36
	Harry H. Woodring	1936–40
	Henry L. Stimson	1940–45
Attorney General	Homer S. Cummings	1933–39
	Frank Murphy	1939–40
	Robert H. Jackson	1940–41
	Francis Biddle	1941–45
Postmaster General	James A. Farley	1933–40
	Frank C. Walker	1940–45
Secretary of the Navy	Claude A. Swanson	1933–40
	Charles Edison	1940
	Frank Knox	1940–44
	James Forrestal	1944–45
Secretary of the Interior	Harold L. Ickes	1933–45
Secretary of Agriculture	Henry A. Wallace	1933–40
	Claude R. Wickard	1940–45
Secretary of Commerce	Daniel C. Roper	1933–38
	Harry L. Hopkins	1938–40
	Jesse H. Jones	1940–45
	Henry A. Wallace	1945
Secretary of Labor	Frances Perkins	1933–45

33rd PRESIDENT HARRY S TRUMAN   1945–1953

Office	Name	Years Served
Chief Justice	Harlan Fiske Stone	1941–46
	Frederick M. Vinson	1946–53
Vice President	Alben W. Barkley	1949–53
Secretary of State	Edward R. Stettinius, Jr.	1945
	James F. Byrnes	1945–47
	George C. Marshall	1947–49
	Dean G. Acheson	1949–53
Secretary of the Treasury	Henry Morgenthau, Jr.	1945
	Frederick M. Vinson	1945–46
	John W. Snyder	1946–53
Secretary of War	Henry L. Stimson	1945
	Robert P. Patterson	1945–47
	Kenneth C. Royall	1947
Secretary of Defense	James V. Forrestal	1947–49
	Louis A. Johnson	1949–50
	George C. Marshall	1950–51
	Robert A. Lovett	1951–53
Attorney General	Francis Biddle	1945
	Thomas C. Clark	1945–49
	J. Howard McGrath	1949–52
	James P. McGranery	1952–53
Postmaster General	Frank C. Walker	1945
	Robert E. Hannegan	1945–47
	Jesse M. Donaldson	1947–53
Secretary of the Navy	James V. Forrestal	1945–47
Secretary of the Interior	Harold L. Ickes	1945–46
	Julius A. Krug	1946–49
	Oscar L. Chapman	1949–53
Secretary of Agriculture	Claude R. Wickard	1945
	Clinton P. Anderson	1945–48
	Charles F. Brannan	1948–53
Secretary of Commerce	Henry A. Wallace	1945–46
	W. Averell Harriman	1946–48
	Charles Sawyer	1948–53

Office	Name	Years Served
Secretary of Labor	Frances Perkins	1945
	Lewis B. Schwellenbach	1945–48
	Maurice J. Tobin	1948–53

34th PRESIDENT DWIGHT D. EISENHOWER 1953–1961

Office	Name	Years Served
Chief Justice	Frederick M. Vinson	1946–53
	Earl Warren	1953–69
Vice President	Richard M. Nixon	1953–61
Secretary of State	John Foster Dulles	1953–59
	Christian A. Herter	1959–61
Secretary of the Treasury	George M. Humphrey	1953–57
	Robert B. Anderson	1957–61
Secretary of Defense	Charles E. Wilson	1953–57
	Neil H. McElroy	1957–59
	Thomas S. Gates, Jr.	1959–61
Attorney General	Herbert Brownell, Jr.	1953–57
	William P. Rogers	1957–61
Postmaster General	Arthur E. Summerfield	1953–61
Secretary of the Interior	Douglas McKay	1953–56
	Fred A. Seaton	1956–61
Secretary of Agriculture	Ezra Taft Benson	1953–61
Secretary of Commerce	Sinclair Weeks	1953–58
	Lewis L. Strauss	1958–59
	Frederick H. Mueller	1959–61
Secretary of Labor	Martin P. Durkin	1953
	James P. Mitchell	1953–61
Secretary of Health, Education, and Welfare	Oveta Culp Hobby	1953–55
	Marion B. Folsom	1955–58
	Arthur S. Flemming	1958–61

35th PRESIDENT JOHN F. KENNEDY 1961–1963

Office	Name	Years Served
Chief Justice	Earl Warren	1953–69
Vice President	Lyndon B. Johnson	1961–63
Secretary of State	Dean Rusk	1961–63

Office	Name	Years Served
Secretary of the Treasury	C. Douglas Dillon	1961–63
Secretary of Defense	Robert S. McNamara	1961–63
Attorney General	Robert F. Kennedy	1961–63
Postmaster General	J. Edward Day	1961–63
	John A. Gronouski, Jr.	1963
Secretary of the Interior	Stewart L. Udall	1961–63
Secretary of Agriculture	Orville L. Freeman	1961–63
Secretary of Commerce	Luther H. Hodges	1961–63
Secretary of Labor	Arthur J. Goldberg	1961–62
	W. Willard Wirtz	1962–63
Secretary of Health, Education, and Welfare	Abraham A. Ribicoff	1961–62
	Anthony J. Celebrezze	1962–63

36th PRESIDENT LYNDON B. JOHNSON   1963–1969

Office	Name	Years Served
Chief Justice	Earl Warren	1953–69
Vice President	Hubert Humphrey	1965–69
Secretary of State	Dean Rusk	1963–69
Secretary of the Treasury	C. Douglas Dillon	1963–65
	Henry H. Fowler	1965–68
	Joseph W. Barr	1968–69
Secretary of Defense	Robert S. McNamara	1963–68
	Clark Clifford	1968–69
Attorney General	Robert F. Kennedy	1963–64
	Nicholas deB. Katzenbach	1964–66
	Ramsey Clark	1967–69
Postmaster General	John A. Gronouski, Jr.	1963–65
	Lawrence Francis O'Brien	1965–68
	W. Marvin Watson	1968–69
Secretary of the Interior	Stewart Lee Udall	1963–69
Secretary of Agriculture	Orville Lothrop Freeman	1963–69
Secretary of Commerce	Luther H. Hodges	1963–64
	John T. Connor	1965–67

Office	Name	Years Served
	Alexander B. Trowbridge	1967–68
	C. R. Smith	1968–69
Secretary of Labor	W. Willard Wirtz	1963–69
Secretary of Health, Education, and Welfare	Anthony J. Celebrezze	1963–65
	John William Gardner	1965–68
	Wilbur J. Cohen	1968–69
Secretary of Housing and Urban Development	Robert C. Weaver	1966–68
	Robert C. Wood	1968–69
Secretary of Transportation	Alan S. Boyd	1966–69

37th PRESIDENT RICHARD M. NIXON 1969–1974

Office	Name	Years Served
Chief Justice	Earl Warren	1953–69
	Warren Earl Burger	1969–86
Vice President	Spiro Agnew	1969–73
	Gerald R. Ford	1973–74
Secretary of State	William P. Rogers	1969–73
	Henry A. Kissinger	1973–74
Secretary of the Treasury	David M. Kennedy	1969–71
	John B. Connally, Jr.	1971–72
	George P. Shultz	1972–74
	William E. Simon	1974
Secretary of Defense	Melvin R. Laird	1969–73
	Elliot L. Richardson	1973
	James R. Schlesinger	1973–74
Attorney General	John N. Mitchell	1969–72
	Richard G. Kleindienst	1972–73
	Elliot L. Richardson	1973
	William B. Saxbe	1974
Postmaster General*	Winton M. Blount	1969–71
Secretary of the Interior	Walter J. Hickel	1969–71
	Rogers C. B. Morton	1971–74
Secretary of Agriculture	Clifford M. Hardin	1969–71
	Earl L. Butz	1971–74

* Abolished as Cabinet position in 1971.

Office	Name	Years Served
Secretary of Commerce	Maurice H. Stans	1969–72
	Peter G. Peterson	1972–73
	Frederick B. Dent	1973–74
Secretary of Labor	George P. Shultz	1969–70
	James D. Hodgson	1970–73
	Peter J. Brennan	1973–74
Secretary of Health, Education, and Welfare	Robert H. Finch	1969–70
	Elliot L. Richardson	1970–73
	Caspar W. Weinberger	1973–74
Secretary of Housing and Urban Development	George Romney	1969–73
	James T. Lynn	1973–74
Secretary of Transportation	John A. Volpe	1969–73
	Claude S. Brinegar	1973–74

38th President GERALD R. FORD   1974–1977

Office	Name	Years Served
Chief Justice	Warren Earl Burger	1969–86
Vice President	Nelson A. Rockefeller	1974–77
Secretary of State	Henry A. Kissinger	1974–77
Secretary of the Treasury	William E. Simon	1974–77
Secretary of Defense	James R. Schlesinger	1974–75
	Donald H. Rumsfeld	1975–77
Attorney General	William B. Saxbe	1974–75
	Edward H. Levi	1975–77
Secretary of the Interior	Rogers C. B. Morton	1974–75
	Stanley K. Hathaway	1975
	Thomas S. Kleppe	1975–77
Secretary of Agriculture	Earl L. Butz	1974–76
	John A. Knebel	1976–77
Secretary of Commerce	Frederick B. Dent	1974–75
	Rogers C. B. Morton	1975–76
	Elliot L. Richardson	1976–77
Secretary of Labor	Peter J. Brennan	1974–75
	John T. Dunlop	1975–76
	William J. Usery, Jr.	1976–77

Office	Name	Years Served
Secretary of Health, Education, and Welfare	Caspar W. Weinberger	1974–75
	F. David Mathews	1975–77
Secretary of Housing and Urban Development	James T. Lynn	1974–75
	Carla Anderson Hills	1975–77
Secretary of Transportation	Claude S. Brinegar	1974–75
	William T. Coleman, Jr.	1975–77

39th PRESIDENT JIMMY CARTER   1977–1981

Office	Name	Years Served
Chief Justice	Warren Earl Burger	1969–86
Vice President	Walter F. Mondale	1977–81
Secretary of State	Cyrus R. Vance	1977–80
	Edmund S. Muskie	1980–81
Secretary of the Treasury	W. Michael Blumenthal	1977–79
	G. William Miller	1979–81
Secretary of Defense	Harold Brown	1977–81
Attorney General	Griffin B. Bell	1977–79
	Benjamin R. Civiletti	1979–81
Secretary of the Interior	Cecil D. Andrus	1977–81
Secretary of Agriculture	Robert S. Bergland	1977–81
Secretary of Commerce	Juanita M. Kreps	1977–79
	Phillip Klutznick	1979–81
Secretary of Labor	F. Ray Marshall	1977–81
Secretary of Health, Education, and Welfare*	Joseph A. Califano, Jr.	1977–79
	Patricia Roberts Harris	1979–81
Secretary of Housing and Urban Development	Patricia Roberts Harris	1977–79
	Moon Landrieu	1979–81
Secretary of Transportation	Brock Adams	1977–79
	Neil E. Goldschmidt	1979–81
Secretary of Energy	James R. Schlesinger	1977–79
	Charles W. Duncan, Jr.	1979–81
Secretary of Education	Shirley M. Hufstedler	1979–81

* Title changed in 1979 to Secretary of Health and Human Services.

40th PRESIDENT RONALD REAGAN 1981–89

Office	Name	Years Served
Chief Justice	Warren Earl Burger	1969–86
	William H. Rehnquist	1986–
Vice President	George Bush	1981–89
Secretary of State	Alexander M. Haig, Jr.	1981–82
	George P. Shultz	1982–89
Secretary of the Treasury	Donald T. Regan	1981–85
	James A. Baker, III	1985–88
	Nicholas Brady	1988–89
Secretary of Defense	Caspar W. Weinberger	1981–87
	Frank C. Carlucci	1987–89
Attorney General	William French Smith	1981–85
	Edwin Meese, III	1985–87
	Richard Thornburgh	1988–89
Secretary of the Interior	James G. Watt	1981–83
	William P. Clark	1983–85
	Donald P. Hodel	1985–89
Secretary of Agriculture	John R. Block	1981–86
	Richard E. Lyng	1986–89
Secretary of Commerce	Malcolm Baldrige	1981–87
	C. William Verity	1987–89
Secretary of Labor	Raymond J. Donovan	1981–85
	William E. Brock, III	1985–87
	Ann Dore McLaughlin	1987–89
Secretary of Health and Human Services	Richard S. Schweiker	1981–83
	Margaret M. Heckler	1983–85
	Otis R. Bowen	1985–89
Secretary of Housing and Urban Development	Samuel R. Pierce, Jr.	1981–89
Secretary of Transportation	Andrew L. Lewis, Jr.	1981–82
	Elizabeth Dole	1983–87
	James H. Burnley, IV	1987–89
Secretary of Energy	James B. Edwards	1981–82
	Donald P. Hodel	1982–85
	John S. Herrington	1985–89

Office	Name	Years Served
Secretary of Education	Terrel H. Bell	1981–84
	William J. Bennett	1985–88
	Lauro F. Cavazos	1988–89

41st PRESIDENT GEORGE BUSH   1989–93

Office	Name	Years Served
Chief Justice	William H. Rehnquist	1986–
Vice President	J. Danforth (Dan) Quayle	1989–93
Secretary of State	James A. Baker, III	1989–92
	Lawrence Eagleburger	1992–93
Secretary of the Treasury	Nicholas F. Brady	1989–93
Secretary of Defense	Richard Cheney	1989–93
Attorney General	Richard Thornburgh	1989–91
	William P. Barr	1991–93
Secretary of the Interior	Manuel Lujan, Jr.	1989–93
Secretary of Agriculture	Clayton K. Yeutter	1989–91
	Edward Madigan	1991–93
Secretary of Commerce	Robert A. Mosbacher	1989–92
	Barbara H. Franklin	1992–93
Secretary of Labor	Elizabeth H. Dole	1989–90
	Lynn Martin	1991–93
Secretary of Health and Human Services	Louis W. Sullivan	1989–93
Secretary of Housing and Urban Development	Jack F. Kemp	1989–93
Secretary of Transportation	Samuel K. Skinner	1989–91
	Andrew H. Card	1992–93
Secretary of Energy	James D. Watkins	1989–93
Secretary of Education	Lauro F. Cavazos	1989–90
	Lamar Alexander	1991–93
Secretary of Veterans Affairs	Edward J. Derwinski	1989–92

42nd President BILL CLINTON 1993–

Office	Name	Years Served
Chief Justice	William H. Rehnquist	1986–
Vice President	Albert Gore, Jr.	1993–
Secretary of State	Warren M. Christopher	1993–
Secretary of the Treasury	Lloyd M. Bentsen	1993–
Secretary of Defense	Les Aspin	1993–
Attorney General	Janet Reno	1993–
Secretary of the Interior	Bruce Babbitt	1993–
Secretary of Agriculture	Mike Espy	1993–
Secretary of Commerce	Ronald H. Brown	1993–
Secretary of Labor	Robert B. Reich	1993–
Secretary of Health and Human Services	Donna E. Shalala	1993–
Secretary of Housing and Urban Development	Henry G. Cisneros	1993–
Secretary of Transportation	Federico F. Peña	1993–
Secretary of Energy	Hazel R. O'Leary	1993–
Secretary of Education	Richard W. Riley	1993–
Secretary of Veterans Affairs	Jesse Brown	1993–

Political party abbreviations: A-F—Anti-Federalist;
DR—Democratic-Republican; Fed—Federalist;
R—Republican;

CONGRESS	YEARS	PRESIDENT AND PARTY	
1st	1789–91	George Washington	Federalist
2d	1791–93	George Washington	Federalist
3d	1793–95	George Washington	Federalist
4th	1795–97	George Washington	Federalist
5th	1797–99	John Adams	Federalist
6th	1799–1801	John Adams	Federalist
7th	1801–3	Thomas Jefferson	Dem-Rep
8th	1803–5	Thomas Jefferson	Dem-Rep
9th	1805–7	Thomas Jefferson	Dem-Rep
10th	1807–9	Thomas Jefferson	Dem-Rep
11th	1809–11	James Madison	Dem-Rep
12th	1811–13	James Madison	Dem-Rep
13th	1813–15	James Madison	Dem-Rep
14th	1815–17	James Madison	Dem-Rep
15th	1817–19	James Monroe	Dem-Rep
16th	1819–21	James Monroe	Dem-Rep
17th	1821–23	James Monroe	Dem-Rep
18th	1823–25	James Monroe	Dem-Rep
19th	1825–27	John Quincy Adams	Coalition
20th	1827–29	John Quincy Adams	Coalition
21st	1829–31	Andrew Jackson	Democrat
22d	1831–33	Andrew Jackson	Democrat
23d	1833–35	Andrew Jackson	Democrat
24th	1835–37	Andrew Jackson	Democrat
25th	1837–39	Martin Van Buren	Democrat
26th	1839–41	Martin Van Buren	Democrat
27th	1841–43	{ William H. Harrison	Whig
		{ John Tyler	Whig
28th	1843–45	John Tyler	Whig
29th	1845–47	James K. Polk	Democrat
30th	1847–49	James K. Polk	Democrat
31st	1849–51	{ Zachary Taylor	Whig
		{ Millard Fillmore	Whig
32d	1851–53	Millard Fillmore	Whig

CONGRESS: 1789–1993

A-M—Anti-Masonic; Co—Coalition; D—Democrat;
Ja—Jacksonian; NR—National Republican;
U—Unionist; W—Whig.

HOUSE OF REPRESENTATIVES			SENATE		
Majority Party	*Minority Party*	*Other*	*Majority Party*	*Minority Party*	*Other*
Fed—38	A-F—26	—	Fed—17	A-F—9	—
Fed—37	DR—33	—	Fed—16	DR—13	—
DR—57	Fed—48	—	Fed—17	DR—13	—
Fed—54	DR—52	—	Fed—19	DR—13	—
Fed—58	DR—48	—	Fed—20	DR—12	—
Fed—64	DR—42	—	Fed—19	DR—13	—
DR—69	Fed—36	—	DR—18	Fed—13	—
DR—102	Fed—39	—	DR—25	Fed—9	—
DR—116	Fed—25	—	DR—27	Fed—7	—
DR—118	Fed—24	—	DR—28	Fed—6	—
DR—94	Fed—48	—	DR—28	Fed—6	—
DR—108	Fed—36	—	DR—30	Fed—6	—
DR—112	Fed—68	—	DR—27	Fed—9	—
DR—117	Fed—65	—	DR—25	Fed—11	—
DR—141	Fed—42	—	DR—34	Fed—10	—
DR—156	Fed—27	—	DR—35	Fed—7	—
DR—158	Fed—25	—	DR—44	Fed—4	—
DR—187	Fed—26	—	DR—44	Fed—4	—
Co—105	Ja—97	—	Co—26	Ja—20	—
Ja—119	Co—94	—	Ja—28	Co—20	—
D—139	NR—74	—	D—26	NR—22	—
D—141	NR—58	14	D—25	NR—21	2
D—147	A-M—53	60	D—20	NR—20	8
D—145	W—98	—	D—27	W—25	—
D—108	W—107	24	D—30	W—18	4
D—124	W—118	—	D—28	W—22	—
W—133	D—102	6	W—28	D—22	2
D—142	W—79	1	W—28	D—25	1
D—143	W—77	6	D—31	W—25	—
W—115	D—108	4	D—36	W—21	1
D—112	W—109	9	D—35	W—25	2
D—140	W—88	5	D—35	W—24	3

CONGRESS	YEARS	PRESIDENT AND PARTY
33d	1853–55	Franklin Pierce.............. Democrat
34th	1855–57	Franklin Pierce.............. Democrat
35th	1857–59	James Buchanan .... Democrat
36th	1859–61	James Buchanan .... Democrat
37th	1861–63	Abraham Lincoln .... Republican
38th	1863–65	Abraham Lincoln .... Republican
39th	1865–67	{ Abraham Lincoln .... Unionist { Andrew Johnson .... Unionist
40th	1867–69	Andrew Johnson .... Unionist
41st	1869–71	Ulysses S. Grant .... Republican
42d	1871–73	Ulysses S. Grant .... Republican
43d	1873–75	Ulysses S. Grant .... Republican
44th	1875–77	Ulysses S. Grant .... Republican
45th	1877–79	Rutherford B. Hayes .... Republican
46th	1879–81	Rutherford B. Hayes .... Republican
47th	1881–83	{ James A. Garfield .... Republican { Chester A. Arthur .... Republican
48th	1883–85	Chester A. Arthur .... Republican
49th	1885–87	Grover Cleveland .... Democrat
50th	1887–89	Grover Cleveland .... Democrat
51st	1889–91	Benjamin Harrison.......... Republican
52d	1891–93	Benjamin Harrison.......... Republican
53d	1893–95	Grover Cleveland .... Democrat
54th	1895–97	Grover Cleveland .... Democrat
55th	1897–99	William McKinley .... Republican
56th	1899–1901	William McKinley .... Republican
57th	1901–3	{ William McKinley .... Republican { Theodore Roosevelt......... Republican
58th	1903–5	Theodore Roosevelt......... Republican
59th	1905–7	Theodore Roosevelt......... Republican
60th	1907–9	Theodore Roosevelt......... Republican
61st	1909–11	William H. Taft............. Republican
62d	1911–13	William H. Taft............. Republican
63d	1913–15	Woodrow Wilson .... Democrat
64th	1915–17	Woodrow Wilson .... Democrat
65th	1917–19	Woodrow Wilson .... Democrat
66th	1919–21	Woodrow Wilson .... Democrat

House of Representatives			Senate		
Majority Party	*Minority Party*	*Other*	*Majority Party*	*Minority Party*	*Other*
D—159	W—71	4	D—38	W—22	2
R—108	D—83	43	D—42	R—15	5
D—131	R—92	14	D—39	R—20	5
R—113	D—101	23	D—38	R—26	2
R—106	D—42	28	R—31	D—11	7
R—103	D—80	—	R—39	D—12	—
U—145	D—46	—	U—42	D—10	—
R—143	D—49	1	R—42	D—11	—
R—170	D—73	—	R—61	D—11	—
R—139	D—104	—	R—57	D—17	—
R—203	D—88	2	R—54	D—19	1
D—181	R—107	5	R—46	D—29	1
D—156	R—137	—	R—39	D—36	1
D—150	R—128	15	D—43	R—33	—
R—152	D—130	11	R—37	D—37	2
D—200	R—119	6	R—40	D—36	—
D—182	R—140	3	R—41	D—34	—
D—170	R—151	4	R—39	D—37	—
R—173	D—156	1	R—47	D—37	—
D—231	R—88	14	R—47	D—39	2
D—220	R—126	10	D—44	R—38	6
R—246	D—104	7	R—44	D—39	5
R—206	D—134	17	R—46	D—34	10
R—185	D—163	9	R—53	D—26	11
R—198	D—153	6	R—56	D—29	5
R—207	D—178	1	R—58	D—32	—
R—250	D—136	—	R—58	D—32	—
R—222	D—164	—	R—61	D—29	2
R—219	D—172	—	R—59	D—32	1
D—228	R—162	1	R—49	D—42	—
D—290	R—127	18	D—51	R—44	1
D—231	R—193	11	D—56	R—39	1
D—210*	R—216	9	D—53	R—42	1
R—237	D—191	7	R—48	D—47	1

* House organized by Democrats with minor parties.

Congress	Years	President and Party
67th	1921–23	Warren G. Harding .... Republican
68th	1923–25	{ Warren G. Harding .... Republican { Calvin Coolidge .... Republican
69th	1925–27	Calvin Coolidge .... Republican
70th	1927–29	Calvin Coolidge .... Republican
71st	1929–31	Herbert C. Hoover.......... Republican
72d	1931–33	Herbert C. Hoover.......... Republican
73d	1933–35	Franklin D. Roosevelt....... Democrat
74th	1935–37	Franklin D. Roosevelt....... Democrat
75th	1937–39	Franklin D. Roosevelt....... Democrat
76th	1939–41	Franklin D. Roosevelt....... Democrat
77th	1941–43	Franklin D. Roosevelt....... Democrat
78th	1943–45	Franklin D. Roosevelt....... Democrat
79th	1945–47	{ Franklin D. Roosevelt....... Democrat { Harry S Truman .... Democrat
80th	1947–49	Harry S Truman .... Democrat
81st	1949–51	Harry S Truman .... Democrat
82d	1951–53	Harry S Truman .... Democrat
83d	1953–55	Dwight D. Eisenhower ..... Republican
84th	1955–57	Dwight D. Eisenhower ..... Republican
85th	1957–59	Dwight D. Eisenhower ..... Republican
86th	1959–61	Dwight D. Eisenhower ..... Republican
87th	1961–63	John F. Kennedy............ Democrat
88th	1963–65	{ John F. Kennedy............ Democrat { Lyndon B. Johnson .... Democrat
89th	1965–67	Lyndon B. Johnson .... Democrat
90th	1967–69	Lyndon B. Johnson .... Democrat
91st	1969–71	Richard M. Nixon .... Republican
92d	1971–73	Richard M. Nixon .... Republican
93d	1973–75	{ Richard M. Nixon .... Republican { Gerald R. Ford.............. Republican
94th	1975–77	Gerald R. Ford.............. Republican
95th	1977–79	Jimmy Carter .... Democrat
96th	1979–81	Jimmy Carter .... Democrat
97th	1981–83	Ronald Reagan.............. Republican
98th	1983–85	Ronald Reagan.............. Republican
99th	1985–87	Ronald Reagan.............. Republican
100th	1987–89	Ronald Reagan.............. Republican

HOUSE OF REPRESENTATIVES			SENATE		
Majority Party	*Minority Party*	*Other*	*Majority Party*	*Minority Party*	*Other*
R—300	D—132	3	R—59	R—37	—
R—225	D—207	3	R—51	D—43	2
R—247	D—183	5	R—54	D—40	2
R—237	D—195	3	R—48	D—47	1
R—267	D—163	5	R—56	D—39	1
D—216*	R—218	1	R—48	D—47	1
D—313	R—117	5	D—59	R—36	1
D—322	R—103	10	D—69	R—25	2
D—333	R—89	13	D—75	R—17	4
D—262	R—169	4	D—69	R—23	4
D—267	R—162	6	D—66	R—28	2
D—222	R—209	4	D—57	R—38	1
D—243	R—190	2	D—57	R—38	1
R—246	D—188	1	R—51	D—45	—
D—263	R—171	1	D—54	R—42	—
D—234	R—199	2	D—48	R—47	1
R—221	D—213	1	R—48	D—46	2
D—232	R—203	—	D—48	R—47	1
D—234	R—201	—	D—49	R—47	—
D—283	R—153	—	D—64	R—34	—
D—262	R—175	—	D—64	R—36	—
D—258	R—176	1	D—67	R—33	—
D—295	R—140	—	D—68	R—32	—
D—248	R—187	—	D—64	R—36	—
D—243	R—192	—	D—57	R—43	—
D—255	R—180	—	D—54	R—44	2
D—242	R—192	1	D—56	R—42	2
D—291	R—144	—	D—60	R—37	2
D—292	R—143	—	D—61	R—38	1
D—277	R—158	—	D—58	R—41	1
D—243	R—192	—	R—53	D—46	1
D—268	R—167	—	R—55	D—45	—
D—253	R—182	—	R—53	D—47	—
D—258	R—177	—	D—54	R—46	—

* Democrats organized because of Republican deaths.

CONGRESS	YEARS	PRESIDENT AND PARTY	
101st	1989–91	George Bush	Republican
102d	1991–93	George Bush	Republican
103d	1993–95	Bill Clinton	Democrat

House of Representatives			Senate		
Majority Party	*Minority Party*	*Other*	*Majority Party*	*Minority Party*	*Other*
D—260	R—175	—	D—55	R—45	—
D—267	R—167	1	D—57	R—43	—
D—258	R—176	1	D—57	R—43	—

PRESIDENTS OF CONGRESS: 1774 to 1789

Although the office of the President of the United States as we know it was created in the Constitution written in 1787, fourteen other men had held the title President before George Washington. These men were chosen President by Congress, and their powers were limited to presiding over that body.

1774	Peyton Randolph, Virginia
1774–75	Henry Middleton, South Carolina
1775	Peyton Randolph, Virginia
1775–77	John Hancock, Massachusetts
1777–78	Henry Laurens, South Carolina
1778–79	John Jay, New York
1779–81	Samuel Huntington, Connecticut
1781	Thomas McKean, Delaware
1781–82	John Hanson, Maryland
1782–83	Elias Boudinot, New Jersey
1783–84	Thomas Mifflin, Pennsylvania
1784–85	Richard Henry Lee, Virginia
1785–86	John Hancock, Massachusetts
1786–87	Nathaniel Gorham, Massachusetts
1787–88	Arthur St. Clair, Pennsylvania
1788–89	Cyrus Griffin, Virginia

THE MAKING OF THE PRESIDENCY

BEFORE THE OFFICE of President of the United States was created by the Founding Fathers, there was no precedent for such a powerful elected official. From the time of the First Continental Congress in 1774 there had been a President of Congress, but he merely was the presiding officer of a legislative body. The best known of the men who held this office was John Hancock, the Boston patriot, who signed his name so defiantly at the bottom of the Declaration of Independence in 1776 that it became synonymous with the word *signature*.

In the Articles of Confederation, under which the United States was governed from 1781 to 1789, the office of President of Congress was so honorific and inconsequential that it was given only this passing mention:

> "The united States in congress assembled shall have authority . . . to appoint such other committees and civil officers as may be necessary for managing the general affairs of the united states under their direction—to appoint one of their number to preside, provided that no person be allowed to serve in the office of president more than one year in any term of three years . . ."

Uneasy at the chaos into which the United States was drifting under the Articles of Confederation, delegates of the states assembled in Philadelphia in May 1787 under the leadership of George Washington to rectify the weaknesses in the national government. Most of them realized the confederation could not continue to exist without a strong executive to carry out the laws of Congress. And most felt that Washington was the only person who could do the job. So the office was tailored to his qualities and abilities. It seems likely that private conversations between Washington and the various delegates molded the words written into the Constitution to describe the office and to enunciate its powers, although there is no direct evidence to support such a speculation.

The Virginia Plan

THE FIRST FORMAL PROPOSAL that a strong "National Executive" be provided for the new federal government was contained in the Virginia Plan presented to the Constitutional Convention by Governor Edmund Randolph of Virginia on May 29, 1787:

Resolved that a National Executive be instituted; to be chosen by the National Legislature for the term of _____ years, to receive punctually at stated times, a fixed compensation for the services rendered, in which no increase or diminution shall be made so as to affect the Magistracy, existing at the time of increase or diminution, and to be ineligible a second time; and that besides a general authority to execute the National laws, it ought to enjoy the Executive rights vested in Congress by the Confederation.

Resolved that the Executive and a convenient number of the National Judiciary, ought to compose a Council of revision with authority to examine every act of the National Legislature before it shall operate, and every act of a particular Legislature before a Negative thereon shall be final; and that the dissent of the said Council shall amount to a rejection, unless the Act of the National Legislature be again passed, or that of a particular Legislature be again negatived by _____ of the members of each branch.

The Pinckney Plan

ON THE SAME DAY Charles Pinckney of South Carolina presented his "Plan of a Federal Constitution." The Pinckney Plan did not figure in the debates during the Convention, but it was one of the documents later used by John Rutledge's committee of detail in drafting a complete constitution. Although the original of Pinckney's Plan was lost, he produced a copy of it for the national archives in 1818. Its Article VIII called for the establishment of the office of President in the following words:

The executive power of the United States shall be vested in a President of the United States of America, which shall be his style; and his title shall be His Excellency. He shall be elected for _____ years; and shall be re-eligible.

He shall from time to time give information to the Legislature, of the State of the Union, and recommend to their consideration the measures he may think necessary. He shall take care that the laws of the United States be duly executed. He shall commission all the officers of the United States; and except as to ambassadors, other ministers, and judges of the Supreme Court, he shall nominate, and, with the consent of the Senate, appoint, all other officers of the United States. He shall receive public ministers from foreign nations; and may correspond with the Executives of the different States. He shall have power to grant pardons and reprieves, except in impeachments. He shall be Commander-in-Chief of the army and navy of the United States, and of the militia of the several States; and shall receive a compensation which shall not be increased or diminished during his continuance in office. At entering on the duties of his office, he shall take an oath faithfully to execute the duties of a President of the United States. He shall be removed from his office on impeachment by the House of Delegates, and conviction in the Supreme Court, of treason, bribery, or corruption. In case of his removal, death, resignation, or disability, the President of the Senate shall exercise the duties of his office until another President be chosen. And in case of the death of the President of the Senate, the Speaker of the House of Delegates shall do so.

Madison Establishes the President's Authority

THE CONSTITUTIONAL CONVENTION began studying the parts of the Virginia Plan concerned with the Chief Executive on Friday, June 1, 1787, and continued to debate them for the next several days. On the first day of the debate the Convention adopted a motion by James Madison of Virginia to fix the extent of the Chief Executive's authority by changing the Resolution to read: "Resolved that a National Executive be instituted with power to carry into effect the national laws, to appoint to offices in cases not otherwise provided for . . ."

Next, the Convention began studying the question of how long the Chief Executive should serve. James Wilson of Pennsylvania and Roger Sherman of Connecticut proposed that the term of office be for three years. But Charles Pinckney of South Carolina and George Mason of Virginia spoke out for a term of seven years. Five states voted aye, four voted no, and one, Massachusetts, was divided. The president of the Convention, George Washington, decided that the motion for a term of seven years had carried.

The Delegates at First Reject an Electoral College

THE CONSTITUTIONAL CONVENTION delegates then turned their attention to deciding whether the Chief Executive should be elected by the people or be appointed by the Congress. James Wilson proposed the establishment of a system of presidential electors to be chosen by the people. But on June 2 this proposal was turned down by a vote of eight to two and by the same number of votes it was decided that the Chief Executive should be elected by Congress.

Benjamin Franklin of Pennsylvania made an impassioned plea that the Chief Executive not be paid a salary, arguing that a higher caliber of man would be found for the office if there was no question of personal gain on his part. His motion was seconded by Alexander Hamilton of New York, but the Convention postponed debate or voting upon it, rather than hurt the old man's feelings by abruptly voting it down.

John Dickinson of Delaware, who had written the Articles of Confederation, moved "That the Executive be made removable by the National Legislature on the request of a majority of the Legislatures of individual States." He believed this would keep the states in a controlling position over the Chief Executive. But his motion was defeated, with all states except Delaware voting against it. The Convention then voted to make the Chief Executive ineligible for re-election after seven years in office.

Hugh Williamson of North Carolina moved to add that the Executive "be removable on impeachment and conviction of malpractice or neglect of duty." This was approved by the delegates.

Should the Executive Be One Man or Three?

TOWARD THE CLOSE OF THE SESSION on Saturday, June 2, John Rutledge of South Carolina, who later was to be appointed Chief Justice by George Washington but then would be rejected by the U. S. Senate, moved that the blank for the number of persons to serve as Executive be filled with the words, "one person." Rutledge said that the reasons were so obvious and conclusive in favor of a single Chief Executive that he believed no one would oppose the motion.

However, Edmund Randolph, who later was to be the first Attorney General of the United States under President Washington, spoke out against the single Chief Executive. He said he believed the people would regard the establishment of a Chief Executive as resembling a monarchy. Instead, he proposed that the Executive be made up of three men on equal footing to be chosen from different parts of the country. The Convention adjourned that day before a vote could be taken on the matter.

After considering the matter over Sunday, the Convention resumed debate on the question of the single Chief Executive on Monday, June 4. James Wilson of Pennsylvania, who later was to be appointed by President Washington as one of the first Associate Justices of the Supreme Court, argued eloquently for a single Chief Executive. He said that with a triumvirate holding the executive power he foresaw "nothing but uncontrolled, continued and violent animosities." He said these quarrels would "diffuse their poison through the other branches of government, through the states, and at length through the people at large."

Finally, the delegates agreed upon a single Chief Executive, although three states opposed the resolution—New York, Delaware, and Maryland.

Establishment of the Veto Power

THE CONVENTION then turned its attention to a discussion of the part of the Virginia Plan that called for the establishment of a "Council of revision" to exercise a veto on legislation.

Elbridge Gerry of Massachusetts, who later was to serve as Vice President under President James Madison, moved that instead of considering the "Council of revision," the delegates should adopt a proposal "that the National Executive shall have a right to negative any legislative act, which shall not be afterwards passed by __ parts of each branch of the National Legislature."

James Wilson and Alexander Hamilton made an effort to obtain an absolute veto for the Chief Executive, eliminating any possibility of Congress overriding a presidential veto. Benjamin Franklin strongly opposed this, pointing out that the Chief Executive could use such a power to extort money from the legislature. He commented that "The Executive will be always increasing here, as elsewhere, till it ends in a monarchy."

The delegations unanimously voted down the idea of giving the Chief Executive an absolute veto, and agreed to fill the blank in Gerry's resolution with the word "two-thirds." In a final vote on the entire resolution giving the Chief Executive a limited veto that could be overridden by a two-thirds vote of each house of Congress, eight states voted for the resolution and two opposed—Connecticut and Maryland.

On Wednesday, June 6, Wilson and Madison made an effort to revive the idea of a "Council of revision" that would include representatives of the judicial branch in the exercise of veto over legislation. But their resolution was voted down, with only Connecticut, New York, and Virginia voting aye.

The question of how the Chief Executive was to be chosen was again brought up for debate on Saturday, June 9. Elbridge Gerry of Massachusetts proposed that the Chief Executive be elected by the governors of the states, instead of by Congress as had been previously agreed upon. He said he believed that the governors, being executives themselves, would be more likely to choose an able Chief Executive than would the legislature. However, the delegates voted down his idea.

The Revised Virginia Plan Resolutions

ON WEDNESDAY, JUNE 13, after the delegates had completed their initial debates on the Virginia Plan, the wording of the two resolutions concerned with the Chief Executive stood as follows:

> Resolved, that a National Executive be instituted, to consist of a single person; to be chosen by the National Legislature, for the term of seven years; with power to carry into execution the national laws; to appoint to offices in cases not otherwise provided for; to be ineligible a second time; and to be removable on impeachment and conviction of malpractices or neglect of duty; to receive a fixed stipend by which he may be compensated for the devotion of his time to the public service, to be paid out of the National Treasury.

> Resolved, that the National Executive shall have a right to negative any legislative act, which shall not be afterwards passed by two-thirds of each branch of the National Legislature.

The New Jersey Plan

SEVERAL OF THE SMALLER STATES had become increasingly concerned that the Convention was moving toward too strong a centralized government. So on Friday, June 15, William Paterson of New Jersey, who would later serve as an Associate Justice of the Supreme Court, presented what became known as the "New Jersey Plan." Its provisions for the executive branch were as follows:

Resolved, that the United States in Congress be authorized to elect a Federal Executive, to consist of ___ persons, to continue in office for the term of ___ years; to receive punctually, at stated times, a fixed compensation for their services, in which no increase nor diminution shall be made so as to affect the persons composing the Executive at the time of such increase or diminution; to be paid out of the Federal treasury; to be incapable of holding any other office or appointment during their time of service, and for ___ years thereafter: to be ineligible a second time, and removable by Congress, on application by a majority of the Executives of the several States; that the Executive, besides their general authority to execute the Federal acts, ought to appoint all Federal officers not otherwise provided for, and to direct all military operations; provided, that none of the persons composing the Federal Executive shall, on any occasion, take command of any troops, so as personally to conduct any military enterprise, as General, or in any other capacity.

Alexander Hamilton's Plan

As THE CONVENTION began to debate the respective merits of the New Jersey Plan versus the Virginia Plan, Alexander Hamilton spoke out against both, saying that neither provided for a strong enough central government. In turn, he presented his own plan. In Hamilton's Plan the provision for the Chief Executive was as follows:

The supreme Executive authority of the United States to be vested in a Governor, to be elected to serve during good behaviour; the election to be made by Electors chosen by the people in the Election Districts aforesaid. The authorities and functions of the Executive to be as follows: to have a negative on all laws about to be passed, and the execution of all laws passed; to have the direction of war when authorized or begun; to have, with the advice and approbation of the Senate, the power of making all treaties; to have the sole appointment of the heads or chief officers of the Departments of Finance, War, and Foreign Affairs; to have the nomination of all other officers (ambassadors to foreign nations included), subject to the approbation or rejection of the Senate; to have the power of pardoning all offences except treason, which he shall not pardon without the approbation of the Senate.

On the death, resignation, or removal of the Governor, his authorities to be exercised by the President of the Senate till a successor be appointed.

The delegates voted to postpone discussion of the New Jersey Plan and ignored Hamilton's Plan. For the next month the delegates devoted their consideration almost entirely to the provisions for the legislative branch of the government. It was not until Tuesday, July 17 that the resolutions concerning the executive branch again came up for discussion.

Rejection of Direct Election by the People

GOUVERNEUR MORRIS of Pennsylvania, who later became a U.S. senator, moved that the Chief Executive be elected by the citizens of the United States, instead of by the national legislature. He said: "If the people should elect, they will never fail to prefer some man of distinguished character, or services . . . If the Legislature elect, it will be the work of intrigue, of cabal, and of faction . . ."

The proposal for direct election by the people was opposed by Roger Sherman of Connecticut, Charles Pinckney of South Carolina, George Mason of Virginia, and Hugh Williamson of North Carolina. Mason said he believed "it would be as unnatural to refer the choice of a proper character for Chief Magistrate to the people, as it would, to refer a trial of colors to a blind man."

When Morris' resolution was put to a motion, only his own state of Pennsylvania voted for it. All the other states voted no.

By a vote of six to four, the delegations voted to strike out the words "to be ineligible a second time." Gouverneur Morris in supporting the motion pointed out that if the Chief Executive was ineligible for re-election it would tend to "destroy the great motive to good behaviour, the hope of being rewarded by a re-appointment. It was saying to him, make hay while the sun shines."

Delegates Fear Development of a Monarchy

THE CONVENTION next spent considerable time discussing whether or not to change the Chief Executive's term of office from seven years to "during good behaviour." Gouverneur Morris and James Madison were among the chief supporters of this proposed change. They saw this as a further way to free the Chief Executive from dependence on the national legislature. George Mason of Virginia made the main speech against the motion, declaring that "an Executive during good behaviour" was "a softer name only for an Executive for life." He said he believed the next easy step was to a hereditary monarchy. The delegates decided by a vote of six to four to retain the seven-year term for the Chief Executive.

Establishment of an Electoral System for Choosing the Chief Executive

ON THURSDAY, JULY 19, the Convention again took up the question of how the Chief Executive should be elected. James Madison made an impassioned address calling upon the delegates to free the Chief Executive from any dependence on the national legislature. He said, "If it be a fundamental principle of free government that the Legislative, Executive and Judiciary powers should be *separately* exercised, it is equally so that they be *independently* exercised."

Oliver Ellsworth of Connecticut, who later was to become the second Chief Justice of the United States, moved to strike out the provision for election of the Chief Executive by the national legislature and substitute, "to be chosen by Electors, appointed by the Legislatures of the States in the following ratio; to wit: one for each State not exceeding two hundred thousand inhabitants; two for each above that number and not exceeding three hundred thousand; and three for each State exceeding three hundred thousand." The Convention voted to accept this motion, but deferred action on the ratio of number of electors for each state.

On motion of Oliver Ellsworth, the Convention decided to reduce the length of the Chief Executive's term from seven years to six years.

On Friday, July 20, Elbridge Gerry moved that the electors for the Chief Executive be allotted to the states in the following ratio: New Hampshire, one; Massachusetts, three; Rhode Island, one; Connecticut, two; New York, two; New Jersey, two; Pennsylvania, three; Delaware, one; Maryland, two; Virginia, three; North Carolina, two; South Carolina, two; Georgia, one. Despite opposition by the smaller states, the Convention adopted Gerry's proposal by a vote of six to four. It was further agreed, "that the Electors of the Executive shall not be members of the National Legislature, nor officers of the United States, nor shall the Electors themselves be eligible to the supreme magistracy."

That same day the delegates spent a substantial amount of time discussing whether the Chief Executive should be made liable to impeachment and removal from office. Benjamin Franklin, James Madison, and Edmund Randolph led the arguments for preserving the right of impeachment. Franklin pointed out that without impeachment the only recourse for removal of a corrupt Chief Executive was assassination. The Convention retained the impeachment clause by a vote of eight to two, with only Massachusetts and South Carolina opposing.

Attempt to Modify the Presidential Veto

ON SATURDAY, JULY 21, James Wilson of Pennsylvania revived the idea that members of the judiciary should be associated with the Chief Executive in exercising the veto power over legislation. James Madison supported the proposition on the basis that it would give the judicial branch "an additional opportunity of defending itself against Legislative encroachments."

Elbridge Gerry opposed Wilson's motion because he felt that it would lead to a "combining and mixing together" of the executive and judiciary. And Nathaniel Gorham, also of Massachusetts, opposed the measure, pointing out that since there would be only one Chief Executive and several judges the proposal would have the effect of taking the veto power "entirely out of the Executive hands, and, instead of enabling him to defend himself, would enable the Judges to sacrifice him."

John Rutledge of South Carolina also opposed the proposition saying that of all men judges were the most unfit to be given the veto power on legislation. He said, "Judges ought never to give their opinion on a law, till it comes before them."

The inclusion of the judiciary in the executive veto power narrowly missed being added to the Constitution. Four states opposed the measure—Massachusetts, Delaware, North Carolina, and South Carolina; three states voted in favor—Connecticut, Maryland, and Virginia; and two states were divided —Pennsylvania and Georgia.

The Convention next began considering a motion by James Madison that the Chief Executive should nominate the members of the judiciary and that these nominations should become appointments unless two thirds of the Senate disagreed. But several delegates objected to taking the power of appointment away from the national legislature, so the motion went down to defeat by a vote of three for and six against.

Choosing of the President Returned to Congress

AFTER SEVERAL DAYS debating other aspects of the Constitution, the delegates on Tuesday, July 24, again took up the question of how the Chief Executive was to be elected. William C. Houston of New Jersey moved that, instead of having the Chief Executive chosen by special electors as had already been agreed to, the national legislature should be given the task. He said he believed the use of electors would cause extreme inconvenience and considerable expense. He also said he believed that capable men would not agree to serve as electors, particularly in the more distant states.

When the delegations were polled on the question, they reversed their previous stand, and by a vote of seven to four agreed to put the election of the Chief Executive back into the hands of the national legislature. Then they fell to arguing about all aspects of the Chief Executive, the length of his term of office, and whether or not he should be eligible for re-election. After two days of wrangling, the Convention decided on Thursday, July 26, by a vote of seven to three to limit the Chief Executive's term to seven years and make him ineligible for a second term. Later that same day the Convention turned all the resulting resolutions over to a Committee of Detail headed by John Rutledge of South Carolina to write them up into the form of a Constitution. In addition the Convention passed along to the Committee the New Jersey Plan and the Pinckney Plan and adjourned for ten days.

Draft by the Committee of Detail

WHEN THE CONVENTION reconvened on Monday, August 6, Rutledge presented the delegates with a draft of the Constitution which apparently had drawn heavily upon the Pinckney Plan for its wording concerning the Chief Executive. Its Article X read as follows:

SECTION 1. The Executive power of the United States shall be vested in a single person. His style shall be, "The President of the United States of America," and his title shall be, "His Excellency." He shall be elected by ballot by the Legislature. He shall hold his office during the term of seven years; but shall not be elected a second time.

SECTION 2. He shall, from time to time, give information to the Legislature of the state of the Union. He may recommend to their consideration such measures as he shall judge necessary, and expedient. He may convene them on extraordinary occasions. In case of disagreement between the two Houses, with regard to the time of adjournment, he may adjourn them to such time as he thinks proper. He shall take care that the laws of the United States be duly and faithfully executed. He shall commission all the officers of the United States; and shall appoint officers in all cases not otherwise provided for by this Constitution. He shall receive Ambassadors, and may correspond with the supreme executives of the several States. He shall have power to grant reprieves and pardons, but his pardon shall not be pleadable in bar of an impeachment. He shall be Commander-in-chief of the army and navy of the United States, and of the militia of the several States. He shall, at stated times, receive for his services a compensation, which shall neither be increased nor diminished during his continuance in office. Before he shall enter on the duties of his department, he shall take the following oath or affirmation, "I _____ solemnly swear, (or affirm) that I will faithfully execute the office of President of the United States of America." He shall be removed from his office on impeachment by the House of Representatives, and conviction in the Supreme Court, of treason, bribery, or corruption. In case of his removal, as aforesaid, death, resignation, or disability to discharge the powers and duties of his office, the President of the Senate shall exercise those powers and duties, until another President of the United States be chosen, or until the disability of the President be removed.

In the new Constitution prepared by the Committee of Detail, the provision for a presidential veto was moved to Article VI, which dealt with the procedures of the two houses of Congress.

The Convention did not take up Article X, relating to the President, until Friday, August 24, and the debate on the provisions extended until Monday, August 27. Most efforts to change the Article, whether by those trying to strengthen the office or by those trying to weaken it, were voted down. On August 31, the Convention turned over to a Committee of Eleven (with one delegate from each state) such knotty problems as how the Chief Executive should be elected.

Report by the Committee of Eleven

ON TUESDAY, SEPTEMBER 4, the Committee of Eleven reported back to the Convention their solutions for the various problems surrounding the office of the President. They recommended creating a Vice President and the establishment of a four-year term of office for both President and Vice President. And the Committee solved the problem of how the President and Vice President should be chosen by drawing up plans for an elaborate electoral system that would leave the method of choosing presidential electors up to the legislatures of the various states. The Committee established the qualifications for being President—a natural-born citizen, at least thirty-five years old, and a resident within the United States for at least fourteen years. Another important change by the Committee gave the President the power to make treaties with the advice and consent of the Senate and to appoint judges of the Supreme Court.

For the rest of the first week of September the Convention debated the changes in the article dealing with the office of the President, making some minor but few major changes. Then on Saturday, September 8, a five-man Committee of Revision was appointed to revise the style and arrangement of the articles that had been agreed to. The Committee included James Madison, Gouverneur Morris, Alexander Hamilton, Rufus King, and William Samuel Johnson.

Final Version of the Constitution

THE COMMITTEE OF REVISION submitted its report on Wednesday, September 12. In the new Constitution prepared by the Committee, the provisions concerning the President became Article II. The wording was approved with a few minor changes on Saturday, September 15. And on Monday, September 17, 1787, the delegates approved and signed the final version of the Constitution of the United States. The wording of Article II follows:

SECTION 1. The executive Power shall be vested in a President of the United States of America. He shall hold his Office during the Term of four Years, and, together with the Vice President, chosen for the same Term, be elected as follows:

Each State shall appoint, in such Manner as the Legislature thereof may direct, a Number of Electors, equal to the whole Number of Senators and Representatives to which the State may be entitled in the Congress: but no Senator or Representative, or Person holding an Office of Trust or Profit under the United States, shall be appointed an Elector.

The Electors shall meet in their respective States, and vote by Ballot for two Persons, of whom one at least shall not be an Inhabitant of the same

State with themselves. And they shall make a List of all the Persons voted for, and of the Number of Votes for each; which List they shall sign and certify, and transmit sealed to the Seat of the Government of the United States, directed to the President of the Senate. The President of the Senate shall, in the Presence of the Senate and House of Representatives, open all the Certificates, and the Votes shall then be counted. The Person having the greatest Number of Votes shall be the President, if such Number be a Majority of the whole Number of Electors appointed; and if there be more than one who have such Majority, and have an equal Number of Votes, then the House of Representatives shall immediately choose by Ballot one of them for President; and if no Person have a Majority, then from the five highest on the List the said House shall in like manner choose the President. But in choosing the President, the Votes shall be taken by States, the Representation from each State having one Vote; a quorum for this Purpose shall consist of a Member or Members from two-thirds of the States, and a Majority of all the States shall be necessary to a Choice. In every Case, after the Choice of the President, the Person having the greatest Number of Votes of the Electors shall be the Vice President. But if there should remain two or more who have equal Votes, the Senate shall choose from them by Ballot the Vice President. *(This procedure was superseded later by Amendment 12.)*

The Congress may determine the Time of choosing the Electors, and the Day on which they shall give their Votes; which Day shall be the same throughout the United States.

No Person except a natural born Citizen, or a Citizen of the United States, at the time of the Adoption of this Constitution, shall be eligible to the Office of President; neither shall any Person be eligible to that Office who shall not have attained to the Age of thirty-five Years, and been fourteen Years a Resident within the United States.

In Case of the Removal of the President from Office, or of his Death, Resignation, or Inability to discharge the Powers and Duties of the said Office, the Same shall devolve on the Vice President, and the Congress may by Law provide for the Case of Removal, Death, Resignation or Inability, both of the President and Vice President, declaring what Officer shall then act as President, and such Officer shall act accordingly, until the Disability be removed, or a President shall be elected.

The President shall, at stated Times, receive for his Services, a Compensation, which shall neither be increased nor diminished during the Period for which he shall have been elected, and he shall not receive within that Period any other Emolument from the United States, or any of them.

Before he enter on the Execution of his Office, he shall take the following Oath or Affirmation:—"I do solemnly swear (or affirm) that I will faithfully execute the Office of President of the United States, and will to the best of my Ability, preserve, protect and defend the Constitution of the United States."

SECTION 2. The President shall be Commander in Chief of the Army and Navy of the United States, and of the Militia of the several States, when called into the actual Service of the United States; he may require the Opinion, in writing, of the principal Officer in each of the executive Departments, upon any Subject relating to the Duties of their respective Offices, and he shall have Power to grant Reprieves and Pardons for Offences against the United States, except in Cases of Impeachment.

He shall have Power, by and with the Advice and Consent of the Senate, to make Treaties, provided two-thirds of the Senators present concur; and he shall nominate, and by and with the Advice and Consent of the Senate, shall appoint Ambassadors, other public Ministers and Consuls, Judges of the supreme Court, and all other Officers of the United States, whose Appointments are not herein otherwise provided for, and which shall be established by Law: but the Congress may by Law vest the Appointment of such inferior Officers, as they think proper, in the President alone, in the Courts of Law, or in the Heads of Departments.

The President shall have Power to fill up all Vacancies that may happen during the Recess of the Senate, by granting Commissions which shall expire at the End of their next Session.

SECTION 3. He shall from time to time give to the Congress Information of the State of the Union, and recommend to their Consideration such Measures as he shall judge necessary and expedient; he may, on extraordinary Occasions, convene both Houses, or either of them, and in Case of Disagreement between them, with Respect to the Time of Adjournment, he may adjourn them to such Time as he shall think proper; he shall receive Ambassadors and other public Ministers; he shall take Care that the Laws be faithfully executed, and shall Commission all the Officers of the United States.

SECTION 4. The President, Vice President and all civil Officers of the United States, shall be removed from Office on Impeachment for, and Conviction of, Treason, Bribery, or other high Crimes and Misdemeanors.

Changing the Presidency by Amendment

ALTHOUGH THE CONSTITUTION as written went into effect in 1789, the making of the presidency had hardly begun. The adoption of amendments to the Constitution have modified the presidency in several ways, although none has directly changed the powers of the Chief Executive.

The need for a change in the electoral system developed from the presidential election of 1800 in which Thomas Jefferson was the Democratic-Republican candidate for President and Aaron Burr was the party's candidate for Vice President. When the electoral votes were counted, Federalist John Adams and his running mate Charles Cotesworth Pinckney had been defeated by the Democratic-Republicans. However, a crisis developed when the electors gave Jefferson and Burr seventy-three electoral votes each without designating which should be President. The Constitution provided that such a tie was to be decided by the House of Representatives. If the Democratic-Republicans had been in control of Congress there might have been no problem. But the Sixth Congress, still in session, was controlled by the Federalists, who saw an opportunity to confound their political enemies. Playing to the ambitions of Burr, they held the presidency in ransom from Jefferson with threats to give it to Burr unless they received guarantees that Federalist officeholders would continue to hold their jobs and that Federalist policies would be followed by the new administration. Jefferson refused to bargain. Finally, the Federalists gave up the game, awarding the presidency to Jefferson on the thirty-sixth ballot.

To ensure that such a deadlock between candidates from the same party never again took place, Amendment Twelve to the Constitution was ratified in 1804. It required the electors to vote separately and specifically for the President and for the Vice President. For a candidate to win an office, the amendment required that he have a majority of the electoral votes. In the event no presidential candidate received an electoral majority, the House of Representatives would choose the President from among the three candidates with the most electoral votes. If a vice-presidential candidate failed to receive a majority, the Senate would decide the winner.

Since the adoption of the amendment, only one President, John Quincy

Adams, has had to be elected by the House of Representatives, and only one Vice President, Richard M. Johnson, has been chosen by the Senate.

Amendments to the Constitution gradually have broadened the electorate eligible to vote for presidential electors. Blacks received the right to vote with Amendment Fifteen to the Constitution in 1870. However, they and many other poor persons continued to be denied their voting rights by poll taxes until that form of discrimination was outlawed by Amendment Twenty-four in 1964. Women won the right to vote in presidential elections for the first time with Amendment Nineteen in 1920. Residents of Washington, D.C., first received the right to vote for President with Amendment Twenty-three in 1961. Youths from eighteen through twenty were enfranchised by Amendment Twenty-six in 1971.

Until 1933 newly elected Presidents and members of Congress did not take office until March 4—four months after the national election. In the early days poor transportation made this a reasonable length of time. Outgoing congressmen and Presidents who remained in office during this four-month period were called *lame ducks*. During the Great Depression a lame-duck President Hoover and a lame-duck Congress held power for four months while the economy suffered and President-elect Franklin D. Roosevelt waited in the wings. As a result, Amendment Twenty, also called the Lame-Duck Amendment, was ratified in 1933. Inauguration Day for the President and Vice President was changed to January 20 and the meeting date of a new Congress to January 3. The first inauguration on the new date occurred when President Roosevelt was sworn in for his second term in 1937. Amendment Twenty also provided that the Vice President-elect should become President if the President-elect died before assuming office.

Republicans had become increasingly infuriated with President Franklin D. Roosevelt as he broke precedent by winning a third term in 1940 and a fourth term in 1944. To prevent such a thing happening again, they obtained ratification of Amendment Twenty-two in 1951, forbidding a person from being elected President more than twice. A President who has served more than two years of a term to which he was not elected cannot run for more than one additional term. Under this amendment, if President Ford had won the election of 1976, he could not have run for re-election in 1980 because he already had served more than two years in filling out President Nixon's term.

Concern was engendered in 1963 by the vacancy left in the office of Vice President after Lyndon B. Johnson succeeded the assassinated President John F. Kennedy. As a result Amendment Twenty-five was adopted in 1967. It gives the President power to fill a vacancy in the office of Vice President by nominating a new Vice President to take office after confirmation by a majority vote of each house of Congress. The amendment first was used after Vice

President Spiro Agnew resigned in October 1973. He was replaced by the appointment of Gerald Ford to the post by President Nixon. After Ford succeeded Nixon upon the latter's resignation, the amendment again was used as Ford appointed Nelson A. Rockefeller to the vice presidency.

Procedures by which the Vice President can take over as Acting President also were established by Amendment Twenty-five as follows:

> "Whenever the Vice President and a majority of either the principal officers of the executive departments or of such other body as Congress may by law provide, transmit to the President pro tempore of the Senate and the Speaker of the House of Representatives their written declaration that the President is unable to discharge the powers and duties of his office, the Vice President shall immediately assume the powers and duties of the office as Acting President.

> "Thereafter, when the President transmits to the President pro tempore of the Senate and the Speaker of the House of Representatives his written declaration that no inability exists, he shall resume the powers and duties of his office unless the Vice President and a majority of either the principal officers of the executive department or of such other body as Congress may by law provide, transmit within four days to the President pro tempore of the Senate and the Speaker of the House of Representatives their written declaration that the President is unable to discharge the powers and duties of his office. Thereupon Congress shall decide the issue, assembling within forty-eight hours for that purpose if not in session. If the Congress, within twenty-one days after receipt of the latter written declaration, or, if Congress is not in session, within twenty-one days after Congress is required to assemble, determines by two-thirds vote of both houses that the President is unable to discharge the powers and duties of his office, the Vice President shall continue to discharge the same as Acting President; otherwise, the President shall resume the powers and duties of his office."

Changes by Precedent and Constitutional Interpretation

THE CONSTITUTION gives the President the combined powers and duties of chief of state, chief executive, director of foreign policy, and commander in chief of the armed forces. In addition he was given veto power over legislation and the right to appoint federal officials, including the justices of the

Supreme Court. The Constitution never says a word about his role as leader of a political party. Yet that role has become an essential part of the presidency through precedent, largely set by Thomas Jefferson. In like manner, scores of other actions of the President have been set by precedent. Whether or not the televised debates between President Ford and his challenger, Jimmy Carter, have set a precedent that will be followed by future Presidents remains to be seen.

A strong President may seize additional power through his interpretation of the Constitution. For example, Andrew Jackson prepared to use federal troops to prevent South Carolina from seceding from the Union in the 1830s, but James Buchanan did not feel he had the power to do the same thing when the Confederate States seceded in the 1860s.

The Supreme Court may modify the President's power by its interpretation of the Constitution. President Truman believed he had the power to seize the steel industry in 1952 when a strike threatened to shut the mills during the Korean War. After he had done so, the Supreme Court ruled that he had acted unconstitutionally, returning the mills to their owners with the consequence that they were shut down by a strike for seven weeks.

Congress and the President often clash with each other in challenges of power, especially when the Chief Executive is of the opposite party from the one controlling Congress. The Radical Republicans that had a majority in Congress in 1867 passed the Tenure of Office Act to prevent Democratic President Andrew Johnson from discharging federal officials without the consent of the Senate. Positive that Congress had acted unconstitutionally, Johnson proceeded to fire a Radical Republican cabinet officer. The House of Representatives impeached him, and the Senate came within one vote of convicting and removing him. Such battles, though seldom so extreme, are likely to continue as long as the Constitution with its system of checks and balances remains the law of the land.

PRESIDENTIAL HISTORIC SITES

OUR NATION has preserved more than a hundred historic sites commemorating and memorializing the Presidents. Visits to these sites give Americans a clearer understanding of the varied economic backgrounds of the Presidents and of the factors that shaped their lives. One or more homes of every President except McKinley have been preserved or restored. Most are open to the public.

Federal Hall National Memorial at Wall and Nassau streets in New York commemorates the nation's first capitol under the Constitution. However, the building which housed the first U.S. Congress and in which George Washington took his first oath of office as President was demolished in 1812. The present building of Greek Revival architecture was built in 1835–42, serving first as the New York City Custom House and then as the U.S. Sub-Treasury. Administered by the National Park Service, it contains many exhibits of historic events.

Independence National Historical Park in Philadelphia provides one of the most extensive exhibits associated with the Presidents. Independence Hall includes the restored Assembly Room where future Presidents Washington, John Adams, Jefferson, Madison, and Monroe helped found the nation and where the Declaration of Independence and the Constitution were debated and adopted. The park also includes Congress Hall, where the U.S. Congress met from 1790 to 1800, where Washington was inaugurated for his second term in 1793, and John Adams for his single term in 1797. The Liberty Bell that announced the adoption of the Declaration of Independence is shown in a separate pavilion. The National Park Service also has reconstructed the Graff House in which Jefferson wrote the Declaration of Independence and the City Tavern where future Presidents and other Founding Fathers lived while in Philadelphia.

In Washington, D.C., visitors can spend many days immersing themselves in the history of the Presidents at such sites as the White House, which has been the residence of all the Presidents except George Washington; the U. S. Capitol, where Presidents have received their oath of office since Thomas

Jefferson in 1801; the Lafayette Square Historic District across Pennsylvania Avenue from the White House, which square includes St. John's Episcopal Church, known as the "Church of the Presidents," and Blair House, which was occupied by President Truman in 1948–52 while the White House was being renovated; and other historic buildings and memorials. About two miles northeast of the White House is the "Corn Riggs" house that was used as a summer home by Presidents Buchanan, Lincoln, Hayes, and Arthur. The Kalorama residential area, about a mile from the White House, has five houses that once were residences of William Howard Taft (2215 Wyoming Street), Woodrow Wilson (2340 S Street), Warren G. Harding (2314 Wyoming Street), Herbert Hoover (2300 S Street), and Franklin D. Roosevelt (2131 R Street).

About seventy miles northwest of Washington, D.C., lies the presidential retreat, Camp David, which was established by President Franklin D. Roosevelt in 1942 as "Shangri-La." Although Camp David is not open to the public, it is surrounded by Maryland's Catoctin Mountain Park that has hiking trails, picnic tables, and camping areas.

Mount Rushmore National Memorial near Keystone, South Dakota, is the most grandiose monument to the Presidents. Huge likenesses of Washington, Jefferson, Lincoln, and Theodore Roosevelt, each sixty feet high, were carved in the granite face of Mount Rushmore by sculptor Gutzon Borglum in 1925 to 1939, and were completed by his son.

Colonial Williamsburg, the capital of Virginia from 1699 to 1780, is a restoration village that attracts more than a million tourists a year. Its many shops, buildings, and costumed guides vividly bring to life the days when George Washington sat in the colonial legislature and when Thomas Jefferson was governor.

George Washington

WAKEFIELD, George Washington's birthplace, was destroyed by fire in about 1779 and was never rebuilt. However, in 1931–32 the Wakefield National Memorial Association and the federal government built a brick Georgian house on the site, about thirty-eight miles east of Fredericksburg, Virginia. The House and surrounding grounds are maintained by the National Park Service as the Washington Birthplace National Monument. About a mile northwest of the memorial home is the Washington family burial plot that contains the graves of the President's father, grandfather, and great-grandfather.

Mount Vernon, Washington's plantation home during most of his life, stands overlooking the Potomac River in Virginia, about fifteen miles south of Washington, D.C. The mansion and its surrounding estate of about five hundred acres are maintained as a national shrine by the Mount Vernon Ladies' Association of the Union. A library on the grounds of Mount Vernon houses Washington's personal papers and documents. The tomb of George and Martha Washington stands to the south of the main house.

The 555-foot Washington Monument rises to the south of the White House in Washington, D.C. It was built in 1848 to 1885 by the Washington National Monument Society and the federal government. Built of white marble quarried in Maryland, the Washington Monument was designed by architect Robert Mills. Visitors may ride to the top in an elevator or climb the 898 steps of the interior stairway.

Fort Necessity National Battlefield near Uniontown, Pennsylvania, preserves the site of a battle Washington led against the French in the French and Indian War.

Valley Forge National Historical Park west of Philadelphia, Pennsylvania, contains the site of the camp where Washington and his troops suffered hardship in the winter of 1777–78 and the stone building that was his headquarters.

John Adams and John Quincy Adams

THE BIRTHPLACE of John Adams, an eight-room New England salt-box house, is maintained by the Quincy Historical Society in Quincy, Massachusetts. The frame house, built about 1681, was purchased by John Adams' father in 1720. It remained in the possession of the Adams family until being given to the city in 1940.

Next door to John Adams' birthplace is the similar eight-room frame house which became his home and law office after his marriage in 1764. Future President John Quincy Adams was born in the house in 1767. It is also preserved by the Quincy Historical Society.

Peacefield, a much larger house that John Adams purchased in 1787, also stands in Quincy, maintained by the National Park Service as the Adams National Historic Site. John Adams retired to this house from the presidency in 1801 and lived there until his death in 1826. John Quincy Adams and other descendants resided there until 1927.

The bodies of John Adams, John Quincy Adams, and their wives lie in a crypt beneath the basement of Quincy's United First Parish Church. This Unitarian church was built in 1827–28 with funds largely provided by John Quincy Adams.

Thomas Jefferson

JEFFERSON was born at his father's plantation house, Shadwell, about two miles southeast of Charlottesville, Virginia, but Shadwell was destroyed by fire in 1770.

The future author of the Declaration of Independence spent seven years of his boyhood, from 1745 to 1752, living with his parents at Tuckahoe, the Randolph family estate about thirteen miles west of Richmond, Virginia. Tuckahoe still stands as an outstanding example of Georgian-style plantation architecture, but because it is privately owned as a residence it is not open to the public.

Jefferson inherited Shadwell and its 1,053-acre plantation when his father died in 1757. After clearing and leveling a nearby hilltop, Jefferson began construction of a new home called Monticello in 1769. He moved into it upon Shadwell's destruction in the following year. He kept making alterations and additions to the house for the rest of his life. Today the thirty-five-room mansion on Route 53 near Charlottesville, Virginia, is maintained by the Thomas Jefferson Memorial Association and is open to the public. Jefferson is buried in a small family graveyard near Monticello.

Poplar Forest, a house designed and built by Jefferson in 1806–19 as a summer home, stands about six miles west of Lynchburg, Virginia. Used as a family residence, it is not open to the public.

The Thomas Jefferson Memorial stands in Washington, D.C., in a beautiful setting of Japanese cherry trees at the edge of the Tidal Basin. Designed in the classic style similar to that used by Jefferson in his construction of Monticello and of the rotunda of the University of Virginia, the memorial contains a nineteen-foot statue of Jefferson sculpted by Rudulph Evans. The memorial was built in 1938–43.

Jefferson National Expansion Memorial in downtown St. Louis, Missouri, commemorates Jefferson's Louisiana Purchase and the westward movement it triggered. The memorial features a 630-foot-high stainless steel arch designed by architect Eero Saarinen. Visitors can ride an elevator to the top of the arch, which was completed in 1965. A museum below the arch exhibits the history of the westward movement.

James Madison

MONTPELIER, Madison's home during most of his life, stands on Route 20 about four miles west of Orange, Virginia. The Georgian-style mansion was built by his father about 1760 and was inherited by the future President in 1801. He and his wife, Dolley, retired to Montpelier in 1817 after he completed his second term as President. Both are buried in Montpelier's family graveyard. Still used as a private residence, Montpelier is not open to the public except for the Madison gravesite. The James Madison Museum in nearby Orange exhibits relics of his life.

The Octagon House at 1799 New York Avenue N.W. in Washington, D.C., was occupied by the Madisons in 1814–15 after the White House was burned by British troops. Standing two blocks west of the White House, the Octagon House has been restored by the American Institute of Architects. Exhibited in the Treaty Room on the second floor is the desk on which Madison signed the Treaty of Ghent that ended the War of 1812.

The Dolley Madison House at the corner of Madison Place and H Street in Washington, D.C., was the residence of the former First Lady from 1837 to 1849 after she returned to the nation's capital following her husband's death. Although owned by the federal government, the house is not open to the public.

James Monroe

MONROE'S BIRTHPLACE near Colonial Beach, Virginia, was destroyed and no one knows its exact location.

Monroe's law office in Fredericksburg, Virginia, a one-story brick building, has been restored. It is open to the public as a museum, exhibiting a collection of his possessions.

Ash Lawn, the home where Monroe and his wife reared their children, is open to the public. It stands near Charlottesville, Virginia, on Route 53.

In 1818, during his first term as President, Monroe began building Oak Hill, a plantation mansion about eight miles south of Leesburg, Virginia. Designed by Thomas Jefferson, the house was completed in 1823. Monroe and his wife retired to Oak Hill after he left the presidency. He was forced to give up the mansion after financial reverses in 1830. Now privately owned, Oak Hill is closed to the public.

Monroe's tomb, a Gothic Revival cast-iron structure, stands in Hollywood Cemetery in Richmond, Virginia. His body, which had been interred in New York City after his death there in 1831, was returned to Virginia for reburial in 1858 to commemorate the centennial of his birth.

During the first six months of Monroe's presidency in 1817, the White House still was being restored from the damage incurred during the War of 1812, so during this time the Monroes resided in a three-and-a-half story row house at 2017 I Street N.W. in Washington, D.C. This house has been renovated by the Arts Club of Washington. It is used as a clubhouse and is not open to the public.

Andrew Jackson

THE HERMITAGE is Jackson's estate about twelve miles northeast of Nashville, Tennessee, on highway U.S. 70N. He acquired the 625-acre plantation in 1804, and lived there with his wife in a two-story log blockhouse until he built a brick house nearby in 1818–19. After fire destroyed the interior in 1834, Jackson rebuilt and expanded the mansion. He and his wife are buried in the garden of the Hermitage. The estate, including the original Jackson log house, is maintained by the Ladies' Hermitage Association and visitors are welcomed.

The 20,000-acre Jean Lafitte National Historic Park in Louisiana marks the site where Jackson, with the aid of Lafitte's pirates defeated the British in the Battle of New Orleans.

Martin Van Buren

LINDENWALD, standing about two miles south of Kinderhook, New York, on Route 9H, was Van Buren's home after he retired from the presidency in 1841. He bought it in 1839 from William Van Ness, who had been Aaron Burr's second in the 1804 duel in which Alexander Hamilton was fatally wounded. Van Buren enlarged the original house that had been built in 1797 by Van Ness' father. The house and its thirty-nine-acre estate was acquired in 1975 by the National Park Service as a national historic site. Van Buren is buried in nearby Kinderhook Cemetery.

In Washington, D.C., the house in which Van Buren resided while he was Secretary of State in 1829–31 is maintained as a museum by the National Trust for Historic Preservation. This townhouse at 748 Jackson Place near the White House was built in 1818 by naval hero Commodore Stephen Decatur.

William Henry Harrison

BERKELEY, about eight miles west of Charles City, Virginia, was the birthplace of Harrison. The brick mansion was built in 1726 by Harrison's grandfather and was the lifelong residence of his father, Benjamin Harrison, a signer of the Declaration of Independence. Although the upper floors of

Berkeley still are used as a private residence, the basement and first floor are open to visitors.

Grouseland at 3 West Scott Street in Vincennes, Indiana, is the mansion that Harrison built in 1803–4 while he was governor of the Indiana Territory. It is maintained as a museum by the Daughters of the American Revolution.

The Harrison Tomb State Memorial in North Bend, Ohio, marks his grave.

John Tyler

TYLER'S BIRTHPLACE, Greenway, in Charles City County, Virginia, is privately owned. The 1,200-acre estate lies about halfway between Richmond and Williamsburg. It includes a 12-room Williamsburg-style house and the remains of Tyler's honeymoon cottage.

Sherwood Forest, on Route 5, about four miles east of Charles City, Virginia, became Tyler's home after he retired from the presidency. Tyler expanded the house, which had been built about 1780. He named it after Robin Hood's hideaway because he considered himself a "political outlaw." Sherwood Forest is open to the public by appointment.

Tyler's grave is in Hollywood Cemetery in Richmond, Virginia.

James K. Polk

THE POLK HOME on Highway 31 four miles north of Columbia, Tennessee, is maintained by the James K. Polk Memorial Association. Built by Polk's father in 1816, the house was Polk's home for only a few years, but it has been decorated with memorabilia from other Polk homes that have been demolished.

Polk and his wife are buried on the grounds of the state capitol in Nashville, Tennessee.

Zachary Taylor

SPRINGFIELD, Taylor's boyhood home, is a brick farmhouse built by his father in about 1790 and later expanded. Located at 5608 Apache Road in Louisville, Kentucky, the house is surrounded by a housing development. Owned privately, the home is closed to the public.

Taylor's birthplace is not definitely known, but some persons claim it is the privately-owned 273-acre farm Montebello, about 80 miles south of Washington, D.C., in Orange County, Virginia.

Taylor is buried in Louisville's Zachary Taylor National Cemetery.

Millard Fillmore

A REPLICA of Fillmore's log cabin birthplace is exhibited in Fillmore Glen State Park at Moravia, New York, a few miles from his actual birthplace.

A frame house built by Millard Fillmore in 1826 exists in East Aurora, New York. However, the house has undergone extension alterations since he lived in it and has been moved to a different location. Owned privately, it is closed to the public.

The Millard Fillmore Museum in East Aurora is maintained by the Aurora Historical Society.

Fillmore's body lies in Forest Lawn Cemetery in Buffalo, New York.

Franklin Pierce

PIERCE HOMESTEAD stands about three miles west of Hillsboro, New Hampshire. Built by his father in 1804, it was Pierce's boyhood home and very likely was his birthplace. Pierce's father ran a tavern in the two-story frame building as well as using it as the family residence. Owned by the state, the house has been restored by the New Hampshire Federation of Women's Clubs.

The Pierce Manse, where Pierce and his family lived in the 1840s, is open to the public in Concord, New Hampshire.

Pierce and his wife are buried in Old North Cemetery in Concord, New Hampshire.

James Buchanan

THE LOG CABIN BIRTHPLACE of James Buchanan is exhibited at Mercersburg, Pennsylvania. A monument in Buchanan's Birthplace State Historical Park, marks its original site nearby.

Wheatland, at 1120 Marietta Avenue on Route 23 on the western outskirts of Lancaster, Pennsylvania, was the home of James Buchanan from the time he was Secretary of State until his death. He purchased the estate in 1848. The large Georgian-style brick house was built in 1828 by a local banker. The mansion is maintained by the James Buchanan Foundation for the Preservation of Wheatland, whose costumed hostesses welcome visitors. The former President is buried in Lancaster's Woodward Hill Cemetery.

Abraham Lincoln

LINCOLN BIRTHPLACE NATIONAL HISTORIC SITE of the National Park Service lies about three miles south of Hodgenville, Kentucky. It includes more than a hundred acres of the farm on which Lincoln was born in 1809. A memorial building contains a restoration of the log cabin that was his birthplace.

Lincoln Boyhood National Memorial, about two miles east of Gentryville, Indiana, commemorates the frontier farm where Lincoln grew to manhood and the place where his mother died. Operated by the National Park Service, the hundred-acre site includes a demonstration farm of the Lincoln era and a memorial building that serves as a museum.

Lincoln New Salem State park, about fifteen miles northwest of Springfield, Illinois, has a restoration of the frontier village where Lincoln lived from 1831 to 1837.

Lincoln Log Cabin State Park lies nine miles south of Charleston, Illinois. It contains the reconstructed, furnished log cabin of the President's father and stepmother who settled here in 1837. Both are buried in nearby Shiloh Cemetery.

Lincoln Home National Historic Site at 526 South Seventh Street in Springfield, Illinois, preserves the house in which he lived from 1844 until he became President. The site, maintained by the National Park Service, also includes four blocks of Lincoln era buildings. Several privately owned buildings in Springfield feature museums of Lincolniana, including the Lincoln-Herndon Building in which Lincoln had his law office. The Old State Capitol in Springfield features a large collection of Lincoln memorabilia owned by the Illinois Historical Library.

Lincoln Tomb in Oak Ridge Cemetery, Springfield, features a 117-foot-high stone obelisk. The tomb, maintained by the state, contains the bodies of Lincoln, his wife, and their sons.

Ford's Theatre National Historic Site in Washington, D.C., preserves the theater in which he was fatally shot and the Petersen house in which he died. The National Park Service has restored both buildings. Visitors can attend a sound-and-light show in the theater that tells the story of the assassination. A museum in the theater's basement has a large collection of Lincoln objects.

Lincoln Memorial stands on the bank of the Potomac River just west of the Washington Monument in Washington, D.C. Resembling the ancient

Parthenon of Greece, the memorial was built in 1914–22. The interior hall of the memorial features a huge statue of a seated Lincoln carved from white marble by sculptor Daniel C. French.

Andrew Johnson

ANDREW JOHNSON National Historic Site on South Main Street in Greene-ville, Tennessee, contains the tailor shop where he worked, the house in which he lived in 1831–51, a larger residence that was his home from 1851 until his death in 1875, and the Andrew Johnson National Cemetery where he and his wife are interred beneath a twenty-six-foot-high marble shaft. The one-room frame tailor shop where Johnson's wife taught him to read and write is preserved inside a memorial building that also serves as a museum and visitor center.

Johnson's birthplace and boyhood home is displayed in Mordecai Historic Park in Raleigh, North Carolina.

Ulysses S. Grant

GRANT BIRTHPLACE in Point Pleasant, Ohio, has been carefully restored. The small frame house is open to the public, exhibiting Grant memorabilia. His boyhood school has been preserved in Georgetown, Ohio.

Grant's farm on Gravois Road at Grant Road in St. Louis, Missouri, pre-serves the log cabin where Grant and his wife lived in the 1850s during his unsuccessful effort to become a farmer.

Grant's home at 510 Bouthillier in Galena, Illinois, is a two-story brick house given to him by the town's citizens in 1865 to show their admiration for his accomplishments in the Civil War. He and his wife lived in this house only for a few brief periods. Maintained as a memorial by the state of Illinois, the house exhibits many of Grant's souvenirs and possessions.

Appomattox National Historical Park in Virginia preserves the McLean House, site of General Robert E. Lee's surrender to Grant on April 9, 1865, ending the Civil War.

General Grant National Memorial on Riverside Drive in New York City overlooking the Hudson River is more commonly known as Grant's Tomb. The 150-foot-high monument designed by architect John H. Duncan was built in 1891–97. The bodies of both Grant and his wife are interred in the tomb. Trophy rooms in the memorial exhibit Civil War battle flags and campaign maps.

Rutherford B. Hayes

SPIEGEL GROVE at 1337 Hayes Avenue in Fremont, Ohio, was the residence of Hayes and his family from 1873 to 1893. The brick house was built by Hayes' uncle in 1859–63. Subsequently Hayes enlarged it to a twenty-room mansion. Near the residence stands the Rutherford B. Hayes Library, a gray sandstone structure that houses Hayes' papers and a museum of memorabilia. Opened in 1916, it was the first presidential library. Hayes and his wife are entombed on the grounds of the estate. The library-museum and the grounds are open to the public, but the residence is still occupied by Hayes' descendants.

James A. Garfield

LAWNFIELD, at 8095 Mentor Avenue in Mentor, Ohio, was Garfield's home from 1876 until he became President in 1881. Built as a small frame farmhouse in 1832, the house was enlarged by Garfield and his widow. Maintained by the National Park Service as a historic site, Lawnfield exhibits many Garfield mementos. A replica of the log cabin in which Garfield was born has been constructed near the main house.

Garfield's body is entombed in a memorial at Lakeview Cemetery in Cleveland, Ohio.

Chester A. Arthur

A REPLICA of the birthplace of Chester A. Arthur is exhibited in Fairfield, Vermont, near the church where his father was the minister.

A five-story brownstone row house at 123 Lexington Avenue in New York City was Arthur's residence from about the 1850s until his death. The building is marked by a bronze plaque, but it is privately owned and closed to the public. None of Arthur's possessions remain in the structure.

Arthur's body was buried in the Albany, New York, Rural Cemetery.

Grover Cleveland

THE BIRTHPLACE of Grover Cleveland is exhibited in the Grover Cleveland Birthplace Historic Site at 207 Bloomfield Avenue in Caldwell, New Jersey.

Westland in Princeton, New Jersey, became Cleveland's home in 1897 after he completed his second term as President. The two-and-a-half story stuccoed stone house was built in the mid-1800s. Privately owned, the house is not open to the public.

Cleveland is buried in Princeton Cemetery.

Benjamin Harrison

HARRISON'S HOME from the 1870s until his death was a two-story brick house at 1230 North Delaware Street in Indianapolis, Indiana. Today the house is maintained as a museum by the Benjamin Harrison Foundation.

Harrison is buried in Indianapolis' Crown Hill Cemetery.

William McKinley

THE ONLY PRESIDENT whose personal residences all have been destroyed, McKinley is honored by the National McKinley Birthplace Memorial in Niles, Ohio, where he was born. The monument exhibits McKinley relics.

The bodies of McKinley and his wife are interred in an elaborate ninety-six-foot-high domed tomb in Canton, Ohio. A bronze statue of McKinley delivering a speech stands in front of the tomb. It was sculpted by Charles H. Niehaus.

The site at which McKinley was fatally shot in Buffalo, New York, is marked by a bronze tablet set into a rock.

Theodore Roosevelt

THEODORE ROOSEVELT BIRTHPLACE NATIONAL HISTORIC SITE of the National Park Service stands at 28 East 20th Street in New York City. The original brownstone townhouse in which Roosevelt was born was destroyed in the early 1900s when the neighborhood turned from residential to commercial. The Woman's Roosevelt Memorial Association reconstructed the birthplace in 1921–23 and established a museum in the adjacent building. In 1963 the birthplace-museum was turned over to the federal government.

Theodore Roosevelt National Memorial Park in North Dakota covers more than seventy thousand acres, encompassing much of the land the future President owned while he engaged in cattle ranching in the 1880s and 1890s. Near the visitor entrance to the park at Medora, North Dakota, one of the original log houses from his Maltese Cross Ranch has been reconstructed.

Theodore Roosevelt Inaugural National Historic Site is the house at 641 Delaware Avenue in Buffalo, New York, where he took the presidential oath after the death of McKinley in 1901. Built as part of the officers' quarters for a military base in the 1830s, the two-story brick house was extensively remodeled and made into a stately mansion by Buffalo lawyer Ansley Wilcox in the 1890s. After its designation by Congress as a national historic site in 1966, the house was restored, redecorated, and opened to the public.

Sagamore Hill National Historic Site stands about two miles northeast of Oyster Bay on Long Island, New York. The rambling twenty-two-room brick and frame house was built by Roosevelt in 1884–85. During his presidency it served as the "summer White House" and he spent many of his happiest days there with his large family. Roosevelt died there and was buried at nearby Oyster Bay Cove. The house and its seventy-eight acres of gardens and grounds are maintained by the National Park Service. Adjacent to Sagamore Hill, the home of his eldest son, Theodore Roosevelt, Jr., has been converted into Old Orchard Museum with exhibits commemorating the former President's contributions to conservation.

Theodore Roosevelt Island National Memorial in Washington, D.C., stands in the Potomac River opposite the Kennedy Center for the Performing Arts. Access to the island can be made only by boat or by footbridge from the Virginia shore. A monument in the center of the island was constructed by the National Park Service in 1963–67, featuring a seventeen-foot bronze statue of Roosevelt sculpted by Paul Manship and four twenty-one-foot-high granite slabs inscribed with quotations of Roosevelt. Most of the eighty-eight acre island is maintained as a wildlife preserve.

William Howard Taft

TAFT NATIONAL HISTORIC SITE at 2038 Auburn Avenue in Cincinnati, Ohio, preserves the two-story home in which Taft was born and grew to manhood. Built in the 1840s, the square brick house was extensively remodeled and enlarged by Taft's father. After the Taft family disposed of the house in 1899 it underwent many remodelings. The home was acquired in 1968 by the National Park Service.

The Taft Museum at 316 Pike Street in downtown Cincinnati is operated by the Cincinnati Institute of Fine Arts.

Taft's grave is in Arlington National Cemetery across the Potomac River from Washington, D.C.

Woodrow Wilson

WILSON BIRTHPLACE in Staunton, Virginia, is the Presbyterian parsonage in which Wilson was born while his father was pastor of the nearby Staunton

Church. The Greek Revival brick house is owned and maintained by the Woodrow Wilson Birthplace Foundation. The house exhibits many of Wilson's possessions, and in the garage is the Pierce Arrow limousine Wilson used while he was President.

A Victorian house where Wilson lived as a teenager is exhibited in Columbia, South Carolina.

Wilson House at 2340 S Street N.W. in Washington, D.C., is the home to which Wilson retired and where he spent his last years. The three-story, redbrick house is owned and exhibited by the National Trust for Historic Preservation.

Wilson's body is interred in the Episcopal National Cathedral in Washington, D.C.—the only President to be buried in the nation's capital.

Warren G. Harding

HARDING HOME at 380 Mount Vernon Avenue in Marion, Ohio, is the large frame house in which he was married in 1891 and from which he conducted his "front porch campaign" for the presidency in 1920. Owned and exhibited by the Harding Memorial Association, the house displays many Harding possessions.

The nearby Harding Memorial in Marion is a circular white marble tomb completed in 1927 in which the bodies of Harding and his wife are interred.

Calvin Coolidge

COOLIDGE HOMESTEAD in Plymouth, Vermont, is the boyhood home of Coolidge and the place where he was sworn into office as President by his notary public father. Owned and exhibited by the state of Vermont, the frame house and connected barn contain the furnishings used by the Coolidge family while they lived there.

Coolidge birthplace, across the street from the homestead, adjoins the general store which was operated by Coolidge's father. This structure also is owned and maintained by the state.

The graves of Coolidge and his wife lie in Plymouth Notch Cemetery, about a mile southwest of the homestead.

Herbert C. Hoover

HOOVER NATIONAL HISTORIC SITE in West Branch, Iowa, is a 186.8-acre park maintained by the National Park Service, containing many buildings that memorialize the President. The tiny three-room cottage in which Hoover was born has been restored. A blacksmith shop like that used by Hoover's father has been constructed nearby. The Herbert Hoover Presidential Library was built in 1962 southwest of the birthplace. The graves of Hoover and his wife lie on a hillside overlooking the site.

Franklin D. Roosevelt

FRANKLIN D. ROOSEVELT NATIONAL HISTORIC SITE stands about two miles south of Hyde Park, New York. The 264-acre estate is maintained and exhibited by the National Park Service. The original eight-room two-story house was built in the early 1800s. After it was purchased by Roosevelt's father in 1867 it underwent many remodelings until it included thirty-five rooms and nine baths. Roosevelt was born in the house and lived there much of his life, using it as a "summer White House" during his presidency. The house is furnished much as it was at his death. The Franklin D. Roosevelt Library, which was built in 1939–40, stands on the Hyde Park estate, housing presidential books and papers and serving as a museum of his memorabilia. The graves of Roosevelt and his wife lie in a rose garden northeast of the house.

Eleanor Roosevelt National Historic Site includes the 180-acre Val-Kill estate two miles east of the Roosevelt home at Hyde Park, New York. The park preserves the cottage built by Roosevelt in 1924 as a retreat for his wife.

Franklin D. Roosevelt Campobello International Park on Campobello Island is in Canada's province of New Brunswick. Lying in the Bay of Fundy, the island is connected to the state of Maine by the Franklin D. Roosevelt Memorial Bridge. Jointly maintained by Canada and the United States, the 2,721-acre park preserves Roosevelt's thirty-four-room Dutch Colonial summer home, where he contracted polio during a visit in 1921.

The Little White House in Warm Springs, Georgia, where Roosevelt underwent treatment for his polio and where he died in 1945, is maintained by the Georgia Warm Springs Foundation, a nonprofit corporation that Roosevelt established in 1927. Visitors are welcomed to the Franklin D. Roosevelt Museum nearby that exhibits memorabilia of the former President.

Franklin D. Roosevelt Memorial in Washington, D.C., is a block of marble standing at the corner of Pennsylvania Avenue and Ninth Street behind the National Archives Building.

Harry S Truman

HARRY S TRUMAN BIRTHPLACE MEMORIAL SHRINE in Lamar, Missouri, exhibits the restored small frame house where the future President was born. He lived there until the age of six when the Trumans moved to Independence, Missouri.

Three of Truman's boyhood homes exist in Independence but are privately owned and are closed to the public. They are at 909 West Waldo Street, 619 South Crysler Street, and 902 North Liberty Street.

The Harry S Truman National Historic Site in Independence was his residence from 1919. He retired there after leaving the White House. The Victorian frame house was built in the 1860s or 1870s by the grandfather of Truman's wife, who willed it to the federal government upon her death in 1982.

The Truman Presidential Library in Independence contains more than five million books and documents relating to his presidency. The library has historical exhibits, including a replica of Truman's White House office.

Truman's grave lies in the courtyard of the Truman Presidential Library.

Dwight D. Eisenhower

EISENHOWER'S BIRTHPLACE, a small white frame house in Denison, Texas, where he lived only as an infant, has been maintained in excellent condition. It is open to public visits.

Eisenhower Center in Abilene, Kansas, is the main national memorial to the thirty-fourth President. His boyhood home in which he lived until he left for West Point has been preserved, furnished as it was in 1946. Adjacent to the house, the Eisenhower Museum displays many of the former President's souvenirs and possessions. The Eisenhower Presidential Library, opposite the museum, contains his official presidential papers and other books and documents relating to his life. His body is interred in a meditation chapel within the fifteen-acre center.

Eisenhower National Historic Site lies adjacent to the southwest boundary of Gettysburg National Military Park in Pennsylvania. Owned by the National Park Service, the 690-acre site includes the estate to which Eisenhower retired after leaving the White House. Purchased by Eisenhower in 1950, the old farmhouse on the property was completely rebuilt and expanded to twenty-two rooms in 1954–55. After Eisenhower's death the government granted his widow lifetime rights to occupy the house, but opened it to the public after her death.

John F. Kennedy

KENNEDY NATIONAL HISTORIC SITE at 83 Beals Street in Brookline, Massachusetts, preserves the nine-room frame house where the future President was born and lived until he was four. The Kennedy family restored and refurnished the first two floors of the house to their 1917 appearance before donating it to the federal government in 1967. A short distance from the birthplace is the home where Kennedy lived from 1921 to 1927, but it is closed to the public because it is privately owned.

Kennedy compound in Hyannis Port, Massachusetts, includes six acres of waterfront along Nantucket Sound and three summer homes owned by the Kennedy family. Kennedy used the compound as headquarters for his presidential campaign and then as a presidential summer retreat. The houses are closed to the public.

Hammersmith Farm at Newport, Rhode Island, was the site for his wedding and was used by him for summer vacations during his presidency.

John F. Kennedy Center for the Performing Arts in Washington, D.C., is operated by the government as a cultural national memorial to the assassinated President. Designed by architect Edward Durell Stone, the center includes three main theaters, an exhibition area, and three restaurants. It began operation in 1971.

The John Fitzgerald Kennedy Library built in Boston, Massachusetts, in 1977–78 contains his presidential papers and displays Kennedy memorabilia.

Kennedy's body and those of his two infant children who died prematurely are buried in Arlington National Cemetery across the Potomac River from Washington, D.C. An eternal flame burns at his grave.

Lyndon B. Johnson

LYNDON B. JOHNSON NATIONAL HISTORICAL PARK west of Austin, Texas, includes on its more than 1,477 acres the three homes most closely associated with his life in Texas. The one-story ranch house near Stonewall, Texas, in which the future President was born has been faithfully reconstructed and furnished with Johnson family items. His boyhood home in Johnson City, Texas, has been restored to its appearance in the early 1920s. The site, owned and managed by the National Park Service, also contains the main two-story ranch house of the LBJ Ranch that served as the "Texas White House" during Johnson's presidency and later as his retirement home. The log house used by Johnson's grandfather as a cattle rancher in the 1880s has been restored as has the one-room school Johnson attended as a child. The grave of the former President lies in the family cemetery next to his birthplace.

The Lyndon B. Johnson Library on the campus of the University of Texas at Austin has in its collection more than thirty million books and documents relating to his presidency. It also displays gifts received by Johnson while he was President.

The Lyndon B. Johnson Memorial Grove across the Potomac River from Washington, D.C., memorializes the thirty-sixth President. Funded by public contributions and dedicated in 1974, the grove of some five hundred white pine trees stands near the Pentagon on what was formerly called Columbia Island. A huge block of granite quarried near Johnson's LBJ Ranch stands at the center of the grove faced by four marble slabs bearing quotations from statements by the President.

Richard M. Nixon

NIXON BIRTHPLACE at 18061 Yorba Linda Boulevard in Yorba Linda, California, is a one-story frame farmhouse built by Nixon's father in the early 1900s. Owned by the local school district, the house has been designated as a historic site.

The palatial home in San Clemente, California, which was used as the "California White House" during Nixon's presidency and to which he retired after resigning, is closed to the public.

Gerald R. Ford

FORD BIRTHPLACE SITE is a city-owned park at the corner of Thirty-second and Woolworth avenues in Omaha, Nebraska. Ford was born in a basement apartment in a building that later was destroyed by fire. A scale model of the original structure is displayed in a memorial building along with engravings of all the Presidents.

Ford's presidential papers are housed in the Gerald R. Ford Library on the Ann Arbor, Michigan, campus of his alma mater, the University of Michigan. Mementos of his presidency are displayed in his home town, Grand Rapids, Michigan, in the Ford Presidential Museum, which cost $12 million to construct.

Jimmy Carter

CARTER was the first President to be born in a hospital, the Wise Sanitarium in Plains, Georgia, a one-story white-painted brick building. At present it is used as a nursing home.

The first home in which Carter lived as an infant stands on the outskirts of Plains. It is a one-story frame house. Privately owned as a residence, it is not open to the public.

The $25 million Carter Presidential Library in Atlanta, Georgia, houses the papers of his administration.

Ronald Reagan

REAGAN'S BIRTHPLACE was a second-floor flat over a store on Main Street in Tampico, Illinois. The brick building has been preserved as the small town's main tourist attraction. In Dixon, Illinois, where Reagan spent much of his boyhood, a rented house in which the Reagan family lived has been restored and is open to the public.

The Ronald Reagan Presidential Library will be located on a site overlooking Stanford University in Palo Alto, California.

Index